FEDERAL CIVIL PROCEDURE

As Amended Through April 1, 1991

Together with:

Appendix: Proposed Rules

(effective date: see page 699)

Westbury, New York
THE FOUNDATION PRESS, INC.
1991

Cover Photos: SUPREME COURT HISTORICAL SOCIETY and USDA Photos

PREFACE

Welcome to the world of the Federal Rules of Civil Procedure. Here is a roadmap to the interior:

1. Federal Rules of Civil Procedure

This booklet begins with the Civil Rules themselves or, more exactly, with (i) the Table of Rules, which allows you to see the structure of the Federal Rules of Civil Procedure, (ii) the main corpus of Civil Rules 1–86, (iii) the Appendix of Forms, as prefaced by its own explanatory Introductory Statement, and (iv) the Supplemental Rules for Certain Admiralty and Maritime Claims.

The most important pointer on use of this portion of the booklet regards the history of amendments. After each amended Rule or Form appears a line listing by year the effective date of all amendments. Details of these amendments appear in and immediately after Federal Rule of Civil Procedure 86—there the booklet tells which particular subdivisions underwent amendment in each year, and it gives both an official citation to the amendatory order or statute and a reference to a readily available source containing any Advisory Committee's Notes. For example, you might want to know how Fed.R.Civ.P. 7(b) read when some 1980 case came down: Rule 7 closes with an indication of amendment in 1948, 1963, and 1983; referring to Rule 86 informs that 1948 and 1963 saw amendments to Rule 7(a) and that only the 1983 changes affected Rule 7(b); for 1983 in particular, the Supreme Court's amendatory order appears at 461 U.S. 1095, while the Advisory Committee's Notes appear at 97 F.R.D. 165; the latter source will tell you exactly how Rule 7(b) looked in 1980.

2. Civil Advisory Committee's Notes

This booklet in fact reprints the most significant of the Advisory Committee's Notes on amendments to the Federal Rules of Civil Procedure. These come right after the booklet's Civil Rules portion, with the primary organization of the Notes being by date of amendment. Thus, the Note on Rule 7(b) lies with the set of 1983 amendments. Each set of reprinted amendments has a separate entry in the thumb index on the booklet's back cover, permitting quick access.

The most important pointer on using this portion of the booklet regards the style of Advisory Committee's Notes. For each amendment, the Rule appears with its changes (new matter is in italics; omitted matter appears with a line through it) and then the following Note allows the Advisory Committee to explain

1

PREFACE

the changes. All this enables you to reconstruct the former Rule. Using the same example, you can see that in 1980 Rule 7(b) lacked a subdivision (3), although its essence came through Rule 7(b)(2)'s former reference to "signing." Indeed, you have reconstructed Rule 7(b) as it existed from the beginning in 1938, and you can find the Advisory Committee's Note on that original Rule 7 in the set of Early Committee's Notes.

3. Federal Rules of Appellate Procedure

This booklet's next portion contains most of the Appellate Rules and Forms. The organization is similar to the booklet's treatment of the Civil Rules.

Also, you can trace the history of amendments in the same way, using the detailed information that appears after Federal Rule of Appellate Procedure 48.

4. Constitution and Procedural Statutes

This booklet next reprints selected provisions of the United States Constitution, title 28 of the United States Code, and other procedural statutes—all preceded by this portion's own table of contents. The editing effort centered on including those provisions most effectively considered in connection with the study of civil procedure. For example, the selection of "other procedural statutes" includes a few key federal statutes that lie outside title 28 (antitrust procedural provisions and civil rights statutes) and also illustrative state statutes in a few key procedural subjects (California's long-arm statute and New York's statute of limitations and jurisdiction, service, and venue provisions).

Title 28 is of course the centerpiece, and accordingly the booklet contains many of its sections. This systematization of statutes on the federal judiciary and judicial procedure comes from the Act of June 25, 1948, ch. 646, § 1, 62 Stat. 869 ("Act to revise, codify, and enact into law title 28 of the United States Code"). After each reprinted statutory section, the booklet lists all amending statutes since the 1948 Act.

5. Federal Rules of Evidence

This booklet sets out finally the complete Rules of Evidence for United States Courts and Magistrates. Although the Evidence Rules constitute a statute, the booklet presents them in a format similar to that of the Civil and Appellate Rules.

Again, you can trace the history of amendments in the same way, using the detailed information that appears after Federal Rule of Evidence 1103.

6. General Comments

PREFACE

The foregoing descriptions evince an editing effort to select thoughtfully a collection of procedural provisions. Also, this preface and the closing consolidated index represent a similarly serious attempt to facilitate the collection's use. We nevertheless want to continue improving this booklet. That does not establish an easy goal, however, because users' widely varying desires are not always obvious. Accordingly, I sincerely request the users to send suggestions for improvement to me.

The booklet also reflects a dedication to keeping it up to date. The Court and Congress are surprisingly active in the procedural arena. We update the Civil Rules through the date shown on the booklet's title page. We update the various other provisions at least through the end of the preceding congressional session, which roughly corresponds to the beginning of the year that appears on the booklet's cover.

> KEVIN M. CLERMONT
> Flanagan Professor of Law
> Myron Taylor Hall
> Cornell Law School
> Ithaca, NY 14853

P.S. Notwithstanding all the above, this booklet still gives you only the raw materials. To get into the immense body of legal doctrine adhering to these materials, you should consult the secondary literature. I especially recommend Charles Alan Wright's single-volume hornbook on Federal Courts and the multivolume Federal Practice and Procedure by Professors Wright and Miller and others. To give you a sample, while also providing you with valuable background information on the Federal Rules that are the subject of the booklet, I close this preface with an excerpt from the former reference work, reprinted here with kind permission:

C. WRIGHT, THE LAW OF FEDERAL COURTS

402–08, 718 (4th ed. 1983).

§ 62. The Federal Rules of Civil Procedure [1]

... An erratic conformity to state procedure, an anachronistic survival of the separation between law and equity, and a

---

1. 4 Wright & Miller, Civil §§ 1003–1008; Tolman, Historical Beginnings of Procedural Reform, 1936, 22 A.B.A.J. 783; Sunderland, The Grant of Rule-Making Power to the Supreme Court of the United States, 1934, 32 Mich.L.Rev. 1116; Holtzoff, Origin and Sources of the Federal Rules of Civil Procedure, 1955, 30 N.Y.U.L.Rev. 1057; Clark, Two Decades of the Federal Civil Rules, 1958, 58 Col.L.Rev. 435; Chandler, Some Major Advances in the Federal Judicial System, 1922–1947, 1963, 31 F.R.D. 307, 477–516; Clark, The Role of the Supreme Court in Federal Rule-Making, 1963, 46 J.Am.Jud.Soc. 250.

failure to take advantage of the possibilities of judicial rulemaking were hallmarks of the system [of federal procedure prior to 1938]. The last of these points, that procedure is better regulated by the courts than by legislative bodies, was seen to be the key to the problem. It is doubtful whether, as some have contended, the legislature lacks constitutional power to regulate procedure.[2] It cannot be doubted that legislative regulation is less satisfactory than regulation by court-made rules.[3]

The fight for court-made rules of civil procedure for the federal courts began in 1911 when the American Bar Association, at the instigation of Thomas Shelton, adopted a resolution favoring such a system. For almost 20 years a bill to give the Supreme Court power to make such rules was introduced in every Congress, but never was passed, despite the gallant efforts of Mr. Shelton. In later years, in response to a suggestion by Chief Justice Taft,[4] the bill included a provision authorizing the Court to unify law and equity. Opposition to the bill was led by Senator Walsh of Montana, and was based in large measure on the fear that grant of the rulemaking power would result in the rather simplified code practice of the western states being superseded by the involved practice that had developed in New York.[5] In 1930 Mr. Shelton died, and the American Bar Association lost interest, even to the point of abolishing its committee that had been pressing for this reform.

Senator Walsh was to have been appointed Attorney General in 1933, which would surely have ended, for the time at least, any hope of obtaining rulemaking power for the Supreme Court. He died, however, on the eve of his appointment, and the new Attorney General, Homer Cummings, assumed sponsorship of the bill authorizing the court to make procedural rules and to unite law and equity. So effective was his leadership that the bill was adopted unanimously by Congress in 1934 with very little discus-

2. Compare Wigmore, Legislative Rules for Judicial Procedure are Void Constitutionally, 1928, 23 Ill.L.Rev. 276, with Kaplan & Greene, The Legislature's Relation to Judicial Rule-Making: An Appraisal of Winberry v. Salisbury, 1951, 65 Harv.L.Rev. 234.

3. 4 Wright & Miller, Civil § 1001; Clark & Wright, The Judicial Council and the Rule-Making Power: A Dissent and a Protest, 1950, 1 Syracuse L.Rev. 346; Joiner & Miller, Rules of Practice and Procedure: A Study of Judicial Rule-Making, 1957, 55 Mich.L.Rev. 623; Levin & Amsterdam, Legislative Control over Judicial Rule-Making: A Problem in Constitutional Revision, 1958, 107 U.Pa.L. Rev. 1.

4. Taft, Three Needed Steps of Progress, 1922, 8 A.B.A.J. 34, 35; Taft, Possible and Needed Reforms in the Administration of Justice in Federal Courts, 1922, 8 A.B.A.J. 601, 604, 607.

5. Walsh, Rule-Making Power on Law Side of Federal Practice, 1927, 13 A.B.A.J. 84. See Clark, Code Pleading, 2d ed. 1947, p. 35.

sion.[6]

It is a long step from a grant of rulemaking power to the adoption of effective rules. Indeed one familiar argument against rulemaking power is that it will not be exercised. For almost a year after the Enabling Act was passed the Supreme Court took no action with regard to it. The Department of Justice and the Conference of Senior Circuit Judges apparently contemplated that no more would be required than the drafting of uniform rules for actions at law to supplement the existing Equity Rules of 1912.

That the reform was not so limited, that law and equity were merged under a single set of simple and effective rules, was due primarily to the efforts of William D. Mitchell, a former Attorney General of the United States, and Charles E. Clark, then Dean of the Yale Law School and later Chief Judge of the Court of Appeals for the Second Circuit. In January 1935, Dean Clark, in collaboration with James Wm. Moore, published a major article summarizing the history of federal procedure and predicting that reform would be a failure unless it included a merger of law and equity.[7] Aroused by this article, General Mitchell wrote Chief Justice Hughes, on February 9, 1935, setting forth powerfully and persuasively the need for the full reform.[8] Three months later the Chief Justice, addressing the American Law Institute, made the dramatic announcement that the rules would not be limited to common-law cases, but would unify the procedure for cases in equity and actions at law "so as to secure one form of civil action and procedure for both."[9] A few weeks later the Court appointed an Advisory Committee of the most distinguished lawyers and law professors in the country to prepare and submit a draft of unified rules. General Mitchell was named by the Court as chairman, a post he filled with distinction until his death in 1955, and Dean Clark was designated as Reporter for the Committee.[10]

The Committee circulated three printed drafts for comment and criticism by the profession. The third draft, which was the Final Report of the Committee, was submitted to the Supreme

6. Act of June 19, 1934, c. 651, 48 Stat. 1064; 4 Wright & Miller, Civil § 1003, p. 43. The Enabling Act, as subsequently revised, is now 28 U.S.C.A. § 2072. See Cummings, Immediate Problems of the Bar, 1934, 20 A.B.A.J. 212.

7. Clark & Moore, A New Federal Civil Procedure: I. The Background, 1935, 44 Yale L.J. 387.

8. The letter appears in full in Mitchell, The Federal Rules of Civil Procedure, in David Dudley Field Centenary Essays, 1949, pp. 73, 76–78.

9. Address of Chief Justice Hughes, 1935, 55 S.Ct. xxxv, xxxvii, 21 A.B.A.J. 340, 12 A.L.I.Proc. 54.

10. Order of June 3, 1935, 295 U.S. 774. For a full list of members of the committee, see 4 Wright & Miller, Civil § 1003, pp. 46–47.

The contributions of Dean—later Judge—Clark are described in Smith, Judge Charles E. Clark and The Federal Rules of Civil Procedure, 1976, 85 Yale L.J. 914.

PREFACE

Court in November 1937, and on December 20, 1937, the Court adopted the rules proposed by the Committee with some changes of its own.[11] The rules were submitted to Congress, as the Enabling Act required, and when Congress adjourned without any adverse legislation,[12] the rules became effective September 16, 1938.

Even the best system of court rules cannot remain static. Experience under the rules, and continued scholarly thinking about problems of procedure, will disclose places in which improvement is possible. Amendment will be necessary in other instances to remove unsound judicial glosses on the rules, or to codify desirable lines of decision. It is essential, therefore, that there be a continuing body charged with the responsibility of examining the rules in action, and recommending change to the Court when this seems desirable.[13] The Advisory Committee that drafted the federal rules was reconstituted in 1942 to serve this function, and did so until its discharge in 1956. Various amendments were made by the Court, on the recommendation of that Committee, but the most significant was the set of amendments adopted in 1946, effective March 19, 1948, which reflected the results of a general study of the rules in operation.

The old Advisory Committee was discharged in 1956. In 1958 Congress amended the act creating the Judicial Conference to include among the duties of that body advising the Supreme Court with regard to necessary changes in the various rules the Court has power to make or amend.[14] An elaborate structure was created to assist the Judicial Conference, and ultimately the Court, in this task. There have been, as needed, advisory committees of practitioners, judges, and scholars for civil procedure, criminal procedure, appellate procedure, admiralty, bankruptcy, and evidence. These report to a standing Committee on Rules of Practice and Procedure and it in turn reports to the Judicial

11. Order of Dec. 20, 1937, 302 U.S. 783. Justice Brandeis dissented from adoption of the rules.

12. There was opposition to the rules in the Senate, but that body took no action, since the House of Representatives favored the rules, and concurrent action of both houses would have been required to delay or defeat adoption of the rules. See Chandler, Some Major Advances in the Federal Judicial System, 1922–1947, 1963, 31 F.R.D. 307, 505–512.

13. Clark, "Clarifying" Amendments to the Federal Rules, 1953, 14 Ohio St.L.J. 241; Wright, Amendments to the Federal Rules: The Function of a Continuing Rules Committee, 1954, 7 Vand.L.Rev. 521; Wright, Rule 56(e): A Case Study on the Need for Amending the Federal Rules, 1956, 69 Harv.L.Rev. 839.

14. 28 U.S.C.A. § 331, as amended by Act of July 11, 1958, 72 Stat. 356. For discussion of this amendment prior to its adoption, see Symposium, 1957, 21 F.R.D. 117.

PREFACE

Conference.[15] The Judicial Conference transmits such of the recommendations as it approves to the Supreme Court, for under this new plan, as under that in effect from 1934 to 1956, the Court retains ultimate responsibility for the adoption of amendments to the rules.

This new machinery led to significant amendments to the Civil Rules in 1961, 1963, 1966, 1970, 1980, and 1983, and to minor corrective or conforming amendments in 1971 and 1975. [There have been further amendments. See Fed.R.Civ.P. 86.]

The success of the Federal Rules of Civil Procedure has been quite phenomenal. They provide for the federal courts a uniform procedure in civil actions. This in itself would be a fine accomplishment, but the rules go beyond this to create a uniform procedure that is flexible, simple, clear, and efficient. It may smack of hyperbole to say, as one commentator has, that the rules are "one of the greatest contributions to the free and unhampered administration of law and justice ever struck off by any group of men since the dawn of civilized law." [16] It is nevertheless true that the chorus of approval of the rules by judges, lawyers, and commentators had been, until very recently, unanimous, unstinted, and spontaneous.[17] In the last few years, however, there has been questioning and reexamination of the assumptions about the proper goals of procedure that are at the heart of the Civil Rules.[18] This questioning has been sparked particularly by what some think is abuse of the discovery procedures made available by the rules.

The impact of the rules has not been limited to the federal courts. The excellence of the rules is such that in more than half the states the rules have been adapted for state use virtually unchanged, and there is not a jurisdiction that has not revised its procedure in some way that reflects the influence of the federal rules.[20]

15. The work of the new committees is described by the chairman of the Judicial Conference's Standing Committee on Rules of Practice and Procedure in Maris, Federal Procedural Rule-Making: The Program of the Judicial Conference, 1961, 37 A.B.A.J. 772. Their members are listed at 4 Wright & Miller, Civil § 1007.

16. Carey, In Favor of Uniformity, 1943, 3 F.R.D. 507, 18 Temp.L.Q. 145.

17. See 4 Wright & Miller, Civil § 1008, and particularly n. 40.

18. Subrin, The New Era in American Civil Procedure, 1981, 67 A.B.A.J. 1648.

20. A commentator has pointed out, however, that certain provisions in the Civil Rules respond to special problems of a federal system and of courts of constitutionally-limited jurisdiction, and that those provisions ought not be blindly adopted by the states. Rowe, A Comment on the Federalism of the Federal Rules, 1979 Duke L.J. 843.

PREFACE

The Enabling Act declares that the rules are to regulate only "practice and procedure" and are not to "abridge, enlarge or modify any substantive rights." [21] Particular rules have been attacked as affecting matters of substance, but the Supreme Court, in a notable series of decisions, has upheld all such rules challenged before it.[22]

The success of the Civil Rules caused many to think that formulation of Federal Rules of Evidence would be desirable. An Advisory Committee on Rules of Evidence was created in 1965 and followed the methods of the committee that had drafted the Civil Rules in its work. Ultimately Federal Rules of Evidence became effective July 1, 1975, but their gestation period was as troubled as it was lengthy. ... [A] draft of Evidence Rules was promulgated by the Supreme Court in 1972, but they caused so much controversy that Congress passed a statute providing that they could not take effect until they were expressly approved by Act of Congress. Congress then made very substantial revisions in the rules as they had been promulgated by the Supreme Court before [enacting] them [as a statute,] to become effective in 1975.

The controversy over the Evidence Rules, and a similar furor over amendments to the Criminal Rules that the Supreme Court had approved in 1974, has led to some reappraisal of the rulemaking process.[25] Although the critics have not been directing themselves particularly to the Civil Rules, insofar as the criticism goes to the methods that the rulemaking committees have used over

---

21. 28 U.S.C.A. § 2072.

22. Sibbach v. Wilson & Co., 1941, 62 S.Ct. 422, 312 U.S. 1, 85 L.Ed. 479 (Rule 35(a)); Mississippi Pub. Co. v. Murphree, 1946, 66 S.Ct. 242, 326 U.S. 438, 90 L.Ed. 185 (Rule 4(f)); Cold Metal Process Co. v. United Engineering & Foundry Co., 1956, 76 S.Ct. 904, 351 U.S. 445, 100 L.Ed. 1311 (amended Rule 54(b)); Hanna v. Plumer, 1965, 85 S.Ct. 1136, 380 U.S. 460, 14 L.Ed.2d 8 (Rule 4(d)(1)).

It has been argued, however, that the Court has been too permissive in upholding rules that do affect substantive rights, contrary to the Enabling Act. Ely, The Irrepressible Myth of Erie, 1974, 87 Harv.L.Rev. 693. Professor Ely's view is rejected, in the course of a thoughtful decision holding that Rule 25(a) is valid, in Boggs v. Blue Diamond Coal Co., D.C.Ky.1980, 497 F.Supp. 1105, 1118–1121, noted 1981, 11 Mem.St.U.L.Rev. 413.

25. Weinstein, Reform of Court Rule-Making Procedures, 1977 (shorter versions of this book appeared in 1977, 63 A.B.A.J. 47, and 1976, 76 Col.L.Rev. 905). See also Wright, Book Review, 1978, 9 St. Mary's L.J. 652; Clinton, Rule 9 of the Federal Habeas Corpus Rules: A Case Study on the Need for Reform of the Rules Enabling Acts, 1977, 63 Iowa L.Rev. 15; Friedenthal, The Rulemaking Power of the Supreme Court: A Contemporary Crisis, 1975, 27 Stan.L.Rev. 673; Lesnick, The Federal Rule-Making Process: Time for Re-examination, 1975, 61 A.B.A.J. 579.

An influential member of the House Judiciary Committee had also said that "few are entirely satisfied with the present process" and suggested that Congress consider whether the Rules Enabling Acts ought to be amended. Hungate, Changes in the Federal Rules of Criminal Procedure, 1975, 61 A.B.A.J. 1203, 1207.

See generally Brown, Federal Rulemaking: Problems and Possibilities, Federal Judicial Center 1981.

the years, they may have an impact on future amendments of the Civil Rules.

Another threat to the integrity of the Civil Rules has come from the proliferation of local rules for particular districts. Although Rule 83 authorizes local rules, it had been expected that these would be few in number and confined to purely housekeeping matters. Instead the use of local rules has been extensive and they cover a great variety of important matters.[26] This in itself is a threat to uniformity of procedure throughout the country, the local rules often provide "a series of traps"[27] for lawyers from other districts, and the very casual manner in which the judges in a district decide to adopt a rule or set of rules is in striking contrast to the care with which the Civil Rules themselves are made and amended. Almost every study of experience with local rules has demonstrated how unsatisfactory it has been.[28]

The Supreme Court sought to provide a check when it ruled in 1960 that the power to make local rules is not to be used to introduce "basic procedural innovations,"[29] but it seemed to retreat from this when it later held that local rules reducing the size of civil juries from 12 to six did not fall afoul of that restriction.[30] Many local rules have been held invalid for this reason, or because they are inconsistent with the Civil Rules, an Act of Congress, or the Constitution,[31] but patently there are many other invalid local rules on the books that have escaped scrutiny in a contested case.

. . . .

26. 12 Wright & Miller, Civil § 3154.

27. Woodham v. American Cystoscope Co. of Pelham, C.A.5th, 1964, 335 F.2d 551, 552.

The difficulty in finding out what local rules are in effect is illustrated by Doran v. U.S., C.A.1st, 1973, 475 F.2d 742, where the United States attorney had no knowledge of a local rule in effect for 20 years. See also U.S. v. Ferretti, C.A.3d, 1980, 635 F.2d 1089, in which the judges in the district were uncertain about the continued existence of a local rule.

28. 12 Wright & Miller, Civil § 3152; Weinstein, note 25 above, at pp. 117–137; Note, Rule 83 and the Local Federal Rules, 1967, 67 Col.L.Rev. 1251; Note, The Local Rules of Civil Procedure in the Federal District Courts—A Survey, 1966 Duke L.J. 1011.

But see Flanders, Local Rules in Federal District Courts: Usurpation, Legislation, or Information?, 1981, 14 Loy.L.A.L.Rev. 213; Flanders, In Praise of Local Rules, 1978, 62 Judicature 28.

29. Miner v. Atlass, 1960, 80 S.Ct. 1300, 1306, 363 U.S. 641, 650, 4 L.Ed.2d 1462.

30. Colgrove v. Battin, 1973, 93 S.Ct. 2448, 2456 n. 23, 413 U.S. 149, 163 n. 23, 37 L.Ed.2d 522.

31. See Carter v. Clark, C.A.5th, 1980, 616 F.2d 228; Rodgers v. United States Steel Corp., C.A.3d, 1975, 508 F.2d 152, noted 1975, 88 Harv.L.Rev. 1911; U.S. v. Columbia Broadcasting System, Inc., C.A.5th, 1974, 497 F.2d 102, 103 n. 3; and cases cited 12 Wright & Miller, Civil § 3153 nn. 53–55.

PREFACE

One of the most striking achievements in the federal rules from the first has been the simplified procedures they introduced for taking appeals. These matters were dealt with until 1968 by Civil Rules 73 to 76 and Criminal Rules 37 to 39. In that year the Federal Rules of Appellate Procedure were adopted, applicable to all cases, and the former civil and criminal provisions were repealed. The Appellate Rules incorporate in general the portions of the Civil Rules and Criminal Rules that they replaced but they also make uniform provision for a number of other matters of appellate practice that prior to 1968 were dealt with in varying ways by the rules of the eleven courts of appeals, though the uniformity that was hoped for has been greatly compromised by the proliferation of local rules for particular circuits.

RULES OF CIVIL PROCEDURE

FOR THE

UNITED STATES DISTRICT COURTS

TABLE OF RULES

RULES OF CIVIL PROCEDURE

RULES OF CIVIL PROCEDURE

RULES OF CIVIL PROCEDURE

RULES OF CIVIL PROCEDURE

RULES OF CIVIL PROCEDURE

RULES OF CIVIL PROCEDURE

RULES OF CIVIL PROCEDURE

RULES OF CIVIL PROCEDURE

RULES OF CIVIL PROCEDURE

RULES OF CIVIL PROCEDURE

APPENDIX OF FORMS

SUPPLEMENTAL RULES FOR CERTAIN ADMIRALTY AND MARITIME CLAIMS

RULES OF CIVIL PROCEDURE

*

RULES OF CIVIL PROCEDURE FOR THE UNITED STATES DISTRICT COURTS

I. SCOPE OF RULES—ONE FORM OF ACTION

Rule 1.

SCOPE OF RULES

These rules govern the procedure in the United States district courts in all suits of a civil nature whether cognizable as cases at law or in equity or in admiralty, with the exceptions stated in Rule 81. They shall be construed to secure the just, speedy, and inexpensive determination of every action.

As amended 1949, 1966.

Rule 2.

ONE FORM OF ACTION

There shall be one form of action to be known as "civil action".

II. COMMENCEMENT OF ACTION; SERVICE OF PROCESS, PLEADINGS, MOTIONS, AND ORDERS

Rule 3.

COMMENCEMENT OF ACTION

A civil action is commenced by filing a complaint with the court.

Rule 4.

PROCESS

(a) **Summons: Issuance.** Upon the filing of the complaint the clerk shall forthwith issue a summons and deliver the summons to the plaintiff or the plaintiff's attorney, who shall be responsible for prompt service of the summons and a copy of the complaint. Upon request of the plaintiff separate or additional summons shall issue against any defendants.

(b) Same: Form. The summons shall be signed by the clerk, be under the seal of the court, contain the name of the court and the names of the parties, be directed to the defendant, state the name and address of the plaintiff's attorney, if any, otherwise the plaintiff's address, and the time within which these rules require the defendant to appear and defend, and shall notify the defendant that in case of the defendant's failure to do so judgment by default will be rendered against the defendant for the relief demanded in the complaint. When, under Rule 4(e), service is made pursuant to a statute or rule of court of a state, the summons, or notice, or order in lieu of summons shall correspond as nearly as may be to that required by the statute or rule.

(c) Service.

(1) Process, other than a subpoena or a summons and complaint, shall be served by a United States marshal or deputy United States marshal, or by a person specially appointed for that purpose.

(2)(A) A summons and complaint shall, except as provided in subparagraphs (B) and (C) of this paragraph, be served by any person who is not a party and is not less than 18 years of age.

(B) A summons and complaint shall, at the request of the party seeking service or such party's attorney, be served by a United States marshal or deputy United States marshal, or by a person specially appointed by the court for that purpose, only—

(i) on behalf of a party authorized to proceed in forma pauperis pursuant to Title 28, U.S.C. § 1915, or of a seaman authorized to proceed under Title 28, U.S.C. § 1916,

(ii) on behalf of the United States or an officer or agency of the United States, or

(iii) pursuant to an order issued by the court stating that a United States marshal or deputy United States marshal, or a person specially appointed for that purpose, is required to serve the summons and complaint in order that service be properly effected in that particular action.

(C) A summons and complaint may be served upon a defendant of any class referred to in paragraph (1) or (3) of subdivision (d) of this rule—

(i) pursuant to the law of the State in which the district court is held for the service of summons or other like process upon such defendant in an action brought in the courts of general jurisdiction of that State, or

(ii) by mailing a copy of the summons and of the complaint (by first-class mail, postage prepaid) to the person to be served, together with two copies of a notice and acknowledgment conforming substantially to form 18–A and a return envelope, postage prepaid, addressed to the sender. If no acknowledgment of service under this subdivision of this rule is received by the sender within 20 days after the date of mailing, service of such summons and complaint shall be made under subparagraph (A) or (B) of this paragraph in the manner prescribed by subdivision (d)(1) or (d)(3).

(D) Unless good cause is shown for not doing so the court shall order the payment of the costs of personal service by the person served if such person does not complete and return within 20 days after mailing, the notice and acknowledgment of receipt of summons.

(E) The notice and acknowledgment of receipt of summons and complaint shall be executed under oath or affirmation.

(3) The court shall freely make special appointments to serve summonses and complaints under paragraph (2)(B) of this subdivision of this rule and all other process under paragraph (1) of this subdivision of this rule.

(d) Summons and Complaint: Person to Be Served. The summons and complaint shall be served together. The plaintiff shall furnish the person making service with such copies as are necessary. Service shall be made as follows:

(1) Upon an individual other than an infant or an incompetent person, by delivering a copy of the summons and of the complaint to the individual personally or by leaving copies thereof at the individual's dwelling house or usual place of abode with some person of suitable age and discretion then residing therein or by delivering a copy of the summons and of the complaint to an agent authorized by appointment or by law to receive service of process.

(2) Upon an infant or an incompetent person, by serving the summons and complaint in the manner prescribed by the law of the state in which the service is made for the service of summons or other like process upon any such defendant in an action brought in the courts of general jurisdiction of that state.

(3) Upon a domestic or foreign corporation or upon a partnership or other unincorporated association which is subject to suit under a common name, by delivering a copy of the summons and of the complaint to an officer, a managing or general agent, or to

any other agent authorized by appointment or by law to receive service of process and, if the agent is one authorized by statute to receive service and the statute so requires, by also mailing a copy to the defendant.

(4) Upon the United States, by delivering a copy of the summons and of the complaint to the United States attorney for the district in which the action is brought or to an assistant United States attorney or clerical employee designated by the United States attorney in a writing filed with the clerk of the court and by sending a copy of the summons and of the complaint by registered or certified mail to the Attorney General of the United States at Washington, District of Columbia, and in any action attacking the validity of an order of an officer or agency of the United States not made a party, by also sending a copy of the summons and of the complaint by registered or certified mail to such officer or agency.

(5) Upon an officer or agency of the United States, by serving the United States and by sending a copy of the summons and of the complaint by registered or certified mail to such officer or agency. If the agency is a corporation the copy shall be delivered as provided in paragraph (3) of this subdivision of this rule.

(6) Upon a state or municipal corporation or other governmental organization thereof subject to suit, by delivering a copy of the summons and of the complaint to the chief executive officer thereof or by serving the summons and complaint in the manner prescribed by the law of that state for the service of summons or other like process upon any such defendant.

(e) Summons: Service upon Party Not Inhabitant of or Found Within State. Whenever a statute of the United States or an order of court thereunder provides for service of a summons, or of a notice, or of an order in lieu of summons upon a party not an inhabitant of or found within the state in which the district court is held, service may be made under the circumstances and in the manner prescribed by the statute or order, or, if there is no provision therein prescribing the manner of service, in a manner stated in this rule. Whenever a statute or rule of court of the state in which the district court is held provides (1) for service of a summons, or of a notice, or of an order in lieu of summons upon a party not an inhabitant of or found within the state, or (2) for service upon or notice to such a party to appear and respond or defend in an action by reason of the attachment or garnishment or similar seizure of the party's property located within the state, service may in either case be made under the circumstances and in the manner prescribed in the statute or rule.

(f) Territorial Limits of Effective Service. All process other than a subpoena may be served anywhere within the territorial limits of the state in which the district court is held, and, when authorized by a statute of the United States or by these rules, beyond the territorial limits of that state. In addition, persons who are brought in as parties pursuant to Rule 14, or as additional parties to a pending action or a counterclaim or cross-claim therein pursuant to Rule 19, may be served in the manner stated in paragraphs (1)–(6) of subdivision (d) of this rule at all places outside the state but within the United States that are not more than 100 miles from the place in which the action is commenced, or to which it is assigned or transferred for trial; and persons required to respond to an order of commitment for civil contempt may be served at the same places. A subpoena may be served within the territorial limits provided in Rule 45.

(g) Return. The person serving the process shall make proof of service thereof to the court promptly and in any event within the time during which the person served must respond to the process. If service is made by a person other than a United States marshal or deputy United States marshal, such person shall make affidavit thereof. If service is made under subdivision (c)(2)(C)(ii) of this rule, return shall be made by the sender's filing with the court the acknowledgment received pursuant to such subdivision. Failure to make proof of service does not affect the validity of the service.

(h) Amendment. At any time in its discretion and upon such terms as it deems just, the court may allow any process or proof of service thereof to be amended, unless it clearly appears that material prejudice would result to the substantial rights of the party against whom the process issued.

(i) Alternative Provisions for Service in a Foreign Country.

(1) *Manner.* When the federal or state law referred to in subdivision (e) of this rule authorizes service upon a party not an inhabitant of or found within the state in which the district court is held, and service is to be effected upon the party in a foreign country, it is also sufficient if service of the summons and complaint is made: (A) in the manner prescribed by the law of the foreign country for service in that country in an action in any of its courts of general jurisdiction; or (B) as directed by the foreign authority in response to a letter rogatory, when service in either case is reasonably calculated to give actual notice; or (C) upon an individual, by delivery to the individual personally, and upon a corporation or partnership or association, by delivery to an officer, a managing or general agent; or (D) by any form of mail, requir-

29

ing a signed receipt, to be addressed and dispatched by the clerk of the court to the party to be served; or (E) as directed by order of the court. Service under (C) or (E) above may be made by any person who is not a party and is not less than 18 years of age or who is designated by order of the district court or by the foreign court. On request, the clerk shall deliver the summons to the plaintiff for transmission to the person or the foreign court or officer who will make the service.

(2) *Return.* Proof of service may be made as prescribed by subdivision (g) of this rule, or by the law of the foreign country, or by order of the court. When service is made pursuant to subparagraph (1)(D) of this subdivision, proof of service shall include a receipt signed by the addressee or other evidence of delivery to the addressee satisfactory to the court.

(j) Summons: Time Limit for Service. If a service of the summons and complaint is not made upon a defendant within 120 days after the filing of the complaint and the party on whose behalf such service was required cannot show good cause why such service was not made within that period, the action shall be dismissed as to that defendant without prejudice upon the court's own initiative with notice to such party or upon motion. This subdivision shall not apply to service in a foreign country pursuant to subdivision (i) of this rule.

As amended 1963, 1966, 1980, 1983, 1987.

Rule 5.

SERVICE AND FILING OF PLEADINGS AND OTHER PAPERS

(a) Service: When Required. Except as otherwise provided in these rules, every order required by its terms to be served, every pleading subsequent to the original complaint unless the court otherwise orders because of numerous defendants, every paper relating to discovery required to be served upon a party unless the court otherwise orders, every written motion other than one which may be heard ex parte, and every written notice, appearance, demand, offer of judgment, designation of record on appeal, and similar paper shall be served upon each of the parties. No service need be made on parties in default for failure to appear except that pleadings asserting new or additional claims for relief against them shall be served upon them in the manner provided for service of summons in Rule 4.

In an action begun by seizure of property, in which no person need be or is named as defendant, any service required to be made prior to the filing of an answer, claim, or appearance shall be made upon the person having custody or possession of the property at the time of its seizure.

(b) **Same: How Made.** Whenever under these rules service is required or permitted to be made upon a party represented by an attorney the service shall be made upon the attorney unless service upon the party is ordered by the court. Service upon the attorney or upon a party shall be made by delivering a copy to the attorney or party or by mailing it to the attorney or party at the attorney's or party's last known address or, if no address is known, by leaving it with the clerk of the court. Delivery of a copy within this rule means: handing it to the attorney or to the party; or leaving it at the attorney's or party's office with a clerk or other person in charge thereof; or, if there is no one in charge, leaving it in a conspicuous place therein; or, if the office is closed or the person to be served has no office, leaving it at the person's dwelling house or usual place of abode with some person of suitable age and discretion then residing therein. Service by mail is complete upon mailing.

(c) **Same: Numerous Defendants.** In any action in which there are unusually large numbers of defendants, the court, upon motion or of its own initiative, may order that service of the pleadings of the defendants and replies thereto need not be made as between the defendants and that any cross-claim, counterclaim, or matter constituting an avoidance or affirmative defense contained therein shall be deemed to be denied or avoided by all other parties and that the filing of any such pleading and service thereof upon the plaintiff constitutes due notice of it to the parties. A copy of every such order shall be served upon the parties in such manner and form as the court directs.

(d) **Filing.** All papers after the complaint required to be served upon a party shall be filed with the court either before service or within a reasonable time thereafter, but the court may on motion of a party or on its own initiative order that depositions upon oral examination and interrogatories, requests for documents, requests for admission, and answers and responses thereto not be filed unless on order of the court or for use in the proceeding.

(e) **Filing with the Court Defined.** The filing of pleadings and other papers with the court as required by these rules shall be made by filing them with the clerk of the court, except that the judge may permit the papers to be filed with the judge, in which event the judge shall note thereon the filing date and forthwith transmit them to the office of the clerk.

As amended 1963, 1970, 1980, 1987.

Rule 6.

TIME

(a) **Computation.** In computing any period of time prescribed or allowed by these rules, by the local rules of any district court, by order of court, or by any applicable statute, the day of the act, event, or default from which the designated period of time begins to run shall not be included. The last day of the period so computed shall be included, unless it is a Saturday, a Sunday, or a legal holiday, or, when the act to be done is the filing of a paper in court, a day on which weather or other conditions have made the office of the clerk of the district court inaccessible, in which event the period runs until the end of the next day which is not one of the aforementioned days. When the period of time prescribed or allowed is less than 11 days, intermediate Saturdays, Sundays, and legal holidays shall be excluded in the computation. As used in this rule and in Rule 77(c), "legal holiday" includes New Year's Day, Birthday of Martin Luther King, Jr., Washington's Birthday, Memorial Day, Independence Day, Labor Day, Columbus Day, Veterans Day, Thanksgiving Day, Christmas Day, and any other day appointed as a holiday by the President or the Congress of the United States, or by the state in which the district court is held.

(b) **Enlargement.** When by these rules or by a notice given thereunder or by order of court an act is required or allowed to be done at or within a specified time, the court for cause shown may at any time in its discretion (1) with or without motion or notice order the period enlarged if request therefor is made before the expiration of the period originally prescribed or as extended by a previous order, or (2) upon motion made after the expiration of the specified period permit the act to be done where the failure to act was the result of excusable neglect; but it may not extend the time for taking any action under Rules 50(b) and (c)(2), 52(b), 59(b), (d) and (e), 60(b), and 74(a), except to the extent and under the conditions stated in them.

(c) **Unaffected by Expiration of Term.** Rescinded Feb. 28, 1966, eff. July 1, 1966.

(d) **For Motions—Affidavits.** A written motion, other than one which may be heard ex parte, and notice of the hearing thereof shall be served not later than 5 days before the time specified for the hearing, unless a different period is fixed by these rules or by order of the court. Such an order may for cause shown be made on ex parte application. When a motion is supported by affidavit, the affidavit shall be served with the motion; and, except as otherwise provided in Rule 59(c), opposing affidavits may be served not later than 1 day before the hearing, unless the court permits them to be served at some other time.

(e) Additional Time After Service by Mail. Whenever a party has the right or is required to do some act or take some proceedings within a prescribed period after the service of a notice or other paper upon the party and the notice or paper is served upon the party by mail, 3 days shall be added to the prescribed period.

As amended 1948, 1963, 1966, 1968, 1971, 1983, 1985, 1987.

III. PLEADINGS AND MOTIONS

Rule 7.

PLEADINGS ALLOWED; FORM OF MOTIONS

(a) Pleadings. There shall be a complaint and an answer; a reply to a counterclaim denominated as such; an answer to a cross-claim, if the answer contains a cross-claim; a third-party complaint, if a person who was not an original party is summoned under the provisions of Rule 14; and a third-party answer, if a third-party complaint is served. No other pleading shall be allowed, except that the court may order a reply to an answer or a third-party answer.

(b) Motions and Other Papers.

(1) An application to the court for an order shall be by motion which, unless made during a hearing or trial, shall be made in writing, shall state with particularity the grounds therefor, and shall set forth the relief or order sought. The requirement of writing is fulfilled if the motion is stated in a written notice of the hearing of the motion.

(2) The rules applicable to captions and other matters of form of pleadings apply to all motions and other papers provided for by these rules.

(3) All motions shall be signed in accordance with Rule 11.

(c) Demurrers, Pleas, etc., Abolished. Demurrers, pleas, and exceptions for insufficiency of a pleading shall not be used.

As amended 1948, 1963, 1983.

Rule 8.

GENERAL RULES OF PLEADING

(a) Claims for Relief. A pleading which sets forth a claim for relief, whether an original claim, counterclaim, cross-claim, or third-party claim, shall contain (1) a short and plain statement of the grounds upon which the court's jurisdiction depends, unless the court already has jurisdiction and the claim needs no new grounds of jurisdiction to support it, (2) a short and plain statement of the claim showing that the pleader is entitled to relief, and (3) a demand for judgment for the relief the pleader seeks. Relief in the alternative or of several different types may be demanded.

(b) Defenses; Form of Denials. A party shall state in short and plain terms the party's defenses to each claim asserted and shall admit or deny the averments upon which the adverse party relies. If a party is without knowledge or information sufficient to form a belief as to the truth of an averment, the party shall so state and this has the effect of a denial. Denials shall fairly meet the substance of the averments denied. When a pleader intends in good faith to deny only a part or a qualification of an averment, the pleader shall specify so much of it as is true and material and shall deny only the remainder. Unless the pleader intends in good faith to controvert all the averments of the preceding pleading, the pleader may make denials as specific denials of designated averments or paragraphs or may generally deny all the averments except such designated averments or paragraphs as the pleader expressly admits; but, when the pleader does so intend to controvert all its averments, including averments of the grounds upon which the court's jurisdiction depends, the pleader may do so by general denial subject to the obligations set forth in Rule 11.

(c) Affirmative Defenses. In pleading to a preceding pleading, a party shall set forth affirmatively accord and satisfaction, arbitration and award, assumption of risk, contributory negligence, discharge in bankruptcy, duress, estoppel, failure of consideration, fraud, illegality, injury by fellow servant, laches, license, payment, release, res judicata, statute of frauds, statute of limitations, waiver, and any other matter constituting an avoidance or affirmative defense. When a party has mistakenly designated a defense as a counterclaim or a counterclaim as a defense, the court on terms, if justice so requires, shall treat the pleading as if there had been a proper designation.

(d) Effect of Failure to Deny. Averments in a pleading to which a responsive pleading is required, other than those as to the amount of damage, are admitted when not denied in the responsive pleading. Averments in a pleading to which no responsive pleading is required or permitted shall be taken as denied or avoided.

(e) Pleading to Be Concise and Direct; Consistency.

(1) Each averment of a pleading shall be simple, concise, and direct. No technical forms of pleading or motions are required.

(2) A party may set forth two or more statements of a claim or defense alternately or hypothetically, either in one count or defense or in separate counts or defenses. When two or more statements are made in the alternative and one of them if made independently would be sufficient, the pleading is not made insufficient by the insufficiency of one or more of the alternative statements. A party may also state as many separate claims or defenses as the party has regardless of consistency and whether based on legal, equitable, or maritime grounds. All statements shall be made subject to the obligations set forth in Rule 11.

(f) Construction of Pleadings. All pleadings shall be so construed as to do substantial justice.

As amended 1966, 1987.

Rule 9.

PLEADING SPECIAL MATTERS

(a) Capacity. It is not necessary to aver the capacity of a party to sue or be sued or the authority of a party to sue or be sued in a representative capacity or the legal existence of an organized association of persons that is made a party, except to the extent required to show the jurisdiction of the court. When a party desires to raise an issue as to the legal existence of any party or the capacity of any party to sue or be sued or the authority of a party to sue or be sued in a representative capacity, the party desiring to raise the issue shall do so by specific negative averment, which shall include such supporting particulars as are peculiarly within the pleader's knowledge.

(b) Fraud, Mistake, Condition of the Mind. In all averments of fraud or mistake, the circumstances constituting fraud or mistake shall be stated with particularity. Malice, intent, knowledge, and other condition of mind of a person may be averred generally.

(c) Conditions Precedent. In pleading the performance or occurrence of conditions precedent, it is sufficient to aver generally that all conditions precedent have been performed or have occurred. A denial of performance or occurrence shall be made specifically and with particularity.

(d) Official Document or Act. In pleading an official document or official act it is sufficient to aver that the document was issued or the act done in compliance with law.

(e) Judgment. In pleading a judgment or decision of a domestic or foreign court, judicial or quasi-judicial tribunal, or of a board or officer, it is sufficient to aver the judgment or decision without setting forth matter showing jurisdiction to render it.

(f) Time and Place. For the purpose of testing the sufficiency of a pleading, averments of time and place are material and shall be considered like all other averments of material matter.

(g) Special Damage. When items of special damage are claimed, they shall be specifically stated.

(h) Admiralty and Maritime Claims. A pleading or count setting forth a claim for relief within the admiralty and maritime jurisdiction that is also within the jurisdiction of the district court on some other ground may contain a statement identifying the claim as an admiralty or maritime claim for the purposes of Rules 14(c), 38(e), 82, and the Supplemental Rules for Certain Admiralty and Maritime Claims. If the claim is cognizable only in admiralty, it is an admiralty or maritime claim for those purposes whether so identified or not. The amendment of a pleading to add or withdraw an identifying statement is governed by the principles of Rule 15. The reference in Title 28, U.S.C., § 1292(a)(3), to admiralty cases shall be construed to mean admiralty and maritime claims within the meaning of this subdivision (h).

As amended 1966, 1968, 1970, 1987.

Rule 10.

FORM OF PLEADINGS

(a) Caption; Names of Parties. Every pleading shall contain a caption setting forth the name of the court, the title of the action, the file number, and a designation as in Rule 7(a). In the complaint the title of the action shall include the names of all the parties, but in other pleadings it is sufficient to state the name of the first party on each side with an appropriate indication of other parties.

(b) Paragraphs; Separate Statements. All averments of claim or defense shall be made in numbered paragraphs, the contents of each of which shall be limited as far as practicable to a statement of a single set of circumstances; and a paragraph may be referred to by number in all succeeding pleadings. Each claim founded upon a separate transaction or occurrence and each defense other than denials shall be stated in a separate count or defense whenever a separation facilitates the clear presentation of the matters set forth.

(c) Adoption by Reference; Exhibits. Statements in a pleading may be adopted by reference in a different part of the same pleading or in another pleading or in any motion. A copy of any written instrument which is an exhibit to a pleading is a part thereof for all purposes.

Rule 11.

SIGNING OF PLEADINGS, MOTIONS, AND OTHER PAPERS; SANCTIONS

Every pleading, motion, and other paper of a party represented by an attorney shall be signed by at least one attorney of record in the attorney's individual name, whose address shall be stated. A party who is not represented by an attorney shall sign the party's pleading, motion, or other paper and state the party's address. Except when otherwise specifically provided by rule or statute, pleadings need not be verified or accompanied by affidavit. The rule in equity that the averments of an answer under oath must be overcome by the testimony of two witnesses or of one witness sustained by corroborating circumstances is abolished. The signature of an attorney or party constitutes a certificate by the signer that the signer has read the pleading, motion, or other paper; that to the best of the signer's knowledge, information, and belief formed after reasonable inquiry it is well grounded in fact and is warranted by existing law or a good faith argument for the extension, modification, or reversal of existing law, and that it is not interposed for any improper purpose, such as to harass or to cause unnecessary delay or needless increase in the cost of litigation. If a pleading, motion, or other paper is not signed, it shall be stricken unless it is signed promptly after the omission is called to the attention of the pleader or movant. If a pleading, motion, or other paper is signed in violation of this rule, the court, upon motion or upon its own initiative, shall impose upon the person who signed it, a represented party, or both, an appropriate sanction, which may include an order to pay to the other party or parties the amount of the reasonable expenses incurred because of the filing of the pleading, motion, or other paper, including a reasonable attorney's fee.

As amended 1983, 1987.

Rule 12.

DEFENSES AND OBJECTIONS—WHEN AND HOW PRE-SENTED—BY PLEADING OR MOTION—MOTION FOR JUDGMENT ON THE PLEADINGS

(a) **When Presented.** A defendant shall serve an answer within 20 days after the service of the summons and complaint upon that defendant, except when service is made under Rule 4(e) and a different time is prescribed in the order of court under the statute of the United States or in the statute or rule of court of the state. A party served with a pleading stating a cross-claim against that party shall serve an answer thereto within 20 days after the service upon that party. The plaintiff shall serve a reply to a counterclaim in the answer within 20 days after service of the answer or, if a reply is ordered by the court, within 20 days after service of the order, unless the order otherwise directs. The United States or an officer or agency thereof shall serve an answer to the complaint or to a cross-claim, or a reply to a counterclaim, within 60 days after the service upon the United States attorney of the pleading in which the claim is asserted. The service of a motion permitted under this rule alters these periods of time as follows, unless a different time is fixed by order of the court: (1) if the court denies the motion or postpones its disposition until the trial on the merits, the responsive pleading shall be served within 10 days after notice of the court's action; (2) if the court grants a motion for a more definite statement the responsive pleading shall be served within 10 days after the service of the more definite statement.

(b) **How Presented.** Every defense, in law or fact, to a claim for relief in any pleading, whether a claim, counterclaim, cross-claim, or third-party claim, shall be asserted in the responsive pleading thereto if one is required, except that the following defenses may at the option of the pleader be made by motion: (1) lack of jurisdiction over the subject matter, (2) lack of jurisdiction over the person, (3) improper venue, (4) insufficiency of process, (5) insufficiency of service of process, (6) failure to state a claim upon which relief can be granted, (7) failure to join a party under Rule 19. A motion making any of these defenses shall be made before pleading if a further pleading is permitted. No defense or objection is waived by being joined with one or more other defenses or objections in a responsive pleading or motion. If a pleading sets forth a claim for relief to which the adverse party is not required to serve a responsive pleading, the adverse party may assert at the trial any defense in law or fact to that claim for relief. If, on a

38

motion asserting the defense numbered (6) to dismiss for failure of the pleading to state a claim upon which relief can be granted, matters outside the pleading are presented to and not excluded by the court, the motion shall be treated as one for summary judgment and disposed of as provided in Rule 56, and all parties shall be given reasonable opportunity to present all material made pertinent to such a motion by Rule 56.

(c) Motion for Judgment on the Pleadings. After the pleadings are closed but within such time as not to delay the trial, any party may move for judgment on the pleadings. If, on a motion for judgment on the pleadings, matters outside the pleadings are presented to and not excluded by the court, the motion shall be treated as one for summary judgment and disposed of as provided in Rule 56, and all parties shall be given reasonable opportunity to present all material made pertinent to such a motion by Rule 56.

(d) Preliminary Hearings. The defenses specifically enumerated (1)–(7) in subdivision (b) of this rule, whether made in a pleading or by motion, and the motion for judgment mentioned in subdivision (c) of this rule shall be heard and determined before trial on application of any party, unless the court orders that the hearing and determination thereof be deferred until the trial.

(e) Motion for More Definite Statement. If a pleading to which a responsive pleading is permitted is so vague or ambiguous that a party cannot reasonably be required to frame a responsive pleading, the party may move for a more definite statement before interposing a responsive pleading. The motion shall point out the defects complained of and the details desired. If the motion is granted and the order of the court is not obeyed within 10 days after notice of the order or within such other time as the court may fix, the court may strike the pleading to which the motion was directed or make such order as it deems just.

(f) Motion to Strike. Upon motion made by a party before responding to a pleading or, if no responsive pleading is permitted by these rules, upon motion made by a party within 20 days after the service of the pleading upon the party or upon the court's own initiative at any time, the court may order stricken from any pleading any insufficient defense or any redundant, immaterial, impertinent, or scandalous matter.

(g) Consolidation of Defenses in Motion. A party who makes a motion under this rule may join with it any other motions herein provided for and then available to the party. If a party makes a motion under this rule but omits therefrom any defense or objection then available to the party which this rule permits to be raised by motion, the party shall not thereafter make a motion based on the defense or objection so omitted, except a motion as provided in subdivision (h)(2) hereof on any of the grounds there stated.

(h) Waiver or Preservation of Certain Defenses.

(1) A defense of lack of jurisdiction over the person, improper venue, insufficiency of process, or insufficiency of service of process is waived (A) if omitted from a motion in the circumstances described in subdivision (g), or (B) if it is neither made by motion under this rule nor included in a responsive pleading or an amendment thereof permitted by Rule 15(a) to be made as a matter of course.

(2) A defense of failure to state a claim upon which relief can be granted, a defense of failure to join a party indispensable under Rule 19, and an objection of failure to state a legal defense to a claim may be made in any pleading permitted or ordered under Rule 7(a), or by motion for judgment on the pleadings, or at the trial on the merits.

(3) Whenever it appears by suggestion of the parties or otherwise that the court lacks jurisdiction of the subject matter, the court shall dismiss the action.

As amended 1948, 1963, 1966, 1987.

Rule 13.

COUNTERCLAIM AND CROSS–CLAIM

(a) **Compulsory Counterclaims.** A pleading shall state as a counterclaim any claim which at the time of serving the pleading the pleader has against any opposing party, if it arises out of the transaction or occurrence that is the subject matter of the opposing party's claim and does not require for its adjudication the presence of third parties of whom the court cannot acquire jurisdiction. But the pleader need not state the claim if (1) at the time the action was commenced the claim was the subject of another pending action, or (2) the opposing party brought suit upon the claim by attachment or other process by which the court did not acquire jurisdiction to render a personal judgment on that claim, and the pleader is not stating any counterclaim under this Rule 13.

(b) **Permissive Counterclaims.** A pleading may state as a counterclaim any claim against an opposing party not arising out of the transaction or occurrence that is the subject matter of the opposing party's claim.

(c) **Counterclaim Exceeding Opposing Claim.** A counterclaim may or may not diminish or defeat the recovery sought by the opposing party. It may claim relief exceeding in amount or different in kind from that sought in the pleading of the opposing party.

(d) Counterclaim Against the United States. These rules shall not be construed to enlarge beyond the limits now fixed by law the right to assert counterclaims or to claim credits against the United States or an officer or agency thereof.

(e) Counterclaim Maturing or Acquired After Pleading. A claim which either matured or was acquired by the pleader after serving a pleading may, with the permission of the court, be presented as a counterclaim by supplemental pleading.

(f) Omitted Counterclaim. When a pleader fails to set up a counterclaim through oversight, inadvertence, or excusable neglect, or when justice requires, the pleader may by leave of court set up the counterclaim by amendment.

(g) Cross-Claim Against Co-Party. A pleading may state as a cross-claim any claim by one party against a co-party arising out of the transaction or occurrence that is the subject matter either of the original action or of a counterclaim therein or relating to any property that is the subject matter of the original action. Such cross-claim may include a claim that the party against whom it is asserted is or may be liable to the cross-claimant for all or part of a claim asserted in the action against the cross-claimant.

(h) Joinder of Additional Parties. Persons other than those made parties to the original action may be made parties to a counterclaim or cross-claim in accordance with the provisions of Rules 19 and 20.

(i) Separate Trials; Separate Judgments. If the court orders separate trials as provided in Rule 42(b), judgment on a counterclaim or cross-claim may be rendered in accordance with the terms of Rule 54(b) when the court has jurisdiction so to do, even if the claims of the opposing party have been dismissed or otherwise disposed of.

As amended 1948, 1963, 1966, 1987.

Rule 14.

THIRD–PARTY PRACTICE

(a) When Defendant May Bring in Third Party. At any time after commencement of the action a defending party, as a third-party plaintiff, may cause a summons and complaint to be served upon a person not a party to the action who is or may be liable to the third-party plaintiff for all or part of the plaintiff's claim against the third-party plaintiff(2)The third-party plaintiff need not obtain leave to make the service if the third-party plaintiff files the third-party complaint not later than 10 days after serving the original answer.(3)Otherwise the third-party plaintiff must obtain leave on motion upon notice to all parties to the action.(4)The person served with the summons and third-party complaint, hereinafter called the third-party defendant, shall make any defenses to the third-party plaintiff's claim as provided in Rule 12 and any counterclaims against the third-party plaintiff and cross-claims against other third-party defendants as provided in Rule 13.(5)The third-party defendant may assert against the plaintiff any defenses which the third-party plaintiff has to the plaintiff's claim(6)The third-party defendant may also assert any claim against the plaintiff arising out of the transaction or occurrence that is the subject matter of the plaintiff's claim against the third-party plaintiff.(7)The plaintiff may assert any claim against the third-party defendant arising out of the transaction or occurrence that is the subject matter of the plaintiff's claim against the third-party plaintiff, and the third-party defendant thereupon shall assert any defenses as provided in Rule 12 and any counterclaims and cross-claims as provided in Rule 13.(8)Any party may move to strike the third-party claim, or for its severance or separate trial.(9)A third-party defendant may proceed under this rule against any person not a party to the action who is or may be liable to the third-party defendant for all or part of the claim made in the action against the third-party defendant.(10)The third-party complaint, if within the admiralty and maritime jurisdiction, may be in rem against a vessel, cargo, or other property subject to admiralty or maritime process in rem, in which case references in this rule to the summons include the warrant of arrest, and references to the third-party plaintiff or defendant include, where appropriate, the claimant of the property arrested.

(b) **When Plaintiff May Bring in Third Party.** When a counterclaim is asserted against a plaintiff, the plaintiff may cause a third party to be brought in under circumstances which under this rule would entitle a defendant to do so.

(c) **Admiralty and Maritime Claims.** When a plaintiff asserts an admiralty or maritime claim within the meaning of Rule 9(h), the defendant or claimant, as a third-party plaintiff, may bring in a third-party defendant who may be wholly or partly liable, either to the plaintiff or to the third-party plaintiff, by way of remedy over, contribution, or otherwise on account of the same transaction, occurrence, or series of transactions or occurrences. In such a case the third-party plaintiff may also demand judgment against the third-party defendant in favor of the plaintiff, in which event the third-party defendant shall make any defenses to the claim of the plaintiff as well as to that of the third-party plaintiff in the manner provided in Rule 12 and the action shall proceed as if the plaintiff had commenced it against the third-party defendant as well as the third-party plaintiff.

As amended 1948, 1963, 1966, 1987.

Rule 15.

AMENDED AND SUPPLEMENTAL PLEADINGS

(a) **Amendments.** A party may amend the party's pleading once as a matter of course at any time before a responsive pleading is served or, if the pleading is one to which no responsive pleading is permitted and the action has not been placed upon the trial calendar, the party may so amend it at any time within 20 days after it is served. Otherwise a party may amend the party's pleading only by leave of court or by written consent of the adverse party; and leave shall be freely given when justice so requires. A party shall plead in response to an amended pleading within the time remaining for response to the original pleading or within 10 days after service of the amended pleading, whichever period may be the longer, unless the court otherwise orders.

(b) **Amendments to Conform to the Evidence.** When issues not raised by the pleadings are tried by express or implied consent of the parties, they shall be treated in all respects as if they had been raised in the pleadings. Such amendment of the pleadings as may be necessary to cause them to conform to the evidence and to raise these issues may be made upon motion of any party at any time, even after judgment; but failure so to amend does not affect the result of the trial of these issues. If evidence is objected to at the trial on the ground that it is not within the issues made by the pleadings, the court may allow the pleadings to be amended and shall do so freely when the presentation of the merits of the action will be subserved thereby and the objecting party fails to satisfy the court that the admission of such evidence would prejudice the party in maintaining the party's action or defense upon the merits. The court may grant a continuance to enable the objecting party to meet such evidence.

(c) **Relation Back of Amendments.** Whenever the claim or defense asserted in the amended pleading arose out of the conduct, transaction, or occurrence set forth or attempted to be set forth in the original pleading, the amendment relates back to the date of the original pleading. An amendment changing the party against whom a claim is asserted relates back if the foregoing provision is satisfied and, within the period provided by law for commencing the action against the party to be brought in by amendment, that

43

party (1) has received such notice of the institution of the action that the party will not be prejudiced in maintaining a defense on the merits, and (2) knew or should have known that, but for a mistake concerning the identity of the proper party, the action would have been brought against the party.

The delivery or mailing of process to the United States Attorney, or the United States Attorney's designee, or the Attorney General of the United States, or an agency or officer who would have been a proper defendant if named, satisfies the requirement of clauses (1) and (2) hereof with respect to the United States or any agency or officer thereof to be brought into the action as a defendant.

(d) Supplemental Pleadings.   Upon motion of a party the court may, upon reasonable notice and upon such terms as are just, permit the party to serve a supplemental pleading setting forth transactions or occurrences or events which have happened since the date of the pleading sought to be supplemented.   Permission may be granted even though the original pleading is defective in its statement of a claim for relief or defense.   If the court deems it advisable that the adverse party plead to the supplemental pleading, it shall so order, specifying the time therefor.

As amended 1963, 1966, 1987.

Rule 16.

PRETRIAL CONFERENCES; SCHEDULING; MANAGEMENT

(a) Pretrial Conferences; Objectives.   In any action, the court may in its discretion direct the attorneys for the parties and any unrepresented parties to appear before it for a conference or conferences before trial for such purposes as

(1) expediting the disposition of the action;

(2) establishing early and continuing control so that the case will not be protracted because of lack of management;

(3) discouraging wasteful pretrial activities;

(4) improving the quality of the trial through more thorough preparation, and;

(5) facilitating the settlement of the case.

(b) Scheduling and Planning.   Except in categories of actions exempted by district court rule as inappropriate, the judge, or a magistrate when authorized by district court rule, shall, after consulting with the attorneys for the parties and any unrepresented parties, by a scheduling conference, telephone, mail, or other suitable means, enter a scheduling order that limits the time

(1) to join other parties and to amend the pleadings;

(2) to file and hear motions; and

(3) to complete discovery.

The scheduling order also may include

(4) the date or dates for conferences before trial, a final pretrial conference, and trial; and

(5) any other matters appropriate in the circumstances of the case.

The order shall issue as soon as practicable but in no event more than 120 days after filing of the complaint. A schedule shall not be modified except by leave of the judge or a magistrate when authorized by district court rule upon a showing of good cause.

(c) Subjects to Be Discussed at Pretrial Conferences. The participants at any conference under this rule may consider and take action with respect to

(1) the formulation and simplification of the issues, including the elimination of frivolous claims or defenses;

(2) the necessity or desirability of amendments to the pleadings;

(3) the possibility of obtaining admissions of fact and of documents which will avoid unnecessary proof, stipulations regarding the authenticity of documents, and advance rulings from the court on the admissibility of evidence;

(4) the avoidance of unnecessary proof and of cumulative evidence;

(5) the identification of witnesses and documents, the need and schedule for filing and exchanging pretrial briefs, and the date or dates for further conferences and for trial;

(6) the advisability of referring matters to a magistrate or master;

(7) the possibility of settlement or the use of extrajudicial procedures to resolve the dispute;

(8) the form and substance of the pretrial order;

(9) the disposition of pending motions;

(10) the need for adopting special procedures for managing potentially difficult or protracted actions that may involve complex issues, multiple parties, difficult legal questions, or unusual proof problems; and

(11) such other matters as may aid in the disposition of the action.

At least one of the attorneys for each party participating in any conference before trial shall have authority to enter into stipulations and to make admissions regarding all matters that the participants may reasonably anticipate may be discussed.

(d) Final Pretrial Conference. Any final pretrial conference shall be held as close to the time of trial as reasonable under the circumstances. The participants at any such conference shall formulate a plan for trial, including a program for facilitating the admission of evidence. The conference shall be attended by at least one of the attorneys who will conduct the trial for each of the parties and by any unrepresented parties.

(e) Pretrial Orders. After any conference held pursuant to this rule, an order shall be entered reciting the action taken. This order shall control the subsequent course of the action unless modified by a subsequent order. The order following a final pretrial conference shall be modified only to prevent manifest injustice.

(f) Sanctions. If a party or party's attorney fails to obey a scheduling or pretrial order, or if no appearance is made on behalf of a party at a scheduling or pretrial conference, or if a party or party's attorney is substantially unprepared to participate in the conference, or if a party or party's attorney fails to participate in good faith, the judge, upon motion or the judge's own initiative, may make such orders with regard thereto as are just, and among others any of the orders provided in Rule 37(b)(2)(B), (C), (D). In lieu of or in addition to any other sanction, the judge shall require the party or the attorney representing the party or both to pay the reasonable expenses incurred because of any noncompliance with this rule, including attorney's fees, unless the judge finds that the noncompliance was substantially justified or that other circumstances make an award of expenses unjust.

As amended 1983, 1987.

IV. PARTIES

Rule 17.

PARTIES PLAINTIFF AND DEFENDANT; CAPACITY

(a) Real Party in Interest. Every action shall be prosecuted in the name of the real party in interest. An executor, administrator, guardian, bailee, trustee of an express trust, a party with whom or in whose name a contract has been made for the benefit of another, or a party authorized by statute may sue in that person's own name without joining the party for whose benefit the action is brought; and when a statute of the United States so provides, an action for the use or benefit of another shall be brought in the name of the United States. No action shall be dismissed on the ground that it is not prosecuted in the name of the real party in interest until a reasonable time has been allowed after objection for ratification of commencement of the action by, or joinder or substitution of, the real party in interest; and such ratification, joinder, or substitution shall have the same effect as if the action had been commenced in the name of the real party in interest.

(b) **Capacity to Sue or Be Sued.** The capacity of an individual, other than one acting in a representative capacity, to sue or be sued shall be determined by the law of the individual's domicile. The capacity of a corporation to sue or be sued shall be determined by the law under which it was organized. In all other cases capacity to sue or be sued shall be determined by the law of the state in which the district court is held, except (1) that a partnership or other unincorporated association, which has no such capacity by the law of such state, may sue or be sued in its common name for the purpose of enforcing for or against it a substantive right existing under the Constitution or laws of the United States, and (2) that the capacity of a receiver appointed by a court of the United States to sue or be sued in a court of the United States is governed by Title 28, U.S.C. §§ 754 and 959(a).

(c) **Infants or Incompetent Persons.** Whenever an infant or incompetent person has a representative, such as a general guardian, committee, conservator, or other like fiduciary, the representative may sue or defend on behalf of the infant or incompetent person. An infant or incompetent person who does not have a duly appointed representative may sue by a next friend or by a guardian ad litem. The court shall appoint a guardian ad litem for an infant or incompetent person not otherwise represented in an action or shall make such other order as it deems proper for the protection of the infant or incompetent person.

As amended 1948, 1949, 1966, 1987, 1988.

Rule 18.

JOINDER OF CLAIMS AND REMEDIES

(a) **Joinder of Claims.** A party asserting a claim to relief as an original claim, counterclaim, cross-claim, or third-party claim, may join, either as independent or as alternate claims, as many claims, legal, equitable, or maritime, as the party has against an opposing party.

(b) Joinder of Remedies; Fraudulent Conveyances. Whenever a claim is one heretofore cognizable only after another claim has been prosecuted to a conclusion, the two claims may be joined in a single action; but the court shall grant relief in that action only in accordance with the relative substantive rights of the parties. In particular, a plaintiff may state a claim for money and a claim to have set aside a conveyance fraudulent as to that plaintiff, without first having obtained a judgment establishing the claim for money.

As amended 1966, 1987.

Rule 19.

JOINDER OF PERSONS NEEDED FOR JUST ADJUDICATION

(a) Persons to Be Joined if Feasible. A person who is subject to service of process and whose joinder will not deprive the court of jurisdiction over the subject matter of the action shall be joined as a party in the action if (1) in the person's absence complete relief cannot be accorded among those already parties, or (2) the person claims an interest relating to the subject of the action and is so situated that the disposition of the action in the person's absence may (i) as a practical matter impair or impede the person's ability to protect that interest or (ii) leave any of the persons already parties subject to a substantial risk of incurring double, multiple, or otherwise inconsistent obligations by reason of the claimed interest. If the person has not been so joined, the court shall order that the person be made a party. If the person should join as a plaintiff but refuses to do so, the person may be made a defendant, or, in a proper case, an involuntary plaintiff. If the joined party objects to venue and joinder of that party would render the venue of the action improper, that party shall be dismissed from the action.

(b) Determination by Court Whenever Joinder Not Feasible. If a person as described in subdivision (a)(1)–(2) hereof cannot be made a party, the court shall determine whether in equity and good conscience the action should proceed among the parties before it, or should be dismissed, the absent person being thus regarded as indispensable. The factors to be considered by the court include: first, to what extent a judgment rendered in the person's absence might be prejudicial to the person or those already parties; second, the extent to which, by protective provisions in the judgment, by the shaping of relief, or other measures, the prejudice can be lessened or avoided; third, whether a judgment rendered in the person's absence will be adequate; fourth, whether the plaintiff will have an adequate remedy if the action is dismissed for nonjoinder.

(c) Pleading Reasons for Nonjoinder. A pleading asserting a claim for relief shall state the names, if known to the pleader, of any persons as described in subdivision (a)(1)–(2) hereof who are not joined, and the reasons why they are not joined.

(d) Exception of Class Actions. This rule is subject to the provisions of Rule 23.

As amended 1966, 1987.

Rule 20.

PERMISSIVE JOINDER OF PARTIES

(a) Permissive Joinder. All persons may join in one action as plaintiffs if they assert any right to relief jointly, severally, or in the alternative in respect of or arising out of the same transaction, occurrence, or series of transactions or occurrences and if any question of law or fact common to all these persons will arise in the action. All persons (and any vessel, cargo or other property subject to admiralty process in rem) may be joined in one action as defendants if there is asserted against them jointly, severally, or in the alternative, any right to relief in respect of or arising out of the same transaction, occurrence, or series of transactions or occurrences and if any question of law or fact common to all defendants will arise in the action. A plaintiff or defendant need not be interested in obtaining or defending against all the relief demanded. Judgment may be given for one or more of the plaintiffs according to their respective rights to relief, and against one or more defendants according to their respective liabilities.

(b) Separate Trials. The court may make such orders as will prevent a party from being embarrassed, delayed, or put to expense by the inclusion of a party against whom the party asserts no claim and who asserts no claim against the party, and may order separate trials or make other orders to prevent delay or prejudice.

As amended 1966, 1987.

Rule 21.

MISJOINDER AND NON–JOINDER OF PARTIES

Misjoinder of parties is not ground for dismissal of an action. Parties may be dropped or added by order of the court on motion of any party or of its own initiative at any stage of the action and on such terms as are just. Any claim against a party may be severed and proceeded with separately.

Rule 22.

INTERPLEADER

(1) Persons having claims against the plaintiff may be joined as defendants and required to interplead when their claims are such that the plaintiff is or may be exposed to double or multiple liability. It is not ground for objection to the joinder that the claims of the several claimants or the titles on which their claims depend do not have a common origin or are not identical but are adverse to and independent of one another, or that the plaintiff avers that the plaintiff is not liable in whole or in part to any or all of the claimants. A defendant exposed to similar liability may obtain such interpleader by way of cross-claim or counterclaim. The provisions of this rule supplement and do not in any way limit the joinder of parties permitted in Rule 20.

(2) The remedy herein provided is in addition to and in no way supersedes or limits the remedy provided by Title 28, U.S.C. §§ 1335, 1397, and 2361. Actions under those provisions shall be conducted in accordance with these rules.

As amended 1949, 1987.

Rule 23.

CLASS ACTIONS

(a) Prerequisites to a Class Action. One or more members of a class may sue or be sued as representative parties on behalf of all only if (1) the class is so numerous that joinder of all members is impracticable, (2) there are questions of law or fact common to the class, (3) the claims or defenses of the representative parties are typical of the claims or defenses of the class, and (4) the representative parties will fairly and adequately protect the interests of the class.

(b) Class Actions Maintainable. An action may be maintained as a class action if the prerequisites of subdivision (a) are satisfied, and in addition:

(1) the prosecution of separate actions by or against individual members of the class would create a risk of

(A) inconsistent or varying adjudications with respect to individual members of the class which would establish incompatible standards of conduct for the party opposing the class, or

(B) adjudications with respect to individual members of the class which would as a practical matter be dispositive of the interests of the other members not parties to the adjudications or substantially impair or impede their ability to protect their interests; or

(2) the party opposing the class has acted or refused to act on grounds generally applicable to the class, thereby making appropriate final injunctive relief or corresponding declaratory relief with respect to the class as a whole; or

(3) the court finds that the questions of law or fact common to the members of the class predominate over any questions affecting only individual members, and that a class action is superior to other available methods for the fair and efficient adjudication of the controversy. The matters pertinent to the findings include: (A) the interest of members of the class in individually controlling the prosecution or defense of separate actions; (B) the extent and nature of any litigation concerning the controversy already commenced by or against members of the class; (C) the desirability or undesirability of concentrating the litigation of the claims in the particular forum; (D) the difficulties likely to be encountered in the management of a class action.

(c) Determination by Order Whether Class Action to Be Maintained; Notice; Judgment; Actions Conducted Partially as Class Actions.

(1) As soon as practicable after the commencement of an action brought as a class action, the court shall determine by order whether it is to be so maintained. An order under this subdivision may be conditional, and may be altered or amended before the decision on the merits.

(2) In any class action maintained under subdivision (b)(3), the court shall direct to the members of the class the best notice practicable under the circumstances, including individual notice to all members who can be identified through reasonable effort. The notice shall advise each member that (A) the court will exclude the member from the class if the member so requests by a specified date; (B) the judgment, whether favorable or not, will include all members who do not request exclusion; and (C) any member who does not request exclusion may, if the member desires, enter an appearance through counsel.

(3) The judgment in an action maintained as a class action under subdivision (b)(1) or (b)(2), whether or not favorable to the class, shall include and describe those whom the court finds to be members of the class. The judgment in an action maintained as a class action under subdivision (b)(3), whether or not favorable to the class, shall include and specify or describe those to whom the

notice provided in subdivision (c)(2) was directed, and who have not requested exclusion, and whom the court finds to be members of the class.

(4) When appropriate (A) an action may be brought or maintained as a class action with respect to particular issues, or (B) a class may be divided into subclasses and each subclass treated as a class, and the provisions of this rule shall then be construed and applied accordingly.

(d) Orders in Conduct of Actions. In the conduct of actions to which this rule applies, the court may make appropriate orders: (1) determining the course of proceedings or prescribing measures to prevent undue repetition or complication in the presentation of evidence or argument; (2) requiring, for the protection of the members of the class or otherwise for the fair conduct of the action, that notice be given in such manner as the court may direct to some or all of the members of any step in the action, or of the proposed extent of the judgment, or of the opportunity of members to signify whether they consider the representation fair and adequate, to intervene and present claims or defenses, or otherwise to come into the action; (3) imposing conditions on the representative parties or on intervenors; (4) requiring that the pleadings be amended to eliminate therefrom allegations as to representation of absent persons, and that the action proceed accordingly; (5) dealing with similar procedural matters. The orders may be combined with an order under Rule 16, and may be altered or amended as may be desirable from time to time.

(e) Dismissal or Compromise. A class action shall not be dismissed or compromised without the approval of the court, and notice of the proposed dismissal or compromise shall be given to all members of the class in such manner as the court directs.

As amended 1966, 1987.

Rule 23.1.

DERIVATIVE ACTIONS BY SHAREHOLDERS

In a derivative action brought by one or more shareholders or members to enforce a right of a corporation or of an unincorporated association, the corporation or association having failed to enforce a right which may properly be asserted by it, the complaint shall be verified and shall allege (1) that the plaintiff was a shareholder or member at the time of the transaction of which the plaintiff complains or that the plaintiff's share or membership thereafter devolved on the plaintiff by operation of law, and (2) that the action is not a collusive one to confer jurisdiction on a court of the United States which it would not otherwise have. The complaint shall also allege with particularity the efforts, if any, made by the plaintiff to obtain the action the plaintiff desires from the directors or comparable authority and, if necessary, from the shareholders or members, and the reasons for the plaintiff's failure to obtain the action or for not making the effort. The derivative action may not be maintained if it appears that the plaintiff does not fairly and adequately represent the interests of the shareholders or members similarly situated in enforcing the right of the corporation or association. The action shall not be dismissed or compromised without the approval of the court, and notice of the proposed dismissal or compromise shall be given to shareholders or members in such manner as the court directs.

Added 1966; as amended 1987.

Rule 23.2.

ACTIONS RELATING TO UNINCORPORATED ASSOCIATIONS

An action brought by or against the members of an unincorporated association as a class by naming certain members as representative parties may be maintained only if it appears that the representative parties will fairly and adequately protect the interests of the association and its members. In the conduct of the action the court may make appropriate orders corresponding with those described in Rule 23(d), and the procedure for dismissal or compromise of the action shall correspond with that provided in Rule 23(e).

Added 1966.

Rule 24.

INTERVENTION

(a) **Intervention of Right.** Upon timely application anyone shall be permitted to intervene in an action: (1) when a statute of the United States confers an unconditional right to intervene; or (2) when the applicant claims an interest relating to the property or transaction which is the subject of the action and the applicant is so situated that the disposition of the action may as a practical matter impair or impede the applicant's ability to protect that interest, unless the applicant's interest is adequately represented by existing parties.

(b) **Permissive Intervention.** Upon timely application anyone may be permitted to intervene in an action: (1) when a statute of the United States confers a conditional right to intervene; or (2) when an applicant's claim or defense and the main action have a question of law or fact in common.   When a party to an action relies for ground of claim or defense upon any statute or executive order administered by a federal or state governmental officer or agency or upon any regulation, order, requirement or agreement issued or made pursuant to the statute or executive order, the officer or agency upon timely application may be permitted to intervene in the action.   In exercising its discretion the court shall consider whether the intervention will unduly delay or prejudice the adjudication of the rights of the original parties.

(c) **Procedure.**   A person desiring to intervene shall serve a motion to intervene upon the parties as provided in Rule 5.   The motion shall state the grounds therefor and shall be accompanied by a pleading setting forth the claim or defense for which intervention is sought.   The same procedure shall be followed when a statute of the United States gives a right to intervene.   When the constitutionality of an act of Congress affecting the public interest is drawn in question in any action to which the United States or an officer, agency, or employee thereof is not a party, the court shall notify the Attorney General of the United States as provided in Title 28, U.S.C. § 2403.

As amended• 1948, 1949, 1963, 1966, 1987.

Rule 25.

SUBSTITUTION OF PARTIES

(a) **Death.**

(1) If a party dies and the claim is not thereby extinguished, the court may order substitution of the proper parties.   The motion for substitution may be made by any party or by the successors or representatives of the deceased party and, together with the notice of hearing, shall be served on the parties as provided in Rule 5 and upon persons not parties in the manner provided in Rule 4 for the service of a summons, and may be served in any judicial district.   Unless the motion for substitution is made not later than 90 days after the death is suggested upon the record by service of a statement of the fact of the death as provided herein for the service of the motion, the action shall be dismissed as to the deceased party.

(2) In the event of the death of one or more of the plaintiffs or of one or more of the defendants in an action in which the right sought to be enforced survives only to the surviving plaintiffs or only against the surviving defendants, the action does not abate.

The death shall be suggested upon the record and the action shall proceed in favor of or against the surviving parties.

(b) Incompetency. If a party becomes incompetent, the court upon motion served as provided in subdivision (a) of this rule may allow the action to be continued by or against the party's representative.

(c) Transfer of Interest. In case of any transfer of interest, the action may be continued by or against the original party, unless the court upon motion directs the person to whom the interest is transferred to be substituted in the action or joined with the original party. Service of the motion shall be made as provided in subdivision (a) of this rule.

(d) Public Officers; Death or Separation from Office.

(1) When a public officer is a party to an action in an official capacity and during its pendency dies, resigns, or otherwise ceases to hold office, the action does not abate and the officer's successor is automatically substituted as a party. Proceedings following the substitution shall be in the name of the substituted party, but any misnomer not affecting the substantial rights of the parties shall be disregarded. An order of substitution may be entered at any time, but the omission to enter such an order shall not affect the substitution.

(2) A public officer who sues or is sued in an official capacity may be described as a party by the officer's official title rather than by name; but the court may require the officer's name to be added.

As amended 1949, 1961, 1963, 1987.

V.   DEPOSITIONS AND DISCOVERY

Rule 26.

GENERAL PROVISIONS GOVERNING DISCOVERY

(a) Discovery Methods. Parties may obtain discovery by one or more of the following methods: depositions upon oral examination or written questions; written interrogatories; production of documents or things or permission to enter upon land or other property, for inspection and other purposes; physical and mental examinations; and requests for admission.

(b) Discovery Scope and Limits. Unless otherwise limited by order of the court in accordance with these rules, the scope of discovery is as follows:

(1) *In General.* Parties may obtain discovery regarding any matter, not privileged, which is relevant to the subject matter

involved in the pending action, whether it relates to the claim or defense of the party seeking discovery or to the claim or defense of any other party, including the existence, description, nature, custody, condition and location of any books, documents, or other tangible things and the identity and location of persons having knowledge of any discoverable matter. It is not ground for objection that the information sought will be inadmissible at the trial if the information sought appears reasonably calculated to lead to the discovery of admissible evidence.

The frequency or extent of use of the discovery methods set forth in subdivision (a) shall be limited by the court if it determines that: (i) the discovery sought is unreasonably cumulative or duplicative, or is obtainable from some other source that is more convenient, less burdensome, or less expensive; (ii) the party seeking discovery has had ample opportunity by discovery in the action to obtain the information sought; or (iii) the discovery is unduly burdensome or expensive, taking into account the needs of the case, the amount in controversy, limitations on the parties' resources, and the importance of the issues at stake in the litigation. The court may act upon its own initiative after reasonable notice or pursuant to a motion under subdivision (c).

(2) *Insurance Agreements.* A party may obtain discovery of the existence and contents of any insurance agreement under which any person carrying on an insurance business may be liable to satisfy part or all of a judgment which may be entered in the action or to indemnify or reimburse for payments made to satisfy the judgment. Information concerning the insurance agreement is not by reason of disclosure admissible in evidence at trial. For purposes of this paragraph, an application for insurance shall not be treated as part of an insurance agreement.

(3) *Trial Preparation: Materials.* Subject to the provisions of subdivision (b)(4) of this rule, a party may obtain discovery of documents and tangible things otherwise discoverable under subdivision (b)(1) of this rule and prepared in anticipation of litigation or for trial by or for another party or by or for that other party's representative (including the other party's attorney, consultant, surety, indemnitor, insurer, or agent) only upon a showing that the party seeking discovery has substantial need of the materials in the preparation of the party's case and that the party is unable without undue hardship to obtain the substantial equivalent of the materials by other means. In ordering discovery of such materials when the required showing has been made, the court shall protect against disclosure of the mental impressions, conclusions, opinions, or legal theories of an attorney or other representative of a party concerning the litigation.

A party may obtain without the required showing a statement concerning the action or its subject matter previously made by that party. Upon request, a person not a party may obtain without the required showing a statement concerning the action or its subject matter previously made by that person. If the request is refused, the person may move for a court order. The provisions of Rule 37(a)(4) apply to the award of expenses incurred in relation to the motion. For purposes of this paragraph, a statement previously made is (A) a written statement signed or otherwise adopted or approved by the person making it, or (B) a stenographic, mechanical, electrical, or other recording, or a transcription thereof, which is a substantially verbatim recital of an oral statement by the person making it and contemporaneously recorded.

(4) *Trial Preparation: Experts.* Discovery of facts known and opinions held by experts, otherwise discoverable under the provisions of subdivision (b)(1) of this rule and acquired or developed in anticipation of litigation or for trial, may be obtained only as follows:

(A)(i) A party may through interrogatories require any other party to identify each person whom the other party expects to call as an expert witness at trial, to state the subject matter on which the expert is expected to testify, and to state the substance of the facts and opinions to which the expert is expected to testify and a summary of the grounds for each opinion. (ii) Upon motion, the court may order further discovery by other means, subject to such restrictions as to scope and such provisions, pursuant to subdivision (b)(4)(C) of this rule, concerning fees and expenses as the court may deem appropriate.

(B) A party may discover facts known or opinions held by an expert who has been retained or specially employed by another party in anticipation of litigation or preparation for trial and who is not expected to be called as a witness at trial, only as provided in Rule 35(b) or upon a showing of exceptional circumstances under which it is impracticable for the party seeking discovery to obtain facts or opinions on the same subject by other means.

(C) Unless manifest injustice would result, (i) the court shall require that the party seeking discovery pay the expert a reasonable fee for time spent in responding to discovery under subdivisions (b)(4)(A)(ii) and (b)(4)(B) of this rule; and (ii) with respect to discovery obtained under subdivision (b)(4)(A)(ii) of this rule the court may require, and with respect to discovery obtained under subdivision (b)(4)(B) of this rule the court shall require, the party seeking discovery to pay the other party a fair portion of the fees and expenses reasonably incurred by the latter party in obtaining facts and opinions from the expert.

(c) **Protective Orders.** Upon motion by a party or by the person from whom discovery is sought, and for good cause shown, the court in which the action is pending or alternatively, on matters relating to a deposition, the court in the district where the deposition is to be taken may make any order which justice requires to protect a party or person from annoyance, embarrassment, oppression, or undue burden or expense, including one or more of the following: (1) that the discovery not be had; (2) that the discovery may be had only on specified terms and conditions, including a designation of the time or place; (3) that the discovery may be had only by a method of discovery other than that selected by the party seeking discovery; (4) that certain matters not be inquired into, or that the scope of the discovery be limited to certain matters; (5) that discovery be conducted with no one present except persons designated by the court; (6) that a deposition after being sealed be opened only by order of the court; (7) that a trade secret or other confidential research, development, or commercial information not be disclosed or be disclosed only in a designated way; (8) that the parties simultaneously file specified documents or information enclosed in sealed envelopes to be opened as directed by the court.

If the motion for a protective order is denied in whole or in part, the court may, on such terms and conditions as are just, order that any party or person provide or permit discovery. The provisions of Rule 37(a)(4) apply to the award of expenses incurred in relation to the motion.

(d) **Sequence and Timing of Discovery.** Unless the court upon motion, for the convenience of parties and witnesses and in the interests of justice, orders otherwise, methods of discovery may be used in any sequence and the fact that a party is conducting discovery, whether by deposition or otherwise, shall not operate to delay any other party's discovery.

(e) **Supplementation of Responses.** A party who has responded to a request for discovery with a response that was complete when made is under no duty to supplement the response to include information thereafter acquired, except as follows:

(1) A party is under a duty seasonally to supplement the response with respect to any question directly addressed to (A) the identity and location of persons having knowledge of discoverable matters, and (B) the identity of each person expected to be called as an expert witness at trial, the subject matter on which the person is expected to testify, and the substance of the person's testimony.

(2) A party is under a duty seasonably to amend a prior response if the party obtains information upon the basis of which (A) the party knows that the response was incorrect when made, or (B) the party knows that the response though correct when made is no longer true and the circumstances are such that a failure to amend the response is in substance a knowing concealment.

(3) A duty to supplement responses may be imposed by order of the court, agreement of the parties, or at any time prior to trial through new requests for supplementation of prior responses.

(f) Discovery Conference. At any time after commencement of an action the court may direct the attorneys for the parties to appear before it for a conference on the subject of discovery. The court shall do so upon motion by the attorney for any party if the motion includes:

(1) A statement of the issues as they then appear;

(2) A proposed plan and schedule of discovery;

(3) Any limitations proposed to be placed on discovery;

(4) Any other proposed orders with respect to discovery; and

(5) A statement showing that the attorney making the motion has made a reasonable effort to reach agreement with opposing attorneys on the matters set forth in the motion. Each party and each party's attorney are under a duty to participate in good faith in the framing of a discovery plan if a plan is proposed by the attorney for any party. Notice of the motion shall be served on all parties. Objections or additions to matters set forth in the motion shall be served not later than 10 days after service of the motion.

Following the discovery conference, the court shall enter an order tentatively identifying the issues for discovery purposes, establishing a plan and schedule for discovery, setting limitations on discovery, if any; and determining such other matters, including the allocation of expenses, as are necessary for the proper management of discovery in the action. An order may be altered or amended whenever justice so requires.

Subject to the right of a party who properly moves for a discovery conference to prompt convening of the conference, the court may combine the discovery conference with a pretrial conference authorized by Rule 16.

(g) Signing of Discovery Requests, Responses, and Objections. Every request for discovery or response or objection thereto made by a party represented by an attorney shall be signed by at least one attorney of record in the attorney's individual name, whose address shall be stated. A party who is not represented by an attorney shall sign the request, response, or objection and state the party's address. The signature of the attorney or party constitutes a certification that the signer has read the request, response, or objection, and that to the best of the signer's knowledge, information, and belief formed after a reasonable inquiry it is: (1) consistent with these rules and warranted by existing law or a good faith argument for the extension, modification, or reversal of existing law; (2) not interposed for any improper purpose, such as to harass or to cause unnecessary delay or needless increase in the cost of litigation; and (3) not unreasonable or unduly burdensome or expensive, given the needs of the case, the discovery already had in the case, the amount in controversy, and the importance of the issues at stake in the litigation. If a request, response, or objection is not signed, it shall be stricken unless it is signed promptly after the omission is called to the attention of the party making the request, response or objection and a party shall not be obligated to take any action with respect to it until it is signed.

If a certification is made in violation of the rule, the court, upon motion or upon its own initiative, shall impose upon the person who made the certification, the party on whose behalf the request, response, or objection is made, or both, an appropriate sanction, which may include an order to pay the amount of the reasonable expenses incurred because of the violation, including a reasonable attorney's fee.

As amended 1948, 1963, 1966, 1970, 1980, 1983, 1987.

Rule 27.

DEPOSITIONS BEFORE ACTION OR PENDING APPEAL

(a) Before Action.

(1) *Petition.* A person who desires to perpetuate testimony regarding any matter that may be cognizable in any court of the United States may file a verified petition in the United States district court in the district of the residence of any expected adverse party. The petition shall be entitled in the name of the petitioner and shall show: 1, that the petitioner expects to be a party to an action cognizable in a court of the United States but is presently unable to bring it or cause it to be brought, 2, the subject matter of the expected action and the petitioner's interest therein, 3, the facts which the petitioner desires to establish by the proposed testimony and the reasons for desiring to perpetuate it,

4, the names or a description of the persons the petitioner expects will be adverse parties and their addresses so far as known, and 5, the names and addresses of the persons to be examined and the substance of the testimony which the petitioner expects to elicit from each, and shall ask for an order authorizing the petitioner to take the depositions of the persons to be examined named in the petition, for the purpose of perpetuating their testimony.

(2) *Notice and Service.* The petitioner shall thereafter serve a notice upon each person named in the petition as an expected adverse party, together with a copy of the petition, stating that the petitioner will apply to the court, at a time and place named therein, for the order described in the petition. At least 20 days before the date of hearing the notice shall be served either within or without the district or state in the manner provided in Rule 4(d) for service of summons; but if such service cannot with due diligence be made upon any expected adverse party named in the petition, the court may make such order as is just for service by publication or otherwise, and shall appoint, for persons not served in the manner provided in Rule 4(d), an attorney who shall represent them, and, in case they are not otherwise represented, shall cross-examine the deponent. If any expected adverse party is a minor or incompetent the provisions of Rule 17(c) apply.

(3) *Order and Examination.* If the court is satisfied that the perpetuation of the testimony may prevent a failure or delay of justice, it shall make an order designating or describing the persons whose depositions may be taken and specifying the subject matter of the examination and whether the depositions shall be taken upon oral examination or written interrogatories. The depositions may then be taken in accordance with these rules; and the court may make orders of the character provided for by Rules 34 and 35. For the purpose of applying these rules to depositions for perpetuating testimony, each reference therein to the court in which the action is pending shall be deemed to refer to the court in which the petition for such deposition was filed.

(4) *Use of Deposition.* If a deposition to perpetuate testimony is taken under these rules or if, although not so taken, it would be admissible in evidence in the courts of the state in which it is taken, it may be used in any action involving the same subject matter subsequently brought in a United States district court, in accordance with the provisions of Rule 32(a).

(b) Pending Appeal. If an appeal has been taken from a judgment of a district court or before the taking of an appeal if the time therefor has not expired, the district court in which the judgment was rendered may allow the taking of the depositions of witnesses to perpetuate their testimony for use in the event of further proceedings in the district court. In such case the party who desires to perpetuate the testimony may make a motion in the district court for leave to take the depositions, upon the same notice and service thereof as if the action was pending in the district court. The motion shall show (1) the names and addresses of persons to be examined and the substance of the testimony which the party expects to elicit from each; (2) the reasons for perpetuating their testimony. If the court finds that the perpetuation of the testimony is proper to avoid a failure or delay of justice, it may make an order allowing the depositions to be taken and may make orders of the character provided for by Rules 34 and 35, and thereupon the depositions may be taken and used in the same manner and under the same conditions as are prescribed in these rules for depositions taken in actions pending in the district court.

(c) Perpetuation by Action. This rule does not limit the power of a court to entertain an action to perpetuate testimony.

As amended 1948, 1949, 1971, 1987.

Rule 28.

PERSONS BEFORE WHOM DEPOSITIONS MAY BE TAKEN

(a) Within the United States. Within the United States or within a territory or insular possession subject to the jurisdiction of the United States, depositions shall be taken before an officer authorized to administer oaths by the laws of the United States or of the place where the examination is held, or before a person appointed by the court in which the action is pending. A person so appointed has power to administer oaths and take testimony. The term officer as used in Rules 30, 31 and 32 includes a person appointed by the court or designated by the parties under Rule 29.

(b) In Foreign Countries. In a foreign country, depositions may be taken (1) on notice before a person authorized to administer oaths in the place in which the examination is held, either by the law thereof or by the law of the United States, or (2) before a person commissioned by the court, and a person so commissioned shall have the power by virtue of the commission to administer any necessary oath and take testimony, or (3) pursuant to a letter rogatory. A commission or a letter rogatory shall be issued on application and notice and on terms that are just and appropriate. It is not requisite to the issuance of a commission or a letter rogatory that the taking of the deposition in any other manner is impracticable or inconvenient; and both a commission and a letter rogatory may be issued in proper cases. A notice or commission may designate the person before whom the deposition is to be taken either by name or descriptive title. A letter rogatory may be addressed "To the Appropriate Authority in [here name the country]." Evidence obtained in response to a letter rogatory need not be excluded merely for the reason that it is not a verbatim transcript or that the testimony was not taken under oath or for any similar departure from the requirements for depositions taken within the United States under these rules.

(c) **Disqualification for Interest.** No deposition shall be taken before a person who is a relative or employee or attorney or counsel of any of the parties, or is a relative or employee of such attorney or counsel, or is financially interested in the action.

As amended 1948, 1963, 1980, 1987.

Rule 29.

STIPULATIONS REGARDING DISCOVERY PROCEDURE

Unless the court orders otherwise, the parties may by written stipulation (1) provide that depositions may be taken before any person, at any time or place, upon any notice, and in any manner and when so taken may be used like other depositions, and (2) modify the procedures provided by these rules for other methods of discovery, except that stipulations extending the time provided in Rules 33, 34, and 36 for responses to discovery may be made only with the approval of the court.

As amended 1970.

Rule 30.

DEPOSITIONS UPON ORAL EXAMINATION

(a) **When Depositions May Be Taken.** After commencement of the action, any party may take the testimony of any person, including a party, by deposition upon oral examination. Leave of court, granted with or without notice, must be obtained only if the plaintiff seeks to take a deposition prior to the expiration of 30 days after service of the summons and complaint upon any defendant or service made under Rule 4(e), except that leave is not required (1) if a defendant has served a notice of taking deposition or otherwise sought discovery, or (2) if special notice is given as provided in subdivision (b)(2) of this rule. The attendance of witnesses may be compelled by subpoena as provided in Rule 45. The deposition of a person confined in prison may be taken only by leave of court on such terms as the court prescribes.

(b) Notice of Examination: General Requirements; Special Notice; Non-Stenographic Recording; Production of Documents and Things; Deposition of Organization; Deposition by Telephone.

(1) A party desiring to take the deposition of any person upon oral examination shall give reasonable notice in writing to every other party to the action. The notice shall state the time and place for taking the deposition and the name and address of each person to be examined, if known, and, if the name is not known, a general description sufficient to identify the person or the particular class or group to which the person belongs. If a subpoena duces tecum is to be served on the person to be examined, the designation of the materials to be produced as set forth in the subpoena shall be attached to or included in the notice.

(2) Leave of court is not required for the taking of a deposition by plaintiff if the notice (A) states that the person to be examined is about to go out of the district where the action is pending and more than 100 miles from the place of trial, or is about to go out of the United States, or is bound on a voyage to sea, and will be unavailable for examination unless the person's deposition is taken before expiration of the 30-day period, and (B) sets forth facts to support the statement. The plaintiff's attorney shall sign the notice, and the attorney's signature constitutes a certification by the attorney that to the best of the attorney's knowledge, information, and belief the statement and supporting facts are true. The sanctions provided by Rule 11 are applicable to the certification.

If a party shows that when the party was served with notice under this subdivision (b)(2) the party was unable through the exercise of diligence to obtain counsel to represent the party at the taking of the deposition, the deposition may not be used against the party.

(3) The court may for cause shown enlarge or shorten the time for taking the deposition.

(4) The parties may stipulate in writing or the court may upon motion order that the testimony at a deposition be recorded by other than stenographic means. The stipulation or order shall designate the person before whom the deposition shall be taken, the manner of recording, preserving, and filing the deposition, and may include other provisions to assure that the recorded testimony will be accurate and trustworthy. A party may arrange to have a stenographic transcription made at the party's own expense. Any objections under subdivision (c), any changes made by the witness, the witness' signature identifying the deposition as the witness' own or the statement of the officer that is required if

64

the witness does not sign, as provided in subdivision (e), and the certification of the officer required by subdivision (f) shall be set forth in a writing to accompany a deposition recorded by non-stenographic means.

(5) The notice to a party deponent may be accompanied by a request made in compliance with Rule 34 for the production of documents and tangible things at the taking of the deposition. The procedure of Rule 34 shall apply to the request.

(6) A party may in the party's notice and in a subpoena name as the deponent a public or private corporation or a partnership or association or governmental agency and describe with reasonable particularity the matters on which examination is requested. In that event, the organization so named shall designate one or more officers, directors, or managing agents, or other persons who consent to testify on its behalf, and may set forth, for each person designated, the matters on which the person will testify. A subpoena shall advise a non-party organization of its duty to make such a designation. The persons so designated shall testify as to matters known or reasonably available to the organization. This subdivision (b)(6) does not preclude taking a deposition by any other procedure authorized in these rules.

(7) The parties may stipulate in writing or the court may upon motion order that a deposition be taken by telephone. For the purposes of this rule and Rules 28(a), 37(a)(1), 37(b)(1) and 45(d), a deposition taken by telephone is taken in the district and at the place where the deponent is to answer questions propounded to the deponent.

(c) **Examination and Cross-Examination; Record of Examination; Oath; Objections.** Examination and cross-examination of witnesses may proceed as permitted at the trial under the provisions of the Federal Rules of Evidence. The officer before whom the deposition is to be taken shall put the witness on oath and shall personally, or by someone acting under the officer's direction and in the officer's presence, record the testimony of the witness. The testimony shall be taken stenographically or recorded by any other means ordered in accordance with subdivision (b)(4) of this rule. If requested by one of the parties, the testimony shall be transcribed. All objections made at the time of the examination to the qualifications of the officer taking the deposition, or to the manner of taking it, or to the evidence presented, or to the conduct of any party, and any other objection to the proceedings, shall be noted by the officer upon the deposition. Evidence objected to shall be taken subject to the objections. In lieu of participating in the oral examination, parties may serve written questions in a sealed envelope on the party taking the deposition and the party taking the deposition shall transmit them to the officer, who shall propound them to the witness and record the answers verbatim.

(d) Motion to Terminate or Limit Examination. At any time during the taking of the deposition, on motion of a party or of the deponent and upon a showing that the examination is being conducted in bad faith or in such manner as unreasonably to annoy, embarrass, or oppress the deponent or party, the court in which the action is pending or the court in the district where the deposition is being taken may order the officer conducting the examination to cease forthwith from taking the deposition, or may limit the scope and manner of the taking of the deposition as provided in Rule 26(c). If the order made terminates the examination, it shall be resumed thereafter only upon the order of the court in which the action is pending. Upon demand of the objecting party or deponent, the taking of the deposition shall be suspended for the time necessary to make a motion for an order. The provisions of Rule 37(a)(4) apply to the award of expenses incurred in relation to the motion.

(e) Submission to Witness; Changes; Signing. When the testimony is fully transcribed the deposition shall be submitted to the witness for examination and shall be read to or by the witness, unless such examination and reading are waived by the witness and by the parties. Any changes in form or substance which the witness desires to make shall be entered upon the deposition by the officer with a statement of the reasons given by the witness for making them. The deposition shall then be signed by the witness, unless the parties by stipulation waive the signing or the witness is ill or cannot be found or refuses to sign. If the deposition is not signed by the witness within 30 days of its submission to the witness, the officer shall sign it and state on the record the fact of the waiver or of the illness or absence of the witness or the fact of the refusal to sign together with the reason, if any, given therefor; and the deposition may then be used as fully as though signed unless on a motion to suppress under Rule 32(d)(4) the court holds that the reasons given for the refusal to sign require rejection of the deposition in whole or in part.

(f) Certification and Filing by Officer; Exhibits; Copies; Notice of Filing.

(1) The officer shall certify on the deposition that the witness was duly sworn by the officer and that the deposition is a true record of the testimony given by the witness. Unless otherwise ordered by the court, the officer shall then securely seal the deposition in an envelope indorsed with the title of the action and marked "Deposition of [here insert name of witness]" and shall

promptly file it with the court in which the action is pending or send it by registered or certified mail to the clerk thereof for filing.

Documents and things produced for inspection during the examination of the witness, shall, upon the request of a party, be marked for identification and annexed to the deposition and may be inspected and copied by any party, except that if the person producing the materials desires to retain them the person may (A) offer copies to be marked for identification and annexed to the deposition and to serve thereafter as originals if the person affords to all parties fair opportunity to verify the copies by comparison with the originals, or (B) offer the originals to be marked for identification, after giving to each party an opportunity to inspect and copy them, in which event the materials may then be used in the same manner as if annexed to the deposition. Any party may move for an order that the original be annexed to and returned with the deposition to the court, pending final disposition of the case.

(2) Upon payment of reasonable charges therefor, the officer shall furnish a copy of the deposition to any party or to the deponent.

(3) The party taking the deposition shall give prompt notice of its filing to all other parties.

(g) Failure to Attend or to Serve Subpoena; Expenses.

(1) If the party giving the notice of the taking of a deposition fails to attend and proceed therewith and another party attends in person or by attorney pursuant to the notice, the court may order the party giving the notice to pay to such other party the reasonable expenses incurred by that party and that party's attorney in attending, including reasonable attorney's fees.

(2) If the party giving the notice of the taking of a deposition of a witness fails to serve a subpoena upon the witness and the witness because of such failure does not attend, and if another party attends in person or by attorney because that party expects the deposition of that witness to be taken, the court may order the party giving the notice to pay to such other party the reasonable expenses incurred by that party and that party's attorney in attending, including reasonable attorney's fees.

As amended 1963, 1970, 1971, 1975, 1980, 1987.

Rule 31.

DEPOSITIONS UPON WRITTEN QUESTIONS

(a) **Serving Questions; Notice.** After commencement of the action, any party may take the testimony of any person, including a party, by deposition upon written questions. The attendance of witnesses may be compelled by the use of subpoena as provided in Rule 45. The deposition of a person confined in prison may be taken only by leave of court on such terms as the court prescribes.

A party desiring to take a deposition upon written questions shall serve them upon every other party with a notice stating (1) the name and address of the person who is to answer them, if known, and if the name is not known, a general description sufficient to identify the person or the particular class or group to which the person belongs, and (2) the name or descriptive title and address of the officer before whom the deposition is to be taken. A deposition upon written questions may be taken of a public or private corporation or a partnership or association or governmental agency in accordance with the provisions of Rule 30(b)(6).

Within 30 days after the notice and written questions are served, a party may serve cross questions upon all other parties. Within 10 days after being served with cross questions, a party may serve redirect questions upon all other parties. Within 10 days after being served with redirect questions, a party may serve recross questions upon all other parties. The court may for cause shown enlarge or shorten the time.

(b) Officer to Take Responses and Prepare Record. A copy of the notice and copies of all questions served shall be delivered by the party taking the deposition to the officer designated in the notice, who shall proceed promptly, in the manner provided by Rule 30(c), (e), and (f), to take the testimony of the witness in response to the questions and to prepare, certify, and file or mail the deposition, attaching thereto the copy of the notice and the questions received by the officer.

(c) Notice of Filing. When the deposition is filed the party taking it shall promptly give notice thereof to all other parties.

As amended 1970, 1987.

Rule 32.

USE OF DEPOSITIONS IN COURT PROCEEDINGS

(a) Use of Depositions. At the trial or upon the hearing of a motion or an interlocutory proceeding, any part or all of a deposition, so far as admissible under the rules of evidence applied as though the witness were then present and testifying, may be used against any party who was present or represented at the taking of the deposition or who had reasonable notice thereof, in accordance with any of the following provisions:

(1) Any deposition may be used by any party for the purpose of contradicting or impeaching the testimony of deponent as a

witness, or for any other purpose permitted by the Federal Rules of Evidence.

(2) The deposition of a party or of anyone who at the time of taking the deposition was an officer, director, or managing agent, or a person designated under Rule 30(b)(6) or 31(a) to testify on behalf of a public or private corporation, partnership or association or governmental agency which is a party may be used by an adverse party for any purpose.

(3) The deposition of a witness, whether or not a party, may be used by any party for any purpose if the court finds: (A) that the witness is dead; or (B) that the witness is at a greater distance than 100 miles from the place of trial or hearing, or is out of the United States, unless it appears that the absence of the witness was procured by the party offering the deposition; or (C) that the witness is unable to attend or testify because of age, illness, infirmity, or imprisonment; or (D) that the party offering the deposition has been unable to procure the attendance of the witness by subpoena; or (E) upon application and notice, that such exceptional circumstances exist as to make it desirable, in the interest of justice and with due regard to the importance of presenting the testimony of witnesses orally in open court, to allow the deposition to be used.

(4) If only part of a deposition is offered in evidence by a party, an adverse party may require the offeror to introduce any other part which ought in fairness to be considered with the part introduced, and any party may introduce any other parts.

Substitution of parties pursuant to Rule 25 does not affect the right to use depositions previously taken; and, when an action has been brought in any court of the United States or of any State and another action involving the same subject matter is afterward brought between the same parties or their representatives or successors in interest, all depositions lawfully taken and duly filed in the former action may be used in the latter as if originally taken therefor. A deposition previously taken may also be used as permitted by the Federal Rules of Evidence.

(b) Objections to Admissibility. Subject to the provisions of Rule 28(b) and subdivision (d)(3) of this rule, objection may be made at the trial or hearing to receiving in evidence any deposition or part thereof for any reason which would require the exclusion of the evidence if the witness were then present and testifying.

(c) Effect of Taking or Using Depositions. Abrogated Nov. 20, 1972, and expressly approved by P.L. 93–595, eff. July 1, 1975.

(d) Effect of Errors and Irregularities in Depositions.

(1) *As to Notice.* All errors and irregularities in the notice for taking a deposition are waived unless written objection is promptly served upon the party giving the notice.

(2) *As to Disqualification of Officer.* Objection to taking a deposition because of disqualification of the officer before whom it is to be taken is waived unless made before the taking of the deposition begins or as soon thereafter as the disqualification becomes known or could be discovered with reasonable diligence.

(3) *As to Taking of Deposition.*

(A) Objections to the competency of a witness or to the competency, relevancy, or materiality of testimony are not waived by failure to make them before or during the taking of the deposition, unless the ground of the objection is one which might have been obviated or removed if presented at that time.

(B) Errors and irregularities occurring at the oral examination in the manner of taking the deposition, in the form of the questions or answers, in the oath or affirmation, or in the conduct of parties, and errors of any kind which might be obviated, removed, or cured if promptly presented, are waived unless seasonable objection thereto is made at the taking of the deposition.

(C) Objections to the form of written questions submitted under Rule 31 are waived unless served in writing upon the party propounding them within the time allowed for serving the succeeding cross or other questions and within 5 days after service of the last questions authorized.

(4) *As to Completion and Return of Deposition.* Errors and irregularities in the manner in which the testimony is transcribed or the deposition is prepared, signed, certified, sealed, indorsed, transmitted, filed, or otherwise dealt with by the officer under Rules 30 and 31 are waived unless a motion to suppress the deposition or some part thereof is made with reasonable promptness after such defect is, or with due diligence might have been, ascertained.

As amended 1970, 1975, 1980, 1987.

Rule 33.

INTERROGATORIES TO PARTIES

(a) **Availability; Procedures for Use.** Any party may serve upon any other party written interrogatories to be answered by the party served or, if the party served is a public or private corporation or a partnership or association or governmental agency, by any officer or agent, who shall furnish such information as is available to the party. Interrogatories may, without leave of court, be served upon the plaintiff after commencement of the action and upon any other party with or after service of the summons and complaint upon that party.

Each interrogatory shall be answered separately and fully in writing under oath, unless it is objected to, in which event the reasons for objection shall be stated in lieu of an answer. The answers are to be signed by the person making them, and the objections signed by the attorney making them. The party upon whom the interrogatories have been served shall serve a copy of the answers, and objections if any, within 30 days after the service of the interrogatories, except that a defendant may serve answers or objections within 45 days after service of the summons and complaint upon that defendant. The court may allow a shorter or longer time. The party submitting the interrogatories may move for an order under Rule 37(a) with respect to any objection to or other failure to answer an interrogatory.

(b) **Scope; Use at Trial.** Interrogatories may relate to any matters which can be inquired into under Rule 26(b), and the answers may be used to the extent permitted by the rules of evidence.

An interrogatory otherwise proper is not necessarily objectionable merely because an answer to the interrogatory involves an opinion or contention that relates to fact or the application of law to fact, but the court may order that such an interrogatory need not be answered until after designated discovery has been completed or until a pre-trial conference or other later time.

(c) **Option to Produce Business Records.** Where the answer to an interrogatory may be derived or ascertained from the business records of the party upon whom the interrogatory has been served or from an examination, audit or inspection of such business records, including a compilation, abstract or summary thereof and the burden of deriving or ascertaining the answer is substantially the same for the party serving the interrogatory as for the party served, it is a sufficient answer to such interrogatory to specify the records from which the answer may be derived or ascertained and to afford to the party serving the interrogatory reasonable opportunity to examine, audit or inspect such records and to make copies, compilations, abstracts or summaries. A specification shall be in sufficient detail to permit the interrogating party to locate and to identify, as readily as can the party served, the records from which the answer may be ascertained.

As amended 1948, 1970, 1980.

Rule 34.

PRODUCTION OF DOCUMENTS AND THINGS AND ENTRY UPON LAND FOR INSPECTION AND OTHER PURPOSES

(a) Scope. Any party may serve on any other party a request (1) to produce and permit the party making the request, or someone acting on the requestor's behalf, to inspect and copy, any designated documents (including writings, drawings, graphs, charts, photographs, phono-records, and other data compilations from which information can be obtained, translated, if necessary, by the respondent through detection devices into reasonably usable form), or to inspect and copy, test, or sample any tangible things which constitute or contain matters within the scope of Rule 26(b) and which are in the possession, custody or control of the party upon whom the request is served; or (2) to permit entry upon designated land or other property in the possession or control of the party upon whom the request is served for the purpose of inspection and measuring, surveying, photographing, testing, or sampling the property or any designated object or operation thereon, within the scope of Rule 26(b).

(b) Procedure. The request may, without leave of court, be served upon the plaintiff after commencement of the action and upon any other party with or after service of the summons and complaint upon that party. The request shall set forth the items to be inspected either by individual item or by category, and describe each item and category with reasonable particularity. The request shall specify a reasonable time, place, and manner of making the inspection and performing the related acts.

The party upon whom the request is served shall serve a written response within 30 days after the service of the request, except that a defendant may serve a response within 45 days after service of the summons and complaint upon that defendant. The court may allow a shorter or longer time. The response shall state, with respect to each item or category, that inspection and related activities will be permitted as requested, unless the request is objected to, in which event the reasons for objection shall be stated. If objection is made to part of an item or category, the part shall be specified. The party submitting the request may move for an order under Rule 37(a) with respect to any objection to or other failure to respond to the request or any part thereof, or any failure to permit inspection as requested.

A party who produces documents for inspection shall produce them as they are kept in the usual course of business or shall organize and label them to correspond with the categories in the request.

(c) Persons Not Parties. This rule does not preclude an independent action against a person not a party for production of documents and things and permission to enter upon land.

As amended 1948, 1970, 1980, 1987.

Rule 35.

PHYSICAL AND MENTAL EXAMINATION OF PERSONS

(a) Order for Examination. When the mental or physical condition (including the blood group) of a party, or of a person in the custody or under the legal control of a party, is in controversy, the court in which the action is pending may order the party to submit to a physical examination by a physician, or mental examination by a physician or psychologist or to produce for examination the person in the party's custody or legal control. The order may be made only on motion for good cause shown and upon notice to the person to be examined and to all parties and shall specify the time, place, manner, conditions, and scope of the examination and the person or persons by whom it is to be made.

(b) Report of Examining Physician or Psychologist.

(1) If requested by the party against whom an order is made under Rule 35(a) or the person examined, the party causing the examination to be made shall deliver to the requestor a copy of a detailed written report of the examining physician or psychologist setting out the physician's findings, including results of all tests made, diagnoses and conclusions, together with like reports of all earlier examinations of the same condition. After delivery the party causing the examination shall be entitled upon request to receive from the party against whom the order is made a like report of any examination, previously or thereafter made, of the same condition, unless, in the case of a report of examination of a person not a party, the party shows that such party is unable to obtain it. The court on motion may make an order against a party requiring delivery of a report on such terms as are just, and if a physician or psychologist fails or refuses to make a report the court may exclude the physician's testimony if offered at the trial.

(2) By requesting and obtaining a report of the examination so ordered or by taking the deposition of the examiner, the party examined waives any privilege the party may have in that action or any other involving the same controversy, regarding the testimony of every other person who has examined or may thereafter

examine the party in respect of the same mental or physical condition.

(3) This subdivision applies to examinations made by agreement of the parties, unless the agreement expressly provides otherwise. This subdivision does not preclude discovery of a report of an examining physician or psychologist or the taking of a deposition of the physician or psychologist in accordance with the provisions of any other rule.

(c) Definitions. For the purpose of this rule, a psychologist is a psychologist licensed or certified by a State or the District of Columbia.

As amended 1970, 1987, 1988.

Rule 36.

REQUESTS FOR ADMISSION

(a) Request for Admission. A party may serve upon any other party a written request for the admission, for purposes of the pending action only, of the truth of any matters within the scope of Rule 26(b) set forth in the request that relate to statements or opinions of fact or of the application of law to fact, including the genuineness of any documents described in the request. Copies of documents shall be served with the request unless they have been or are otherwise furnished or made available for inspection and copying. The request may, without leave of court, be served upon the plaintiff after commencement of the action and upon any other party with or after service of the summons and complaint upon that party.

Each matter of which an admission is requested shall be separately set forth. The matter is admitted unless, within 30 days after service of the request, or within such shorter or longer time as the court may allow, the party to whom the request is directed serves upon the party requesting the admission a written answer or objection addressed to the matter, signed by the party or by the party's attorney, but, unless the court shortens the time, a defendant shall not be required to serve answers or objections before the expiration of 45 days after service of the summons and complaint upon that defendant. If objection is made, the reasons therefor shall be stated. The answer shall specifically deny the matter or set forth in detail the reasons why the answering party cannot truthfully admit or deny the matter. A denial shall fairly meet the substance of the requested admission, and when good faith requires that a party qualify an answer or deny only a part of the matter of which an admission is requested, the party shall specify so much of it as is true and qualify or deny the remainder. An answering party may not give lack of information or knowledge as a reason for failure to admit or deny unless the party states that the party has made reasonable inquiry and that the information known or readily obtainable by the party is insufficient to enable the party to admit or deny. A party who considers that a matter of which an admission has been requested presents a genuine issue for trial may not, on that ground alone, object to the request; the party may, subject to the provisions of Rule 37(c), deny the matter or set forth reasons why the party cannot admit or deny it.

The party who has requested the admissions may move to determine the sufficiency of the answers or objections. Unless the court determines that an objection is justified, it shall order that an answer be served. If the court determines that an answer does not comply with the requirements of this rule, it may order either that the matter is admitted or that an amended answer be served. The court may, in lieu of these orders, determine that final disposition of the request be made at a pre-trial conference or at a designated time prior to trial. The provisions of Rule 37(a)(4) apply to the award of expenses incurred in relation to the motion.

(b) Effect of Admission. Any matter admitted under this rule is conclusively established unless the court on motion permits withdrawal or amendment of the admission. Subject to the provisions of Rule 16 governing amendment of a pre-trial order, the court may permit withdrawal or amendment when the presentation of the merits of the action will be subserved thereby and the party who obtained the admission fails to satisfy the court that withdrawal or amendment will prejudice that party in maintaining the action or defense on the merits. Any admission made by a party under this rule is for the purpose of the pending action only and is not an admission for any other purpose nor may it be used against the party in any other proceeding.

As amended 1948, 1970, 1987.

Rule 37.

FAILURE TO MAKE OR COOPERATE IN DISCOVERY: SANCTIONS

(a) Motion for Order Compelling Discovery. A party, upon reasonable notice to other parties and all persons affected thereby, may apply for an order compelling discovery as follows:

(1) *Appropriate Court.* An application for an order to a party may be made to the court in which the action is pending, or, on

matters relating to a deposition, to the court in the district where the deposition is being taken.   An application for an order to a deponent who is not a party shall be made to the court in the district where the deposition is being taken.

(2) *Motion.*   If a deponent fails to answer a question propounded or submitted under Rule 30 or 31, or a corporation or other entity fails to make a designation under Rule 30(b) (6) or 31(a), or a party fails to answer an interrogatory submitted under Rule 33, or if a party, in response to a request for inspection submitted under Rule 34, fails to respond that inspection will be permitted as requested or fails to permit inspection as requested, the discovering party may move for an order compelling an answer, or a designation, or an order compelling inspection in accordance with the request.   When taking a deposition on oral examination, the proponent of the question may complete or adjourn the examination before applying for an order.

If the court denies the motion in whole or in part, it may make such protective order as it would have been empowered to make on a motion made pursuant to Rule 26(c).

(3) *Evasive or Incomplete Answer.*   For purposes of this subdivision an evasive or incomplete answer is to be treated as a failure to answer.

(4) *Award of Expenses of Motion.*   If the motion is granted, the court shall, after opportunity for hearing, require the party or deponent whose conduct necessitated the motion or the party or attorney advising such conduct or both of them to pay to the moving party the reasonable expenses incurred in obtaining the order, including attorney's fees, unless the court finds that the opposition to the motion was substantially justified or that other circumstances make an award of expenses unjust.

If the motion is denied, the court shall, after opportunity for hearing, require the moving party or the attorney advising the motion or both of them to pay to the party or deponent who opposed the motion the reasonable expenses incurred in opposing the motion, including attorney's fees, unless the court finds that the making of the motion was substantially justified or that other circumstances make an award of expenses unjust.

If the motion is granted in part and denied in part, the court may apportion the reasonable expenses incurred in relation to the motion among the parties and persons in a just manner.

(b) Failure to Comply with Order.

(1) *Sanctions by Court in District Where Deposition Is Taken.* If a deponent fails to be sworn or to answer a question after being directed to do so by the court in the district in which the deposi-

tion is being taken, the failure may be considered a contempt of that court.

(2) *Sanctions by Court in Which Action Is Pending.* If a party or an officer, director, or managing agent of a party or a person designated under Rule 30(b)(6) or 31(a) to testify on behalf of a party fails to obey an order to provide or permit discovery, including an order made under subdivision (a) of this rule or Rule 35, or if a party fails to obey an order entered under Rule 26(f), the court in which the action is pending may make such orders in regard to the failure as are just, and among others the following:

(A) An order that the matters regarding which the order was made or any other designated facts shall be taken to be established for the purposes of the action in accordance with the claim of the party obtaining the order;

(B) An order refusing to allow the disobedient party to support or oppose designated claims or defenses, or prohibiting that party from introducing designated matters in evidence;

(C) An order striking out pleadings or parts thereof, or staying further proceedings until the order is obeyed, or dismissing the action or proceeding or any part thereof, or rendering a judgment by default against the disobedient party;

(D) In lieu of any of the foregoing orders or in addition thereto, an order treating as a contempt of court the failure to obey any orders except an order to submit to a physical or mental examination;

(E) Where a party has failed to comply with an order under Rule 35(a) requiring that party to produce another for examination, such orders as are listed in paragraphs (A), (B), and (C) of this subdivision, unless the party failing to comply shows that that party is unable to produce such person for examination.

In lieu of any of the foregoing orders or in addition thereto, the court shall require the party failing to obey the order or the attorney advising that party or both to pay the reasonable expenses, including attorney's fees, caused by the failure, unless the court finds that the failure was substantially justified or that other circumstances make an award of expenses unjust.

(c) **Expenses on Failure to Admit.** If a party fails to admit the genuineness of any document or the truth of any matter as requested under Rule 36, and if the party requesting the admissions thereafter proves the genuineness of the document or the truth of the matter, the requesting party may apply to the court for an order requiring the other party to pay the reasonable expenses incurred in making that proof, including reasonable attorney's fees. The court shall make the order unless it finds that (1) the request was held objectionable pursuant to Rule 36(a), or (2) the admission sought was of no substantial importance, or (3) the party failing to admit had reasonable ground to believe that the party might prevail on the matter, or (4) there was other good reason for the failure to admit.

(d) Failure of Party to Attend at Own Deposition or Serve Answers to Interrogatories or Respond to Request for Inspection. If a party or an officer, director, or managing agent of a party or a person designated under Rule 30(b)(6) or 31(a) to testify on behalf of a party fails (1) to appear before the officer who is to take the deposition, after being served with a proper notice, or (2) to serve answers or objections to interrogatories submitted under Rule 33, after proper service of the interrogatories, or (3) to serve a written response to a request for inspection submitted under Rule 34, after proper service of the request, the court in which the action is pending on motion may make such orders in regard to the failure as are just, and among others it may take any action authorized under paragraphs (A), (B), and (C) of subdivision (b)(2) of this rule. In lieu of any order or in addition thereto, the court shall require the party failing to act or the attorney advising that party or both to pay the reasonable expenses, including attorney's fees, caused by the failure, unless the court finds that the failure was substantially justified or that other circumstances make an award of expenses unjust.

The failure to act described in this subdivision may not be excused on the ground that the discovery sought is objectionable unless the party failing to act has applied for a protective order as provided by Rule 26(c).

(e) Subpoena of Person in Foreign Country. Abrogated Apr. 29, 1980, eff. Aug. 1, 1980.

(f) Expenses Against United States. Repealed by P.L. 96–481, eff. Oct. 1, 1981.

(g) Failure to Participate in the Framing of a Discovery Plan. If a party or a party's attorney fails to participate in good faith in the framing of a discovery plan by agreement as is required by Rule 26(f), the court may, after opportunity for hearing, require such party or attorney to pay to any other party the reasonable expenses, including attorney's fees, caused by the failure.

As amended 1949, 1970, 1980, 1981, 1987.

VI. TRIALS

Rule 38.

JURY TRIAL OF RIGHT

(a) Right Preserved. The right of trial by jury as declared by the Seventh Amendment to the Constitution or as given by a statute of the United States shall be preserved to the parties inviolate.

(b) Demand. Any party may demand a trial by jury of any issue triable of right by a jury by serving upon the other parties a demand therefor in writing at any time after the commencement of the action and not later than 10 days after the service of the last pleading directed to such issue. Such demand may be indorsed upon a pleading of the party.

(c) Same: Specification of Issues. In the demand a party may specify the issues which the party wishes so tried; otherwise the party shall be deemed to have demanded trial by jury for all the issues so triable. If the party has demanded trial by jury for only some of the issues, any other party within 10 days after service of the demand or such lesser time as the court may order, may serve a demand for trial by jury of any other or all of the issues of fact in the action.

(d) Waiver. The failure of a party to serve a demand as required by this rule and to file it as required by Rule 5(d) constitutes a waiver by the party of trial by jury. A demand for trial by jury made as herein provided may not be withdrawn without the consent of the parties.

(e) Admiralty and Maritime Claims. These rules shall not be construed to create a right to trial by jury of the issues in an admiralty or maritime claim within the meaning of Rule 9(h).

As amended 1966, 1987.

Rule 39.

TRIAL BY JURY OR BY THE COURT

(a) By Jury. When trial by jury has been demanded as provided in Rule 38, the action shall be designated upon the docket as a jury action. The trial of all issues so demanded shall be by jury, unless (1) the parties or their attorneys of record, by written stipulation filed with the court or by an oral stipulation made in open court and entered in the record, consent to trial by the court sitting without a jury or (2) the court upon motion or of its own initiative finds that a right of trial by jury of some or all of those issues does not exist under the Constitution or statutes of the United States.

(b) By the Court. Issues not demanded for trial by jury as provided in Rule 38 shall be tried by the court; but, notwithstanding the failure of a party to demand a jury in an action in which such a demand might have been made of right, the court in its discretion upon motion may order a trial by a jury of any or all issues.

(c) Advisory Jury and Trial by Consent. In all actions not triable of right by a jury the court upon motion or of its own initiative may try any issue with an advisory jury or, except in actions against the United States when a statute of the United States provides for trial without a jury, the court, with the consent of both parties, may order a trial with a jury whose verdict has the same effect as if trial by jury had been a matter of right.

Rule 40.

ASSIGNMENT OF CASES FOR TRIAL

The district courts shall provide by rule for the placing of actions upon the trial calendar (1) without request of the parties or (2) upon request of a party and notice to the other parties or (3) in such other manner as the courts deem expedient. Precedence shall be given to actions entitled thereto by any statute of the United States.

Rule 41.

DISMISSAL OF ACTIONS

(a) Voluntary Dismissal; Effect Thereof.

(1) *By Plaintiff; by Stipulation.* Subject to the provisions of Rule 23(e), of Rule 66, and of any statute of the United States, an action may be dismissed by the plaintiff without order of court (i) by filing a notice of dismissal at any time before service by the adverse party of an answer or of a motion for summary judgment, whichever first occurs, or (ii) by filing a stipulation of dismissal signed by all parties who have appeared in the action. Unless otherwise stated in the notice of dismissal or stipulation, the dismissal is without prejudice, except that a notice of dismissal operates as an adjudication upon the merits when filed by a plaintiff who has once dismissed in any court of the United States or of any state an action based on or including the same claim.

(2) *By Order of Court.* Except as provided in paragraph (1) of this subdivision of this rule, an action shall not be dismissed at the plaintiff's instance save upon order of the court and upon such terms and conditions as the court deems proper. If a counterclaim has been pleaded by a defendant prior to the service upon the defendant of the plaintiff's motion to dismiss, the action shall not be dismissed against the defendant's objection unless the counterclaim can remain pending for independent adjudication by the court. Unless otherwise specified in the order, a dismissal under this paragraph is without prejudice.

(b) Involuntary Dismissal: Effect Thereof. For failure of the plaintiff to prosecute or to comply with these rules or any order of court, a defendant may move for dismissal of an action or of any claim against the defendant. After the plaintiff, in an action tried by the court without a jury, has completed the presentation of evidence, the defendant, without waiving the right to offer evidence in the event the motion is not granted, may move for a dismissal on the ground that upon the facts and the law the plaintiff has shown no right to relief. The court as trier of the facts may then determine them and render judgment against the plaintiff or may decline to render any judgment until the close of all the evidence. If the court renders judgment on the merits against the plaintiff, the court shall make findings as provided in Rule 52(a). Unless the court in its order for dismissal otherwise specifies, a dismissal under this subdivision and any dismissal not provided for in this rule, other than a dismissal for lack of jurisdiction, for improper venue, or for failure to join a party under Rule 19, operates as an adjudication upon the merits.

(c) Dismissal of Counterclaim, Cross-Claim, or Third-Party Claim. The provisions of this rule apply to the dismissal of any counterclaim, cross-claim, or third-party claim. A voluntary dismissal by the claimant alone pursuant to paragraph (1) of subdivision (a) of this rule shall be made before a responsive pleading is served or, if there is none, before the introduction of evidence at the trial or hearing.

(d) Costs of Previously Dismissed Action. If a plaintiff who has once dismissed an action in any court commences an action based upon or including the same claim against the same defendant, the court may make such order for the payment of costs of the action previously dismissed as it may deem proper and may stay the proceedings in the action until the plaintiff has complied with the order.

As amended 1948, 1963, 1966, 1968, 1987.

Rule 42.

CONSOLIDATION; SEPARATE TRIALS

(a) **Consolidation.** When actions involving a common question of law or fact are pending before the court, it may order a joint hearing or trial of any or all the matters in issue in the actions; it may order all the actions consolidated; and it may make such orders concerning proceedings therein as may tend to avoid unnecessary costs or delay.

(b) **Separate Trials.** The court, in furtherance of convenience or to avoid prejudice, or when separate trials will be conducive to expedition and economy, may order a separate trial of any claim, cross-claim, counterclaim, or third-party claim, or of any separate issue or of any number of claims, cross-claims, counterclaims, third-party claims, or issues, always preserving inviolate the right of trial by jury as declared by the Seventh Amendment to the Constitution or as given by a statute of the United States.

As amended 1966.

Rule 43.

TAKING OF TESTIMONY

(a) **Form.** In all trials the testimony of witnesses shall be taken orally in open court, unless otherwise provided by an Act of Congress or by these rules, the Federal Rules of Evidence, or other rules adopted by the Supreme Court.

(b) **Scope of Examination and Cross-Examination.** Abrogated Dec. 18, 1972, and expressly approved by P.L. 93–595, eff. July 1, 1975.

(c) **Record of Excluded Evidence.** Abrogated Dec. 18, 1972, and expressly approved by P.L. 93–595, eff. July 1, 1975.

(d) **Affirmation in Lieu of Oath.** Whenever under these rules an oath is required to be taken, a solemn affirmation may be accepted in lieu thereof.

(e) **Evidence on Motions.** When a motion is based on facts not appearing of record the court may hear the matter on affidavits presented by the respective parties, but the court may direct that the matter be heard wholly or partly on oral testimony or deposition.

(f) **Interpreters.** The court may appoint an interpreter of its own selection and may fix the interpreter's reasonable compensation. The compensation shall be paid out of funds provided by law or by one or more of the parties as the court may direct, and may be taxed ultimately as costs, in the discretion of the court.

As amended 1966, 1975, 1987.

Rule 44.

PROOF OF OFFICIAL RECORD

(a) **Authentication.**

(1) *Domestic.* An official record kept within the United States, or any state, district, commonwealth, territory, or insular possession thereof, or within the Panama Canal Zone, the Trust Territory of the Pacific Islands, or the Ryukyu Islands, or an entry therein, when admissible for any purpose, may be evidenced by an official publication thereof or by a copy attested by the officer having the legal custody of the record, or by the officer's deputy, and accompanied by a certificate that such officer has the custody. The certificate may be made by a judge of a court of record of the district or political subdivision in which the record is kept, authenticated by the seal of the court, or may be made by any public officer having a seal of office and having official duties in the district or political subdivision in which the record is kept, authenticated by the seal of the officer's office.

(2) *Foreign.* A foreign official record, or an entry therein, when admissible for any purpose, may be evidenced by an official publication thereof; or a copy thereof, attested by a person authorized to make the attestation, and accompanied by a final certification as to the genuineness of the signature and official position (i) of the attesting person, or (ii) of any foreign official whose certificate of genuineness of signature and official position relates to the attestation or is in a chain of certificates of genuineness of signature and official position relating to the attestation. A final certification may be made by a secretary of embassy or legation, consul general, consul, vice consul, or consular agent of the United States, or a diplomatic or consular official of the foreign country assigned or accredited to the United States. If reasonable opportunity has been given to all parties to investigate the authenticity and accuracy of the documents, the court may, for good cause shown, (i) admit an attested copy without final certification or (ii) permit the foreign official record to be evidenced by an attested summary with or without a final certification.

(b) **Lack of Record.** A written statement that after diligent search no record or entry of a specified tenor is found to exist in the records designated by the statement, authenticated as provided in subdivision (a)(1) of this rule in the case of a domestic record, or complying with the requirements of subdivision (a)(2) of this rule for a summary in the case of a foreign record, is admissible as evidence that the records contain no such record or entry.

(c) **Other Proof.** This rule does not prevent the proof of official records or of entry or lack of entry therein by any other method authorized by law.

As amended 1966, 1987.

Rule 44.1.

DETERMINATION OF FOREIGN LAW

A party who intends to raise an issue concerning the law of a foreign country shall give notice by pleadings or other reasonable written notice. The court, in determining foreign law, may consider any relevant material or source, including testimony, whether or not submitted by a party or admissible under the Federal Rules of Evidence. The court's determination shall be treated as a ruling on a question of law.

Added 1966; as amended 1975, 1987.

Rule 45.

SUBPOENA

(a) **For Attendance of Witnesses; Form; Issuance.** Every subpoena shall be issued by the clerk under the seal of the court, shall state the name of the court and the title of the action, and shall command each person to whom it is directed to attend and give testimony at a time and place therein specified. The clerk shall issue a subpoena, or a subpoena for the production of documentary evidence, signed and sealed but otherwise in blank, to a party requesting it, who shall fill it in before service.

(b) **For Production of Documentary Evidence.** A subpoena may also command the person to whom it is directed to produce the books, papers, documents, or tangible things designated therein; but the court, upon motion made promptly and in any event at or before the time specified in the subpoena for compliance therewith, may (1) quash or modify the subpoena if it is unreasonable and oppressive or (2) condition denial of the motion upon the advancement by the person in whose behalf the subpoena is issued of the reasonable cost of producing the books, papers, documents, or tangible things.

(c) **Service.** A subpoena may be served by the marshal, by a deputy marshal, or by any other person who is not a party and is not less than 18 years of age. Service of a subpoena upon a person named therein shall be made by delivering a copy thereof to such person and by tendering to that person the fees for one day's attendance and the mileage allowed by law. When the subpoena is issued on behalf of the United States or an officer or agency thereof, fees and mileage need not be tendered.

(d) Subpoena for Taking Depositions; Place of Examination.

(1) Proof of service of a notice to take a deposition as provided in Rules 30(b) and 31(a) constitutes a sufficient authorization for the issuance by the clerk of the district court for the district in which the deposition is to be taken of subpoenas for the persons named or described therein. Proof of service may be made by filing with the clerk of the district court for the district in which the deposition is to be taken a copy of the notice together with a statement of the date and manner of service and of the names of the persons served, certified by the person who made service. The subpoena may command the person to whom it is directed to produce and permit inspection and copying of designated books, papers, documents, or tangible things which constitute or contain matters within the scope of the examination permitted by Rule 26(b), but in that event the subpoena will be subject to the provisions of Rule 26(c) and subdivision (b) of this rule.

The person to whom the subpoena is directed may, within 10 days after the service thereof or on or before the time specified in the subpoena for compliance if such time is less than 10 days after service, serve upon the attorney designated in the subpoena written objection to inspection or copying of any or all of the designated materials. If objection is made, the party serving the subpoena shall not be entitled to inspect and copy the materials except pursuant to an order of the court from which the subpoena was issued. The party serving the subpoena may, if objection has been made, move upon notice to the deponent for an order at any time before or during the taking of the deposition.

(2) A person to whom a subpoena for the taking of a deposition is directed may be required to attend at any place within 100 miles from the place where that person resides, is employed or transacts business in person, or is served, or at such other convenient place as is fixed by an order of court.

(e) Subpoena for a Hearing or Trial.

(1) At the request of any party subpoenas for attendance at a hearing or trial shall be issued by the clerk of the district court for the district in which the hearing or trial is held. A subpoena requiring the attendance of a witness at a hearing or trial may be served at any place within the district, or at any place without the

district that is within 100 miles of the place of the hearing or trial specified in the subpoena, or at a place within the state where a state statute or rule of court permits service of a subpoena issued by a state court of general jurisdiction sitting in the place where the district court is held.   When a statute of the United States provides therefor, the court upon proper application and cause shown may authorize the service of a subpoena at any other place.

(2) A subpoena directed to a witness in a foreign country shall issue under the circumstances and in the manner and be served as provided in Title 28, U.S.C. § 1783.

(f) Contempt.   Failure by any person without adequate excuse to obey a subpoena served upon that person may be deemed a contempt of the court from which the subpoena issued.

As amended 1948, 1949, 1970, 1980, 1985, 1987.

Rule 46.

EXCEPTIONS UNNECESSARY

Formal exceptions to rulings or orders of the court are unnecessary; but for all purposes for which an exception has heretofore been necessary it is sufficient that a party, at the time the ruling or order of the court is made or sought, makes known to the court the action which the party desires the court to take or the party's objection to the action of the court and the grounds therefor; and, if a party has no opportunity to object to a ruling or order at the time it is made, the absence of an objection does not thereafter prejudice the party.

As amended 1987.

Rule 47.

JURORS

(a) Examination of Jurors.   The court may permit the parties or their attorneys to conduct the examination of prospective jurors or may itself conduct the examination.   In the latter event, the court shall permit the parties or their attorneys to supplement the examination by such further inquiry as it deems proper or shall itself submit to the prospective jurors such additional questions of the parties or their attorneys as it deems proper.

(b) Alternate Jurors.   The court may direct that not more than six jurors in addition to the regular jury be called and impanelled to sit as alternate jurors.   Alternate jurors in the order in which they are called shall replace jurors who, prior to the time the jury retires to consider its verdict, become or are found to be unable or disqualified to perform their duties. Alternate jurors shall be drawn in the same manner, shall have the same qualifications, shall be subject to the same examination and challenges, shall take the same oath, and shall have the same functions, powers, facilities, and privileges as the regular jurors. An alternate juror who does not replace a regular juror shall be discharged after the jury retires to consider its verdict. Each side is entitled to 1 peremptory challenge in addition to those otherwise allowed by law if 1 or 2 alternate jurors are to be impanelled, 2 peremptory challenges if 3 or 4 alternate jurors are to be impanelled, and 3 peremptory challenges if 5 or 6 alternate jurors are to be impanelled. The additional peremptory challenges may be used against an alternate juror only, and the other peremptory challenges allowed by law shall not be used against an alternate juror.

As amended 1966.

Rule 48.

JURIES OF LESS THAN TWELVE—MAJORITY VERDICT

The parties may stipulate that the jury shall consist of any number less than twelve or that a verdict or a finding of a stated majority of the jurors shall be taken as the verdict or finding of the jury.

Rule 49.

SPECIAL VERDICTS AND INTERROGATORIES

(a) **Special Verdicts.** The court may require a jury to return only a special verdict in the form of a special written finding upon each issue of fact. In that event the court may submit to the jury written questions susceptible of categorical or other brief answer or may submit written forms of the several special findings which might properly be made under the pleadings and evidence; or it may use such other method of submitting the issues and requiring the written findings thereon as it deems most appropriate. The court shall give to the jury such explanation and instruction concerning the matter thus submitted as may be necessary to enable the jury to make its findings upon each issue. If in so doing the court omits any issue of fact raised by the pleadings or by the evidence, each party waives the right to a trial by jury of the issue so omitted unless before the jury retires the party demands its submission to the jury. As to an issue omitted without such demand the court may make a finding; or, if it fails to do so, it shall be deemed to have made a finding in accord with the judgment on the special verdict.

(b) **General Verdict Accompanied by Answer to Interrogatories.** The court may submit to the jury, together with appropriate forms for a general verdict, written interrogatories upon one or more issues of fact the decision of which is necessary to a verdict. The court shall give such explanation or instruction as may be necessary to enable the jury both to make answers to the interrogatories and to render a general verdict, and the court shall direct the jury both to make written answers and to render a general verdict. When the general verdict and the answers are harmonious, the appropriate judgment upon the verdict and answers shall be entered pursuant to Rule 58. When the answers are consistent with each other but one or more is inconsistent with the general verdict, judgment may be entered pursuant to Rule 58 in accordance with the answers, notwithstanding the general verdict, or the court may return the jury for further consideration of its answers and verdict or may order a new trial. When the answers are inconsistent with each other and one or more is likewise inconsistent with the general verdict, judgment shall not be entered, but the court shall return the jury for further consideration of its answers and verdict or shall order a new trial.

As amended 1963, 1987.

Rule 50.

MOTION FOR A DIRECTED VERDICT AND FOR JUDGMENT NOTWITHSTANDING THE VERDICT

(a) **Motion for Directed Verdict: When Made; Effect.** A party who moves for a directed verdict at the close of the evidence offered by an opponent may offer evidence in the event that the motion is not granted, without having reserved the right so to do and to the same extent as if the motion had not been made. A motion for a directed verdict which is not granted is not a waiver of trial by jury even though all parties to the action have moved for directed verdicts. A motion for a directed verdict shall state the specific grounds therefor. The order of the court granting a motion for a directed verdict is effective without any assent of the jury.

(b) **Motion for Judgment Notwithstanding the Verdict.** Whenever a motion for a directed verdict made at the close of all the evidence is denied or for any reason is not granted, the court is deemed to have submitted the action to the jury subject to a later determination of the legal questions raised by the motion. Not later than 10 days after entry of judgment, a party who has moved for a directed verdict may move to have the verdict and any judgment entered thereon set aside and to have judgment entered in accordance with the party's motion for a directed verdict; or if a verdict was not returned such party, within 10 days after the jury has been discharged, may move for judgment in accordance with the party's motion for a directed verdict. A motion for a new trial may be joined with this motion, or a new trial may be prayed for in the alternative. If a verdict was returned the court may allow the judgment to stand or may reopen the judgment and either order a new trial or direct the entry of judgment as if the requested verdict had been directed. If no verdict was returned the court may direct the entry of judgment as if the requested verdict had been directed or may order a new trial.

(c) Same: Conditional Rulings on Grant of Motion.

(1) If the motion for judgment notwithstanding the verdict, provided for in subdivision (b) of this rule, is granted, the court shall also rule on the motion for a new trial, if any, by determining whether it should be granted if the judgment is thereafter vacated or reversed, and shall specify the grounds for granting or denying the motion for the new trial. If the motion for a new trial is thus conditionally granted, the order thereon does not affect the finality of the judgment. In case the motion for a new trial has been conditionally granted and the judgment is reversed on appeal, the new trial shall proceed unless the appellate court has otherwise ordered. In case the motion for a new trial has been conditionally denied, the appellee on appeal may assert error in that denial; and if the judgment is reversed on appeal, subsequent proceedings shall be in accordance with the order of the appellate court.

(2) The party whose verdict has been set aside on motion for judgment notwithstanding the verdict may serve a motion for a new trial pursuant to Rule 59 not later than 10 days after entry of the judgment notwithstanding the verdict.

(d) Same: Denial of Motion. If the motion for judgment notwithstanding the verdict is denied, the party who prevailed on that motion may, as appellee, assert grounds entitling the party to a new trial in the event the appellate court concludes that the trial court erred in denying the motion for judgment notwithstanding the verdict. If the appellate court reverses the judgment, nothing in this rule precludes it from determining that the appellee is entitled to a new trial, or from directing the trial court to determine whether a new trial shall be granted.

As amended 1963, 1987.

Rule 51.

INSTRUCTIONS TO JURY: OBJECTION

At the close of the evidence or at such earlier time during the trial as the court reasonably directs, any party may file written requests that the court instruct the jury on the law as set forth in the requests. The court shall inform counsel of its proposed action upon the requests prior to their arguments to the jury. The court, at its election, may instruct the jury before or after argument, or both. No party may assign as error the giving or the failure to give an instruction unless that party objects thereto before the jury retires to consider its verdict, stating distinctly the matter objected to and the grounds of the objection. Opportunity shall be given to make the objection out of the hearing of the jury.

As amended 1987.

Rule 52.

FINDINGS BY THE COURT

(a) **Effect.** In all actions tried upon the facts without a jury or with an advisory jury, the court shall find the facts specially and state separately its conclusions of law thereon, and judgment shall be entered pursuant to Rule 58; and in granting or refusing interlocutory injunctions the court shall similarly set forth the findings of fact and conclusions of law which constitute the grounds of its action. Requests for findings are not necessary for purposes of review. Findings of fact, whether based on oral or documentary evidence, shall not be set aside unless clearly erroneous, and due regard shall be given to the opportunity of the trial court to judge of the credibility of the witnesses. The findings of a master, to the extent that the court adopts them, shall be considered as the findings of the court. It will be sufficient if the findings of fact and conclusions of law are stated orally and recorded in open court following the close of the evidence or appear in an opinion or memorandum of decision filed by the court. Findings of fact and conclusions of law are unnecessary on decisions of motions under Rules 12 or 56 or any other motion except as provided in Rule 41(b).

(b) **Amendment.** Upon motion of a party made not later than 10 days after entry of judgment the court may amend its findings or make additional findings and may amend the judgment accordingly. The motion may be made with a motion for a new trial pursuant to Rule 59. When findings of fact are made in actions tried by the court without a jury, the question of the sufficiency of the evidence to support the findings may thereafter be raised whether or not the party raising the question has made in the district court an objection to such findings or has made a motion to amend them or a motion for judgment.

As amended 1948, 1963, 1983, 1985.

Rule 53.

MASTERS

(a) **Appointment and Compensation.** The court in which any action is pending may appoint a special master therein. As used in these rules the word "master" includes a referee, an auditor, an examiner, and an assessor. The compensation to be allowed to a master shall be fixed by the court, and shall be charged upon such of the parties or paid out of any fund or subject matter of the action, which is in the custody and control of the court as the court may direct; provided that this provision for compensation shall not apply when a United States magistrate is designated to serve as a master pursuant to Title 28, U.S.C. § 636(b)(2). The master shall not retain the master's report as security for the master's compensation; but when the party ordered to pay the compensation allowed by the court does not pay it after notice and within the time prescribed by the court, the master is entitled to a writ of execution against the delinquent party.

(b) **Reference.** A reference to a master shall be the exception and not the rule. In actions to be tried by a jury, a reference shall be made only when the issues are complicated; in actions to be tried without a jury, save in matters of account and of difficult computation of damages, a reference shall be made only upon a showing that some exceptional condition requires it. Upon the consent of the parties, a magistrate may be designated to serve as a special master without regard to the provisions of this subdivision.

(c) **Powers.** The order of reference to the master may specify or limit the master's powers and may direct the master to report only upon particular issues or to do or perform particular acts or to receive and report evidence only and may fix the time and place for beginning and closing the hearings and for the filing of the master's report. Subject to the specifications and limitations stated in the order, the master has and shall exercise the power to regulate all proceedings in every hearing before the master and to do all acts and take all measures necessary or proper for the efficient performance of the master's duties under the order. The master may require the production before the master of evidence upon all matters embraced in the reference, including the production of all books, papers, vouchers, documents, and writings applicable thereto. The master may rule upon the admissibility of evidence unless otherwise directed by the order of reference and has the authority to put witnesses on oath and may examine them and may call the parties to the action and examine them upon oath. When a party so requests, the master shall make a record of the evidence offered and excluded in the same manner and subject to the same limitations as provided in the Federal Rules of Evidence for a court sitting without a jury.

(d) Proceedings.

(1) *Meetings.* When a reference is made, the clerk shall forthwith furnish the master with a copy of the order of reference. Upon receipt thereof unless the order of reference otherwise provides, the master shall forthwith set a time and place for the first meeting of the parties or their attorneys to be held within 20 days after the date of the order of reference and shall notify the parties or their attorneys. It is the duty of the master to proceed with all reasonable diligence. Either party, on notice to the parties and master, may apply to the court for an order requiring the master to speed the proceedings and to make the report. If a party fails to appear at the time and place appointed, the master may proceed ex parte or, in the master's discretion, adjourn the proceedings to a future day, giving notice to the absent party of the adjournment.

(2) *Witnesses.* The parties may procure the attendance of witnesses before the master by the issuance and service of subpoenas as provided in Rule 45. If without adequate excuse a witness fails to appear or give evidence, the witness may be punished as for a contempt and be subjected to the consequences, penalties, and remedies provided in Rules 37 and 45.

(3) *Statement of Accounts.* When matters of accounting are in issue before the master, the master may prescribe the form in which the accounts shall be submitted and in any proper case may require or receive in evidence a statement by a certified public accountant who is called as a witness. Upon objection of a party to any of the items thus submitted or upon a showing that the form of statement is insufficient, the master may require a different form of statement to be furnished, or the accounts or specific items thereof to be proved by oral examination of the accounting parties or upon written interrogatories or in such other manner as the master directs.

(e) Report.

(1) *Contents and Filing.* The master shall prepare a report upon the matters submitted to the master by the order of reference and, if required to make findings of fact and conclusions of law, the master shall set them forth in the report. The master shall file the report with the clerk of the court and in an action to be tried without a jury, unless otherwise directed by the order of reference, shall file with it a transcript of the proceedings and of the evidence and the original exhibits. The clerk shall forthwith mail to all parties notice of the filing.

(2) *In Non-Jury Actions.* In an action to be tried without a jury the court shall accept the master's findings of fact unless clearly erroneous. Within 10 days after being served with notice of the filing of the report any party may serve written objections thereto upon the other parties. Application to the court for action upon the report and upon objections thereto shall be by motion and upon notice as prescribed in Rule 6(d). The court after hearing may adopt the report or may modify it or may reject it in whole or in part or may receive further evidence or may recommit it with instructions.

(3) *In Jury Actions.* In an action to be tried by a jury the master shall not be directed to report the evidence. The master's findings upon the issues submitted to the master are admissible as evidence of the matters found and may be read to the jury, subject to the ruling of the court upon any objections in point of law which may be made to the report.

(4) *Stipulation as to Findings.* The effect of a master's report is the same whether or not the parties have consented to the reference; but, when the parties stipulate that a master's findings of fact shall be final, only questions of law arising upon the report shall thereafter be considered.

(5) *Draft Report.* Before filing the master's report a master may submit a draft thereof to counsel for all parties for the purpose of receiving their suggestions.

(f) [Application to Magistrate]. A magistrate is subject to this rule only when the order referring a matter to the magistrate expressly provides that the reference is made under this Rule.

As amended 1966, 1983, 1987.

VII. JUDGMENT

Rule 54.

JUDGMENTS; COSTS

(a) Definition; Form. "Judgment" as used in these rules includes a decree and any order from which an appeal lies. A judgment shall not contain a recital of pleadings, the report of a master, or the record of prior proceedings.

(b) Judgment upon Multiple Claims or Involving Multiple Parties. When more than one claim for relief is presented in an action, whether as a claim, counterclaim, cross-claim, or third-party claim, or when multiple parties are involved, the court may direct the entry of a final judgment as to one or more but fewer than all of the claims or parties only upon an express determination that there is no just reason for delay and upon an express direction for the entry of judgment. In the absence of such determination and direction, any order or other form of decision, however designated, which adjudicates fewer than all the claims or the rights and liabilities of fewer than all the parties shall not terminate the action as to any of the claims or parties, and the order or other form of decision is subject to revision at any time before the entry of judgment adjudicating all the claims and the rights and liabilities of all the parties.

(c) Demand for Judgment. A judgment by default shall not be different in kind from or exceed in amount that prayed for in the demand for judgment. Except as to a party against whom a judgment is entered by default, every final judgment shall grant the relief to which the party in whose favor it is rendered is entitled, even if the party has not demanded such relief in the party's pleadings.

(d) Costs. Except when express provision therefor is made either in a statute of the United States or in these rules, costs shall be allowed as of course to the prevailing party unless the court otherwise directs; but costs against the United States, its officers, and agencies shall be imposed only to the extent permitted by law. Costs may be taxed by the clerk on one day's notice. On motion served within 5 days thereafter, the action of the clerk may be reviewed by the court.

As amended 1948, 1961, 1987.

Rule 55.

DEFAULT

(a) Entry. When a party against whom a judgment for affirmative relief is sought has failed to plead or otherwise defend as provided by these rules and that fact is made to appear by affidavit or otherwise, the clerk shall enter the party's default.

(b) Judgment. Judgment by default may be entered as follows:

(1) *By the Clerk.* When the plaintiff's claim against a defendant is for a sum certain or for a sum which can by computation

be made certain, the clerk upon request of the plaintiff and upon affidavit of the amount due shall enter judgment for that amount and costs against the defendant, if the defendant has been default-ed for failure to appear and is not an infant or incompetent person.

(2) *By the Court.*   In all other cases the party entitled to a judgment by default shall apply to the court therefor; but no judgment by default shall be entered against an infant or incompe-tent person unless represented in the action by a general guardi-an, committee, conservator, or other such representative who has appeared therein.   If the party against whom judgment by default is sought has appeared in the action, the party (or, if appearing by representative, the party's representative) shall be served with written notice of the application for judgment at least 3 days prior to the hearing on such application.   If, in order to enable the court to enter judgment or to carry it into effect, it is necessary to take an account or to determine the amount of damages or to establish the truth of any averment by evidence or to make an investigation of any other matter, the court may conduct such hearings or order such references as it deems necessary and proper and shall accord a right of trial by jury to the parties when and as required by any statute of the United States.

(c) Setting Aside Default.   For good cause shown the court may set aside an entry of default and, if a judgment by default has been entered, may likewise set it aside in accordance with Rule 60(b).

(d) Plaintiffs, Counterclaimants, Cross-Claimants.   The provisions of this rule apply whether the party entitled to the judgment by default is a plaintiff, a third-party plaintiff, or a party who has pleaded a cross-claim or counterclaim.   In all cases a judgment by default is subject to the limitations of Rule 54(c).

(e) Judgment Against the United States.   No judgment by default shall be entered against the United States or an officer or agency thereof unless the claimant establishes a claim or right to relief by evidence satisfactory to the court.

As amended 1987.

Rule 56.

SUMMARY JUDGMENT

(a) For Claimant.   A party seeking to recover upon a claim, counterclaim, or cross-claim or to obtain a declaratory judgment may, at any time after the expiration of 20 days from the com-mencement of the action or after service of a motion for summary judgment by the adverse party, move with or without supporting affidavits for a summary judgment in the party's favor upon all or any part thereof.

(b) For Defending Party. A party against whom a claim, counterclaim, or cross-claim is asserted or a declaratory judgment is sought may, at any time, move with or without supporting affidavits for a summary judgment in the party's favor as to all or any part thereof.

(c) Motion and Proceedings Thereon. The motion shall be served at least 10 days before the time fixed for the hearing. The adverse party prior to the day of hearing may serve opposing affidavits. The judgment sought shall be rendered forthwith if the pleadings, depositions, answers to interrogatories, and admissions on file, together with the affidavits, if any, show that there is no genuine issue as to any material fact and that the moving party is entitled to a judgment as a matter of law. A summary judgment, interlocutory in character, may be rendered on the issue of liability alone although there is a genuine issue as to the amount of damages.

(d) Case Not Fully Adjudicated on Motion. If on motion under this rule judgment is not rendered upon the whole case or for all the relief asked and a trial is necessary, the court at the hearing of the motion, by examining the pleadings and the evidence before it and by interrogating counsel, shall if practicable ascertain what material facts exist without substantial controversy and what material facts are actually and in good faith controverted. It shall thereupon make an order specifying the facts that appear without substantial controversy, including the extent to which the amount of damages or other relief is not in controversy, and directing such further proceedings in the action as are just. Upon the trial of the action the facts so specified shall be deemed established, and the trial shall be conducted accordingly.

(e) Form of Affidavits; Further Testimony; Defense Required. Supporting and opposing affidavits shall be made on personal knowledge, shall set forth such facts as would be admissible in evidence, and shall show affirmatively that the affiant is competent to testify to the matters stated therein. Sworn or certified copies of all papers or parts thereof referred to in an affidavit shall be attached thereto or served therewith. The court may permit affidavits to be supplemented or opposed by depositions, answers to interrogatories, or further affidavits. When a motion for summary judgment is made and supported as provided in this rule, an adverse party may not rest upon the mere allegations or denials of the adverse party's pleading, but the adverse party's response, by affidavits or as otherwise provided in this rule, must set forth specific facts showing that there is a genuine issue for trial. If the adverse party does not so respond, summary judgment, if appropriate, shall be entered against the adverse party.

(f) When Affidavits Are Unavailable. Should it appear from the affidavits of a party opposing the motion that the party cannot for reasons stated present by affidavit facts essential to justify the party's opposition, the court may refuse the application for judgment or may order a continuance to permit affidavits to be obtained or depositions to be taken or discovery to be had or may make such other order as is just.

(g) Affidavits Made in Bad Faith. Should it appear to the satisfaction of the court at any time that any of the affidavits presented pursuant to this rule are presented in bad faith or solely for the purpose of delay, the court shall forthwith order the party employing them to pay to the other party the amount of the reasonable expenses which the filing of the affidavits caused the other party to incur, including reasonable attorney's fees, and any offending party or attorney may be adjudged guilty of contempt.

As amended 1948, 1963, 1987.

Rule 57.

DECLARATORY JUDGMENTS

The procedure for obtaining a declaratory judgment pursuant to Title 28 U.S.C. § 2201, shall be in accordance with these rules, and the right to trial by jury may be demanded under the circumstances and in the manner provided in Rules 38 and 39. The existence of another adequate remedy does not preclude a judgment for declaratory relief in cases where it is appropriate. The court may order a speedy hearing of an action for a declaratory judgment and may advance it on the calendar.

As amended 1949.

Rule 58.

ENTRY OF JUDGMENT

Subject to the provisions of Rule 54(b): (1) upon a general verdict of a jury, or upon a decision by the court that a party shall recover only a sum certain or costs or that all relief shall be denied, the clerk, unless the court otherwise orders, shall forthwith prepare, sign, and enter the judgment without awaiting any direction by the court; (2) upon a decision by the court granting other relief, or upon a special verdict or a general verdict accompanied by answers to interrogatories, the court shall promptly approve the form of the judgment, and the clerk shall thereupon enter it. Every judgment shall be set forth on a separate document. A judgment is effective only when so set forth and when entered as provided in Rule 79(a). Entry of the judgment shall not be delayed for the taxing of costs. Attorneys shall not submit forms of judgment except upon direction of the court, and these directions shall not be given as a matter of course.

As amended 1948, 1963.

Rule 59.

NEW TRIALS; AMENDMENT OF JUDGMENTS

(a) Grounds. A new trial may be granted to all or any of the parties and on all or part of the issues (1) in an action in which there has been a trial by jury, for any of the reasons for which new trials have heretofore been granted in actions at law in the courts of the United States; and (2) in an action tried without a jury, for any of the reasons for which rehearings have heretofore been granted in suits in equity in the courts of the United States. On a motion for a new trial in an action tried without a jury, the court may open the judgment if one has been entered, take additional testimony, amend findings of fact and conclusions of law or make new findings and conclusions, and direct the entry of a new judgment.

(b) Time for Motion. A motion for a new trial shall be served not later than 10 days after the entry of the judgment.

(c) Time for Serving Affidavits. When a motion for new trial is based upon affidavits they shall be served with the motion. The opposing party has 10 days after such service within which to serve opposing affidavits, which period may be extended for an additional period not exceeding 20 days either by the court for good cause shown or by the parties by written stipulation. The court may permit reply affidavits.

(d) On Initiative of Court. Not later than 10 days after entry of judgment the court of its own initiative may order a new trial for any reason for which it might have granted a new trial on motion of a party. After giving the parties notice and an opportunity to be heard on the matter, the court may grant a motion for a new trial, timely served, for a reason not stated in the motion. In either case, the court shall specify in the order the grounds therefor.

(e) **Motion to Alter or Amend a Judgment.** A motion to alter or amend the judgment shall be served not later than 10 days after entry of the judgment.

As amended 1948, 1966.

Rule 60.

RELIEF FROM JUDGMENT OR ORDER

(a) **Clerical Mistakes.** Clerical mistakes in judgments, orders or other parts of the record and errors therein arising from oversight or omission may be corrected by the court at any time of its own initiative or on the motion of any party and after such notice, if any, as the court orders. During the pendency of an appeal, such mistakes may be so corrected before the appeal is docketed in the appellate court, and thereafter while the appeal is pending may be so corrected with leave of the appellate court.

(b) **Mistakes; Inadvertence; Excusable Neglect; Newly Discovered Evidence; Fraud, etc.** On motion and upon such terms as are just, the court may relieve a party or a party's legal representative from a final judgment, order, or proceeding for the following reasons: (1) mistake, inadvertence, surprise, or excusable neglect; (2) newly discovered evidence which by due diligence could not have been discovered in time to move for a new trial under Rule 59(b); (3) fraud (whether heretofore denominated intrinsic or extrinsic), misrepresentation, or other misconduct of an adverse party; (4) the judgment is void; (5) the judgment has been satisfied, released, or discharged, or a prior judgment upon which it is based has been reversed or otherwise vacated, or it is no longer equitable that the judgment should have prospective application; or (6) any other reason justifying relief from the operation of the judgment. The motion shall be made within a reasonable time, and for reasons (1), (2), and (3) not more than one year after the judgment, order, or proceeding was entered or taken. A motion under this subdivision (b) does not affect the finality of a judgment or suspend its operation. This rule does not limit the power of a court to entertain an independent action to relieve a party from a judgment, order, or proceeding, or to grant relief to a defendant not actually personally notified as provided in Title 28, U.S.C., § 1655, or to set aside a judgment for fraud upon the court. Writs of coram nobis, coram vobis, audita querela, and bills of review and bills in the nature of a bill of review, are abolished, and the procedure for obtaining any relief from a judgment shall be by motion as prescribed in these rules or by an independent action.

As amended 1948, 1949, 1987.

Rule 61.

HARMLESS ERROR

No error in either the admission or the exclusion of evidence and no error or defect in any ruling or order or in anything done or omitted by the court or by any of the parties is ground for granting a new trial or for setting aside a verdict or for vacating, modifying or otherwise disturbing a judgment or order, unless refusal to take such action appears to the court inconsistent with substantial justice. The court at every stage of the proceeding must disregard any error or defect in the proceeding which does not affect the substantial rights of the parties.

Rule 62.

STAY OF PROCEEDINGS TO ENFORCE A JUDGMENT

(a) **Automatic Stay; Exceptions—Injunctions, Receiverships, and Patent Accountings.** Except as stated herein, no execution shall issue upon a judgment nor shall proceedings be taken for its enforcement until the expiration of 10 days after its entry. Unless otherwise ordered by the court, an interlocutory or final judgment in an action for an injunction or in a receivership action, or a judgment or order directing an accounting in an action for infringement of letters patent, shall not be stayed during the period after its entry and until an appeal is taken or during the pendency of an appeal. The provisions of subdivision (c) of this rule govern the suspending, modifying, restoring, or granting of an injunction during the pendency of an appeal.

(b) **Stay on Motion for New Trial or for Judgment.** In its discretion and on such conditions for the security of the adverse party as are proper, the court may stay the execution of or any proceedings to enforce a judgment pending the disposition of a motion for a new trial or to alter or amend a judgment made pursuant to Rule 59, or of a motion for relief from a judgment or order made pursuant to Rule 60, or of a motion for judgment in accordance with a motion for a directed verdict made pursuant to Rule 50, or of a motion for amendment to the findings or for additional findings made pursuant to Rule 52(b).

(c) **Injunction Pending Appeal.** When an appeal is taken from an interlocutory or final judgment granting, dissolving, or denying an injunction, the court in its discretion may suspend, modify, restore, or grant an injunction during the pendency of the appeal upon such terms as to bond or otherwise as it considers proper for the security of the rights of the adverse party. If the judgment appealed from is rendered by a district court of three judges specially constituted pursuant to a statute of the United States, no such order shall be made except (1) by such court sitting in open court or (2) by the assent of all the judges of such court evidenced by their signatures to the order.

(d) Stay upon Appeal. When an appeal is taken the appellant by giving a supersedeas bond may obtain a stay subject to the exceptions contained in subdivision (a) of this rule. The bond may be given at or after the time of filing the notice of appeal or of procuring the order allowing the appeal, as the case may be. The stay is effective when the supersedeas bond is approved by the court.

(e) Stay in Favor of the United States or Agency Thereof. When an appeal is taken by the United States or an officer or agency thereof or by direction of any department of the Government of the United States and the operation or enforcement of the judgment is stayed, no bond, obligation, or other security shall be required from the appellant.

(f) Stay According to State Law. In any state in which a judgment is a lien upon the property of the judgment debtor and in which the judgment debtor is entitled to a stay of execution, a judgment debtor is entitled, in the district court held therein, to such stay as would be accorded the judgment debtor had the action been maintained in the courts of that state.

(g) Power of Appellate Court Not Limited. The provisions in this rule do not limit any power of an appellate court or of a judge or justice thereof to stay proceedings during the pendency of an appeal or to suspend, modify, restore, or grant an injunction during the pendency of an appeal or to make any order appropriate to preserve the status quo or the effectiveness of the judgment subsequently to be entered.

(h) Stay of Judgment as to Multiple Claims or Multiple Parties. When a court has ordered a final judgment under the conditions stated in Rule 54(b), the court may stay enforcement of that judgment until the entering of a subsequent judgment or judgments and may prescribe such conditions as are necessary to secure the benefit thereof to the party in whose favor the judgment is entered.

As amended 1948, 1949, 1961, 1987.

Rule 63.

DISABILITY OF A JUDGE

If by reason of death, sickness, or other disability, a judge before whom an action has been tried is unable to perform the duties to be performed by the court under these rules after a verdict is returned or findings of fact and conclusions of law are filed, then any other judge regularly sitting in or assigned to the court in which the action was tried may perform those duties; but if such other judge is satisfied that such other judge cannot perform those duties because such other judge did not preside at the trial or for any other reason, such other judge may in such other judge's discretion grant a new trial.

As amended 1987.

VIII.   PROVISIONAL AND FINAL REMEDIES AND SPECIAL PROCEEDINGS

Rule 64.

SEIZURE OF PERSON OR PROPERTY

At the commencement of and during the course of an action, all remedies providing for seizure of person or property for the purpose of securing satisfaction of the judgment ultimately to be entered in the action are available under the circumstances and in the manner provided by the law of the state in which the district court is held, existing at the time the remedy is sought, subject to the following qualifications: (1) any existing statute of the United States governs to the extent to which it is applicable; (2) the action in which any of the foregoing remedies is used shall be commenced and prosecuted or, if removed from a state court, shall be prosecuted after removal, pursuant to these rules. The remedies thus available include arrest, attachment, garnishment, replevin, sequestration, and other corresponding or equivalent remedies, however designated and regardless of whether by state procedure the remedy is ancillary to an action or must be obtained by an independent action.

Rule 65.

INJUNCTIONS

(a) Preliminary Injunction.

(1) *Notice.* No preliminary injunction shall be issued without notice to the adverse party.

(2) *Consolidation of Hearing with Trial on Merits.* Before or after the commencement of the hearing of an application for a preliminary injunction, the court may order the trial of the action on the merits to be advanced and consolidated with the hearing of the application. Even when this consolidation is not ordered, any evidence received upon an application for a preliminary injunction which would be admissible upon the trial on the merits becomes part of the record on the trial and need not be repeated upon the trial. This subdivision (a)(2) shall be so construed and applied as to save to the parties any rights they may have to trial by jury.

(b) Temporary Restraining Order; Notice; Hearing; Duration. A temporary restraining order may be granted without written or oral notice to the adverse party or that party's attorney only if (1) it clearly appears from specific facts shown by affidavit or by the verified complaint that immediate and irreparable injury, loss, or damage will result to the applicant before the adverse party or that party's attorney can be heard in opposition, and (2) the applicant's attorney certifies to the court in writing the efforts, if any, which have been made to give the notice and the reasons supporting the claim that notice should not be required. Every temporary restraining order granted without notice shall be indorsed with the date and hour of issuance; shall be filed forthwith in the clerk's office and entered of record; shall define the injury and state why it is irreparable and why the order was granted without notice; and shall expire by its terms within such time after entry, not to exceed 10 days, as the court fixes, unless within the time so fixed the order, for good cause shown, is extended for a like period or unless the party against whom the order is directed consents that it may be extended for a longer period. The reasons for the extension shall be entered of record. In case a temporary restraining order is granted without notice, the motion for a preliminary injunction shall be set down for hearing at the earliest possible time and takes precedence of all matters except older matters of the same character; and when the motion comes on for hearing the party who obtained the temporary restraining order shall proceed with the application for a preliminary injunction and, if the party does not do so, the court shall dissolve the temporary restraining order. On 2 days' notice to the party who obtained the temporary restraining order without notice or on such shorter notice to that party as the court may prescribe, the adverse party may appear and move its dissolution or modification and in that event the court shall proceed to hear and determine such motion as expeditiously as the ends of justice require.

(c) Security. No restraining order or preliminary injunction shall issue except upon the giving of security by the applicant, in such sum as the court deems proper, for the payment of such costs and damages as may be incurred or suffered by any party who is found to have been wrongfully enjoined or restrained. No such security shall be required of the United States or of an officer or agency thereof.

The provisions of Rule 65.1 apply to a surety upon a bond or undertaking under this rule.

(d) Form and Scope of Injunction or Restraining Order. Every order granting an injunction and every restraining order shall set forth the reasons for its issuance; shall be specific in terms; shall describe in reasonable detail, and not by reference to the complaint or other document, the act or acts sought to be restrained; and is binding only upon the parties to the action, their officers, agents, servants, employees, and attorneys, and upon those persons in active concert or participation with them who receive actual notice of the order by personal service or otherwise.

(e) Employer and Employee; Interpleader; Constitutional Cases. These rules do not modify any statute of the United States relating to temporary restraining orders and preliminary injunctions in actions affecting employer and employee; or the provisions of Title 28, U.S.C., § 2361, relating to preliminary injunctions in actions of interpleader or in the nature of interpleader; or Title 28, U.S.C., § 2284, relating to actions required by Act of Congress to be heard and determined by a district court of three judges.

As amended 1948, 1949, 1966, 1987.

Rule 65.1.

SECURITY: PROCEEDINGS AGAINST SURETIES

Whenever these rules, including the Supplemental Rules for Certain Admiralty and Marine Claims, require or permit the giving of security by a party, and security is given in the form of a bond or stipulation or other undertaking with one or more sureties, each surety submits to the jurisdiction of the court and irrevocably appoints the clerk of the court as the surety's agent upon whom any papers affecting the surety's liability on the bond or undertaking may be served. The surety's liability may be enforced on motion without the necessity of an independent action. The motion and such notice of the motion as the court prescribes may be served on the clerk of the court, who shall forthwith mail copies to the sureties if their addresses are known.

Added 1966; as amended 1987.

Rule 66.

RECEIVERS APPOINTED BY FEDERAL COURTS

An action wherein a receiver has been appointed shall not be dismissed except by order of the court. The practice in the administration of estates by receivers or by other similar officers appointed by the court shall be in accordance with the practice heretofore followed in the courts of the United States or as provided in rules promulgated by the district courts. In all other respects the action in which the appointment of a receiver is sought or which is brought by or against a receiver is governed by these rules.

As amended 1948, 1949.

Rule 67.

DEPOSIT IN COURT

In an action in which any part of the relief sought is a judgment for a sum of money or the disposition of a sum of money or the disposition of any other thing capable of delivery, a party, upon notice to every other party, and by leave of court, may deposit with the court all or any part of such sum or thing, whether or not that party claims all or any part of the sum or thing. The party making the deposit shall serve the order permitting deposit on the clerk of the court. Money paid into court under this rule shall be deposited and withdrawn in accordance with the provisions of Title 28, U.S.C., §§ 2041, and 2042; the Act of June 26, 1934, c. 756, § 23, as amended (48 Stat. 1236, 58 Stat. 845), U.S.C., Title 31, § 725v; or any like statute. The fund shall be deposited in an interest-bearing account or invested in an interest-bearing instrument approved by the court.

As amended 1949, 1983.

Rule 68.

OFFER OF JUDGMENT

At any time more than 10 days before the trial begins, a party defending against a claim may serve upon the adverse party an offer to allow judgment to be taken against the defending party for the money or property or to the effect specified in the offer, with costs then accrued. If within 10 days after the service of the offer the adverse party serves written notice that the offer is accepted, either party may then file the offer and notice of acceptance together with proof of service thereof and thereupon the clerk shall enter judgment. An offer not accepted shall be deemed withdrawn and evidence thereof is not admissible except in a proceeding to determine costs. If the judgment finally obtained by the offeree is not more favorable than the offer, the offeree must pay the costs incurred after the making of the offer. The fact that an offer is made but not accepted does not preclude a subsequent offer. When the liability of one party to another has been determined by verdict or order or judgment, but the amount or extent of the liability remains to be determined by further proceedings, the party adjudged liable may make an offer of judgment, which shall have the same effect as an offer made before trial if it is served within a reasonable time not less than 10 days prior to the commencement of hearings to determine the amount or extent of liability.

As amended 1948, 1966, 1987.

Rule 69.

EXECUTION

(a) **In General.** Process to enforce a judgment for the payment of money shall be a writ of execution, unless the court directs otherwise. The procedure on execution, in proceedings supplementary to and in aid of a judgment, and in proceedings on and in aid of execution shall be in accordance with the practice and procedure of the state in which the district court is held, existing at the time the remedy is sought, except that any statute of the United States governs to the extent that it is applicable. In aid of the judgment or execution, the judgment creditor or a successor in interest when that interest appears of record, may obtain discovery from any person, including the judgment debtor, in the manner provided in these rules or in the manner provided by the practice of the state in which the district court is held.

(b) **Against Certain Public Officers.** When a judgment has been entered against a collector or other officer of revenue under the circumstances stated in Title 28, U.S.C., § 2006, or against an officer of Congress in an action mentioned in the Act of March 3, 1875, c. 130, § 8 (18 Stat. 401), U.S.C., Title 2, § 118, and when the court has given the certificate of probable cause for the officer's act as provided in those statutes, execution shall not issue against the officer or the officer's property but the final judgment shall be satisfied as provided in such statutes.

As amended 1949, 1970, 1987.

Rule 70.

JUDGMENT FOR SPECIFIC ACTS; VESTING TITLE

If a judgment directs a party to execute a conveyance of land or to deliver deeds or other documents or to perform any other specific act and the party fails to comply within the time specified, the court may direct the act to be done at the cost of the disobedient party by some other person appointed by the court and the act when so done has like effect as if done by the party. On application of the party entitled to performance, the clerk shall issue a writ of attachment or sequestration against the property of the disobedient party to compel obedience to the judgment. The court may also in proper cases adjudge the party in contempt. If real or personal property is within the district, the court in lieu of directing a conveyance thereof may enter a judgment divesting the title of any party and vesting it in others and such judgment has the effect of a conveyance executed in due form of law. When any order or judgment is for the delivery of possession, the party in whose favor it is entered is entitled to a writ of execution or assistance upon application to the clerk.

Rule 71.

PROCESS IN BEHALF OF AND AGAINST PERSONS NOT PARTIES

When an order is made in favor of a person who is not a party to the action, that person may enforce obedience to the order by the same process as if a party; and, when obedience to an order may be lawfully enforced against a person who is not a party, that person is liable to the same process for enforcing obedience to the order as if a party.

As amended 1987.

Rule 71A.

CONDEMNATION OF PROPERTY

(a) **Applicability of Other Rules.** The Rules of Civil Procedure for the United States District Courts govern the procedure for the condemnation of real and personal property under the power of eminent domain, except as otherwise provided in this rule.

(b) **Joinder of Properties.** The plaintiff may join in the same action one or more separate pieces of property, whether in

107

the same or different ownership and whether or not sought for the same use.

(c) Complaint.

(1) *Caption.* The complaint shall contain a caption as provided in Rule 10(a), except that the plaintiff shall name as defendants the property, designated generally by kind, quantity, and location, and at least one of the owners of some part of or interest in the property.

(2) *Contents.* The complaint shall contain a short and plain statement of the authority for the taking, the use for which the property is to be taken, a description of the property sufficient for its identification, the interests to be acquired, and as to each separate piece of property a designation of the defendants who have been joined as owners thereof or of some interest therein. Upon the commencement of the action, the plaintiff need join as defendants only the persons having or claiming an interest in the property whose names are then known, but prior to any hearing involving the compensation to be paid for a piece of property, the plaintiff shall add as defendants all persons having or claiming an interest in that property whose names can be ascertained by a reasonably diligent search of the records, considering the character and value of the property involved and the interests to be acquired, and also those whose names have otherwise been learned. All others may be made defendants under the designation "Unknown Owners." Process shall be served as provided in subdivision (d) of this rule upon all defendants, whether named as defendants at the time of the commencement of the action or subsequently added, and a defendant may answer as provided in subdivision (e) of this rule. The court meanwhile may order such distribution of a deposit as the facts warrant.

(3) *Filing.* In addition to filing the complaint with the court, the plaintiff shall furnish to the clerk at least one copy thereof for the use of the defendants and additional copies at the request of the clerk or of a defendant.

(d) Process.

(1) *Notice; Delivery.* Upon the filing of the complaint the plaintiff shall forthwith deliver to the clerk joint or several notices directed to the defendants named or designated in the complaint. Additional notices directed to defendants subsequently added shall be so delivered. The delivery of the notice and its service have the same effect as the delivery and service of the summons under Rule 4.

(2) *Same; Form.* Each notice shall state the court, the title of the action, the name of the defendant to whom it is directed, that

the action is to condemn property, a description of the defendant's property sufficient for its identification, the interest to be taken, the authority for the taking, the uses for which the property is to be taken, that the defendant may serve upon the plaintiff's attorney an answer within 20 days after service of the notice, and that the failure so to serve an answer constitutes a consent to the taking and to the authority of the court to proceed to hear the action and to fix the compensation. The notice shall conclude with the name of the plaintiff's attorney and an address within the district in which action is brought where the attorney may be served. The notice need contain a description of no other property than that to be taken from the defendants to whom it is directed.

(3) *Service of Notice.*

(i) *Personal Service.* Personal service of the notice (but without copies of the complaint) shall be made in accordance with Rule 4(c) and (d) upon a defendant who resides within the United States or its territories or insular possessions and whose residence is known.

(ii) *Service by Publication.* Upon the filing of a certificate of the plaintiff's attorney stating that the attorney believes a defendant cannot be personally served, because after diligent inquiry within the state in which the complaint is filed the defendant's place of residence cannot be ascertained by the plaintiff or, if ascertained, that it is beyond the territorial limits of personal service as provided in this rule, service of the notice shall be made on this defendant by publication in a newspaper published in the county where the property is located, or if there is no such newspaper, then in a newspaper having a general circulation where the property is located, once a week for not less than three successive weeks. Prior to the last publication, a copy of the notice shall also be mailed to a defendant who cannot be personally served as provided in this rule but whose place of residence is then known. Unknown owners may be served by publication in like manner by a notice addressed to "Unknown Owners."

Service by publication is complete upon the date of the last publication. Proof of publication and mailing shall be made by certificate of the plaintiff's attorney, to which shall be attached a printed copy of the published notice with the name and dates of the newspaper marked thereon.

(4) *Return; Amendment.* Proof of service of the notice shall be made and amendment of the notice or proof of its service allowed in the manner provided for the return and amendment of the summons under Rule 4(g) and (h).

(e) **Appearance or Answer.** If a defendant has no objection or defense to the taking of the defendant's property, the defendant may serve a notice of appearance designating the property in which the defendant claims to be interested. Thereafter, the defendant shall receive notice of all proceedings affecting it. If a defendant has any objection or defense to the taking of the property, the defendant shall serve an answer within 20 days after the service of notice upon the defendant. The answer shall identify the property in which the defendant claims to have an interest, state the nature and extent of the interest claimed, and state all the defendant's objections and defenses to the taking of the property. A defendant waives all defenses and objections not so presented, but at the trial of the issue of just compensation, whether or not the defendant has previously appeared or answered, the defendant may present evidence as to the amount of the compensation to be paid for the property, and the defendant may share in the distribution of the award. No other pleading or motion asserting any additional defense or objection shall be allowed.

(f) **Amendment of Pleadings.** Without leave of court, the plaintiff may amend the complaint at any time before the trial of the issue of compensation and as many times as desired, but no amendment shall be made which will result in a dismissal forbidden by subdivision (i) of this rule. The plaintiff need not serve a copy of an amendment, but shall serve notice of the filing, as provided in Rule 5(b), upon any party affected thereby who has appeared and, in the manner provided in subdivision (d) of this rule, upon any party affected thereby who has not appeared. The plaintiff shall furnish to the clerk of the court for the use of the defendants at least one copy of each amendment and shall furnish additional copies on the request of the clerk or of a defendant. Within the time allowed by subdivision (e) of this rule a defendant may serve an answer to the amended pleading, in the form and manner and with the same effect as there provided.

(g) **Substitution of Parties.** If a defendant dies or becomes incompetent or transfers an interest after the defendant's joinder, the court may order substitution of the proper party upon motion and notice of hearing. If the motion and notice of hearing are to be served upon a person not already a party, service shall be made as provided in subdivision (d)(3) of this rule.

(h) **Trial.** If the action involves the exercise of the power of eminent domain under the law of the United States, any tribunal specially constituted by an Act of Congress governing the case for the trial of the issue of just compensation shall be the tribunal for the determination of that issue; but if there is no such specially constituted tribunal any party may have a trial by jury of the issue of just compensation by filing a demand therefor within the time allowed for answer or within such further time as the court may fix, unless the court in its discretion orders that, because of the character, location, or quantity of the property to be condemned, or for other reasons in the interest of justice, the issue of compensation shall be determined by a commission of three persons appointed by it.

In the event that a commission is appointed the court may direct that not more than two additional persons serve as alternate commissioners to hear the case and replace commissioners who, prior to the time when a decision is filed, are found by the court to be unable or disqualified to perform their duties. An alternate who does not replace a regular commissioner shall be discharged after the commission renders its final decision. Before appointing the members of the commission and alternates the court shall advise the parties of the identity and qualifications of each prospective commissioner and alternate and may permit the parties to examine each such designee. The parties shall not be permitted or required by the court to suggest nominees. Each party shall have the right to object for valid cause to the appointment of any person as a commissioner or alternate. If a commission is appointed it shall have the powers of a master provided in subdivision (c) of Rule 53 and proceedings before it shall be governed by the provisions of paragraphs (1) and (2) of subdivision (d) of Rule 53. Its action and report shall be determined by a majority and its findings and report shall have the effect, and be dealt with by the court in accordance with the practice, prescribed in paragraph (2) of subdivision (e) of Rule 53. Trial of all issues shall otherwise be by the court.

(i) Dismissal of Action.

(1) *As of Right.* If no hearing has begun to determine the compensation to be paid for a piece of property and the plaintiff has not acquired the title or a lesser interest in or taken possession, the plaintiff may dismiss the action as to that property, without an order of the court, by filing a notice of dismissal setting forth a brief description of the property as to which the action is dismissed.

(2) *By Stipulation.* Before the entry of any judgment vesting the plaintiff with title or a lesser interest in or possession of property, the action may be dismissed in whole or in part, without an order of the court, as to any property by filing a stipulation of dismissal by the plaintiff and the defendant affected thereby; and, if the parties so stipulate, the court may vacate any judgment that has been entered.

(3) *By Order of the Court.* At any time before compensation for a piece of property has been determined and paid and after motion and hearing, the court may dismiss the action as to that

property, except that it shall not dismiss the action as to any part of the property of which the plaintiff has taken possession or in which the plaintiff has taken title or a lesser interest, but shall award just compensation for the possession, title or lesser interest so taken. The court at any time may drop a defendant unnecessarily or improperly joined.

(4) *Effect.*   Except as otherwise provided in the notice, or stipulation of dismissal, or order of the court, any dismissal is without prejudice.

(j) **Deposit and Its Distribution.** The plaintiff shall deposit with the court any money required by law as a condition to the exercise of the power of eminent domain; and, although not so required, may make a deposit when permitted by statute. In such cases the court and attorneys shall expedite the proceedings for the distribution of the money so deposited and for the ascertainment and payment of just compensation. If the compensation finally awarded to any defendant exceeds the amount which has been paid to that defendant on distribution of the deposit, the court shall enter judgment against the plaintiff and in favor of that defendant for the deficiency. If the compensation finally awarded to any defendant is less than the amount which has been paid to that defendant, the court shall enter judgment against that defendant and in favor of the plaintiff for the overpayment.

(k) **Condemnation Under a State's Power of Eminent Domain.** The practice as herein prescribed governs in actions involving the exercise of the power of eminent domain under the law of a state, provided that if the state law makes provision for trial of any issue by jury, or for trial of the issue of compensation by jury or commission or both, that provision shall be followed.

(*l*) **Costs.** Costs are not subject to Rule 54(d).

Added 1951; as amended 1963, 1985, 1987, 1988.

Rule 72.

MAGISTRATES; PRETRIAL MATTERS

(a) **Nondispositive Matters.** A magistrate to whom a pretrial matter not dispositive of a claim or defense of a party is referred to hear and determine shall promptly conduct such proceedings as are required and when appropriate enter into the record a written order setting forth the disposition of the matter. The district judge to whom the case is assigned shall consider objections made by the parties, provided they are served and filed within 10 days after the entry of the order, and shall modify or set aside any portion of the magistrate's order found to be clearly erroneous or contrary to law.

(b) **Dispositive Motions and Prisoner Petitions.** A magistrate assigned without consent of the parties to hear a pretrial matter dispositive of a claim or defense of a party or a prisoner petition challenging the conditions of confinement shall promptly conduct such proceedings as are required. A record shall be made of all evidentiary proceedings before the magistrate, and a record may be made of such other proceedings as the magistrate deems necessary. The magistrate shall enter into the record a recommendation for disposition of the matter, including proposed findings of fact when appropriate. The clerk shall forthwith mail copies to all parties.

A party objecting to the recommended disposition of the matter shall promptly arrange for the transcription of the record, or portions of it as all parties may agree upon or the magistrate deems sufficient, unless the district judge otherwise directs. Within 10 days after being served with a copy of the recommended disposition, a party may serve and file specific, written objections to the proposed findings and recommendations. A party may respond to another party's objections within 10 days after being served with a copy thereof. The district judge to whom the case is assigned shall make a de novo determination upon the record, or after additional evidence, of any portion of the magistrate's disposition to which specific written objection has been made in accordance with this rule. The district judge may accept, reject, or modify the recommended decision, receive further evidence, or recommit the matter to the magistrate with instructions.

Added 1983.

Rule 73.

MAGISTRATES; TRIAL BY CONSENT AND APPEAL OPTIONS

(a) **Powers; Procedure.** When specially designated to exercise such jurisdiction by local rule or order of the district court and when all parties consent thereto, a magistrate may exercise the authority provided by Title 28, U.S.C. § 636(c) and may conduct any or all proceedings, including a jury or nonjury trial, in a civil case. A record of the proceedings shall be made in accordance with the requirements of Title 28, U.S.C. § 636(c)(7).

(b) **Consent.** When a magistrate has been designated to exercise civil trial jurisdiction, the clerk shall give written notice to the parties of their opportunity to consent to the exercise by a magistrate of civil jurisdiction over the case, as authorized by Title 28, U.S.C. § 636(c). If, within the period specified by local rule, the parties agree to a magistrate's exercise of such authority, they shall execute and file a joint form of consent or separate forms of consent setting forth such election.

No district judge, magistrate, or other court official shall attempt to persuade or induce a party to consent to a reference of a civil matter to a magistrate under this rule, nor shall a district judge or magistrate be informed of a party's response to the clerk's notification, unless all parties have consented to the referral of the matter to a magistrate.

The district judge, for good cause shown on the judge's motion, or under extraordinary circumstances shown by a party, may vacate a reference of a civil matter to a magistrate under this subdivision.

(c) Normal Appeal Route. In accordance with Title 28, U.S.C. § 636(c)(3), unless the parties otherwise agree to the optional appeal route provided for in subdivision (d) of this rule, appeal from a judgment entered upon direction of a magistrate in proceedings under this rule will lie to the court of appeals as it would from a judgment of the district court.

(d) Optional Appeal Route. In accordance with Title 28, U.S.C. § 636(c)(4), at the time of reference to a magistrate, the parties may consent to appeal on the record to a judge of the district court and thereafter, by petition only, to the court of appeals.

Added 1983; as amended 1987.

Rule 74.

METHOD OF APPEAL FROM MAGISTRATE TO DISTRICT JUDGE UNDER TITLE 28, U.S.C. § 636(c)(4) AND RULE 73(d)

(a) When Taken. When the parties have elected under Rule 73(d) to proceed by appeal to a district judge from an appealable decision made by a magistrate under the consent provisions of Title 28, U.S.C. § 636(c)(4), an appeal may be taken from the decision of a magistrate by filing with the clerk of the district court a notice of appeal within 30 days of the date of entry of the judgment appealed from; but if the United States or an officer or agency thereof is a party, the notice of appeal may be filed by any party within 60 days of such entry. If a timely notice of appeal is filed by a party, any other party may file a notice of appeal within 14 days thereafter, or within the time otherwise prescribed by this subdivision, whichever period last expires.

The running of the time for filing a notice of appeal is terminated as to all parties by the timely filing of any of the following motions with the magistrate by any party, and the full time for appeal from the judgment entered by the magistrate commences to run anew from entry of any of the following orders: (1) granting or denying a motion for judgment under Rule 50(b); (2) granting or denying a motion under Rule 52(b) to amend or make additional findings of fact, whether or not an alteration of the judgment would be required if the motion is granted; (3) granting or denying a motion under Rule 59 to alter or amend the judgment; (4) denying a motion for a new trial under Rule 59.

An interlocutory decision or order by a magistrate which, if made by a judge of the district court, could be appealed under any provision of law, may be appealed to a judge of the district court by filing a notice of appeal within 15 days after entry of the decision or order, provided the parties have elected to appeal to a judge of the district court under Rule 73(d). An appeal of such interlocutory decision or order shall not stay the proceedings before the magistrate unless the magistrate or judge shall so order.

Upon a showing of excusable neglect, the magistrate may extend the time for filing a notice of appeal upon motion filed not later than 20 days after the expiration of the time otherwise prescribed by this rule.

(b) Notice of Appeal; Service. The notice of appeal shall specify the party or parties taking the appeal, designate the judgment, order or part thereof appealed from, and state that the appeal is to a judge of the district court. The clerk shall mail copies of the notice to all other parties and note the date of mailing in the civil docket.

(c) Stay Pending Appeal. Upon a showing that the magistrate has refused or otherwise failed to stay the judgment pending appeal to the district judge under Rule 73(d), the appellant may make application for a stay to the district judge with reasonable notice to all parties. The stay may be conditioned upon the filing in the district court of a bond or other appropriate security.

(d) Dismissal. For failure to comply with these rules or any local rule or order, the district judge may take such action as is deemed appropriate, including dismissal of the appeal. The district judge also may dismiss the appeal upon the filing of a stipulation signed by all parties, or upon motion and notice by the appellant.

Added 1983.

Rule 75.

PROCEEDINGS ON APPEAL FROM MAGISTRATE TO DISTRICT JUDGE UNDER RULE 73(d)

(a) **Applicability.** In proceedings under Title 28, U.S.C. § 636(c), when the parties have previously elected under Rule 73(d) to appeal to a district judge rather than to the court of appeals, this rule shall govern the proceedings on appeal.

(b) **Record on Appeal.**

(1) *Composition.* The original papers and exhibits filed with the clerk of the district court, the transcript of the proceedings, if any, and the docket entries shall constitute the record on appeal. In lieu of this record the parties, within 10 days after the filing of the notice of appeal, may file a joint statement of the case showing how the issues presented by the appeal arose and were decided by the magistrate, and setting forth only so many of the facts averred and proved or sought to be proved as are essential to a decision of the issues presented.

(2) *Transcript.* Within 10 days after filing the notice of appeal the appellant shall make arrangements for the production of a transcript of such parts of the proceedings as the appellant deems necessary. Unless the entire transcript is to be included, the appellant, within the time provided above, shall serve on the appellee and file with the court a description of the parts of the transcript which the appellant intends to present on the appeal. If the appellee deems a transcript of other parts of the proceedings to be necessary, within 10 days after the service of the statement of the appellant, the appellee shall serve on the appellant and file with the court a designation of additional parts to be included. The appellant shall promptly make arrangements for the inclusion of all such parts unless the magistrate, upon motion, exempts the appellant from providing certain parts, in which case the appellee may provide for their transcription.

(3) *Statement in Lieu of Transcript.* If no record of the proceedings is available for transcription, the parties shall, within 10 days after the filing of the notice of appeal, file a statement of the evidence from the best available means to be submitted in lieu of the transcript. If the parties cannot agree they shall submit a statement of their differences to the magistrate for settlement.

(c) **Time for Filing Briefs.** Unless a local rule or court order otherwise provides, the following time limits for filing briefs shall apply.

(1) The appellant shall serve and file the appellant's brief within 20 days after the filing of the transcript, statement of the case, or statement of the evidence.

(2) The appellee shall serve and file the appellee's brief within 20 days after service of the brief of the appellant.

(3) The appellant may serve and file a reply brief within 10 days after service of the brief of the appellee.

(4) If the appellee has filed a cross-appeal, the appellee may file a reply brief limited to the issues on the cross-appeal within 10 days after service of the reply brief of the appellant.

(d) **Length and Form of Briefs.** Briefs may be typewritten. The length and form of briefs shall be governed by local rule.

(e) **Oral Argument.** The opportunity for the parties to be heard on oral argument shall be governed by local rule.

Added 1983; as amended 1987.

Rule 76.

JUDGMENT OF THE DISTRICT JUDGE ON THE APPEAL UNDER RULE 73(d) AND COSTS

(a) **Entry of Judgment.** When the parties have elected under Rule 73(d) to appeal from a judgment of the magistrate to a district judge, the clerk shall prepare, sign, and enter judgment in accordance with the order or decision of the district judge following an appeal from a judgment of the magistrate, unless the district judge directs otherwise. The clerk shall mail to all parties a copy of the order or decision of the district judge.

(b) **Stay of Judgments.** The decision of the district judge shall be stayed for 10 days during which time a party may petition the district judge for rehearing, and a timely petition shall stay the decision of the district judge pending disposition of a petition for rehearing. Upon the motion of a party, the decision of the district judge may be stayed in order to allow a party to petition the court of appeals for leave to appeal.

(c) **Costs.** Except as otherwise provided by law or ordered by the district judge, costs shall be taxed against the losing party; if a judgment of the magistrate is affirmed in part or reversed in part, or is vacated, costs shall be allowed only as ordered by the district judge. The cost of the transcript, if necessary for the determination of the appeal, and the premiums paid for bonds to preserve rights pending appeal shall be taxed as costs by the clerk.

Added 1983.

IX. APPEALS

ABROGATED DEC. 4, 1967, EFF. JULY 1, 1968

PRIOR PROVISIONS

The heading "IX. APPEALS" and Rules 72 to 76, formerly constituting the provisions of IX, were abrogated December 4, 1967, effective July 1, 1968. Former Rules 72 to 76 were the civil rules relating to appeals, the provisions of which, except for Rule 73(h), were transferred to and covered by the Federal Rules of Appellate Procedure and (in the case of Rule 72) the Rules of the Supreme Court. The substance of Rule 73(h) was transferred to Rule 9(h) of these Rules.

X. DISTRICT COURTS AND CLERKS

Rule 77.

DISTRICT COURTS AND CLERKS

(a) **District Courts Always Open.** The district courts shall be deemed always open for the purpose of filing any pleading or other proper paper, of issuing and returning mesne and final process, and of making and directing all interlocutory motions, orders, and rules.

(b) **Trials and Hearings; Orders in Chambers.** All trials upon the merits shall be conducted in open court and so far as convenient in a regular court room. All other acts or proceedings may be done or conducted by a judge in chambers, without the attendance of the clerk or other court officials and at any place either within or without the district; but no hearing, other than one ex parte, shall be conducted outside the district without the consent of all parties affected thereby.

(c) **Clerk's Office and Orders by Clerk.** The clerk's office with the clerk or a deputy in attendance shall be open during business hours on all days except Saturdays, Sundays, and legal holidays, but a district court may provide by local rule or order that its clerk's office shall be open for specified hours on Saturdays or particular legal holidays other than New Year's Day, Birthday of Martin Luther King, Jr., Washington's Birthday, Memorial Day, Independence Day, Labor Day, Columbus Day, Veterans Day, Thanksgiving Day, and Christmas Day. All motions and applications in the clerk's office for issuing mesne process, for issuing final process to enforce and execute judgments, for entering defaults or judgments by default, and for other proceedings which do not require allowance or order of the court are grantable of course by the clerk; but the clerk's action may be suspended or altered or rescinded by the court upon cause shown.

(d) Notice of Orders or Judgments. Immediately upon the entry of an order or judgment the clerk shall serve a notice of the entry by mail in the manner provided for in Rule 5 upon each party who is not in default for failure to appear, and shall make a note in the docket of the mailing. Such mailing is sufficient notice for all purposes for which notice of the entry of an order is required by these rules; but any party may in addition serve a notice of such entry in the manner provided in Rule 5 for the service of papers. Lack of notice of the entry by the clerk does not affect the time to appeal or relieve or authorize the court to relieve a party for failure to appeal within the time allowed, except as permitted in Rule 4(a) of the Federal Rules of Appellate Procedure.

As amended 1948, 1963, 1968, 1971, 1987.

Rule 78.

MOTION DAY

Unless local conditions make it impracticable, each district court shall establish regular times and places, at intervals sufficiently frequent for the prompt dispatch of business, at which motions requiring notice and hearing may be heard and disposed of; but the judge at any time or place and on such notice, if any, as the judge considers reasonable may make orders for the advancement, conduct, and hearing of actions.

To expedite its business, the court may make provision by rule or order for the submission and determination of motions without oral hearing upon brief written statements of reasons in support and opposition.

As amended 1987.

Rule 79.

BOOKS AND RECORDS KEPT BY THE CLERK AND ENTRIES THEREIN

(a) Civil Docket. The clerk shall keep a book known as "civil docket" of such form and style as may be prescribed by the Director of the Administrative Office of the United States Courts with the approval of the Judicial Conference of the United States, and shall enter therein each civil action to which these rules are made applicable. Actions shall be assigned consecutive file numbers. The file number of each action shall be noted on the folio of the docket whereon the first entry of the action is made. All papers filed with the clerk, all process issued and returns made thereon, all appearances, orders, verdicts, and judgments shall be entered chronologically in the civil docket on the folio assigned to the action and shall be marked with its file number. These entries shall be brief but shall show the nature of each paper filed or writ issued and the substance of each order or judgment of the court and of the returns showing execution of process. The entry of an order or judgment shall show the date the entry is made. When in an action trial by jury has been properly demanded or ordered the clerk shall enter the word "jury" on the folio assigned to that action.

(b) **Civil Judgments and Orders.** The clerk shall keep, in such form and manner as the Director of the Administrative Office of the United States Courts with the approval of the Judicial Conference of the United States may prescribe, a correct copy of every final judgment or appealable order, or order affecting title to or lien upon real or personal property, and any other order which the court may direct to be kept.

(c) **Indices; Calendars.** Suitable indices of the civil docket and of every civil judgment and order referred to in subdivision (b) of this rule shall be kept by the clerk under the direction of the court. There shall be prepared under the direction of the court calendars of all actions ready for trial, which shall distinguish "jury actions" from "court actions."

(d) **Other Books and Records of the Clerk.** The clerk shall also keep such other books and records as may be required from time to time by the Director of the Administrative Office of the United States Courts with the approval of the Judicial Conference of the United States.

As amended 1948, 1949, 1963.

Rule 80.

STENOGRAPHER; STENOGRAPHIC REPORT OR TRANSCRIPT AS EVIDENCE

(a) **Stenographer.** Abrogated Dec. 27, 1946, eff. Mar. 19, 1948.

(b) **Official Stenographer.** Abrogated Dec. 27, 1946, eff. Mar. 19, 1948.

(c) **Stenographic Report or Transcript as Evidence.** Whenever the testimony of a witness at a trial or hearing which was stenographically reported is admissible in evidence at a later trial, it may be proved by the transcript thereof duly certified by the person who reported the testimony.

As amended 1948.

XI. GENERAL PROVISIONS

Rule 81.

APPLICABILITY IN GENERAL

(a) To What Proceedings Applicable.

(1) These rules do not apply to prize proceedings in admiralty governed by Title 10, U.S.C. §§ 7651–7681. They do not apply to proceedings in bankruptcy or proceedings in copyright under Title 17, U.S.C., except in so far as they may be made applicable thereto by rules promulgated by Supreme Court of the United States. They do not apply to mental health proceedings in the United States District Court for the District of Columbia.

(2) These rules are applicable to proceedings for admission to citizenship, habeas corpus, and quo warranto, to the extent that the practice in such proceedings is not set forth in statutes of the United States and has heretofore conformed to the practice in civil actions. The writ of habeas corpus, or order to show cause, shall be directed to the person having custody of the person detained. It shall be returned within 3 days unless for good cause shown additional time is allowed which in cases brought under 28 U.S.C. § 2254 shall not exceed 40 days, and in all other cases shall not exceed 20 days.

(3) In proceedings under Title 9, U.S.C., relating to arbitration, or under the Act of May 20, 1926, ch. 347, § 9 (44 Stat. 585), U.S.C., Title 45, § 159, relating to boards of arbitration of railway labor disputes, these rules apply only to the extent that matters of procedure are not provided for in those statutes. These rules apply to proceedings to compel the giving of testimony or production of documents in accordance with a subpoena issued by an officer or agency of the United States under any statute of the United States except as otherwise provided by statute or by rules of the district court or by order of the court in the proceedings.

(4) These rules do not alter the method prescribed by the Act of February 18, 1922, c. 57, § 2 (42 Stat. 388), U.S.C., Title 7, § 292; or by the Act of June 10, 1930, c. 436, § 7 (46 Stat. 534), as amended, U.S.C., Title 7, § 499g(c), for instituting proceedings in the United States district courts to review orders of the Secretary of Agriculture; or prescribed by the Act of June 25, 1934, c. 742,

§ 2 (48 Stat. 1214), U.S.C., Title 15, § 522, for instituting proceedings to review orders of the Secretary of the Interior; or prescribed by the Act of February 22, 1935, c. 18, § 5 (49 Stat. 31), U.S.C., Title 15, § 715d(c), as extended, for instituting proceedings to review orders of petroleum control boards; but the conduct of such proceedings in the district courts shall be made to conform to these rules as far as applicable.

(5) These rules do not alter the practice in the United States district courts prescribed in the Act of July 5, 1935, c. 372, §§ 9 and 10 (49 Stat. 453), as amended, U.S.C., Title 29, §§ 159 and 160, for beginning and conducting proceedings to enforce orders of the National Labor Relations Board; and in respects not covered by those statutes, the practice in the district courts shall conform to these rules so far as applicable.

(6) These rules apply to proceedings for enforcement or review of compensation orders under the Longshoremen's and Harbor Workers' Compensation Act, Act of March 4, 1927, c. 509, §§ 18, 21 (44 Stat. 1434, 1436), as amended, U.S.C., Title 33, §§ 918, 921, except to the extent that matters of procedure are provided for in that Act. The provisions for service by publication and for answer in proceedings to cancel certificates of citizenship under the Act of June 27, 1952, c. 477, Title III, c. 2, § 340 (66 Stat. 260), U.S.C., Title 8, § 1451, remain in effect.

(7) Abrogated Apr. 30, 1951, eff. Aug. 1, 1951.

(b) Scire Facias and Mandamus. The writs of scire facias and mandamus are abolished. Relief heretofore available by mandamus or scire facias may be obtained by appropriate action or by appropriate motion under the practice prescribed in these rules.

(c) Removed Actions. These rules apply to civil actions removed to the United States district courts from the state courts and govern procedure after removal. Repleading is not necessary unless the court so orders. In a removed action in which the defendant has not answered, the defendant shall answer or present the other defenses or objections available under these rules within 20 days after the receipt through service or otherwise of a copy of the initial pleading setting forth the claim for relief upon which the action or proceeding is based, or within 20 days after the service of summons upon such initial pleading, then filed, or within 5 days after the filing of the petition for removal, whichever period is longest. If at the time of removal all necessary pleadings have been served, a party entitled to trial by jury under Rule 38 shall be accorded it, if the party's demand therefor is served within 10 days after the petition for removal is filed if the party is the petitioner, or if not the petitioner within 10 days

122

after service on the party of the notice of filing the petition. A party who, prior to removal, has made an express demand for trial by jury in accordance with state law, need not make a demand after removal. If state law applicable in the court from which the case is removed does not require the parties to make express demands in order to claim trial by jury, they need not make demands after removal unless the court directs that they do so within a specified time if they desire to claim trial by jury. The court may make this direction on its own motion and shall do so as a matter of course at the request of any party. The failure of a party to make demand as directed constitutes a waiver by that party of trial by jury.

(d) **District of Columbia; Courts and Judges.** Abrogated Dec. 29, 1948, eff. Oct. 20, 1949.

(e) **Law Applicable.** Whenever in these rules the law of the state in which the district court is held is made applicable, the law applied in the District of Columbia governs proceedings in the United States District Court for the District of Columbia. When the word "state" is used, it includes, if appropriate, the District of Columbia. When the term "statute of the United States" is used, it includes, so far as concerns proceedings in the United States District Court for the District of Columbia, any Act of Congress locally applicable to and in force in the District of Columbia. When the law of a state is referred to, the word "law" includes the statutes of that state and the state judicial decisions construing them.

(f) **References to Officer of the United States.** Under any rule in which reference is made to an officer or agency of the United States, the term "officer" includes a district director of internal revenue, a former district director or collector of internal revenue, or the personal representative of a deceased district director or collector of internal revenue.

As amended 1941, 1948, 1949, 1951, 1963, 1966, 1968, 1971, 1987.

Rule 82.

JURISDICTION AND VENUE UNAFFECTED

These rules shall not be construed to extend or limit the jurisdiction of the United States district courts or the venue of actions therein. An admiralty or maritime claim within the meaning of Rule 9(h) shall not be treated as a civil action for the purposes of Title 28, U.S.C. §§ 1391-93.

As amended 1949, 1966.

Rule 83.

RULES BY DISTRICT COURTS

Each district court by action of a majority of the judges thereof may from time to time, after giving appropriate public notice and an opportunity to comment, make and amend rules governing its practice not inconsistent with these rules. A local rule so adopted shall take effect upon the date specified by the district court and shall remain in effect unless amended by the district court or abrogated by the judicial council of the circuit in which the district is located. Copies of rules and amendments so made by any district court shall upon their promulgation be furnished to the judicial council and the Administrative Office of the United States Courts and be made available to the public. In all cases not provided for by rule, the district judges and magistrates may regulate their practice in any manner not inconsistent with these rules or those of the district in which they act.

As amended 1985.

Rule 84.

FORMS

The forms contained in the Appendix of Forms are sufficient under the rules and are intended to indicate the simplicity and brevity of statement which the rules contemplate.

As amended 1948.

Rule 85.

TITLE

These rules may be known and cited as the Federal Rules of Civil Procedure.

Rule 86.

EFFECTIVE DATE

(a) [**Effective Date of Original Rules**]. These rules will take effect on the day which is 3 months subsequent to the adjournment of the second regular session of the 75th Congress, but if that day is prior to September 1, 1938, then these rules will take effect on September 1, 1938. They govern all proceedings in actions brought after they take effect and also all further proceedings in actions then pending, except to the extent that in the opinion of the court their application in a particular action pending when the rules take effect would not be feasible or would work injustice, in which event the former procedure applies.

[The order of the Supreme Court of December 20, 1937, adopted the rules, to be known as the Federal Rules of Civil Procedure. The Rules became effective on September 16, 1938. 302 U.S. 783, 308 U.S. 645; see 12 C. Wright & A. Miller, Federal Practice and Procedure app. C.]

[Rule 81(a) was amended by the order of the Supreme Court of December 28, 1939, to be effective February 3, 1941. 308 U.S. 642; see 1 F.R.D. 79.]

(b) **Effective Date of Amendments.** The amendments adopted by the Supreme Court on December 27, 1946, and transmitted to the Attorney General on January 2, 1947, shall take effect on the day which is three months subsequent to the adjournment of the first regular session of the 80th Congress, but, if that day is prior to September 1, 1947, then these amendments shall take effect on September 1, 1947. They govern all proceedings in actions brought after they take effect and also all further proceedings in actions then pending, except to the extent that in the opinion of the court their application in a particular action pending when the amendments take effect would not be feasible or would work injustice, in which event the former procedure applies.

[Rules 6(b) and (c), 7(a), 12(a), (b), (c), (d), (e), (f), (g), and (h), 13(a), (g), and (i), 14(a), 17(b), 24(a) and (b), 26, 27(a) and (b), 28(a), 33, 34, 36(a), 41(a) and (b), 45(b) and (d), 52(a), 54(b), 56(a) and (c), 58, 59(b) and (e), 60 (a) and (b), 62(b) and (h), 65(c), 66, 68, 73, 75, 77(d), 79(a), (b), (c), and (d), 80(a) and (b), 81(a), (c), and (f), 84, and 86 and Forms 17, 20, 22, and 25 were amended by the order of the Supreme Court of December 27, 1946, to be effective March 19, 1948. 329 U.S. 839; cf. 5 F.R.D. 433.]

(c) **Effective Date of Amendments.** The amendments adopted by the Supreme Court on December 29, 1948, and transmitted to the Attorney General on December 31, 1948, shall take effect on the day following the adjournment of the first regular session of the 81st Congress.

[Rules 1, 17(b), 22(2), 24(c), 25(d), 27(a), 37(e), 45(e), 57, 60(b), 62(g), 65(e), 66, 67, 69(b), 72, 73, 74, 75, 76, 79(a), (b), and (d), 81(a), (c), (d), and (e), 82, and 86(c) and Forms 1, 19, 22, 23, and 27 were amended by the order of the Supreme Court of December 29, 1948, to be effective October 20, 1949. 335 U.S. 919; see 8 F.R.D. 591.]

[Rule 81(a) was amended, and Rule 71A and Forms 28 and 29 added, by the order of the Supreme Court of April 30, 1951, to be effective August 1, 1951. 341 U.S. 959; see 11 F.R.D. 213.]

(d) **Effective Date of Amendments.** The amendments adopted by the Supreme Court on April 17, 1961, and transmitted to the Congress on April 18, 1961, shall take effect on July 19,

1961. They govern all proceedings in actions brought after they take effect and also all further proceedings in actions then pending, except to the extent that in the opinion of the court their application in a particular action pending when the amendments take effect would not be feasible or would work injustice, in which event the former procedure applies.

[Rules 25(d), 54(b), 62(h), and 86(d) and Forms 2 and 19 were amended by the order of the Supreme Court of April 17, 1961, to be effective July 19, 1961. 368 U.S. 1009; see 12 C. Wright & A. Miller, Federal Practice and Procedure app. C.]

(e) Effective Date of Amendments. The amendments adopted by the Supreme Court on January 21, 1963, and transmitted to the Congress on January 21, 1963, shall take effect on July 1, 1963. They govern all proceedings in actions brought after they take effect and also all further proceedings in actions then pending, except to the extent that in the opinion of the court their application in a particular action pending when the amendments take effect would not be feasible or would work injustice, in which event the former procedure applies.

[Rules 4(b), (d), (e), (f), and (i), 5(a), 6(a) and (b), 7(a), 12(a), 13(a), 14(a), 15(d), 24(c), 25(a), 26, 28(b), 30(f), 41(b), 49(b), 50(a), (b), (c), and (d), 52(a), 56(c) and (e), 58, 71A(d), 77(c) and (d), 79(a), 81(a), (c), and (f), and 86(e) and Forms 3, 4, 5, 6, 7, 8, 9, 10, 11, 12, 13, 16, 18, and 21 were amended, Form 22 eliminated, and Forms 22–A, 22–B, 30, 31, and 32 added, by the orders of the Supreme Court of January 21, 1963, and March 18, 1963, to be effective July 1, 1963. 374 U.S. 861; see 31 F.R.D. 587.]

As amended 1948, 1949, 1961, 1963.

[Rules 1, 4(f), 6(c), 8(e), 9(h), 12(b), (g), and (h), 13(h), 14(a) and (c), 15(c), 17(a), 18(a), 19, 20(a), 23, 24(a), 26, 38(e), 41(b), 42(b), 43(f), 44(a), (b), and (c), 47(b), 53(a) and (b), 59(d), 65(a), (b), and (c), 68, 73, 74, 75, 81(a), and 82 and Forms 2 and 15 were amended, and Rules 23.1, 23.2, 44.1, and 65.1 and Supplemental Rules A–F added, by the order of the Supreme Court of February 28, 1966, to be effective July 1, 1966. 383 U.S. 1029; see 39 F.R.D. 69.]

[Rules 6(b), 9(h), 41(a), 77(d), and 81(a) were amended, and former Rules 72–76 and Form 27 abrogated, by the order of the Supreme Court of December 4, 1967, to be effective July 1, 1968. 389 U.S. 1121; see 43 F.R.D. 163.]

[Rules 5(a), 9(h), 26, 29, 30, 31, 32, 33, 34, 35, 36, 37, 45(d), and 69(a) and Form 24 were amended by the order of the Supreme Court of March 30, 1970, to be effective July 1, 1970. 398 U.S. 977; see 48 F.R.D. 485.]

———

[Rules 6(a), 27(a), 30(b), 77(c), and 81(a) were amended by the order of the Supreme Court of March 1, 1971, to be effective July 1, 1971. 401 U.S. 1017; see 52 F.R.D. 79.]

———

[Rules 30(c), 32(c), 43(a), (b), and (c), and 44.1 were amended by the orders of the Supreme Court of November 20, 1972, and December 18, 1972. 419 U.S. 1133; see 56 F.R.D. 355. Those amendments were expressly approved by Congress January 2, 1975, Pub.L. 93–595, § 3, 88 Stat. 1949, to be effective July 1, 1975.]

———

[Rules 4(a) and (c), 5(d), 26(f), 28(a), 30(b) and (f), 32(a), 33(c), 34(b), 37(b), (e), and (g), and 45(d) and (e) were amended by the order of the Supreme Court of April 29, 1980, to be effective August 1, 1980. 446 U.S. 995; see 85 F.R.D. 521.]

———

[Rule 37(f) was repealed October 21, 1980, Pub.L. 96–481, Title II, § 205(a), 94 Stat. 2330, to be effective October 1, 1981.]

———

[Rule 4(a), (c), (d), (e), (g), and (j) was amended by the order of the Supreme Court of April 28, 1982, to be effective August 1, 1982. 456 U.S. 1013; see 93 F.R.D. 255. That amendment was suspended by Congress August 2, 1982, Pub.L. 97–227, 96 Stat. 246, effective August 1, 1982. See 94 F.R.D. 221. Rule 4(a), (c), (d), (e), (g), and (j) was then amended, and Form 18–A added, January 12, 1983, Pub.L. 97–462, 96 Stat. 2527, to be effective February 26, 1983. See 96 F.R.D. 75.]

———

[Rules 6(b), 7(b), 11, 16, 26(a), (b), and (g), 52(a), 53(a), (b), (c), and (f), and 67 were amended, and Rules 72–76 and Forms 33 and 34 added, by the order of the Supreme Court of April 28, 1983, to be effective August 1, 1983. 461 U.S. 1095; see 97 F.R.D. 165.]

———

[Rules 6(a), 45(d), 52(a), 71A(h), and 83, Form 18–A, and Supplemental Rules B(1), C(3), and E(4) were amended by the order of the Supreme Court of April 29, 1985, to be effective August 1, 1985. 471 U.S. 1153; see 105 F.R.D. 202.]

————

[Rules 51 and 77(c) were amended, and gender-specific language was neutralized in numerous Rules and Supplemental Rules, by the order of the Supreme Court of March 2, 1987, to be effective August 1, 1987. 480 U.S. 953; see 113 F.R.D. 189.]

————

[Technical corrections to Rules 17(a) and 71A(e) were made by the order of the Supreme Court of April 25, 1988, to be effective August 1, 1988. 485 U.S. 1043; see 119 F.R.D. 261.]

————

[Rule 35 was amended November 18, 1988, Pub.L. 100–690, Title VII, § 7047, 102 Stat. 4401. See 122 F.R.D. 276.]

APPENDIX OF FORMS

(See Rule 84)

Introductory Statement [1938]

1. The following forms are intended for illustration only. They are limited in number. No attempt is made to furnish a manual of forms. Each form assumes the action to be brought in the Southern District of New York. If the district in which an action is brought has divisions, the division should be indicated in the caption.

2. Except where otherwise indicated each pleading, motion, and other paper should have a caption similar to that of the summons, with the designation of the particular paper substituted for the word "Summons". In the caption of the summons and in the caption of the complaint all parties must be named but in other pleadings and papers, it is sufficient to state the name of the first party on either side, with an appropriate indication of other parties. See Rules 4(b), 7(b)(2), and 10(a).

3. In Form 3 and the forms following, the words, "Allegation of jurisdiction", are used to indicate the appropriate allegation in Form 2.

4. Each pleading, motion, and other paper is to be signed in his individual name by at least one attorney of record (Rule 11). The attorney's name is to be followed by his address as indicated in Form 3. In forms following Form 3 the signature and address are not indicated.

5. If a party is not represented by an attorney, the signature and address of the party are required in place of those of the attorney.

Form 1.

SUMMONS

UNITED STATES DISTRICT COURT FOR THE SOUTHERN DISTRICT OF NEW YORK

Civil Action, File Number _____

A. B., Plaintiff   )
        v.   ) *Summons*
C. D., Defendant   )

Form 1   RULES OF CIVIL PROCEDURE

To the above-named Defendant:

You are hereby summoned and required to serve upon _____, plaintiff's attorney, whose address is _____, an answer to the complaint which is herewith served upon you, within 20 [1] days after service of this summons upon you, exclusive of the day of service. If you fail to do so, judgment by default will be taken against you for the relief demanded in the complaint.

_____,

Clerk of Court.

[Seal of the U. S. District Court]

Dated _____

(This summons is issued pursuant to
Rule 4 of the Federal Rules of
Civil Procedure).

As amended 1949.

Form 2.

ALLEGATION OF JURISDICTION

(a) Jurisdiction founded on diversity of citizenship and amount.

Plaintiff is a [citizen of the State of Connecticut] [2] [corporation incorporated under the laws of the State of Connecticut having its principal place of business in the State of Connecticut] and defendant is a corporation incorporated under the laws of the State of New York having its principal place of business in a State other than the State of Connecticut. The matter in controversy exceeds, exclusive of interest and costs, the sum of ten thousand dollars.

(b) Jurisdiction founded on the existence of a Federal question and amount in controversy.

The action arises under [the Constitution of the United States, Article ____, Section ____]; [the ____ Amendment to the Constitution of the United States, Section ____]; [the Act of ____, ____ Stat. ____; U.S.C., Title ____, § ____]; [the Treaty of the United States

---

[1] If the United States or an officer or agency thereof is a defendant, the time to be inserted as to it is 60 days.

[2] Form for natural person.

130

(here describe the treaty)],[3] as hereinafter more fully appears. The matter in controversy exceeds, exclusive of interest and costs, the sum of ten thousand dollars.

(c) Jurisdiction founded on the existence of a question arising under particular statutes.

The action arises under the Act of ___, ___ Stat. ___; U.S.C., Title ___, § ___, as hereinafter more fully appears.

(d) Jurisdiction founded on the admiralty or maritime character of the claim.

This is a case of admiralty and maritime jurisdiction, as hereinafter more fully appears. [If the pleader wishes to invoke the distinctively maritime procedures referred to in Rule 9(h), add the following or its substantial equivalent: This is an admiralty or maritime claim within the meaning of Rule 9(h).]

As amended 1961, 1966.

Note

1. **Diversity of Citizenship.** U.S.C., Title 28, § 1332 (Diversity of citizenship; amount in controversy; costs), as amended by PL 85–554, 72 Stat. 415, July 25, 1958, states in subsection (c) that "For the purposes of this section and section 1441 of this title [removable actions], a corporation shall be deemed a citizen of any State by which it has been incorporated and of the State where it has its principal place of business." Thus if the defendant corporation in Form 2(a) had its principal place of business in Connecticut, diversity of citizenship would not exist. An allegation regarding the principal place of business of each corporate party must be made in addition to an allegation regarding its place of incorporation.

2. **Jurisdictional Amount.** U.S.C., Title 28, § 1331 (Federal question; amount in controversy; costs) and § 1332 (Diversity of citizenship; amount in controversy; costs), as amended by PL 85–554, 72 Stat. 415, July 25, 1958, require that the amount in controversy, exclusive of interest and costs, be in excess of $10,000. The allegation as to the amount in controversy may be omitted in any case where by law no jurisdictional amount is required. See, for example, U.S.C., Title 28, § 1338 (Patents, copyrights, trademarks, and unfair competition), § 1343 (Civil rights and elective franchise).

3. **Pleading Venue.** Since improper venue is a matter of defense, it is not necessary for plaintiff to include allegations showing the venue to be proper. See 1 Moore's Federal Practice, par. 0.140[1.–4.] (2d ed. 1959).

[3] Use the appropriate phrase or phrases. The general allegation of the existence of a Federal question is ineffective unless the matters constituting the claim for relief as set forth in the complaint raise a Federal question.

Form 2   RULES OF CIVIL PROCEDURE

Editor's Note

Since this official Form was last amended, the statutory provisions regarding jurisdictional amount have changed in important ways. See 28 U.S.C. §§ 1331–1332.

Form 3.

COMPLAINT ON A PROMISSORY NOTE

1. Allegation of jurisdiction.

2. Defendant on or about June 1, 1935, executed and delivered to plaintiff a promissory note [in the following words and figures: (here set out the note verbatim)]; [a copy of which is hereto annexed as Exhibit A]; [whereby defendant promised to pay to plaintiff or order on June 1, 1936 the sum of _____ dollars with interest thereon at the rate of six percent per annum].

3. Defendant owes to plaintiff the amount of said note and interest.

Wherefore plaintiff demands judgment against defendant for the sum of _____ dollars, interest, and costs.

Signed: _____

Attorney for Plaintiff.

Address: _____

As amended 1963.

Note

1. The pleader may use the material in one of the three sets of brackets. His choice will depend upon whether he desires to plead the document verbatim, or by exhibit, or according to its legal effect.

2. Under the rules free joinder of claims is permitted. See rules 8(e) and 18. Consequently the claims set forth in each and all of the following forms may be joined with this complaint or with each other. Ordinarily each claim should be stated in a separate division of the complaint, and the divisions should be designated as counts successively numbered. In particular the rules permit alternative and inconsistent pleading. See Form 10.

Form 4.

COMPLAINT ON AN ACCOUNT

1. Allegation of jurisdiction.

2. Defendant owes plaintiff _____ dollars according to the account hereto annexed as Exhibit A.

Wherefore (etc. as in Form 3).

As amended 1963.

Form 5.

COMPLAINT FOR GOODS SOLD AND DELIVERED

1. Allegation of jurisdiction.

2. Defendant owes plaintiff _____ dollars for goods sold and delivered by plaintiff to defendant between June 1, 1936 and December 1, 1936.

Wherefore (etc. as in Form 3).

As amended 1963.

Note

This form may be used where the action is for an agreed price or for the reasonable value of the goods.

Form 6.

COMPLAINT FOR MONEY LENT

1. Allegation of jurisdiction.

2. Defendant owes plaintiff _____ dollars for money lent by plaintiff to defendant on June 1, 1936.

Wherefore (etc. as in Form 3).

As amended 1963.

Form 7.

COMPLAINT FOR MONEY PAID BY MISTAKE

1. Allegation of jurisdiction.

2. Defendant owes plaintiff _____ dollars for money paid by plaintiff to defendant by mistake on June 1, 1936, under the following circumstances: [here state the circumstances with particularity—see Rule 9(b)].

Wherefore (etc. as in Form 3).

As amended 1963.

Form 8.

COMPLAINT FOR MONEY HAD AND RECEIVED

1. Allegation of jurisdiction.

2. Defendant owes plaintiff _____ dollars for money had and received from one G. H. on June 1, 1936, to be paid by defendant to plaintiff.

Wherefore (etc. as in Form 3).

As amended 1963.

Form 9.

COMPLAINT FOR NEGLIGENCE

1.   Allegation of jurisdiction.

2.   On June 1, 1936, in a public highway called Boylston Street in Boston, Massachusetts, defendant negligently drove a motor vehicle against plaintiff who was then crossing said highway.

3.   As a result plaintiff was thrown down and had his leg broken and was otherwise injured, was prevented from transacting his business, suffered great pain of body and mind, and incurred expenses for medical attention and hospitalization in the sum of one thousand dollars.

Wherefore plaintiff demands judgment against defendant in the sum of _____ dollars and costs.

As amended 1963.

Note

Since contributory negligence is an affirmative defense, the complaint need contain no allegation of due care of plaintiff.

Form 10.

COMPLAINT FOR NEGLIGENCE WHERE PLAINTIFF IS UNABLE TO DETERMINE DEFINITELY WHETHER THE PERSON RESPONSIBLE IS C. D. OR E. F. OR WHETHER BOTH ARE RESPONSIBLE AND WHERE HIS EVIDENCE MAY JUSTIFY A FINDING OF WILFULNESS OR OF RECKLESSNESS OR OF NEGLIGENCE

A. B., Plaintiff   )
                v.   ) *Complaint*
C. D. and E. F., Defendants)

1.   Allegation of jurisdiction.

2.   On June 1, 1936, in a public highway called Boylston Street in Boston, Massachusetts, defendant C. D. or defendant E. F., or both defendants C. D. and E. F. wilfully or recklessly or negligently drove or caused to be driven a motor vehicle against plaintiff who was then crossing said highway.

3.   As a result plaintiff was thrown down and had his leg broken and was otherwise injured, was prevented from transacting

his business, suffered great pain of body and mind, and incurred expenses for medical attention and hospitalization in the sum of one thousand dollars.

Wherefore plaintiff demands judgment against C. D. or against E. F. or against both in the sum of _____ dollars and costs.

As amended 1963.

Form 11.

COMPLAINT FOR CONVERSION

1. Allegation of jurisdiction.

2. On or about December 1, 1936, defendant converted to his own use ten bonds of the _____ Company (here insert brief identification as by number and issue) of the value of _____ dollars, the property of plaintiff.

Wherefore plaintiff demands judgment against defendant in the sum of _____ dollars, interest, and costs.

As amended 1963.

Form 12.

COMPLAINT FOR SPECIFIC PERFORMANCE OF CONTRACT TO CONVEY LAND

1. Allegation of jurisdiction.

2. On or about December 1, 1936, plaintiff and defendant entered into an agreement in writing a copy of which is hereto annexed as Exhibit A.

3. In accord with the provisions of said agreement plaintiff tendered to defendant the purchase price and requested a conveyance of the land, but defendant refused to accept the tender and refused to make the conveyance.

4. Plaintiff now offers to pay the purchase price.

Wherefore plaintiff demands (1) that defendant be required specifically to perform said agreement, (2) damages in the sum of one thousand dollars, and (3) that if specific performance is not granted plaintiff have judgment against defendant in the sum of _____ dollars.

As amended 1963.

Note

Here, as in Form 3, plaintiff may set forth the contract verbatim in the complaint or plead it, as indicated, by exhibit, or plead it according to its legal effect. Furthermore, plaintiff may seek legal or equitable relief or both even though this was impossible under the system in operation before these rules.

Form 13.

COMPLAINT ON CLAIM FOR DEBT AND TO SET ASIDE FRAUDULENT CONVEYANCE UNDER RULE 18(b)

A. B., Plaintiff   )
         v.   ) *Complaint*
C. D. and E. F., Defendants   )

1. Allegation of jurisdiction.

2. Defendant C. D. on or about _____ executed and delivered to plaintiff a promissory note [in the following words and figures: (here set out the note verbatim)]; [a copy of which is hereto annexed as Exhibit A]; [whereby defendant C. D. promised to pay to plaintiff or order on _____ the sum of five thousand dollars with interest thereon at the rate of __ percent. per annum].

3. Defendant C. D. owes to plaintiff the amount of said note and interest.

4. Defendant C. D. on or about _____ conveyed all his property, real and personal [or specify and describe] to defendant E. F. for the purpose of defrauding plaintiff and hindering and delaying the collection of the indebtedness evidenced by the note above referred to.

Wherefore plaintiff demands:

(1) That plaintiff have judgment against defendant C. D. for _____ dollars and interest; (2) that the aforesaid conveyance to defendant E. F. be declared void and the judgment herein be declared a lien on said property; (3) that plaintiff have judgment against the defendants for costs.

As amended 1963.

Form 14.

COMPLAINT FOR NEGLIGENCE UNDER FEDERAL EMPLOYERS' LIABILITY ACT

1. Allegation of jurisdiction.

2. During all the times herein mentioned defendant owned and operated in interstate commerce a railroad which passed through a tunnel located at _____ and known as Tunnel No. _____.

3. On or about June 1, 1936, defendant was repairing and enlarging the tunnel in order to protect interstate trains and passengers and freight from injury and in order to make the tunnel more conveniently usable for interstate commerce.

4. In the course of thus repairing and enlarging the tunnel on said day defendant employed plaintiff as one of its workmen, and negligently put plaintiff to work in a portion of the tunnel which defendant had left unprotected and unsupported.

5. By reason of defendant's negligence in thus putting plaintiff to work in that portion of the tunnel, plaintiff was, while so working pursuant to defendant's orders, struck and crushed by a rock, which fell from the unsupported portion of the tunnel, and was (here describe plaintiff's injuries).

6. Prior to these injuries, plaintiff was a strong, able-bodied man, capable of earning and actually earning _____ dollars per day. By these injuries he has been made incapable of any gainful activity, has suffered great physical and mental pain, and has incurred expense in the amount of _____ dollars for medicine, medical attendance, and hospitalization.

Wherefore plaintiff demands judgment against defendant in the sum of _____ dollars and costs.

Form 15.

COMPLAINT FOR DAMAGES UNDER MERCHANT MARINE ACT

1. Allegation of jurisdiction. [If the pleader wishes to invoke the distinctively maritime procedures referred to in Rule 9(h), add the following or its substantial equivalent: This is an admiralty or maritime claim within the meaning of Rule 9(h).]

2. During all the times herein mentioned defendant was the owner of the steamship _____ and used it in the transportation of freight for hire by water in interstate and foreign commerce.

3. During the first part of (month and year) at _____ plaintiff entered the employ of defendant as an able seaman on said steamship under seamen's articles of customary form for a voyage from _____ ports to the Orient and return at a wage of _____ dollars per month and found, which is equal to a wage of _____ dollars per month as a shore worker.

4. On June 1, 1936, said steamship was about _____ days out of the port of _____ and was being navigated by the master and crew on the return voyage to _____ ports. (Here describe weather conditions and the condition of the ship and state as in an

ordinary complaint for personal injuries the negligent conduct of defendant.)

5. By reason of defendant's negligence in thus (brief statement of defendant's negligent conduct) and the unseaworthiness of said steamship, plaintiff was (here describe plaintiff's injuries).

6. Prior to these injuries, plaintiff was a strong, able-bodied man, capable of earning and actually earning _____ dollars per day. By these injuries he has been made incapable of any gainful activity; has suffered great physical and mental pain, and has incurred expense in the amount of _____ dollars for medicine, medical attendance, and hospitalization.

Wherefore plaintiff demands judgment against defendant in the sum of _____ dollars and costs.

As amended 1966.

Form 16.

COMPLAINT FOR INFRINGEMENT OF PATENT

1. Allegation of jurisdiction.

2. On May 16, 1934, United States Letters Patent No. _____ were duly and legally issued to plaintiff for an invention in an electric motor; and since that date plaintiff has been and still is the owner of those Letters Patent.

3. Defendant has for a long time past been and still is infringing those Letters Patent by making, selling, and using electric motors embodying the patented invention, and will continue to do so unless enjoined by this court.

4. Plaintiff has placed the required statutory notice on all electric motors manufactured and sold by him under said Letters Patent, and has given written notice to defendant of his said infringement.

Wherefore plaintiff demands a preliminary and final injunction against continued infringement, an accounting for damages, and an assessment of interest and costs against defendant.

As amended 1963.

Form 17.

COMPLAINT FOR INFRINGEMENT OF COPYRIGHT AND UNFAIR COMPETITION

1. Allegation of jurisdiction.

2. Prior to March, 1936, plaintiff, who then was and ever since has been a citizen of the United States, created and wrote an original book, entitled _____.

3. This book contains a large amount of material wholly original with plaintiff and is copyrightable subject matter under the laws of the United States.

4. Between March 2, 1936, and March 10, 1936, plaintiff complied in all respects with the Act of (give citation) and all other laws governing copyright, and secured the exclusive rights and privileges in and to the copyright of said book, and received from the Register of Copyrights a certificate of registration, dated and identified as follows: "March 10, 1936, Class _____, No. _____."

5. Since March 10, 1936, said book has been published by plaintiff and all copies of it made by plaintiff or under his authority or license have been printed, bound, and published in strict conformity with the provisions of the Act of _____ and all other laws governing copyright.

6. Since March 10, 1936, plaintiff has been and still is the sole proprietor of all rights, title, and interest in and to the copyright in said book.

7. After March 10, 1936, defendant infringed said copyright by publishing and placing upon the market a book entitled _____, which was copied largely from plaintiff's copyrighted book, entitled _____.

8. A copy of plaintiff's copyrighted book is hereto attached as "Exhibit 1"; and a copy of defendant's infringing book is hereto attached as "Exhibit 2."

9. Plaintiff has notified defendant that defendant has infringed the copyright of plaintiff, and defendant has continued to infringe the copyright.

10. After March 10, 1936, and continuously since about _____, defendant has been publishing, selling and otherwise marketing the book entitled _____, and has thereby been engaging in unfair trade practices and unfair competition against plaintiff to plaintiff's irreparable damage.

Wherefore plaintiff demands:

(1) That defendant, his agents, and servants be enjoined during the pendency of this action and permanently from infringing said copyright of said plaintiff in any manner, and from publishing, selling, marketing or otherwise disposing of any copies of the book entitled _____.

(2) That defendant be required to pay to plaintiff such damages as plaintiff has sustained in consequence of defendant's infringement of said copyright and said unfair trade practices and unfair competition and to account for

(a) all gains, profits and advantages derived by defendant by said trade practices and unfair competition and

(b) all gains, profits, and advantages derived by defendant by his infringement of plaintiff's copyright or such damages as to the court shall appear proper within the provisions of the copyright statutes, but not less than two hundred and fifty dollars.

(3) That defendant be required to deliver up to be impounded during the pendency of this action all copies of said book entitled _____ in his possession or under his control and to deliver up for destruction all infringing copies and all plates, molds, and other matter for making such infringing copies.

(4) That defendant pay to plaintiff the costs of this action and reasonable attorney's fees to be allowed to the plaintiff by the court.

(5) That plaintiff have such other and further relief as is just.

As amended 1948.

Form 18.

COMPLAINT FOR INTERPLEADER AND DECLARATORY RELIEF

1.   Allegation of jurisdiction.

2.   On or about June 1, 1935, plaintiff issued to G. H. a policy of life insurance whereby plaintiff promised to pay to K. L. as beneficiary the sum of _____ dollars upon the death of G. H. The policy required the payment by G. H. of a stipulated premium on June 1, 1936, and annually thereafter as a condition precedent to its continuance in force.

3.   No part of the premium due June 1, 1936, was ever paid and the policy ceased to have any force or effect on July 1, 1936.

4.   Thereafter, on September 1, 1936, G. H. and K. L. died as the result of a collision between a locomotive and the automobile in which G. H. and K. L. were riding.

5.   Defendant C. D. is the duly appointed and acting executor of the will of G. H.; defendant E. F. is the duly appointed and acting executor of the will of K. L.; defendant X. Y. claims to have been duly designated as beneficiary of said policy in place of K. L.

140

6. Each of defendants, C. D., E. F., and X. Y. is claiming that the above-mentioned policy was in full force and effect at the time of the death of G. H.; each of them is claiming to be the only person entitled to receive payment of the amount of the policy and has made demand for payment thereof.

7. By reason of these conflicting claims of the defendants, plaintiff is in great doubt as to which defendant is entitled to be paid the amount of the policy, if it was in force at the death of G. H.

Wherefore plaintiff demands that the court adjudge:

(1) That none of the defendants is entitled to recover from plaintiff the amount of said policy or any part thereof.

(2) That each of the defendants be restrained from instituting any action against plaintiff for the recovery of the amount of said policy or any part thereof.

(3) That, if the court shall determine that said policy was in force at the death of G. H., the defendants be required to interplead and settle between themselves their rights to the money due under said policy, and that plaintiff be discharged from all liability in the premises except to the person whom the court shall adjudge entitled to the amount of said policy.

(4) That plaintiff recover its costs.

As amended 1963.

Form 18–A.

NOTICE AND ACKNOWLEDGMENT FOR SERVICE BY MAIL

United States District Court for the Southern District of New York

Civil Action, File Number _____

A. B., Plaintiff	)	Notice and Acknowledgment
v.	)	of Receipt of Summons
C. D., Defendant	)	and Complaint

NOTICE

To: (insert the name and address of the person to be served.)

The enclosed summons and complaint are served pursuant to Rule 4(c)(2)(C)(ii) of the Federal Rules of Civil Procedure.

You must complete the acknowledgment part of this form and return one copy of the completed form to the sender within 20 days.

Form 18–A RULES OF CIVIL PROCEDURE

You must sign and date the acknowledgment. If you are served on behalf of a corporation, unincorporated association (including a partnership), or other entity, you must indicate under your signature your relationship to that entity. If you are served on behalf of another person and you are authorized to receive process, you must indicate under your signature your authority.

If you do not complete and return the form to the sender within 20 days, you (or the party on whose behalf you are being served) may be required to pay any expenses incurred in serving a summons and complaint in any other manner permitted by law.

If you do complete and return this form, you (or the party on whose behalf you are being served) must answer the complaint within 20 days. If you fail to do so, judgment by default will be taken against you for the relief demanded in the complaint.

I declare, under penalty of perjury, that this Notice and Acknowledgment of Receipt of Summons and Complaint will have been mailed on (insert date).

_____

Signature

_____

Date of Signature

ACKNOWLEDGMENT OF RECEIPT OF SUMMONS AND COMPLAINT

I declare, under penalty of perjury, that I received a copy of the summons and of the complaint in the above-captioned matter at (insert address).

_____

Signature

_____

Relationship to Entity/ Authority to Receive Service of Process

_____

Date of Signature

Added 1983; as amended 1985.

Form 19.

MOTION TO DISMISS, PRESENTING DEFENSES OF FAILURE TO STATE A CLAIM, OF LACK OF SERVICE OF PROCESS, OF IMPROPER VENUE, AND OF LACK OF JURISDICTION UNDER RULE 12(b)

The defendant moves the court as follows:

1. To dismiss the action because the complaint fails to state a claim against defendant upon which relief can be granted. *#6*

2. To dismiss the action or in lieu thereof to quash the return of service of summons on the grounds (a) that the defen- *#2* dant is a corporation organized under the laws of Delaware and was not and is not subject to service of process within the Southern District of New York, and (b) that the defendant has not been properly served with process in this action, all of which more clearly appears in the affidavits of M. N. and X. Y. hereto annexed *#5* as Exhibit A and Exhibit B, respectively.

3. To dismiss the action on the ground that it is in the wrong district because (a) the jurisdiction of this court is invoked solely *#3* on the ground that the action arises under the Constitution and laws of the United States and (b) the defendant is a corporation incorporated under the laws of the State of Delaware and is not *#1* licensed to do or doing business in the Southern District of New York, all of which more clearly appears in the affidavits of K. L. and V. W. hereto annexed as Exhibits C and D, respectively.

4. To dismiss the action on the ground that the court lacks jurisdiction because the amount actually in controversy is less than ten thousand dollars exclusive of interest and costs.

Signed: _____

                                Attorney for Defendant.

Address: _____

Notice of Motion

To:_____

   Attorney for Plaintiff.

_____

Please take notice, that the undersigned will bring the above motion on for hearing before this Court at Room _____, United States Court House, Foley Square, City of New York, on the _____ day of _____, 19__, at 10 o'clock in the forenoon of that day or as soon thereafter as counsel can be heard.

Signed: _____

Attorney for Defendant.

Address: _____

As amended 1949, 1961.

Note

1. The above motion and notice of motion may be combined and denominated Notice of Motion. See Rule 7(b).

2. As to paragraph 3, see U.S.C., Title 28, § 1391 (Venue generally), subsections (b) and (c).

3. As to paragraph 4, see U.S.C., Title 28, § 1331 (Federal question; amount in controversy; costs), as amended by P.L. 85–554, 72 Stat. 415, July 25, 1958, requiring that the amount in controversy, exclusive of interest and costs, be in excess of $10,000.

Form 20.

ANSWER PRESENTING DEFENSES UNDER RULE 12(b)

First Defense

The complaint fails to state a claim against defendant upon which relief can be granted.

Second Defense

If defendant is indebted to plaintiffs for the goods mentioned in the complaint, he is indebted to them jointly with G. H. G. H. is alive; is a citizen of the State of New York and a resident of this district, is subject to the jurisdiction of this court, as to both service of process and venue; can be made a party without depriving this court of jurisdiction of the present parties, and has not been made a party.

Third Defense

Defendant admits the allegation contained in paragraphs 1 and 4 of the complaint; alleges that he is without knowledge or information sufficient to form a belief as to the truth of the allegations contained in paragraph 2 of the complaint; and denies each and every other allegation contained in the complaint.

Fourth Defense

The right of action set forth in the complaint did not accrue within six years next before the commencement of this action.

Counterclaim

(Here set forth any claim as a counterclaim in the manner in which a claim is pleaded in a complaint. No statement of the grounds on which the court's jurisdiction depends need be made unless the counterclaim requires independent grounds of jurisdiction.)

Cross-Claim Against Defendant M. N.

(Here set forth the claim constituting a cross-claim against defendant M. N. in the manner in which a claim is pleaded in a complaint. The statement of grounds upon which the court's jurisdiction depends need not be made unless the cross-claim requires independent grounds of jurisdiction.)

As amended 1948.

Note

The above form contains examples of certain defenses provided for in Rule 12(b). The first defense challenges the legal sufficiency of the complaint. It is a substitute for a general demurrer or a motion to dismiss.

The second defense embodies the old plea in abatement; the decision thereon, however, may well provide under Rules 19 and 21 for the citing in of the party rather than an abatement of the action.

The third defense is an answer on the merits.

The fourth defense is one of the affirmative defenses provided for in Rule 8(c).

The answer also includes a counterclaim and a cross-claim.

Form 21.

ANSWER TO COMPLAINT SET FORTH IN FORM 8, WITH COUNTERCLAIM FOR INTERPLEADER

Defense

Defendant admits the allegations stated in paragraph 1 of the complaint; and denies the allegations stated in paragraph 2 to the extent set forth in the counterclaim herein.

Counterclaim for Interpleader

1. Defendant received the sum of _____ dollars as a deposit from E. F.

2. Plaintiff has demanded the payment of such deposit to him by virtue of an assignment of it which he claims to have received from E. F.

3. E. F. has notified the defendant that he claims such deposit, that the purported assignment is not valid, and that he holds the defendant responsible for the deposit.

Wherefore defendant demands:

(1) That the court order E. F. to be made a party defendant to respond to the complaint and to this counterclaim.[4]

(2) That the court order the plaintiff and E. F. to interplead their respective claims.

(3) That the court adjudge whether the plaintiff or E. F. is entitled to the sum of money.

(4) That the court discharge defendant from all liability in the premises except to the person it shall adjudge entitled to the sum of money.

(5) That the court award to the defendant its costs and attorney's fees.

As amended 1963.

Form 22.

MOTION TO BRING IN THIRD–PARTY DEFENDANT

Abrogated Jan. 21, 1963, eff. July 1, 1963

Form 22–A.

SUMMONS AND COMPLAINT AGAINST THIRD–PARTY DEFENDANT

UNITED STATES DISTRICT COURT FOR THE SOUTHERN DISTRICT OF NEW YORK

Civil Action, File Number _____

A. B., Plaintiff   )
                    v.   )
C. D., Defendant and   )
Third-Party Plaintiff   ) Summons
                    v.   )
E. F., Third-Party   )
Defendant   )

To the above-named Third-Party Defendant:

You are hereby summoned and required to serve upon _____, plaintiff's attorney whose address is _____, and upon _____, who is attorney for C. D., defendant and third-party plaintiff, and whose address is _____, an answer to the third-party complaint which is herewith served upon you within 20 days

---

[4] Rule 13(h) provides for the court ordering parties to a counterclaim, but who are not parties to the original action, to be brought in as defendants.

after the service of this summons upon you exclusive of the day of service. If you fail to do so, judgment by default will be taken against you for the relief demanded in the third-party complaint. There is also served upon you herewith a copy of the complaint of the plaintiff which you may but are not required to answer.

_____

Clerk of Court.

[Seal of District Court]

Dated _____

UNITED STATES DISTRICT COURT FOR THE SOUTHERN DISTRICT OF NEW YORK

Civil Action, File Number _____

A. B., Plaintiff	)
v.	)
C. D., Defendant and	)
Third-Party Plaintiff	) Third-Party Complaint
v.	)
E. F., Third-Party	)
Defendant	)

1. Plaintiff A. B. has filed against defendant C. D. a complaint, a copy of which is hereto attached as "Exhibit A."

2. (Here state the grounds upon which C. D. is entitled to recover from E. F., all or part of what A. B. may recover from C. D. The statement should be framed as in an original complaint.)

Wherefore C. D. demands judgment against third-party defendant E. F. for all sums [5] that may be adjudged against defendant C. D. in favor of plaintiff A. B.

Signed: _____

Attorney for C. D.,
Third-Party Plaintiff.

Address: _____

Added 1963.

[5] Make appropriate change where C. D. is entitled to only partial recovery-over against E. F.

Form 22–B.

MOTION TO BRING IN THIRD–PARTY DEFENDANT

Defendant moves for leave, as third-party plaintiff, to cause to be served upon E. F. a summons and third-party complaint, copies of which are hereto attached as Exhibit X.

Signed: _____

Attorney for Defendant C.D.

Address: _____

Notice of Motion

(Contents the same as in Form 19. The notice should be addressed to all parties to the action.)

Exhibit X

(Contents the same as in Form 22–A.)

Added 1963.

Form 23.

MOTION TO INTERVENE AS A DEFENDANT UNDER RULE 24

(Based upon the complaint, Form 16)

United States District Court for the Southern District of New York

Civil Action, File Number _____

A. B., Plaintiff	)
v.	) *Motion to intervene as*
C. D., Defendant	) *a defendant*
E. F., Applicant for Intervention	)

E. F. moves for leave to intervene as a defendant in this action, in order to assert the defenses set forth in his proposed answer, of which a copy is hereto attached, on the ground that he is the manufacturer and vendor to the defendant, as well as to others, of the articles alleged in the complaint to be an infringement of plaintiff's patent, and as such has a defense to plaintiff's claim presenting both questions of law and of fact which are common to the main action.[6]

Signed: _____,

*Attorney for E. F.,
Applicant for Intervention.*

Address: _____.

Notice of Motion

(Contents the same as in Form 19)

United States District Court for the Southern
District of New York

Civil Action, File Number _____

A. B., Plaintiff)
      v.   ) *Intervener's answer*
C. D., Defendant)
E. F., Intervener)

First Defense

Intervener admits the allegations stated in paragraphs 1 and 4 of the complaint; denies the allegations in paragraph 3, and denies the allegations in paragraph 2 in so far as they assert the legality of the issuance of the Letters Patent to plaintiff.

Second Defense

Plaintiff is not the first inventor of the articles covered by the Letters Patent specified in his complaint, since articles substantially identical in character were previously patented in Letters Patent granted to intervener on January 5, 1920.

Signed: _____,

*Attorney for
E. F., Intervener.*

Address: _____.

As amended 1949.

Form 24.

REQUEST FOR PRODUCTION OF DOCUMENTS, ETC., UNDER RULE 34

[6] For other grounds of intervention, either of right or in the discretion of the court, see Rule 24(a) and (b).

Plaintiff A. B. requests defendant C. D. to respond within _____ days to the following requests:

(1) That defendant produce and permit plaintiff to inspect and to copy each of the following documents:

(Here list the documents either individually or by category and describe each of them.)

(Here state the time, place, and manner of making the inspection and performance of any related acts.)

(2) That defendant produce and permit plaintiff to inspect and to copy, test, or sample each of the following objects:

(Here list the objects either individually or by category and describe each of them.)

(Here state the time, place, and manner of making the inspection and performance of any related acts.)

(3) That defendant permit plaintiff to enter (here describe property to be entered) and to inspect and to photograph, test or sample (here describe the portion of the real property and the objects to be inspected).

(Here state the time, place, and manner of making the inspection and performance of any related acts.)

Signed: _____
Attorney for Plaintiff.

Address: _____

As amended 1970.

Form 25.

REQUEST FOR ADMISSION UNDER RULE 36

Plaintiff A. B. requests defendant C. D. within _____ days after service of this request to make the following admissions for the purpose of this action only and subject to all pertinent objections to admissibility which may be interposed at the trial:

1. That each of the following documents, exhibited with this request, is genuine.

(Here list the documents and describe each document.)

2. That each of the following statements is true.

(Here list the statements.)

Signed: _____,
Attorney for Plaintiff.

Address: _____

As amended 1948.

Form 26.

ALLEGATION OF REASON FOR OMITTING PARTY

When it is necessary, under Rule 19(c), for the pleader to set forth in his pleading the names of persons who ought to be made parties, but who are not so made, there should be an allegation such as the one set out below:

John Doe named in this complaint is not made a party to this action [because he is not subject to the jurisdiction of this court]; [because he cannot be made a party to this action without depriving this court of jurisdiction].

Form 27.

NOTICE OF APPEAL TO COURT OF APPEALS UNDER RULE 73(b)

Abrogated Dec. 4, 1967, eff. July 1, 1968

Form 28.

NOTICE: CONDEMNATION

United States District Court for the Southern
District of New York

Civil Action, File Number _____

UNITED STATES OF AMERICA, Plaintiff	)
v.	)
1,000 ACRES OF LAND IN [here insert a gener-	)
al location as "City of _____" or	) *Notice.*
"County of _____"], JOHN DOE ET AL.,	)
AND UNKNOWN OWNERS, Defendants	)

To (here insert the names of the defendants to whom the notice is directed):

You are hereby notified that a complaint in condemnation has heretofore been filed in the office of the clerk of the United States District Court for the Southern District of New York, in the United States Court House in New York City, New York, for the taking (here state the interest to be acquired, as "an estate in fee simple") for use (here state briefly the use, "as a site for a post-office building") of the following described property in which you have or claim an interest.

> (Here insert brief description of the property in which the defendants, to whom the notice is directed, have or claim an interest.)

The authority for the taking is (here state briefly, as "the Act of _____, _____ Stat. _____, U.S.C., Title _____, § _____".)[7]

You are further notified that if you desire to present any objection or defense to the taking of your property you are required to serve your answer on the plaintiff's attorney at the address herein designated within twenty days after _____.[8]

Your answer shall identify the property in which you claim to have an interest, state the nature and extent of the interest you claim, and state all of your objections and defenses to the taking of your property. All defenses and objections not so presented are waived. And in case of your failure so to answer the complaint, judgment of condemnation of that part of the above-described property in which you have or claim an interest will be rendered.

But without answering, you may serve on the plaintiff's attorney a notice of appearance designating the property in which you claim to be interested. Thereafter you will receive notice of all proceedings affecting it. At the trial of the issue of just compensation, whether or not you have previously appeared or answered, you may present evidence as to the amount of the compensation to be paid for your property, and you may share in the distribution of the award.

_____
United States Attorney.

Address _____

> (Here state an address within the district where the United States Attorney may be served, as "United States Court House, New York, N. Y.")

Dated _____

Added 1951.

[7] And where appropriate add a citation to any applicable Executive Order.

[8] Here insert the words "personal service of this notice upon you," if personal service is to be made pursuant to subdivision (d)(3)(i) of this rule [Rule 71A]; or, insert the date of the last publication of notice, if service by publication is to be made pursuant to subdivision (d)(3)(ii) of this rule.

Form 29.

COMPLAINT: CONDEMNATION

United States District Court for the Southern
District of New York

Civil Action, File Number _____

UNITED STATES OF AMERICA, Plaintiff	)
v.	)
1,000 ACRES OF LAND IN [here insert a gener-	) *Complaint.*
al location as "City of _____" or	)
"County of _____"], JOHN DOE ET AL.,	)
AND UNKNOWN OWNERS, Defendants	)

1. This is an action of a civil nature brought by the United States of America for the taking of property under the power of eminent domain and for the ascertainment and award of just compensation to the owners and parties in interest.[9]

2. The authority for the taking is (here state briefly, as "the Act of _____, _____ Stat. _____, U.S.C., Title _____, § _____").[10]

3. The use for which the property is to be taken is (here state briefly the use, "as a site for a post-office building").

4. The interest to be acquired in the property is (here state the interest as "an estate in fee simple").

5. The property so to be taken is (here set forth a description of the property sufficient for its identification) or (described in Exhibit A hereto attached and made a part hereof).

6. The persons known to the plaintiff to have or claim an interest in the property [11] are:

(Here set forth the names of such persons and the

---

[9] If the plaintiff is not the United States, but is, for example, a corporation invoking the power of eminent domain delegated to it by the state, then this paragraph 1 of the complaint should be appropriately modified and should be preceded by a paragraph appropriately alleging federal jurisdiction for the action, such as diversity. See Form 2.

[10] And where appropriate add a citation to any applicable Executive Order.

[11] At the commencement of the action the plaintiff need name as defendants only the persons having or claiming an interest in the property whose names are then known, but prior to any hearing involving the compensation to be paid for a particular piece of property the plaintiff must add as defendants all persons having or claiming an interest in that property whose names can be ascertained by an appropriate search of the records and also those whose names have otherwise been learned. See Rule 71A(c)(2).

interests claimed.)[12]

7. In addition to the persons named, there are or may be others who have or may claim some interest in the property to be taken, whose names are unknown to the plaintiff and on diligent inquiry have not been ascertained. They are made parties to the action under the designation "Unknown Owners."

Wherefore the plaintiff demands judgment that the property be condemned and that just compensation for the taking be ascertained and awarded and for such other relief as may be lawful and proper.

United States Attorney.

Address _____

(Here state an address within the district where the United States Attorney may be served, as "United States Court House, New York, N. Y.").

Added 1951.

Form 30.

SUGGESTION OF DEATH UPON THE RECORD UNDER RULE 25(a)(1)

A. B. [describe as a party, or as executor, administrator, or other representative or successor of C. D., the deceased party] suggests upon the record, pursuant to Rule 25(a)(1), the death of C. D. [describe as party] during the pendency of this action.

Added 1963.

Form 31.

JUDGMENT ON JURY VERDICT

UNITED STATES DISTRICT COURT FOR THE SOUTHERN DISTRICT OF NEW YORK

Civil Action, File Number _____

A. B., Plaintiff   )
      v.   ) Judgment
C. D., Defendant)

[12] The plaintiff should designate, as to each separate piece of property, the defendants who have been joined as owners thereof or of some interest therein. See Rule 71A(c)(2).

This action came on for trial before the Court and a jury, Honorable John Marshall, District Judge, presiding, and the issues having been duly tried and the jury having duly rendered its verdict,

It is Ordered and Adjudged

[that the plaintiff A. B. recover of the defendant C. D. the sum of _____, with interest thereon at the rate of _____ per cent as provided by law, and his costs of action.]

[that the plaintiff take nothing, that the action be dismissed on the merits, and that the defendant C. D. recover of the plaintiff A. B. his costs of action.]

Dated at New York, New York, this _____ day of _____, 19__.

_____
Clerk of Court.

Added 1963.

Note

1. This Form is illustrative of the judgment to be entered upon the general verdict of a jury. It deals with the cases where there is a general jury verdict awarding the plaintiff money damages or finding for the defendant, but is adaptable to other situations of jury verdicts.

2. The clerk, unless the court otherwise orders, is required forthwith to prepare, sign, and enter the judgment upon a general jury verdict without awaiting any direction by the court. The form of the judgment upon a spe- cial verdict or a general verdict accompanied by answers to interrogatories shall be promptly approved by the court, and the clerk shall thereupon enter it. See Rule 58, as amended.

3. The Rules contemplate a simple judgment promptly entered. See Rule 54(a). Every judgment shall be set forth on a separate document. See Rule 58, as amended.

4. Attorneys are not to submit forms of judgment unless directed in exceptional cases to do so by the court. See Rule 58, as amended.

Form 32.

JUDGMENT ON DECISION BY THE COURT

UNITED STATES DISTRICT COURT FOR THE SOUTHERN DISTRICT OF NEW YORK

Civil Action, File Number _____

A. B., Plaintiff)
v.) Judgment
C. D., Defendant)

This action came on for [trial] [hearing] before the Court, Honorable John Marshall, District Judge, presiding, and the issues having been duly [tried] [heard] and a decision having been duly rendered,

It is Ordered and Adjudged

[that the plaintiff A. B. recover of the defendant C. D. the sum of _____, with interest thereon at the rate of _____ per cent as provided by law, and his costs of action.]

[that the plaintiff take nothing, that the action be dismissed on the merits, and that the defendant C. D. recover of the plaintiff A. B. his costs of action.]

Dated at New York, New York, this _____ day of _____, 19__.

_____
Clerk of Court.

Added 1963.

Note

1. This Form is illustrative of the judgment to be entered upon a decision of the court. It deals with the cases of decisions by the court awarding a party only money damages or costs, but is adaptable to other decisions by the court.

2. The clerk, unless the court otherwise orders, is required forthwith, without awaiting any direction by the court, to prepare, sign, and enter the judgment upon a decision by the court that a party shall recover only a sum certain or costs or that all relief shall be denied. The form of the judgment upon a decision by the court granting other relief shall be promptly approved by the court, and the clerk shall thereupon enter it. See Rule 58, as amended.

3. See also paragraphs 3–4 of the Explanatory Note to Form 31.

Form 33.

NOTICE OF RIGHT TO CONSENT TO THE EXERCISE OF CIVIL JURISDICTION BY A MAGISTRATE AND APPEAL OPTION

In accordance with the provisions of Title 28, U.S.C. § 636(c), you are hereby notified that the United States magistrates of this district court, in addition to their other duties, upon the consent of all parties in a civil case, may conduct any or all proceedings in a civil case including a jury or nonjury trial, and order the entry of a final judgment.

You should be aware that your decision to consent, or not to consent, to the referral of your case to a United States magistrate must be entirely voluntary. Only if all the parties to the case consent to the reference to a magistrate will either the judge or magistrate to whom the case has been assigned be informed of your decision.

An appeal from a judgment entered by a magistrate may be taken directly to the United States court of appeals for this judicial circuit in the same manner as an appeal from any other judgment of a district court. Alternatively, upon consent of all parties, an appeal from a judgment entered by a magistrate may be taken directly to a district judge. Cases in which an appeal is taken to a district judge may be reviewed by the United States court of appeals for this judicial circuit only by way of petition for leave to appeal.

Copies of the Form for the "Consent to Proceed Before a United States Magistrate" and "Election of Appeal to a District Judge" are available from the clerk of the court.

Added 1983.

Form 34.

CONSENT TO PROCEED BEFORE A UNITED STATES MAGISTRATE, ELECTION OF APPEAL TO DISTRICT JUDGE, AND ORDER OF REFERENCE

UNITED STATES DISTRICT COURT FOR THE _____

DISTRICT OF _____

Plaintiff,	)	
vs.	)	Docket No. _____
Defendant.	)	

CONSENT TO PROCEED BEFORE A UNITED STATES MAGISTRATE

In accordance with the provisions of Title 28, U.S.C. § 636(c), the parties to the above-captioned civil matter hereby voluntarily waive their rights to proceed before a judge of the United States district court and consent to have a United States magistrate conduct any and all further proceedings in the case, including trial, and order the entry of a final judgment.

_____

_____

_____
Date

ELECTION OF APPEAL TO DISTRICT JUDGE

[Do not execute this portion of the Consent Form if the parties desire that the appeal lie directly to the court of appeals.]

157

In accordance with the provisions of Title 28, U.S.C. § 636(c)(4), the parties elect to take any appeal in this case to a district judge.

_____

_____

_____

Date

ORDER OF REFERENCE

IT IS HEREBY ORDERED that the above-captioned matter be referred to United States Magistrate _____ for all further proceedings and the entry of judgment in accordance with Title 28, U.S.C. § 636(c) and the foregoing consent of the parties.

_____
U.S. District Judge

Note: Return this form to the Clerk of the Court only if all parties have consented to proceed before a magistrate.

Added 1983.

SUPPLEMENTAL RULES FOR CERTAIN ADMIRALTY AND MARITIME CLAIMS

Adopted February 28, 1966, effective July 1, 1966

Rule A.

SCOPE OF RULES

These Supplemental Rules apply to the procedure in admiralty and maritime claims within the meaning of Rule 9(h) with respect to the following remedies:

(1) Maritime attachment and garnishment;

(2) Actions in rem;

(3) Possessory, petitory, and partition actions;

(4) Actions for exoneration from or limitation of liability.

These rules also apply to the procedure in statutory condemnation proceedings analogous to maritime actions in rem, whether within the admiralty and maritime jurisdiction or not. Except as otherwise provided, references in these Supplemental Rules to actions in rem include such analogous statutory condemnation proceedings.

The general Rules of Civil Procedure for the United States District Courts are also applicable to the foregoing proceedings except to the extent that they are inconsistent with these Supplemental Rules.

Rule B.

ATTACHMENT AND GARNISHMENT: SPECIAL PROVISIONS

(1) **When Available; Complaint, Affidavit, Judicial Authorization, and Process.** With respect to any admiralty or maritime claim in personam a verified complaint may contain a prayer for process to attach the defendant's goods and chattels, or credits and effects in the hands of garnishees to be named in the process to the amount sued for, if the defendant shall not be found within the district. Such a complaint shall be accompanied by an

affidavit signed by the plaintiff or the plaintiff's attorney that, to the affiant's knowledge, or to the best of the affiant's information and belief, the defendant cannot be found within the district. The verified complaint and affidavit shall be reviewed by the court and, if the conditions set forth in this rule appear to exist, an order so stating and authorizing process of attachment and garnishment shall issue. Supplemental process enforcing the court's order may be issued by the clerk upon application without further order of the court. If the plaintiff or the plaintiff's attorney certifies that exigent circumstances make review by the court impracticable, the clerk shall issue a summons and process of attachment and garnishment and the plaintiff shall have the burden on a post-attachment hearing under Rule E(4)(f) to show that exigent circumstances existed. In addition, or in the alternative, the plaintiff may, pursuant to Rule 4(e), invoke the remedies provided by state law for attachment and garnishment or similar seizure of the defendant's property. Except for Rule E(8) these Supplemental Rules do not apply to state remedies so invoked.

(2) **Notice to Defendant.** No judgment by default shall be entered except upon proof, which may be by affidavit, (a) that the plaintiff or the garnishee has given notice of the action to the defendant by mailing to the defendant a copy of the complaint, summons, and process of attachment or garnishment, using any form of mail requiring a return receipt, or (b) that the complaint, summons, and process of attachment or garnishment have been served on the defendant in a manner authorized by Rule 4(d) or (i), or (c) that the plaintiff or the garnishee has made diligent efforts to give notice of the action to the defendant and has been unable to do so.

(3) **Answer.**

(a) By Garnishee. The garnishee shall serve an answer, together with answers to any interrogatories served with the complaint, within 20 days after service of process upon the garnishee. Interrogatories to the garnishee may be served with the complaint without leave of court. If the garnishee refuses or neglects to answer on oath as to the debts, credits, or effects of the defendant in the garnishee's hands, or any interrogatories concerning such debts, credits, and effects that may be propounded by the plaintiff, the court may award compulsory process against the garnishee. If the garnishee admits any debts, credits, or effects, they shall be held in the garnishee's hands or paid into the registry of the court, and shall be held in either case subject to the further order of the court.

(b) By Defendant. The defendant shall serve an answer within 30 days after process has been executed, whether by attachment of property or service on the garnishee.

As amended 1985, 1987.

Rule C.

ACTIONS IN REM: SPECIAL PROVISIONS

(1) When Available. An action in rem may be brought:

(a) To enforce any maritime lien;

(b) Whenever a statute of the United States provides for a maritime action in rem or a proceeding analogous thereto.

Except as otherwise provided by law a party who may proceed in rem may also, or in the alternative, proceed in personam against any person who may be liable.

Statutory provisions exempting vessels or other property owned or possessed by or operated by or for the United States from arrest or seizure are not affected by this rule. When a statute so provides, an action against the United States or an instrumentality thereof may proceed on in rem principles.

(2) Complaint. In actions in rem the complaint shall be verified on oath or solemn affirmation. It shall describe with reasonable particularity the property that is the subject of the action and state that it is within the district or will be during the pendency of the action. In actions for the enforcement of forfeitures for violation of any statute of the United States the complaint shall state the place of seizure and whether it was on land or on navigable waters, and shall contain such allegations as may be required by the statute pursuant to which the action is brought.

(3) Judicial Authorization and Process. Except in actions by the United States for forfeitures for federal statutory violations, the verified complaint and any supporting papers shall be reviewed by the court and, if the conditions for an action in rem appear to exist, an order so stating and authorizing a warrant for the arrest of the vessel or other property that is the subject of the action shall issue and be delivered to the clerk who shall prepare the warrant and deliver it to the marshal for service. If the property that is the subject of the action consists in whole or in part of freight, or the proceeds of property sold, or other intangible property, the clerk shall issue a summons directing any person having control of the funds to show cause why they should not be paid into court to abide the judgment. Supplemental process enforcing the court's order may be issued by the clerk upon application without further order of the court. If the plaintiff or the plaintiff's attorney certifies that exigent circumstances make review by the court impracticable, the clerk shall issue a summons and warrant for the arrest and the plaintiff shall have the burden on a post-arrest hearing under Rule E(4)(f) to show that exigent circumstances existed. In actions by the United States for forfeitures for federal statutory violations, the clerk, upon filing of the complaint, shall forthwith issue a summons and warrant for the arrest of the vessel or other property without requiring a certification of exigent circumstances.

(4) Notice. No notice other than the execution of the process is required when the property that is the subject of the action has been released in accordance with Rule E(5). If the property is not released within 10 days after execution of process, the plaintiff shall promptly or within such time as may be allowed by the court cause public notice of the action and arrest to be given in a newspaper of general circulation in the district, designated by order of the court. Such notice shall specify the time within which the answer is required to be filed as provided by subdivision (6) of this rule. This rule does not affect the requirements of notice in actions to foreclose a preferred ship mortgage pursuant to the Act of June 5, 1920, ch. 250, § 30, as amended.

(5) Ancillary Process. In any action in rem in which process has been served as provided by this rule, if any part of the property that is the subject of the action has not been brought within the control of the court because it has been removed or sold, or because it is intangible property in the hands of a person who has not been served with process, the court may, on motion, order any person having possession or control of such property or its proceeds to show cause why it should not be delivered into the custody of the marshal or paid into court to abide the judgment; and, after hearing, the court may enter such judgment as law and justice may require.

(6) Claim and Answer; Interrogatories. The claimant of property that is the subject of an action in rem shall file a claim within 10 days after process has been executed, or within such additional time as may be allowed by the court, and shall serve an answer within 20 days after the filing of the claim. The claim shall be verified on oath or solemn affirmation, and shall state the interest in the property by virtue of which the claimant demands its restitution and the right to defend the action. If the claim is made on behalf of the person entitled to possession by an agent, bailee, or attorney, it shall state that the agent, bailee, or attorney is duly authorized to make the claim. At the time of answering the claimant shall also serve answers to any interrogatories served with the complaint. In actions in rem interrogatories may be so served without leave of court.

As amended 1985, 1987.

Rule D.

POSSESSORY, PETITORY, AND PARTITION ACTIONS

In all actions for possession, partition, and to try title maintainable according to the course of the admiralty practice with respect to a vessel, in all actions so maintainable with respect to the possession of cargo or other maritime property, and in all actions by one or more part owners against the others to obtain security for the return of the vessel from any voyage undertaken without their consent, or by one or more part owners against the others to obtain possession of the vessel for any voyage on giving security for its safe return, the process shall be by a warrant of arrest of the vessel, cargo, or other property, and by notice in the manner provided by Rule B(2) to the adverse party or parties.

Rule E.

ACTIONS IN REM AND QUASI IN REM: GENERAL PROVISIONS

(1) Applicability. Except as otherwise provided, this rule applies to actions in personam with process of maritime attachment and garnishment, actions in rem, and petitory, possessory, and partition actions, supplementing Rules B, C, and D.

(2) Complaint; Security.

(a) Complaint. In actions to which this rule is applicable the complaint shall state the circumstances from which the claim arises with such particularity that the defendant or claimant will be able, without moving for a more definite statement, to commence an investigation of the facts and to frame a responsive pleading.

(b) Security for Costs. Subject to the provisions of Rule 54(d) and of relevant statutes, the court may, on the filing of the complaint or on the appearance of any defendant, claimant, or any other party, or at any later time, require the plaintiff, defendant, claimant, or other party to give security, or additional security, in such sum as the court shall direct to pay all costs and expenses that shall be awarded against the party by any interlocutory order or by the final judgment, or on appeal by any appellate court.

(3) Process.

(a) Territorial Limits of Effective Service. Process in rem and of maritime attachment and garnishment shall be served only within the district.

(b) Issuance and Delivery. Issuance and delivery of process in rem, or of maritime attachment and garnishment, shall be held in abeyance if the plaintiff so requests.

(4) Execution of Process; Marshal's Return; Custody of Property; Procedures for Release.

(a) In General. Upon issuance and delivery of the process or, in the case of summons with process of attachment and garnishment, when it appears that the defendant cannot be found within the district, the marshal shall forthwith execute the process in accordance with this subdivision (4), making due and prompt return.

(b) Tangible Property. If tangible property is to be attached or arrested, the marshal shall take it into the marshal's possession for safe custody. If the character or situation of the property is such that the taking of actual possession is impracticable, the marshal shall execute the process by affixing a copy thereof to the property in a conspicuous place and by leaving a copy of the complaint and process with the person having possession or the person's agent. In furtherance of the marshal's custody of any vessel the marshal is authorized to make a written request to the collector of customs not to grant clearance to such vessel until notified by the marshal or a deputy marshal or by the clerk that the vessel has been released in accordance with these rules.

(c) Intangible Property. If intangible property is to be attached or arrested the marshal shall execute the process by leaving with the garnishee or other obligor a copy of the complaint and process requiring the garnishee or other obligor to answer as provided in Rules B(3)(a) and C(6); or the marshal may accept for payment into the registry of the court the amount owed to the extent of the amount claimed by the plaintiff with interest and costs, in which event the garnishee or other obligor shall not be required to answer unless alias process shall be served.

(d) Directions with Respect to Property in Custody. The marshal may at any time apply to the court for directions with respect to property that has been attached or arrested, and shall give notice of such application to any or all of the parties as the court may direct.

(e) Expenses of Seizing and Keeping Property; Deposit. These rules do not alter the provisions of Title 28, U.S.C., § 1921, as amended, relative to the expenses of seizing and keeping property attached or arrested and to the requirement of deposits to cover such expenses.

(f) Procedure for Release from Arrest or Attachment. Whenever property is arrested or attached, any person claiming an inter-

est in it shall be entitled to a prompt hearing at which the plaintiff shall be required to show why the arrest or attachment should not be vacated or other relief granted consistent with these rules. This subdivision shall have no application to suits for seamen's wages when process is issued upon a certification of sufficient cause filed pursuant to Title 46, U.S.C. §§ 603 and 604 or to actions by the United States for forfeitures for violation of any statute of the United States.

(5) Release of Property.

(a) Special Bond. Except in cases of seizures for forfeiture under any law of the United States, whenever process of maritime attachment and garnishment or process in rem is issued the execution of such process shall be stayed, or the property released, on the giving of security, to be approved by the court or clerk, or by stipulation of the parties, conditioned to answer the judgment of the court or of any appellate court. The parties may stipulate the amount and nature of such security. In the event of the inability or refusal of the parties so to stipulate the court shall fix the principal sum of the bond or stipulation at an amount sufficient to cover the amount of the plaintiff's claim fairly stated with accrued interest and costs; but the principal sum shall in no event exceed (i) twice the amount of the plaintiff's claim or (ii) the value of the property on due appraisement, whichever is smaller. The bond or stipulation shall be conditioned for the payment of the principal sum and interest thereon at 6 per cent per annum.

(b) General Bond. The owner of any vessel may file a general bond or stipulation, with sufficient surety, to be approved by the court, conditioned to answer the judgment of such court in all or any actions that may be brought thereafter in such court in which the vessel is attached or arrested. Thereupon the execution of all such process against such vessel shall be stayed so long as the amount secured by such bond or stipulation is at least double the aggregate amount claimed by plaintiffs in all actions begun and pending in which such vessel has been attached or arrested. Judgments and remedies may be had on such bond or stipulation as if a special bond or stipulation had been filed in each of such actions. The district court may make necessary orders to carry this rule into effect, particularly as to the giving of proper notice of any action against or attachment of a vessel for which a general bond has been filed. Such bond or stipulation shall be indorsed by the clerk with a minute of the actions wherein process is so stayed. Further security may be required by the court at any time.

If a special bond or stipulation is given in a particular case, the liability on the general bond or stipulation shall cease as to that case.

(c) Release by Consent or Stipulation; Order of Court or Clerk; Costs. Any vessel, cargo, or other property in the custody of the marshal may be released forthwith upon the marshal's acceptance and approval of a stipulation, bond, or other security, signed by the party on whose behalf the property is detained or the party's attorney and expressly authorizing such release, if all costs and charges of the court and its officers shall have first been paid. Otherwise no property in the custody of the marshal or other officer of the court shall be released without an order of the court; but such order may be entered as of course by the clerk, upon the giving of approved security as provided by law and these rules, or upon the dismissal or discontinuance of the action; but the marshal shall not deliver any property so released until the costs and charges of the officers of the court shall first have been paid.

(d) Possessory, Petitory, and Partition Actions. The foregoing provisions of this subdivision (5) do not apply to petitory, possessory, and partition actions. In such cases the property arrested shall be released only by order of the court, on such terms and conditions and on the giving of such security as the court may require.

(6) Reduction or Impairment of Security. Whenever security is taken the court may, on motion and hearing, for good cause shown, reduce the amount of security given; and if the surety shall be or become insufficient, new or additional sureties may be required on motion and hearing.

(7) Security on Counterclaim. Whenever there is asserted a counterclaim arising out of the same transaction or occurrence with respect to which the action was originally filed, and the defendant or claimant in the original action has given security to respond in damages, any plaintiff for whose benefit such security has been given shall give security in the usual amount and form to respond in damages to the claims set forth in such counterclaim, unless the court, for cause shown, shall otherwise direct; and proceedings on the original claim shall be stayed until such security is given, unless the court otherwise directs. When the United States or a corporate instrumentality thereof as defendant is relieved by law of the requirement of giving security to respond in damages it shall nevertheless be treated for the purposes of this subdivision E(7) as if it had given such security if a private person so situated would have been required to give it.

(8) Restricted Appearance. An appearance to defend against an admiralty and maritime claim with respect to which there has issued process in rem, or process of attachment and garnishment whether pursuant to these Supplemental Rules or to Rule 4(e), may be expressly restricted to the defense of such claim, and in that event shall not constitute an appearance for the purposes of any other claim with respect to which such process is not available or has not been served.

(9) Disposition of Property; Sales.

(a) Actions for Forfeitures. In any action in rem to enforce a forfeiture for violation of a statute of the United States the property shall be disposed of as provided by statute.

(b) Interlocutory Sales. If property that has been attached or arrested is perishable, or liable to deterioration, decay, or injury by being detained in custody pending the action, or if the expense of keeping the property is excessive or disproportionate, or if there is unreasonable delay in securing the release of property, the court, on application of any party or of the marshal, may order the property or any portion thereof to be sold; and the proceeds, or so much thereof as shall be adequate to satisfy any judgment, may be ordered brought into court to abide the event of the action; or the court may, on motion of the defendant or claimant, order delivery of the property to the defendant or claimant, upon the giving of security in accordance with these rules.

(c) Sales; Proceeds. All sales of property shall be made by the marshal or a deputy marshal, or other proper officer assigned by the court where the marshal is a party in interest; and the proceeds of sale shall be forthwith paid into the registry of the court to be disposed of according to law.

As amended 1985, 1987.

Rule F.

LIMITATION OF LIABILITY

(1) Time for Filing Complaint; Security. Not later than six months after receipt of a claim in writing, any vessel owner may file a complaint in the appropriate district court, as provided in subdivision (9) of this rule, for limitation of liability pursuant to statute. The owner (a) shall deposit with the court, for the benefit of claimants, a sum equal to the amount or value of the owner's interest in the vessel and pending freight, or approved security therefor, and in addition such sums, or approved security therefor, as the court may from time to time fix as necessary to carry out the provisions of the statutes as amended; or (b) at the owner's option shall transfer to a trustee to be appointed by the court, for the benefit of claimants, the owner's interest in the vessel and pending freight, together with such sums, or approved security therefor, as the court may from time to time fix as necessary to carry out the provisions of the statutes as amended. The plaintiff shall also give security for costs and, if the plaintiff elects to give security, for interest at the rate of 6 percent per annum from the date of the security.

(2) Complaint. The complaint shall set forth the facts on the basis of which the right to limit liability is asserted, and all facts necessary to enable the court to determine the amount to which the owner's liability shall be limited. The complaint may demand exoneration from as well as limitation of liability. It shall state the voyage, if any, on which the demands sought to be limited arose, with the date and place of its termination; the amount of all demands including all unsatisfied liens or claims of lien, in contract or in tort or otherwise, arising on that voyage, so far as known to the plaintiff, and what actions and proceedings, if any, are pending thereon; whether the vessel was damaged, lost, or abandoned, and, if so, when and where; the value of the vessel at the close of the voyage or, in case of wreck, the value of her wreckage, strippings, or proceeds, if any, and where and in whose possession they are; and the amount of any pending freight recovered or recoverable. If the plaintiff elects to transfer the plaintiff's interest in the vessel to a trustee, the complaint must further show any prior paramount liens thereon, and what voyages or trips, if any, she has made since the voyage or trip on which the claims sought to be limited arose, and any existing liens arising upon any such subsequent voyage or trip, with the amounts and causes thereof, and the names and addresses of the lienors, so far as known; and whether the vessel sustained any injury upon or by reason of such subsequent voyage or trip.

(3) Claims Against Owner; Injunction. Upon compliance by the owner with the requirements of subdivision (1) of this rule all claims and proceedings against the owner or the owner's property with respect to the matter in question shall cease. On application of the plaintiff the court shall enjoin the further prosecution of any action or proceeding against the plaintiff or the plaintiff's property with respect to any claim subject to limitation in the action.

(4) Notice to Claimants. Upon the owner's compliance with subdivision (1) of this rule the court shall issue a notice to all persons asserting claims with respect to which the complaint seeks limitation, admonishing them to file their respective claims with the clerk of the court and to serve on the attorneys for the plaintiff a copy thereof on or before a date to be named in the notice. The date so fixed shall not be less than 30 days after issuance of the notice. For cause shown, the court may enlarge the time within which claims may be filed. The notice shall be published in such newspaper or newspapers as the court may direct once a week for four successive weeks prior to the date fixed for the filing of claims. The plaintiff not later than the day of second publication shall also mail a copy of the notice to every person known to have made any claim against the vessel or the plaintiff arising out the voyage or trip on which the claims sought to be limited arose. In cases involving death a copy of such notice shall be mailed to the decedent at the decedent's last known address, and also to any person who shall be known to have made any claim on account of such death.

(5) **Claims and Answer.** Claims shall be filed and served on or before the date specified in the notice provided for in subdivision (4) of this rule. Each claim shall specify the facts upon which the claimant relies in support of the claim, the items thereof, and the dates on which the same accrued. If a claimant desires to contest either the right to exoneration from or the right to limitation of liability the claimant shall file and serve an answer to the complaint unless the claim has included an answer.

(6) **Information to Be Given Claimants.** Within 30 days after the date specified in the notice for filing claims, or within such time as the court thereafter may allow, the plaintiff shall mail to the attorney for each claimant (or if the claimant has no attorney to the claimant) a list setting forth (a) the name of each claimant, (b) the name and address of the claimant's attorney (if the claimant is known to have one), (c) the nature of the claim, i. e., whether property loss, property damage, death, personal injury, etc., and (d) the amount thereof.

(7) **Insufficiency of Fund or Security.** Any claimant may by motion demand that the funds deposited in court or the security given by the plaintiff be increased on the ground that they are less than the value of the plaintiff's interest in the vessel and pending freight. Thereupon the court shall cause due appraisement to be made of the value of the plaintiff's interest in the vessel and pending freight; and if the court finds that the deposit or security is either insufficient or excessive it shall order its increase or reduction. In like manner any claimant may demand that the deposit or security be increased on the ground that it is insufficient to carry out the provisions of the statutes relating to claims in respect of loss of life or bodily injury; and, after notice and hearing, the court may similarly order that the deposit or security be increased or reduced.

(8) **Objections to Claims: Distribution of Fund.** Any interested party may question or controvert any claim without filing an objection thereto. Upon determination of liability the fund deposited or secured, or the proceeds of the vessel and pending freight, shall be divided pro rata, subject to all relevant provisions of law, among the several claimants in proportion to the amounts

of their respective claims, duly proved, saving, however, to all parties any priority to which they may be legally entitled.

(9) **Venue; Transfer.** The complaint shall be filed in any district in which the vessel has been attached or arrested to answer for any claim with respect to which the plaintiff seeks to limit liability; or, if the vessel has not been attached or arrested, then in any district in which the owner has been sued with respect to any such claim. When the vessel has not been attached or arrested to answer the matters aforesaid, and suit has not been commenced against the owner, the proceedings may be had in the district in which the vessel may be, but if the vessel is not within any district and no suit has been commenced in any district, then the complaint may be filed in any district. For the convenience of parties and witnesses, in the interest of justice, the court may transfer the action to any district; if venue is wrongly laid the court shall dismiss or, if it be in the interest of justice, transfer the action to any district in which it could have been brought. If the vessel shall have been sold, the proceeds shall represent the vessel for the purposes of these rules.

As amended 1987.

CERTAIN OF THE EARLY CIVIL ADVISORY COMMIT- TEE'S NOTES FROM 1938, 1948, AND 1961

Rule 4.   Process

Advisory Committee's Note to Original Rule

Note to Subdivision (a).   With the provision permitting additional summons upon request of the plaintiff, compare Equity Rule 14 (Alias Subpoena) and the last sentence of Equity Rule 12 (Issue of Subpoena—Time for Answer).

Note to Subdivision (b).   This rule prescribes a form of summons which follows substantially the requirements stated in Equity Rules 12 (Issue of Subpoena—Time for Answer) and 7 (Process, Mesne and Final).

U.S.C., Title 28, § 721 [now § 1691] (Sealing and testing of writs) is substantially continued in so far as it applies to a summons, but its requirements as to teste of process are superseded.   U.S.C., Title 28, § 722 [1946 ed.] (Teste of process, day of) is superseded.

See Rule 12(a) for a statement of the time within which the defendant is required to appear and defend.

Note to Subdivision (c).   This Rule does not affect U.S.C., Title 28, § 503, as amended June 15, 1935 [1946 ed.] (Marshals; duties) and such statutes as the following in so far as they provide for service of process by a marshal, but modifies them in so far as they may imply service by a marshal only:

U.S.C., Title 15:

   § 5 (Bringing in additional parties) (Sherman Act)

   § 10 (Bringing in additional parties)

   § 25 (Restraining violations; procedure)

U.S.C., Title 28:

   § 45 [1946 ed.] (Practice and procedure in certain cases under the interstate commerce laws)

Compare Equity Rule 15 (Process, by Whom Served).

Note to Subdivision (d).   Under this rule the complaint must always be served with the summons.

Paragraph (1).   For an example of a statute providing for service upon an agent of an individual see U.S.C., Title 28, § 109 [now §§ 1400, 1694] (Patent cases).

Paragraph (3).   This enumerates the officers and agents of a corporation or of a partnership or other unincorporated association upon whom service of process may be made, and permits service of process only upon the officers, managing or general agents, or agents authorized by appointment or by law, of the corporation, partnership or unincorporated association against which the action is brought. See *Christian v. International Ass'n of Machinists,* 7 F.(2d) 481 (D.C.Ky.,1925) and *Singleton v. Order of Railway Conductors of America,* 9 F.Supp. 417 (D.C.Ill.,1935).

New matter is shown in italics; matter to be omitted is lined through

Compare *Operative Plasterers' and Cement Finishers' International Ass'n of the United States and Canada v. Case,* 93 F.(2d) 56 (App.D.C.,1937).

For a statute authorizing service upon a specified agent and requiring mailing to the defendant, see U.S.C., Title 6, § 7 (Surety companies as sureties; appointment of agents; service of process).

Paragraphs (4) and (5) provide a uniform and comprehensive method of service for all actions against the United States or an officer or agency thereof. For statutes providing for such service, see U.S.C., Title 7, §§ 217 (Proceedings for suspension of orders), 499k (Injunctions; application of injunction laws governing orders of Interstate Commerce Commission), 608c(15)(B) (Court review of ruling of Secretary of Agriculture), and 855 (making § 608c(15)(B) applicable to orders of the Secretary of Agriculture as to handlers of anti-hog-cholera serum and hog-cholera virus); U.S.C., Title 26, § 1569 (Bill in chancery to clear title to realty on which the United States has a lien for taxes); U.S.C., Title 28, §§ 45 [1946 ed.] (District Courts; practice and procedure in certain cases under the interstate commerce laws), 763 [1946 ed.] (Petition in suit against the United States; service; appearance by district attorney), 766 [now § 2409] (Partition suits where United States is tenant in common or joint tenant), 902 [now § 2410] (Foreclosure of mortgages or other liens on property in which the United States has an interest). These and similar statutes are modified in so far as they prescribe a different method of service or dispense with the service of a summons.

For the Equity Rule on service, see Equity Rule 13 (Manner of Serving Subpoena).

Note to Subdivision (e). The provisions for the service of a summons or of notice or of an order in lieu of summons contained in U.S.C., Title 8, § 405 (Cancellation of certificates of citizenship fraudulently or illegally procured) (service by publication in accordance with state law); U.S.C., Title 28, § 118 [now § 1655] (Absent defendants in suits to enforce liens); U.S.C., Title 35, § 72a (Jurisdiction of District Court of United States for the District of Columbia in certain equity suits where adverse parties reside elsewhere) (service by publication against parties residing in foreign countries); U.S.C., Title 38, § 445 (Action against the United States on a veteran's contract of insurance) (parties not inhabitants of or not found within the district may be served with an order of the court, personally or by publication) and similar statutes are continued by this rule. Title 24, § 378 of the Code of the District of Columbia (Publication against non-resident; those absent for six months; unknown heirs or devisees; for divorce or in rem; actual service beyond District) is continued by this rule.

Note to Subdivision (f). This rule enlarges to some extent the present rule as to where service may be made. It does not, however, enlarge the jurisdiction of the district courts.

U.S.C., Title 28, §§ 113 [now § 1392] (Suits in States containing more than one district) (where there are two or more defendants residing in different districts), 115 [1946 ed.] (Suits of a local nature), 116 [now § 1392] (Property in different districts in same state), 838 [1946 ed.] (Executions run in all districts of state); U.S.C., Title 47, § 13 (Action for damages against a railroad or telegraph company whose officer or agent in control of a telegraph line refuses or fails to operate such line in a certain manner—"upon any agent of the company found in such state"); U.S.C., Title 49, § 321(c) (Requiring designation of a process agent by interstate motor carriers and in case of failure so to do, service may be made upon any agent in the state) and similar statutes, allowing the running of process throughout a state, are substantially continued.

New matter is shown in italics; matter to be omitted is lined through

U.S.C., Title 15, §§ 5 (Bringing in additional parties) (Sherman Act), 25 (Restraining violations; procedure); U.S.C., Title 28, §§ 44 [now § 2321] (Procedure in certain cases under interstate commerce laws; service of processes of court), 117 [now §§ 754, 1692] (Property in different states in same circuit; jurisdiction of receiver), 839 [now § 2413] (Executions; run in every State and Territory) and similar statutes, providing for the running of process beyond the territorial limits of a state, are expressly continued.

Note to Subdivision (g). With the second sentence compare Equity Rule 15 (Process, by Whom Served).

Note to Subdivision (h). This rule substantially continues U.S.C., Title 28, § 767 [1946 ed.] (Amendment of process).

Rule 7. Pleadings Allowed; Form of Motions

Advisory Committee's Note to Original Rule

1. A provision designating pleadings and defining a motion is common in the state practice acts. See Ill.Rev.Stat. (1937) ch. 110, § 156 (Designation and order of pleadings); 2 Minn.Stat. (Mason, 1927) § 9246 (Definition of motion); and N.Y.C. P.A. (1937) § 113 (Definition of motion). Equity Rules 18 (Pleadings—Technical Forms Abrogated), 29 (Defenses—How Presented), and 33 (Testing Sufficiency of Defense) abolished technical forms of pleading, demurrers, and pleas, and exceptions for insufficiency of an answer.

2. *Note to Subdivision (a).* This preserves the substance of Equity Rule 31 (Reply—When Required—When Cause at Issue). Compare the English practice, English Rules Under the Judicature Act (The Annual Practice, 1937) O. 23, r. r. 1, 2 (Reply to counterclaim; amended, 1933, to be subject to the rules applicable to defenses, O. 21). See O. 21, r. r. 1–14; O. 27, r. 13 (When pleadings deemed denied and put in issue). Under the codes the pleadings are generally limited. A reply is sometimes required to an affirmative defense in the answer. 1 Colo.Stat.Ann. (1935) § 66; Ore.Code Ann. (1930) §§ 1–614, 1–616. In other jurisdictions no reply is necessary to an affirmative defense in the answer, but a reply may be ordered by the court. N.C.Code Ann. (1935) § 525; 1 S.D.Comp.Laws (1929) § 2357. A reply to a counterclaim is usually required. Ark.Civ.Code (Crawford, 1934) §§ 123–125; Wis.Stat. (1935) §§ 263.20, 263.21. U.S.C., Title 28, § 45 [1946 ed.] (District courts; practice and procedure in certain cases) is modified in so far as it may dispense with a reply to a counterclaim.

For amendment of pleadings, see Rule 15 dealing with amended and supplemental pleadings.

3. All statutes which use the words "petition", "bill of complaint", "plea", "demurrer", and other such terminology are modified in form by this rule.

(a) **Pleadings.** There shall be a complaint and an answer; and there shall be a reply, if the answer contains *to* a counterclaim denominated as such; an answer to a cross-claim, if the answer contains a cross-claim; a third-party complaint, if leave is given under Rule 14 to summon a person who was not an original party; and there shall be a third-party answer, if a third-party

New matter is shown in italics; matter to be omitted is lined through

complaint is served. No other pleading shall be allowed, except that the court may order a reply to an answer or a third-party answer.

Advisory Committee's Note to 1948 Amendment

This amendment eliminates any question as to whether the compulsory reply, where a counterclaim is pleaded, is a reply only to the counterclaim or is a general reply to the answer containing the counterclaim. See Commentary, *Scope of Reply Where Defendant Has Pleaded Counterclaim,* 1939, 1 Fed.Rules Serv. 672; *Fort Chartres and Ivy Landing Drainage and Levee District No. Five v. Thompson,* E.D.Ill.1945, 8 Fed.Rules Serv. 13.32, Case 1.

Rule 12. Defenses and Objections—When and How Presented—By Pleading or Motion—Motion for Judgment on Pleadings

Advisory Committee's Note to Original Rule

Note to Subdivision (a). 1. Compare Equity Rules 12 (Issue of Subpoena—Time for Answer) and 31 (Reply—When Required—When Cause at Issue); 4 Mont.Rev. Codes Ann. (1935) §§ 9107, 9158; N.Y.C.P.A. (1937) § 263; N.Y.R.C.P. (1937) Rules 109–111.

2. U.S.C., Title 28, § 763 [1946 ed.] (Petition in action against United States; service; appearance by district attorney) provides that the United States as a defendant shall have 60 days within which to answer or otherwise defend. This and other statutes which provide 60 days for the United States or an officer or agency thereof to answer or otherwise defend are continued by this rule. In so far as any statutes not excepted in Rule 81 provide a different time for a defendant to defend, such statutes are modified. See U.S.C., Title 28, § 45 [1946 ed.] (District courts; practice and procedure in certain cases under the interstate commerce laws) (30 days).

3. Compare the last sentence of Equity Rule 29 (Defenses—How Presented) and N.Y.C.P.A. (1937) § 283. See Rule 15(a) for time within which to plead to an amended pleading.

Note to Subdivisions (b) and (d). 1. See generally Equity Rules 29 (Defenses— How Presented), 33 (Testing Sufficiency of Defense), 43 (Defect of Parties—Resisting Objection), and 44 (Defect of Parties—Tardy Objection); N.Y.C.P.A. (1937) §§ 277–280; N.Y.R.C.P. (1937) Rules 106–112; English Rules Under the Judicature Act (The Annual Practice, 1937) O. 25, r. r. 1–4; Clark, Code Pleading (1928) pp. 371–381.

2. For provisions authorizing defenses to be made in the answer or reply see English Rules Under the Judicature Act (The Annual Practice, 1937) O. 25, r. r. 1–4; 1 Miss.Code Ann. (1930) §§ 378, 379. Compare Equity Rule 29 (Defenses— How Presented); U.S.C., Title 28, § 45 [1946 ed.] (District Courts; practice and procedure in certain cases under the interstate commerce laws). U.S.C., Title 28, § 45, [1946 ed.] substantially continued by this rule, provides: "No replication need be filed to the answer, and objections to the sufficiency of the petition or answer as not setting forth a cause of action or defense must be taken at the final hearing or by motion to dismiss the petition based on said grounds, which motion may be made at any time before answer is filed." Compare Calif.Code Civ.Proc. (Deering,

---

New matter is shown in italics; matter to be omitted is lined through

1937) § 433; 4 Nev.Comp.Laws (Hillyer, 1929) § 8600. For provisions that the defendant may demur and answer at the same time, see Calif.Code Civ.Proc. (Deering, 1937) § 431; 4 Nev.Comp.Laws (Hillyer, 1929) § 8598.

3. Equity Rule 29 (Defenses—How Presented) abolished demurrers and provided that defenses in point of law arising on the face of the bill should be made by motion to dismiss or in the answer, with further provision that every such point of law going to the whole or material part of the cause or causes stated might be called up and disposed of before final hearing "at the discretion of the court." Likewise many state practices have abolished the demurrer, or retain it only to attack substantial and not formal defects. See 6 Tenn.Code Ann. (Williams, 1934) § 8784; Ala.Code Ann. (Michie, 1928) § 9479; 2 Mass.Gen.Laws (Ter.Ed., 1932) ch. 231, §§ 15–18; Kansas Gen.Stat.Ann. (1935) §§ 60–705, 60–706.

Note to Subdivision (c). Compare Equity Rule 33 (Testing Sufficiency of Defense); N.Y.R.C.P. (1937) Rules 111 and 112.

Note to Subdivisions (e) and (f). Compare Equity Rules 20 (Further and Particular Statement in Pleading May Be Required) and 21 (Scandal and Impertinence); English Rules Under the Judicature Act (The Annual Practice, 1937) O. 19, r. r. 7, 7a, 7b, 8; 4 Mont.Rev.Codes Ann. (1935) §§ 9166, 9167; N.Y.C.P.A. (1937) § 247; N.Y.R.C.P. (1937) Rules 103, 115, 116, 117; Wyo.Rev.Stat.Ann. (Courtright, 1931) §§ 89–1033, 89–1034.

Note to Subdivision (g). Compare Rules of the District Court of the United States for the District of Columbia (1937), Equity Rule 11; N.M. Rules of Pleading, Practice and Procedure, 38 N.M.Rep. vii [105–408] (1934); Wash.Gen.Rules of the Superior Courts, 1 Wash.Rev.Stat.Ann. (Remington, 1932) p. 160, Rule VI(e) and (f).

Note to Subdivision (h). Compare Calif.Code Civ.Proc. (Deering, 1937) § 434; 2 Minn.Stat. (Mason, 1927) § 9252; N.Y.C.P.A. (1937) §§ 278 and 279; Wash.Gen. Rules of the Superior Courts, 1 Wash.Rev.Stat.Ann. (Remington, 1932) p. 160, Rule VI(e). This rule continues U.S.C., Title 28, § 80 [now §§ 1359, 1447, 1919] (Dismissal or remand) (of action over which district court lacks jurisdiction), while U.S.C., Title 28, § 399 [now § 1653] (Amendments to show diverse citizenship) is continued by Rule 15.

(a) **When Presented.** A defendant shall serve his answer within 20 days after the service of the summons and complaint upon him, unless the court directs otherwise when service of process is made pursuant to Rule 4(e). A party served with a pleading stating a cross-claim against him shall serve an answer thereto within 20 days after the service upon him. The plaintiff shall serve his reply to a counterclaim in the answer within 20 days after service of the answer or, if a reply is ordered by the court, within 20 days after service of the order, unless the order otherwise directs. The United States or an officer or agency thereof shall serve an answer to the complaint or to a cross-claim, or a reply to a counterclaim, within 60 days after the service upon the United States attorney of the pleading in which the claim is asserted. The service of ~~any~~ *a* motion ~~provided for in~~ *permitted under* this rule alters ~~the time fixed by these rules for serving any~~

New matter is shown in italics; matter to be omitted is lined through

175

~~required responsive pleading~~ *these periods of time* as follows, unless a different time is fixed by order of the court: (1) if the court denies the motion or postpones its disposition until the trial on the merits, the responsive pleading ~~may~~ *shall* be served within 10 days after notice of the court's action; (2) if the court grants a motion for a more definite statement ~~or for a bill of particulars,~~ the responsive pleading ~~may~~ *shall* be served within ~~ten~~ *10* days after the service of the more definite statement ~~or bill of particu-lars. In either case the time for service of the responsive pleading shall be not less than remains of the time which would have been allowed under these rules if the motion had not been made.~~

(b) **How Presented.** Every defense, in law or fact, to a claim for relief in any pleading, whether a claim, counterclaim, cross-claim, or third-party claim, shall be asserted in the responsive pleading thereto if one is required, except that the following defenses may at the option of the pleader be made by motion: (1) lack of jurisdiction over the subject matter, (2) lack of jurisdiction over the person, (3) improper venue, (4) insufficiency of process, (5) insufficiency of service of process, (6) failure to state a claim upon which relief can be granted, *(7) failure to join an indispensable party.* A motion making any of these defenses shall be made before pleading if a further pleading is permitted. No defense or objection is waived by being joined with one or more other defenses or objections in a responsive pleading or motion. If a pleading sets forth a claim for relief to which the adverse party is not required to serve a responsive pleading, he may assert at the trial any defense in law or fact to that claim for relief. *If, on a motion asserting the defense numbered (6) to dismiss for failure of the pleading to state a claim upon which relief can be granted, matters outside the pleading are presented to and not excluded by the court, the motion shall be treated as one for summary judgment and disposed of as provided in Rule 56, and all parties shall be given reasonable opportunity to present all material made pertinent to such a motion by Rule 56.*

(c) **Motion for Judgment on the Pleadings.** After the pleadings are closed but within such time as not to delay the trial, any party may move for judgment on the pleadings. *If, on a motion for judgment on the pleadings, matters outside the plead-ings are presented to and not excluded by the court, the motion shall be treated as one for summary judgment and disposed of as provided in Rule 56, and all parties shall be given reasonable opportunity to present all material made pertinent to such a motion by Rule 56.*

New matter is shown in italics; matter to be omitted is lined through

(d) Preliminary Hearings. The defenses specifically enumerated (1)-(6) *(7)* in subdivision (b) of this rule, whether made in a pleading or by motion, and the motion for judgment mentioned in subdivision (c) of this rule shall be heard and determined before trial on application of any party, unless the court orders that the hearing and determination thereof be deferred until the trial.

(e) Motion for More Definite Statement ~~or for Bill of Particulars~~. ~~Before responding to a pleading or, if no responsive pleading is permitted by these rules, within 20 days after the service of the pleading upon him, a party may move for a more definite statement or for a bill of particulars of any matter which is not averred with sufficient definiteness or particularity to enable him properly to prepare his responsive pleading or to prepare for trial.~~ *If a pleading to which a responsive pleading is permitted is so vague or ambiguous that a party cannot reasonably be required to frame a responsive pleading, he may move for a more definite statement before interposing his responsive pleading.* The motion shall point out the defects complained of and the details desired. If the motion is granted and the order of the court is not obeyed within 10 days after notice of the order or within such other time as the court may fix, the court may strike the pleading to which the motion was directed or make such order as it deems just. ~~A bill of particulars becomes part of the pleading which it supplements.~~

(f) Motion to Strike. Upon motion made by a party before responding to a pleading or, if no responsive pleading is permitted by these rules, upon motion made by a party within 20 days after the service of the pleading upon him or upon the court's own initiative at any time, the court may order *stricken from any pleading any insufficient defense or* any redundant, immaterial, impertinent, or scandalous matter ~~stricken from any pleading~~.

(g) Consolidation of ~~Motions~~ *Defenses*. A party who makes a motion under this rule may join with it the other motions herein provided for and then available to him. If a party makes a motion under this rule and does not include therein all defenses and objections then available to him which this rule permits to be raised by motion, he shall not thereafter make a motion based on any of the defenses or objections so omitted, except ~~that prior to making any other motions under this rule he may make a motion in which are joined all the defenses numbered (1) to (5) in subdivision (b) of this rule which he cares to assert~~ *as provided in subdivision (h) of this rule.*

(h) Waiver of Defenses. A party waives all defenses and objections which he does not present either by motion as herein-

---

New matter is shown in italics; matter to be omitted is lined through

before provided or, if he has made no motion, in his answer or reply, except (1) that the defense of failure to state a claim upon which relief can be granted, *the defense of failure to join an indispensable party,* and the objection of failure to state a legal defense to a claim may also be made by a later pleading, if one is permitted, or by motion for judgment on the pleadings or at the trial on the merits, and except (2) that, whenever it appears by suggestion of the parties or otherwise that the court lacks jurisdiction of the subject matter, the court shall dismiss the action. The objection or defense, if made at the trial, shall be disposed of as provided in Rule 15(b) in the light of any evidence that may have been received.

Advisory Committee's Note to 1948 Amendment

Subdivision (a). Various minor alterations in language have been made to improve the statement of the rule. All references to bills of particulars have been stricken in accordance with changes made in subdivision (e).

Subdivision (b). The addition of defense (7), "failure to join an indispensable party", cures an omission in the rules, which are silent as to the mode of raising such failure. See Commentary, *Manner of Raising Objection of Non-Joinder of Indispensable Party,* 1940, 2 Fed.Rules Serv. 658 and, 1942, 5 Fed.Rules Serv. 820. In one case, *United States v. Metropolitan Life Ins. Co.,* E.D.Pa.1941, 36 F.Supp. 399, the failure to join an indispensable party was raised under Rule 12(c).

Rule 12(b)(6), permitting a motion to dismiss for failure of the complaint to state a claim on which relief can be granted, is substantially the same as the old demurrer for failure of a pleading to state a cause of action. Some courts have held that as the rule by its terms refers to statements in the complaint, extraneous matter on affidavits, depositions or otherwise, may not be introduced in support of the motion, or to resist it. On the other hand, in many cases the district courts have permitted the introduction of such material. When these cases have reached circuit courts of appeals in situations where the extraneous material so received shows that there is no genuine issue as to any material question of fact and that on the undisputed facts as disclosed by the affidavits or depositions, one party or the other is entitled to judgment as a matter of law, the circuit courts, properly enough, have been reluctant to dispose of the case merely on the face of the pleading, and in the interest of prompt disposition of the action have made a final disposition of it. In dealing with such situations the Second Circuit has made the sound suggestion that whatever its label or original basis, the motion may be treated as a motion for summary judgment and disposed of as such. *Samara v. United States,* C.C.A.2d, 1942, 129 F.2d 594, cert. den., 1942, 317 U.S. 686, 63 S.Ct. 258; *Boro Hall Corp. v. General Motors Corp.,* C.C.A.2d, 1942, 124 F.2d 822, cert. den., 1943, 317 U.S. 695, 63 S.Ct. 436. See also *Kithcart v. Metropolitan Life Ins. Co.,* C.C.A.8th, 1945, 150 F.2d 997, aff'g 62 F.Supp. 93.

It has also been suggested that this practice could be justified on the ground that the federal rules permit "speaking" motions. The Committee entertains the view that on motion under Rule 12(b)(6) to dismiss for failure of the complaint to state a good claim, the trial court should have authority to permit the introduction of extraneous matter, such as may be offered on a motion for summary judgment, and if it does not exclude such matter the motion should then be treated as a motion for summary judgment and disposed of in the manner and on the conditions

---

New matter is shown in italics; matter to be omitted is lined through

stated in Rule 56 relating to summary judgments, and, of course, in such a situation, when the case reaches the circuit court of appeals, that court should treat the motion in the same way. The Committee believes that such practice, however, should be tied to the summary judgment rule. The term "speaking motion" is not mentioned in the rules, and if there is such a thing its limitations are undefined. Where extraneous matter is received, by tying further proceedings to the summary judgment rule the courts have a definite basis in the rules for disposing of the motion.

The Committee emphasizes particularly the fact that the summary judgment rule does not permit a case to be disposed of by judgment on the merits on affidavits, which disclose a conflict on a material issue of fact, and unless this practice is tied to the summary judgment rule, the extent to which a court, on the introduction of such extraneous matter, may resolve questions of fact on conflicting proof would be left uncertain.

The decisions dealing with this general situation may be generally grouped as follows: (1) cases dealing with the use of affidavits and other extraneous material on motions; (2) cases reversing judgments to prevent final determination on mere pleading allegations alone.

Under group (1) are: *Boro Hall Corp. v. General Motors Corp.*, C.C.A.2d, 1942, 124 F.2d 822, cert. den., 1943, 317 U.S. 695, 63 S.Ct. 436; *Gallup v. Caldwell*, C.C.A.3d, 1941, 120 F.2d 90; *Central Mexico Light & Power Co. v. Munch*, C.C.A.2d, 1940, 116 F.2d 85; *National Labor Relations Board v. Montgomery Ward & Co.*, App.D.C.1944, 79 U.S.App.D.C. 200, 144 F.2d 528, cert. den., 1944, 65 S.Ct. 134; *Urquhart v. American–La France Foamite Corp.*, App.D.C.1944, 79 U.S.App.D.C. 219, 144 F.2d 542; *Samara v. United States*, C.C.A.2d, 1942, 129 F.2d 594; *Cohen v. American Window Glass Co.*, C.C.A.2d, 1942, 126 F.2d 111; *Sperry Products Inc. v. Association of American Railroads*, C.C.A.2d, 1942, 132 F.2d 408; *Joint Council Dining Car Employees Local 370 v. Delaware, Lackawanna and Western R. Co.*, C.C.A.2d, 1946, 157 F.2d 417; *Weeks v. Bareco Oil Co.*, C.C.A.7th, 1941, 125 F.2d 84; *Carroll v. Morrison Hotel Corp.*, C.C.A.7th, 1945, 149 F.2d 404; *Victory v. Manning*, C.C.A.3rd, 1942, 128 F.2d 415; *Locals No. 1470, No. 1469, and No. 1512 of International Longshoremen's Association v. Southern Pacific Co.*, C.C.A.5th, 1942, 131 F.2d 605; *Lucking v. Delano*, C.C.A.6th, 1942, 129 F.2d 283; *San Francisco Lodge No. 68 of International Association of Machinists v. Forrestal*, N.D.Cal.1944, 58 F.Supp. 466; *Benson v. Export Equipment Corp.*, N.Mex.1945, 164 P.2d 380, construing New Mexico rule identical with Rule 12(b)(6); *F.E. Myers & Bros. Co. v. Gould Pumps, Inc.*, W.D.N.Y.1946, 9 Fed.Rules Serv. 12b.33, Case 2, 5 F.R.D. 132. Cf. *Kohler v. Jacobs*, C.C.A.5th, 1943, 138 F.2d 440; *Cohen v. United States*, C.C.A.8th, 1942, 129 F.2d 733.

Under group (2) are: *Sparks v. England*, C.C.A.8th, 1940, 113 F.2d 579; *Continental Collieries, Inc. v. Shober*, C.C.A.3d, 1942, 130 F.2d 631; *Downey v. Palmer*, C.C.A.2d, 1940, 114 F.2d 116; *DeLoach v. Crowley's Inc.*, C.C.A.5th, 1942, 128 F.2d 378; *Leimer v. State Mutual Life Assurance Co. of Worcester, Mass.*, C.C.A.8th, 1940, 108 F.2d 302; *Rossiter v. Vogel*, C.C.A.2d, 1943, 134 F.2d 908, compare s.c., C.C.A.2d, 1945, 148 F.2d 292; *Karl Kiefer Machine Co. v. United States Bottlers Machinery Co.*, C.C.A.7th, 1940, 113 F.2d 356; *Chicago Metallic Mfg. Co. v. Edward Katzinger Co.*, C.C.A.7th, 1941, 123 F.2d 518; *Louisiana Farmers' Protective Union, Inc. v. Great Atlantic & Pacific Tea Co. of America, Inc.*, C.C.A.8th, 1942, 131 F.2d 419; *Publicity Bldg. Realty Corp. v. Hannegan*, C.C.A.8th, 1943, 139 F.2d 583; *Dioguardi v. Durning*, C.C.A.2d, 1944, 139 F.2d 774; *Package Closure Corp. v. Sealright Co., Inc.*, C.C.A.2d, 1944, 141 F.2d 972; *Tahir Erk v. Glenn L. Martin Co.*, C.C.A.4th, 1941, 116 F.2d 865; *Bell v. Preferred Life Assurance Society of Montgomery, Ala.*, 1943, 320 U.S. 238, 64 S.Ct. 5.

New matter is shown in italics; matter to be omitted is lined through

The addition at the end of subdivision (b) makes it clear that on a motion under Rule 12(b)(6) extraneous material may not be considered if the court excludes it, but that if the court does not exclude such material the motion shall be treated as a motion for summary judgment and disposed of as provided in Rule 56. It will also be observed that if a motion under Rule 12(b)(6) is thus converted into a summary judgment motion, the amendment insures that both parties shall be given a reasonable opportunity to submit affidavits and extraneous proofs to avoid taking a party by surprise through the conversion of the motion into a motion for summary judgment. In this manner and to this extent the amendment regularizes the practice above described. As the courts are already dealing with cases in this way, the effect of this amendment is really only to define the practice carefully and apply the requirements of the summary judgment rule in the disposition of the motion.

Subdivision (c). The sentence appended to subdivision (c) performs the same function and is grounded on the same reasons as the corresponding sentence added in subdivision (b).

Subdivision (d). The change here was made necessary because of the addition of defense (7) in subdivision (b).

Subdivision (e). References in this subdivision to a bill of particulars have been deleted, and the motion provided for is confined to one for a more definite statement, to be obtained only in cases where the movant cannot reasonably be required to frame an answer or other responsive pleading to the pleading in question. With respect to preparations for trial, the party is properly relegated to the various methods of examination and discovery provided in the rules for that purpose. *Slusher v. Jones,* E.D.Ky.1943, 7 Fed.Rules Serv. 12e.231, Case 5, 3 F.R.D. 168; *Best Foods, Inc. v. General Mills, Inc.,* D.Del.1943, 7 Fed.Rules Serv. 12e.231, Case 7, 3 F.R.D. 275; *Braden v. Callaway,* E.D.Tenn.1943, 8 Fed.Rules Serv. 12e.231, Case 1 (". . . most courts . . . conclude that the definiteness required is only such as will be sufficient for the party to prepare responsive pleadings"). Accordingly, the reference to the 20 day time limit has also been eliminated, since the purpose of this present provision is to state a time period where the motion for a bill is made for the purpose or preparing for trial.

Rule 12(e) as originally drawn has been the subject of more judicial rulings than any other part of the rules, and has been much criticized by commentators, judges and members of the bar. See general discussion and cases cited in 1 *Moore's Federal Practice,* 1938, Cum.Supplement § 12.07, under "Page 657"; also, Holtzoff, *New Federal Procedure and the Courts,* 1940, 35–41. And compare vote of Second Circuit Conference of Circuit and District Judges, June 1940, recommending the abolition of the bill of particulars; *Sun Valley Mfg. Co. v. Mylish,* E.D.Pa.1944, 8 Fed.Rules Serv. 12e.231, Case 6 ("Our experience . . . has demonstrated not only that 'the office of the bill of particulars is fast becoming obsolete' . . . but that in view of the adequate discovery procedure available under the Rules, motions for bills of particulars should be abolished altogether."); *Walling v. American Steamship Co.,* W.D.N.Y.1945, 4 F.R.D. 355, 8 Fed.Rules Serv. 12e.244, Case 8 (". . . the adoption of the rule was ill advised. It has led to confusion, duplication and delay.") The tendency of some courts freely to grant extended bills of particulars has served to neutralize any helpful benefits derived from Rule 8, and has overlooked the intended use of the rules on depositions and discovery. The words "or to prepare for trial"—eliminated by the proposed amendment—have sometimes been seized upon as grounds for compulsory statement in the opposing pleading of all the details which the movant would have to meet at the trial. On the other hand, many courts have in effect read these words out of the rule. See *Walling v. Alabama Pipe Co.,* W.D.Mo.1942, 3 F.R.D. 159, 6 Fed.Rules Serv. 12e.244, Case 7;

New matter is shown in italics; matter to be omitted is lined through

Fleming v. Mason & Dixon Lines, Inc., E.D.Tenn.1941, 42 F.Supp. 230; *Kellogg Co. v. National Biscuit Co.,* D.N.J.1941, 38 F.Supp. 643; *Brown v. H.L. Green Co.,* S.D.N.Y.1943, 7 Fed.Rules Serv. 12e.231, Case 6; *Pedersen v. Standard Accident Ins. Co.,* W.D.Mo.1945, 8 Fed.Rules Serv. 12e.231, Case 8; *Bowles v. Ohse,* D.Neb. 1945, 4 F.R.D. 403, 9 Fed.Rules Serv. 12e.231, Case 1; *Klages v. Cohen,* E.D.N.Y. 1945, 9 Fed.Rules Serv. 8a.25, Case 4; *Bowles v. Lawrence,* D.Mass.1945, 8 Fed. Rules Serv. 12e.231, Case 19; *McKinney Tool & Mfg. Co. v. Hoyt,* N.D.Ohio 1945, 9 Fed.Rules Serv. 12e.235, Case 1; *Bowles v. Jack,* D.Minn.1945, 5 F.R.D. 1, 9 Fed.Rules Serv. 12e.244, Case 9. And it has been urged from the bench that the phrase be stricken. *Poole v. White,* N.D.W.Va.1941, 5 Fed.Rules Serv. 12e.231, Case 4, 2 F.R.D. 40. See also *Bowles v. Gabel,* W.D.Mo.1946, 9 Fed.Rules Serv. 12e.244, Case 10 ("The courts have never favored that portion of the rules which undertook to justify a motion of this kind for the purpose of aiding counsel in preparing his case for trial.").

Subdivision (f). This amendment affords a specific method of raising the insufficiency of a defense, a matter which has troubled some courts, although attack has been permitted in one way or another. See *Dysart v. Remington–Rand, Inc.,* D.Conn.1939, 31 F.Supp. 296; *Eastman Kodak Co. v. McAuley,* S.D.N.Y.1941, 4 Fed.Rules Serv. 12f.21, Case 8, 2 F.R.D. 21; *Schenley Distillers Corp. v. Renken,* E.D.S.C.1940, 34 F.Supp. 678; *Yale Transport Corp. v. Yellow Truck & Coach Mfg. Co.,* S.D.N.Y.1944, 3 F.R.D. 440; *United States v. Turner Milk Co.,* N.D.Ill.1941, 4 Fed.Rules Serv. 12b.51, Case 3, 1 F.R.D. 643; *Teiger v. Stephan Oderwald, Inc.,* S.D.N.Y.1940, 31 F.Supp. 626; *Teplitsky v. Pennsylvania R. Co.,* N.D.Ill.1941, 38 F.Supp. 535; *Gallagher v. Carroll,* E.D.N.Y.1939, 27 F.Supp. 568; *United States v. Palmer,* S.D.N.Y.1939, 28 F.Supp. 936. And see *Indemnity Ins. Co. of North America v. Pan American Airways, Inc.,* S.D.N.Y.1944, 58 F.Supp. 338; Commentary, *Modes of Attacking Insufficient Defenses in the Answer,* 1939, 1 Fed.Rules Serv. 669, 1940, 2 Fed.Rules Serv. 640.

Subdivision (g). The change in title conforms with the companion provision in subdivision (h).

The alteration of the "except" clause requires that other than provided in subdivision (h) a party who resorts to a motion to raise defenses specified in the rule, must include in one motion all that are then available to him. Under the original rule defenses which could be raised by motion were divided into two groups which could be the subjects of two successive motions.

Subdivision (h). The addition of the phrase relating to indispensable parties is one of necessity.

Rule 13. Counterclaim and Cross-Claim

Advisory Committee's Note to Original Rule

1. This is substantially Equity Rule 30 (Answer—Contents—Counterclaim), broadened to include legal as well as equitable counterclaims.

2. Compare the English practice, English Rules Under the Judicature Act (The Annual Practice, 1937) O. 19, r. r. 2 and 3, and O. 21, r. r. 10–17; *Beddall v. Maitland,* L.R. 17 Ch.Div. 174, 181, 182 (1881).

3. Certain states have also adopted almost unrestricted provisions concerning both the subject matter of and the parties to a counterclaim. This seems to be the modern tendency. Ark.Civ.Code (Crawford, 1934) §§ 117 (as amended) and 118; N.J.Comp.Stat., (2 Cum.Supp. 1911–1924) tit. 163, § 288; N.Y.C.P.A. (1937) §§ 262,

New matter is shown in italics; matter to be omitted is lined through

266, 267 (all as amended, Laws of 1936, ch. 324), 268, 269, and 271; Wis.Stat. (1935) § 263.14(1)(c).

4. Most codes do not expressly provide for a counterclaim in the reply. Clark, *Code Pleading* (1928), p. 486. Ky.Codes (Carroll, 1932) Civ.Pract. § 98 does provide, however, for such counterclaim.

5. The provisions of this rule respecting counterclaims are subject to Rule 82 (Jurisdiction and Venue Unaffected). For a discussion of federal jurisdiction and venue in regard to counterclaims and cross-claims, see Shulman and Jaegerman, *Some Jurisdictional Limitations in Federal Procedure* (1936), 45 Yale L.J. 393, 410 *et seq.*

6. This rule does not affect such statutes of the United States as U.S.C., Title 28, § 41(1) [now §§ 1331, 1332, 1341, 1342, 1345, 1354, 1359] (United States as plaintiff; civil suits at common law and in equity), relating to assigned claims in actions based on diversity of citizenship.

7. If the action proceeds to judgment without the interposition of a counterclaim as required by subdivision (a) of this rule, the counterclaim is barred. See *American Mills Co. v. American Surety Co.*, 260 U.S. 360, 43 S.Ct. 149, 67 L.Ed. 306 (1922); *Marconi Wireless Telegraph Co. v. National Electric Signalling Co.*, 206 Fed. 295 (E.D.N.Y., 1913); Hopkins, *Federal Equity Rules* (8th ed., 1933), p. 213; Simkins, *Federal Practice* (1934), p. 663.

8. For allowance of credits against the United States see U.S.C., Title 26, §§ 1672–1673 (Suits for refunds of internal revenue taxes—limitations); U.S.C., Title 28, §§ 774 [now § 2406] (Suits by United States against individuals; credits), 775 [1946 ed.] (Suits under postal laws; credits); U.S.C., Title 31, § 227 (Offsets against judgments and claims against United States).

————————

(a) **Compulsory Counterclaims.** A pleading shall state as a counterclaim any claim, not the subject of a pending action, which at the time of filing *serving* the pleading the pleader has against any opposing party, if it arises out of the transaction or occurrence that is the subject matter of the opposing party's claim and does not require for its adjudication the presence of third parties of whom the court cannot acquire jurisdiction, *except that such a claim need not be so stated if at the time the action was commenced the claim was the subject of another pending action.*

(g) **Cross–Claim Against Co–Party.** A pleading may state as a cross-claim any claim by one party against a co-party arising out of the transaction or occurrence that is the subject matter either of the original action or of a counterclaim therein *or relating to any property that is the subject matter of the original action.* Such cross-claim may include a claim that the party against whom it is asserted is or may be liable to the cross-claimant for all or part of a claim asserted in the action against the cross-claimant.

New matter is shown in italics; matter to be omitted is lined through

(i) **Separate Trials; Separate Judgments.** If the court orders separate trials as provided in Rule 42(b), judgment on a counterclaim or cross-claim may be rendered *in accordance with the terms of Rule 54(b)* when the court has jurisdiction so to do, even if the claims of the opposing party have been dismissed or otherwise disposed of.

Advisory Committee's Note to 1948 Amendment

Subdivision (a). The use of the word "filing" was inadvertent. The word "serving" conforms with subdivision (e) and with usage generally throughout the rules.

The removal of the phrase "not the subject of a pending action" and the addition of the new clause at the end of the subdivision is designed to eliminate the ambiguity noted in *Prudential Insurance Co. of America v. Saxe,* App.D.C.1943, 77 U.S.App.D.C. 144, 134 F.2d 16, 33–34, cert. den., 1943, 319 U.S. 745, 63 S.Ct. 1033. The rewording of the subdivision in this respect insures against an undesirable possibility presented under the original rule whereby a party having a claim which would be the subject of a compulsory counterclaim could avoid stating it as such by bringing an independent action in another court after the commencement of the federal action but before serving his pleading in the federal action.

Subdivision (g). The amendment is to care for a situation such as where a second mortgagee is made defendant in a foreclosure proceeding and wishes to file a cross-complaint against the mortgagor in order to secure a personal judgment for the indebtedness and foreclose his lien. A claim of this sort by the second mortgagee may not necessarily arise out of the transaction or occurrence that is the subject matter of the original action under the terms of Rule 13(g).

Subdivision (i). The change clarifies the interdependence of Rules 13(i) and 54(b).

Rule 15.   Amended and Supplemental Pleadings

Advisory Committee's Note to Original Rule

See generally for the present federal practice, Equity Rules 19 (Amendments Generally), 28 (Amendment of Bill as of Course), 32 (Answer to Amended Bill), 34 (Supplemental Pleading), and 35 (Bills of Revivor and Supplemental Bills—Form); U.S.C., Title 28, §§ 399 [now § 1653] (Amendments to show diverse citizenship) and 777 [1946 ed.] (Defects of form; amendments). See English Rules Under the Judicature Act (The Annual Practice, 1937) O. 28, r. r. 1–13; O. 20, r. 4; O. 24, r. r. 1–3.

Note to Subdivision (a). The right to serve an amended pleading once as of course is common. 4 Mont.Rev.Codes Ann. (1935) § 9186; 1 Ore.Code Ann. (1930) § 1–904; 1 S.C.Code (Michie, 1932) § 493; English Rules Under the Judicature Act (The Annual Practice, 1937) O. 28, r. 2. Provision for amendment of pleading before trial, by leave of court, is in almost every code. If there is no statute the power of the court to grant leave is said to be inherent. Clark, *Code Pleading* (1928), pp. 498, 509.

Note to Subdivision (b). Compare Equity Rule 19 (Amendments Generally) and code provisions which allow an amendment "at any time in furtherance of justice," (e.g., Ark.Civ.Code (Crawford, 1934) § 155) and which allow an amendment of

---

New matter is shown in italics; matter to be omitted is lined through

pleadings to conform to the evidence, where the adverse party has not been misled and prejudiced (e.g., N.M. Stat.Ann. (Courtright, 1929) §§ 105–601, 105–602).

Note to Subdivision (c). "Relation back" is a well recognized doctrine of recent and now more frequent application. Compare Ala.Code Ann. (Michie, 1928) § 9513; Ill.Rev.Stat. (1937) ch. 110, § 170(2); 2 Wash.Rev.Stat.Ann. (Remington, 1932) § 308–3(4). See U.S.C., Title 28, § 399 [now § 1653] (Amendments to show diverse citizenship) for a provision for "relation back".

Note to Subdivision (d). This is an adaptation of Equity Rule 34 (Supplemental Pleading).

Rule 16. Pre–Trial Procedure; Formulating Issues

Advisory Committee's Note to Original Rule

1. Similar rules of pre-trial procedure are now in force in Boston, Cleveland, Detroit, and Los Angeles, and a rule substantially like this one has been proposed for the urban centers of New York state. For a discussion of the successful operation of pre-trial procedure in relieving the congested condition of trial calendars of the courts in such cities and for the proposed New York plan, see *A Proposal for Minimizing Calendar Delay in Jury Cases* (Dec. 1936—published by The New York Law Society); *Pre–Trial Procedure and Administration,* Third Annual Report of the Judicial Council of the State of New York (1937), pages 207–243; *Report of the Commission on the Administration of Justice in New York State* (1934), pp. (288)–(290). See also *Pre–trial Procedure in the Wayne Circuit Court, Detroit, Michigan,* Sixth Annual Report of the Judicial Council of Michigan (1936), pp. 63–75; and Sunderland, *The Theory and Practice of Pre–Trial Procedure* (Dec. 1937) 36 Mich.L.Rev. 215–226, 21 J.Am.Jud.Soc. 125. Compare the English procedure known as the "summons for directions", English Rules Under the Judicature Act (The Annual Practice, 1937) O. 38a; and a similar procedure in New Jersey, N.J.Comp.Stat. (2 Cum.Supp. 1911–1924) tit. 163, § 293, (Supp. 1925–1930) tit. 163, § 347a, N.J.Supreme Court Rules, 2 N.J.Misc.Rep. (1924) 1230, Rules 94, 92, 93, 95 (the last three as amended 1933, 11 N.J.Misc.Rep. (1933) 955).

2. Compare the similar procedure under rule 56(d) (Summary Judgment—Case Not Fully Adjudicated on Motion). Rule 12(g) (Consolidation of Motions), by requiring to some extent the consolidation of motions dealing with matters preliminary to trial, is a step in the same direction. In connection with clause (5) of this rule, see Rules 53(b) (Masters; Reference) and 53(e)(3) (Master's Report: In Jury Actions).

Rule 19. Necessary Joinder of Parties

Advisory Committee's Note to Original Rule

Note to Subdivision (a). The first sentence with verbal differences (e.g., "united" interest for "joint" interest) is to be found in Equity Rule 37 (Parties Generally—Intervention). Such compulsory joinder provisions are common. Compare Alaska Comp.Laws (1933) § 3392 (containing in same sentence a "class suit" provision); Wyo.Rev.Stat.Ann. (Courtright, 1931) § 89–515 (immediately followed by "class suit" provisions, § 89–516). See also Equity Rule 42 (Joint and Several Demands). For example of a proper case for involuntary plaintiff, see *Independent Wireless Telegraph Co. v. Radio Corp. of America,* 269 U.S. 459, 46 S.Ct. 166, 70 L.Ed. 357 (1926).

New matter is shown in italics; matter to be omitted is lined through

The joinder provisions of this rule are subject to Rule 82 (Jurisdiction and Venue Unaffected).

Note to Subdivision (b). For the substance of this rule see Equity Rule 39 (Absence of Persons who Would be Proper Parties) and U.S.C., Title 28, § 111 [now § 1391] (When part of several defendants cannot be served); *Camp v. Gress,* 250 U.S. 308, 39 S.Ct. 478, 63 L.Ed. 997 (1919). See also the second and third sentences of Equity Rule 37 (Parties Generally—Intervention).

Note to Subdivision (c). For the substance of this rule see the fourth subdivision of Equity Rule 25 (Bill of Complaint—Contents).

Rule 23.   Class Actions

Advisory Committee's Note to Original Rule

Note to Subdivision (a). This is a substantial restatement of Equity Rule 38 (Representatives of Class) as that rule has been construed. It applies to all actions, whether formerly denominated legal or equitable. For a general analysis of class actions, effect of judgment, and requisites of jurisdiction see Moore, *Federal Rules of Civil Procedure: Some Problems Raised by the Preliminary Draft,* 25 Georgetown L.J. 551, 570 *et seq.* (1937); Moore and Cohn, *Federal Class Actions,* 32 Ill.L.Rev. 307 (1937); Moore and Cohn, *Federal Class Actions—Jurisdiction and Effect of Judgment,* 32 Ill.L.Rev. 555–567 (1938); Lesar, *Class Suits and the Federal Rules,* 22 Minn.L.Rev. 34 (1937); *cf.* Arnold and James, *Cases on Trials, Judgments and Appeals* (1936) 175; and see Blume, *Jurisdictional Amount in Representative Suits,* 15 Minn.L.Rev. 501 (1931).

The general test of Equity Rule 38 (Representatives of Class) that the question should be "one of common or general interest to many persons constituting a class so numerous as to make it impracticable to bring them all before the court," is a common test. For states which require the two elements of a common or general interest *and* numerous persons, as provided for in Equity Rule 38, see Del.Ch.Rule 113; Fla.Comp.Gen.Laws Ann. (Supp., 1936) § 4918(7); Georgia Code (1933) § 37–1002, and see English Rules Under the Judicature Act (The Annual Practice, 1937) O. 16, r. 9. For statutory provisions providing for class actions when the question is one of common or general interest *or* when the parties are numerous, see Ala.Code Ann. (Michie, 1928) § 5701; 2 Ind.Stat.Ann. (Burns, 1933) § 2–220; N.Y.C.P.A. (1937) § 195; Wis.Stat. (1935) § 260.12. These statutes have, however, been uniformly construed as though phrased in the conjunctive. See *Garfein v. Stiglitz,* 260 Ky. 430, 86 S.W.(2d) 155 (1935). The rule adopts the test of Equity Rule 38, but defines what constitutes a "common or general interest". Compare with code provisions which make the action dependent upon the propriety of joinder of the parties. See Blume, *The "Common Questions" Principle in the Code Provision for Representative Suits,* 30 Mich.L.Rev. 878 (1932). For discussion of what constitutes "numerous persons" see Wheaton, *Representative Suits Involving Numerous Litigants,* 19 Corn.L.Q. 399 (1934); Note, 36 Harv.L.Rev. 89 (1922).

Clause (1). Joint, Common, or Secondary Right. This clause is illustrated in actions brought by or against representatives of an unincorporated association. See *Oster v. Brotherhood of Locomotive Firemen and Enginemen,* 271 Pa. 419, 114 Atl. 377 (1921); *Pickett v. Walsh,* 192 Mass 572, 78 N.E. 753, 6 L.R.A.(N.S.) 1067 (1906); *Colt v. Hicks,* 97 Ind.App. 177, 179 N.E. 335 (1932). Compare Rule 17(b) as to when an unincorporated association has capacity to sue or be sued in its common name; *United Mine Workers of America v. Coronado Coal Co.,* 259 U.S. 344, 42 S.Ct. 570, 66 L.Ed. 975, 27 A.L.R. 762 (1922) (an unincorporated association was

New matter is shown in italics; matter to be omitted is lined through

sued as an entity for the purpose of enforcing against it a federal substantive right); Moore, *Federal Rules of Civil Procedure: Some Problems Raised by the Preliminary Draft,* 25 Georgetown L.J. 551, 566 (for discussion of jurisdictional requisites when an unincorporated association sues or is sued in its common name and jurisdiction is founded upon diversity of citizenship). For an action brought by representatives of one group against representatives of another group for distribution of a fund held by an unincorporated association, see *Smith v. Swormstedt,* 16 How. 288, 14 L.Ed. 942 (U.S., 1853). Compare *Christopher, et al. v. Brusselback,* 302 U.S. 500, 58 S.Ct. 350, 82 L.Ed. 388 (1938).

For an action to enforce rights held in common by policyholders against the corporate issuer of the policies, see *Supreme Tribe of Ben Hur v. Cauble,* 255 U.S. 356, 41 S.Ct. 338, 65 L.Ed. 673 (1921). See also *Terry v. Little,* 101 U.S. 216, 25 L.Ed. 864 (1880); *John A. Roebling's Sons Co. v. Kinnicutt,* 248 Fed. 596 (D.C.N.Y., 1917) dealing with the right held in common by creditors to enforce the statutory liability of stockholders.

Typical of a secondary action is a suit by stockholders to enforce a corporate right. For discussion of the general nature of these actions see *Ashwander v. Tennessee Valley Authority,* 297 U.S. 288, 56 S.Ct. 466, 80 L.Ed. 688 (1936); Glenn, *The Stockholder's Suit—Corporate and Individual Grievances,* 33 Yale L.J. 580 (1924); McLaughlin, *Capacity of Plaintiff–Stockholder to Terminate a Stockholder's Suit,* 46 Yale L.J. 421 (1937). See also Subdivision (b) of this rule which deals with Shareholder's Action; note, 15 Minn.L.Rev. 453 (1931).

Clause (2). A creditor's action for liquidation or reorganization of a corporation is illustrative of this clause. An action by a stockholder against certain named defendants as representatives of numerous claimants presents a situation converse to the creditor's action.

Clause (3). See *Everglades Drainage League v. Napoleon Broward Drainage Dist.,* 253 Fed. 246 (D.C.Fla., 1918); *Gramling v. Maxwell,* 52 F.2d 256 (D.C.N.C., 1931), approved in 30 Mich.L.Rev. 624 (1932); *Skinner v. Mitchell,* 108 Kan. 861, 197 Pac. 569 (1921); *Duke of Bedford v. Ellis* (1901) A.C. 1, for class actions when there were numerous persons and there was only a question of law or fact common to them; and see Blume, *The "Common Questions" Principle in the Code Provision for Representative Suits,* 30 Mich.L.Rev. 878 (1932).

Note to Subdivision (b). This is Equity Rule 27 (Stockholder's Bill) with verbal changes. See also *Hawes v. Oakland,* 104 U.S. 450, 26 L.Ed. 827 (1882) and former Equity Rule 94, promulgated January 23, 1882, 104 U.S. IX.

Note to Subdivision (c). See McLaughlin, *Capacity of Plaintiff–Stockholder to Terminate a Stockholder's Suit,* 46 Yale L.J. 421 (1937).

Rule 50.   Motion for a Directed Verdict

Advisory Committee's Note to Original Rule

Note to Subdivision (a). The present federal rule is changed to the extent that the formality of an express reservation of rights against waiver is no longer necessary. See *Sampliner v. Motion Picture Patents Co.,* 254 U.S. 233, 41 S.Ct. 79, 65 L.Ed. 240 (1920); *Union Indemnity Co. v. United States,* 74 F.(2d) 645 (C.C.A.6th, 1935). The requirement that specific grounds for the motion for a directed verdict must be stated settles a conflict in the federal cases. See Simkins, *Federal Practice* (1934) § 189.

Note to Subdivision (b). For comparable state practice upheld under the conformity act, see *Baltimore and Carolina Line v. Redman,* 295 U.S. 654, 55 S.Ct.

New matter is shown in italics; matter to be omitted is lined through

890, 79 L.Ed. 1636 (1935); compare *Slocum v. New York Life Ins. Co.*, 228 U.S. 364, 33 S.Ct. 523, 57 L.Ed. 879, Ann.Cas.1914D, 1029 (1913).

See *Northern Ry. Co. v. Page*, 274 U.S. 65, 47 S.Ct. 491, 71 L.Ed. 929 (1927), following the Massachusetts practice of alternative verdicts, explained in Thorndike, *Trial by Jury in United States Courts*, 26 Harv.L.Rev. 732 (1913). See also Thayer, *Judicial Administration*, 63 U. of Pa.L.Rev. 585, 600–601, and note 32 (1915); Scott, *Trial by Jury and the Reform of Civil Procedure*, 31 Harv.L.Rev. 669, 685 (1918); Comment, 34 Mich.L.Rev. 93, 98 (1935).

Rule 54. Judgments; Costs

Advisory Committee's Note to Original Rule

Note to Subdivision (a). The second sentence is derived substantially from Equity Rule 71 (Form of Decree).

Note to Subdivision (b). This provides for the separate judgment of equity and code practice. See Wis.Stat. (1935) § 270.54; Compare N.Y.C.P.A. (1937) § 476.

Note to Subdivision (c). For the limitation on default contained in the first sentence, see 2 N.D.Comp.Laws Ann. (1913) § 7680; N.Y.C.P.A. (1937) § 479. Compare English Rules Under the Judicature Act (The Annual Practice, 1937) O. 13, r. r. 3–12. The remainder is a usual code provision. It makes clear that a judgment should give the relief to which a party is entitled, regardless of whether it is legal or equitable or both. This necessarily includes the deficiency judgment in foreclosure cases formerly provided for by Equity Rule 10 (Decree for Deficiency in Foreclosures, Etc.).

Note to Subdivision (d). For the present rule in common law actions, see *Ex parte Peterson*, 253 U.S. 300, 40 S.Ct. 543, 64 L.Ed. 919 (1920); Payne, *Costs in Common Law Actions in the Federal Courts* (1935), 21 Va.L.Rev. 397.

The provisions as to costs in actions in forma pauperis contained in U.S.C., Title 28, §§ 832–836 [now § 1915] are unaffected by this rule. Other sections of U.S.C., Title 28, which are unaffected by this rule are: §§ 815 [1946 ed.] (Costs; plaintiff not entitled to, when), 821 [now § 1928] (Costs; infringement of patent; disclaimer), 825 [1946 ed.] (Costs; several actions), 829 [now § 1927] (Costs; attorney liable for, when), and 830 [now § 1920] (Costs; bill of; taxation).

The provisions of the following and similar statutes as to costs against the United States and its officers and agencies are specifically continued:

U.S.C., Title 15, §§ 77v(a), 78aa, 79y (Securities and Exchange Commission)

U.S.C., Title 16, § 825p (Federal Power Commission)

U.S.C., Title 26, §§ 1569(d) and 1645(d) (Internal revenue actions)

U.S.C., Title 26, § 1670(b)(2) (Reimbursement of costs of recovery against revenue officers)

U.S.C., Title 28, § 817 [1946 ed.] (Internal revenue actions)

U.S.C., Title 28, § 836 [now § 1915] (United States—actions in forma pauperis)

U.S.C., Title 28, § 842 [now § 2006] (Actions against revenue officers)

U.S.C., Title 28, § 870 [now § 2408] (United States—in certain cases)

U.S.C., Title 28, § 906 [1946 ed.] (United States—foreclosure actions)

New matter is shown in italics; matter to be omitted is lined through

U.S.C., Title 47, § 401 (Communications Commission)

The provisions of the following and similar statutes as to costs are unaffected:

U.S.C., Title 7, § 210(f) (Actions for damages based on an order of the Secretary of Agriculture under Stockyards Act)

U.S.C., Title 7, § 499g(c) (Appeals from reparations orders of Secretary of Agriculture under Perishable Commodities Act)

U.S.C., Title 8, § 45 (Action against district attorneys in certain cases)

U.S.C., Title 15, § 15 (Actions for injuries due to violation of antitrust laws)

U.S.C., Title 15, § 72 (Actions for violation of law forbidding importation or sale of articles at less than market value or wholesale prices)

U.S.C., Title 15, § 77k (Actions by persons acquiring securities registered with untrue statements under Securities Act of 1933)

U.S.C., Title 15, § 78i(e) (Certain actions under the Securities Exchange Act of 1934)

U.S.C., Title 15, § 78r (Similar to 78i(e))

U.S.C., Title 15, § 96 (Infringement of trade-mark—damages)

U.S.C., Title 15, § 99 (Infringement of trade-mark—injunctions)

U.S.C., Title 15, § 124 (Infringement of trade-mark—damages)

U.S.C., Title 19, § 274 (Certain actions under customs law)

U.S.C., Title 30, § 32 (Action to determine right to possession of mineral lands in certain cases)

U.S.C., Title 31, §§ 232 and 234 (Action for making false claims upon United States)

U.S.C., Title 33, § 926 (Actions under Harbor Workers' Compensation Act)

U.S.C., Title 35, § 67 (Infringement of patent—damages)

U.S.C., Title 35, § 69 (Infringement of patent—pleading and proof)

U.S.C., Title 35, § 71 (Infringement of patent—when specification too broad)

U.S.C., Title 45, § 153p (Actions for non-compliance with an order of National R.R. Adjustment Board for payment of money)

U.S.C., Title 46, § 38 (Action for penalty for failure to register vessel)

U.S.C., Title 46, § 829 (Action based on non-compliance with an order of Maritime Commission for payment of money)

U.S.C., Title 46, § 941 (Certain actions under Ship Mortgage Act)

U.S.C., Title 46, § 1227 (Actions for damages for violation of certain provisions of the Merchant Marine Act, 1936)

U.S.C., Title 47, § 206 (Actions for certain violations of Communications Act of 1934)

U.S.C., Title 49, § 16(2) (Action based on non-compliance with an order of I.C.C. for payment of money)

New matter is shown in italics; matter to be omitted is lined through

(b) ~~Judgment at Various Stages.~~ ~~When more than one~~
~~claim for relief is presented in an action, the court at any stage,~~
~~upon a determination of the issues material to a particular claim~~
~~and all counterclaims arising out of the transaction or occurrence~~
~~which is the subject matter of the claim, may enter a judgment~~
~~disposing of such claim.~~ ~~The judgment shall terminate the action~~
~~with respect to the claim so disposed of and the action shall~~
~~proceed as to the remaining claims.~~ ~~In case a separate judgment~~
~~is so entered, the court by order may stay its enforcement until~~
~~the entering of a subsequent judgment or judgments and may~~
~~prescribe such conditions as are necessary to secure the benefit~~
~~thereof to the party in whose favor the judgment is entered.~~
Judgment Upon Multiple Claims. *When more than one claim*
for relief is presented in an action, whether as a claim, counter-
claim, cross-claim, or third-party claim, the court may direct the
entry of a final judgment upon one or more but less than all of the
claims only upon an express determination that there is no just
reason for delay and upon an express direction for the entry of
judgment. In the absence of such determination and direction, any
order or other form of decision, however designated, which adjudi-
cates less than all the claims shall not terminate the action as to
any of the claims, and the order or other form of decision is subject
to revision at any time before the entry of judgment adjudicating
all the claims.

Advisory Committee's Note to 1948 Amendment

The historic rule in the federal courts has always prohibited piecemeal disposal
of litigation and permitted appeals only from final judgments except in those
special instances covered by statute. *Hohorst v. Hamburg-American Packet Co.,*
1893, 148 U.S. 262, 13 S.Ct. 590; *Rexford v. Brunswick-Balke-Collender Co.,* 1913,
228 U.S. 339, 33 S.Ct. 515; *Collins v. Miller,* 1920, 252 U.S. 364, 40 S.Ct. 347. Rule
54(b) was originally adopted in view of the wide scope and possible content of the
newly created "civil action" in order to avoid the possible injustice of a delay in
judgment of a distinctly separate claim to await adjudication of the entire case. It
was not designed to overturn the settled federal rule stated above, which, indeed,
has more recently been reiterated in *Catlin v. United States,* 1945, 324 U.S. 229, 65
S.Ct. 631. See also *United States v. Florian,* 1941, 312 U.S. 656, 61 S.Ct. 713, rev'g,
and restoring the first opinion in, *Florian v. United States,* C.C.A.7th, 1940, 114
F.2d 990; *Reeves v. Beardall,* 1942, 316 U.S. 283, 62 S.Ct. 1085.

Unfortunately, this was not always understood, and some confusion ensued.
Hence situations arose where district courts made a piecemeal disposition of an
action and entered what the parties thought amounted to a judgment, although a
trial remained to be had on other claims similar or identical with those disposed of.
In the interim the parties did not know their ultimate rights, and accordingly took
an appeal, thus putting the finality of the partial judgment in question. While
most appellate courts have reached a result generally in accord with the intent of
the rule, yet there have been divergent precedents and division of views which
have served to render the issues more clouded to the parties appellant. It hardly
seems a case where multiplicity of precedents will tend to remove the problem

---

New matter is shown in italics; matter to be omitted is lined through

from debate. The problem is presented and discussed in the following cases: *Atwater v. North American Coal Corp.*, C.C.A.2d, 1940, 111 F.2d 125; *Rosenblum v. Dingfelder*, C.C.A.2d, 1940, 111 F.2d 406; *Audi-Vision, Inc. v. RCA Mfg. Co., Inc.*, C.C.A.2d, 1943, 136 F.2d 621; *Zalkind v. Scheinman*, C.C.A.2d, 1943, 139 F.2d 895; *Oppenheimer v. F.J. Young & Co., Inc.*, C.C.A.2d, 1944, 144 F.2d 387; *Libbey-Owens-Ford Glass Co. v. Sylvania Industrial Corp.*, C.C.A.2d, 1946, 154 F.2d 814, cert. den., 1946, 66 S.Ct. 1353; *Zarati Steamship Co. v. Park Bridge Corp.*, C.C.A.2d, 1946, 154 F.2d 377; *Baltimore and Ohio R. Co. v. United Fuel Gas Co.*, C.C.A.4th, 1946, 154 F.2d 545; *Jefferson Electric Co. v. Sola Electric Co.*, C.C.A.7th, 1941, 122 F.2d 124; *Leonard v. Socony-Vacuum Oil Co.*, C.C.A.7th, 1942, 130 F.2d 535; *Markham v. Kasper*, C.C.A.7th, 1945, 152 F.2d 270; *Hanney v. Franklin Fire Ins. Co. of Philadelphia*, C.C.A.9th, 1944, 142 F.2d 864; *Toomey v. Toomey*, App.D.C.1945, 80 U.S.App.D.C. 77, 149 F.2d 19.

In view of the difficulty thus disclosed, the Advisory Committee in its two preliminary drafts of proposed amendments attempted to redefine the original rule with particular stress upon the interlocutory nature of partial judgments which did not adjudicate all claims arising out of a single transaction or occurrence. This attempt appeared to meet with almost universal approval from those of the profession commenting upon it, although there were, of course, helpful suggestions for additional changes in language or clarification of detail. But *cf.* Circuit Judge Frank's dissenting opinion in *Libbey-Owens-Ford Glass Co. v. Sylvania Industrial Corp., supra,* n. 21 of the dissenting opinion. The Committee, however, became convinced on careful study of its own proposals that the seeds of ambiguity still remained, and that it had not completely solved the problem of piecemeal appeals. After extended consideration, it concluded that a retention of the older federal rule was desirable, and that this rule needed only the exercise of a discretionary power to afford a remedy in the infrequent harsh case to provide a simple, definite, workable rule. This is afforded by amended Rule 54(b). It re-establishes an ancient policy with clarity and precision. For the possibility of staying execution where not all claims are disposed of under Rule 54(b), see amended Rule 62(h).

(b) Judgment Upon Multiple Claims *or Involving Multiple Parties.* When more than one claim for relief is presented in an action, whether as a claim, counterclaim, cross-claim, or third-party claim, *or when multiple parties are involved,* the court may direct the entry of a final judgment ~~upon~~ *as to* one or more but ~~less~~ *fewer* than all of the claims *or parties* only upon an express determination that there is no just reason for delay and upon an express direction for the entry of judgment. In the absence of such determination and direction, any order or other form of decision, however designated, which adjudicates ~~less~~ *fewer* than all the claims *or the rights and liabilities of fewer than all the parties* shall not terminate the action as to any of the claims *or parties,* and the order or other form of decision is subject to revision at any time before the entry of judgment adjudicating all the claims *and the rights and liabilities of all the parties.*

New matter is shown in italics; matter to be omitted is lined through

Advisory Committee's Note to 1961 Amendment

This rule permitting appeal, upon the trial court's determination of "no just reason for delay," from a judgment upon one or more but fewer than all the claims in an action, has generally been given a sympathetic construction by the courts and its validity is settled. *Reeves v. Beardall,* 316 U.S. 283 (1942); *Sears, Roebuck & Co. v. Mackey,* 351 U.S. 427 (1956); *Cold Metal Process Co. v. United Engineering & Foundry Co.,* 351 U.S. 445 (1956).

A serious difficulty has, however, arisen because the rule speaks of claims but nowhere mentions parties. A line of cases has developed in the circuits consistently holding the rule to be inapplicable to the dismissal, even with the requisite trial court determination, of one or more but fewer than all defendants jointly charged in an action, *i.e.,* charged with various forms of concerted or related wrongdoing or related liability. See *Mull v. Ackerman,* 279 F.2d 25 (2d Cir.1960); *Richards v. Smith,* 276 F.2d 652 (5th Cir.1960); *Hardy v. Bankers Life & Cas. Co.,* 222 F.2d 827 (7th Cir.1955); *Steiner v. 20th Century-Fox Film Corp.,* 220 F.2d 105 (9th Cir.1955). For purposes of Rule 54(b) it was arguable that there were as many "claims" as there were parties defendant and that the rule in its present text applied where fewer than all of the parties were dismissed, *cf. United Artists Corp. v. Masterpiece Productions, Inc.,* 221 F.2d 213, 215 (2d Cir.1955); *Bowling Machines, Inc. v. First Nat. Bank,* 283 F.2d 39 (1st Cir.1960); but the Courts of Appeals are now committed to an opposite view.

The danger of hardship through delay of appeal until the whole action is concluded may be at least as serious in the multiple-parties situations as in multiple-claims cases, see *Pabellon v. Grace Line, Inc.,* 191 F.2d 169, 179 (2d Cir.1951), *cert. denied,* 342 U.S. 893 (1951), and courts and commentators have urged that Rule 54(b) be changed to take in the former. See *Reagan v. Traders & General Ins. Co.,* 255 F.2d 845 (5th Cir.1958); *Meadows v. Greyhound Corp.,* 235 F.2d 233 (5th Cir.1956); *Steiner v. 20th Century-Fox Film Corp., supra;* 6 *Moore's Federal Practice* ¶ 54.34[2] (2d ed. 1953); 3 Barron & Holtzoff, *Federal Practice & Procedure* § 1193.2 (Wright ed. 1958); *Developments in the Law—Multiparty Litigation,* 71 Harv.L.Rev. 874, 981 (1958); Note, 62 Yale L.J. 263, 271 (1953); Ill.Ann. Stat. ch. 110, § 50(2) (Smith-Hurd 1956). The amendment accomplishes this purpose by referring explicitly to parties.

There has been some recent indication that interlocutory appeal under the provisions of 28 U.S.C. § 1292(b), added in 1958, may now be available for the multiple-parties cases here considered. See *Jaftex Corp. v. Randolph Mills, Inc.,* 282 F.2d 508 (2d Cir.1960). The Rule 54(b) procedure seems preferable for those cases, and § 1292(b) should be held inapplicable to them when the rule is enlarged as here proposed. See *Luckenbach Steamship Co., Inc., v. H. Muehlstein & Co., Inc.,* 280 F.2d 755, 757 (2d Cir.1960); 1 Barron & Holtzoff, *supra,* § 58.1, p. 321 (Wright ed. 1960).

Rule 56. Summary Judgment

Advisory Committee's Note to Original Rule

This rule is applicable to all actions, including those against the United States or an officer or agency thereof.

Summary judgment procedure is a method for promptly disposing of actions in which there is no genuine issue as to any material fact. It has been extensively used in England for more than 50 years and has been adopted in a number of

---

New matter is shown in italics; matter to be omitted is lined through

American states. New York, for example, has made great use of it. During the first nine years after its adoption there, the records of New York county alone show 5,600 applications for summary judgments. *Report of the Commission on the Administration of Justice in New York State* (1934), p. 383. See also Third Annual Report of the Judicial Council of the State of New York (1937), p. 30.

In England it was first employed only in cases of liquidated claims, but there has been a steady enlargement of the scope of the remedy until it is now used in actions to recover land or chattels and in all other actions at law, for liquidated or unliquidated claims, except for a few designated torts and breach of promise of marriage. English Rules Under the Judicature Act (The Annual Practice, 1937) O. 3, r. 6; Orders 14, 14A, and 15; see also O. 32, r. 6, authorizing an application for judgment at any time upon admissions. In Michigan (3 Comp.Laws (1929) § 14260) and Illinois (Ill.Rev.Stat. (1937) ch. 110, §§ 181, 259.15, 259.16), it is not limited to liquidated demands. New York (N.Y.R.C.P. (1937) Rule 113; see also Rule 107) has brought so many classes of actions under the operation of the rule that the Commission on Administration of Justice in New York State (1934) recommend that all restrictions be removed and that the remedy be available "in any action" (p. 287). For the history and nature of the summary judgment procedure and citations of state statutes, see Clark and Samenow, *The Summary Judgment* (1929), 38 Yale L.J. 423.

Note to Subdivision (d). See Rule 16 (Pre-Trial Procedure; Formulating Issues) and the Note thereto.

Note to Subdivisions (e) and (f). These are similar to rules in Michigan. Mich.Court Rules Ann. (Searl, 1933) Rule 30.

(a) For Claimant. A party seeking to recover upon a claim, counterclaim, or cross-claim or to obtain a declaratory judgment may, at any time after the ~~pleading in answer thereto has been served,~~ *expiration of 20 days from the commencement of the action or after service of a motion for summary judgment by the adverse party*, move with or without supporting affidavits for summary judgment in his favor upon all or any part thereof.

(c) Motion and Proceedings Thereon. The motion shall be served at least 10 days before the time ~~specified~~ *fixed* for the hearing. The adverse party prior to the day of hearing may serve opposing affidavits. The judgment sought shall be rendered forthwith if the pleadings, depositions, and admissions on file, together with the affidavits, if any, show that, ~~except as to the amount of damages,~~ there is no genuine issue as to any material fact and that the moving party is entitled to a judgment as a matter of law. *A summary judgment, interlocutory in character, may be rendered on the issue of liability alone although there is a genuine issue as to the amount of damages.*

New matter is shown in italics; matter to be omitted is lined through

Advisory Committee's Note to 1948 Amendment

Subdivision (a). The amendment allows a claimant to move for a summary judgment at any time after the expiration of 20 days from the commencement of the action or after service of a motion for summary judgment by the adverse party. This will normally operate to permit an earlier motion by the claimant than under the original rule, where the phrase "at any time after the pleading in answer thereto has been served" operates to prevent a claimant from moving for summary judgment, even in a case clearly proper for its exercise, until a former answer has been filed. Thus in *Peoples Bank v. Federal Reserve Bank of San Francisco*, N.D.Cal.1944, 58 F.Supp. 25, the plaintiff's counter-motion for a summary judgment was stricken as premature, because the defendant had not filed an answer. Since Rule 12(a) allows at least 20 days for an answer, that time plus the 10 days required in Rule 56(c) means that under original Rule 56(a) a minimum period of 30 days necessarily has to elapse in every case before the claimant can be heard on his right to a summary judgment. An extension of time by the court or the service of preliminary motions of any kind will prolong that period even further. In many cases this merely represents unnecessary delay. See *United States v. Adler's Creamery, Inc.*, C.C.A.2d, 1939, 107 F.2d 987. The changes are in the interest of more expeditious litigation. The 20-day period, as provided, gives the defendant an opportunity to secure counsel and determine a course of action. But in a case where the defendant himself serves a motion for summary judgment within that time, there is no reason to restrict the plaintiff and the amended rule so provides.

Subdivision (c). The amendment of Rule 56(c), by the addition of the final sentence, resolves a doubt expressed in *Sartor v. Arkansas Natural Gas Corp.*, 1944, 321 U.S. 620, 64 S.Ct. 724. See also Commentary, *Summary Judgment as to Damages*, 1944, 7 Fed.Rules Serv. 974; *Madeirense Do Brasil S/A v. Stulman-Emrick Lumber Co.*, C.C.A.2d, 1945, 147 F.2d 399, cert. den., 1945, 325 U.S. 861, 65 S.Ct. 1201. It makes clear that although the question of recovery depends on the amount of damages, the summary judgment rule is applicable and summary judgment may be granted in a proper case. If the case is not fully adjudicated it may be dealt with as provided in subdivision (d) of Rule 56, and the right to summary recovery determined by a preliminary order, interlocutory in character, and the precise amount of recovery left for trial.

Subdivision (d). Rule 54(a) defines "judgment" as including a decree and "any order from which an appeal lies." Subdivision (d) of Rule 56 indicates clearly, however, that a partial summary "judgment" is not a final judgment, and, therefore, that it is not appealable, unless in the particular case some statute allows an appeal from the interlocutory order involved. The partial summary judgment is merely a pre-trial adjudication that certain issues shall be deemed established for the trial of the case. This adjudication is more nearly akin to the preliminary order under Rule 16, and likewise serves the purpose of speeding up litigation by eliminating before trial matters wherein there is no genuine issue of fact. See *Leonard v. Socony-Vacuum Oil Co.*, C.C.A.7th, 1942, 130 F.2d 535; *Biggins v. Oltmer Iron Works*, C.C.A.7th, 1946, 154 F.2d 214; 3 *Moore's Federal Practice*, 1938, 3190–3192. Since interlocutory appeals are not allowed, except where specifically provided by statute, see 3 *Moore, op. cit. supra*, 3155–3156, this interpretation is in line with that policy, *Leonard v. Socony-Vacuum Oil Co., supra.* See also *Audi Vision Inc. v. RCA Mfg. Co.*, C.C.A.2d, 1943, 136 F.2d 621; *Toomey v. Toomey*, App.D.C.1945, 80 U.S.App.D.C. 77, 149 F.2d 19; *Biggins v. Oltmer Iron Works, supra*; *Catlin v. United States*, 1945, 324 U.S. 229, 65 S.Ct. 631.

*

New matter is shown in italics; matter to be omitted is lined through

CERTAIN OF THE AMENDMENTS OF FEDERAL RULES OF CIVIL PROCEDURE ADOPTED BY THE SUPREME COURT OF THE UNITED STATES ON JANUARY 21, 1963, EFFECTIVE JULY 1, 1963, WITH ADVISORY COMMITTEE'S NOTES THEREON

[Amendments here omitted: Changes in Rule 86 and Forms 3, 4, 5, 6, 7, 8, 9, 10, 11, 12, 13, 16, 18, and 21; elimination of Form 22; and addition of new Forms 22–A, 22–B, 30, 31, and 32.]

Rule 4. Process

(b) Same: Form. The summons shall be signed by the clerk, be under the seal of the court, contain the name of the court and the names of the parties, be directed to the defendant, state the name and address of the plaintiff's attorney, if any, otherwise the plaintiff's address, and the time within which these rules require the defendant to appear and defend, and shall notify him that in case of his failure to do so judgment by default will be rendered against him for the relief demanded in the complaint. *When, under Rule 4(e), service is made pursuant to a statute or rule of court of a state, the summons, or notice, or order in lieu of summons shall correspond as nearly as may be to that required by the statute or rule.*

(d) Summons: Personal Service.

(4) Upon the United States, by delivering a copy of the summons and of the complaint to the United States attorney for the district in which the action is brought or to an assistant United States attorney or clerical employee designated by the United States attorney in a writing filed with the clerk of the court and by sending a copy of the summons and of the complaint by registered *or certified* mail to the Attorney General of the United States at Washington, District of Columbia, and in any action attacking the validity of an order of an officer or agency of the United States not made a party, by also sending a copy of the summons and of the complaint by registered *or certified* mail to such officer or agency.

(7) Upon a defendant of any class referred to in paragraph (1) or (3) of this subdivision of this rule, it is also sufficient if the

---

New matter is shown in italics; matter to be omitted is lined through

195

summons and complaint are served in the manner prescribed by any statute of the United States or in the manner prescribed by the law of the state in which the ~~service is made~~ *district court is held* for the service of summons or other like process upon any such defendant in an action brought in the courts of general jurisdiction of that state.

(e) Same: ~~Other Service~~ *Service Upon Party Not Inhabitant of or Found Within State.* Whenever a statute of the United States or an order of court *thereunder* provides for service of a summons, or of a notice, or of an order in lieu of summons upon a party not an inhabitant of or found within the state *in which the district court is held,* service ~~shall~~ *may* be made under the circumstances and in the manner prescribed by the statute~~, rule,~~ or order.~~,~~ *or, if there is no provision therein prescribing the manner of service, in a manner stated in this rule. Whenever a statute or rule of court of the state in which the district court is held provides (1) for service of a summons, or of a notice, or of an order in lieu of summons upon a party not an inhabitant of or found within the state, or (2) for service upon or notice to him to appear and respond or defend in an action by reason of the attachment or garnishment or similar seizure of his property located within the state, service may in either case be made under the circumstances and in the manner prescribed in the statute or rule.*

(f) Territorial Limits of Effective Service. All process other than a subpoena may be served anywhere within the territorial limits of the state in which the district court is held, and, when *authorized by* a statute of the United States *or by these rules,* ~~so provides,~~ beyond the territorial limits of that state. *In addition, persons who are brought in as parties pursuant to Rule 13(h) or Rule 14, or as additional parties to a pending action pursuant to Rule 19, may be served in the manner stated in paragraphs (1)–(6) of subdivision (d) of this rule at all places outside the state but within the United States that are not more than 100 miles from the place in which the action is commenced, or to which it is assigned or transferred for trial; and persons required to respond to an order of commitment for civil contempt may be served at the same places.* A subpoena may be served within the territorial limits provided in Rule 45.

(i) Alternative Provisions for Service in a Foreign Country.*

---

* This subdivision was developed collaboratively by the Commission and Advisory Committee on International Rules of Judicial Procedure, a statutory organization established pursuant to Act of September 2, 1958, 72 Stat. 1743, and the Advisory Committee on Civil Rules.

New matter is shown in italics; matter to be omitted is lined through

(1) Manner. When the federal or state law referred to in subdivision (e) of this rule authorizes service upon a party not an inhabitant of or found within the state in which the district court is held, and service is to be effected upon the party in a foreign country, it is also sufficient if service of the summons and complaint is made: (A) in the manner prescribed by the law of the foreign country for service in that country in an action in any of its courts of general jurisdiction, or (B) as directed by the foreign authority in response to a letter rogatory, when service in either case is reasonably calculated to give actual notice; or (C) upon an individual, by delivery to him personally, and upon a corporation or partnership or association, by delivery to an officer, a managing or general agent; or (D) by any form of mail, requiring a signed receipt, to be addressed and dispatched by the clerk of the court to the party to be served; or (E) as directed by order of the court. Service under (C) or (E) above may be made by any person who is not a party and is not less than 18 years of age or who is designated by order of the district court or by the foreign court. On request, the clerk shall deliver the summons to the plaintiff for transmission to the person or the foreign court or officer who will make the service.

(2) Return. Proof of service may be made as prescribed by subdivision (g) of this rule, or by the law of the foreign country, or by order of the court. When service is made pursuant to subparagraph (1)(D) of this subdivision, proof of service shall include a receipt signed by the addressee or other evidence of delivery to the addressee satisfactory to the court.

Advisory Committee's Note

Subdivision (b). Under amended subdivision (e) of this rule, an action may be commenced against a nonresident of the State in which the district court is held by complying with State procedures. Frequently the form of the summons or notice required in these cases by State law differs from the Federal form of summons described in present subdivision (b) and exemplified in Form 1. To avoid confusion, the amendment of subdivision (b) states that a form of summons or notice, corresponding "as nearly as may be" to the State form, shall be employed. See also a corresponding amendment of Rule 12(a) with regard to the time to answer.

Subdivision (d)(4). This paragraph, governing service upon the United States, is amended to allow the use of certified mail as an alternative to registered mail for sending copies of the papers to the Attorney General or to a United States officer or agency. *Cf.* N.J. Rule 4:5–2. See also the amendment of Rule 30(f)(1).

Subdivision (d)(7). Formerly a question was raised whether this paragraph, in the context of the rule as a whole, authorized service in original Federal actions pursuant to State statutes permitting service on a State official as a means of bringing a nonresident motorist defendant into court. It was argued in *McCoy v. Siler,* 205 F.2d 498, 501–2 (3d Cir.) (concurring opinion), *cert. denied,* 346 U.S. 872, 74 S.Ct. 120, 98 L.Ed. 380 (1953), that the effective service in those cases occurred

---

New matter is shown in italics; matter to be omitted is lined through

not when the State official was served but when notice was given to the defendant outside the State, and that subdivision (f) (Territorial limits of effective service), as then worded, did not authorize out-of-State service. This contention found little support. A considerable number of cases held the service to be good, either by fixing upon the service on the official within the State as the effective service, thus satisfying the wording of subdivision (f) as it then stood, see *Holbrook v. Cafiero,* 18 F.R.D. 218 (D.Md.1955); *Pasternack v. Dalo,* 17 F.R.D. 420 (W.D.Pa.1955); *cf. Super Prods. Corp. v. Parkin,* 20 F.R.D. 377 (S.D.N.Y.1957), or by reading paragraph (7) as not limited by subdivision (f). See *Giffin v. Ensign,* 234 F.2d 307 (3d Cir.1956); 2 *Moore's Federal Practice,* ¶ 4.19 (2d ed. 1948); 1 Barron & Holtzoff, *Federal Practice & Procedure* § 182.1 (Wright ed. 1960); Comment, 27 U. of Chi.L.Rev. 751 (1960). See also *Olberding v. Illinois Central R. R.,* 201 F.2d 582 (6th Cir.), *rev'd on other grounds,* 346 U.S. 338, 74 S.Ct. 83, 98 L.Ed. 39 (1953); *Feinsinger v. Bard,* 195 F.2d 45 (7th Cir. 1952).

An important and growing class of State statutes base personal jurisdiction over nonresidents on the doing of acts or on other contacts within the State, and permit notice to be given the defendant outside the State without any requirement of service on a local State official. See, *e.g.,* Ill.Ann.Stat., c. 110, §§ 16, 17 (Smith-Hurd 1956); Wis.Stat. § 262.06 (1959). This service, employed in original Federal actions pursuant to paragraph (7), has also been held proper. See *Farr & Co. v. Cia. Intercontinental de Nav. de Cuba,* 243 F.2d 342 (2d Cir. 1957); *Kappus v. Western Hills Oil, Inc.,* 24 F.R.D. 123 (E.D.Wis.1959); *Star v. Rogalny,* 162 F.Supp. 181 (E.D.Ill.1957). It has also been held that the clause of paragraph (7) which permits service "in the manner prescribed by the law of the state," etc., is not limited by subdivision (c) requiring that service of all process be made by certain designated persons. See *Farr & Co. v. Cia. Intercontinental de Nav. de Cuba, supra.* But *cf. Sappia v. Lauro Lines,* 130 F.Supp. 810 (S.D.N.Y.1955).

The salutary results of these cases are intended to be preserved. See paragraph (7), with a clarified reference to State law, and amended subdivisions (e) and (f).

Subdivision (e). For the general relation between subdivisions (d) and (e), see 2 Moore, *supra,* ¶ 4.32.

The amendment of the first sentence inserting the word "thereunder" supports the original intention that the "order of court" must be authorized by a specific United States statute. See 1 Barron & Holtzoff, *supra,* at 731. The clause added at the end of the first sentence expressly adopts the view taken by commentators that, if no manner of service is prescribed in the statute or order, the service may be made in a manner stated in Rule 4. See 2 Moore, *supra,* ¶ 4.32, at 1004; Smit, *International Aspects of Federal Civil Procedure,* 61 Colum.L.Rev. 1031, 1036–39 (1961). *But see* Commentary, 5 Fed. Rules Serv. 791 (1942).

Examples of the statutes to which the first sentence relates are 28 U.S.C. § 2361 (Interpleader; process and procedure); 28 U.S.C. § 1655 (Lien enforcement; absent defendants).

The second sentence, added by amendment, expressly allows resort in original Federal actions to the procedures provided by State law for effecting service on nonresident parties (as well as on domiciliaries not found within the State). See, as illustrative, the discussion under amended subdivision (d)(7) of service pursuant to State nonresident motorist statutes and other comparable State statutes. Of particular interest is the change brought about by the reference in this sentence to State procedures for commencing actions against nonresidents by attachment and the like, accompanied by notice. Although an action commenced in a State court by attachment may be removed to the Federal court if ordinary conditions for

---

New matter is shown in italics; matter to be omitted is lined through

removal are satisfied, see 28 U.S.C. § 1450; *Rorick v. Devon Syndicate, Ltd.*, 307 U.S. 299, 59 S.Ct. 877, 83 L.Ed. 1303 (1939); Clark v. Wells, 203 U.S. 164, 27 S.Ct. 43, 51 L.Ed. 138 (1906), there has heretofore been no provision recognized by the courts for commencing an original Federal civil action by attachment. See Currie, *Attachment and Garnishment in the Federal Courts*, 59 Mich.L.Rev. 337 (1961), arguing that this result came about through historical anomaly. Rule 64, which refers to attachment, garnishment, and similar procedures under State law, furnishes only provisional remedies in actions otherwise validly commenced. See *Big Vein Coal Co. v. Read*, 229 U.S. 31, 33 S.Ct. 694, 57 L.Ed. 1053 (1913); *Davis v. Ensign-Bickford Co.*, 139 F.2d 624 (8th Cir. 1944); 7 *Moore's Federal Practice* ¶ 64.05 (2d ed. 1954); 3 Barron & Holtzoff, *Federal Practice & Procedure* § 1423 (Wright ed. 1958); *but cf.* Note, 13 So.Calif.L.Rev. 361 (1940). The amendment will now permit the institution of original Federal actions against nonresidents through the use of familiar State procedures by which property of these defendants is brought within the custody of the court and some appropriate service is made upon them.

The necessity of satisfying subject-matter jurisdictional requirements and requirements of venue will limit the practical utilization of these methods of effecting service. Within those limits, however, there appears to be no reason for denying plaintiffs means of commencing actions in Federal courts which are generally available in the State courts. See 1 Barron & Holtzoff, *supra*, at 374–80; Nordbye, *Comments on Proposed Amendments to Rules of Civil Procedure for the United States District Courts*, 18 F.R.D. 105, 106 (1956); Note, 34 Corn.L.Q. 103 (1948); Note, 13 So.Calif.L.Rev. 361 (1940).

If the circumstances of a particular case satisfy the applicable Federal law (first sentence of Rule 4(e), as amended) and the applicable State law (second sentence), the party seeking to make the service may proceed under the Federal or the State law, at his option.

See also amended Rule 13(a), and the Advisory Committee's Note thereto.

Subdivision (f). The first sentence is amended to assure the effectiveness of service outside the territorial limits of the State in all the cases in which any of the rules authorize service beyond those boundaries. Besides the preceding provisions of Rule 4, see Rule 71A(d)(3). In addition, the new second sentence of the subdivision permits effective service within a limited area outside the State in certain special situations, namely, to bring in additional parties to a counterclaim or cross-claim (Rule 13(h)), impleaded parties (Rule 14), and indispensable or conditionally necessary parties to a pending action (Rule 19); and to secure compliance with an order of commitment for civil contempt. In those situations effective service can be made at points not more than 100 miles distant from the courthouse in which the action is commenced, or to which it is assigned or transferred for trial.

The bringing in of parties under the 100-mile provision in the limited situations enumerated is designed to promote the objective of enabling the court to determine entire controversies. In the light of present-day facilities for communication and travel, the territorial range of the service allowed, analogous to that which applies to the service of a subpoena under Rule 45(e)(1), can hardly work hardship on the parties summoned. The provision will be especially useful in metropolitan areas spanning more than one State. Any requirements of subject-matter jurisdiction and venue will still have to be satisfied as to the parties brought in, although these requirements will be eased in some instances when the parties can be regarded as "ancillary." See *Pennsylvania R.R. v. Erie Avenue Warehouse Co.*, 5 F.R. Serv. 2d 14a.62, Case 2 (3d Cir. 1962); *Dery v. Wyer*, 265 F.2d

---

New matter is shown in italics; matter to be omitted is lined through

804 (2d Cir. 1959); *United Artists Corp. v. Masterpiece Productions, Inc.*, 221 F.2d 213 (2d Cir. 1955); *Lesnik v. Public Industrials Corp.*, 144 F.2d 968 (2d Cir. 1944); *Vaughn v. Terminal Transp. Co.*, 162 F.Supp. 647 (E.D.Tenn.1957); and compare the fifth paragraph of the Advisory Committee's Note to Rule 4(e), as amended. The amendment is but a moderate extension of the territorial reach of Federal process and has ample practical justification. See 2 Moore, *supra*, § 4.01[13] (Supp.1960); 1 Barron & Holtzoff, *supra*, § 184; Note, 51 Nw.U.L.Rev. 354 (1956). *But cf.* Nordbye, *Comments on Proposed Amendments to Rules of Civil Procedure for the United States District Courts*, 18 F.R.D. 105, 106 (1956).

As to the need for enlarging the territorial area in which orders of commitment for civil contempt may be served, see *Graber v. Graber*, 93 F.Supp. 281 (D.D.C.1950); *Teele Soap Mfg. Co. v. Pine Tree Products Co., Inc.*, 8 F.Supp. 546 (D.N.H.1934); *Mitchell v. Dexter*, 244 Fed. 926 (1st Cir.1917); *In re Graves*, 29 Fed. 60 (N.D.Iowa 1886).

As to the Court's power to amend subdivisions (e) and (f) as here set forth, see *Mississippi Pub. Corp. v. Murphree*, 326 U.S. 438, 66 S.Ct. 242, 90 L.Ed. 185 (1946).

Subdivision (i). The continual increase of civil litigation having international elements makes it advisable to consolidate, amplify, and clarify the provisions governing service upon parties in foreign countries. See generally Jones, *International Judicial Assistance: Procedural Chaos and a Program for Reform*, 62 Yale L.J. 515 (1953); Longley, *Serving Process, Subpoenas and Other Documents in Foreign Territory*, Proc.A.B.A., Sec.Int'l & Comp.L. 34 (1959); Smit, *International Aspects of Federal Civil Procedure*, 61 Colum.L.Rev. 1031 (1961).

As indicated in the opening lines of new subdivision (i), referring to the provisions of subdivision (e), the authority for effecting foreign service must be found in a statute of the United States or a statute or rule of court of the State in which the district court is held providing in terms or upon proper interpretation for service abroad upon persons not inhabitants of or found within the State. See the Advisory Committee's Note to amended Rule 4(d)(7) and Rule 4(e). For examples of Federal and State statutes expressly authorizing such service, see 8 U.S.C. § 1451(b); 35 U.S.C. §§ 146, 293; Me.Rev.Stat., ch. 22, § 70 (Supp.1961); Minn.Stat.Ann. § 303.13 (1947); N.Y.Veh. & Tfc. Law § 253. Several decisions have construed statutes to permit service in foreign countries, although the matter is not expressly mentioned in the statutes. See, *e.g., Chapman v. Superior Court*, 162 Cal.App.2d 421, 328 P.2d 23 (Dist.Ct.App.1958); *Sperry v. Fliegers*, 194 Misc. 438, 86 N.Y.S.2d 830 (Sup.Ct.1949); *Ewing v. Thompson*, 233 N.C. 564, 65 S.E.2d 17 (1951); *Rushing v. Bush*, 260 S.W.2d 900 (Tex.Ct.Civ.App.1953). Federal and State statutes authorizing service on nonresidents in such terms as to warrant the interpretation that service abroad is permissible include 15 U.S.C. §§ 77v(a), 78aa, 79y; 28 U.S.C. § 1655; 38 U.S.C. § 784(a); Ill.Ann.Stat., c. 110, §§ 16, 17 (Smith-Hurd 1956); Wis.Stat. § 262.06 (1959).

Under subdivisions (e) and (i), when authority to make foreign service is found in a Federal statute or statute or rule of court of a State, it is always sufficient to carry out the service in the manner indicated therein. Subdivision (i) introduces considerable further flexibility by permitting the foreign service and the return thereof to be carried out in any of a number of other alternative ways that are also declared to be sufficient. Other aspects of foreign service continue to be governed by the other provisions of Rule 4. Thus, for example, subdivision (i) effects no change in the form of the summons, or the issuance of separate or additional summons, or the amendment of service.

Service of process beyond the territorial limits of the United States may involve difficulties not encountered in the case of domestic service. Service abroad

---

New matter is shown in italics; matter to be omitted is lined through

may be considered by a foreign country to require the performance of judicial, and therefore "sovereign," acts within its territory, which that country may conceive to be offensive to its policy or contrary to its law. See Jones, *supra*, at 537. For example, a person not qualified to serve process according to the law of the foreign country may find himself subject to sanctions if he attempts service therein. See Inter-American Juridical Committee, *Report on Uniformity of Legislation on International Cooperation in Judicial Procedures* 20 (1952). The enforcement of a judgment in the foreign country in which the service was made may be embarrassed or prevented if the service did not comport with the law of that country. See *ibid.*

One of the purposes of subdivision (i) is to allow accommodation to the policies and procedures of the foreign country. It is emphasized, however, that the attitudes of foreign countries vary considerably and that the question of recognition of United States judgments abroad is complex. Accordingly, if enforcement is to be sought in the country of service, the foreign law should be examined before a choice is made among the methods of service allowed by subdivision (i).

Subdivision (i)(1). Subparagraph (a) of paragraph (1), permitting service by the method prescribed by the law of the foreign country for service on a person in that country in a civil action in any of its courts of general jurisdiction, provides an alternative that is likely to create least objection in the place of service and also is likely to enhance the possibilities of securing ultimate enforcement of the judgment abroad. See *Report on Uniformity of Legislation on International Cooperation in Judicial Procedures, supra.*

In certain foreign countries service in aid of litigation pending in other countries can lawfully be accomplished only upon request to the foreign court, which in turn directs the service to be made. In many countries this has long been a customary way of accomplishing the service. See *In re Letters Rogatory out of First Civil Court of City of Mexico,* 261 Fed. 652 (S.D.N.Y.1919); Jones, *supra*, at 543; Comment, 44 Colum.L.Rev. 72 (1944); Note, 58 Yale L.J. 1193 (1949). Subparagraph (B) of paragraph (1), referring to a letter rogatory, validates this method. A proviso, applicable to this subparagraph and the preceding one, requires, as a safeguard, that the service made shall be reasonably calculated to give actual notice of the proceedings to the party. See *Milliken v. Meyer,* 311 U.S. 457, 61 S.Ct. 339, 85 L.Ed. 278 (1940).

Subparagraph (C) of paragraph (1), permitting foreign service by personal delivery on individuals and corporations, partnerships, and associations, provides for a manner of service that is not only traditionally preferred, but also is most likely to lead to actual notice. Explicit provision for this manner of service was thought desirable because a number of Federal and State statutes permitting foreign service do not specifically provide for service by personal delivery abroad, see *e.g.,* 35 U.S.C. §§ 146, 293; 46 U.S.C. § 1292; Calif.Ins.Code § 1612; N.Y.Veh. & Tfc. Law § 253, and it also may be unavailable under the law of the country in which the service is made.

Subparagraph (D) of paragraph (1), permitting service by certain types of mail, affords a manner of service that is inexpensive and expeditious, and requires a minimum of activity within the foreign country. Several statutes specifically provide for service in a foreign country by mail, *e.g.,* Hawaii Rev. Laws §§ 230–31, 230–32 (1955); Minn.Stat.Ann. § 303.13 (1947); N.Y.Civ.Prac. Act, § 229–b; N.Y. Veh. & Tfc. Law § 253, and it has been sanctioned by the courts even in the absence of statutory provision specifying that form of service. *Zurini v. United States,* 189 F.2d 722 (8th Cir. 1951); *United States v. Cardillo,* 135 F.Supp. 798 (W.D.Pa.1955); *Autogiro Co. v. Kay Gyroplanes, Ltd.,* 55 F.Supp. 919 (D.D.C.1944).

New matter is shown in italics; matter to be omitted is lined through

Since the reliability of postal service may vary from country to country, service by mail is proper only when it is addressed to the party to be served and a form of mail requiring a signed receipt is used. An additional safeguard is provided by the requirement that the mailing be attended to by the clerk of the court. See also the provisions of paragraph (2) of this subdivision (i) regarding proof of service by mail.

Under the applicable law it may be necessary, when the defendant is an infant or incompetent person, to deliver the summons and complaint to a guardian, committee, or similar fiduciary. In such a case it would be advisable to make service under subparagraph (A), (B), or (E).

Subparagraph (E) of paragraph (1) adds flexibility by permitting the court by order to tailor the manner of service to fit the necessities of a particular case or the peculiar requirements of the law of the country in which the service is to be made. A similar provision appears in a number of statutes, *e.g.*, 35 U.S.C. §§ 146, 293; 38 U.S.C. § 784(a); 46 U.S.C. § 1292.

The next-to-last sentence of paragraph (1) permits service under (C) and (E) to be made by any person who is not a party and is not less than 18 years of age or who is designated by court order or by the foreign court. *Cf.* Rule 45(c); N.Y.Civ. Prac.Act §§ 233, 235. This alternative increases the possibility that the plaintiff will be able to find a process server who can proceed unimpeded in the foreign country; it also may improve the chances of enforcing the judgment in the country of service. Especially is this alternative valuable when authority for the foreign service is found in a statute or rule of court that limits the group of eligible process servers to designated officials or special appointees who, because directly connected with another "sovereign," may be particularly offensive to the foreign country. See generally Smit, *supra*, at 1040–41. When recourse is had to subparagraph (A) or (B) the identity of the process server always will be determined by the law of the foreign country in which the service is made.

The last sentence of paragraph (1) sets forth an alternative manner for the issuance and transmission of the summons for service. After obtaining the summons from the clerk, the plaintiff must ascertain the best manner of delivering the summons and complaint to the person, court, or officer who will make the service. Thus the clerk is not burdened with the task of determining who is permitted to serve process under the law of a particular country or the appropriate governmental or nongovernmental channel for forwarding a letter rogatory. Under (D), however, the papers must always be posted by the clerk.

Subdivision (i)(2). When service is made in a foreign country, paragraph (2) permits methods for proof of service in addition to those prescribed by subdivision (g). Proof of service in accordance with the law of the foreign country is permitted because foreign process servers, unaccustomed to the form or the requirement of return of service prevalent in the United States, have on occasion been unwilling to execute the affidavit required by Rule 4(g). See Jones, *supra*, at 537; Longley, *supra*, at 35. As a corollary of the alternate manner of service in subdivision (i)(1)(E), proof of service as directed by order of the court is permitted. The special provision for proof of service by mail is intended as an additional safeguard when that method is used. On the type of evidence of delivery that may be satisfactory to a court in lieu of a signed receipt, see *Aero Associates, Inc. v. La Metropolitana*, 183 F.Supp. 357 (S.D.N.Y.1960).

Rule 5. Service and Filing of Pleadings and Other Papers

(a) **Service: When Required.** *Except as otherwise provided in these rules,* ~~E~~every order required by its terms to be served,

---

New matter is shown in italics; matter to be omitted is lined through

every pleading subsequent to the original complaint unless the court otherwise orders because of numerous defendants, every written motion other than one which may be heard ex parte, and every written notice, appearance, demand, offer of judgment, designation of record on appeal, and similar paper shall be served upon each of the parties. ~~affected thereby, but n~~*N*o service need be made on parties in default for failure to appear except that pleadings asserting new or additional claims for relief against them shall be served upon them in the manner provided for service of summons in Rule 4.

Advisory Committee's Note

The words "affected thereby," stricken out by the amendment, introduced a problem of interpretation. See 1 Barron & Holtzoff, *Federal Practice & Procedure* 760–61 (Wright ed. 1960). The amendment eliminates this difficulty and promotes full exchange of information among the parties by requiring service of papers on all the parties to the action, except as otherwise provided in the rules. See also subdivision (c) of Rule 5. So, for example, a third-party defendant is required to serve his answer to the third-party complaint not only upon the defendant but also upon the plaintiff. See amended Form 22–A and the Advisory Committee's Note thereto.

As to the method of serving papers upon a party whose address is unknown, see Rule 5(b).

Rule 6.   Time

(a) **Computation.**   In computing any period of time pre-scribed or allowed by these rules, *by the local rules of any district court,* by order of court, or by any applicable statute, the day of the act, event, or default ~~after~~ *from* which the designated period of time begins to run ~~is~~ *shall* not ~~to~~ be included. The last day of the period so computed ~~is to~~ *shall* be included, unless it is *a Saturday,* a Sunday, or a legal holiday, in which event the period runs until the end of the next day which is ~~neither~~ *not a Saturday*, a Sunday, ~~nor~~ *or* a *legal* holiday. When the period of time prescribed or allowed is less than 7 days, intermediate *Saturdays*, Sundays, and *legal* holidays shall be excluded in the computation. ~~A half holiday shall be considered as other days and not as a holiday.~~ *As used in this rule and in rule 77(c), "legal holiday" includes New Year's Day, Washington's Birthday, Memorial Day, Independence Day, Labor Day, Veterans Day, Thanksgiving Day, Christmas Day, and any other day appointed as a holiday by the President or the Congress of the United States, or by the state in which the district court is held.*

(b) **Enlargement.**   When by these rules or by a notice given thereunder or by order of court an act is required or allowed to be

---

New matter is shown in italics; matter to be omitted is lined through

done at or within a specified time, the court for cause shown may at any time in its discretion (1) with or without motion or notice order the period enlarged if request therefor is made before the expiration of the period originally prescribed or as extended by a previous order or (2) upon motion made after the expiration of the specified period permit the act to be done where the failure to act was the result of excusable neglect; but it may not extend the time for taking any action under Rules ~~25,~~ 50(b), 52(b), 59(b), (d) and (e), 60(b), and 73(a) and (g), except to the extent and under the conditions stated in them.

Advisory Committee's Note

Subdivision (a). This amendment is related to the amendment of Rule 77(c) changing the regulation of the days on which the clerk's office shall be open.

The wording of the first sentence of Rule 6(a) is clarified and the subdivision is made expressly applicable to computing periods of time set forth in local rules.

Saturday is to be treated in the same way as Sunday or a "legal holiday" in that it is not to be included when it falls on the last day of a computed period, nor counted as an intermediate day when the period is less than 7 days. "Legal holiday" is defined for purposes of this subdivision and amended Rule 77(c). Compare the definition of "holiday" in 11 U.S.C. § 1(18); also 5 U.S.C. § 86a; Executive Order No. 10358, "Observance of Holidays," June 9, 1952, 17 Fed.Reg. 5269. In the light of these changes the last sentence of the present subdivision, dealing with half holidays, is eliminated.

With Saturdays and State holidays made "dies non" in certain cases by the amended subdivision, computation of the usual 5-day notice of motion or the 2-day notice to dissolve or modify a temporary restraining order may work out so as to cause embarrassing delay in urgent cases. The delay can be obviated by applying to the court to shorten the time, see Rules 6(d) and 65(b).

Subdivision (b). The prohibition against extending the time for taking action under Rule 25 (Substitution of parties) is eliminated. The only limitation of time provided for in amended Rule 25 is the 90-day period following a suggestion upon the record of the death of a party within which to make a motion to substitute the proper parties for the deceased party. See Rule 25(a) (1), as amended, and the Advisory Committee's Note thereto. It is intended that the court shall have discretion to enlarge that period.

Rule 7. Pleadings Allowed; Form of Motions

(a) **Pleadings.** There shall be a complaint and an answer; ~~and there shall be~~ a reply to a counterclaim denominated as such; an answer to a cross-claim, if the answer contains a cross-claim; a third-party complaint, if ~~leave is given under Rule 14 to summon~~ a person who was not an original party *is summoned under the provisions of Rule 14;* and ~~there shall be~~ a third-party answer, if a third-party complaint is served. No other pleading shall be allowed, except that the court may order a reply to an answer or a third-party answer.

New matter is shown in italics; matter to be omitted is lined through

Advisory Committee's Note

Certain redundant words are eliminated and the subdivision is modified to reflect the amendment of Rule 14(a) which in certain cases eliminates the requirement of obtaining leave to bring in a third-party defendant.

Rule 12. Defenses and Objections—When and How Presented—By Pleading or Motion—Motion for Judgment on Pleadings

(a) **When Presented.** A defendant shall serve his answer within 20 days after the service of the summons and complaint upon him, ~~unless the court directs otherwise when service is made pursuant to Rule 4(e)~~ *except when service is made under Rule 4(e) and a different time is prescribed in the order of court under the statute of the United States or in the statute or rule of court of the state.* A party served with a pleading stating a cross-claim against him shall serve an answer thereto within 20 days after the service upon him. The plaintiff shall serve his reply to a counterclaim in the answer within 20 days after service of the answer or, if a reply is ordered by the court, within 20 days after service of the order, unless the order otherwise directs. The United States or an officer or agency thereof shall serve an answer to the complaint or to a cross-claim, or a reply to a counterclaim, within 60 days after the service upon the United States attorney of the pleading in which the claim is asserted. The service of a motion permitted under this rule alters these periods of time as follows, unless a different time is fixed by order of the court: (1) if the court denies the motion or postpones its disposition until the trial on the merits, the responsive pleading shall be served within 10 days after notice of the court's action; (2) if the court grants a motion for a more definite statement the responsive pleading shall be served within 10 days after the service of the more definite statement.

Advisory Committee's Note

This amendment conforms to the amendment of Rule 4(e). See also the Advisory Committee's Note to amended Rule 4(b).

Rule 13. Counterclaim and Cross-Claim

(a) **Compulsory Counterclaims.** A pleading shall state as a counterclaim any claim which at the time of serving the pleading the pleader has against any opposing party, if it arises out of the transaction or occurrence that is the subject matter of the opposing party's claim and does not require for its adjudication the

---

New matter is shown in italics; matter to be omitted is lined through

presence of third parties of whom the court cannot acquire juris-diction,. ~~except that such a claim need not be so stated~~ *But the pleader need not state the claim* if *(1)* at the time the action was commenced the claim was the subject of another pending action.-, *or (2) the opposing party brought suit upon his claim by attachment or other process by which the court did not acquire jurisdiction to render a personal judgment on that claim, and the pleader is not stating any counterclaim under this Rule 13.*

Advisory Committee's Note

When a defendant, if he desires to defend his interest in property, is obliged to come in and litigate in a court to whose jurisdiction he could not ordinarily be subjected, fairness suggests that he should not be required to assert counterclaims, but should rather be permitted to do so at his election. If, however, he does elect to assert a counterclaim, it seems fair to require him to assert any other which is compulsory within the meaning of Rule 13(a). Clause (2), added by amendment to Rule 13(a), carries out this idea. It will apply to various cases described in Rule 4(e), as amended, where service is effected through attachment or other process by which the court does not acquire jurisdiction to render a personal judgment against the defendant. Clause (2) will also apply to actions commenced in State courts jurisdictionally grounded on attachment or the like, and removed to the Federal courts.

Rule 14. Third-Party Practice

(a) **When Defendant May Bring in Third Party.** ~~Before the service of his answer~~ *At any time after commencement of the action* a defendant, ~~may move ex parte or, after the service of his answer, on notice to the plaintiff for leave~~ as a third-party plain-tiff, ~~to serve~~ *may cause* a summons and complaint *to be served* upon a person not a party to the action who is or may be liable to him for all or part of the plaintiff's claim against him. *The third-party plaintiff need not obtain leave to make the service if he files the third-party complaint not later than 10 days after he serves his original answer. Otherwise he must obtain leave on motion upon notice to all parties to the action.* ~~If the motion is granted and the summons and complaint are served, t~~*T*he person ~~so~~ served *with the summons and third-party complaint,* herein-after called the third-party defendant, shall make his defenses to the third-party plaintiff's claim as provided in Rule 12 and his counterclaims against the third-party plaintiff and cross-claims against other third-party defendants as provided in Rule 13. The third-party defendant may assert against the plaintiff any defens-es which the third-party plaintiff has to the plaintiff's claim. The third-party defendant may also assert any claim against the plain-tiff arising out of the transaction or occurrence that is the subject matter of the plaintiff's claim against the third-party plaintiff.

New matter is shown in italics; matter to be omitted is lined through

The plaintiff may assert any claim against the third-party defendant arising out of the transaction or occurrence that is the subject matter of the plaintiff's claim against the third-party plaintiff, and the third-party defendant thereupon shall assert his defenses as provided in Rule 12 and his counterclaims and cross-claims as provided in Rule 13. *Any party may move to strike the third-party claim, or for its severance or separate trial.* A third-party defendant may proceed under this rule against any person not a party to the action who is or may be liable to him for all or part of the claim made in the action against the third-party defendant.

Advisory Committee's Note

Under the amendment of the initial sentences of the subdivision, a defendant as third-party plaintiff may freely and without leave of court bring in a third-party defendant if he files the third-party complaint not later than 10 days after he serves his original answer. When the impleader comes so early in the case, there is little value in requiring a preliminary ruling by the court on the propriety of the impleader.

After the third-party defendant is brought in, the court has discretion to strike the third-party claim if it is obviously unmeritorious and can only delay or prejudice the disposition of the plaintiff's claim, or to sever the third-party claim or accord it separate trial if confusion or prejudice would otherwise result. This discretion, applicable not merely to the cases covered by the amendment where the third-party defendant is brought in without leave, but to all impleaders under the rule, is emphasized in the next-to-last sentence of the subdivision, added by amendment.

In dispensing with leave of court for an impleader filed not later than 10 days after serving the answer, but retaining the leave requirement for impleaders sought to be effected thereafter, the amended subdivision takes a moderate position on the lines urged by some commentators, see Note, 43 Minn.L.Rev. 115 (1958); *cf.* Pa.R.Civ.P. 2252–53 (60 days after service on the defendant); Minn.R.Civ.P. 14.01 (45 days). Other commentators would dispense with the requirement of leave regardless of the time when impleader is effected, and would rely on subsequent action by the court to dismiss the impleader if it would unduly delay or complicate the litigation or would be otherwise objectionable. See 1A Barron & Holtzoff, *Federal Practice & Procedure* 649–50 (Wright ed. 1960); Comment, 58 Colum.L.Rev. 532, 546 (1958); *cf.* N.Y.Civ.Prac.Act § 193–a; Me.R.Civ.P. 14. The amended subdivision preserves the value of a preliminary screening, through the leave procedure, of impleaders attempted after the 10–day period.

The amendment applies also when an impleader is initiated by a third-party defendant against a person who may be liable to him, as provided in the last sentence of the subdivision.

Rule 15.   Amended and Supplemental Pleadings

(d) Supplemental Pleadings. Upon motion of a party the court may, upon reasonable notice and upon such terms as are just, permit him to serve a supplemental pleading setting forth

New matter is shown in italics; matter to be omitted is lined through

transactions or occurrences or events which have happened since the date of the pleading sought to be supplemented. *Permission may be granted even though the original pleading is defective in its statement of a claim for relief or defense.* If the court deems it advisable that the adverse party plead ~~thereto~~ *to the supplemental pleading,* it shall so order, specifying the time therefor.

Advisory Committee's Note

Rule 15(d) is intended to give the court broad discretion in allowing a supplemental pleading. However, some cases, opposed by other cases and criticized by the commentators, have taken the rigid and formalistic view that where the original complaint fails to state a claim upon which relief can be granted, leave to serve a supplemental complaint must be denied. See *Bonner v. Elizabeth Arden, Inc.,* 177 F.2d 703 (2d Cir. 1949); *Bowles v. Senderowitz,* 65 F.Supp. 548 (E.D.Pa.), *rev'd on other grounds,* 158 F.2d 435 (3d Cir.1946), *cert. denied, Senderowitz v. Fleming,* 330 U.S. 848, 67 S.Ct. 1091, 91 L.Ed. 1292 (1947); *cf. LaSalle Nat. Bank v. 222 East Chestnut St. Corp.,* 267 F.2d 247 (7th Cir.), *cert. denied,* 361 U.S. 836, 80 S.Ct. 88, 4 L.Ed.2d 77 (1959). *But see Camilla Cotton Oil Co. v. Spencer Kellogg & Sons,* 257 F.2d 162 (5th Cir. 1958); *Genuth v. National Biscuit Co.,* 81 F.Supp. 213 (S.D.N.Y.1948), *app. dism.,* 177 F.2d 962 (2d Cir. 1949); 3 *Moore's Federal Practice* ¶ 15.01[5] (Supp.1960); 1A Barron & Holtzoff, *Federal Practice & Procedure* 820–21 (Wright ed. 1960). Thus plaintiffs have sometimes been needlessly remitted to the difficulties of commencing a new action even though events occurring after the commencement of the original action have made clear the right to relief.

Under the amendment the court has discretion to permit a supplemental pleading despite the fact that the original pleading is defective. As in other situations where a supplemental pleading is offered, the court is to determine in the light of the particular circumstances whether filing should be permitted, and if so, upon what terms. The amendment does not attempt to deal with such questions as the relation of the statute of limitations to supplemental pleadings, the operation of the doctrine of laches, or the availability of other defenses. All these questions are for decision in accordance with the principles applicable to supplemental pleadings generally. *Cf. Blau v. Lamb,* 191 F.Supp. 906 (S.D.N.Y. 1961); *Lendonsol Amusement Corp. v. B. & Q. Assoc., Inc.,* 23 F.R.Serv. 15d.3, Case 1 (D.Mass.1957).

Rule 24.   Intervention

(c) Procedure. A person desiring to intervene shall serve a motion to intervene upon ~~all~~ *the* parties ~~affected thereby~~ *as provided in Rule 5.* The motion shall state the grounds therefor and shall be accompanied by a pleading setting forth the claim or defense for which intervention is sought. The same procedure shall be followed when a statute of the United States gives a right to intervene. When the constitutionality of an act of Congress affecting the public interest is drawn in question in any action to which the United States or an officer, agency, or employee thereof is not a party, the court shall notify the Attorney General of the United States as provided in Title 28, U.S.C., § 2403.

New matter is shown in italics; matter to be omitted is lined through

This amendment conforms to the amendment of Rule 5(a). See the Advisory Committee's Note to that amendment.

Rule 25.   Substitution of Parties

(a) Death.

(1) If a party dies and the claim is not thereby extinguished, the court ~~within 2 years after the death~~ may order substitution of the proper parties. ~~If substitution is not so made, the action shall be dismissed as to the deceased party.~~ The motion for substitution my be made by *any party or by* the successors or representatives of the deceased party ~~or by any party~~ and, together with the notice of hearing, shall be served on the parties as provided in Rule 5 and upon persons not parties in the manner provided in Rule 4 for the service of a summons, and may be served in any judicial district. *Unless the motion for substitution is made not later than 90 days after the death is suggested upon the record by service of a statement of the fact of the death as provided herein for the service of the motion, the action shall be dismissed as to the deceased party.*

Advisory Committee's Note

Present Rule 25(a)(1), together with present Rule 6(b), results in an inflexible requirement that an action be dismissed as to a deceased party if substitution is not carried out within a fixed period measured from the time of the death. The hardships and inequities of this unyielding requirement plainly appear from the cases. See, *e. g., Anderson v. Yungkau,* 329 U.S. 482, 67 S.Ct. 428, 91 L.Ed. 436 (1947); *Iovino v. Waterson,* 274 F.2d 41 (1959), *cert. denied, Carlin v. Sovino,* 362 U.S. 949, 80 S.Ct. 860, 4 L.Ed.2d 867 (1960); *Perry v. Allen,* 239 F.2d 107 (5th Cir. 1956); *Starnes v. Pennsylvania R. R.,* 26 F.R.D. 625 (E.D.N.Y.), *aff'd per curiam,* 295 F.2d 704 (2d Cir. 1961), *cert. denied,* 369 U.S. 813, 82 S.Ct. 688, 7 L.Ed.2d 612 (1962); *Zdanok v. Glidden Co.,* 28 F.R.D. 346 (S.D.N.Y.1961). See also 4 *Moore's Federal Practice* ¶ 25.01[9] (Supp.1960); 2 Barron & Holtzoff, *Federal Practice & Procedure,* § 621, at 420–21 (Wright ed. 1961).

The amended rule establishes a time limit for the motion to substitute based not upon the time of the death, but rather upon the time information of the death is provided by means of a suggestion of death upon the record, *i. e.* service of a statement of the fact of the death. *Cf.* Ill.Ann.Stat., c. 110, § 54(2) (Smith-Hurd 1956). The motion may not be made later than 90 days after the service of the statement unless the period is extended pursuant to Rule 6(b), as amended. See the Advisory Committee's Note to amended Rule 6(b). See also the new Official Form 30.

A motion to substitute may be made by any party or by the representative of the deceased party without awaiting the suggestion of death. Indeed, the motion will usually be so made. If a party or the representative of the deceased party

New matter is shown in italics; matter to be omitted is lined through

desires to limit the time within which another may make the motion, he may do so by suggesting the death upon the record.

A motion to substitute made within the prescribed time will ordinarily be granted, but under the permissive language of the first sentence of the amended rule ("the court may order") it may be denied by the court in the exercise of a sound discretion if made long after the death—as can occur if the suggestion of death is not made or is delayed—and circumstances have arisen rendering it unfair to allow substitution. *Cf. Anderson v. Yungkau, supra,* 329 U.S. at 485, 486, 67 S.Ct. at 430, 431, 91 L.Ed. 436, where it was noted under the present rule that settlement and distribution of the estate of a deceased defendant might be so far advanced as to warrant denial of a motion for substitution even though made within the time limit prescribed by that rule. Accordingly, a party interested in securing substitution under the amended rule should not assume that he can rest indefinitely awaiting the suggestion of death before he makes his motion to substitute.

Rule 26. Depositions Pending Action

(e) **Objections to Admissibility.** Subject to the provisions of Rules *28(b) and* 32(c), objection may be made at the trial or hearing to receiving in evidence any deposition or part thereof for any reason which would require the exclusion of the evidence if the witness were then present and testifying.

Advisory Committee's Note

This amendment conforms to the amendment of Rule 28(b). See the next-to-last paragraph of the Advisory Committee's Note to that amendment.

Rule 28. Persons Before Whom Depositions May Be Taken

(b) **In Foreign Countries.*** In a foreign ~~state or~~ country, depositions ~~shall~~ *may* be taken (1) on notice before a ~~secretary of embassy or legation, consul general, consul, vice consul, or consular agent of the United States~~ *person authorized to administer oaths in the place in which the examination is held, either by the law thereof or by the law of the United States,* or (2) before ~~such~~ *a* person ~~or officer as may be appointed by commission~~ *commissioned by the court, and a person so commissioned shall have the power by virtue of his commission to administer any necessary oath and take testimony,* or *(3)* ~~under~~ *pursuant to a* letters rogatory. A commission or *a* letters rogatory shall be issued ~~only when necessary or convenient,~~ on application and notice~~,~~ and on ~~such~~ terms ~~and with such directions as~~ *that* are just and appropriate. *It is*

---

* The amendments of this subdivision and of Rule 26(e) were developed collaboratively by the Commission and Advisory Committee on International Rules of Judicial Procedure, a statutory organization established pursuant to Act of September 2, 1958, 72 Stat. 1743, and the Advisory Committee on Civil Rules.

New matter is shown in italics; matter to be omitted is lined through

not requisite to the issuance of a commission or a letter rogatory that the taking of the deposition in any other manner is impracticable or inconvenient; and both a commission and a letter rogatory may be issued in proper cases. ~~Officers may be designated in notices or commissions~~ *A notice or commission may designate the person before whom the deposition is to be taken* either by name or descriptive title. ~~and~~ *A* letters rogatory may be addressed "To the Appropriate ~~Judicial~~ Authority in [here name the country]." *Evidence obtained in response to a letter rogatory need not be excluded merely for the reason that it is not a verbatim transcript or that the testimony was not taken under oath or for any similar departure from the requirements for depositions taken within the United States under these rules.*

Advisory Committee's Note

The amendment of clause (1) is designed to facilitate depositions in foreign countries by enlarging the class of persons before whom the depositions may be taken on notice. The class is no longer confined, as at present, to a secretary of embassy or legation, consul general, consul, vice consul, or consular agent of the United States. In a country that regards the taking of testimony by a foreign official in aid of litigation pending in a court of another country as an infringement upon its sovereignty, it will be expedient to notice depositions before officers of the country in which the examination is taken. See generally *Symposium Letters Rogatory* (Grossman ed. 1956); Doyle, *Taking Evidence by Deposition and Letters Rogatory and Obtaining Documents in Foreign Territory,* Proc.A.B.A., Sec. Int'l & Comp.L. 37 (1959); Heilpern, *Procuring Evidence Abroad,* 14 Tul.L.Rev. 29 (1939); Jones, *International Judicial Assistance: Procedural Chaos and a Program for Reform,* 62 Yale L.J. 515, 526–29 (1953); Smit, *International Aspects of Federal Civil Procedure,* 61 Colum.L.Rev. 1031, 1056–58 (1961).

Clause (2) of amended subdivision (b), like the corresponding provision of subdivision (a) dealing with depositions taken in the United States, makes it clear that the appointment of a person by commission in itself confers power upon him to administer any necessary oath.

It has been held that a letter rogatory will not be issued unless the use of a notice or commission is shown to be impossible or impractical. See, *e. g., United States v. Matles,* 154 F.Supp. 574 (E.D.N.Y.1957); *The Edmund Fanning,* 89 F.Supp. 282 (E.D.N.Y.1950); *Branyan v. Koninklijke Luchtvaart Maatschappij,* 13 F.R.D. 425 (S.D.N.Y.1953). See also *Ali Akber Kiachif v. Philco International Corp.,* 10 F.R.D. 277 (S.D.N.Y.1950). The intent of the fourth sentence of the amended subdivision is to overcome this judicial antipathy and to permit a sound choice between depositions under a letter rogatory and on notice or by commission in the light of all the circumstances. In a case in which the foreign country will compel a witness to attend or testify in aid of a letter rogatory but not in aid of a commission, a letter rogatory may be preferred on the ground that it is less expensive to execute, even if there is plainly no need for compulsive process. A letter rogatory may also be preferred when it cannot be demonstrated that a witness will be recalcitrant or when the witness states that he is willing to testify voluntarily, but the contingency exists that he will change his mind at the last moment. In the latter case, it may be advisable to issue both a commission and a letter rogatory, the latter to be executed if the former fails. The choice between a

---

New matter is shown in italics; matter to be omitted is lined through

letter rogatory and a commission may be conditioned by other factors, including the nature and extent of the assistance that the foreign country will give to the execution of either.

In executing a letter rogatory the courts of other countries may be expected to follow their customary procedure for taking testimony. See *United States v. Paraffin Wax, 2255 Bags,* 23 F.R.D. 289 (E.D.N.Y.1959). In many noncommon-law countries the judge questions the witness, sometimes without first administering an oath, the attorneys put any supplemental questions either to the witness or through the judge, and the judge dictates a summary of the testimony, which the witness acknowledges as correct. See Jones, *supra,* at 530–32; Doyle, *supra,* at 39–41. The last sentence of the amended subdivision provides, contrary to the implications of some authority, that evidence recorded in such a fashion need not be excluded on that account. See *The Mandu,* 11 F.Supp. 845 (E.D.N.Y.1935). *But cf. Nelson v. United States,* 17 Fed.Cas. 1340 (No. 10,116) (C.C.D.Pa.1816); *Winthrop v. Union Ins. Co.,* 30 Fed.Cas. 376 (No. 17,901) (C.C.D.Pa.1807). The specific reference to the lack of an oath or a verbatim transcript is intended to be illustrative. Whether or to what degree the value or weight of the evidence may be affected by the method of taking or recording the testimony is left for determination according to the circumstances of the particular case, *cf. Uebersee Finanz-Korporation, A. G. v. Brownell,* 121 F.Supp. 420 (D.D.C.1954); *Danisch v. Guardian Life Ins. Co.,* 19 F.R.D. 235 (S.D.N.Y.1956); the testimony may indeed be so devoid of substance or probative value as to warrant its exclusion altogether.

Some foreign countries are hostile to allowing a deposition to be taken in their country, especially by notice or commission, or to lending assistance in the taking of a deposition. Thus compliance with the terms of amended subdivision (b) may not in all cases ensure completion of a deposition abroad. Examination of the law and policy of the particular foreign country in advance of attempting a deposition is therefore advisable. See 4 *Moore's Federal Practice* ¶¶ 28.05–28.08 (2d ed. 1950).

Rule 30.   Depositions Upon Oral Examination

(f) Certification and Filing by Officer; Copies; Notice of Filing.

(1) The officer shall certify on the deposition that the witness was duly sworn by him and that the deposition is a true record of the testimony given by the witness. He shall then securely seal the deposition in an envelope indorsed with the title of the action and marked "Deposition of [here insert name of witness]" and shall promptly file it with the court in which the action is pending or send it by registered *or certified* mail to the clerk thereof for filing.

Advisory Committee's Note

This amendment corresponds to the change in Rule 4(d)(4). See the Advisory Committee's Note to that amendment.

Rule 41.   Dismissal of Actions

(b) Involuntary Dismissal: Effect Thereof. For failure of the plaintiff to prosecute or to comply with these rules or any

---

New matter is shown in italics; matter to be omitted is lined through

order of court, a defendant may move for dismissal of an action or of any claim against him. After the plaintiff, *in an action tried by the court without a jury,* has completed the presentation of his evidence the defendant, without waiving his right to offer evidence in the event the motion is not granted, may move for a dismissal on the ground that upon the facts and the law the plaintiff has shown no right to relief. ~~In an action tried by the court without a jury t~~*T*he court as trier of the facts may then determine them and render judgment against the plaintiff or may decline to render any judgment until the close of all the evidence. If the court renders judgment on the merits against the plaintiff, the court shall make findings as provided in Rule 52(a). Unless the court in its order for dismissal otherwise specifies, a dismissal under this subdivision and any dismissal not provided for in this rule, other than a dismissal for lack of jurisdiction or for improper venue *or for lack of an indispensable party,* operates as an adjudication upon the merits.

Advisory Committee's Note

Under the present text of the second sentence of this subdivision, the motion for dismissal at the close of the plaintiff's evidence may be made in a case tried to a jury as well as in a case tried without a jury. But, when made in a jury-tried case, this motion overlaps the motion for a directed verdict under Rule 50(a), which is also available in the same situation. It has been held that the standard to be applied in deciding the Rule 41(b) motion at the close of the plaintiff's evidence in a jury-tried case is the same as that used upon a motion for a directed verdict made at the same stage; and, just as the court need not make findings pursuant to Rule 52(a) when it directs a verdict, so in a jury-tried case it may omit these findings in granting the Rule 41(b) motion. See generally *O'Brien v. Westinghouse Electric Corp.,* 293 F.2d 1, 5–10 (3d Cir. 1961).

As indicated by the discussion in the *O'Brien* case, the overlap has caused confusion. Accordingly, the second and third sentences of Rule 41(b) are amended to provide that the motion for dismissal at the close of the plaintiff's evidence shall apply only to non-jury cases (including cases tried with an advisory jury). Hereafter the correct motion in jury-tried cases will be the motion for a directed verdict. This involves no change of substance. It should be noted that the court upon a motion for a directed verdict may in appropriate circumstances deny that motion and grant instead a new trial, or a voluntary dismissal without prejudice under Rule 41(a)(2). See 6 *Moore's Federal Practice* ¶ 59.08[5] (2d ed. 1954); *cf. Cone v. West Virginia Pulp & Paper Co.,* 330 U.S. 212, 217, 67 S.Ct. 752, 91 L.Ed. 849 (1947).

The first sentence of Rule 41(b), providing for dismissal for failure to prosecute or to comply with the Rules or any order of court, and the general provisions of the last sentence remain applicable in jury as well as non-jury cases.

The amendment of the last sentence of Rule 41(b) indicates that a dismissal for lack of an indispensable party does not operate as an adjudication on the merits. Such a dismissal does not bar a new action, for it is based merely "on a plaintiff's failure to comply with a precondition requisite to the Court's going forward to determine the merits of his substantive claim." See *Costello v. United States,* 365 U.S. 265, 284–288, 81 S.Ct. 534, 5 L.Ed.2d 551 & n. 5 (1961); *Mallow v. Hinde,* 12

New matter is shown in italics; matter to be omitted is lined through

Wheat. (25 U.S.) 193, 6 L.Ed. 599 (1827); Clark, *Code Pleading* 602 (2d ed. 1947); *Restatement of Judgments* § 49, comm. a, b (1942). This amendment corrects an omission from the rule and is consistent with an earlier amendment, effective in 1948, adding "the defense of failure to join an indispensable party" to clause (1) of Rule 12(h).

Rule 49. Special Verdicts and Interrogatories

(b) General Verdict Accompanied by Answer to Interrogatories. The court may submit to the jury, together with appropriate forms for a general verdict, written interrogatories upon one or more issues of fact the decision of which is necessary to a verdict. The court shall give such explanation or instruction as may be necessary to enable the jury both to make answers to the interrogatories and to render a general verdict, and the court shall direct the jury both to make written answers and to render a general verdict. When the general verdict and the answers are harmonious, ~~the court shall direct the entry of~~ the appropriate judgment upon the verdict and answers *shall be entered pursuant to Rule 58*. When the answers are consistent with each other but one or more is inconsistent with the general verdict, ~~the court may direct the entry of~~ judgment *may be entered pursuant to Rule 58* in accordance with the answers, notwithstanding the general verdict, or *the court* may return the jury for further consideration of its answers and verdict or may order a new trial. When the answers are inconsistent with each other and one or more is likewise inconsistent with the general verdict, ~~the court shall not direct the entry of~~ judgment *shall not be entered,* but *the court* ~~may~~ *shall* return the jury for further consideration of its answers and verdict or ~~may~~ *shall* order a new trial.

Advisory Committee's Note

This amendment conforms to the amendment of Rule 58. See the Advisory Committee's Note to Rule 58, as amended.

Rule 50. Motion for a Directed Verdict *and for Judgment Notwithstanding the Verdict*

(a) *Motion for Directed Verdict:* **When Made~~;~~ Effect.** A party who moves for a directed verdict at the close of the evidence offered by an opponent may offer evidence in the event that the motion is not granted, without having reserved the right so to do and to the same extent as if the motion had not been made. A motion for a directed verdict which is not granted is not a waiver of trial by jury even though all parties to the action have moved for directed verdicts. A motion for a directed verdict shall state

---

New matter is shown in italics; matter to be omitted is lined through

the specific grounds therefor. *The order of the court granting a motion for a directed verdict is effective without any assent of the jury.*

(b) Reservation of Decision on Motion. *Motion for Judgment Notwithstanding the Verdict.* Whenever a motion for a directed verdict made at the close of all the evidence is denied or for any reason is not granted, the court is deemed to have submitted the action to the jury subject to a later determination of the legal questions raised by the motion. Within 10 days after the reception of a verdict *Not later than 10 days after entry of judgment,* a party who has moved for a directed verdict may move to have the verdict and any judgment entered thereon set aside and to have judgment entered in accordance with his motion for a directed verdict; or if a verdict was not returned such party, within 10 days after the jury has been discharged, may move for judgment in accordance with his motion for a directed verdict. A motion for a new trial may be joined with this motion, or a new trial may be prayed for in the alternative. If a verdict was returned the court may allow the judgment to stand or may reopen the judgment and either order a new trial or direct the entry of judgment as if the requested verdict had been directed. If no verdict was returned the court may direct the entry of judgment as if the requested verdict had been directed or may order a new trial.

(c) Same: Conditional Rulings on Grant of Motion.

(1) If the motion for judgment notwithstanding the verdict, provided for in subdivision (b) of this rule, is granted, the court shall also rule on the motion for a new trial, if any, by determining whether it should be granted if the judgment is thereafter vacated or reversed, and shall specify the grounds for granting or denying the motion for the new trial. If the motion for a new trial is thus conditionally granted, the order thereon does not affect the finality of the judgment. In case the motion for a new trial has been conditionally granted and the judgment is reversed on appeal, the new trial shall proceed unless the appellate court has otherwise ordered. In case the motion for a new trial has been conditionally denied, the appellee on appeal may assert error in that denial; and if the judgment is reversed on appeal, subsequent proceedings shall be in accordance with the order of the appellate court.

(2) The party whose verdict has been set aside on motion for judgment notwithstanding the verdict may serve a motion for a new trial pursuant to Rule 59 not later than 10 days after entry of the judgment notwithstanding the verdict.

New matter is shown in italics; matter to be omitted is lined through

(d) Same: Denial of Motion. If the motion for judgment notwithstanding the verdict is denied, the party who prevailed on that motion may, as appellee, assert grounds entitling him to a new trial in the event the appellate court concludes that the trial court erred in denying the motion for judgment notwithstanding the verdict. If the appellate court reverses the judgment, nothing in this rule precludes it from determining that the appellee is entitled to a new trial, or from directing the trial court to determine whether a new trial shall be granted.

Advisory Committee's Note

Subdivision (a). The practice, after the court has granted a motion for a directed verdict, of requiring the jury to express assent to a verdict they did not reach by their own deliberations serves no useful purpose and may give offense to the members of the jury. See 2B Barron & Holtzoff, *Federal Practice & Procedure* § 1072, at 367 (Wright ed. 1961); Blume, *Origin and Development of the Directed Verdict,* 48 Mich.L.Rev. 555, 582–85, 589–90 (1950). The final sentence of the subdivision, added by amendment, provides that the court's order granting a motion for a directed verdict is effective in itself, and that no action need be taken by the foreman or other members of the jury. See Ariz.R.Civ.P. 50(c); *cf.* Fed.R. Crim.P. 29(a). No change is intended in the standard to be applied in deciding the motion. To assure this interpretation, and in the interest of simplicity, the traditional term, "directed verdict," is retained.

Subdivision (b). A motion for judgment notwithstanding the verdict will not lie unless it was preceded by a motion for a directed verdict made at the close of all the evidence.

The amendment of the second sentence of this subdivision sets the time limit for making the motion for judgment n. o. v. at 10 days after the entry of judgment, rather than 10 days after the reception of the verdict. Thus the time provision is made consistent with that contained in Rule 59(b) (time for motion for new trial) and Rule 52(b) (time for motion to amend findings by the court).

Subdivision (c) deals with the situation where a party joins a motion for a new trial with his motion for judgment n. o. v., or prays for a new trial in the alternative, and the motion for judgment n. o. v. is granted. The procedure to be followed in making rulings on the motion for the new trial, and the consequences of the rulings thereon, were partly set out in *Montgomery Ward & Co. v. Duncan,* 311 U.S. 243, 253, 61 S.Ct. 189, 85 L.Ed. 147 (1940), and have been further elaborated in later cases. See *Cone v. West Virginia Pulp & Paper Co.,* 330 U.S. 212, 67 S.Ct. 752, 91 L.Ed. 849 (1947); *Globe Liquor Co., Inc. v. San Roman,* 332 U.S. 571, 68 S.Ct. 246, 92 L.Ed. 177 (1948); *Fountain v. Filson,* 336 U.S. 681, 69 S.Ct. 754, 93 L.Ed. 971 (1949); *Johnson v. New York, N. H. & H. R. R. Co.,* 344 U.S. 48, 73 S.Ct. 125, 97 L.Ed. 77 (1952). However, courts as well as counsel have often misunderstood the procedure, and it will be helpful to summarize the proper practice in the text of the rule. The amendments do not alter the effects of a jury verdict or the scope of appellate review.

In the situation mentioned, *subdivision (c)(1)* requires that the court make a "conditional" ruling on the new-trial motion, *i. e.,* a ruling which goes on the assumption that the motion for judgment n. o. v. was erroneously granted and will be reversed or vacated; and the court is required to state its grounds for the conditional ruling. Subdivision (c)(1) then spells out the consequences of a reversal of the judgment in the light of the conditional ruling on the new-trial motion.

If the motion for new trial has been conditionally granted, and the judgment is reversed, "the new trial shall proceed unless the appellate court has otherwise ordered." The party against whom the judgment n. o. v. was entered below may, as appellant, besides seeking to overthrow that judgment, also attack the conditional grant of the new trial. And the appellate court, if it reverses the judgment n. o. v., may in an appropriate case also reverse the conditional grant of the new trial and direct that judgment be entered on the verdict. See *Bailey v. Slentz,* 189 F.2d 406 (10th Cir. 1951); *Moist Cold Refrigerator Co. v. Lou Johnson Co.,* 249 F.2d 246 (9th Cir. 1957), *cert. denied,* 356 U.S. 968, 78 S.Ct. 1008, 2 L.Ed.2d 1074 (1958); *Peters v. Smith,* 221 F.2d 721 (3d Cir. 1955); *Dailey v. Timmer,* 292 F.2d 824 (3d Cir. 1961), explaining *Lind v. Schenley Industries, Inc.,* 278 F.2d 79 (3d Cir.), *cert. denied,* 364 U.S. 835, 81 S.Ct. 58, 5 L.Ed.2d 60 (1960); *Cox v. Pennsylvania R. R.,* 120 A.2d 214 (D.C.Mun.Ct.App.1956); 3 Barron & Holtzoff, *Federal Practice & Procedure* § 1302.1 at 346–47 (Wright ed. 1958); 6 *Moore's Federal Practice* ¶ 59.16 at 3915 n. 8a (2d ed. 1954).

If the motion for a new trial has been conditionally denied, and the judgment is reversed, "subsequent proceedings shall be in accordance with the order of the appellate court." The party in whose favor judgment n. o. v. was entered below may, as appellee, besides seeking to uphold that judgment, also urge on the appellate court that the trial court committed error in conditionally denying the new trial. The appellee may assert this error in his brief, without taking a cross-appeal. *Cf. Patterson v. Pennsylvania R. R.,* 238 F.2d 645, 650 (6th Cir. 1956); *Hughes v. St. Louis Nat. L. Baseball Club, Inc.,* 359 Mo. 993, 997, 224 S.W.2d 989, 992 (1949). If the appellate court concludes that the judgment cannot stand, but accepts the appellee's contention that there was error in the conditional denial of the new trial, it may order a new trial in lieu of directing the entry of judgment upon the verdict.

Subdivision (c)(2), which also deals with the situation where the trial court has granted the motion for judgment n. o. v., states that the verdict-winner may apply to the trial court for a new trial pursuant to Rule 59 after the judgment n. o. v. has been entered against him. In arguing to the trial court in opposition to the motion for judgment n. o. v., the verdict-winner may, and often will, contend that he is entitled, at the least, to a new trial, and the court has a range of discretion to grant a new trial or (where plaintiff won the verdict) to order a dismissal of the action without prejudice instead of granting judgment n. o. v. See *Cone v. West Virginia Pulp & Paper Co., supra,* 330 U.S. at 217, 218, 67 S.Ct. at 755, 756, 91 L.Ed. 849. Subdivision (c)(2) is a reminder that the verdict-winner is entitled, even after entry of judgment n. o. v. against him, to move for a new trial in the usual course. If in these circumstances the motion is granted, the judgment is superseded.

In some unusual circumstances, however, the grant of the new-trial motion may be only conditional, and the judgment will not be superseded. See the situation in *Tribble v. Bruin,* 279 F.2d 424 (4th Cir. 1960) (upon a verdict for plaintiff, defendant moves for and obtains judgment n. o. v.; plaintiff moves for a new trial on the ground of inadequate damages; trial court might properly have granted plaintiff's motion, conditional upon reversal of the judgment n. o. v.).

Even if the verdict-winner makes no motion for a new trial, he is entitled upon his appeal from the judgment n. o. v. not only to urge that that judgment should be reversed and judgment entered upon the verdict, but that errors were committed during the trial which at the least entitle him to a new trial.

New matter is shown in italics; matter to be omitted is lined through

Subdivision (d) deals with the situation where judgment has been entered on the jury verdict, the motion for judgment n. o. v. and any motion for a new trial having been denied by the trial court. The verdict-winner, as appellee, besides seeking to uphold the judgment, may urge upon the appellate court that in case the trial court is found to have erred in entering judgment on the verdict, there are grounds for granting him a new trial instead of directing the entry of judgment for his opponent. In appropriate cases the appellate court is not precluded from itself directing that a new trial be had. See *Weade v. Dichmann, Wright & Pugh, Inc.,* 337 U.S. 801, 69 S.Ct. 1326, 93 L.Ed. 1704 (1949). Nor is it precluded in proper cases from remanding the case for a determination by the trial court as to whether a new trial should be granted. The latter course is advisable where the grounds urged are suitable for the exercise of trial court discretion.

Subdivision (d) does not attempt a regulation of all aspects of the procedure where the motion for judgment n. o. v. and any accompanying motion for a new trial are denied, since the problems have not been fully canvassed in the decisions and the procedure is in some respects still in a formative stage. It is, however, designed to give guidance on certain important features of the practice.

Rule 52.   Findings by the Court

(a) **Effect.** In all actions tried upon the facts without a jury or with an advisory jury, the court shall find the facts specially and state separately its conclusions of law thereon, and ~~direct the entry of the appropriate~~ judgment *shall be entered pursuant to Rule 58;* and in granting or refusing interlocutory injunctions the court shall similarly set forth the findings of fact and conclusions of law which constitute the grounds of its action. Requests for findings are not necessary for purposes of review. Findings of fact shall not be set aside unless clearly erroneous, and due regard shall be given to the opportunity of the trial court to judge of the credibility of the witnesses. The findings of a master, to the extent that the court adopts them, shall be considered as the findings of the court. If an opinion or memorandum of decision is filed, it will be sufficient if the findings of fact and conclusions of law appear therein. Findings of fact and conclusions of law are unnecessary on decisions of motions under Rules 12 or 56 or any other motion except as provided in Rule 41(b).

Advisory Committee's Note

This amendment conforms to the amendment of Rule 58. See the Advisory Committee's Note to Rule 58, as amended.

Rule 56.   Summary Judgment

(c) **Motion and Proceedings Thereon.** The motion shall be served at least 10 days before the time fixed for the hearing. The adverse party prior to the day of hearing may serve opposing

---

New matter is shown in *italics;* matter to be omitted is lined through

affidavits. The judgment sought shall be rendered forthwith if the pleadings, depositions, *answers to interrogatories,* and admissions on file, together with the affidavits, if any, show that there is no genuine issue as to any material fact and that the moving party is entitled to a judgment as a matter of law. A summary judgment, interlocutory in character, may be rendered on the issue of liability alone although there is a genuine issue as to the amount of damages.

(e) **Form of Affidavits; Further Testimony;** *Defense Required.* Supporting and opposing affidavits shall be made on personal knowledge, shall set forth such facts as would be admissible in evidence, and shall show affirmatively that the affiant is competent to testify to the matters stated therein. Sworn or certified copies of all papers or parts thereof referred to in an affidavit shall be attached thereto or served therewith. The court may permit affidavits to be supplemented or opposed by depositions, *answers to interrogatories,* or by further affidavits. *When a motion for summary judgment is made and supported as provided in this rule, an adverse party may not rest upon the mere allegations or denials of his pleading, but his response, by affidavits or as otherwise provided in this rule, must set forth specific facts showing that there is a genuine issue for trial. If he does not so respond, summary judgment, if appropriate, shall be entered against him.*

Advisory Committee's Note

Subdivision (c). By the amendment "answers to interrogatories" are included among the materials which may be considered on motion for summary judgment. The phrase was inadvertently omitted from the rule, see 3 Barron & Holtzoff, *Federal Practice & Procedure* 159–60 (Wright ed. 1958), and the courts have generally reached by interpretation the result which will hereafter be required by the text of the amended rule. See Annot., 74 A.L.R.2d 984 (1960).

Subdivision (e). The words "answers to interrogatories" are added in the third sentence of this subdivision to conform to the amendment of subdivision (c).

The last two sentences are added to overcome a line of cases, chiefly in the Third Circuit, which has impaired the utility of the summary judgment device. A typical case is as follows: A party supports his motion for summary judgment by affidavits or other evidentiary matter sufficient to show that there is no genuine issue as to a material fact. The adverse party, in opposing the motion, does not produce any evidentiary matter, or produces some but not enough to establish that there is a genuine issue for trial. Instead, the adverse party rests on averments of his pleadings which on their face present an issue. In this situation Third Circuit cases have taken the view that summary judgment must be denied, at least if the averments are "well-pleaded," and not supposititious, conclusory, or ultimate. See *Frederick Hart & Co., Inc. v. Recordgraph Corp.,* 169 F.2d 580 (3d Cir. 1948); *United States ex rel. Kolton v. Halpern,* 260 F.2d 590 (3d Cir. 1958); *United States ex rel. Nobles v. Ivey Bros. Constr. Co., Inc.,* 191 F.Supp. 383 (D.Del.1961); *Jamison v. Pennsylvania Salt Mfg. Co.,* 22 F.R.D. 238 (W.D.Pa.1958); *Bunny Bear, Inc. v.*

New matter is shown in italics; matter to be omitted is lined through

Dennis Mitchell Industries, 139 F.Supp. 542 (E.D.Pa.1956); *Levy v. Equitable Life Assur. Society,* 18 F.R.D. 164 (E.D.Pa.1955).

The very mission of the summary judgment procedure is to pierce the pleadings and to assess the proof in order to see whether there is a genuine need for trial. The Third Circuit doctrine, which permits the pleadings themselves to stand in the way of granting an otherwise justified summary judgment, is incompatible with the basic purpose of the rule. See 6 *Moore's Federal Practice* 2069 (2d ed. 1953); 3 Barron & Holtzoff, *supra,* § 1235.1.

It is hoped that the amendment will contribute to the more effective utilization of the salutary device of summary judgment.

The amendment is not intended to derogate from the solemnity of the pleadings. Rather it recognizes that, despite the best efforts of counsel to make his pleadings accurate, they may be overwhelmingly contradicted by the proof available to his adversary.

Nor is the amendment designed to affect the ordinary standards applicable to the summary judgment motion. So, for example: Where an issue as to a material fact cannot be resolved without observation of the demeanor of witnesses in order to evaluate their credibility, summary judgment is not appropriate. Where the evidentiary matter in support of the motion does not establish the absence of a genuine issue, summary judgment must be denied even if no opposing evidentiary matter is presented. And summary judgment may be inappropriate where the party opposing it shows under subdivision (f) that he cannot at the time present facts essential to justify his opposition.

Rule 58. Entry of Judgment

~~Unless the court otherwise directs and subject to the provisions of Rule 54(b), judgment upon the verdict of a jury shall be entered forthwith by the clerk; but the court shall direct the appropriate judgment to be entered upon a special verdict or upon a general verdict accompanied by answers to interrogatories returned by a jury pursuant to Rule 40. When the court directs that a party recover only money or costs or that all relief be denied, the clerk shall enter judgment forthwith upon receipt by him of the direction; but when the court directs entry of judgment for other relief, the judge shall promptly settle or approve the form of the judgment and direct that it be entered by the clerk. The notation of a judgment in the civil docket as provided by Rule 79(a) constitutes the entry of the judgment; and the judgment is not effective before such entry. The entry of the judgment shall not be delayed for the taxing of costs.~~

Subject to the provisions of Rule 54(b): (1) upon a general verdict of a jury, or upon a decision by the court that a party shall recover only a sum certain or costs or that all relief shall be denied, the clerk, unless the court otherwise orders, shall forthwith prepare, sign, and enter the judgment without awaiting any direction by the court; (2) upon a decision by the court granting other relief,

---

New matter is shown in italics; matter to be omitted is lined through

or upon a special verdict or a general verdict accompanied by answers to interrogatories, the court shall promptly approve the form of the judgment, and the clerk shall thereupon enter it. Every judgment shall be set forth on a separate document. A judgment is effective only when so set forth and when entered as provided in Rule 79(a). Entry of the judgment shall not be delayed for the taxing of costs. Attorneys shall not submit forms of judgment except upon direction of the court, and these directions shall not be given as a matter of course.

Advisory Committee's Note

Under the present rule a distinction has sometimes been made between judgments on general jury verdicts, on the one hand, and, on the other, judgments upon decisions of the court that a party shall recover only money or costs or that all relief shall be denied. In the first situation, it is clear that the clerk should enter the judgment without awaiting a direction by the court unless the court otherwise orders. In the second situation it was intended that the clerk should similarly enter the judgment forthwith upon the court's decision; but because of the separate listing in the rule, and the use of the phrase "upon receipt . . . of the direction," the rule has sometimes been interpreted as requiring the clerk to await a separate direction of the court. All these judgments are usually uncomplicated, and should be handled in the same way. The amended rule accordingly deals with them as a single group in clause (1) (substituting the expression "only a sum certain" for the present expression "only money"), and requires the clerk to prepare, sign, and enter them forthwith, without awaiting court direction, unless the court makes a contrary order. (The clerk's duty is ministerial and may be performed by a deputy clerk in the name of the clerk. See 28 U.S.C. § 956; *cf. Gilbertson v. United States,* 168 Fed. 672 (7th Cir. 1909).) The more complicated judgments described in clause (2) must be approved by the court before they are entered.

Rule 58 is designed to encourage all reasonable speed in formulating and entering the judgment when the case has been decided. Participation by the attorneys through the submission of forms of judgment involves needless expenditure of time and effort and promotes delay, except in special cases where counsel's assistance can be of real value. See *Matteson v. United States,* 240 F.2d 517, 518–19 (2d Cir. 1956). Accordingly, the amended rule provides that attorneys shall not submit forms of judgment unless directed to do so by the court. This applies to the judgments mentioned in clause (2) as well as clause (1).

Hitherto some difficulty has arisen, chiefly where the court has written an opinion or memorandum containing some apparently directive or dispositive words, *e.g.,* "the plaintiff's motion [for summary judgment] is granted," see *United States v. F. & M. Schaefer Brewing Co.,* 356 U.S. 227, 229, 78 S.Ct. 674, 2 L.Ed.2d 721 (1958). Clerks on occasion have viewed these opinions or memoranda as being in themselves a sufficient basis for entering judgment in the civil docket as provided by Rule 79(a). However, where the opinion or memorandum has not contained all the elements of a judgment, or where the judge has later signed a formal judgment, it has become a matter of doubt whether the purported entry of judgment was effective, starting the time running for post-verdict motions and for the purpose of appeal. See *id.*; and *compare Blanchard v. Commonwealth Oil Co.,* 294 F.2d 834 (5th Cir. 1961); *United States v. Higginson,* 238 F.2d 439 (1st Cir. 1956); *Danzig v. Virgin Isle Hotel, Inc.,* 278 F.2d 580 (3d Cir. 1960); *Sears v. Austin,* 282 F.2d 340

New matter is shown in italics; matter to be omitted is lined through

(9th Cir. 1960), *with Matteson v. United States, supra; Erstling v. Southern Bell Tel. & Tel. Co.,* 255 F.2d 93 (5th Cir. 1958); *Barta v. Oglala Sioux Tribe,* 259 F.2d 553 (8th Cir. 1958), *cert. denied,* 358 U.S. 932, 79 S.Ct. 320, 3 L.Ed.2d 304 (1959); *Beacon Fed. S. & L. Assn. v. Federal Home L. Bank Bd.,* 266 F.2d 246 (7th Cir.), *cert. denied,* 361 U.S. 823, 80 S.Ct. 70, 4 L.Ed.2d 67 (1959); *Ram v. Paramount Film D. Corp.,* 278 F.2d 191 (4th Cir. 1960).

The amended rule eliminates these uncertainties by requiring that there be a judgment set out on a separate document—distinct from any opinion or memorandum—which provides the basis for the entry of judgment. That judgments shall be on separate documents is also indicated in Rule 79(b); and see General Rule 10 of the U. S. District Courts for the Eastern and Southern Districts of New York; *Ram v. Paramount Film D. Corp., supra,* at 194.

See the amendment of Rule 79(a) and the new specimen forms of judgment, Forms 31 and 32.

See also Rule 55(b)(1) and (2) covering the subject of judgments by default.

Rule 71A.   Condemnation of Property

(d) Process.

(3) Service of Notice.   (i) Personal service. Personal service of the notice (but without copies of the complaint) shall be made in accordance with Rule 4(c) and (d) upon a defendant who resides within the United States or its territories or insular possessions and whose residence is known. ~~The provisions of Rule 4(f) shall not be applicable.~~

Advisory Committee's Note

This amendment conforms to the amendment of Rule 4(f).

Rule 77.   District Courts and Clerks

(c) Clerk's Office and Orders by Clerk. The clerk's office with the clerk or a deputy in attendance shall be open during business hours on all days except *Saturdays,* Sundays, and legal holidays~~,~~ *but a district court may provide by local rule or order that its clerk's office shall be open for specified hours on Saturdays or particular legal holidays other than New Year's Day, Washington's Birthday, Memorial Day, Independence Day, Labor Day, Veterans Day, Thanksgiving Day, and Christmas Day.* All motions and applications in the clerk's office for issuing mesne process, for issuing final process to enforce and execute judgments, for entering defaults or judgments by default, and for other proceedings which do not require allowance or order of the court are grantable of course by the clerk; but his action may be suspended or altered or rescinded by the court upon cause shown.

New matter is shown in italics; matter to be omitted is lined through

(d) Notice of Orders or Judgments. Immediately upon the entry of an order or judgment the clerk shall serve a notice of the entry by mail in the manner provided for in Rule 5 upon ~~every~~ *each* party ~~affected thereby~~ who is not in default for failure to appear, and shall make a note in the docket of the mailing. Such mailing is sufficient notice for all purposes for which notice of the entry of an order is required by these rules; but any party may in addition serve a notice of such entry in the manner provided in Rule 5 for the service of papers. Lack of notice of the entry by the clerk does not affect the time to appeal or relieve or authorize the court to relieve a party for failure to appeal within the time allowed, except as permitted in Rule 73(a).

Advisory Committee's Note

Subdivision (c). The amendment authorizes closing of the clerk's office on Saturday as far as civil business is concerned. However, a district court may require its clerk's office to remain open for specified hours on Saturdays or "legal holidays" other than those enumerated. ("Legal holiday" is defined in Rule 6(a), as amended.) The clerk's offices of many district courts have customarily remained open on some of the days appointed as holidays by State law. This practice could be continued by local rule or order.

Subdivision (d). This amendment conforms to the amendment of Rule 5(a). See the Advisory Committee's Note to that amendment.

Rule 79.   Books and Records Kept by the Clerk and Entries Therein

(a) Civil Docket. The clerk shall keep a book known as "civil docket" of such form and style as may be prescribed by the Director of the Administrative Office of the United States Courts with the approval of the Judicial Conference of the United States, and shall enter therein each civil action to which these rules are made applicable. Actions shall be assigned consecutive file numbers. The file number of each action shall be noted on the folio of the docket whereon the first entry of the action is made. All papers filed with the clerk, all process issued and returns made thereon, all appearances, orders, verdicts, and judgments shall be ~~noted~~ *entered* chronologically in the civil docket on the folio assigned to the action and shall be marked with its file number. These ~~notations~~ *entries* shall be brief but shall show the nature of each paper filed or writ issued and the substance of each order or judgment of the court and of the returns showing execution of process. The ~~notation~~ *entry* of an order or judgment shall show the date the ~~notation~~ *entry* is made. When in an action trial by jury has been properly demanded or ordered the clerk shall enter the word "jury" on the folio assigned to that action.

New matter is shown in italics; matter to be omitted is lined through

Advisory Committee's Note

The terminology is clarified without any change of the prescribed practice. See amended Rule 58, and the Advisory Committee's Note thereto.

Rule 81. Applicability in General

(a) To What Proceedings Applicable.

(4) These rules do not alter the method prescribed by the Act of February 18, 1922, c. 57, § 2 (42 Stat. 388), U.S.C., Title 7, § 292; or by the Act of June 10, 1930, c. 436, § 7 (46 Stat. 534), as amended, U.S.C., Title 7, § 499g(c), for instituting proceedings in the United States district courts to review orders of the Secretary of Agriculture; or prescribed by the Act of June 25, 1934, c. 742, § 2 (48 Stat. 1214), U.S.C., Title 15, § 522, for instituting proceedings to review orders of the Secretary of ~~Commerce~~ *the Interior*; or prescribed by the Act of February 22, 1935, c. 18, § 5 (49 Stat. 31), U.S.C., Title 15, § 715d(c), as extended, for instituting proceedings to review orders of petroleum control boards; but the conduct of such proceedings in the district courts shall be made to conform to these rules so far as applicable.

(6) These rules apply to proceedings for enforcement or review of compensation orders under the Longshoremen's and Harbor Workers' Compensation Act, Act of March 4, 1927, c. 509, §§ 18, 21 (44 Stat. 1434, 1436), as amended, U.S.C., Title 33, §§ 918, 921, except to the extent that matters of procedure are provided for in that Act. The provisions for service by publication and for answer in proceedings to cancel certificates of citizenship under the ~~Act of October 14, 1940, c. 876, § 338 (54 Stat. 1158), U.S.C., Title 8, § 738,~~ *Act of June 27, 1952, c. 477, Title III, c. 2, § 340 (66 Stat. 260), U.S.C., Title 8, § 1451,* remain in effect.

(c) Removed Actions. These rules apply to civil actions removed to the United States district courts from the state courts and govern procedure after removal. Repleading is not necessary unless the court so orders. In a removed action in which the defendant has not answered, he shall answer or present the other defenses or objections available to him under these rules within 20 days after the receipt through service or otherwise of a copy of the initial pleading setting forth the claim for relief upon which the action or proceeding is based, or within 20 days after the service of summons upon such initial pleading, then filed, or within 5 days after the filing of the petition for removal, whichever period is longest. If at the time of removal all necessary pleadings have been served, a party entitled to trial by jury under Rule 38 shall be accorded it, if his demand therefor is served within 10 days

---

New matter is shown in italics; matter to be omitted is lined through

after the petition for removal is filed if he is the petitioner, or if he is not the petitioner within 10 days after service on him of the notice of filing the petition. *A party who, prior to removal, has made an express demand for trial by jury in accordance with state law, need not make a demand after removal. If state law applicable in the court from which the case is removed does not require the parties to make express demands in order to claim trial by jury, they need not make demands after removal unless the court directs that they do so within a specified time if they desire to claim trial by jury. The court may make this direction on its own motion and shall do so as a matter of course at the request of any party. The failure of a party to make demand as directed constitutes a waiver by him of trial by jury.*

(f) References to Officer of the United States. Under any rule in which reference is made to an officer or agency of the United States, the term "officer" includes a ~~collector~~ *district director* of internal revenue, a former *district director or* collector of internal revenue, or the personal representative of a deceased *district director or* collector of internal revenue.

Advisory Committee's Note

Subdivision (a)(4). This change reflects the transfer of functions from the Secretary of Commerce to the Secretary of the Interior made by 1939 Reorganization Plan No. II, § 4(e), 53 Stat. 1433.

Subdivision (a)(6). The proper current reference is to the 1952 statute superseding the 1940 statute.

Subdivision (c). Most of the cases have held that a party who has made a proper express demand for jury trial in the State court is not required to renew the demand after removal of the action. *Zakoscielny v. Waterman Steamship Corp.,* 16 F.R.D. 314 (D.Md.1954); *Talley v. American Bakeries Co.,* 15 F.R.D. 391 (E.D.Tenn. 1954); *Rehrer v. Service Trucking Co.,* 15 F.R.D. 113 (D.Del.1953); 5 *Moore's Federal Practice* ¶ 38.39[3] (2d ed. 1951); 1 Barron & Holtzoff, *Federal Practice & Procedure* § 132 (Wright ed. 1960). But there is some authority to the contrary. *Petsel v. Chicago, B. & Q. R. Co.,* 101 F.Supp. 1006 (S.D.Iowa 1951); *Nelson v. American Nat. Bank & Trust Co.,* 9 F.R.D. 680 (E.D.Tenn.1950). The amendment adopts the preponderant view.

In order still further to avoid unintended waivers of jury trial, the amendment provides that where by State law applicable in the court from which the case is removed a party is entitled to jury trial without making an express demand, he need not make a demand after removal. However, the district court for calendar or other purposes may on its own motion direct the parties to state whether they demand a jury, and the court must make such a direction upon the request of any party. Under the amendment a district court may find it convenient to establish a routine practice of giving these directions to the parties in appropriate cases.

Subdivision (f). The amendment recognizes the change of nomenclature made by Treasury Dept. Order 150–26(2), 18 Fed.Reg. 3499 (1953).

As to a special problem arising under Rule 25 (Substitution of parties) in actions for refund of taxes, see the Advisory Committee's Note to the amendment of Rule 25(d), effective July 19, 1961; and 4 *Moore's Federal Practice* ¶ 25.09 at 531 (2d ed. 1950).

*

New matter is shown in italics; matter to be omitted is lined through

CERTAIN OF THE AMENDMENTS OF FEDERAL RULES OF CIVIL PROCEDURE ADOPTED BY THE SUPREME COURT OF THE UNITED STATES ON FEBRUARY 28, 1966, EFFECTIVE JULY 1, 1966, WITH ADVISORY COMMITTEE'S NOTES THEREON

[Amendments here omitted: Changes in Rules 4, 6, 8, 14, 26, 38, 41, 42, 43, 44, 47, 53, 68, 73, 74, 75, 81 and Forms 2 and 15; and addition of new Rule 65.1 and Supplemental Rules A, B, C, D, E, and F for Certain Admiralty and Maritime Claims.]

Rule 1.

SCOPE OF RULES

These rules govern the procedure in the United States district courts in all suits of a civil nature whether cognizable as cases at law or in equity *or in admiralty,* with the exceptions stated in Rule 81. They shall be construed to secure the just, speedy, and inexpensive determination of every action.

Advisory Committee's Note

This is the fundamental change necessary to effect unification of the civil and admiralty procedure. Just as the 1938 rules abolished the distinction between actions at law and suits in equity, this change would abolish the distinction between civil actions and suits in admiralty. See also Rule 81.

Rule 9.

PLEADING SPECIAL MATTERS

(h) Admiralty and Maritime Claims. A pleading or count setting forth a claim for relief within the admiralty and maritime jurisdiction that is also within the jurisdiction of the district court on some other ground may contain a statement identifying the claim as an admiralty or maritime claim for the purposes of Rules 14(c), 26(a), 38(e), 73(h), 82, and the Supplemental Rules for Certain Admiralty and Maritime Claims. If the claim is cognizable only in admiralty it is an admiralty or maritime claim for those purposes whether so identified or not. The amendment of a plead-

---

New matter is shown in italics; matter to be omitted is lined through

ing to add or withdraw an identifying statement is governed by the principles of Rule 15.

Advisory Committee's Note

Certain distinctive features of the admiralty practice must be preserved for what are now suits in admiralty. This raises the question: After unification, when a single form of action is established, how will the counterpart of the present suit in admiralty be identifiable? In part the question is easily answered. Some claims for relief can only be suits in admiralty, either because the admiralty jurisdiction is exclusive or because no nonmaritime ground of federal jurisdiction exists. Many claims, however, are cognizable by the district courts whether asserted in admiralty or in a civil action, assuming the existence of a nonmaritime ground of jurisdiction. Thus at present the pleader has power to determine procedural consequences by the way in which he exercises the classic privilege given by the saving-to-suitors clause (28 U.S.C. § 1333) or by equivalent statutory provisions. For example, a longshoreman's claim for personal injuries suffered by reason of the unseaworthiness of a vessel may be asserted in a suit in admiralty or, if diversity of citizenship exists, in a civil action. One of the important procedural consequences is that in the civil action either party may demand a jury trial, while in the suit in admiralty there is no right to jury trial except as provided by statute.

It is no part of the purpose of unification to inject a right to jury trial into those admiralty cases in which that right is not provided by statute. Similarly, as will be more specifically noted below, there is no disposition to change the present law as to interlocutory appeals in admiralty, or as to the venue of suits in admiralty; and, of course, there is no disposition to inject into the civil practice as it now is the distinctively maritime remedies (maritime attachment and garnishment, actions in rem, possessory, petitory, and partition actions and limitation of liability). The unified rules must therefore provide some device for preserving the present power of the pleader to determine whether these historically maritime procedures shall be applicable to his claim or not; the pleader must be afforded some means of designating his claim as the counterpart of the present suit in admiralty, where its character as such is not clear.

The problem is different from the similar one concerning the identification of claims that were formerly suits in equity. While that problem is not free from complexities, it is broadly true that the modern counterpart of the suit in equity is distinguishable from the former action at law by the character of the relief sought. This mode of identification is possible in only a limited category of admiralty cases. In large numbers of cases the relief sought in admiralty is simple money damages, indistinguishable from the remedy afforded by the common law. This is true, for example, in the case of the longshoreman's action for personal injuries stated above. After unification has abolished the distinction between civil actions and suits in admiralty, the complaint in such an action would be almost completely ambiguous as to the pleader's intentions regarding the procedure invoked. The allegation of diversity of citizenship might be regarded as a clue indicating an intention to proceed as at present under the saving-to-suitors clause; but this, too, would be ambiguous if there were also reference to the admiralty jurisdiction, and the pleader ought not to be required to forego mention of all available jurisdictional grounds.

Other methods of solving the problem were carefully explored, but the Advisory Committee concluded that the preferable solution is to allow the pleader who now has power to determine procedural consequences by filing a suit in admiralty to exercise that power under unification, for the limited instances in which

---

New matter is shown in italics; matter to be omitted is lined through

procedural differences will remain, by a simple statement in his pleading to the effect that the claim is an admiralty or maritime claim.

The choice made by the pleader in identifying or in failing to identify his claim as an admiralty or maritime claim is not an irrevocable election. The rule provides that the amendment of a pleading to add or withdraw an identifying statement is subject to the principles of Rule 15.

Rule 12.

DEFENSES AND OBJECTIONS—WHEN AND HOW PRE-SENTED—BY PLEADING OR MOTION—MOTION FOR JUDGMENT ON THE PLEADINGS

(b) How Presented. Every defense, in law or fact, to a claim for relief in any pleading, whether a claim, counterclaim, cross-claim, or third-party claim, shall be asserted in the responsive pleading thereto if one is required, except that the following defenses may at the option of the pleader be made by motion: (1) lack of jurisdiction over the subject matter, (2) lack of jurisdiction over the person, (3) improper venue, (4) insufficiency of process, (5) insufficiency of service of process, (6) failure to state a claim upon which relief can be granted, (7) failure to join ~~an indispensable~~ *a* party *under Rule 19*. A motion making any of these defenses shall be made before pleading if a further pleading is permitted. No defense or objection is waived by being joined with one or more other defenses or objections in a responsive pleading or motion. If a pleading sets forth a claim for relief to which the adverse party is not required to serve a responsive pleading, he may assert at the trial any defense in law or fact to that claim for relief. If, on a motion asserting the defense numbered (6) to dismiss for failure of the pleading to state a claim upon which relief can be granted, matters outside the pleading are presented to and not excluded by the court, the motion shall be treated as one for summary judgment and disposed of as provided in Rule 56, and all parties shall be given reasonable opportunity to present all material made pertinent to such a motion by Rule 56.

(g) Consolidation of Defenses *in Motion.* A party who makes a motion under this rule may join with it any other motions herein provided for and then available to him. If a party makes a motion under this rule but ~~does not include therein all defenses and objections~~ *omits therefrom any defense or objection* then available to him which this rule permits to be raised by motion, he shall not thereafter make a motion based on ~~any of the defenses or objections~~ *the defense or objection* so omitted, except *a motion* as provided in subdivision (h)*(2)* ~~of this rule~~ *hereof on any of the grounds there stated.*

New matter is shown in italics; matter to be omitted is lined through

(h) Waiver or Preservation of Certain Defenses. ~~A party waives all defenses and objections which he does not present either by motion as hereinbefore provided or, if he has made no motion, in his answer or reply, except (1) that the defense of failure to state a claim upon which relief can be granted, the defense of failure to join an indispensable party, and the objection of failure to state a legal defense to a claim may also be made by a later pleading, if one is permitted, or by motion for judgment on the pleadings or at the trial on the merits, and except (2) that, whenever it appears by suggestion of the parties or otherwise that the court lacks jurisdiction of the subject matter, the court shall dismiss the action. The objection or defense, if made at the trial, shall be disposed of as provided in Rule 15(b) in the light of any evidence that may have been received.~~ *(1) A defense of lack of jurisdiction over the person, improper venue, insufficiency of process, or insufficiency of service of process is waived (A) if omitted from a motion in the circumstances described in subdivision (g), or (B) if it is neither made by motion under this rule nor included in a responsive pleading or an amendment thereof permitted by Rule 15(a) to be made as a matter of course.*

(2) A defense of failure to state a claim upon which relief can be granted, a defense of failure to join a party indispensable under Rule 19, and an objection of failure to state a legal defense to a claim may be made in any pleading permitted or ordered under Rule 7(a), or by motion for judgment on the pleadings, or at the trial on the merits.

(3) Whenever it appears by suggestion of the parties or otherwise that the court lacks jurisdiction of the subject matter, the court shall dismiss the action.

Advisory Committee's Note

Subdivision (b)(7). The terminology of this subdivision is changed to accord with the amendment of Rule 19. See the Advisory Committee's Note to Rule 19, as amended, especially the third paragraph therein before the caption "Subdivision (c)."

Subdivision (g). Subdivision (g) has forbidden a defendant who makes a preanswer motion under this rule from making a further motion presenting any defense or objection which was available to him at the time he made the first motion and which he could have included, but did not in fact include therein. Thus if the defendant moves before answer to dismiss the complaint for failure to state a claim, he is barred from making a further motion presenting the defense of improper venue, if that defense was available to him when he made his original motion. Amended subdivision (g) is to the same effect. This required consolidation of defenses and objections in a Rule 12 motion is salutary in that it works against piecemeal consideration of a case. For exceptions to the requirement of consolidation, see the last clause of subdivision (g), referring to new subdivision (h)(2).

New matter is shown in italics; matter to be omitted is lined through

Subdivision (h). The question has arisen whether an omitted defense which cannot be made the basis of a second motion may nevertheless be pleaded in the answer. Subdivision (h) called for waiver of "* * * defenses and objections which he [defendant] does not present * * * by motion * * * or, if he has made no motion, in his answer * * *." If the clause "if he has made no motion," was read literally, it seemed that the omitted defense was waived and could not be pleaded in the answer. On the other hand, the clause might be read as adding nothing of substance to the preceding words; in that event it appeared that a defense was not waived by reason of being omitted from the motion and might be set up in the answer. The decisions were divided. Favoring waiver, see *Keefe v. Derounian,* 6 F.R.D. 11 (N.D.Ill.1946); *Elbinger v. Precision Metal Workers Corp.,* 18 F.R.D. 467 (E.D.Wis.1956); see also *Rensing v. Turner Aviation Corp.,* 166 F.Supp. 790 (N.D.Ill. 1958); *P. Beiersdorf & Co. v. Duke Laboratories, Inc.,* 10 F.R.D. 282 (S.D.N.Y.1950); *Neset v. Christensen,* 92 F.Supp. 78 (E.D.N.Y.1950). Opposing waiver, see *Phillips v. Baker,* 121 F.2d 752 (9th Cir.1941); *Crum v. Graham,* 32 F.R.D. 173 (D.Mont. 1963) (regretfully following the Phillips case); see also *Birnbaum v. Birrell,* 9 F.R.D. 72 (S.D.N.Y.1948); *Johnson v. Joseph Schlitz Brewing Co.,* 33 F.Supp. 176 (E.D.Tenn.1940); *cf. Carter v. American Bus Lines, Inc.,* 22 F.R.D. 323 (D.Neb.1958).

Amended subdivision (h)(1)(A) eliminates the ambiguity and states that certain specified defenses which were available to a party when he made a preanswer motion, but which he omitted from the motion, are waived. The specified defenses are lack of jurisdiction over the person, improper venue, insufficiency of process, and insufficiency of service of process (see Rule 12(b)(2)–(5)). A party who by motion invites the court to pass upon a threshold defense should bring forward all the specified defenses he then has and thus allow the court to do a reasonably complete job. The waiver reinforces the policy of subdivision (g) forbidding successive motions.

By amended subdivision (h)(1)(B), the specified defenses, even if not waived by the operation of (A), are waived by the failure to raise them by a motion under Rule 12 or in the responsive pleading or any amendment thereof to which the party is entitled as a matter of course. The specified defenses are of such a character that they should not be delayed and brought up for the first time by means of an application to the court to amend the responsive pleading.

Since the language of the subdivisions is made clear, the party is put on fair notice of the effect of his actions and omissions and can guard himself against unintended waiver. It is to be noted that while the defenses specified in subdivision (h)(1) are subject to waiver as there provided, the more substantial defenses of failure to state a claim upon which relief can be granted, failure to join a party indispensible under Rule 19, and failure to state a legal defense to a claim (see Rule 12(b)(6), (7), (f)), as well as the defense of lack of jurisdiction over the subject matter (see Rule 12(b)(1)), are expressly preserved against waiver by amended subdivision (h)(2) and (3).

Rule 13.

COUNTERCLAIM AND CROSS-CLAIM

(h) ~~Additional Parties May Be Brought in~~ *Joinder of Additional Parties.* ~~When the presence of parties other than those to the original action is required for the granting of complete relief in the determination of a counterclaim or cross-claim, the court~~

New matter is shown in italics; matter to be omitted is lined through

~~shall order them to be brought in as defendants as provided in~~
~~these rules, if jurisdiction of them can be obtained and their~~
~~joinder will not deprive the court of jurisdiction of the action.~~
Persons other than those made parties to the original action may be
made parties to a counterclaim or cross-claim in accordance with
the provisions of Rules 19 and 20.

Advisory Committee's Note

Rule 13(h), dealing with the joinder of additional parties to a counterclaim or cross-claim, has partaken of some of the textual difficulties of Rule 19 on necessary joinder of parties. See Advisory Committee's Note to Rule 19, as amended; *cf.* 3 *Moore's Federal Practice* ¶ 13.39 (2d ed. 1963), and Supp. thereto; 1A Barron & Holtzoff, *Federal Practice and Procedure* § 399 (Wright ed. 1960). Rule 13(h) has also been inadequate in failing to call attention to the fact that a party pleading a counterclaim or cross-claim may join additional persons when the conditions for permissive joinder of parties under Rule 20 are satisfied.

The amendment of Rule 13(h) supplies the latter omission by expressly referring to Rule 20, as amended, and also incorporates by direct reference the revised criteria and procedures of Rule 19, as amended. Hereafter, for the purpose of determining who must or may be joined as additional parties to a counterclaim or cross-claim, the party pleading the claim is to be regarded as a plaintiff and the additional parties as plaintiffs or defendants as the case may be, and amended Rules 19 and 20 are to be applied in the usual fashion. See also Rules 13(a) (compulsory counterclaims) and 22 (interpleader).

The amendment of Rule 13(h), like the amendment of Rule 19, does not attempt to regulate Federal jurisdiction or venue. See Rule 82. It should be noted, however, that in some situations the decisional law has recognized "ancillary" Federal jurisdiction over counterclaims and cross-claims and "ancillary" venue as to parties to these claims.

Rule 15.

AMENDED AND SUPPLEMENTAL PLEADINGS

(c) Relation Back of Amendments. Whenever the claim or defense asserted in the amended pleading arose out of the conduct, transaction, or occurrence set forth or attempted to be set forth in the original pleading, the amendment relates back to the date of the original pleading. *An amendment changing the party against whom a claim is asserted relates back if the foregoing provision is satisfied and, within the period provided by law for commencing the action against him, the party to be brought in by amendment (1) has received such notice of the institution of the action that he will not be prejudiced in maintaining his defense on the merits, and (2) knew or should have known that, but for a mistake concerning the identity of the proper party, the action would have been brought against him.*

The delivery or mailing of process to the United States Attorney, or his designee, or the Attorney General of the United States,

---

New matter is shown in italics; matter to be omitted is lined through

or an agency or officer who would have been a proper defendant if named, satisfies the requirement of clauses (1) and (2) hereof with respect to the United States or any agency or officer thereof to be brought into the action as a defendant.

Advisory Committee's Note

Rule 15(c) is amplified to state more clearly when an amendment of a pleading changing the party against whom a claim is asserted (including an amendment to correct a misnomer or misdescription of a defendant) shall "relate back" to the date of the original pleading.

The problem has arisen most acutely in certain actions by private parties against officers or agencies of the United States. Thus an individual denied social security benefits by the Secretary of Health, Education, and Welfare may secure review of the decision by bringing a civil action against that officer within sixty days. 42 U.S.C. § 405(g) (Supp. III, 1962). In several recent cases the claimants instituted timely action but mistakenly named as defendant the United States, the Department of HEW, the "Federal Security Administration" (a nonexistent agency), and a Secretary who had retired from the office nineteen days before. Discovering their mistakes, the claimants moved to amend their complaints to name the proper defendant; by this time the statutory sixty-day period had expired. The motions were denied on the ground that the amendment "would amount to the commencement of a new proceeding and would not relate back in time so as to avoid the statutory provision * * * that suit be brought within sixty days. * * *" *Cohn v. Federal Security Adm.*, 199 F.Supp. 884, 885 (W.D.N.Y.1961); see also *Cunningham v. United States*, 199 F.Supp. 541 (W.D.Mo.1958); *Hall v. Department of HEW*, 199 F.Supp. 833 (S.D.Tex.1960); *Sandridge v. Folsom, Secretary of HEW*, 200 F.Supp. 25 (M.D.Tenn.1959). [The Secretary of Health, Education, and Welfare has approved certain ameliorative regulations under 42 U.S.C. § 405(g). See 29 Fed.Reg. 8209 (June 30, 1964); Jacoby, *The Effect of Recent Changes in the Law of "Nonstatutory" Judicial Review*, 53 Geo.L.J. 19, 42–43 (1964); see also *Simmons v. United States Dept. HEW*, 328 F.2d 86 (3d Cir.1964).]

Analysis in terms of "new proceeding" is traceable to *Davis v. L. L. Cohen & Co.*, 268 U.S. 638 (1925), and *Mellon v. Arkansas Land & Lumber Co.*, 275 U.S. 460 (1928), but those cases antedate the adoption of the rules which import different criteria for determining when an amendment is to "relate back". As lower courts have continued to rely on the *Davis* and *Mellon* cases despite the contrary intent of the rules, clarification of Rule 15(c) is considered advisable.

Relation back is intimately connected with the policy of the statute of limitations. The policy of the statute limiting the time for suit against the Secretary of HEW would not have been offended by allowing relation back in the situations described above. For the government was put on notice of the claim within the stated period—in the particular instances, by means of the initial delivery of process to a responsible government official (see Rule 4(d)(4) and (5)). In these circumstances, characterization of the amendment as a new proceeding is not responsive to the reality, but is merely question-begging; and to deny relation back is to defeat unjustly the claimant's opportunity to prove his case. See the full discussion by Byse, *Suing the "Wrong" Defendant in Judicial Review of Federal Administrative Action: Proposals for Reform*, 77 Harv.L.Rev. 40 (1963); see also Ill.Civ.P.Act § 46(4).

Much the same question arises in other types of actions against the government (see Byse, *supra*, at 45 n. 15). In actions between private parties, the problem

New matter is shown in italics; matter to be omitted is lined through

of relation back of amendments changing defendants has generally been better handled by the courts, but incorrect criteria have sometimes been applied, leading sporadically to doubtful results. See 1A Barron & Holtzoff, *Federal Practice & Procedure* § 451 (Wright ed. 1960); 1 *id.* § 186 (1960); 2 *id.* § 543 (1961); 3 *Moore's Federal Practice* ¶ 15.15 (Cum.Supp.1962); Annot., *Change in Party After Statute of Limitations Has Run,* 8 A.L.R.2d 6 (1949). Rule 15(c) has been amplified to provide a general solution. An amendment changing the party against whom a claim is asserted relates back if the amendment satisfies the usual condition of Rule 15(c) of "arising out of the conduct * * * set forth * * * in the original pleading," and if, within the applicable limitations period, the party brought in by amendment, *first,* received such notice of the institution of the action—the notice need not be formal—that he would not be prejudiced in defending the action, and, *second,* knew or should have known that the action would have been brought against him initially had there not been a mistake concerning the identity of the proper party. Revised Rule 15(c) goes on to provide specifically in the government cases that the *first* and *second* requirements are satisfied when the government has been notified in the manner there described (see Rule 4(d)(4) and (5)). As applied to the government cases, revised Rule 15(c) further advances the objectives of the 1961 amendment of Rule 25(d) (substitution of public officers).

The relation back of amendments changing plaintiffs is not expressly treated in revised Rule 15(c) since the problem is generally easier. Again the chief consideration of policy is that of the statute of limitations, and the attitude taken in revised Rule 15(c) toward change of defendants extends by analogy to amendments changing plaintiffs. Also relevant is the amendment of Rule 17(a) (real party in interest). To avoid forfeitures of just claims, revised Rule 17(a) would provide that no action shall be dismissed on the ground that it is not prosecuted in the name of the real party in interest until a reasonable time has been allowed for correction of the defect in the manner there stated.

Rule 17.

PARTIES PLAINTIFF AND DEFENDANT; CAPACITY

(a) **Real Party in Interest.** Every action shall be prosecuted in the name of the real party in interest;. ~~but a~~An executor, administrator, guardian, *bailee,* trustee of an express trust, a party with whom or in whose name a contract has been made for the benefit of another, or a party authorized by statute may sue in his own name without joining with him the party for whose benefit the action is brought; and when a statute of the United States so provides, an action for the use or benefit of another shall be brought in the name of the United States. *No action shall be dismissed on the ground that it is not prosecuted in the name of the real party in interest until a reasonable time has been allowed after objection for ratification of commencement of the action by, or joinder or substitution of, the real party in interest; and such ratification, joinder, or substitution shall have the same effect as if the action had been commenced in the name of the real party in interest.*

New matter is shown in italics; matter to be omitted is lined through

Advisory Committee's Note

The minor change in the text of the rule is designed to make it clear that the specific instances enumerated are not exceptions to, but illustrations of, the rule. These illustrations, of course, carry no negative implication to the effect that there are not other instances of recognition as the real party in interest of one whose standing as such may be in doubt. The enumeration is simply of cases in which there might be substantial doubt as to the issue but for the specific enumeration. There are other potentially arguable cases that are not excluded by the enumeration. For example, the enumeration states that the promisee in a contract for the benefit of a third party may sue as real party in interest; it does not say, because it is obvious, that the third-party beneficiary may sue (when the applicable law gives him that right.)

The rule adds to the illustrative list of real parties in interest a bailee—meaning, of course, a bailee suing on behalf of the bailor with respect to the property bailed. (When the possessor of property other than the owner sues for an invasion of the possessory interest he is the real party in interest.) The word "bailee" is added primarily to preserve the admiralty practice whereby the owner of a vessel as bailee of the cargo, or the master of the vessel as bailee of both vessel and cargo, sues for damage to either property interest or both. But there is no reason to limit such a provision to maritime situations. The owner of a warehouse in which household furniture is stored is equally entitled to sue on behalf of the numerous owners of the furniture stored. *Cf. Gulf Oil Corp. v. Gilbert*, 330 U.S. 501 (1947).

The provision that no action shall be dismissed on the ground that it is not prosecuted in the name of the real party in interest until a reasonable time has been allowed, after the objection has been raised, for ratification, substitution, etc., is added simply in the interests of justice. In its origin the rule concerning the real party in interest was permissive in purpose: it was designed to *allow* an assignee to sue in his own name. That having been accomplished, the modern function of the rule in its negative aspect is simply to protect the defendant against a subsequent action by the party actually entitled to recover, and to insure generally that the judgment will have its proper effect as res judicata.

This provision keeps pace with the law as it is actually developing. Modern decisions are inclined to be lenient when an honest mistake has been made in choosing the party in whose name the action is to be filed—in both maritime and nonmaritime cases. See *Levinson v. Deupree*, 345 U.S. 648 (1953); *Link Aviation, Inc. v. Downs*, 325 F.2d 613 (D.C.Cir.1963). The provision should not be misunderstood or distorted. It is intended to prevent forfeiture when determination of the proper party to sue is difficult or when an understandable mistake has been made. It does not mean, for example, that, following an airplane crash in which all aboard were killed, an action may be filed in the name of John Doe (a fictitious person), as personal representative of Richard Roe (another fictitious person), in the hope that at a later time the attorney filing the action may substitute the real name of the real personal representative of a real victim, and have the benefit of suspension of the limitation period. It does not even mean, when an action is filed by the personal representative of John Smith, of Buffalo, in the good faith belief that he was aboard the flight, that upon discovery that Smith is alive and well, having missed the fatal flight, the representative of James Brown, of San Francisco, an actual victim, can be substituted to take advantage of the suspension of the limitation period. It is, in cases of this sort, intended to insure against forfeiture and injustice—in short, to codify in broad terms the salutary principle of *Levinson v. Deupree*, 345 U.S. 648 (1953), and *Link Aviation, Inc. v. Downs*, 325 F.2d 613 (D.C.Cir.1963).

New matter is shown in italics; matter to be omitted is lined through

Rule 18.

JOINDER OF CLAIMS AND REMEDIES

(a) **Joinder of Claims.** ~~The plaintiff in his complaint or in a reply setting forth a counterclaim may join either as independent or as alternate claims as many claims either legal or equitable or both as he may have against an opposing party. There may be a like joinder of claims when there are multiple parties if the requirements of Rules 19, 20, and 22 are satisfied. There may be a like joinder of cross-claims or third-party claims if the requirements of Rule 13 and 14 respectively are satisfied.~~ *A party asserting a claim to relief as an original claim, counterclaim, cross-claim, or third-party claim, may join, either as independent or as alternate claims, as many claims, legal, equitable, or maritime, as he has against an opposing party.*

Advisory Committee's Note

The rules "proceed upon the theory that no inconvenience can result from the joinder of any two or more matters in the pleadings, but only from trying two or more matters together which have little or nothing in common." Sunderland, *The New Federal Rules,* 45 W.Va.L.Q. 5, 13 (1938); see Clark, *Code Pleading,* 58 (2d ed. 1947). Accordingly, Rule 18(a) has permitted a party to plead multiple claims of all types against an opposing party, subject to the court's power to direct an appropriate procedure for trying the claims. See Rules 42(b), 20(b), 21.

The liberal policy regarding joinder of claims in the pleadings extends to cases with multiple parties. However, the language used in the second sentence of Rule 18(a)—"if the requirements of Rules 19 [necessary joinder of parties], 20 [permissive joinder of parties], and 22 [interpleader] are satisfied"—has led some courts to infer that the rules regulating joinder of parties are intended to carry back to Rule 18(a) and to impose some special limits on joinder of claims in multiparty cases. In particular, Rule 20(a) has been read as restricting the operation of Rule 18(a) in certain situations in which a number of parties have been permissively joined in an action. In *Federal Housing Admr. v. Christianson,* 26 F.Supp. 419 (D.Conn.1939), the indorsee of two notes sued the three co-makers of one note, and sought to join in the action a count on a second note which had been made by two of the three defendants. There was no doubt about the propriety of the joinder of the three parties defendant, for a right to relief was being asserted against all three defendants which arose out of a single "transaction" (the first note) and a question of fact or law "common" to all three defendants would arise in the action. See the text of Rule 20(a). The court, however, refused to allow the joinder of the count on the second note, on the ground that this right to relief, assumed to arise from a distinct transaction, did not involve a question common to all the defendants but only two of them. For analysis of the *Christianson* case and other authorities, see 2 Barron & Holtzoff, *Federal Practice & Procedure,* § 533.1 (Wright ed. 1961); 3 *Moore's Federal Practice* ¶ 18.04[3] (2d ed. 1963).

If the court's view is followed, it becomes necessary to enter at the pleading stage into speculations about the exact relation between the claim sought to be joined against fewer than all the defendants properly joined in the action, and the

---

New matter is shown in italics; matter to be omitted is lined through

claims asserted against all the defendants. *Cf.* Wright, *Joinder of Claims and Parties Under Modern Pleading Rules,* 36 Minn.L.Rev. 580, 605–06 (1952). Thus if it could be found in the *Christianson* situation that the claim on the second note arose out of the same transaction as the claim on the first or out of a transaction forming part of a "series," and that any question of fact or law with respect to the second note also arose with regard to the first, it would be held that the claim on the second note could be joined in the complaint. See 2 Barron & Holtzoff, *supra,* at 199; see also *id.* at 198 n. 60.4; *cf.* 3 *Moore's Federal Practice, supra,* at 1811. Such pleading niceties provide a basis for delaying and wasteful maneuver. It is more compatible with the design of the rules to allow the claim to be joined in the pleading, leaving the question of possible separate trial of that claim to be later decided. See 2 Barron & Holtzoff, *supra,* § 533.1; Wright, *supra,* 36 Minn.L.Rev. at 604–11; *Developments in the Law—Multiparty Litigation in the Federal Courts,* 71 Harv. 874, 970–71 (1958); Commentary, *Relation Between Joinder of Parties and Joinder of Claims,* 5 F.R.Serv. 822 (1942). It is instructive to note that the court in the *Christianson* case, while holding that the claim on the second note could not be joined as a matter of pleading, held open the possibility that both claims would later be consolidated for trial under Rule 42(a). See 26 F.Supp. 419.

Rule 18(a) is now amended not only to overcome the *Christianson* decision and similar authority, but also to state clearly, as a comprehensive proposition, that a party asserting a claim (an original claim, counterclaim, cross-claim, or third-party claim) may join as many claims as he has against an opposing party. See *Noland Co., Inc. v. Graver Tank & Mfg. Co.,* 301 F.2d 43, 49–51 (4th Cir.1962); but *cf. C. W. Humphrey Co. v. Security Alum. Co.,* 31 F.R.D. 41 (E.D.Mich.1962). This permitted joinder of claims is not affected by the fact there are multiple parties in the action. The joinder of parties is governed by other rules operating independently.

It is emphasized that amended Rule 18(a) deals only with pleading. As already indicated, a claim properly joined as a matter of pleading need not be proceeded with together with the other claims if fairness or convenience justifies separate treatment.

Amended Rule 18(a), like the rule prior to amendment, does not purport to deal with questions of jurisdiction or venue which may arise with respect to claims properly joined as a matter of pleading. See Rule 82.

See also the amendment of Rule 20(a) and the Advisory Committee's Note thereto.

Free joinder of claims and remedies is one of the basic purposes of unification of the admiralty and civil procedure. The amendment accordingly provides for the inclusion in the rule of maritime claims as well as those which are legal and equitable in character.

Rule 19.

NECESSARY JOINDER OF PARTIES

(a) Necessary Joinder. Subject to the provisions of Rule 23 and of subdivision (b) of this rule, persons having a joint interest shall be made parties and be joined on the same side as plaintiffs or defendants. When a person who should join as a plaintiff refuses to do so, he may be made a defendant or, in proper cases, an involuntary plaintiff.

New matter is shown in italics; matter to be omitted is lined through

~~(b) **Effect of Failure to Join.** When persons who are not indispensable, but who ought to be parties if complete relief is to be accorded between those already parties, have not been made parties and are subject to the jurisdiction of the court as to both service of process and venue and can be made parties without depriving the court of jurisdiction of the parties before it, the court shall order them summoned to appear in the action. The court in its discretion may proceed in the action without making such persons parties, if its jurisdiction over them as to either service of process or venue can be acquired only by their consent or voluntary appearance or if, though they are subject to its jurisdiction, their joinder would deprive the court of jurisdiction of the parties before it, but the judgment rendered therein does not affect the rights or liabilities of absent persons.~~

~~(c) **Same: Names of Omitted Persons and Reasons for Non-Joinder to be Pleaded.** In any pleading in which relief is asked, the pleader shall set forth the names, if known to him, of persons who ought to be parties if complete relief is to be accorded between those already parties, but who are not joined, and shall state why they are omitted.~~

Rule 19.

JOINDER OF PERSONS NEEDED FOR JUST ADJUDICATION

(a) Persons to be Joined if Feasible. A person who is subject to service of process and whose joinder will not deprive the court of jurisdiction over the subject matter of the action shall be joined as a party in the action if (1) in his absence complete relief cannot be accorded among those already parties, or (2) he claims an interest relating to the subject of the action and is so situated that the disposition of the action in his absence may (i) as a practical matter impair or impede his ability to protect that interest or (ii) leave any of the persons already parties subject to a substantial risk of incurring double, multiple, or otherwise inconsistent obligations by reason of his claimed interest. If he has not been so joined, the court shall order that he be made a party. If he should join as a plaintiff but refuses to do so, he may be made a defendant, or, in a proper case, an involuntary plaintiff. If the joined party objects to venue and his joinder would render the venue of the action improper, he shall be dismissed from the action.

(b) Determination by Court Whenever Joinder Not Feasible. If a person as described in subdivision (a)(1)–(2) hereof cannot be made a party, the court shall determine whether in equity and good conscience the action should proceed among the parties before it, or should be dismissed, the absent person being thus regarded as

New matter is shown in italics; matter to be omitted is lined through

indispensable.   The factors to be considered by the court include: first, to what extent a judgment rendered in the person's absence might be prejudicial to him, or those already parties; second, the extent to which, by protective provisions in the judgment, by the shaping of relief, or other measures, the prejudice can be lessened or avoided; third, whether a judgment rendered in the person's absence will be adequate; fourth, whether the plaintiff will have an adequate remedy if the action is dismissed for nonjoinder.

(c) Pleading Reasons for Nonjoinder.   A pleading asserting a claim for relief shall state the names, if known to the pleader, of any persons as described in subdivision (a)(1)–(2) hereof who are not joined, and the reasons why they are not joined.

(d) Exception of Class Actions.   This rule is subject to the provisions of Rule 23.

Advisory Committee's Note

General Considerations

Whenever feasible, the persons materially interested in the subject of an action—see the more detailed description of these persons in the discussion of new subdivision (a) below—should be joined as parties so that they may be heard and a complete disposition made.   When this comprehensive joinder cannot be accomplished—a situation which may be encountered in Federal courts because of limitations on service of process, subject matter jurisdiction, and venue—the case should be examined pragmatically and a choice made between the alternatives of proceeding with the action in the absence of particular interested persons, and dismissing the action.

Even if the court is mistaken in its decision to proceed in the absence of an interested person, it does not by that token deprive itself of the power to adjudicate as between the parties already before it through proper service of process.   But the court can make a legally binding adjudication only between the parties actually joined in the action.   It is true that an adjudication between the parties before the court may on occasion adversely affect the absent person as a practical matter, or leave a party exposed to a later inconsistent recovery by the absent person.   These are factors which should be considered in deciding whether the action should proceed, or should rather be dismissed; but they do not themselves negate the court's power to adjudicate as between the parties who have been joined.

Defects in the Original Rule

The foregoing propositions were well understood in the older equity practice, see Hazard, *Indispensable Party: The Historical Origin of a Procedural Phantom,* 61 Colum.L.Rev. 1254 (1961), and Rule 19 could be and often was applied in consonance with them.   But experience showed that the rule was defective in its phrasing and did not point clearly to the proper basis of decision.

Textual defects.   (1) The expression "persons * * * who ought to be parties if complete relief is to be accorded between those already parties," appearing in original subdivision (b), was apparently intended as a description of the persons whom it would be desirable to join in the action, all questions of feasibility of

New matter is shown in italics; matter to be omitted is lined through

joinder being put to one side; but it was not adequately descriptive of those persons.

(2) The word "indispensable," appearing in original subdivision (b), was apparently intended as an inclusive reference to the interested persons in whose absence it would be advisable, all factors having been considered, to dismiss the action. Yet the sentence implied that there might be interested persons, not "indispensable," in whose absence the action ought also to be dismissed. Further, it seemed at least superficially plausible to equate the word "indispensable" with the expression "having a joint interest," appearing in subdivision (a). See *United States v. Washington Inst. of Tech., Inc.*, 138 F.2d 25, 26 (3d Cir.1943); *cf. Chidester v. City of Newark*, 162 F.2d 598 (3d Cir.1947). But persons holding an interest technically "joint" are not always so related to an action that it would be unwise to proceed without joining all of them, whereas persons holding an interest not technically "joint" may have this relation to an action. See Reed, *Compulsory Joinder of Parties in Civil Actions*, 55 Mich.L.Rev. 327, 356 ff., 483 (1957).

(3) The use of "indispensable" and "joint interest" in the context of original Rule 19 directed attention to the technical or abstract character of the rights or obligations of the persons whose joinder was in question, and correspondingly distracted attention from the pragmatic considerations which should be controlling.

(4) The original rule, in dealing with the feasibility of joining a person as a party to the action, besides referring to whether the person was "subject to the jurisdiction of the court as to both service of process and venue," spoke of whether the person could be made a party "without depriving the court of jurisdiction of the parties before it." The second quoted expression used "jurisdiction" in the sense of the competence of the court over the subject matter of the action, and in this sense the expression was apt. However, by a familiar confusion, the expression seems to have suggested to some that the absence from the lawsuit of a person who was "indispensable" or "who ought to be [a] part[y]" itself deprived the court of the power to adjudicate as between the parties already joined. See *Samuel Goldwyn, Inc. v. United Artists Corp.*, 113 F.2d 703, 707 (3d Cir. 1940); *McArthur v. Rosenbaum Co. of Pittsburgh*, 180 F.2d 617, 621 (3d Cir. 1949); *cf. Calcote v. Texas Pac. Coal & Oil Co.*, 157 F.2d 216 (5th Cir. 1946), *cert. denied*, 329 U.S. 782 (1946), noted in 56 Yale L.J. 1088 (1947); Reed, *supra*, 55 Mich.L.Rev. at 332–34.

Failure to point to correct basis of decision. The original rule did not state affirmatively what factors were relevant in deciding whether the action should proceed or be dismissed when joinder of interested persons was infeasible. In some instances courts did not undertake the relevant inquiry or were misled by the "jurisdiction" fallacy. In other instances there was undue preoccupation with abstract classifications of rights or obligations, as against consideration of the particular consequences of proceeding with the action and the ways by which these consequences might be ameliorated by the shaping of final relief or other precautions.

Although these difficulties cannot be said to have been general, analysis of the cases showed that there was good reason for attempting to strengthen the rule. The literature also indicated how the rule should be reformed. See Reed, *supra* (discussion of the important case of *Shields v. Barrow*, 17 How. (58 U.S.) 130 (1854), appears at 55 Mich.L.Rev., p. 340 ff.); Hazard, *supra*; N.Y. Temporary Comm. on Courts, *First Preliminary Report*, Legis.Doc. 1957, No. 6(b), pp. 28, 233; N.Y. Judicial Council, *Twelfth Ann.Rep.*, Legis.Doc. 1946, No. 17, p. 163; Joint Comm. on Michigan Procedural Revision, *Final Report*, Pt. III, p. 69 (1960); Note, *Indispensable Parties in the Federal Courts*, 65 Harv.L.Rev. 1050 (1952); *Developments in the Law—Multiparty Litigation in the Federal Courts*, 71 Harv.L.Rev. 874, 879

New matter is shown in italics; matter to be omitted is lined through

(1958); Mich.Gen. Court Rules, R. 205 (effective Jan. 1, 1963); N.Y.Civ.Prac. Law & Rules, § 1001 (effective Sept. 1, 1963).

The Amended Rule

New *subdivision (a)* defines the persons whose joinder in the action is desirable. Clause (1) stresses the desirability of joining those persons in whose absence the court would be obliged to grant partial or "hollow" rather than complete relief to the parties before the court. The interests that are being furthered here are not only those of the parties, but also that of the public in avoiding repeated lawsuits on the same essential subject matter. Clause (2)(i) recognizes the importance of protecting the person whose joinder is in question against the practical prejudice to him which may arise through a disposition of the action in his absence. Clause (2)(ii) recognizes the need for considering whether a party may be left, after the adjudication, in a position where a person not joined can subject him to a double or otherwise inconsistent liability. See Reed, *supra,* 55 Mich.L.Rev. at 330, 338; Note, *supra,* 65 Harv.L.Rev. at 1052–57; *Developments in the Law, supra,* 71 Harv.L.Rev. at 881–85.

The subdivision (a) definition of persons to be joined is not couched in terms of the abstract nature of their interests—"joint," "united," "separable," or the like. See N.Y. Temporary Comm. on Courts, *First Preliminary Report, supra; Developments in the Law, supra,* at 880. It should be noted particularly, however, that the description is not at variance with the settled authorities holding that a tortfeasor with the usual "joint-and-several" liability is merely a permissive party to an action against another with like liability. See 3 *Moore's Federal Practice,* § 2153 (2d ed. 1963); 2 Barron & Holtzoff, *Federal Practice & Procedure* § 513.8 (Wright ed. 1961). Joinder of these tortfeasors continues to be regulated by Rule 20; compare Rule 14 on third-party practice.

If a person as described in subdivision (a)(1)–(2) is amenable to service of process and his joinder would not deprive the court of jurisdiction in the sense of competence over the action, he should be joined as a party; and if he has not been joined, the court should order him to be brought into the action. If a party joined has a valid objection to the venue and chooses to assert it, he will be dismissed from the action.

Subdivision (b). When a person as described in subdivision (a)(1)–(2) cannot be made a party, the court is to determine whether in equity and good conscience the action should proceed among the parties already before it, or should be dismissed. That this decision is to be made in the light of pragmatic considerations has often been acknowledged by the courts. See *Roos v. Texas Co.,* 23 F.2d 171 (2d Cir. 1927), *cert. denied,* 277 U.S. 587 (1928); *Niles-Bement-Pond Co. v. Iron Moulders' Union,* 254 U.S. 77, 80 (1920). The subdivision sets out four relevant considerations drawn from the experience revealed in the decided cases. The factors are to a certain extent overlapping, and they are not intended to exclude other considerations which may be applicable in particular situations.

The *first factor* brings in a consideration of what a judgment in the action would mean to the absentee. Would the absentee by adversely affected in a practical sense, and if so, would the prejudice be immediate and serious, or remote and minor? The possible collateral consequences of the judgment upon the parties already joined are also to be appraised. Would any party be exposed to a fresh action by the absentee, and if so, how serious is the threat? See the elaborate discussion in Reed, *supra; cf. A. L. Smith Iron Co. v. Dickson,* 141 F.2d 3 (2d Cir. 1944); *Caldwell Mfg. Co. v. Unique Balance Co.,* 18 F.R.D. 258 (S.D.N.Y.1955).

New matter is shown in italics; matter to be omitted is lined through

The *second factor* calls attention to the measures by which prejudice may be averted or lessened. The "shaping of relief" is a familiar expedient to this end. See, *e. g.,* the award of money damages in lieu of specific relief where the latter might affect an absentee adversely. *Ward v. Deavers,* 203 F.2d 72 (D.C.Cir. 1953); *Miller & Lux, Inc. v. Nickel,* 141 F.Supp. 41 (N.D.Calif.1956). On the use of "protective provisions," see *Roos v. Texas Co., supra; Atwood v. Rhode Island Hosp. Trust Co.,* 275 Fed. 513, 519 (1st Cir. 1921), *cert. denied,* 257 U.S. 661 (1922); *cf. Stumpf v. Fidelity Gas Co.,* 294 F.2d 886 (9th Cir. 1961); and the general statement in *National Licorice Co. v. Labor Board,* 309 U.S. 350, 363 (1940).

Sometimes the party is himself able to take measures to avoid prejudice. Thus a defendant faced with a prospect of a second suit by an absentee may be in a position to bring the latter into the action by defensive interpleader. See *Hudson v. Newell,* 172 F.2d 848, 852, *mod.,* 176 F.2d 546 (5th Cir. 1949); *Gauss v. Kirk,* 198 F.2d 83, 86 (D.C.Cir. 1952); *Abel v. Brayton Flying Service, Inc.,* 248 F.2d 713, 716 (5th Cir. 1957) (suggestion of possibility of counterclaim under Rule 13(h)); *cf. Parker Rust-Proof Co. v. Western Union Tel. Co.,* 105 F.2d 976 (2d Cir. 1939), *cert. denied,* 308 U.S. 597 (1939). So also the absentee may sometimes be able to avert prejudice to himself by voluntarily appearing in the action or intervening on an ancillary basis. See *Developments in the Law, supra,* 71 Harv.L.Rev. at 882; Annot., *Intervention or Subsequent Joinder of Parties as Affecting Jurisdiction of Federal Court Based on Diversity of Citizenship,* 134 A.L.R. 335 (1941); *Johnson v. Middleton,* 175 F.2d 535 (7th Cir. 1949); *Kentucky Nat. Gas Corp. v. Duggins,* 165 F.2d 1011 (6th Cir. 1948); *McComb v. McCormack,* 159 F.2d 219 (5th Cir. 1947). The court should consider whether this, in turn, would impose undue hardship on the absentee. (For the possibility of the court's informing an absentee of the pendency of the action, see comment under subdivision (c) below.)

The *third factor*—whether an "adequate" judgment can be rendered in the absence of a given person—calls attention to the extent of the relief that can be accorded among the parties joined. It meshes with the other factors, especially the "shaping of relief" mentioned under the second factor. *Cf. Kroese v. General Steel Castings Corp.,* 179 F.2d 760 (3d Cir. 1949), *cert. denied,* 339 U.S. 983 (1950).

The *fourth factor,* looking to the practical effects of a dismissal, indicates that the court should consider whether there is any assurance that the plaintiff, if dismissed, could sue effectively in another forum where better joinder would be possible. See *Fitzgerald v. Haynes,* 241 F.2d 417, 420 (3d Cir. 1957); *Fouke v. Schenewerk,* 197 F.2d 234, 236 (5th Cir. 1952); *cf. Warfield v. Marks,* 190 F.2d 178 (5th Cir. 1951).

The subdivision uses the word "indispensable" only in a conclusory sense, that is, a person is "regarded as indispensable" when he cannot be made a party and, upon consideration of the factors above-mentioned, it is determined that in his absence it would be preferable to dismiss the action, rather than to retain it.

A person may be added as a party at any stage of the action on motion or on the court's initiative (see Rule 21); and a motion to dismiss, on the ground that a person has not been joined and justice requires that the action should not proceed in his absence, may be made as late as the trial on the merits (see Rule 12(h)(2), as amended; *cf.* Rule 12(b)(7), as amended). However, when the moving party is seeking dismissal in order to protect himself against a later suit by the absent person (subdivision (a)(2)(ii)), and is not seeking vicariously to protect the absent person against a prejudicial judgment (subdivision (a)(2)(i)), his undue delay in making the motion can properly be counted against him as a reason for denying the motion. A joinder question should be decided with reasonable promptness, but decision may properly be deferred if adequate information is not available at the

---

New matter is shown in italics; matter to be omitted is lined through

time. Thus the relationship of an absent person to the action, and the practical effects of an adjudication upon him and others, may not be sufficiently revealed at the pleading state; in such a case it would be appropriate to defer decision until the action was further advanced. *Cf.* Rule 12(d).

The amended rule makes no special provision for the problem arising in suits against subordinate Federal officials where it has often been set up as a defense that some superior officer must be joined. Frequently this defense has been accompanied by or intermingled with defenses of sovereign immunity or lack of consent of the United States to suit. So far as the issue of joinder can be isolated from the rest, the new subdivision seems better adapted to handle it than the predecessor provision. See the discussion in *Johnson v. Kirkland,* 290 F.2d 440, 446–47 (5th Cir. 1961) (stressing the practical orientation of the decisions); *Shaughnessy v. Pedreiro,* 349 U.S. 48, 54 (1955). Recent legislation, P.L. 87–748, 76 Stat. 744, approved October 5, 1962, adding §§ 1361, 1391(e) to Title 28, U.S.C., vests original jurisdiction in the district courts over actions in the nature of mandamus to compel officials of the United States to perform their legal duties, and extends the range of service of process and liberalizes venue in these actions. If, then, it is found that a particular official should be joined in the action, the legislation will make it easy to bring him in.

Subdivision (c) parallels the predecessor subdivision (c) of Rule 19. In some situations it may be desirable to advise a person who has not been joined of the fact that the action is pending, and in particular cases the court in its discretion may itself convey this information by directing a letter or other informal notice to the absentee.

Subdivision (d) repeats the exception contained in the first clause of the predecessor subdivision (a).

Rule 20.

PERMISSIVE JOINDER OF PARTIES

(a) **Permissive Joinder.** All persons may join in one action as plaintiffs if they assert any right to relief jointly, severally, or in the alternative in respect of or arising out of the same transaction, occurrence, or series of transactions or occurrences and if any question of law or fact common to all ~~of them~~ *these persons* will arise in the action. All persons *(and any vessel, cargo or other property subject to admiralty process in rem)* may be joined in one action as defendants if there is asserted against them jointly, severally, or in the alternative, any right to relief in respect of or arising out of the same transaction, occurrence, or series of transactions or occurrences and if any question of law or fact common to all ~~of them~~ *defendants* will arise in the action. A plaintiff or defendant need not be interested in obtaining or defending against all the relief demanded. Judgment may be given for one or more of the plaintiffs according to their respective rights to relief, and against one or more defendants according to their respective liabilities.

New matter is shown in italics; matter to be omitted is lined through

See the amendment of Rule 18(a) and the Advisory Committee's Note thereto. It has been thought that a lack of clarity in the antecedent of the word "them," as it appeared in two places in Rule 20(a), contributed to the view, taken by some courts, that this rule limited the joinder of claims in certain situations of permissive party-joinder. Although the amendment of Rule 18(a) should make clear that this view is untenable, it has been considered advisable to amend Rule 20(a) to eliminate any ambiguity. See 2 Barron & Holtzoff, *Federal Practice & Procedure* 202 (Wright ed. 1961).

A basic purpose of unification of admiralty and civil procedure is to reduce barriers to joinder; hence the reference to "any vessel," etc.

~~Rule 23.~~

~~CLASS ACTIONS~~

~~**(a) Representation.** If persons constituting a class are so numerous as to make it impracticable to bring them all before the court, such of them, one or more, as will fairly insure the adequate representation of all may, on behalf of all, sue or be sued, when the character of the right sought to be enforced for or against the class is~~

~~(1) joint or common, or secondary in the sense that the owner of a primary right refuses to enforce that right and a member of the class thereby becomes entitled to enforce it;~~

~~(2) several, and the object of the action is the adjudication of claims which do or may affect specific property involved in the action; or~~

~~(3) several, and there is a common question of law or fact affecting the several rights and a common relief is sought.~~

~~**(b) Secondary Action by Shareholders.** In an action brought to enforce a secondary right on the part of one or more shareholders in an association, incorporated or unincorporated, because the association refuses to enforce rights which may properly be asserted by it, the complaint shall be verified by oath and shall aver (1) that the plaintiff was a shareholder at the time of the transaction of which he complains or that his share thereafter devolved on him by operation of law and (2) that the action is not a collusive one to confer on a court of the United States jurisdiction of any action of which it would not otherwise have jurisdiction. The complaint shall also set forth with particularity the efforts of the plaintiff to secure from the managing directors or trustees and, if necessary, from the shareholders such action as he desires, and the reasons for his failure to obtain such action or the reasons for not making such effort.~~

New matter is shown in italics; matter to be omitted is lined through

~~(c) **Dismissal or Compromise.** A class action shall not be dismissed or compromised without the approval of the court. If the right sought to be enforced is one defined in paragraph (1) of subdivision (a) of this rule notice of the proposed dismissal or compromise shall be given to all members of the class in such manner as the court directs. If the right is one defined in paragraphs (2) or (3) of subdivision (a) notice shall be given only if the court requires it.~~

Rule 23.

CLASS ACTIONS

(a) Prerequisites to a Class Action. One or more members of a class may sue or be sued as representative parties on behalf of all only if (1) the class is so numerous that joinder of all members is impracticable, (2) there are questions of law or fact common to the class, (3) the claims or defenses of the representative parties are typical of the claims or defenses of the class, and (4) the representative parties will fairly and adequately protect the interests of the class.

(b) Class Actions Maintainable. An action may be maintained as a class action if the prerequisites of subdivision (a) are satisfied, and in addition:

(1) the prosecution of separate actions by or against individual members of the class would create a risk of

(A) inconsistent or varying adjudications with respect to individual members of the class which would establish incompatible standards of conduct for the party opposing the class, or

(B) adjudications with respect to individual members of the class which would as a practical matter be dispositive of the interests of the other members not parties to the adjudications or substantially impair or impede their ability to protect their interests; or

(2) the party opposing the class has acted or refused to act on grounds generally applicable to the class, thereby making appropriate final injunctive relief or corresponding declaratory relief with respect to the class as a whole; or

(3) the court finds that the questions of law or fact common to the members of the class predominate over any questions affecting only individual members, and that a class action is superior to other available methods for the fair and efficient adjudication of the controversy. The matters pertinent to the findings include: (A)

New matter is shown in italics; matter to be omitted is lined through

the interest of members of the class in individually controlling the prosecution or defense of separate actions; (B) the extent and nature of any litigation concerning the controversy already commenced by or against members of the class; (C) the desirability or undesirability of concentrating the litigation of the claims in the particular forum; (D) the difficulties likely to be encountered in the management of a class action.

(c) Determination by Order Whether Class Action to be Maintained; Notice; Judgment; Actions Conducted Partially as Class Actions.

(1) As soon as practicable after the commencement of an action brought as a class action, the court shall determine by order whether it is to be so maintained. An order under this subdivision may be conditional, and may be altered or amended before the decision on the merits.

(2) In any class action maintained under subdivision (b)(3), the court shall direct to the members of the class the best notice practicable under the circumstances, including individual notice to all members who can be identified through reasonable effort. The notice shall advise each member that (A) the court will exclude him from the class if he so requests by a specified date; (B) the judgment, whether favorable or not, will include all members who do not request exclusion; and (C) any member who does not request exclusion may, if he desires, enter an appearance through his counsel.

(3) The judgment in an action maintained as a class action under subdivision (b)(1) or (b)(2), whether or not favorable to the class, shall include and describe those whom the court finds to be members of the class. The judgment in an action maintained as a class action under subdivision (b)(3), whether or not favorable to the class, shall include and specify or describe those to whom the notice provided in subdivision (c)(2) was directed, and who have not requested exclusion, and whom the court finds to be members of the class.

(4) When appropriate (A) an action may be brought or maintained as a class action with respect to particular issues, or (B) a class may be divided into subclasses and each subclass treated as a class, and the provisions of this rule shall then be construed and applied accordingly.

(d) Orders in Conduct of Actions. In the conduct of actions to which this rule applies, the court may make appropriate orders: (1) determining the course of proceedings or prescribing measures to prevent undue repetition or complication in the presentation of

---

New matter is shown in italics; matter to be omitted is lined through

evidence or argument; (2) requiring, for the protection of the members of the class or otherwise for the fair conduct of the action, that notice be given in such manner as the court may direct to some or all of the members of any step in the action, or of the proposed extent of the judgment, or of the opportunity of members to signify whether they consider the representation fair and adequate, to intervene and present claims or defenses, or otherwise to come into the action; (3) imposing conditions on the representative parties or on intervenors; (4) requiring that the pleadings be amended to eliminate therefrom allegations as to representation of absent persons, and that the action proceed accordingly; (5) dealing with similar procedural matters. The orders may be combined with an order under Rule 16, and may be altered or amended as may be desirable form time to time.

(e) Dismissal or Compromise. A class action shall not be dismissed or compromised without the approval of the court, and notice of the proposed dismissal or compromise shall be given to all members of the class in such manner as the court directs.

Advisory Committee's Note

Difficulties with the original rule. The categories of class actions in the original rule were defined in terms of the abstract nature of the rights involved: the so-called "true" category was defined as involving "joint, common, or secondary rights"; the "hybrid" category, as involving "several" rights related to "specific property"; the "spurious" category, as involving "several" rights affected by a common question and related to common relief. It was thought that the definitions accurately described the situations amenable to the class-suit device, and also would indicate the proper extent of the judgment in each category, which would in turn help to determine the *res judicata* effect of the judgment if questioned in a later action. Thus the judgments in "true" and "hybrid" class actions would extend to the class (although in somewhat different ways); the judgment in a "spurious" class action would extend only to the parties including intervenors. See Moore, *Federal Rules of Civil Procedure: Some Problems Raised by the Preliminary Draft,* 25 Geo.L.J. 551, 570–76 (1937).

In practice the terms "joint," "common," etc., which were used as the basis of the Rule 23 classification proved obscure and uncertain. See Chafee, *Some Problems of Equity* 245–46, 256–57 (1950); Kalven & Rosenfield, *The Contemporary Function of the Class Suit,* 8 U. of Chi.L.Rev. 684, 707 & n. 73 (1941); Keeffe, Levy & Donovan, *Lee Defeats Ben Hur,* 33 Corn.L.Q. 327, 329–36 (1948); *Developments in the Law: Multiparty Litigation in the Federal Courts,* 71 Harv.L.Rev. 874, 931 (1958); Advisory Committee's Note to Rule 19, as amended. The courts had considerable difficulty with these terms. See, *e. g., Gullo v. Veterans' Coop. H. Assn.,* 13 F.R.D. 11 (D.D.C.1952); *Shipley v. Pittsburgh & L. E. R. Co.,* 70 F.Supp. 870 (W.D.Pa.1947); *Deckert v. Independence Shares Corp.,* 27 F.Supp. 763 (E.D.Pa. 1939), *rev'd,* 108 F.2d 51 (3d Cir. 1939), *rev'd,* 311 U.S. 282 (1940), *on remand,* 39 F.Supp. 592 (E.D.Pa.1941), *rev'd sub nom. Pennsylvania Co. for Ins. on Lives v. Deckert,* 123 F.2d 979 (3d Cir. 1941) (see Chafee, *supra,* at 264–65).

Nor did the rule provide an adequate guide to the proper extent of the judgments in class actions. First, we find instances of the courts classifying actions

New matter is shown in italics; matter to be omitted is lined through

as "true" or intimating that the judgments would be decisive for the class where these results seemed appropriate but were reached by dint of depriving the word "several" of coherent meaning. See, *e. g., System Federation No. 91 v. Reed,* 180 F.2d 991 (6th Cir. 1950); *Wilson v. City of Paducah,* 100 F.Supp. 116 (W.D.Ky.1951); *Citizens Banking Co. v. Monticello State Bank,* 143 F.2d 261 (8th Cir. 1944); *Redmond v. Commerce Trust Co.,* 144 F.2d 140 (8th Cir. 1944), *cert. denied,* 323 U.S. 776 (1944); *United States v. American Optical Co.,* 97 F.Supp. 66 (N.D.Ill.1951); *National Hairdressers' & C. Assn. v. Philad Co.,* 34 F.Supp. 264 (D.Del.1940); 41 F.Supp. 701 (D.Del.1940), *aff'd mem.,* 129 F.2d 1020 (3d Cir. 1942). Second, we find cases classified by the courts as "spurious" in which, on a realistic view, it would seem fitting for the judgments to extend to the class. See, *e. g., Knapp v. Bankers Sec. Corp.,* 17 F.R.D. 245 (E.D.Pa.1954), *aff'd,* 230 F.2d 717 (3d Cir. 1956); *Giesecke v. Denver Tramway Corp.,* 81 F.Supp. 957 (D.Del.1949); *York v. Guaranty Trust Co.,* 143 F.2d 503 (2d Cir. 1944), *rev'd on grounds not here relevant,* 326 U.S. 99 (1945) (see Chafee, *supra,* at 208); *cf. Webster Eisenlohr, Inc. v. Kalodner,* 145 F.2d 316, 320 (3d Cir. 1944), *cert. denied,* 325 U.S. 867 (1945). But *cf.* the early decisions, *Duke of Bedford v. Ellis,* [1901] A.C. 1; *Sheffield Waterworks v. Yeomans,* L.R. 2 Ch.App. 8 (1866); *Brown v. Vermuden,* 1 Ch.Cas. 272, 22 Eng.Rep. 796 (1676).

The "spurious" action envisaged by original Rule 23 was in any event an anomaly because, although denominated a "class" action and pleaded as such, it was supposed not to adjudicate the rights or liabilities of any person not a party. It was believed to be an advantage of the "spurious" category that it would invite decisions that a member of the "class" could, like a member of the class in a "true" or "hybrid" action, intervene on an ancillary basis without being required to show an independent basis of Federal jurisdiction, and have the benefit of the date of the commencement of the action for purposes of the statute of limitations. See 3 *Moore's Federal Practice* ¶¶ 23.10[1], 23.12 (2d ed. 1963). These results were attained in some instances but not in others. On the statute of limitations, see *Union Carbide & Carbon Corp. v. Nisley,* 300 F.2d 561 (10th Cir. 1961), *pet. cert. dism.,* 371 U.S. 801 (1963); but *cf. P. W. Husserl, Inc. v. Newman,* 25 F.R.D. 264 (S.D.N.Y.1960); *Athas v. Day,* 161 F.Supp. 916 (D.Colo.1958). On ancillary intervention, see *Amen v. Black,* 234 F.2d 12 (10th Cir. 1956), *cert. granted,* 352 U.S. 888 (1956), *dism. on stip.,* 355 U.S. 600 (1958); but *cf. Wagner v. Kemper,* 13 F.R.D. 128 (W.D.Mo.1952). The results, however, can hardly depend upon the mere appearance of a "spurious" category in the rule; they should turn on more basic considerations. See discussion of subdivision (c)(1) below.

Finally, the original rule did not squarely address itself to the question of the measures that might be taken during the course of the action to assure procedural fairness, particularly giving notice to members of the class, which may in turn be related in some instances to the extension of the judgment to the class. See Chafee, *supra,* at 230–31; Keeffe, Levy & Donovan, *supra; Developments in the Law, supra,* 71 Harv.L.Rev. at 937–38; Note, *Binding Effect of Class Actions,* 67 Harv.L.Rev. 1059, 1062–65 (1954); Note, *Federal Class Actions: A Suggested Revision of Rule 23,* 46 Colum.L.Rev. 818, 833–36 (1946); Mich.Gen.Court R. 208.4 (effective Jan. 1, 1963); Idaho R.Civ.P. 23(d); Minn.R.Civ.P. 23.04; N.Dak.R.Civ.P. 23(d).

The amended rule describes in more practical terms the occasions for maintaining class action; provides that all class actions maintained to the end as such will result in judgments including those whom the court finds to be members of the class, whether or not the judgment is favorable to the class; and refers to the measures which can be taken to assure the fair conduct of these actions.

Subdivision (a) states the prerequisites for maintaining any class action in terms of the numerousness of the class making joinder of the members impractica-

---

New matter is shown in italics; matter to be omitted is lined through

ble, the existence of questions common to the class, and the desired qualifications of the representative parties. See Weinstein, *Revision of Procedure: Some Problems in Class Actions,* 9 Buffalo L.Rev. 433, 458–59 (1960); 2 Barron & Holtzoff, *Federal Practice & Procedure* § 562, at 265, § 572, at 351–52 (Wright ed. 1961). These are necessary but not sufficient conditions for a class action. See *e. g., Giordano v. Radio Corp. of Am.,* 183 F.2d 558, 560 (3d Cir. 1950); *Zachman v. Erwin,* 186 F.Supp. 681 (S.D.Tex.1959); *Baim & Blank, Inc. v. Warren-Connelly Co., Inc.,* 19 F.R.D. 108 (S.D.N.Y.1956). Subdivision (b) describes the additional elements which in varying situations justify the use of a class action.

Subdivision (b)(1). The difficulties which would be likely to arise if resort were had to separate actions by or against the individual members of the class here furnish the reasons for, and the principal key to, the propriety and value of utilizing the class-action device. The considerations stated under clauses (A) and (B) are comparable to certain of the elements which define the persons whose joinder in an action is desirable as stated in Rule 19(a), as amended. See amended Rule 19(a)(2)(i) and (ii), and the Advisory Committee's Note thereto; Hazard, *Indispensable Party: The Historical Origin of a Procedural Phantom,* 61 Colum.L. Rev. 1254, 1259–60 (1961); *cf.* 3 Moore, *supra,* ¶ 23.08, at 3435.

Clause (A): One person may have rights against, or be under duties toward, numerous persons constituting a class, and be so positioned that conflicting or varying adjudications in lawsuits with individual members of the class might establish incompatible standards to govern his conduct. The class action device can be used effectively to obviate the actual or virtual dilemma which would thus confront the party opposing the class. The matter has been stated thus: "The felt necessity for a class action is greatest when the courts are called upon to order or sanction the alteration of the status quo in circumstances such that a large number of persons are in a position to call on a single person to alter the status quo, or to complain if it is altered, and the possibility exists that [the] actor might be called upon to act in inconsistent ways." Louisell & Hazard, *Pleading and Procedure: State and Federal* 719 (1962); see *Supreme Tribe of Ben-Hur v. Cauble,* 255 U.S. 356, 366–67 (1921). To illustrate: Separate actions by individuals against a municipality to declare a bond issue invalid or condition or limit it, to prevent or limit the making of a particular appropriation or to compel or invalidate an assessment, might create a risk of inconsistent or varying determinations. In the same way, individual litigations of the rights and duties of riparian owners, or of landowners' rights and duties respecting a claimed nuisance, could create a possibility of incompatible adjudications. Actions by or against a class provide a ready and fair means of achieving unitary adjudication. See *Maricopa County Mun. Water Con. Dist. v. Looney,* 219 F.2d 529 (9th Cir. 1955); *Rank v. Krug,* 142 F.Supp. 1, 154–59 (S.D.Calif.1956), *on app., State of California v. Rank,* 293 F.2d 340, 348 (9th Cir. 1961); *Gart v. Cole,* 263 F.2d 244 (2d Cir. 1959), *cert. denied,* 359 U.S. 978 (1959); *cf. Martinez v. Maverick Cty. Water Con. & Imp. Dist.,* 219 F.2d 666 (5th Cir. 1955); 3 Moore, *supra,* ¶ 23.11[2], at 3458–59.

Clause (B): This clause takes in situations where the judgment in a nonclass action by or against an individual member of the class, while not technically concluding the other members, might do so as a practical matter. The vice of an individual action would lie in the fact that the other members of the class, thus practically concluded, would have had no representation in the lawsuit. In an action by policy holders against a fraternal benefit association attacking a financial reorganization of the society, it would hardly have been practical, if indeed it would have been possible, to confine the effects of a validation of the reorganization to the individual plaintiffs. Consequently a class action was called for with adequate representation of all members of the class. See *Supreme Tribe of Ben-Hur v.*

New matter is shown in italics; matter to be omitted is lined through

Cauble, 255 U.S. 356 (1921); *Waybright v. Columbian Mut. Life Ins. Co.,* 30 F.Supp. 885 (W.D.Tenn.1939); *cf. Smith v. Swormstedt,* 16 How. (57 U.S.) 288 (1853). For much the same reason actions by shareholders to compel the declaration of a dividend, the proper recognition and handling of redemption or pre-emption rights, or the like (or actions by the corporation for corresponding declaration of rights), should ordinarily be conducted as class actions, although the matter has been much obscured by the insistence that each shareholder has an individual claim. See *Knapp v. Bankers Securities Corp.* 17 F.R.D. 245 (E.D.Pa.1954), *aff'd,* 230 F.2d 717 (3d Cir. 1956); *Giesecke v. Denver Tramway Corp.,* 81 F.Supp. 957 (D.Del.1949); *Zahn v. Transamerica Corp.,* 162 F.2d 36 (3d Cir. 1947); *Speed v. Transamerica Corp.,* 100 F.Supp. 461 (D.Del.1951); *Sobel v. Whittier Corp.,* 95 F.Supp. 643 (E.D.Mich.1951), *app. dism.,* 195 F.2d 361 (6th Cir. 1952); *Goldberg v. Whittier Corp.,* 111 F.Supp. 382 (E.D.Mich.1953); *Dann v. Studebaker-Packard Corp.,* 288 F.2d 201 (6th Cir. 1961); *Edgerton v. Armour & Co.,* 94 F.Supp. 549 (S.D.Calif.1950); *Ames v. Mengel Co.,* 190 F.2d 344 (2d Cir. 1951). (These shareholders' actions are to be distinguished from derivative actions by shareholders dealt with in new Rule 23.1). The same reasoning applies to an action which charges a breach of trust by an indenture trustee or other fiduciary similarly affecting the members of a large class of security holders or other beneficiaries, and which requires an accounting or like measures to restore the subject of the trust. See *Boesenberg v. Chicago T. & T. Co.,* 128 F.2d 245 (7th Cir. 1942); *Citizens Banking Co. v. Monticello State Bank,* 143 F.2d 261 (8th Cir. 1944); *Redmond v. Commerce Trust Co.* 144 F.2d 140 (8th Cir. 1944), *cert. denied,* 323 U.S. 776 (1944); *cf. York v. Guaranty Trust Co.,* 143 F.2d 503 (2d Cir. 1944), *rev'd on grounds not here relevant,* 326 U.S. 99 (1945).

In various situations an adjudication as to one or more members of the class will necessarily or probably have an adverse practical effect on the interests of other members who should therefore be represented in the lawsuit. This is plainly the case when claims are made by numerous persons against a fund insufficient to satisfy all claims. A class action by or against representative members to settle the validity of the claims as a whole, or in groups, followed by separate proof of the amount of each valid claim and proportionate distribution of the fund, meets the problem. *Cf. Dickinson v. Burnham,* 197 F.2d 973 (2d Cir. 1952), *cert. denied,* 344 U.S. 875 (1952); 3 Moore, *supra,* at ¶ 23.09. The same reasoning applies to an action by a creditor to set aside a fraudulent conveyance by the debtor and to appropriate the property to his claim, when the debtor's assets are insufficient to pay all creditors' claims. See *Heffernan v. Bennett & Armour,* 110 Cal.App.2d 564, 243 P.2d 846 (1952); *cf. City & County of San Francisco v. Market Street Ry.,* 95 Cal.App.2d 648, 213 P.2d 780 (1950). Similar problems, however, can arise in the absence of a fund either present or potential. A negative or mandatory injunction secured by one of a numerous class may disable the opposing party from performing claimed duties toward the other members of the class or materially affect his ability to do so. An adjudication as to movie "clearances and runs" nominally affecting only one exhibitor would often have practical effects on all the exhibitors in the same territorial area. *Cf. United States v. Paramount Pictures, Inc.,* 66 F.Supp. 323, 341–46 (S.D.N.Y.1946); 334 U.S. 131, 144–48 (1948). Assuming a sufficiently numerous class of exhibitors, a class action would be advisable. (Here representation of subclasses of exhibitors could become necessary; see subdivision (c)(3)(B).)

Subdivision (b)(2). This subdivision is intended to reach situations where a party has taken action or refused to take action with respect to a class, and final relief of an injunctive nature or of a corresponding declaratory nature, settling the legality of the behavior with respect to the class as a whole, is appropriate. Declaratory relief "corresponds" to injunctive relief when as a practical matter it affords injunctive relief or serves as a basis for later injunctive relief. The

---

New matter is shown in italics; matter to be omitted is lined through

subdivision does not extend to cases in which the appropriate final relief relates exclusively or predominantly to money damages. Action or inaction is directed to a class within the meaning of this subdivision even if it has taken effect or is threatened only as to one or a few members of the class, provided it is based on grounds which have general application to the class.

Illustrative are various actions in the civil-rights field where a party is charged with discriminating unlawfully against a class, usually one whose members are incapable of specific enumeration. See *Potts v. Flax,* 313 F.2d 284 (5th Cir. 1963); *Bailey v. Patterson,* 323 F.2d 201 (5th Cir. 1963), *cert. denied,* 377 U.S. 972 (1964); *Brunson v. Board of Trustees of School District No. 1, Clarendon Cty., S. C.,* 311 F.2d 107 (4th Cir. 1962), *cert. denied,* 373 U.S. 933 (1963); *Green v. School Bd. of Roanoke, Va.,* 304 F.2d 118 (4th Cir. 1962); *Orleans Parish School Bd. v. Bush,* 242 F.2d 156 (5th Cir. 1957), *cert denied,* 354 U.S. 921 (1957); *Mannings v. Board of Public Inst. of Hillsborough County, Fla.,* 277 F.2d 370 (5th Cir. 1960); *Northcross v. Board of Ed. of City of Memphis,* 302 F.2d 818 (6th Cir. 1962), *cert. denied,* 370 U.S. 944 (1962); *Frasier v. Board of Trustees of Univ. of N. C.,* 134 F.Supp. 589 (M.D.N.C.1955, 3-judge court), *aff'd,* 350 U.S. 979 (1956). Subdivision (b)(2) is not limited to civil-rights cases. Thus an action looking to specific or declaratory relief could be brought by a numerous class of purchasers, say retailers of a given description, against a seller alleged to have undertaken to sell to that class at prices higher than those set for other purchasers, say retailers of another description, when the applicable law forbids such a pricing differential. So also a patentee of a machine, charged with selling or licensing the machine on condition that purchasers or licensees also purchase or obtain licenses to use an ancillary unpatented machine, could be sued on a class basis by a numerous group of purchasers or licensees, or by a numerous group of competing sellers or licensors of the unpatented machine, to test the legality of the "tying" condition.

Subdivision (b)(3). In the situations to which this subdivision relates, class-action treatment is not as clearly called for as in those described above, but it may nevertheless be convenient and desirable depending upon the particular facts. Subdivision (b)(3) encompasses those cases in which a class action would achieve economies of time, effort, and expense, and promote uniformity of decision as to persons similarly situated, without sacrificing procedural fairness or bringing about other undesirable results. *Cf.* Chafee, *supra,* at 201.

The court is required to find, as a condition of holding that a class action may be maintained under this subdivision, that the questions common to the class predominate over the questions affecting individual members. It is only where this predominance exists that economies can be achieved by means of the class-action device. In this view, a fraud perpetrated on numerous persons by the use of similar misrepresentations may be an appealing situation for a class action, and it may remain so despite the need, if liability is found, for separate determination of the damages suffered by individuals within the class. On the other hand, although having some common core, a fraud case may be unsuited for treatment as a class action if there was material variation in the representations made or in the kinds or degrees of reliance by the persons to whom they were addressed. See *Oppenheimer v. F. J. Young & Co., Inc.,* 144 F.2d 387 (2d Cir. 1944); *Miller v. National City Bank of N. Y.,* 166 F.2d 723 (2d Cir. 1948); and for like problems in other contexts, see *Hughes v. Encyclopaedia Britannica,* 199 F.2d 295 (7th Cir. 1952); *Sturgeon v. Great Lakes Steel Corp.,* 143 F.2d 819 (6th Cir. 1944). A "mass accident" resulting in injuries to numerous persons is ordinarily not appropriate for a class action because of the likelihood that significant questions, not only of damages but of liability and defenses to liability, would be present, affecting the individuals in different ways. In these circumstances an action conducted nom-

New matter is shown in italics; matter to be omitted is lined through

inally as a class action would degenerate in practice into multiple lawsuits separately tried. See *Pennsylvania R. R. v. United States,* 111 F.Supp. 80 (D.N.J. 1953); *cf.* Weinstein, *supra,* 9 Buffalo L.Rev. at 469. Private damage claims by numerous individuals arising out of concerted antitrust violations may or may not involve predominating common questions. See *Union Carbide & Carbon Corp. v. Nisley,* 300 F.2d 561 (10th Cir. 1961), *pet. cert. dism.,* 371 U.S. 801 (1963); *cf. Weeks v. Bareco Oil Co.,* 125 F.2d 84 (7th Cir. 1941); *Kainz v. Anheuser-Busch, Inc.,* 194 F.2d 737 (7th Cir. 1952); *Hess v. Anderson, Clayton & Co.,* 20 F.R.D. 466 (S.D.Calif. 1957).

That common questions predominate is not itself sufficient to justify a class action under subdivision (b)(3), for another method of handling the litigious situation may be available which has greater practical advantages. Thus one or more actions agreed to by the parties as test or model actions may be preferable to a class action; or it may prove feasible and preferable to consolidate actions. *Cf.* Weinstein, *supra,* 9 Buffalo L.Rev. at 438–54. Even when a number of separate actions are proceeding simultaneously, experience shows that the burdens on the parties and the courts can sometimes be reduced by arrangements for avoiding repetitious discovery or the like. Currently the Coordinating Committee on Multiple Litigation in the United States District Courts (a subcommittee of the Committee on Trial Practice and Technique of the Judicial Conference of the United States) is charged with developing methods for expediting such massive litigation. To reinforce the point that the court with the aid of the parties ought to assess the relative advantages of alternative procedures for handling the total controversy, subdivision (b)(3) requires, as a further condition of maintaining the class action, that the court shall find that that procedure is "superior" to the others in the particular circumstances.

Factors (A)–(D) are listed, non-exhaustively, as pertinent to the findings. The court is to consider the interests of individual members of the class in controlling their own litigations and carrying them on as they see fit. See *Weeks v. Bareco Oil Co.,* 125 F.2d 84, 88–90, 93–94 (7th Cir.1941) (anti-trust action); see also *Pentland v. Dravo Corp.,* 152 F.2d 851 (3d Cir.1945), and Chafee, *supra,* at 273–75, regarding policy of Fair Labor Standards Act of 1938, § 16(b), 29 U.S.C. § 216(b), prior to amendment by Portal-to-Portal Act of 1947, § 5(a). [The present provisions of 29 U.S.C. § 216(b) are not intended to be affected by Rule 23, as amended.] In this connection the court should inform itself of any litigation actually pending by or against the individuals. The interests of individuals in conducting separate lawsuits may be so strong as to call for denial of a class action. On the other hand, these interests may be theoretic rather than practical: the class may have a high degree of cohesion and prosecution of the action through representatives would be quite unobjectionable, or the amounts at stake for individuals may be so small that separate suits would be impracticable. The burden that separate suits would impose on the party opposing the class, or upon the court calendars, may also fairly be considered. (See the discussion, under subdivision (c)(2) below, of the right of members to be excluded from the class upon their request.)

Also pertinent is the question of the desirability of concentrating the trial of the claims in the particular forum by means of a class action, in contrast to allowing the claims to be litigated separately in forums to which they would ordinarily be brought. Finally, the court should consider the problems of management which are likely to arise in the conduct of a class action.

Subdivision (c)(1). In order to give clear definition to the action, this provision requires the court to determine, as early in the proceedings as may be practicable, whether an action brought as a class action is to be so maintained. The determina-

---

New matter is shown in italics; matter to be omitted is lined through

tion depends in each case on satisfaction of the terms of subdivision (a) and the relevant provisions of subdivision (b).

An order embodying a determination can be conditional; the court may rule, for example, that a class action may be maintained only if the representation is improved through intervention of additional parties of a stated type. A determination once made can be altered or amended before the decision on the merits if, upon full development of the facts, the original determination appears unsound. A negative determination means that the action should be stripped of its character as a class action. See subdivision (d)(4). Although an action thus becomes a nonclass action, the court may still be receptive to interventions before the decision on the merits so that the litigation may cover as many interests as can be conveniently handled; the questions whether the intervenors in the nonclass action shall be permitted to claim "ancillary" jurisdiction or the benefit of the date of the commencement of the action for purposes of the statute of limitations are to be decided by reference to the laws governing jurisdiction and limitations as they apply in particular contexts.

Whether the court should require notice to be given to members of the class of its intention to make a determination, or of the order embodying it, is left to the court's discretion under subdivision (d)(2).

Subdivision (c)(2) makes special provision for class actions maintained under subdivision (b)(3). As noted in the discussion of the latter subdivision, the interests of the individuals in pursuing their own litigations may be so strong here as to warrant denial of a class action altogether. Even when a class action is maintained under subdivision (b)(3), this individual interest is respected. Thus the court is required to direct notice to the members of the class of the right of each member to be excluded from the class upon his request. A member who does not request exclusion may, if he wishes, enter an appearance in the action through his counsel; whether or not he does so, the judgment in the action will embrace him.

The notice, setting forth the alternatives open to the members of the class, is to be the best practicable under the circumstances, and shall include individual notice to the members who can be identified through reasonable effort. (For further discussion of this notice, see the statement under subdivision (d)(2) below.)

Subdivision (c)(3). The judgment in a class action maintained as such to the end will embrace the class, that is, in a class action under subdivision (b)(1) or (b)(2), those found by the court to be class members; in a class action under subdivision (b)(3), those to whom the notice prescribed by subdivision (c)(2) was directed, excepting those who requested exclusion or who are ultimately found by the court not to be members of the class. The judgment has this scope whether it is favorable or unfavorable to the class. In a (b)(1) or (b)(2) action the judgment "describes" the members of the class, but need not specify the individual members; in a (b)(3) action the judgment "specifies" the individual members who have been identified and describes the others.

Compare subdivision (c)(4) as to actions conducted as class actions only with respect to particular issues. Where the class-action character of the lawsuit is based solely on the existence of a "limited fund," the judgment, while extending to all claims of class members against the fund, has ordinarily left unaffected the personal claims of nonappearing members against the debtor. See 3 Moore, *supra,* ¶ 23.11[4].

Hitherto, in a few actions conducted as "spurious" class actions and thus nominally designed to extend only to parties and others intervening *before* the determination of liability, courts have held or intimated that class members might be permitted to intervene *after* a decision on the merits favorable to their interests,

---

New matter is shown in italics; matter to be omitted is lined through

in order to secure the benefits of the decision for themselves, although they would presumably be unaffected by an unfavorable decision. See, as to the propriety of this so-called "one-way" intervention in "spurious" actions, the conflicting views expressed in *Union Carbide & Carbon Corp. v. Nisley,* 300 F.2d 561 (10th Cir.1961), *pet. cert. dism.,* 371 U.S. 801 (1963); *York v. Guaranty Trust Co.,* 143 F.2d 503, 529 (2d Cir.1944), *rev'd on grounds not here relevant,* 326 U.S. 99 (1945); *Pentland v. Dravo Corp.,* 152 F.2d 851, 856 (3d Cir.1945); *Speed v. Transamerica Corp.,* 100 F.Supp. 461, 463 (D.Del.1951); *State Wholesale Grocers v. Great Atl. & Pac. Tea Co.,* 24 F.R.D. 510 (N.D.Ill.1959); *Alabama Ind. Serv. Stat. Assn. v. Shell Pet. Corp.,* 28 F.Supp. 386, 390 (N.D.Ala.1939); *Tolliver v. Cudahy Packing Co.,* 39 F.Supp. 337, 339 (E.D.Tenn.1941); *Kalven & Rosenfield, supra,* 8 U. of Chi.L.Rev. 684 (1941); Comment, 53 Nw.U.L.Rev. 627, 632–33 (1958); *Developments in the Law, supra,* 71 Harv.L.Rev. at 935; 2 Barron & Holtzoff, *supra,* § 568; but *cf. Lockwood v. Hercules Powder Co.,* 7 F.R.D. 24, 28–29 (W.D.Mo.1947); *Abram v. San Joaquin Cotton Oil Co.,* 46 F.Supp. 969, 976–77 (S.D.Calif.1942); Chafee, *supra,* at 280, 285; 3 Moore, *supra,* ¶ 23.12, at 3476. Under proposed subdivision (c)(3), one-way intervention is excluded; the action will have been early determined to be a class or nonclass action, and in the former case the judgment, whether or not favorable, will include the class, as above stated.

Although thus declaring that the judgment in a class action includes the class, as defined, subdivision (c)(3) does not disturb the recognized principle that the court conducting the action cannot predetermine the *res judicata* effect of the judgment; this can be tested only in a subsequent action. See Restatement, *Judgments* § 86, comment (h), § 116 (1942). The court, however, in framing the judgment in any suit brought as a class action, must decide what its extent or coverage shall be, and if the matter is carefully considered, questions of *res judicata* are less likely to be raised at a later time and if raised will be more satisfactorily answered. See Chafee, *supra,* at 294; Weinstein, *supra,* 9 Buffalo L.Rev. at 460.

Subdivision (c)(4). This provision recognizes that an action may be maintained as a class action as to particular issues only. For example, in a fraud or similar case the action may retain its "class" character only through the adjudication of liability to the class; the members of the class may thereafter be required to come in individually and prove the amounts of their respective claims.

Two or more classes may be represented in a single action. Where a class is found to include subclasses divergent in interest, the class may be divided correspondingly, and each subclass treated as a class.

Subdivision (d) is concerned with the fair and efficient conduct of the action and lists some types of orders which may be appropriate.

The court should consider how the proceedings are to be arranged in sequence, and what measures should be taken to simplify the proof and argument. See subdivision (d)(1). The orders resulting from this consideration, like the others referred to in subdivision (d), may be combined with a pretrial order under Rule 16, and are subject to modification as the case proceeds.

Subdivision (d)(2) sets out a non-exhaustive list of possible occasions for orders requiring notice to the class. Such notice is not a novel conception. For example, in "limited fund" cases, members of the class have been notified to present individual claims after the basic class decision. Notice has gone to members of a class so that they might express any opposition to the representation, see *United States v. American Optical Co.,* 97 F.Supp. 66 (N.D.Ill.1951), and 1950–51 CCH Trade Cases 64573–74 (¶ 62869); *cf. Weeks v. Bareco Oil Co.,* 125 F.2d 84, 94 (7th Cir.1941), and notice may encourage interventions to improve the representation of the class. *Cf. Oppenheimer v. F.J. Young & Co.,* 144 F.2d 387 (2d Cir.1944). Notice

---

New matter is shown in italics; matter to be omitted is lined through

has been used to poll members on a proposed modification of a consent decree. See record in *Sam Fox Publishing Co. v. United States,* 366 U.S. 683 (1961).

Subdivision (d)(2) does not require notice at any stage, but rather calls attention to its availability and invokes the court's discretion. In the degree that there is cohesiveness or unity in the class and the representation is effective, the need for notice to the class will tend toward a minimum. These indicators suggest that notice under subdivision (d)(2) may be particularly useful and advisable in certain class actions maintained under subdivision (b)(3), for example, to permit members of the class to object to the representation. Indeed, under subdivision (c)(2), notice must be ordered, and is not merely discretionary, to give the members in a subdivision (b)(3) class action an opportunity to secure exclusion from the class. This mandatory notice pursuant to subdivision (c)(2), together with any discretionary notice which the court may find it advisable to give under subdivision (d)(2), is designed to fulfill requirements of due process to which the class action procedure is of course subject. See *Hansberry v. Lee,* 311 U.S. 32 (1940); *Mullane v. Central Hanover Bank & Trust Co.,* 339 U.S. 306 (1950); *cf. Dickinson v. Burnham,* 197 F.2d 973, 979 (2d Cir.1952), and studies cited at 979 n. 4; see also *All American Airways, Inc. v. Eldered,* 209 F.2d 247, 249 (2d Cir.1954); *Gart v. Cole,* 263 F.2d 244, 248–49 (2d Cir.1959), *cert. denied,* 359 U.S. 978 (1959).

Notice to members of the class, whenever employed under amended Rule 23, should be accommodated to the particular purpose but need not comply with the formalities for service of process. See Chafee, *supra,* at 230–31; *Brendle v. Smith,* 7 F.R.D. 119 (S.D.N.Y.1946). The fact that notice is given at one stage of the action does not mean that it must be given at subsequent stages. Notice is available fundamentally "for the protection of the members of the class or otherwise for the fair conduct of the action" and should not be used merely as a device for the undesirable solicitation of claims. See the discussion in *Cherner v. Transitron Electronic Corp.,* 201 F.Supp. 934 (D.Mass.1962); *Hormel v. United States,* 17 F.R.D. 303 (S.D.N.Y.1955).

In appropriate cases the court should notify interested government agencies of the pendency of the action or of particular steps therein.

Subdivision (d)(3) reflects the possibility of conditioning the maintenance of a class action, *e. g.,* on the strengthening of the representation, see subdivision (c)(1) above; and recognizes that the imposition of conditions on intervenors may be required for the proper and efficient conduct of the action.

As to orders under subdivision (d)(4), see subdivision (c)(1) above.

Subdivision (e) requires approval of the court, after notice, for the dismissal or compromise of any class action.

Rule 23.1 [New].

DERIVATIVE ACTIONS BY SHAREHOLDERS

In a derivative action brought by one or more shareholders or members to enforce a right of a corporation or of an unincorporated association, the corporation or association having failed to enforce a right which may properly be asserted by it, the complaint shall be verified and shall allege (1) that the plaintiff was a shareholder or member at the time of the transaction of which he complains or that his share or membership thereafter devolved on him by operation of law, and (2) that the action is not a collusive one to confer

New matter is shown in italics; matter to be omitted is lined through

jurisdiction on a court of the United States which it would not otherwise have. The complaint shall also allege with particularity the efforts, if any, made by the plaintiff to obtain the action he desires from the directors or comparable authority and, if necessary, from the shareholders or members, and the reasons for his failure to obtain the action or for not making the effort. The derivative action may not be maintained if it appears that the plaintiff does not fairly and adequately represent the interests of the shareholders or members similarly situated in enforcing the right of the corporation or association. The action shall not be dismissed or compromised without the approval of the court, and notice of the proposed dismissal or compromise shall be given to shareholders or members in such manner as the court directs.

Advisory Committee's Note

A derivative action by a shareholder of a corporation or by a member of an unincorporated association has distinctive aspects which require the special provisions set forth in the new rule. The next-to-the-last sentence recognizes that the question of adequacy of representation may arise when the plaintiff is one of a group of shareholders or members. *Cf.* 3 *Moore's Federal Practice* ¶ 23.08 (2d ed.1963).

The court has inherent power to provide for the conduct of the proceedings in a derivative action, including the power to determine the course of the proceedings and require that any appropriate notice be given to shareholders or members.

Rule 23.2 [New].

ACTIONS RELATING TO UNINCORPORATED ASSOCIATIONS

An action brought by or against the members of an unincorporated association as a class by naming certain members as representative parties may be maintained only if it appears that the representative parties will fairly and adequately protect the interests of the association and its members. In the conduct of the action the court may make appropriate orders corresponding with those described in Rule 23(d), and the procedure for dismissal or compromise of the action shall correspond with that provided in Rule 23(e).

Advisory Committee's Note

Although an action by or against representatives of the membership of an unincorporated association has often been viewed as a class action, the real or main purpose of this characterization has been to give "entity treatment" to the association when for formal reasons it cannot sue or be sued as a jural person under Rule 17(b). See Louisell & Hazard, *Pleading and Procedure: State and Federal* 718 (1962); 3 *Moore's Federal Practice* ¶ 23.08 (2d ed.1963); Story, J. in *West v. Randall*, 29 Fed.Cas. 718, 722–23, No. 17,424 (C.C.D.R.I.1820); and, for

---

New matter is shown in italics; matter to be omitted is lined through

examples, *Gibbs v. Buck*, 307 U.S. 66 (1939); *Tunstall v. Brotherhood of Locomotive F. & E.*, 148 F.2d 403 (4th Cir.1945); *Oskoian v. Canuel*, 269 F.2d 311 (1st Cir.1959). Rule 23.2 deals separately with these actions, referring where appropriate to Rule 23.

Rule 24.

INTERVENTION

(a) **Intervention of Right.** Upon timely application anyone shall be permitted to intervene in an action: (1) when a statute of the United States confers an unconditional right to intervene; or (2) when the ~~representation of the applicant's interest by existing parties is or may be inadequate and the applicant is or may be bound by a judgment in the action; or (3) when the applicant is so situated as to be adversely affected by a distribution or other disposition of property which is in the custody or subject to the control or disposition of the court or an officer thereof.~~ *applicant claims an interest relating to the property or transaction which is the subject of the action and he is so situated that the disposition of the action may as a practical matter impair or impede his ability to protect that interest, unless the applicant's interest is adequately represented by existing parties.*

Advisory Committee's Note

In attempting to overcome certain difficulties which have arisen in the application of present Rule 24(a)(2) and (3), this amendment draws upon the revision of the related Rules 19 (joinder of persons needed for just adjudication) and 23 (class actions), and the reasoning underlying that revision.

Rule 24(a)(3) as amended in 1948 provided for intervention of right where the applicant established that he would be adversely affected by the distribution or disposition of property involved in an action to which he had not been made a party. Significantly, some decided cases virtually disregarded the language of this provision. Thus Professor Moore states: "The concept of a fund has been applied so loosely that it is possible for a court to find a fund in almost any in personam action." 4 *Moore's Federal Practice,* ¶ 24.09[3], at 55 (2d ed. 1962), and see, *e.g., Formulabs, Inc. v. Hartley Pen Co.*, 275 F.2d 52 (9th Cir.1960). This development was quite natural, for Rule 24(a)(3) was unduly restricted. If an absentee would be substantially affected in a practical sense by the determination made in an action, he should, as a general rule, be entitled to intervene, and his right to do so should not depend on whether there is a fund to be distributed or otherwise disposed of. Intervention of right is here seen to be a kind of counterpart to Rule 19(a)(2)(i) on joinder of persons needed for a just adjudication: where, upon motion of a party in an action, an absentee should be joined so that he may protect his interest which as a practical matter may be substantially impaired by the disposition of the action, he ought to have a right to intervene in the action on his own motion. See Louisell & Hazard, *Pleading and Procedure: State and Federal* 749–50 (1962).

The general purpose of original Rule 24(a)(2) was to entitle an absentee, purportedly represented by a party, to intervene in the action if he could establish

---

New matter is shown in italics; matter to be omitted is lined through

with fair probability that the representation was inadequate. Thus, where an action is being prosecuted or defended by a trustee, a beneficiary of the trust should have a right to intervene if he can show that the trustee's representation of his interest probably is inadequate; similarly a member of a class should have the right to intervene in a class action if he can show the inadequacy of the representation of his interest by the representative parties before the court.

Original Rule 24(a)(2), however, made it a condition of intervention that "the applicant is or may be bound by a judgment in the action," and this created difficulties with intervention in class actions. If the "bound" language was read literally in the sense of res judicata, it could defeat intervention in some meritorious cases. A member of a class to whom a judgment in a class action extended by its terms (see Rule 23(c)(3), as amended) might be entitled to show in a later action, when the judgment in the class action was claimed to operate as res judicata against him, that the "representative" in the class action had not in fact adequately represented him. If he could make this showing, the class-action judgment might be held not to bind him. See *Hansberry v. Lee*, 311 U.S. 32 (1940). If a class member sought to intervene in the class action proper, while it was still pending, on grounds of inadequacy of representation, he could be met with the argument: if the representation was in fact inadequate, he would not be "bound" by the judgment when it was subsequently asserted against him as res judicata, hence he was not entitled to intervene; if the representation was in fact adequate, there was no occasion or ground for intervention. See *Sam Fox Publishing Co. v. United States*, 366 U.S. 683 (1961); *cf. Sulphen Estates, Inc. v. United States*, 342 U.S. 19 (1951). This reasoning might be linguistically justified by original Rule 24(a)(2); but it could lead to poor results. Compare the discussion in *International M. & I. Corp. v. Von Clemm*, 301 F.2d 857 (2d Cir.1962); *Atlantic Refining Co. v. Standard Oil Co.*, 304 F.2d 387 (D.C.Cir.1962). A class member who claims that his "representative" does not adequately represent him, and is able to establish that proposition with sufficient probability should not be put to the risk of having a judgment entered in the action which by its terms extends to him, and be obliged to test the validity of the judgment as applied to his interest by a later collateral attack. Rather he should, as a general rule, be entitled to intervene in the action.

The amendment provides that an applicant is entitled to intervene in an action when his position is comparable to that of a person under Rule 19(a)(2)(i), as amended, unless his interest is already adequately represented in the action by existing parties. The Rule 19(a)(2)(i) criterion imports practical considerations, and the deletion of the "bound" language similarly frees the rule from undue preoccupation with strict considerations of res judicata.

The representation whose adequacy comes into question under the amended rule is not confined to formal representation like that provided by a trustee for his beneficiary or a representative party in a class action for a member of the class. A party to an action may provide practical representation to the absentee seeking intervention although no such formal relationship exists between them, and the adequacy of this practical representation will then have to be weighed. See *International M. & I. Corp. v. Von Clemm*, and *Atlantic Refining Co. v. Standard Oil Co.*, both supra; *Wolpe v. Poretsky*, 144 F.2d 505 (D.C.Cir.1944), cert. denied, 323 U.S. 777 (1944); *cf. Ford Motor Co. v. Bisanz Bros.*, 249 F.2d 22 (8th Cir.1957); and generally Annot., 84 A.L.R.2d 1412 (1962).

An intervention of right under the amended rule may be subject to appropriate conditions or restrictions responsive among other things to the requirements of efficient conduct of the proceedings.

New matter is shown in italics; matter to be omitted is lined through

Rule 44.1 [New].

DETERMINATION OF FOREIGN LAW *

A party who intends to raise an issue concerning the law of a foreign country shall give notice in his pleadings or other reasonable written notice. The court, in determining foreign law, may consider any relevant material or source, including testimony, whether or not submitted by a party or admissible under Rule 43. The court's determination shall be treated as a ruling on a question of law.

Advisory Committee's Note

Rule 44.1 is added by amendment to furnish Federal courts with a uniform and effective procedure for raising and determining an issue concerning the law of a foreign country.

To avoid unfair surprise, the *first sentence* of the new rule requires that a party who intends to raise an issue of foreign law shall give notice thereof. The uncertainty under Rule 8(a) about whether foreign law must be pleaded—*compare Siegelman v. Cunard White Star, Ltd.*, 221 F.2d 189 (2d Cir.1955), and *Pedersen v. United States*, 191 F.Supp. 95 (D.Guam 1961) *with Harrison v. United Fruit Co.*, 143 F.Supp. 598 (S.D.N.Y.1956)—is eliminated by the provision that the notice shall be "written" and "reasonable." It may, but need not be, incorporated in the pleadings. In some situations the pertinence of foreign law is apparent from the outset; accordingly the necessary investigation of that law will have been accomplished by the party at the pleading stage, and the notice can be given conveniently in the pleadings. In other situations the pertinence of foreign law may remain doubtful until the case is further developed. A requirement that notice of foreign law be given only through the medium of the pleadings would tend in the latter instances to force the party to engage in a peculiarly burdensome type of investigation which might turn out to be unnecessary; and correspondingly the adversary would be forced into a possibly wasteful investigation. The liberal provisions for amendment of the pleadings afford help if the pleadings are used as the medium of giving notice of the foreign law; but it seems best to permit a written notice to be given outside of and later than the pleadings, provided the notice is reasonable.

The new rule does not attempt to set any definite limit on the party's time for giving the notice of an issue of foreign law; in some cases the issue may not become apparent until the trial, and notice then given may still be reasonable. The stage which the case has reached at the time of the notice, the reason proffered by the party for his failure to give earlier notice, and the importance to the case as a whole of the issue of foreign law sought to be raised, are among the factors which the court should consider in deciding a question of the reasonableness of a notice. If notice is given by one party it need not be repeated by any other and serves as a basis for presentation of material on the foreign law by all parties.

The *second sentence* of the new rule describes the materials to which the court may resort in determining an issue of foreign law. Heretofore the district courts, applying Rule 43(a), have looked in certain cases to State law to find the rules of

* This rule was developed collaboratively by the Advisory Committee on Civil Rules, the Commission and Advisory Committee on International Rules of Judicial Procedure (see Act of Sept. 2, 1958, 72 Stat. 1743), and the Columbia Law School Project on International Procedure.

New matter is shown in italics; matter to be omitted is lined through

evidence by which the content of foreign-country law is to be established. The State laws vary; some embody procedures which are inefficient, time consuming, and expensive. See, generally, Nussbaum, *Proving the Law of Foreign Countries*, 3 Am.J.Comp.L. 60 (1954). In all events the ordinary rules of evidence are often inapposite to the problem of determining foreign law and have in the past prevented examination of material which could have provided a proper basis for the determination. The new rule permits consideration by the court of any relevant material, including testimony, without regard to its admissibility under Rule 43. *Cf.* N.Y.Civ.Prac.Law & Rules, R. 4511 (effective Sept. 1, 1963); 2 Va.Code Ann. tit. 8, § 8–273; 2 W.Va.Code Ann. § 5711.

In further recognition of the peculiar nature of the issue of foreign law, the new rule provides that in determining this law the court is not limited by material presented by the parties; it may engage in its own research and consider any relevant material thus found. The court may have at its disposal better foreign law materials than counsel have presented, or may wish to reexamine and amplify material that has been presented by counsel in partisan fashion or in insufficient detail. On the other hand, the court is free to insist on a complete presentation by counsel.

There is no requirement that the court give formal notice to the parties of its intention to engage in its own research on an issue of foreign law which has been raised by them, or of its intention to raise and determine independently an issue not raised by them. Ordinarily the court should inform the parties of material it has found diverging substantially from the material which they have presented; and in general the court should give the parties an opportunity to analyze and counter new points upon which it proposes to rely. See Schlesinger, *Comparative Law* 142 (2d ed. 1959); Wyzanski, *A Trial Judge's Freedom and Responsibility*, 65 Harv.L.Rev. 1281, 1296 (1952); *cf. Siegelman v. Cunard White Star, Ltd., supra*, 221 F.2d at 197. To require, however, that the court give formal notice from time to time as it proceeds with its study of the foreign law would add an element of undesirable rigidity to the procedure for determining issues of foreign law.

The new rule refrains from imposing an obligation on the court to take "judicial notice" of foreign law because this would put an extreme burden on the court in many cases; and it avoids use of the concept of "judicial notice" in any form because of the uncertain meaning of that concept as applied to foreign law. See, *e.g.*, Stern, *Foreign Law in the Courts: Judicial Notice and Proof*, 45 Calif.L. Rev. 23, 43 (1957). Rather the rule provides flexible procedures for presenting and utilizing material on issues of foreign law by which a sound result can be achieved with fairness to the parties.

Under the *third sentence*, the court's determination of an issue of foreign law is to be treated as a ruling on a question of "law," not "fact," so that appellate review will not be narrowly confined by the "clearly erroneous" standard of Rule 52(a). *Cf.* Uniform Judicial Notice of Foreign Law Act § 3; Note, 72 Harv.L.Rev. 318 (1958).

The new rule parallels Article IV of the Uniform Interstate and International Procedure Act, approved by the Commissioners on Uniform State Laws in 1962, except that section 4.03 of Article IV states that "[t]he court, not the jury" shall determine foreign law. The new rule does not address itself to this problem, since the rules refrain from allocating functions as between the court and the jury. See Rule 38(a). It has long been thought, however, that the jury is not the appropriate body to determine issues of foreign law. See, *e.g.*, Story, *Conflict of Laws* § 638 (1st ed. 1834, 8th ed. 1883); 1 Greenleaf, *Evidence* § 486 (1st ed. 1842, 16th ed. 1899); 4 Wigmore, *Evidence* § 2558 (1st ed. 1905); 9 *id.* § 2558 (3d ed. 1940). The majority

---

New matter is shown in italics; matter to be omitted is lined through

of the States have committed such issues to determination by the court. See Article 5 of the Uniform Judicial Notice of Foreign Law Act, adopted by twenty-six states, 9A U.L.A. 318 (1957) (Supp.1961, at 134); N.Y.Civ.Prac.Law & Rules, R. 4511 (effective Sept. 1, 1963); Wigmore, *loc. cit.* And Federal courts that have considered the problem in recent years have reached the same conclusion without reliance on statute. See *Jansson v. Swedish American Line*, 185 F.2d 212, 216 (1st Cir. 1950); *Bank of Nova Scotia v. San Miguel*, 196 F.2d 950, 957 n. 6 (1st Cir.1952); *Liechti v. Roche*, 198 F.2d 174 (5th Cir.1952); *Daniel Lumber Co. v. Empresas Hondurenas, S.A.*, 215 F.2d 465 (5th Cir.1954).

Rule 59.

NEW TRIALS; AMENDMENT OF JUDGMENTS

(d) On Initiative of Court. Not later than 10 days after entry of judgment the court of its own initiative may order a new trial for any reason for which it might have granted a new trial on motion of a party, ~~and in the order shall specify the grounds therefor~~. *After giving the parties notice and an opportunity to be heard on the matter, the court may grant a motion for a new trial, timely served, for a reason not stated in the motion. In either case, the court shall specify in the order the grounds therefor.*

Advisory Committee's Note

By narrow interpretation of Rule 59(b) and (d), it has been held that the trial court is without power to grant a motion for a new trial, timely served, by an order made more than 10 days after the entry of judgment, based upon a ground not stated in the motion but perceived and relied on by the trial court *sua sponte*. *Freid v. McGrath*, 133 F.2d 350 (D.C.Cir.1942); *National Farmers Union Auto. & Cas. Co. v. Wood*, 207 F.2d 659 (10th Cir.1953); *Bailey v. Slentz*, 189 F.2d 406 (10th Cir.1951); *Marshall's U.S. Auto Supply, Inc. v. Cashman*, 111 F.2d 140 (10th Cir.1940), *cert. denied*, 311 U.S. 667 (1940); but see *Steinberg v. Indemnity Ins. Co.*, 36 F.R.D. 253 (E.D.La.1964).

The result is undesirable. Just as the court has power under Rule 59(d) to grant a new trial of its own initiative within the 10 days, so it should have power, when an effective new trial motion has been made and is pending, to decide it on grounds thought meritorious by the court although not advanced in the motion. The second sentence added by amendment to Rule 59(d) confirms the court's power in the latter situation, with provision that the parties be afforded a hearing before the power is exercised. See 6 *Moore's Federal Practice* ¶ 59.09[2] (2d ed. 1953).

In considering whether a given ground has or has not been advanced in the motion made by the party, it should be borne in mind that the particularity called for in stating the grounds for a new-trial motion is the same as that required for all motions by Rule 7(b)(1). The latter rule does not require ritualistic detail but rather a fair indication to court and counsel of the substance of the grounds relied on. See *Lebeck v. William A. Jarvis Co.*, 250 F.2d 285 (3d Cir.1957); *Tsai v. Rosenthal*, 297 F.2d 614 (8th Cir.1961); *General Motors Corp. v. Perry*, 303 F.2d 544 (7th Cir.1962); *cf. Grimm v. California Spray-Chemical Corp.*, 264 F.2d 145 (9th Cir.1959); *Cooper v. Midwest Feed Products Co.*, 271 F.2d 177 (8th Cir.1959).

New matter is shown in italics; matter to be omitted is lined through

Rule 65.

INJUNCTIONS

(a) Preliminary; ~~Notice~~ *Injunction.*

(1) Notice. No preliminary injunction shall be issued without notice to the adverse party.

(2) Consolidation of Hearing With Trial on Merits. Before or after the commencement of the hearing of an application for a preliminary injunction, the court may order the trial of the action on the merits to be advanced and consolidated with the hearing of the application. Even when this consolidation is not ordered, any evidence received upon an application for a preliminary injunction which would be admissible upon the trial on the merits becomes part of the record on the trial and need not be repeated upon the trial. This subdivision (a)(2) shall be so construed and applied as to save to the parties any rights they may have to trial by jury.

(b) Temporary Restraining Order; Notice; Hearing; Duration. ~~No~~ *A* temporary restraining order ~~shall~~ *may* be granted without *written or oral* notice to the adverse party *or his attorney* ~~unless~~ *only if (1)* it clearly appears from specific facts shown by affidavit or by the verified complaint that immediate and irreparable injury, loss, or damage will result to the applicant before ~~notice can be served and a hearing had thereon.~~ *the adverse party or his attorney can be heard in opposition, and (2) the applicant's attorney certifies to the court in writing the efforts, if any, which have been made to give the notice and the reasons supporting his claim that notice should not be required.* Every temporary restraining order granted without notice shall be indorsed with the date and hour of issuance; shall be filed forthwith in the clerk's office and entered of record; shall define the injury and state why it is irreparable and why the order was granted without notice; and shall expire by its terms within such time after entry, not to exceed 10 days, as the court fixes, unless within the time so fixed the order, for good cause shown, is extended for a like period or unless the party against whom the order is directed consents that it may be extended for a longer period. The reasons for the extension shall be entered of record. In case a temporary restraining order is granted without notice, the motion for a preliminary injunction shall be set down for hearing at the earliest possible time and takes precedence of all matters except older matters of the same character; and when the motion comes on for hearing the party who obtained the temporary restraining order

---

New matter is shown in italics; matter to be omitted is lined through

shall proceed with the application for a preliminary injunction and, if he does not do so, the court shall dissolve the temporary restraining order. On 2 days' notice to the party who obtained the temporary restraining order without notice or on such shorter notice to that party as the court may prescribe, the adverse party may appear and move its dissolution or modification and in that event the court shall proceed to hear and determine such motion as expeditiously as the ends of justice require.

(c) **Security.** No restraining order or preliminary injunction shall issue except upon the giving of security by the applicant, in such sum as the court deems proper, for the payment of such costs and damages as may be incurred or suffered by any party who is found to have been wrongfully enjoined or restrained. No such security shall be required of the United States or of an officer or agency thereof.

~~A surety upon a bond or undertaking under this rule submits himself to the jurisdiction of the court and irrevocably appoints the clerk of the court as his agent upon whom any papers affecting his liability on the bond or undertaking may be served. His liability may be enforced on motion without the necessity of an independent action. The motion and such notice of the motion as the court prescribes may be served on the clerk of the court who shall forthwith mail copies to the persons giving the security if their addresses are known.~~ *The provisions of Rule 65.1 apply to a surety upon a bond or undertaking under this rule.*

Advisory Committee's Note

Subdivision (a)(2). This new subdivision provides express authority for consolidating the hearing of an application for a preliminary injunction with the trial on the merits. The authority can be exercised with particular profit when it appears that a substantial part of the evidence offered on the application will be relevant to the merits and will be presented in such form as to qualify for admission on the trial proper. Repetition of evidence is thereby avoided. The fact that the proceedings have been consolidated should cause no delay in the disposition of the application for the preliminary injunction, for the evidence will be directed in the first instance to that relief, and the preliminary injunction, if justified by the proof, may be issued in the course of the consolidated proceedings. Furthermore, to consolidate the proceeding will tend to expedite the final disposition of the action. It is believed that consolidation can be usefully availed of in many cases.

The subdivision further provides that even when consolidation is not ordered, evidence received in connection with an application for a preliminary injunction which would be admissible on the trial on the merits forms part of the trial record. This evidence need not be repeated on the trial. On the other hand, repetition is not altogether prohibited. That would be impractical and unwise. For example, a witness testifying comprehensively on the trial who has previously testified upon the application for a preliminary injunction might sometimes be hamstrung in telling his story if he could not go over some part of his prior testimony to connect it with his present testimony. So also, some repetition of testimony may be called

---

New matter is shown in italics; matter to be omitted is lined through

for where the trial is conducted by a judge who did not hear the application for the preliminary injunction. In general, however, repetition can be avoided with an increase of efficiency in the conduct of the case and without any distortion of the presentation of evidence by the parties.

Since an application for a preliminary injunction may be made in an action in which, with respect to all or part of the merits, there is a right to trial by jury, it is appropriate to add the caution appearing in the last sentence of the subdivision. In such a case the jury will have to hear all the evidence bearing on its verdict, even if some part of the evidence has already been heard by the judge alone on the application for the preliminary injunction.

The subdivision is believed to reflect the substance of the best current practice and introduces no novel conception.

Subdivision (b). In view of the possibly drastic consequences of a temporary restraining order, the opposition should be heard, if feasible, before the order is granted. Many judges have properly insisted that, when time does not permit of formal notice of the application to the adverse party, some expedient, such as telephonic notice to the attorney for the adverse party, be resorted to if this can reasonably be done. On occasion, however, temporary restraining orders have been issued without any notice when it was feasible for some fair, although informal, notice to be given. See the emphatic criticisms in *Pennsylvania Rd. Co. v. Transport Workers Union*, 278 F.2d 693, 694 (3d Cir.1960); *Arvida Corp. v. Sugarman*, 259 F.2d 428, 429 (2d Cir.1958); *Lummus Co. v. Commonwealth Oil Ref. Co., Inc.*, 297 F.2d 80, 83 (2d Cir.1961), *cert. denied*, 368 U.S. 986 (1962).

Heretofore the first sentence of subdivision (b), in referring to a notice "served" on the "adverse party" on which a "hearing" could be held, perhaps invited the interpretation that the order might be granted without notice if the circumstances did not permit of a formal hearing on the basis of a formal notice. The subdivision is amended to make it plain that informal notice, which may be communicated to the attorney rather than the adverse party, is to be preferred to no notice at all.

Before notice can be dispensed with, the applicant's counsel must give his certificate as to any efforts made to give notice and the reasons why notice should not be required. This certificate is in addition to the requirement of an affidavit or verified complaint setting forth the facts as to the irreparable injury which would result before the opposition could be heard.

The amended subdivision continues to recognize that a temporary restraining order may be issued without any notice when the circumstances warrant.

Subdivision (c). Original Rules 65 and 73 contained substantially identical provisions for summary proceedings against sureties on bonds required or permitted by the rules. There was fragmentary coverage of the same subject in the Admiralty Rules. Clearly, a single comprehensive rule is required, and is incorporated as Rule 65.1.

Rule 82.

JURISDICTION AND VENUE UNAFFECTED

These rules shall not be construed to extend or limit the jurisdiction of the United States district courts or the venue of actions therein. *An admiralty or maritime claim within the meaning of Rule 9(h) shall not be treated as a civil action for the purposes of Title 28, U.S.C., §§ 1391–93.*

New matter is shown in italics; matter to be omitted is lined through

Advisory Committee's Note

Title 28, U.S.C., § 1391(b) provides: "A civil action wherein jurisdiction is not founded solely on diversity of citizenship may be brought only in the judicial district where all defendants reside, except as otherwise provided by law." This provision cannot appropriately be applied to what were formerly suits in admiralty. The rationale of decisions holding it inapplicable rests largely on the use of the term "civil action": i.e., a suit in admiralty is not a "civil action" within the statute. By virtue of the amendment to Rule 1, the provisions of Rule 2 convert suits in admiralty into civil actions. The added sentence is necessary to avoid an undesirable change in existing law with respect to venue.

*

CERTAIN OF THE AMENDMENTS OF FEDERAL RULES OF CIVIL PROCEDURE ADOPTED BY THE SUPREME COURT OF THE UNITED STATES ON MARCH 30, 1970, EFFECTIVE JULY 1, 1970, WITH ADVISORY COMMITTEE'S NOTES THEREON

[Amendments here omitted: Changes in Form 24.]

Advisory Committee's Explanatory Statement Concerning Amendments of the Discovery Rules

This statement is intended to serve as a general introduction to the amendments of Rules 26–37, concerning discovery, as well as related amendments of other rules. A separate note of customary scope is appended to amendments proposed for each rule. This statement provides a framework for the consideration of individual rule changes.

Changes in the Discovery Rules

The discovery rules, as adopted in 1938, were a striking and imaginative departure from tradition. It was expected from the outset that they would be important, but experience has shown them to play an even larger role than was initially foreseen. Although the discovery rules have been amended since 1938, the changes were relatively few and narrowly focused, made in order to remedy specific defects. The amendments now proposed reflect the first comprehensive review of the discovery rules undertaken since 1938. These amendments make substantial changes in the discovery rules. Those summarized here are among the more important changes.

Scope of Discovery. New provisions are made and existing provisions changed affecting the scope of discovery: (1) The contents of insurance policies are made discoverable (Rule 26(b)(2)). (2) A showing of good cause is no longer required for discovery of documents and things and entry upon land (Rule 34). However, a showing of need is required for discovery of "trial preparation" materials other than a party's discovery of his own statement and a witness' discovery of his own statement; and protection is afforded against disclosure in such documents of mental impressions, conclusions, opinions, or legal theories concerning the litiga-

---

New matter is shown in italics; matter to be omitted is lined through

267

tion (Rule 26(b)(3)). (3) Provision is made for discovery with respect to experts retained for trial preparation, and particularly those experts who will be called to testify at trial (Rule 26(b)(4)). (4) It is provided that interrogatories and requests for admission are not objectionable simply because they relate to matters of opinion or contention, subject of course to the supervisory power of the court (Rules 33(b), 36(a)). (5) Medical examination is made available as to certain nonparties (Rule 35(a)).

Mechanics of Discovery. A variety of changes are made in the mechanics of the discovery process, affecting the sequence and timing of discovery, the respective obligations of the parties with respect to requests, responses, and motions for court orders, and the related powers of the court to enforce discovery requests and to protect against their abusive use. A new provision eliminates the automatic grant of priority in discovery to one side (Rule 26(d)). Another provides that a party is not under a duty to supplement his responses to requests for discovery, except as specified (Rule 26(e)).

Other changes in the mechanics of discovery are designed to encourage extrajudicial discovery with a minimum of court intervention. Among these are the following: (1) The requirement that a plaintiff seek leave of court for early discovery requests is eliminated or reduced, and motions for a court order under Rule 34 are made unnecessary. Motions under Rule 35 are continued. (2) Answers and objections are to be served together and an enlargement of the time for response is provided. (3) The party seeking discovery, rather than the objecting party, is made responsible for invoking judicial determination of discovery disputes not resolved by the parties. (4) Judicial sanctions are tightened with respect to unjustified insistence upon or objection to discovery. These changes bring Rules 33, 34, and 36 substantially into line with the procedure now provided for depositions.

Failure to amend Rule 35 in the same way is based upon two considerations. First, the Columbia Survey (described below) finds that only about 5 percent of medical examinations require court motions, of which about half result in court orders. Second and of greater importance, the interest of the person to be examined in the privacy of his person was recently stressed by the Supreme Court in *Schlagenhauf v. Holder*, 379 U.S. 104 (1964). The court emphasized the trial judge's responsibility to assure that the medical examination was justified, particularly as to its scope.

Rearrangement of Rules. A limited rearrangement of the discovery rules has been made, whereby certain provisions are transferred from one rule to another. The reasons for this rear-

---

New matter is shown in italics; matter to be omitted is lined through

rangement are discussed below in a separate section of this statement, and the details are set out in a table at the end of this statement.

Optional Procedures. In two instances, new optional procedures have been made available. A new procedure is provided to a party seeking to take the deposition of a corporation or other organization (Rule 30(b)(6)). A party on whom interrogatories have been served requesting information derivable from his business records may under specified circumstances produce the records rather than give answers (Rule 33(c)).

Other Changes. This summary of changes is by no means exhaustive. Various changes have been made in order to improve, tighten, or clarify particular provisions, to resolve conflicts in the case law, and to improve language. All changes, whether mentioned here or not, are discussed in the appropriate note for each rule.

A Field Survey of Discovery Practice

Despite widespread acceptance of discovery as an essential part of litigation, disputes have inevitably arisen concerning the values claimed for discovery and abuses alleged to exist. Many disputes about discovery relate to particular rule provisions or court decisions and can be studied in traditional fashion with a view to specific amendment. Since discovery is in large measure extrajudicial, however, even these disputes may be enlightened by a study of discovery "in the field." And some of the larger questions concerning discovery can be pursued only by a study of its operation at the law office level and in unreported cases.

The Committee, therefore, invited the Project for Effective Justice of Columbia Law School to conduct a field survey of discovery. Funds were obtained from the Ford Foundation and the Walter E. Meyer Research Institute of Law, Inc. The survey was carried on under the direction of Prof. Maurice Rosenberg of Columbia Law School. The Project for Effective Justice has submitted a report to the Committee entitled "Field Survey of Federal Pretrial Discovery" (hereafter referred to as the Columbia Survey). The Committee is deeply grateful for the benefit of this extensive undertaking and is most appreciative of the cooperation of the Project and the funding organizations. The Committee is particularly grateful to Professor Rosenberg who not only directed the survey but has given much time in order to assist the Committee in assessing the results.

The Columbia Survey concludes, in general, that there is no empirical evidence to warrant a fundamental change in the philos-

---

New matter is shown in italics; matter to be omitted is lined through

ophy of the discovery rules. No widespread or profound failings are disclosed in the scope or availability of discovery. The costs of discovery do not appear to be oppressive, as a general matter, either in relation to ability to pay or to the stakes of the litigation. Discovery frequently provides evidence that would not otherwise be available to the parties and thereby makes for a fairer trial or settlement. On the other hand, no positive evidence is found that discovery promotes settlement.

More specific findings of the Columbia Survey are described in other Committee notes, in relation to particular rule provisions and amendments. Those interested in more detailed information may obtain it from the Project for Effective Justice.

Rearrangement of the Discovery Rules

The present discovery rules are structured entirely in terms of individual discovery devices, except for Rule 27 which deals with perpetuation of testimony, and Rule 37 which provides sanctions to enforce discovery. Thus, Rules 26 and 28 to 32 are in terms addressed only to the taking of a deposition of a party or third person. Rules 33 to 36 then deal in succession with four additional discovery devices: Written interrogatories to parties, production for inspection of documents and things, physical or mental examination and requests for admission.

Under the rules as promulgated in 1938, therefore, each of the discovery devices was separate and self-contained. A defect of this arrangement is that there is no natural location in the discovery rules for provisions generally applicable to all discovery or to several discovery devices. From 1938 until the present, a few amendments have applied a discovery provision to several rules. For example, in 1948, the scope of deposition discovery in Rule 26(b) and the provision for protective orders in Rule 30(b) were incorporated by reference in Rules 33 and 34. The arrangement was adequate so long as there were few provisions governing discovery generally and these provisions were relatively simple.

As will be seen, however, a series of amendments are now proposed which govern most or all of the discovery devices. Proposals of a similar nature will probably be made in the future. Under these circumstances, it is very desirable, even necessary, that the discovery rules contain one rule addressing itself to discovery generally.

Rule 26 is obviously the most appropriate rule for this purpose. One of its subdivisions, Rule 26(b), in terms governs only scope of deposition discovery, but it has been expressly incorporated by reference in Rules 33 and 34 and is treated by courts as

---

New matter is shown in italics; matter to be omitted is lined through

setting a general standard. By means of a transfer to Rule 26 of the provisions for protective orders now contained in Rule 30(b), and a transfer from Rule 26 of provisions addressed exclusively to depositions, Rule 26 is converted into a rule concerned with discovery generally. It becomes a convenient vehicle for the inclusion of new provisions dealing with the scope, timing, and regulation of discovery. Few additional transfers are needed. See table showing rearrangement of rules, set out below.

There are, to be sure, disadvantages in transferring any provision from one rule to another. Familiarity with the present pattern, reinforced by the references made by prior court decisions and the various secondary writings about the rules, is not lightly to be sacrificed. Revision of treatises and other reference works is burdensome and costly. Moreover, many States have adopted the existing pattern as a model for their rules.

On the other hand, the amendments now proposed will in any event require revision of texts and reference works as well as reconsideration by States following the Federal model. If these amendments are to be incorporated in an understandable way, a rule with general discovery provisions is needed. As will be seen, the proposed rearrangement produces a more coherent and intelligible pattern for the discovery rules taken as a whole. The difficulties described are those encountered whenever statutes are reexamined and revised. Failure to rearrange the discovery rules now would freeze the present scheme, making future change even more difficult.

Table Showing Rearrangement of Rules

Existing Rule No.	*New Rule No.*
26(a)	30(a), 31(a)
26(c)	30(c)
26(d)	32(a)
26(e)	32(b)
26(f)	32(c)
30(a)	30(b)
30(b)	26(c)
32	32(d)

Rule 5. Service and Filing of Pleadings and Other Papers

(a) Service: When Required. Except as otherwise provided in these rules, every order required by its terms to be served, every pleading subsequent to the original complaint unless the court otherwise orders because of numerous defendants, *every*

New matter is shown in italics; matter to be omitted is lined through

paper relating to discovery required to be served upon a party unless the court otherwise orders, every written motion other than one which may be heard ex parte, and every written notice, appearance, demand, offer of judgment, designation of record on appeal, and similar paper shall be served upon each of the parties. No service need be made on parties in default for failure to appear except that pleadings asserting new or additional claims for relief against them shall be served upon them in the manner provided for service of summons in Rule 4.

In an action begun by seizure of property, in which no person need be or is named as defendant, any service required to be made prior to the filing of an answer, claim, or appearance shall be made upon the person having custody or possession of the property at the time of the seizure.

Advisory Committee's Note

The amendment makes clear that all papers relating to discovery which are required to be served on any party must be served on all parties, unless the court orders otherwise. The present language expressly includes notices and demands, but it is not explicit as to answers or responses as provided in Rules 33, 34, and 36. Discovery papers may be voluminous or the parties numerous, and the court is empowered to vary the requirement if in a given case it proves needlessly onerous.

In actions begun by seizure of property, service will at times have to be made before the absent owner of the property has filed an appearance. For example, a prompt deposition may be needed in a maritime action in rem. See Rules 30(a) and 30(b)(2) and the related notes. A provision is added authorizing service on the person having custody or possession of the property at the time of its seizure.

Rule 9. Pleading Special Matters

(h) Admiralty and Maritime Claims. A pleading or count setting forth a claim for relief within the admiralty and maritime jurisdiction that is also within the jurisdiction of the district court on some other ground may contain a statement identifying the claim as an admiralty or maritime claim for the purposes of Rules 14(c), 26(a), 38(e), 82, and the Supplemental Rules for Certain Admiralty and Maritime Claims. If the claim is cognizable only in admiralty it is an admiralty or maritime claim for those purposes whether so identified or not. The amendment of a pleading to add or withdraw an identifying statement is governed by the principles of Rule 15. The reference in Title 28, U.S.C., § 1292(a)(3), to admiralty cases shall be construed to mean admiralty and maritime claims within the meaning of this subdivision (h).

New matter is shown in italics; matter to be omitted is lined through

Advisory Committee's Note

The reference to Rule 26(a) is deleted, in light of the transfer of that subdivision to Rule 30(a) and the elimination of the de bene esse procedure therefrom. See the Advisory Committee's note to Rule 30(a).

Rule 26. ~~Depositions Pending Action~~ *General Provisions Governing Discovery*

~~(a) When Depositions May Be Taken.~~ ~~Any party may take the testimony of any person, including a party, by deposition upon oral examination or written interrogatories for the purpose of discovery or for use as evidence in the action or for both purposes. After commencement of the action the deposition may be taken without leave of court, except that leave, granted with or without notice, must be obtained if notice of the taking is served by the plaintiff within 20 days after commencement of the action. The attendance of witnesses may be compelled by the use of subpoena as provided in Rule 45. Depositions shall be taken only in accordance with these rules, except that in admiralty and maritime claims within the meaning of Rule 9(h) depositions may also be taken under and used in accordance with sections 863, 864, and 865 of the Revised Statutes (see note preceding 28 U.S.C. § 1781). The deposition of a person confined in prison may be taken only by leave of court on such terms as the court prescribes.~~

(a) Discovery Methods. Parties may obtain discovery by one or more of the following methods: depositions upon oral examination or written questions; written interrogatories; production of documents or things or permission to enter upon land or other property, for inspection and other purposes; physical and mental examinations; and requests for admission. Unless the court orders otherwise under subdivision (c) of this rule, the frequency of use of these methods is not limited.

(b) Scope of ~~Examination~~ *Discovery.* Unless otherwise ~~ordered by~~ *limited by order of* the court ~~as provided by Rule 30(b) or (d), the deponent may be examined~~ *in accordance with these rules, the scope of discovery is as follows:*

(1) In General. Parties may obtain discovery regarding any matter, not privileged, which is relevant to the subject matter involved in the pending action, whether it relates to the claim or defense of the ~~examining~~ party *seeking discovery* or to the claim or defense of any other party, including the existence, description, nature, custody, condition and location of any books, documents, or other tangible things and the identity and location of persons having knowledge of *any discoverable matter* ~~relevant facts.~~ It is

---

New matter is shown in italics; matter to be omitted is lined through

not ground for objection that the ~~testimony~~ *information sought will be inadmissible at the trial if the* ~~testimony~~ *information sought appears reasonably calculated to lead to the discovery of admissible evidence.*

(2) Insurance Agreements. A party may obtain discovery of the existence and contents of any insurance agreement under which any person carrying on an insurance business may be liable to satisfy part or all of a judgment which may be entered in the action or to indemnify or reimburse for payments made to satisfy the judgment. Information concerning the insurance agreement is not by reason of disclosure admissible in evidence at trial. For purposes of this paragraph, an application for insurance shall not be treated as part of an insurance agreement.

(3) Trial Preparation: Materials. Subject to the provisions of subdivision (b)(4) of this rule, a party may obtain discovery of documents and tangible things otherwise discoverable under subdivision (b)(1) of this rule and prepared in anticipation of litigation or for trial by or for another party or by or for that other party's representative (including his attorney, consultant, surety, indemnitor, insurer, or agent) only upon a showing that the party seeking discovery has substantial need of the materials in the preparation of his case and that he is unable without undue hardship to obtain the substantial equivalent of the materials by other means. In ordering discovery of such materials when the required showing has been made, the court shall protect against disclosure of the mental impressions, conclusions, opinions, or legal theories of an attorney or other representative of a party concerning the litigation.

A party may obtain without the required showing a statement concerning the action or its subject matter previously made by that party. Upon request, a person not a party may obtain without the required showing a statement concerning the action or its subject matter previously made by that person. If the request is refused, the person may move for a court order. The provisions of Rule 37(a)(4) apply to the award of expenses incurred in relation to the motion. For purposes of this paragraph, a statement previously made is (A) a written statement signed or otherwise adopted or approved by the person making it, or (B) a stenographic, mechanical, electrical, or other recording, or a transcription thereof, which is a substantially verbatim recital of an oral statement by the person making it and contemporaneously recorded.

(4) Trial Preparation: Experts. Discovery of facts known and opinions held by experts, otherwise discoverable under the provisions of subdivision (b)(1) of this rule and acquired or developed in

---

New matter is shown in italics; matter to be omitted is lined through

anticipation of litigation or for trial, may be obtained only as follows:

(A)(i) A party may through interrogatories require any other party to identify each person whom the other party expects to call as an expert witness at trial, to state the subject matter on which the expert is expected to testify, and to state the substance of the facts and opinions to which the expert is expected to testify and a summary of the grounds for each opinion. (ii) Upon motion the court may order further discovery by other means, subject to such restrictions as to scope and such provisions, pursuant to subdivision (b)(4)(C) of this rule, concerning fees and expenses as the court may deem appropriate.

(B) A party may discover facts known or opinions held by an expert who has been retained or specially employed by another party in anticipation of litigation or preparation for trial and who is not expected to be called as a witness at trial, only as provided in Rule 35(b) or upon a showing of exceptional circumstances under which it is impracticable for the party seeking discovery to obtain facts or opinions on the same subject by other means.

(C) Unless manifest injustice would result, (i) the court shall require that the party seeking discovery pay the expert a reasonable fee for time spent in responding to discovery under subdivisions (b)(4)(A)(ii) and (b)(4)(B) of this rule; and (ii) with respect to discovery obtained under subdivision (b)(4)(A)(ii) of this rule the court may require, and with respect to discovery obtained under subdivision (b)(4)(B) of this rule the court shall require, the party seeking discovery to pay the other party a fair portion of the fees and expenses reasonably incurred by the latter party in obtaining facts and opinions from the expert.

(c) Examination and Cross Examination. Examination and cross examination of deponents may proceed as permitted at the trial under the provisions of Rule 43(b).

(d) Use of Depositions. At the trial or upon the hearing of a motion or an interlocutory proceeding, any part or all of a deposition, so far as admissible under the rules of evidence, may be used against any party who was present or represented at the taking of the deposition or who had due notice thereof, in accordance with any one of the following provisions:

(1) Any deposition may be used by any party for the purpose of contradicting or impeaching the testimony of deponent as a witness.

(2) The deposition of a party or of any one who at the time of taking the deposition was an officer, director, or managing agent

New matter is shown in italics; matter to be omitted is lined through

of a public or private corporation, partnership, or association which is a party may be used by an adverse party for any purpose.

(3) The deposition of a witness, whether or not a party, may be used by any party for any purpose if the court finds: 1, that the witness is dead; or 2, that the witness is at a greater distance than 100 miles from the place of trial or hearing, or is out of the United States, unless it appears that the absence of the witness was procured by the party offering the deposition; or 3, that the witness is unable to attend or testify because of age, sickness, infirmity, or imprisonment; or 4, that the party offering the deposition has been unable to procure the attendance of the witness by subpoena; or 5, upon application and notice, that such exceptional circumstances exist as to make it desirable, in the interest of justice and with due regard to the importance of presenting the testimony of witnesses orally in open court, to allow the deposition to be used.

(4) If only part of a deposition is offered in evidence by a party, an adverse party may require him to introduce all of it which is relevant to the part introduced, and any party may introduce any other parts.

Substitution of parties does not affect the right to use depositions previously taken; and, when an action in any court of the United States or of any state has been dismissed and another action involving the same subject matter is afterward brought between the same parties or their representatives or successors in interest, all depositions lawfully taken and duly filed in the former action may be used in the latter as if originally taken therefor.

(e) **Objections to Admissibility.** Subject to the provisions of Rules 28(b) and 32(c) objection may be made at the trial or hearing to receiving in evidence any deposition or part thereof for any reason which would require the exclusion of the evidence if the witness were then present and testifying.

(f) **Effect of Taking or Using Depositions.** A party shall not be deemed to make a person his own witness for any purpose by taking his deposition. The introduction in evidence of the deposition or any part thereof for any purpose other than that of contradicting or impeaching the deponent makes the deponent the witness of the party introducing the deposition, but this shall not apply to the use by an adverse party of a deposition as described in paragraph (2) of subdivision (d) of this rule. At the trial or hearing any party may rebut any relevant evidence contained in a deposition whether introduced by him or by any other party.

New matter is shown in italics; matter to be omitted is lined through

(c) Protective Orders. Upon motion by a party or by the person from whom discovery is sought, and for good cause shown, the court in which the action is pending or alternatively, on matters relating to a deposition, the court in the district where the deposition is to be taken may make any order which justice requires to protect a party or person from annoyance, embarrassment, oppression, or undue burden or expense, including one or more of the following: (1) that the discovery not be had; (2) that the discovery may be had only on specified terms and conditions, including a designation of the time or place; (3) that the discovery may be had only by a method of discovery other than that selected by the party seeking discovery; (4) that certain matters not be inquired into, or that the scope of the discovery be limited to certain matters; (5) that discovery be conducted with no one present except persons designated by the court; (6) that a deposition after being sealed be opened only by order of the court; (7) that a trade secret or other confidential research, development, or commercial information not be disclosed or be disclosed only in a designated way; (8) that the parties simultaneously file specified documents or information enclosed in sealed envelopes to be opened as directed by the court.

If the motion for a protective order is denied in whole or in part, the court may, on such terms and conditions as are just, order that any party or person provide or permit discovery. The provisions of Rule 37(a)(4) apply to the award of expenses incurred in relation to the motion.

(d) Sequence and Timing of Discovery. Unless the court upon motion, for the convenience of parties and witnesses and in the interests of justice, orders otherwise, methods of discovery may be used in any sequence and the fact that a party is conducting discovery, whether by deposition or otherwise, shall not operate to delay any other party's discovery.

(e) Supplementation of Responses. A party who has responded to a request for discovery with a response that was complete when made is under no duty to supplement his response to include information thereafter acquired, except as follows:

(1) A party is under a duty seasonably to supplement his response with respect to any question directly addressed to (A) the identity and location of persons having knowledge of discoverable matters, and (B) the identity of each person expected to be called as an expert witness at trial, the subject matter on which he is expected to testify, and the substance of his testimony.

(2) A party is under a duty seasonably to amend a prior response if he obtains information upon the basis of which (A) he knows that the response was incorrect when made, or (B) he knows

---

New matter is shown in italics; matter to be omitted is lined through

that the response though correct when made is no longer true and the circumstances are such that a failure to amend the response is in substance a knowing concealment.

(3) A duty to supplement responses may be imposed by order of the court, agreement of the parties, or at any time prior to trial through new requests for supplementation of prior responses.

Advisory Committee's Note

A limited rearrangement of the discovery rules is made, whereby certain rule provisions are transferred, as follows: Existing Rule 26(a) is transferred to Rules 30(a) and 31(a). Existing Rule 26(c) is transferred to Rule 30(c). Existing Rules 26(d), (e), and (f) are transferred to Rule 32. Revisions of the transferred provisions, if any, are discussed in the notes appended to Rules 30, 31, and 32. In addition, Rule 30(b) is transferred to Rule 26(c). The purpose of this rearrangement is to establish Rule 26 as a rule governing discovery in general. (The reasons are set out in the Advisory Committee's explanatory statement.)

Subdivision (a)—Discovery Devices. This is a new subdivision listing all of the discovery devices provided in the discovery rules and establishing the relationship between the general provisions of Rule 26 and the specific rules for particular discovery devices. The provision that the frequency of use of these methods is not limited confirms existing law. It incorporates in general form a provision now found in Rule 33.

Subdivision (b)—Scope of Discovery. This subdivision is recast to cover the scope of discovery generally. It regulates the discovery obtainable through any of the discovery devices listed in Rule 26(a).

All provisions as to scope of discovery are subject to the initial qualification that the court may limit discovery in accordance with these rules. Rule 26(c) (transferred from 30(b)) confers broad powers on the courts to regulate or prevent discovery even though the materials sought are within the scope of 26(b), and these powers have always been freely exercised. For example, a party's income tax return is generally held not privileged, 2A Barron & Holtzoff, *Federal Practice and Procedure,* § 651.2 (Wright ed. 1961), and yet courts have recognized that interests in privacy may call for a measure of extra protection. *E.g., Wiesenberger v. W. E. Hutton & Co.,* 35 F.R.D. 556 (S.D.N.Y.1964). Similarly, the courts have in appropriate circumstances protected materials that are primarily of an impeaching character. These two types of materials merely illustrate the many situations, not capable of governance by precise rule, in which courts must exercise judgment. The new subsections in Rule 26(b) do not change existing law with respect to such situations.

Subdivision (b)(1)—In General. The language is changed to provide for the scope of discovery in general terms. The existing subdivision, although in terms applicable only to depositions, is incorporated by reference in existing Rules 33 and 34. Since decisions as to relevance to the subject matter of the action are made for discovery purposes well in advance of trial, a flexible treatment of relevance is required and the making of discovery, whether voluntary or under court order, is not a concession or determination of relevance for purposes of trial. *Cf.* 4 *Moore's Federal Practice* ¶ 26–16[1] (2d ed. 1966).

Subdivision (b)(2)—Insurance Policies. Both the cases and commentators are sharply in conflict on the question whether defendant's liability insurance coverage is subject to discovery in the usual situation when the insurance coverage is not

New matter is shown in italics; matter to be omitted is lined through

itself admissible and does not bear on another issue in the case. Examples of Federal cases requiring disclosure and supporting comments: *Cook v. Welty,* 253 F.Supp. 875 (D.D.C.1966) (cases cited); *Johanek v. Aberle,* 27 F.R.D. 272 (D.Mont. 1961); Williams, *Discovery of Dollar Limits in Liability Policies in Automobile Tort Cases,* 10 Ala.L.Rev. 355 (1958); Thode, *Some Reflections on the 1957 Amendments to the Texas Rules,* 37 Tex.L.Rev. 33, 40–42 (1958). Examples of Federal cases refusing disclosure and supporting comments: *Bisserier v. Manning,* 207 F.Supp. 476 (D.N.J.1962); *Cooper v. Stender,* 30 F.R.D. 389 (E.D.Tenn.1962); Frank, *Discovery and Insurance, Coverage* 1959 Ins.L.J. 281; Fournier, *Pre-Trial Discovery of Insurance Coverage and Limits,* 28 Ford.L.Rev. 215 (1959).

The division in reported cases is close. State decisions based on provisions similar to the federal rules are similarly divided. See cases collected in 2A Barron & Holtzoff, *Federal Practice and Procedure* § 647.1, nn. 45.5, 45.6 (Wright ed. 1961). It appears to be difficult if not impossible to obtain appellate review of the issue. Resolution by rule amendment is indicated. The question is essentially procedural in that it bears upon preparation for trial and settlement before trial, and courts confronting the question, however they have decided it, have generally treated it as procedural and governed by the rules.

The amendment resolves this issue in favor of disclosure. Most of the decisions denying discovery, some explicitly, reason from the text of Rule 26(b) that it permits discovery only of matters which will be admissible in evidence or appear reasonably calculated to lead to such evidence; they avoid considerations of policy, regarding them as foreclosed. See *Bisserier v. Manning, supra.* Some note also that facts about a defendant's financial status are not discoverable as such, prior to judgment with execution unsatisfied, and fear that, if courts hold insurance coverage discoverable, they must extend the principle to other aspects of the defendant's financial status. The cases favoring disclosure rely heavily on the practical significance of insurance in the decisions lawyers make about settlement and trial preparation. In *Clauss v. Danker,* 264 F.Supp. 246 (S.D.N.Y.1967), the court held that the rules forbid disclosure but called for an amendment to permit it.

Disclosure of insurance coverage will enable counsel for both sides to make the same realistic appraisal of the case, so that settlement and litigation strategy are based on knowledge and not speculation. It will conduce to settlement and avoid protracted litigation in some cases, though in others it may have an opposite effect. The amendment is limited to insurance coverage, which should be distinguished from any other facts concerning defendant's financial status (1) because insurance is an asset created specifically to satisfy the claim; (2) because the insurance company ordinarily controls the litigation; (3) because information about coverage is available only from defendant or his insurer; and (4) because disclosure does not involve a significant invasion of privacy.

Disclosure is required when the insurer "may be liable" on part or all of the judgment. Thus, an insurance company must disclose even when it contests liability under the policy, and such disclosure does not constitute a waiver of its claim. It is immaterial whether the liability is to satisfy the judgment directly or merely to indemnify or reimburse another after he pays the judgment.

The provision applies only to persons "carrying on an insurance business" and thus covers insurance companies and not the ordinary business concern that enters into a contract of indemnification. *Cf.* N.Y.Ins.Law § 41. Thus, the provision makes no change in existing law on discovery of indemnity agreements other than insurance agreements by persons carrying on an insurance business. Similarly,

New matter is shown in italics; matter to be omitted is lined through

the provision does not cover the business concern that creates a reserve fund for purposes of self-insurance.

For some purposes other than discovery, an application for insurance is treated as a part of the insurance agreement. The provision makes clear that, for discovery purposes, the application is not to be so treated. The insurance application may contain personal and financial information concerning the insured, discovery of which is beyond the purpose of this provision.

In no instance does disclosure make the facts concerning insurance coverage admissible in evidence.

Subdivision (b)(3)—Trial Preparation: Materials. Some of the most controversial and vexing problems to emerge from the discovery rules have arisen out of requests for the production of documents or things prepared in anticipation of litigation or for trial. The existing rules make no explicit provision for such materials. Yet, two verbally distinct doctrines have developed, each conferring a qualified immunity on these materials—the "good cause" requirement in Rule 34 (now generally held applicable to discovery of documents via deposition under Rule 45 and interrogatories under Rule 33) and the work-product doctrine of *Hickman v. Taylor,* 329 U.S. 495 (1947). Both demand a showing of justification before production can be had, the one of "good cause" and the other variously described in the *Hickman* case: "necessity or justification," "denial * * * would unduly prejudice the preparation of petitioner's case," or "cause hardship or injustice" 329 U.S. at 509–510.

In deciding the *Hickman* case, the Supreme Court appears to have expressed a preference in 1947 for an approach to the problem of trial preparation materials by judicial decision rather than by rule. Sufficient experience has accumulated, however, with lower court applications of the *Hickman* decision to warrant a reappraisal.

The major difficulties visible in the existing case law are (1) confusion and disagreement as to whether "good cause" is made out by a showing of relevance and lack of privilege, or requires an additional showing of necessity, (2) confusion and disagreement as to the scope of the *Hickman* work-product doctrine, particularly whether it extends beyond work actually performed by lawyers, and (3) the resulting difficulty of relating the "good cause" required by Rule 34 and the "necessity or justification" of the work-product doctrine, so that their respective roles and the distinctions between them are understood.

Basic Standard.—Since Rule 34 in terms requires a showing of "good cause" for the production of all documents and things, whether or not trial preparation is involved, courts have felt that a single formula is called for and have differed over whether a showing of relevance and lack of privilege is enough or whether more must be shown. When the facts of the cases are studied, however, a distinction emerges based upon the type of materials. With respect to documents not obtained or prepared with an eye to litigation, the decisions, while not uniform, reflect a strong and increasing tendency to relate "good cause" to a showing that the documents are relevant to the subject matter of the action. *E.g., Connecticut Mutual Life Ins. Co. v. Shields,* 17 F.R.D. 273 (S.D.N.Y.1959), with cases cited; *Houdry Process Corp. v. Commonwealth Oil Refining Co.,* 24 F.R.D. 58 (S.D.N.Y. 1955); see *Bell v. Commercial Ins. Co.,* 280 F.2d 514, 517 (3d Cir.1960). When the party whose documents are sought shows that the request for production is unduly burdensome or oppressive, courts have denied discovery for lack of "good cause", although they might just as easily have based their decision on the protective provisions of existing Rule 30(b) (new Rule 26(c)). *E.g., Lauer v. Tankrederi,* 39 F.R.D. 334 (E.D.Pa.1966).

New matter is shown in italics; matter to be omitted is lined through

As to trial-preparation materials, however, the courts are increasingly interpreting "good cause" as requiring more than relevance. When lawyers have prepared or obtained the materials for trial, all courts require more than relevance; so much is clearly commanded by *Hickman*. But even as to the preparatory work of nonlawyers, while some courts ignore work-product and equate "good cause" with relevance, *e.g.*, *Brown v. New York, N.H. & H.R.R.*, 17 F.R.D. 324 (S.D.N.Y.1955), the more recent trend is to read "good cause" as requiring inquiry into the importance of and need for the materials, as well as into alternative sources for securing the same information. In *Guilford Nat'l Bank v. Southern Ry.*, 297 F.2d 921 (4th Cir.1962), statements of witnesses obtained by claim agents were held not discoverable because both parties had had equal access to the witnesses at about the same time, shortly after the collision in question. The decision was based solely on Rule 34 and "good cause"; the court declined to rule on whether the statements were work-product. The court's treatment of "good cause" is quoted at length and with approval in *Schlagenhauf v. Holder*, 379 U.S. 104, 117–118 (1964). See also *Mitchell v. Bass*, 252 F.2d 513 (8th Cir.1958); *Hauger v. Chicago, R.I. & Pac. R.R.*, 216 F.2d 501 (7th Cir.1954); *Burke v. United States*, 32 F.R.D. 213 (E.D.N.Y.1963). While the opinions dealing with "good cause" do not often draw an explicit distinction between trial preparation materials and other materials, in fact an overwhelming proportion of the cases in which a special showing is required are cases involving trial preparation materials.

The rules are amended by eliminating the general requirement of "good cause" from Rule 34 but retaining a requirement of a special showing for trial preparation materials in this subdivision. The required showing is expressed, not in terms of "good cause" whose generality has tended to encourage confusion and controversy, but in terms of the elements of the special showing to be made: substantial need of the materials in the preparation of the case and inability without undue hardship to obtain the substantial equivalent of the materials by other means.

These changes conform to the holdings of the cases, when viewed in light of their facts. Apart from trial preparation, the fact that the materials sought are documentary does not in and of itself require a special showing beyond relevance and absence of privilege. The protective provisions are of course available, and if the party from whom production is sought raises a special issue of privacy (as with respect to income tax returns or grand jury minutes) or points to evidence primarily impeaching, or can show serious burden or expense, the court will exercise its traditional power to decide whether to issue a protective order. On the other hand, the requirement of a special showing for discovery of trial preparation materials reflects the view that each side's informal evaluation of its case should be protected, that each side should be encouraged to prepare independently, and that one side should not automatically have the benefit of the detailed preparatory work of the other side. See Field and McKusick, *Maine Civil Practice* 264 (1959).

Elimination of a "good cause" requirement from Rule 34 and the establishment of a requirement of a special showing in this subdivision will eliminate the confusion caused by having two verbally distinct requirements of justification that the courts have been unable to distinguish clearly. Moreover, the language of the subdivision suggests the factors which the courts should consider in determining whether the requisite showing has been made. The importance of the materials sought to the party seeking them in preparation of his case and the difficulty he will have obtaining them by other means are factors noted in the *Hickman* case. The courts should also consider the likelihood that the party, even if he obtains the information by independent means, will not have the substantial equivalent of the documents the production of which he seeks.

New matter is shown in italics; matter to be omitted is lined through

Consideration of these factors may well lead the court to distinguish between witness statements taken by an investigator, on the one hand, and other parts of the investigative file, on the other. The court in *Southern Ry. v. Lanham*, 403 F.2d 119 (5th Cir.1968), while it naturally addressed itself to the "good cause" requirements of Rule 34, set forth as controlling considerations the factors contained in the language of this subdivision. The analysis of the court suggests circumstances under which witness statements will be discoverable. The witness may have given a fresh and contemporaneous account in a written statement while he is available to the party seeking discovery only a substantial time thereafter. *Lanham, supra* at 127–128; *Guilford, supra* at 926. Or he may be reluctant or hostile, *Lanham, supra* at 128–129; *Brookshire v. Pennsylvania RR*, 14 F.R.D. 154 (N.D.Ohio 1953); *Diamond v. Mohawk Rubber Co.*, 33 F.R.D. 264 (D.Colo.1963). Or he may have a lapse of memory. *Tannenbaum v. Walker*, 16 F.R.D. 570 (E.D.Pa.1954). Or he may probably be deviating from his prior statement. *Cf. Hauger v. Chicago, R. I. & Pac. RR*, 216 F.2d 501 (7th Cir.1954). On the other hand, a much stronger showing is needed to obtain evaluative materials in an investigator's reports. *Lanham, supra* at 131–133; *Pickett v. L. R. Ryan, Inc.*, 237 F.Supp. 198 (E.D.S.C.1965).

Materials assembled in the ordinary course of business, or pursuant to public requirements unrelated to litigation, or for other nonlitigation purposes are not under the qualified immunity provided by this subdivision. *Goosman v. A. Duie Pyle, Inc.*, 320 F.2d 45 (4th Cir.1963); *cf. United States v. New York Foreign Trade Zone Operators, Inc.*, 304 F.2d 792 (2d Cir.1962). No change is made in the existing doctrine, noted in the *Hickman* case, that one party may discover relevant facts known or available to the other party, even though such facts are contained in a document which is not itself discoverable.

Treatment of Lawyers; Special Protection of Mental Impressions, Conclusions, Opinions, and Legal Theories Concerning the Litigation.—The courts are divided as to whether the work-product doctrine extends to the preparatory work only of lawyers. The *Hickman* case left this issue open since the statements in that case were taken by a lawyer. As to courts of appeals, *compare Alltmont v. United States*, 177 F.2d 971, 976 (3d Cir.1949), *cert. denied*, 339 U.S. 967 (1950) (*Hickman* applied to statements obtained by FBI agents on theory it should apply to "all statements of prospective witnesses which a party has obtained for his trial counsel's use"), with *Southern Ry. v. Campbell*, 309 F.2d 569 (5th Cir.1962) (statements taken by claim agents not work-product), and *Guilford Nat'l Bank v. Southern Ry.*, 297 F.2d 921 (4th Cir.1962) (avoiding issue of work-product as to claim agents, deciding case instead under Rule 34 "good cause"). Similarly, the district courts are divided on statements obtained by claim agents, *compare, e.g., Brown v. New York, N.H. & H. R.R.*, 17 F.R.D. 324 (S.D.N.Y 1955) with *Hanke v. Milwaukee Electric Ry. & Transp. Co.*, 7 F.R.D. 540 (E.D.Wis.1947); investigators, *compare Burke v. United States*, 32 F.R.D. 213 (E.D.N.Y.1963) with *Snyder v. United States*, 20 F.R.D. 7 (E.D.N.Y.1956); and insurers, *compare Gottlieb v. Bresler*, 24 F.R.D. 371 (D.D.C.1959) with *Burns v. Mulder*, 20 F.R.D. 605 (E.D.Pa.1957). See 4 *Moore's Federal Practice* ¶ 26.23[8.1] (2d ed. 1966); 2A Barron & Holtzoff, *Federal Practice and Procedure* § 652.2 (Wright ed. 1961).

A complication is introduced by the use made by courts of the "good cause" requirement of Rule 34, as described above. A court may conclude that trial preparation materials are not work-product because not the result of lawyer's work and yet hold that they are not producible because "good cause" has not been shown. *Cf. Guilford Nat'l Bank v. Southern Ry.*, 297 F.2d 921 (4th Cir.1962), cited and described above. When the decisions on "good cause" are taken into account, the weight of authority affords protection of the preparatory work of both lawyers

---

New matter is shown in italics; matter to be omitted is lined through

and nonlawyers (though not necessarily to the same extent) by requiring more than a showing of relevance to secure production.

Subdivision (b)(3) reflects the trend of the cases by requiring a special showing, not merely as to materials prepared by an attorney, but also as to materials prepared in anticipation of litigation or preparation for trial by or for a party or any representative acting on his behalf. The subdivision then goes on to protect against disclosure the mental impressions, conclusions, opinions, or legal theories concerning the litigation of an attorney or other representative of a party. The *Hickman* opinion drew special attention to the need for protecting an attorney against discovery of memoranda prepared from recollection of oral interviews. The courts have steadfastly safeguarded against disclosure of lawyers' mental impressions and legal theories, as well as mental impressions and subjective evaluations of investigators and claim-agents. In enforcing this provision of the subdivision, the courts will sometimes find it necessary to order disclosure of a document but with portions deleted.

Rules 33 and 36 have been revised in order to permit discovery calling for opinions, contentions, and admissions relating not only to fact but also to the application of law to fact. Under those rules, a party and his attorney or other representative may be required to disclose, to some extent, mental impressions, opinions, or conclusions. But documents or parts of documents containing these matters are protected against discovery by this subdivision. Even though a party may ultimately have to disclose in response to interrogatories or requests to admit, he is entitled to keep confidential documents containing such matters prepared for internal use.

Party's Right to Own Statement.—An exception to the requirement of this subdivision enables a party to secure production of his own statement without any special showing. The cases are divided. *Compare, e. g., Safeway Stores, Inc. v. Reynolds*, 176 F.2d 476 (D.C.Cir.1949); *Shupe v. Pennsylvania R. R.*, 19 F.R.D. 144 (W.D.Pa.1956); with *e. g., New York Central R. R. v. Carr*, 251 F.2d 433 (4th Cir.1957); *Belback v. Wilson Freight Forwarding Co.*, 40 F.R.D. 16 (W.D.Pa.1966).

Courts which treat a party's statement as though it were that of any witness overlook the fact that the party's statement is, without more, admissible in evidence. Ordinarily, a party gives a statement without insisting on a copy because he does not yet have a lawyer and does not understand the legal consequences of his actions. Thus, the statement is given at a time when he functions at a disadvantage. Discrepancies between his trial testimony and earlier statement may result from lapse of memory or ordinary inaccuracy; a written statement produced for the first time at trial may give such discrepancies a prominence which they do not deserve. In appropriate cases the court may order a party to be deposed before his statement is produced. *E.g., Smith v. Central Linen Service Co.*, 39 F.R.D. 15 (D.Md.1966); *McCoy v. General Motors Corp.*, 33 F.R.D. 354 (W.D.Pa.1963).

Commentators strongly support the view that a party be able to secure his statement without a showing. 4 *Moore's Federal Practice* ¶ 26.23[8.4] (2d ed. 1966); 2A Barron & Holtzoff, *Federal Practice and Procedure* § 652.3 (Wright ed. 1961); see also Note, *Developments in the Law—Discovery*, 74 Harv.L.Rev. 940, 1039 (1961). The following states have by statute or rule taken the same position: *Statutes:* Fla.Stat.Ann. § 92.33; Ga.Code Ann. § 38–2109(b); La.Stat.Ann.R.S. 13:3732; Mass.Gen.Laws Ann. c. 271, § 44; Minn.Stat.Ann. § 602.01; N.Y.C.P.L.R. § 3101(e). *Rules:* Mo.R.C.P. 56.01(a); N.Dak.R.C.P. 34(b); Wyo.R.C.P. 34(b); *cf.* Mich.G.C.R. 306.2.

New matter is shown in italics; matter to be omitted is lined through

In order to clarify and tighten the provision on statements by a party, the term "statement" is defined. The definition is adapted from 18 U.S.C. § 3500(e) (Jencks Act). The statement of a party may of course be that of plaintiff or defendant, and it may be that of an individual or of a corporation or other organization.

Witness' Right to Own Statement.—A second exception to the requirement of this subdivision permits a non-party witness to obtain a copy of his own statement without any special showing. Many, though not all, of the considerations supporting a party's right to obtain his statement apply also to the non-party witness. Insurance companies are increasingly recognizing that a witness is entitled to a copy of his statement and are modifying their regular practice accordingly.

Subdivision (b)(4)—Trial Preparation: Experts. This is a new provision dealing with discovery of information (including facts and opinions) obtained by a party from an expert retained by that party in relation to litigation or obtained by the expert and not yet transmitted to the party. The subdivision deals separately with those experts whom the party expects to call as trial witnesses and with those experts who have been retained or specially employed by the party but who are not expected to be witnesses. It should be noted that the subdivision does not address itself to the expert whose information was not acquired in preparation for trial but rather because he was an actor or viewer with respect to transactions or occurrences that are part of the subject matter of the lawsuit. Such an expert should be treated as an ordinary witness.

Subsection (b)(4)(A) deals with discovery of information obtained by or through experts who will be called as witnesses at trial. The provision is responsive to problems suggested by a relatively recent line of authorities. Many of these cases present intricate and difficult issues as to which expert testimony is likely to be determinative. Prominent among them are food and drug, patent, and condemnation cases. See, *e. g., United States v. Nysco Laboratories, Inc.,* 26 F.R.D. 159, 162 (E.D.N.Y.1960) (food and drug); *E. I. du Pont de Nemours & Co. v. Phillips Petroleum Co.,* 24 F.R.D. 416, 421 (D.Del.1959) (patent); *Cold Metal Process Co. v. Aluminum Co. of America,* 7 F.R.D. 425 (N.D.Ohio 1947), aff'd, *Sachs v. Aluminum Co. of America,* 167 F.2d 570 (6th Cir.1948) (same); *United States v. 50.34 Acres of Land,* 13 F.R.D. 19 (E.D.N.Y.1952) (condemnation).

In cases of this character, a prohibition against discovery of information held by expert witnesses produces in acute form the very evils that discovery has been created to prevent. Effective cross-examination of an expert witness requires advance preparation. The lawyer even with the help of his own experts frequently cannot anticipate the particular approach his adversary's expert will take or the data on which he will base his judgment on the stand. McGlothlin, *Some Practical Problems in Proof of Economic, Scientific, and Technical Facts,* 23 F.R.D. 467, 478 (1958). A California study of discovery and pretrial in condemnation cases notes that the only substitute for discovery of experts' valuation materials is "lengthy—and often fruitless—cross-examination during trial," and recommends pretrial exchange of such material. Calif.Law Rev.Comm'n, *Discovery in Eminent Domain Proceedings* 707–710 (Jan.1963). Similarly, effective rebuttal requires advance knowledge of the line of testimony of the other side. If the latter is foreclosed by a rule against discovery, then the narrowing of issues and elimination of surprise which discovery normally produces are frustrated.

These considerations appear to account for the broadening of discovery against experts in the cases cited where expert testimony was central to the case. In some instances, the opinions are explicit in relating expanded discovery to improved cross-examination and rebuttal at trial. *Franks v. National Dairy Products Corp.,* 41 F.R.D. 234 (W.D.Tex.1966); *United States v. 23.76 Acres,* 32 F.R.D. 593 (D.Md.

New matter is shown in italics; matter to be omitted is lined through

1963); see also an unpublished opinion of Judge Hincks, quoted in *United States v. 48 Jars, etc.*, 23 F.R.D. 192, 198 (D.D.C.1958). On the other hand, the need for new provision is shown by the many cases in which discovery of expert trial witnesses is needed for effective cross-examination and rebuttal, and yet courts apply the traditional doctrine and refuse disclosure. *E.g., United States v. Certain Parcels of Land*, 25 F.R.D. 192 (N.D.Cal.1959); *United States v. Certain Acres*, 18 F.R.D. 98 (M.D.Ga.1955).

Although the trial problems flowing from lack of discovery of expert witnesses are most acute and noteworthy when the case turns largely on experts, the same problems are encountered when a single expert testifies. Thus, subdivision (b)(4)(A) draws no line between complex and simple cases, or between cases with many experts and those with but one. It establishes by rule substantially the procedure adopted by decision of the court in *Knighton v. Villian & Fassio*, 39 F.R.D. 11 (D.Md.1965). For a full analysis of the problem and strong recommendations to the same effect, see Friedenthal, *Discovery and Use of an Adverse Party's Expert Information*, 14 Stan.L.Rev. 455, 485–488 (1962); Long, *Discovery and Experts under the Federal Rules of Civil Procedure*, 38 F.R.D. 111 (1965).

Past judicial restrictions on discovery of an adversary's expert, particularly as to his opinions, reflect the fear that one side will benefit unduly from the other's better preparation. The procedure established in subsection (b)(4)(A) holds the risk to a minimum. Discovery is limited to trial witnesses, and may be obtained only at a time when the parties know who their expert witnesses will be. A party must as a practical matter prepare his own case in advance of that time, for he can hardly hope to build his case out of his opponent's experts.

Subdivision (b)(4)(A) provides for discovery of an expert who is to testify at the trial. A party can require one who intends to use the expert to state the substance of the testimony that the expert is expected to give. The court may order further discovery, and it has ample power to regulate its timing and scope and to prevent abuse. Ordinarily, the order for further discovery shall compensate the expert for his time, and may compensate the party who intends to use the expert for past expenses reasonably incurred in obtaining facts or opinions from the expert. Those provisions are likely to discourage abusive practices.

Subdivision (b)(4)(B) deals with an expert who has been retained or specially employed by the party in anticipation of litigation or preparation for trial (thus excluding an expert who is simply a general employee of the party not specially employed on the case), but who is not expected to be called as a witness. Under its provisions, a party may discover facts known or opinions held by such an expert only on a showing of exceptional circumstances under which it is impracticable for the party seeking discovery to obtain facts or opinions on the same subject by other means.

Subdivision (b)(4)(B) is concerned only with experts retained or specially consulted in relation to trial preparation. Thus the subdivision precludes discovery against experts who were informally consulted in preparation for trial, but not retained or specially employed. As an ancillary procedure, a party may on a proper showing require the other party to name experts retained or specially employed, but not those informally consulted.

These new provisions of subdivision (b)(4) repudiate the few decisions that have held an expert's information privileged simply because of his status as an expert, *e. g., American Oil Co. v. Pennsylvania Petroleum Products Co.*, 23 F.R.D. 680, 685–686 (D.R.I.1959). See Louisell, *Modern California Discovery* 315–316 (1963). They also reject as ill-considered the decisions which have sought to bring expert information within the work-product doctrine. See *United States v. McKay*, 372

New matter is shown in italics; matter to be omitted is lined through

F.2d 174, 176–177 (5th Cir.1967). The provisions adopt a form of the more recently developed doctrine of "unfairness". See *e. g., United States v. 23.76 Acres of Land*, 32 F.R.D. 593, 597 (D.Md.1963); Louisell, *supra*, at 317–318; 4 *Moore's Federal Practice* ¶ 26.24 (2d ed. 1966).

Under subdivision (b)(4)(C), the court is directed or authorized to issue protective orders, including an order that the expert be paid a reasonable fee for time spent in responding to discovery, and that the party whose expert is made subject to discovery be paid a fair portion of the fees and expenses that the party incurred in obtaining information from the expert. The court may issue the latter order as a condition of discovery, or it may delay the order until after discovery is completed. These provisions for fees and expenses meet the objection that it is unfair to permit one side to obtain without cost the benefit of an expert's work for which the other side has paid, often a substantial sum. *E. g., Lewis v. United Air Lines Transp. Corp.*, 32 F.Supp. 21 (W.D.Pa.1940); *Walsh v. Reynolds Metal Co.*, 15 F.R.D. 376 (D.N.J.1954). On the other hand, a party may not obtain discovery simply by offering to pay fees and expenses. *Cf. Boynton v. R. J. Reynolds Tobacco Co.*, 36 F.Supp. 593 (D.Mass.1941).

In instances of discovery under subdivision (b)(4)(B), the court is directed to award fees and expenses to the other party, since the information is of direct value to the discovering party's preparation of his case. In ordering discovery under (b)(4)(A)(ii), the court has discretion whether to award fees and expenses to the other party; its decision should depend upon whether the discovering party is simply learning about the other party's case or is going beyond this to develop his own case. Even in cases where the court is directed to issue a protective order, it may decline to do so if it finds that manifest injustice would result. Thus, the court can protect, when necessary and appropriate, the interests of an indigent party.

Subdivision (c)—Protective Orders. The provisions of existing Rule 30(b) are transferred to this subdivision (c), as part of the rearrangement of Rule 26. The language has been changed to give it application to discovery generally. The subdivision recognizes the power of the court in the district where a deposition is being taken to make protective orders. Such power is needed when the deposition is being taken far from the court where the action is pending. The court in the district where the deposition is being taken may, and frequently will, remit the deponent or party to the court where the action is pending.

In addition, drafting changes are made to carry out and clarify the sense of the rule. Insertions are made to avoid any possible implication that a protective order does not extend to "time" as well as to "place" or may not safeguard against "undue burden or expense."

The new reference to trade secrets and other confidential commercial information reflects existing law. The courts have not given trade secrets automatic and complete immunity against disclosure, but have in each case weighed their claim to privacy against the need for disclosure. Frequently, they have been afforded a limited protection. See, *e.g., Covey Oil Co. v. Continental Oil Co.*, 340 F.2d 993 (10th Cir.1965); *Julius M. Ames Co. v. Bostitch, Inc.*, 235 F.Supp. 856 (S.D.N.Y. 1964).

The subdivision contains new matter relating to sanctions. When a motion for a protective order is made and the court is disposed to deny it, the court may go a step further and issue an order to provide or permit discovery. This will bring the sanctions of Rule 37(b) directly into play. Since the court has heard the contentions of all interested persons, an affirmative order is justified. See Rosenberg, *Sanctions to Effectuate Pretrial Discovery*, 58 Col.L.Rev. 480, 492–493 (1958). In

New matter is shown in italics; matter to be omitted is lined through

addition, the court may require the payment of expenses incurred in relation to the motion.

Subdivision (d)—Sequence and Priority. This new provision is concerned with the sequence in which parties may proceed with discovery and with related problems of timing. The principal effects of the new provision are first, to eliminate any fixed priority in the sequence of discovery, and second, to make clear and explicit the court's power to establish priority by an order issued in a particular case.

A priority rule developed by some courts, which confers priority on the party who first serves notice of taking a deposition, is unsatisfactory in several important respects:

First, this priority rule permits a party to establish a priority running to all depositions as to which he has given earlier notice. Since he can on a given day serve notice of taking many depositions he is in a position to delay his adversary's taking of depositions for an inordinate time. Some courts have ruled that deposition priority also permits a party to delay his answers to interrogatories and production of documents. *E.g., E. I. du Pont de Nemours & Co. v. Phillips Petroleum Co.*, 23 F.R.D. 237 (D.Del.1959); *but cf. Sturdevant v. Sears, Roebuck & Co.*, 32 F.R.D. 426 (W.D.Mo.1963).

Second, since notice is the key to priority, if both parties wish to take depositions first a race results. See *Caldwell-Clements, Inc. v. McGraw-Hill Pub. Co.*, 11 F.R.D. 156 (S.D.N.Y.1951) (description of tactics used by parties). But the existing rules on notice of deposition create a race with runners starting from different positions. The plaintiff may not give notice without leave of court until 20 days after commencement of the action, whereas the defendant may serve notice at any time after commencement. Thus, a careful and prompt defendant can almost always secure priority. This advantage of defendants is fortuitous, because the purpose of requiring plaintiff to wait 20 days is to afford defendant an opportunity to obtain counsel, not to confer priority.

Third, although courts have ordered a change in the normal sequence of discovery on a number of occasions, *e. g., Kaeppler v. James H. Matthews & Co.*, 200 F.Supp. 229 (E.D.Pa.1961); *Park & Tilford Distillers Corp. v. Distillers Co.*, 19 F.R.D. 169 (S.D.N.Y.1956), and have at all times avowed discretion to vary the usual priority, most commentators are agreed that courts in fact grant relief only for "the most obviously compelling reasons." 2A Barron & Holtzoff, *Federal Practice and Procedure* 44–47 (Wright ed. 1961); see also Younger, *Priority of Pretrial Examination in the Federal Courts—A Comment*, 34 N.Y.U.L.Rev. 1271 (1959); Freund, *The Pleading and Pretrial of an Antitrust Claim*, 46 Corn.L.Q. 555, 564 (1964). Discontent with the fairness of actual practice has been evinced by other observers. Comment, 59 Yale L.J. 117, 134–136 (1949); Yudkin, *Some Refinements in Federal discovery Procedure*, 11 Fed.B.J. 289, 296–297 (1951); *Developments in the Law-Discovery*, 74 Harv.L.Rev. 940, 954–958 (1961).

Despite these difficulties, some courts have adhered to the priority rule, presumably because it provides a test which is easily understood and applied by the parties without much court intervention. It thus permits deposition discovery to function extrajudicially, which the rules provide for and the courts desire. For these same reasons, courts are reluctant to make numerous exceptions to the rule.

The Columbia Survey makes clear that the problem of priority does not affect litigants generally. It found that most litigants do not move quickly to obtain discovery. In over half of the cases, both parties waited at least 50 days. During the first 20 days after commencement of the action—the period when defendant might assure his priority by noticing depositions—16 percent of the defendants

New matter is shown in italics; matter to be omitted is lined through

acted to obtained discovery. A race could not have occurred in more than 16 percent of the cases and it undoubtedly occurred in fewer. On the other hand, five times as many defendants as plaintiffs served notice of deposition during the first 19 days. To the same effect, see Comment, *Tactical Use and Abuse of Depositions Under the Federal Rules*, 59 Yale L.J. 117, 134 (1949).

These findings do not mean, however, that the priority rule is satisfactory or that a problem of priority does not exist. The court decisions show that parties do battle on this issue and carry their disputes to court. The statistics show that these court cases are not typical. By the same token, they reveal that more extensive exercise of judicial discretion to vary the priority will not bring a flood of litigation, and that a change in the priority rule will in fact affect only a small fraction of the cases.

It is contended by some that there is no need to alter the existing priority practice. In support, it is urged that there is no evidence that injustices in fact result from present practice and that, in any event, the courts can and do promulgate local rules, as in New York, to deal with local situations and issue orders to avoid possible injustice in particular cases.

Subdivision (d) is based on the contrary view that the rule of priority based on notice is unsatisfactory and unfair in its operation. Subdivision (d) follows an approach adapted from Civil Rule 4 of the District Court for the Southern District of New York. That rule provides that starting 40 days after commencement of the action, unless otherwise ordered by the court, the fact that one party is taking a deposition shall not prevent another party from doing so "concurrently." In practice, the depositions are not usually taken simultaneously; rather, the parties work out arrangements for alternation in the taking of depositions. One party may take a complete deposition and then the other, or, if the depositions are extensive, one party deposes for a set time, and then the other. See *Caldwell-Clements, Inc. v. McGraw-Hill Pub. Co.*, 11 F.R.D. 156 (S.D.N.Y.1951).

In principle, one party's initiation of discovery should not wait upon the other's completion, unless delay is dictated by special considerations. Clearly the principle is feasible with respect to all methods of discovery other than depositions. And the experience of the Southern District of New York shows that the principle can be applied to depositions as well. The courts have not had an increase in motion business on this matter. Once it is clear to lawyers that they bargain on an equal footing, they are usually able to arrange for an orderly succession of depositions without judicial intervention. Professor Moore has called attention to Civil Rule 4 and suggested that it may usefully be extended to other areas. 4 *Moore's Federal Practice* 1154 (2d ed. 1966).

The court may upon motion and by order grant priority in a particular case. But a local court rule purporting to confer priority in certain classes of cases would be inconsistent with this subdivision and thus void.

Subdivision (e)—Supplementation of Responses. The rules do not now state whether interrogatories (and questions at deposition as well as requests for inspection and admissions) impose a "continuing burden" on the responding party to supplement his answers if he obtains new information. The issue is acute when new information renders substantially incomplete or inaccurate an answer which was complete and accurate when made. It is essential that the rules provide an answer to this question. The parties can adjust to a rule either way, once they know what it is. See 4 *Moore's Federal Practice* ¶ 33.25[4] (2d ed. 1966).

Arguments can be made both ways. Imposition of a continuing burden reduces the proliferation of additional sets of interrogatories. Some courts have adopted local rules establishing such a burden. *E.g.*, E.D.Pa.R. 20(f), quoted in

---

New matter is shown in italics; matter to be omitted is lined through

Taggart v. Vermont Transp. Co., 32 F.R.D. 587 (E.D.Pa.1963); D.Me.R.15(c). Others have imposed the burden by decision. *E.g., Chenault v. Nebraska Farm Products, Inc.*, 9 F.R.D. 529, 533 (D.Nebr.1949). On the other hand, there are serious objections to the burden, especially in protracted cases. Although the party signs the answers, it is his lawyer who understands their significance and bears the responsibility to bring answers up to date. In a complex case all sorts of information reaches the party, who little understands its bearing on answers previously given to interrogatories. In practice, therefore, the lawyer under a continuing burden must periodically recheck all interrogatories and canvass all new information. But a full set of new answers may no longer be needed by the interrogating party. Some issues will have been dropped from the case, some questions are now seen as unimportant, and other questions must in any event by reformulated. See *Novick v. Pennsylvania R. R.*, 18 F.R.D. 296, 298 (W.D.Pa.1955).

Subdivision (e) provides that a party is not under a continuing burden except as expressly provided. *Cf.* Note, 68 Harv.L.Rev. 673, 677 (1955). An exception is made as to the identity of persons having knowledge of discoverable matters, because of the obvious importance to each side of knowing all witnesses and because information about witnesses routinely comes to each lawyer's attention. Many of the decisions on the issue of a continuing burden have in fact concerned the identity of witnesses. An exception is also made as to expert trial witnesses in order to carry out the provisions of Rule 26(b)(4). See *Diversified Products Corp. v. Sports Center Co.*, 42 F.R.D. 3 (D.Md.1967).

Another exception is made for the situation in which a party, or more frequently his lawyer, obtains actual knowledge that a prior response is incorrect. This exception does not impose a duty to check the accuracy of prior responses, but it prevents knowing concealment by a party or attorney. Finally, a duty to supplement may be imposed by order of the court in a particular case (including an order resulting from a pretrial conference) or by agreement of the parties. A party may of course make a new discovery request which requires supplementation of prior responses.

The duty will normally be enforced, in those limited instances where it is imposed, through sanctions imposed by the trial court, including exclusion of evidence, continuance, or other action, as the court may deem appropriate.

Rule 29. Stipulations Regarding ~~the Taking of Depositions~~ *Discovery Procedure*

Unless the court orders otherwise, ~~If the parties so stipulate in writing,~~ *the parties may by written stipulation (1) provide that* depositions may be taken before any person, at any time or place, upon any notice, and in any manner and when so taken may be used like other depositions~~,~~ *and (2) modify the procedures provided by these rules for other methods of discovery, except that stipulations extending the time provided in Rules 33, 34, and 36 for responses to discovery may be made only with the approval of the court.*

Advisory Committee's Note

There is no provision for stipulations varying the procedures by which methods of discovery other than depositions are governed. It is common practice for parties

---

New matter is shown in italics; matter to be omitted is lined through

to agree on such variations, and the amendment recognizes such agreements and provides a formal mechanism in the rules for giving them effect. Any stipulation varying the procedures may be superseded by court order, and stipulations extending the time for response to discovery under Rules 33, 34, and 36 require court approval.

Rule 30. Depositions Upon Oral Examination

(a) When Depositions May Be Taken. After commencement of the action, any party may take the testimony of any person, including a party, by deposition upon oral examination. Leave of court, granted with or without notice, must be obtained only if the plaintiff seeks to take a deposition prior to the expiration of 30 days after service of the summons and complaint upon any defendant or service made under Rule 4(e), except that leave is not required (1) if a defendant has served a notice of taking deposition or otherwise sought discovery, or (2) if special notice is given as provided in subdivision (b)(2) of this rule. The attendance of witnesses may be compelled by subpoena as provided in Rule 45. The deposition of a person confined in prison may be taken only by leave of court on such terms as the court prescribes.

~~(a)~~*(b) Notice of Examination:* ~~**Time and Place**~~ *General Requirements; Special Notice; Non-Stenographic Recording; Production of Documents and Things; Deposition of Organization.*

(1) A party desiring to take the deposition of any person upon oral examination shall give reasonable notice in writing to every other party to the action. The notice shall state the time and place for taking the deposition and the name and address of each person to be examined, if known, and, if the name is not known, a general description sufficient to identify him or the particular class or group to which he belongs. *If a subpoena duces tecum is to be served on the person to be examined, a designation of the materials to be produced as set forth in the subpoena shall be attached to or included in the notice.*

(2) Leave of court is not required for the taking of a deposition by plaintiff if the notice (A) states that the person to be examined is about to go out of the district where the action is pending and more than 100 miles from the place of trial, or is about to go out of the United States, or is bound on a voyage to sea, and will be unavailable for examination unless his deposition is taken before expiration of the 30-day period, and (B) sets forth facts to support the statement. The plaintiff's attorney shall sign the notice, and his signature constitutes a certification by him that to the best of his knowledge, information, and belief the statement and supporting

facts are true.   The sanctions provided by Rule 11 are applicable to the certification.

If a party shows that when he was served with notice under this subdivision (b)(2) he was unable through the exercise of diligence to obtain counsel to represent him at the taking of the deposition, the deposition may not be used against him.

(3) ~~On motion of any party upon whom the notice is served, the~~ *The* court may for cause shown enlarge or shorten the time~~.~~ *for taking the deposition.*

(4) The court may upon motion order that the testimony at a deposition be recorded by other than stenographic means, in which event the order shall designate the manner of recording, preserving, and filing the deposition, and may include other provisions to assure that the recorded testimony will be accurate and trustworthy.   If the order is made, a party may nevertheless arrange to have a stenographic transcription made at his own expense.

(5) The notice to a party deponent may be accompanied by a request made in compliance with Rule 34 for the production of documents and tangible things at the taking of the deposition. The procedure of Rule 34 shall apply to the request.

(6) A party may in his notice name as the deponent a public or private corporation or a partnership or association or governmental agency and designate with reasonable particularity the matters on which examination is requested.   The organization so named shall designate one or more officers, directors, or managing agents, or other persons who consent to testify on its behalf, and may set forth, for each person designated, the matters on which he will testify.   The persons so designated shall testify as to matters known or reasonably available to the organization.   This subdivision (b)(6) does not preclude taking a deposition by any other procedure authorized in these rules.

(b) Orders for the Protection of Parties and Deponents. ~~After notice is served for taking a deposition by oral examination, upon motion seasonably made by any party or by the person to be examined and upon notice and for good cause shown, the court in which the action is pending may make an order that the deposition shall not be taken, or that it may be taken only at some designated place other than that stated in the notice, or that it may be taken only on written interrogatories, or that certain matters shall not be inquired into, or that the scope of the examination shall be limited to certain matters, or that the examination shall be held with no one present except the parties to the action and their officers or counsel, or that after being~~

sealed the deposition shall be opened only by order of the court, or
that secret processes, developments, or research need not be disclosed, or that the parties shall simultaneously file specified documents or information enclosed in sealed envelopes to be opened
as directed by the court; or the court may make any other order
which justice requires to protect the party or witness from annoyance, embarrassment, or oppression.

(c) *Examination and Cross-Examination;* **Record of Examination; Oath; Objections.** *Examination and cross-examination
of witnesses may proceed as permitted at the trial under the
provisions of Rule 43(b).* The officer before whom the deposition is
to be taken shall put the witness on oath and shall personally, or
by some one acting under his direction and in his presence, record
the testimony of the witness. The testimony shall be taken
stenographically *or recorded by any other means ordered in accordance with subdivision (b)(4) of this rule.* and *If requested by one of
the parties, the testimony shall be* transcribed unless the parties
agree otherwise.

All objections made at the time of the examination to the
qualifications of the officer taking the deposition, or to the manner
of taking it, or to the evidence presented, or to the conduct of any
party, and any other objection to the proceedings, shall be noted
by the officer upon the deposition. Evidence objected to shall be
taken subject to the objections. In lieu of participating in the oral
examination, parties served with notice of taking a deposition may
transmit *serve* written interrogatories *questions in a sealed envelope on the party taking the deposition and he shall transmit
them* to the officer, who shall propound them to the witness and
record the answers verbatim.

(d) **Motion To Terminate or Limit Examination.** At any
time during the taking of the deposition, on motion of any *a* party
or of the deponent and upon a showing that the examination is
being conducted in bad faith or in such manner as unreasonably to
annoy, embarrass, or oppress the deponent or party, the court in
which the action is pending or the court in the district where the
deposition is being taken may order the officer conducting the
examination to cease forthwith from taking the deposition, or may
limit the scope and manner of the taking of the deposition as
provided in subdivision (b) *Rule 26(c).* If the order made terminates the examination, it shall be resumed thereafter only upon
the order of the court in which the action is pending. Upon
demand of the objecting party or deponent, the taking of the
deposition shall be suspended for the time necessary to make a
motion for an order. In granting or refusing such order the court

New matter is shown in italics; matter to be omitted is lined through

may impose upon either party or upon the witness the requirement to pay such costs or expenses as the court may deem
reasonable. *The provisions of Rule 37(a)(4) apply to the award of
expenses incurred in relation to the motion.*

(e) **Submission to Witness; Changes; Signing.** When the
testimony is fully transcribed the deposition shall be submitted to
the witness for examination and shall be read to or by him, unless
such examination and reading are waived by the witness and by
the parties. Any changes in form or substance which the witness
desires to make shall be entered upon the deposition by the officer
with a statement of the reasons given by the witness for making
them. The deposition shall then be signed by the witness, unless
the parties by stipulation waive the signing or the witness is ill or
cannot be found or refuses to sign. If the deposition is not signed
by the witness *within 30 days of its submission to him,* the officer
shall sign it and state on the record the fact of the waiver or of the
illness or absence of the witness or the fact of the refusal to sign
together with the reason, if any, given therefor; and the deposition may then be used as fully as though signed, unless on a
motion to suppress under Rule 32(d)*(4)* the court holds that the
reasons given for the refusal to sign require rejection of the
deposition in whole or in part.

(f) **Certification and Filing by Officer;** *Exhibits;* **Copies;
Notice of Filing.**

(1) The officer shall certify on the deposition that the witness
was duly sworn by him and that the deposition is a true record of
the testimony given by the witness. He shall then securely seal
the deposition in an envelope indorsed with the title of the action
and marked "Deposition of [here insert name of witness]" and
shall promptly file it with the court in which the action is pending
or send it by registered or certified mail to the clerk thereof for
filing.

*Documents and things produced for inspection during the
examination of the witness, shall, upon the request of a party, be
marked for identification and annexed to and returned with the
deposition, and may be inspected and copied by any party, except
that (A) the person producing the materials may substitute copies to
be marked for identification, if he affords to all parties fair
opportunity to verify the copies by comparison with the originals,
and (B) if the person producing the materials requests their return,
the officer shall mark them, give each party an opportunity to
inspect and copy them, and return them to the person producing
them, and the materials, may then be used in the same manner as
if annexed to and returned with the deposition. Any party may*

New matter is shown in italics; matter to be omitted is lined through

293

move for an order that the original be annexed to and returned with the deposition to the court, pending final disposition of the case.

(2) Upon payment of reasonable charges therefor, the officer shall furnish a copy of the deposition to any party or to the deponent.

(3) The party taking the deposition shall give prompt notice of its filing to all other parties.

(g) Failure To Attend or To Serve Subpoena; Expenses.

(1) If the party giving the notice of the taking of a deposition fails to attend and proceed therewith and another party attends in person or by attorney pursuant to the notice, the court may order the party giving the notice to pay to such other party the ~~amount of the~~ reasonable expenses incurred by him and his attorney in ~~so~~ attending, including reasonable attorney's fees.

(2) If the party giving the notice of the taking of a deposition of a witness fails to serve a subpoena upon him and the witness because of such failure does not attend, and if another party attends in person or by attorney because he expects the deposition of that witness to be taken, the court may order the party giving the notice to pay to such other party the ~~amount of the~~ reasonable expenses incurred by him and his attorney in ~~so~~ attending, including reasonable attorney's fees.

Advisory Committee's Note

Subdivision (a). This subdivision contains the provisions of the existing Rule 26(a), transferred here as part of the rearrangement relating to Rule 26. Existing Rule 30(a) is transferred to 30(b). Changes in language have been made to conform to the new arrangement.

This subdivision is further revised in regard to the requirement of leave of court for taking a deposition. The present procedure, requiring a plaintiff to obtain leave of court if he serves notice of taking a deposition within 20 days after commencement of the action, is changed in several respects. First, leave is required by reference to the time the deposition is to be taken rather than the date of serving notice of taking. Second, the 20–day period is extended to 30 days and runs from the service of summons and complaint on any defendant, rather than the commencement of the action. *Cf.* Ill.S.Ct.R. 19–1, S—H Ill.Ann.Stat. § 101.19–1. Third, leave is not required beyond the time that defendant initiates discovery, thus showing that he has retained counsel. As under the present practice, a party not afforded a reasonable opportunity to appear at a deposition, because he has not yet been served with process, is protected against use of the deposition at trial against him. See Rule 32(a), transferred from 26(d). Moreover, he can later redepose the witness if he so desires.

The purpose of requiring the plaintiff to obtain leave of court is, as stated by the Advisory Committee that proposed the present language of Rule 26(a), to protect "a defendant who has not had an opportunity to retain counsel and inform

---

New matter is shown in italics; matter to be omitted is lined through

himself as to the nature of the suit." Note to 1948 amendment of Rule 26(a), quoted in 3A Barron & Holtzoff, *Federal Practice and Procedure* 455–456 (Wright ed. 1958). In order to assure defendant of this opportunity, the period is lengthened to 30 days. This protection, however, is relevant to the time of taking the deposition, not to the time that notice is served. Similarly, the protective period should run from the service of process rather than the filing of the complaint with the court. As stated in the note to Rule 26(d), the courts have used the service of notice as a convenient reference point for assigning priority in taking depositions, but with the elimination of priority in new Rule 26(d) the reference point is no longer needed. The new procedure is consistent in principle with the provisions of Rules 33, 34, and 36 as revised.

Plaintiff is excused from obtaining leave even during the initial 30-day period if he gives the special notice provided in subdivision (b)(2). The required notice must state that the person to be examined is about to go out of the district where the action is pending and more than 100 miles from the place of trial, or out of the United States, or on a voyage to sea, and will be unavailable for examination unless deposed within the 30-day period. These events occur most often in maritime litigation, when seamen are transferred from one port to another or are about to go to sea. Yet, there are analogous situations in nonmaritime litigation, and although the maritime problems are more common, a rule limited to claims in the admiralty and maritime jurisdiction is not justified.

In the recent unification of the civil and admiralty rules, this problem was temporarily met through addition in Rule 26(a) of a provision that depositions de bene esse may continue to be taken as to admiralty and maritime claims within the meaning of Rule 9(h). It was recognized at the time that "a uniform rule applicable alike to what are now civil actions and suits in admiralty" was clearly preferable, but the de bene esse procedure was adopted "for the time being at least." See Advisory Committee's note in *Report of the Judicial Conference: Proposed Amendments to Rules of Civil Procedure* 43–44 (1966).

The changes in Rule 30(a) and the new Rule 30(b)(2) provide a formula applicable to ordinary civil as well as maritime claims. They replace the provision for depositions de bene esse. They authorize an early deposition without leave of court where the witness is about to depart and, unless his deposition is promptly taken, (1) it will be impossible or very difficult to depose him before trial or (2) his deposition can later be taken but only with substantially increased effort and expense. *Cf.* S. S. Hai Chang, 1966 A.M.C. 2239 (S.D.N.Y.1966), in which the deposing party is required to prepay expenses and counsel fees of the other party's lawyer when the action is pending in New York and depositions are to be taken on the West Coast. Defendant is protected by a provision that the deposition cannot be used against him if he was unable through exercise of diligence to obtain counsel to represent him.

The distance of 100 miles from place of trial is derived from the de bene esse provision and also conforms to the reach of a subpoena of the trial court, as provided in Rule 45(e). See also S.D.N.Y.Civ.R. 5(a). Some parts of the de bene esse provision are omitted from Rule 30(b)(2). Modern deposition practice adequately covers the witness who lives more than 100 miles away from place of trial. If a witness is aged or infirm, leave of court can be obtained.

Subdivision (b). Existing Rule 30(b) on protective orders has been transferred to Rule 26(c), and existing Rule 30(a) relating to the notice of taking deposition has been transferred to this subdivision. Because new material has been added, subsection numbers have been inserted.

New matter is shown in italics; matter to be omitted is lined through

Subdivision (b)(1). If a subpoena duces tecum is to be served, a copy thereof or a designation of the materials to be produced must accompany the notice. Each party is thereby enabled to prepare for the deposition more effectively.

Subdivision (b)(2). This subdivision is discussed in the note to subdivision (a), to which it relates.

Subdivision (b)(3). This provision is derived from existing Rule 30(a), with a minor change of language.

Subdivision (b)(4). In order to facilitate less expensive procedures, provision is made for the recording of testimony by other than stenographic means—*e.g.*, by mechanical, electronic, or photographic means. Because these methods give rise to problems of accuracy and trustworthiness, the party taking the deposition is required to apply for a court order. The order is to specify how the testimony is to be recorded, preserved, and filed, and it may contain whatever additional safeguards the court deems necessary.

Subdivision (b)(5). A provision is added to enable a party, through service of notice, to require another party to produce documents or things at the taking of his deposition. This may now be done as to a nonparty deponent through use of a subpoena duces tecum as authorized by Rule 45, but some courts have held that documents may be secured from a party only under Rule 34. See 2A Barron & Holtzoff, *Federal Practice and Procedure* § 644.1 n. 83.2, § 792 n. 16 (Wright ed. 1961). With the elimination of "good cause" from Rule 34, the reason for this restrictive doctrine has disappeared. *Cf.* N.Y.C.P.L.R. § 3111.

Whether production of documents or things should be obtained directly under rule 34 or at the deposition under this rule will depend on the nature and volume of the documents or things. Both methods are made available. When the documents are few and simple, and closely related to the oral examination, ability to proceed via this rule will facilitate discovery. If the discovering party insists on examining many and complex documents at the taking of the deposition, thereby causing undue burdens on others, the latter may, under Rules 26(c) or 30(d), apply for a court order that the examining party proceed via Rule 34 alone.

Subdivision (b)(6). A new provision is added, whereby a party may name a corporation, partnership, association, or governmental agency as the deponent and designate the matters on which he requests examination, and the organization shall then name one or more of its officers, directors, or managing agents, or other persons consenting to appear and testify on its behalf with respect to matters known or reasonably available to the organization. *Cf.* Alberta Sup.Ct. R. 255. The organization may designate persons other than officers, directors, and managing agents, but only with their consent. Thus, an employee or agent who has an independent or conflicting interest in the litigation—for example, in a personal injury case—can refuse to testify on behalf of the organization.

This procedure supplements the existing practice whereby the examining party designates the corporate official to be deposed. Thus, if the examining party believes that certain officials who have not testified pursuant to this subdivision have added information, he may depose them. On the other hand, a court's decision whether to issue a protective order may take account of the availability and use made of the procedures provided in this subdivision.

The new procedure should be viewed as an added facility for discovery, one which may be advantageous to both sides as well as an improvement in the deposition process. It will reduce the difficulties now encountered in determining, prior to the taking of a deposition, whether a particular employee or agent is a "managing agent." See Note, *Discovery Against Corporations Under the Federal*

New matter is shown in italics; matter to be omitted is lined through

Rules, 47 Iowa L.Rev. 1006–1016 (1962). It will curb the "bandying" by which officers or managing agents of a corporation are deposed in turn but each disclaims knowledge of facts that are clearly known to persons in the organization and thereby to it. *Cf. Haney v. Woodward & Lothrop, Inc.,* 330 F.2d 940, 944 (4th Cir.1964). The provision should also assist organizations which find that an unnecessarily large number of their officers and agents are being deposed by a party uncertain of who in the organization has knowledge. Some courts have held that under the existing rules a corporation should not be burdened with choosing which person is to appear for it. *E.g., United States v. Gahagan Dredging Corp.,* 24 F.R.D. 328, 329 (S.D.N.Y.1958). This burden is not essentially different from that of answering interrogatories under Rule 33, and is in any case lighter than that of an examining party ignorant of who in the corporation has knowledge.

Subdivision (c). A new sentence is inserted at the beginning, representing the transfer of existing Rule 26(c) to this subdivision. Another addition conforms to the new provision in subdivision (b)(4).

The present rule provides that transcription shall be carried out unless all parties waive it. In view of the many depositions taken from which nothing useful is discovered, the revised language provides that transcription is to be performed if any party requests it. The fact of the request is relevant to the exercise of the court's discretion in determining who shall pay for transcription.

Parties choosing to serve written questions rather than participate personally in an oral deposition are directed to serve their questions on the party taking the deposition, since the officer is often not identified in advance. Confidentiality is preserved, since the questions may be served in a sealed envelope.

Subdivision (d). The assessment of expenses incurred in relation to motions made under this subdivision (d) is made subject to the provisions of Rule 37(a). The standards for assessment of expenses are more fully set out in Rule 37(a), and these standards should apply to the essentially similar motions of this subdivision.

Subdivision (e). The provision relating to the refusal of a witness to sign his deposition is tightened through insertion of a 30-day time period.

Subdivision (f)(1). A provision is added which codifies in a flexible way the procedure for handling exhibits related to the deposition and at the same time assures each party that he may inspect and copy documents and things produced by a nonparty witness in response to a subpoena duces tecum. As a general rule and in the absence of agreement to the contrary or order of the court, exhibits produced without objection are to be annexed to and returned with the deposition, but a witness may substitute copies for purposes of marking and he may obtain return of the exhibits. The right of the parties to inspect exhibits for identification and to make copies is assured. *Cf.* N.Y.C.P.L.R. § 3116(c).

Rule 31.   Depositions ~~of Witnesses~~ Upon Written ~~Interrogatories~~ *Questions*

(a) **Serving ~~Interrogatories~~** *Questions*; **Notice.** *After commencement of the action, any party may take the testimony of any person, including a party, by deposition upon written questions. The attendance of witnesses may be compelled by the use of subpoena as provided in Rule 45. The deposition of a person confined in prison may be taken only by leave of court on such terms as the court prescribes.*

New matter is shown in italics; matter to be omitted is lined through

A party desiring to take ~~the~~ *a* deposition ~~of any person~~ upon written ~~interrogatories~~ *questions* shall serve them upon every other party with a notice stating *(1)* the name and address of the person who is to answer them, *if known, and if the name is not known, a general description sufficient to identify him or the particular class or group to which he belongs,* and *(2)* the name or descriptive title and address of the officer before whom the deposition is to be taken. *A deposition upon written questions may be taken of a public or private corporation or a partnership or association or governmental agency in accordance with the provisions of Rule 30(b)(6).*

Within ~~10~~ *30* days ~~thereafter~~ *after the notice and written questions are served,* a party ~~so served~~ may serve cross ~~interrogatories~~ *questions* upon ~~the party proposing to take the deposition.~~ *all other parties.* Within ~~5~~ *10* days ~~thereafter the latter~~ *after being served with cross questions, a party* may serve redirect ~~interrogatories~~ *questions* upon *all other parties.* ~~a party who has served cross interrogatories.~~ Within ~~3~~ *10* days after being served with redirect ~~interrogatories~~ *questions,* a party may serve recross ~~interrogatories~~ *questions* upon *all other parties.* ~~the party proposing to take the deposition.~~ *The court may for cause shown enlarge or shorten the time.*

(b) Officer To Take Responses and Prepare Record. A copy of the notice and copies of all ~~interrogatories~~ *questions* served shall be delivered by the party taking the deposition to the officer designated in the notice, who shall proceed promptly, in the manner provided by Rule 30(c), (e), and (f), to take the testimony of the witness in response to the ~~interrogatories~~ *questions* and to prepare, certify, and file or mail the deposition, attaching thereto the copy of the notice and the ~~interrogatories~~ *questions* received by him.

(c) Notice of Filing. When the deposition is filed the party taking it shall promptly give notice thereof to all other parties.

~~(d) Orders for the Protection of Parties and Deponents. After the service of interrogatories and prior to the taking of the testimony of the deponent, the court in which the action is pending, on motion promptly made by a party or a deponent, upon notice and good cause shown, may make any order specified in Rule 30 which is appropriate and just or an order that the deposition shall not be taken before the officer designated in the notice or that it shall not be taken except upon oral examination.~~

Advisory Committee's Note

Confusion is created by the use of the same terminology to describe both the taking of a deposition upon "written interrogatories" pursuant to this rule and the

---

New matter is shown in italics; matter to be omitted is lined through

serving of "written interrogatories" upon parties pursuant to Rule 33. The distinction between these two modes of discovery will be more readily and clearly grasped through substitution of the word "questions" for "interrogatories" throughout this rule.

Subdivision (a). A new paragraph is inserted at the beginning of this subdivision to conform to the rearrangement of provisions in Rules 26(a), 30(a), and 30(b).

The revised subdivision permits designation of the deponent by general description or by class or group. This conforms to the practice for depositions on oral examination.

The new procedure provided in Rule 30(b)(6) for taking the deposition of a corporation or other organization through persons designated by the organization is incorporated by reference.

The service of all questions, including cross, redirect, and recross, is to be made on all parties. This will inform the parties and enable them to participate fully in the procedure.

The time allowed for service of cross, redirect, and recross questions has been extended. Experience with the existing time limits shows them to be unrealistically short. No special restriction is placed on the time for serving the notice of taking the deposition and the first set of questions. Since no party is required to serve cross questions less than 30 days after the notice and questions are served, the defendant has sufficient time to obtain counsel. The court may for cause shown enlarge or shorten the time.

Subdivision (d). Since new Rule 26(c) provides for protective orders with respect to all discovery, and expressly provides that the court may order that one discovery device be used in place of another, subdivision (d) is eliminated as unnecessary.

Rule 32.   ~~Effect of Errors and Irregularities in Depositions~~ *Use of Depositions in Court Proceedings*

[*Special Note:* The provisions of Rule 32(a), (b), and (c) set out below represent the transfer of Rules 26(d), (e), and (f) with a few amendments. To enable the reader to distinguish easily between transferred material and amendments of material, the provisions are presented within brackets and in roman type as they have heretofore appeared in Rule 26, with line deletions and italics representing the changes made.]

[~~(d)~~ *(a)* **Use of Depositions.** At the trial or upon the hearing of a motion or an interlocutory proceeding, any part or all of a deposition, so far as admissible under the rules of evidence *applied as though the witness were then present and testifying,* may be used against any party who was present or represented at the taking of the deposition or who had ~~due~~ *reasonable* notice thereof, in accordance with any ~~one~~ of the following provisions:

(1) Any deposition may be used by any party for the purpose of contradicting or impeaching the testimony of deponent as a witness.

(2) The deposition of a party or of any one who at the time of taking the deposition was an officer, director, or managing agent,

New matter is shown in italics; matter to be omitted is lined through

or a person designated under Rule 30(b)(6) or 31(a) to testify on behalf of a public or private corporation, partnership or association *or governmental agency* which is a party may be used by an adverse party for any purpose.

(3) The deposition of a witness, whether or not a party, may be used by any party for any purpose if the court finds: ~~1,~~ *(A)* that the witness is dead; or ~~2,~~ *(B)* that the witness is at a greater distance than 100 miles from the place of trial or hearing, or is out of the United States, unless it appears that the absence of the witness was procured by the party offering the deposition; or ~~3,~~ *(C)* that the witness is unable to attend or testify because of age, *illness* ~~sickness~~, infirmity, or imprisonment; or ~~4,~~ *(D)* that the party offering the deposition has been unable to procure the attendance of the witness by subpoena; or ~~5,~~ *(E)* upon application and notice, that such exceptional circumstances exist as to make it desirable, in the interest of justice and with due regard to the importance of presenting the testimony of witnesses orally in open court, to allow the deposition to be used.

(4) If only part of a deposition is offered in evidence by a party, an adverse party may require him to introduce ~~all of it which is relevant to~~ *any other part which ought in fairness to be considered with* the part introduced, and any party may introduce any other parts.

Substitution of parties *pursuant to Rule 25* does not affect the right to use depositions previously taken; and, when an action in any court of the United States or of any state has been dismissed and another action involving the same subject matter is afterward brought between the same parties or their representatives or successors in interest, all depositions lawfully taken and duly filed in the former action may be used in the latter as if originally taken therefor.

~~(e)~~ *(b)* **Objections to Admissibility.** Subject to the provisions of Rules 28(b) and ~~32(c)~~ *subdivision (d)(3) of this rule,* objection may be made at the trial or hearing to receiving in evidence any deposition or part thereof for any reason which would require the exclusion of the evidence if the witness were then present and testifying.

~~(f)~~ *(c)* **Effect of Taking or Using Depositions.** A party ~~shall~~ *does* not ~~be deemed to~~ make a person his own witness for any purpose by taking his deposition. The introduction in evidence of the deposition or any part thereof for any purpose other than that of contradicting or impeaching the deponent makes the deponent the witness of the party introducing the deposition, but this shall not apply to the use by an adverse party of a deposition *under* ~~as~~

New matter is shown in italics; matter to be omitted is lined through

~~described in paragraph (2) of subdivision (d)~~ *subdivision (a)(2)* of this rule. At the trial or hearing any party may rebut any relevant evidence contained in a deposition whether introduced by him or by any other party.]

(d) Effect of Errors and Irregularities in Depositions.

~~(a)~~ *(1) As to Notice.* All errors and irregularities in the notice for taking a deposition are waived unless written objection is promptly served upon the party giving the notice.

~~(b)~~ *(2) As to Disqualification of Officer.* Objection to taking a deposition because of disqualification of the officer before whom it is to be taken is waived unless made before the taking of the deposition begins or as soon thereafter as the disqualification becomes known or could be discovered with reasonable diligence.

~~(c)~~ *(3) As to Taking of Deposition.*

~~(1)~~ *(A)* Objections to the competency of a witness or to the competency, relevancy, or materiality of testimony are not waived by failure to make them before or during the taking of the deposition, unless the ground of the objection is one which might have been obviated or removed if presented at that time.

~~(2)~~ *(B)* Errors and irregularities occurring at the oral examination in the manner of taking the deposition, in the form of the questions or answers, in the oath or affirmation, or in the conduct of parties and errors of any kind which might be obviated, removed, or cured if promptly presented, are waived unless seasonable objection thereto is made at the taking of the deposition.

~~(3)~~ *(C)* Objections to the form of written ~~interrogatories~~ *questions* submitted under Rule 31 are waived unless served in writing upon the party propounding them within the time allowed for serving the succeeding cross or other ~~interrogatories~~ *questions* and within ~~3~~ *5* days after service of the last ~~interrogatories~~ *questions* authorized.

~~(d)~~ *(4) As to Completion and Return of Deposition.* Errors and irregularities in the manner in which the testimony is transcribed or the deposition is prepared, signed, certified, sealed, indorsed, transmitted, filed, or otherwise dealt with by the officer under Rules 30 and 31 are waived unless a motion to suppress the deposition or some part thereof is made with reasonable promptness after such defect is, or with due diligence might have been, ascertained.

Advisory Committee's Note

As part of the rearrangement of the discovery rules, existing subdivisions (d), (e), and (f) of Rule 26 are transferred to Rule 32 as new subdivisions (a), (b), and (c).

New matter is shown in italics; matter to be omitted is lined through

The provisions of Rule 32 are retained as subdivision (d) of Rule 32 with appropriate changes in the lettering and numbering of subheadings. The new rule is given a suitable new title. A beneficial byproduct of the rearrangement is that provisions which are naturally related to one another are placed in one rule.

A change is made in new Rule 32(a), whereby it is made clear that the rules of evidence are to be applied to depositions offered at trial as though the deponent were then present and testifying at trial. This eliminates the possibility of certain technical hearsay objections which are based, not on the contents of deponent's testimony, but on his absence from court. The language of present Rule 26(d) does not appear to authorize these technical objections, but it is not entirely clear. Note present Rule 26(e), transferred to Rule 32(b); see 2A Barron & Holtzoff, *Federal Practice and Procedure* 164–166 (Wright ed. 1961).

An addition in Rule 32(a)(2) provides for use of a deposition of a person designated by a corporation or other organization, which is a party, to testify on its behalf. This complements the new procedure for taking the deposition of a corporation or other organization provided in Rules 30(b)(6) and 31(a). The addition is appropriate, since the deposition is in substance and effect that of the corporation or other organization which is a party.

A change is made in the standard under which a party offering part of a deposition in evidence may be required to introduce additional parts of the deposition. The new standard is contained in a proposal made by the Advisory Committee on Rules of Evidence. See Rule 1–07 and accompanying Note, Preliminary Draft of Proposed Rules of Evidence for the United States District Courts and Magistrates 21–22 (March, 1969).

References to other rules are changed to conform to the rearrangement, and minor verbal changes have been made for clarification. The time for objecting to written questions served under Rule 31 is slightly extended.

Rule 33.   Interrogatories to Parties

(a) Availability; Procedures for Use.   Any party may serve upon any ~~adverse~~ *other* party written interrogatories to be answered by the party served or, if the party served is a public or private corporation or a partnership or association *or governmental agency,* by any officer or agent, who shall furnish such information as is available to the party. Interrogatories may, *without leave of court,* be served *upon the plaintiff* after commencement of the action *and upon any other party with or after service of the summons and complaint upon that party.* ~~and without leave of court, except that, if service is made by the plaintiff within 10 days after such commencement, leave of court granted with or without notice must first be obtained. The interrogatories~~

Each interrogatory shall be answered separately and fully in writing under oath~~.~~, *unless it is objected to, in which event the reasons for objection shall be stated in lieu of an answer.* The answers ~~shall~~ *are to* be signed by the person making them~~,~~, *and the objections signed by the attorney making them.* ~~t~~*T*he party upon whom the interrogatories have been served shall serve a

---

New matter is shown in italics; matter to be omitted is lined through

copy of the answers, *and objections if any,* ~~on the party submitting the interrogatories within 15 days after the service of the interrogatories, unless the court, on motion and notice and for good cause shown, enlarges or shortens the time.~~ *within 30 days after the service of the interrogatories, except that a defendant may serve answers or objections within 45 days after service of the summons and complaint upon that defendant. The court may allow a shorter or longer time.* ~~Within 10 days after service of interrogatories a party may serve written objections thereto together with a notice of hearing the objections at the earliest practicable time. Answers to interrogatories to which objection is made shall be deferred until the objections are determined.~~ *The party submitting the interrogatories may move for an order under Rule 37(a) with respect to any objection to or other failure to answer an interrogatory.*

(b) *Scope; Use at Trial.* Interrogatories may relate to any matters which can be inquired into under Rule 26(b), and the answers may be used to the ~~same~~ extent *permitted by the rules of evidence.* ~~as provided in Rule 26(d) for the use of the deposition of a party. Interrogatories may be served after a deposition has been taken, and a deposition may be sought after interrogatories have been answered, but the court, on motion of the deponent or the party interrogated, may make such protective order as justice may require. The number of interrogatories or of sets of interrogatories to be served is not limited except as justice requires to protect the party from annoyance, expense, embarrassment, or oppression. The provisions of Rule 30(b) are applicable for the protection of the party from whom answers to interrogatories are sought under this rule.~~

An interrogatory otherwise proper is not necessarily objectionable merely because an answer to the interrogatory involves an opinion or contention that relates to fact or the application of law to fact, but the court may order that such an interrogatory need not be answered until after designated discovery has been completed or until a pre-trial conference or other later time.

(c) Option to Produce Business Records. *Where the answer to an interrogatory may be derived or ascertained from the business records of the party upon whom the interrogatory has been served or from an examination, audit or inspection of such business records, or from a compilation, abstract or summary based thereon, and the burden of deriving or ascertaining the answer is substantially the same for the party serving the interrogatory as for the party served, it is a sufficient answer to such interrogatory to specify the records from which the answer may be derived or*

New matter is shown in italics; matter to be omitted is lined through

ascertained and to afford to the party serving the interrogatory reasonable opportunity to examine, audit or inspect such records and to make copies, compilations, abstracts or summaries.

Advisory Committee's Note

Subdivision (a). The mechanics of the operation of Rule 33 are substantially revised by the proposed amendment, with a view to reducing court intervention. There is general agreement that interrogatories spawn a greater percentage of objections and motions than any other discovery device. The Columbia Survey shows that, although half of the litigants resorted to depositions and about one-third used interrogatories, about 65 percent of the objections were made with respect to interrogatories and 26 percent related to depositions. See also Speck, *The Use of Discovery in United States District Courts,* 60 Yale L.J. 1132, 1144, 1151 (1951); Note, 36 Minn.L.Rev. 364, 379 (1952).

The procedures now provided in Rule 33 seem calculated to encourage objections and court motions. The time periods now allowed for responding to interrogatories—15 days for answers and 10 days for objections—are too short. The Columbia Survey shows that tardy response to interrogatories is common, virtually expected. The same was reported in Speck, *supra,* 60 Yale L.J. 1132, 1144. The time pressures tend to encourage objections as a means of gaining time to answer.

The time for objections is even shorter than for answers, and the party runs the risk that if he fails to object in time he may have waived his objections. *E.g., Cleminshaw v. Beech Aircraft Corp.,* 21 F.R.D 300 (D.Del.1957); see 4 *Moore's Federal Practice,* ¶ 33.27 (2d ed. 1966); 2A Barron & Holtzoff, *Federal Practice and Procedure* 372–373 (Wright ed. 1961). It often seems easier to object than to seek an extension of time. Unlike Rules 30(d) and 37(a), Rule 33 imposes no sanction of expenses on a party whose objections are clearly unjustified.

Rule 33 assures that the objections will lead directly to court, through its requirement that they be served with a notice of hearing. Although this procedure does not preclude an out-of-court resolution of the dispute, the procedure tends to discourage informal negotiations. If answers are served and they are thought inadequate, the interrogating party may move under Rule 37(a) for an order compelling adequate answers. There is no assurance that the hearing on objections and that on inadequate answers will be heard together.

The amendment improves the procedure of Rule 33 in the following respects:

(1) The time allowed for response is increased to 30 days and this time period applies to both answers and objections, but a defendant need not respond in less than 45 days after service of the summons and complaint upon him. As is true under existing law, the responding party who believes that some parts or all of the interrogatories are objectionable may choose to seek a protective order under new Rule 26(c) or may serve objections under this rule. Unless he applies for a protective order, he is required to serve answers or objections in response to the interrogatories, subject to the sanctions provided in Rule 37(d). Answers and objections are served together, so that a response to each interrogatory is encouraged, and any failure to respond is easily noted.

(2) In view of the enlarged time permitted for response, it is no longer necessary to require leave of court for service of interrogatories. The purpose of this requirement—that defendant have time to obtain counsel before a response must be made—is adequately fulfilled by the requirement that interrogatories be served upon a party with or after service of the summons and complaint upon him.

New matter is shown in italics; matter to be omitted is lined through

Some would urge that the plaintiff nevertheless not be permitted to serve interrogatories with the complaint. They fear that a routine practice might be invited, whereby form interrogatories would accompany most complaints. More fundamentally, they feel that, since very general complaints are permitted in present-day pleading, it is fair that the defendant have a right to take the lead in serving interrogatories. (These views apply also to Rule 36.) The amendment of Rule 33 rejects these views, in favor of allowing both parties to go forward with discovery, each free to obtain the information he needs respecting the case.

(3) If objections are made, the burden is on the interrogating party to move under Rule 37(a) for a court order compelling answers, in the course of which the court will pass on the objections. The change in the burden of going forward does not alter the existing obligation of an objecting party to justify his objections. *E.g., Pressley v. Boehlke,* 33 F.R.D. 316 (W.D.N.C. 1963). If the discovering party asserts that an answer is incomplete or evasive, again he may look to Rule 37(a) for relief, and he should add this assertion to his motion to overrule objections. There is no requirement that the parties consult informally concerning their differences, but the new procedure should encourage consultation, and the court may by local rule require it.

The proposed changes are similar in approach to those adopted by California in 1961. See Calif.Code Civ.Proc. § 2030(a). The experience of the Los Angeles Superior Court is informally reported as showing that the California amendment resulted in a significant reduction in court motions concerning interrogatories. Rhode Island takes a similar approach. See R. 33, R.I.R. Civ.Proc. Official Draft, p. 74 (Boston Law Book Co.).

A change is made in subdivision (a) which is not related to the sequence of procedures. The restriction to "adverse" parties is eliminated. The courts have generally construed this restriction as precluding interrogatories unless an issue between the parties is disclosed by the pleadings—even though the parties may have conflicting interests. *E.g., Mozeika v. Kaufman Construction Co.,* 25 F.R.D. 233 (E.D.Pa.1960) (plaintiff and third-party defendant); *Biddle v. Hutchinson,* 24 F.R.D. 256 (M.D.Pa.1959) (codefendants). The resulting distinctions have often been highly technical. In *Schlagenhauf v. Holder,* 379 U.S. 104 (1964), the Supreme Court rejected a contention that examination under Rule 35 could be had only against an "opposing" party, as not in keeping "with the aims of a liberal, nontechnical application of the Federal Rules." 379 U.S. at 116. Eliminating the requirement of "adverse" parties from Rule 33 brings it into line with all other discovery rules.

A second change in subdivision (a) is the addition of the term "governmental agency" to the listing of organizations whose answers are to be made by any officer or agent of the organization. This does not involve any change in existing law. Compare the similar listing in Rule 30(b)(6).

The duty of a party to supplement his answers to interrogatories is governed by a new provision in Rule 26(e).

Subdivision (b). There are numerous and conflicting decisions on the question whether and to what extent interrogatories are limited to matters "of fact," or may elicit opinions, contentions, and legal conclusions. *Compare, e.g., Payer, Hewitt & Co. v. Bellanca Corp.,* 26 F.R.D. 219 (D.Del.1960) (opinions bad); *Zinsky v. New York Central R. R.,* 36 F.R.D. 680 (N.D.Ohio 1964) (factual opinion or contention good, but legal theory bad); *United States v. Carter Products, Inc.,* 28 F.R.D. 373 (S.D.N.Y.1961) (factual contentions and legal theories bad) *with Taylor v. Sound Steamship Lines, Inc.,* 100 F.Supp. 388 (D.Conn.1951) (opinions good); *Bynum v. United States,* 36 F.R.D. 14 (E.D.La.1964) (contentions as to facts constituting

New matter is shown in italics; matter to be omitted is lined through

negligence good). For lists of the many conflicting authorities, see 4 *Moore's Federal Practice* ¶ 33.17 (2d ed. 1966); 2A Barron & Holtzoff, *Federal Practice and Procedure* § 768 (Wright ed. 1961).

Rule 33 is amended to provide that an interrogatory is not objectionable merely because it calls for an opinion or contention that relates to fact or the application of law to fact. Efforts to draw sharp lines between facts and opinions have invariably been unsuccessful, and the clear trend of the cases is to permit "factual" opinions. As to requests for opinions or contentions that call for the application of law to fact, they can be most useful in narrowing and sharpening the issues, which is a major purpose of discovery. See *Diversified Products Corp. v. Sports Center Co.,* 42 F.R.D. 3 (D.Md.1967); Moore, *supra*; Field & McKusick, *Maine Civil Practice* § 26.18 (1959). On the other hand, under the new language interrogatories may not extend to issues of "pure law," *i.e.,* legal issues unrelated to the facts of the case. *Cf. United States v. Maryland & Va. Milk Producers Assn., Inc.,* 22 F.R.D. 300 (D.D.C.1958).

Since interrogatories involving mixed questions of law and fact may create disputes between the parties which are best resolved after much or all of the other discovery has been completed, the court is expressly authorized to defer an answer. Likewise, the court may delay determination until pretrial conference, if it believes that the dispute is best resolved in the presence of the judge.

The principal question raised with respect to the cases permitting such interrogatories is whether they reintroduce undesirable aspects of the prior pleading practice, whereby parties were chained to misconceived contentions or theories, and ultimate determination on the merits was frustrated. See James, *The Revival of Bills of Particulars under the Federal Rules,* 71 Harv.L.Rev. 1473 (1958). But there are few if any instances in the recorded cases demonstrating that such frustration has occurred. The general rule governing the use of answers to interrogatories is that under ordinary circumstances they do not limit proof. See, *e.g., McElroy v. United Air Lines, Inc.,* 21 F.R.D. 100 (W.D.Mo.1967); *Pressley v. Boehlke,* 33 F.R.D. 316, 317 (W.D.N.C.1963). Although in exceptional circumstances reliance on an answer may cause such prejudice that the court will hold the answering party bound to his answer, *e.g., Zielinski v. Philadelphia Piers, Inc.,* 139 F.Supp. 408 (E.D.Pa.1956), the interrogating party will ordinarily not be entitled to rely on the unchanging character of the answers he receives and cannot base prejudice on such reliance. The rule does not affect the power of a court to permit withdrawal or amendment of answers to interrogatories.

The use of answers to interrogatories at trial is made subject to the rules of evidence. The provisions governing use of depositions, to which Rule 33 presently refers, are not entirely apposite to answers to interrogatories, since deposition practice contemplates that all parties will ordinarily participate through cross-examination. See 4 *Moore's Federal Practice* ¶ 33.29[1] (2d ed. 1966).

Certain provisions are deleted from subdivision (b) because they are fully covered by new Rule 26(c) providing for protective orders and Rules 26(a) and 26(d). The language of the subdivision is thus simplified without any change of substance.

Subdivision (c). This is a new subdivision, adapted from Calif.Code Civ.Proc. § 2030(c), relating especially to interrogatories which require a party to engage in burdensome or expensive research into his own business records in order to give an answer. The subdivision gives the party an option to make the records available and place the burden of research on the party who seeks the information. "This provision, without undermining the liberal scope of interrogatory discovery, places the burden of discovery upon its potential benefitee," Louisell, *Modern California Discovery,* 124–125 (1963), and alleviates a problem which in the past has troubled

---

New matter is shown in italics; matter to be omitted is lined through

Federal courts. See Speck, *The Use of Discovery in United States District Courts*, 60 Yale L.J. 1132, 1142–1144 (1951). The interrogating party is protected against abusive use of this provision through the requirement that the burden of ascertaining the answer be substantially the same for both sides. A respondent may not impose on an interrogating party a mass of records as to which research is feasible only for one familiar with the records. At the same time, the respondent unable to invoke this subdivision does not on that account lose the protection available to him under new Rule 26(c) against oppressive or unduly burdensome or expensive interrogatories. And even when the respondent successfully invokes the subdivision, the court is not deprived of its usual power, in appropriate cases, to require that the interrogating party reimburse the respondent for the expense of assembling his records and making them intelligible.

~~Rule 34. Discovery and Production of Documents and Things for Inspection, Copying, or Photographing~~

~~Upon motion of any party showing good cause therefor and upon notice to all other parties, and subject to the provisions of Rule 30(b), the court in which an action is pending may (1) order any party to produce and permit the inspection and copying or photographing, by or on behalf of the moving party, of any designated documents, papers, books, accounts, letters, photographs, objects, or tangible things, not privileged, which constitute or contain evidence relating to any of the matters within the scope of the examination permitted by Rule 26(b) and which are in his possession, custody, or control; or (2) order any party to permit entry upon designated land or other property in his possession or control for the purpose of inspecting, measuring, surveying, or photographing the property or any designated object or operation thereon within the scope of the examination permitted by Rule 26(b). The order shall specify the time, place, and manner of making the inspection and taking the copies and photographs and may prescribe such terms and conditions as are just.~~

Rule 34.   Production of Documents and Things and Entry Upon Land for Inspection and Other Purposes

(a) Scope. Any party may serve on any other party a request (1) to produce and permit the party making the request, or someone acting on his behalf, to inspect and copy, any designated documents (including writings, drawings, graphs, charts, photographs, phonorecords, and other data compilations from which information can be obtained, translated, if necessary, by the respondent through detection devices into reasonable usable form), or to inspect and copy, test, or sample any tangible things which constitute or contain matters within the scope of Rule 26(b) and which are in the possession, custody or control of the party upon whom the request is served; or (2) to permit entry upon designated land or other

---

New matter is shown in italics; matter to be omitted is lined through

property in the possession or control of the party upon whom the request is served for the purpose of inspection and measuring, surveying, photographing, testing, or sampling the property or any designated objection or operation thereon, within the scope of Rule 26(b).

(b) Procedure. The request may, without leave of court, be served upon the plaintiff after commencement of the action and upon any other party with or after service of the summons and complaint upon that party. The request shall set forth the items to be inspected either by individual item or by category, and describe each item and category with reasonable particularity. The request shall specify a reasonable time, place, and manner of making the inspection and performing the related acts.

The party upon whom the request is served shall serve a written response within 30 days after the service of the request, except that a defendant may serve a response within 45 days after service of the summons and complaint upon that defendant. The court may allow a shorter or longer time. The response shall state, with respect to each item or category, that inspection and related activities will be permitted as requested, unless the request is objected to, in which event the reasons for objection shall be stated. If objection is made to part of an item or category, the part shall be specified. The party submitting the request may move for an order under Rule 37(a) with respect to any objection to or other failure to respond to the request or any part thereof, or any failure to permit inspection as requested.

(c) Persons Not Parties. This rule does not preclude an independent action against a person not a party for production of documents and things and permission to enter upon land.

Advisory Committee's Note

Rule 34 is revised to accomplish the following major changes in the existing rule: (1) to eliminate the requirement of good cause; (2) to have the rule operate extrajudicially; (3) to include testing and sampling as well as inspecting or photographing tangible things; and (4) to make clear that the rule does not preclude an independent action for analogous discovery against persons not parties.

Subdivision (a). Good cause is eliminated because it has furnished an uncertain and erratic protection to the parties from whom production is sought and is now rendered unnecessary by virtue of the more specific provisions added to Rule 26(b) relating to materials assembled in preparation for trial and to experts retained or consulted by parties.

The good cause requirement was originally inserted in Rule 34 as a general protective provision in the absence of experience with the specific problems that would arise thereunder. As the note to Rule 26(b)(3) on trial preparation materials makes clear, good cause has been applied differently to varying classes of documents, though not without confusion. It has often been said in court opinions

---

New matter is shown in italics; matter to be omitted is lined through

that good cause requires a consideration of need for the materials and of alternative means of obtaining them, *i. e.*, something more than relevance and lack of privilege. But the overwhelming proportion of the cases in which the formula of good cause has been applied to require a special showing are those involving trial preparation. In practice, the courts have not treated documents as having a special immunity to discovery simply because of their being documents. Protection may be afforded to claims of privacy or secrecy or of undue burden or expense under what is now Rule 26(c) (previously Rule 30(b)). To be sure, an appraisal of "undue" burden inevitably entails consideration of the needs of the party seeking discovery. With special provisions added to govern trial preparation materials and experts, there is no longer any occasion to retain the requirement of good cause.

The revision of Rule 34 to have it operate extrajudicially, rather than by court order, is to a large extent a reflection of existing law office practice. The Columbia Survey shows that of the litigants seeking inspection of documents or things, only about 25 percent filed motions for court orders. This minor fraction nevertheless accounted for a significant number of motions. About half of these motions were uncontested and in almost all instances the party seeking production ultimately prevailed. Although an extrajudicial procedure will not drastically alter existing practice under Rule 34—it will conform to it in most cases—it has the potential of saving court time in a substantial though proportionately small number of cases tried annually.

The inclusion of testing and sampling of tangible things and objects or operations on land reflects a need frequently encountered by parties in preparation for trial. If the operation of a particular machine is the basis of a claim for negligent injury, it will often be necessary to test its operating parts or to sample and test the products it is producing. *Cf.* Mich.Gen.Ct.R. 310.1(1) (1963) (testing authorized).

The inclusive description of "documents" is revised to accord with changing technology. It makes clear that Rule 34 applies to electronic data compilations from which information can be obtained only with the use of detection devices, and that when the data can as a practical matter be made usable by the discovering party only through respondent's devices, respondent may be required to use his devices to translate the data into usable form. In many instances, this means that respondent will have to supply a print-out of computer data. The burden thus placed on respondent will vary from case to case, and the courts have ample power under Rule 26(c) to protect respondent against undue burden or expense, either by restricting discovery or requiring that the discovering party pay costs. Similarly, if the discovering party needs to check the electronic source itself, the court may protect respondent with respect to preservation of his records, confidentiality of nondiscoverable matters, and costs.

Subdivision (b). The procedure provided in Rule 34 is essentially the same as that in Rule 33, as amended, and the discussion in the note appended to that rule is relevant to Rule 34 as well. Problems peculiar to Rule 34 relate to the specific arrangements that must be worked out for inspection and related acts of copying, photographing, testing, or sampling. The rule provides that a request for inspection shall set forth the items to be inspected either by item or category, describing each with reasonable particularity, and shall specify a reasonable time, place, and manner of making the inspection.

Subdivision (c). Rule 34 as revised continues to apply only to parties. Comments from the bar make clear that in the preparation of cases for trial it is occasionally necessary to enter land or inspect large tangible things in the possession of a person not a party, and that some courts have dismissed indepen-

---

New matter is shown in italics; matter to be omitted is lined through

dent actions in the nature of bills in equity for such discovery on the ground that Rule 34 is preemptive. While an ideal solution to this problem is to provide for discovery against persons not parties in Rule 34, both the jurisdictional and procedural problems are very complex. For the present, this subdivision makes clear that Rule 34 does not preclude independent actions for discovery against persons not parties.

Rule 35. Physical and Mental Examination of Persons

(a) **Order for Examination.** ~~In an action in which~~ *When* the mental or physical condition *(including the blood group)* of a party, *or of a person in the custody or under the legal control of a party,* is in controversy, the court in which the action is pending may order ~~him~~ *the party* to submit to a physical or mental examination by a physician *or to produce for examination the person in his custody or legal control.* The order may be made only on motion for good cause shown and upon notice to the ~~party~~ *person* to be examined and to all ~~other~~ parties and shall specify the time, place, manner, conditions, and scope of the examination and the person or persons by whom it is to be made.

(b) **Report of** *Examining Physician* ~~**Findings.**~~

(1) If requested by the *party against whom an order is made under Rule 35(a) or the* person examined, the party causing the examination to be made shall deliver to him a copy of a detailed written report of the examining physician setting out his findings, *including results of all tests made, diagnoses* and conclusions~~.~~, *together with like reports of all earlier examinations of the same condition.* After ~~such request and~~ delivery the party causing the examination ~~to be made~~ shall be entitled upon request to receive from the party ~~examined~~ *against whom the order is made* a like report of any examination, previously or thereafter made, of the same ~~mental or physical~~ condition~~.~~, *unless, in the case of a report of examination of a person not a party, the party shows that he is unable to obtain it.* ~~If the party examined refuses to deliver such report t~~*T*he court on motion ~~and notice~~ may make an order *against a party* requiring delivery of a *report* on such terms as are just, and if a physician fails or refuses to make ~~such~~ a report the court may exclude his testimony if offered at the trial.

(2) By requesting and obtaining a report of the examination so ordered or by taking the deposition of the examiner, the party examined waives any privilege he may have in that action or any other involving the same controversy, regarding the testimony of every other person who has examined or may thereafter examine him in respect of the same mental or physical condition.

New matter is shown in italics; matter to be omitted is lined through

(3) This subdivision applies to examinations made by agreement of the parties, unless the agreement expressly provides otherwise. This subdivision does not preclude discovery of a report of an examining physician or the taking of a deposition of the physician in accordance with the provisions of any other rule.

Advisory Committee's Note

Subdivision (a). Rule 35(a) has hitherto provided only for an order requiring a party to submit to an examination. It is desirable to extend the rule to provide for an order against the party for examination of a person in his custody or under his legal control. As appears from the provisions of amended Rule 37(b)(2) and the comment under that rule, an order to "produce" the third person imposes only an obligation to use good faith efforts to produce the person.

The amendment will settle beyond doubt that a parent or guardian suing to recover for injuries to a minor may be ordered to produce the minor for examination. Further, the amendment expressly includes blood examination within the kinds of examinations that can be ordered under the rule. See *Beach v. Beach,* 114 F.2d 479 (D.C.Cir.1940). Provisions similar to the amendment have been adopted in at least 10 States: Calif.Code Civ.Proc. § 2032; Ida.R.Civ.P. 35; Ill. S–H Ann. c. 110A, § 215; Md.R.P. 420; Mich.Gen.Ct.R. 311; Minn.R.Civ.P. 35; Mo.Vern.Ann.R. Civ.P. 60.01; N.Dak.R.Civ.P. 35; N.Y.C.P.L. § 3121; Wyo.R.Civ.R. 35.

The amendment makes no change in the requirements of Rule 35 that, before a court order may issue, the relevant physical or mental condition must be shown to be "in controversy" and "good cause" must be shown for the examination. Thus, the amendment has no effect on the recent decision of the Supreme Court in *Schlagenhauf v. Holder,* 379 U.S. 104 (1964), stressing the importance of these requirements and applying them to the facts of the case. The amendment makes no reference to employees of a party. Provisions relating to employees in the State statutes and rules cited above appear to have been virtually unused.

Subdivision (b)(1). This subdivision is amended to correct an imbalance in Rule 35(b)(1) as heretofore written. Under that text, a party causing a Rule 35(a) examination to be made is required to furnish to the party examined, on request, a copy of the examining physician's report. If he delivers this copy, he is in turn entitled to receive from the party examined reports of all examinations of the same condition previously or later made. But the rule has not in terms entitled the examined party to receive from the party causing the Rule 35(a) examination any reports of earlier examinations of the same condition to which the latter may have access. The amendment cures this defect. See La.Stat.Ann., Civ.Proc. art. 1495 (1960); Utah R.Civ.P. 35(c).

The amendment specifies that the written report of the examining physician includes results of all tests made, such as results of X-rays and cardiograms. It also embodies changes required by the broadening of Rule 35(a) to take in persons who are not parties.

Subdivision (b)(3). This new subdivision removes any possible doubt that reports of examination may be obtained although no order for examination has been made under Rule 35(a). Examinations are very frequently made by agreement, and sometimes before the party examined has an attorney. The courts have uniformly ordered that reports be supplied, see 4 *Moore's Federal Practice* ¶ 35.06, n. 1 (2d ed. 1966); 2A Barron & Holtzoff, *Federal Practice and Procedure* § 823, n. 22 (Wright ed. 1961), and it appears best to fill the technical gap in the present rule.

New matter is shown in italics; matter to be omitted is lined through

The subdivision also makes clear that reports of examining physicians are discoverable not only under Rule 35(b) but under other rules as well. To be sure, if the report is privileged, then discovery is not permissible under any rule other than Rule 35(b) and it is permissible under Rule 35(b) only if the party requests a copy of the report of examination made by the other party's doctor. *Sher v. De Haven,* 199 F.2d 777 (D.C.Cir.1952), *cert. denied* 345 U.S. 936 (1953). But if the report is unprivileged and is subject to discovery under the provisions of rules other than Rule 35(b)—such as Rules 34 or 26(b)(3) or (4)—discovery should not depend upon whether the person examined demands a copy of the report. Although a few cases have suggested the contrary, *e. g., Galloway v. National Dairy Products Corp.,* 24 F.R.D. 362 (E.D.Pa.1959), the better considered district court decisions hold that Rule 35(b) is not preemptive. *E. g., Leszynski v. Russ,* 29 F.R.D. 10, 12 (D.Md.1961) and cases cited. The question was recently given full consideration in *Buffington v. Wood,* 351 F.2d 292 (3d Cir.1965), holding that Rule 35(b) is not preemptive.

Rule 36. *Requests for* Admission ~~of Facts and of~~ ~~Genuineness of Documents~~

(a) **Request for Admission.** ~~After commencement of an action a party may serve upon any other party a written request for the admission by the latter of the genuineness of any relevant documents described in and exhibited with the request or of the truth of any relevant matters of fact set forth in the request. If a plaintiff desires to serve a request within 10 days after commencement of the action leave of court, granted with or without notice, must be obtained. Copies of the documents shall be served with the request unless copies have already been furnished.~~ *A party may serve upon any other party a written request for the admission, for purposes of the pending action only, of the truth of any matters within the scope of Rule 26(b) set forth in the request that relate to statements or opinions of fact or of the application of law to fact, including the genuineness of any documents described in the request. Copies of documents shall be served with the request unless they have been or are otherwise furnished or made available for inspection and copying. The request may, without leave of court, be served upon the plaintiff after commencement of the action and upon any other party with or after service of the summons and complaint upon that party.*

Each ~~of the matters~~ *matter* of which an admission is requested *shall be separately set forth.* ~~shall be deemed~~ *The matter is* admitted unless, within ~~a period designated in the request, not less than 10~~ *30* days after service ~~thereof~~ *of the request,* or within such shorter or longer time as the court may allow ~~on motion and notice~~, the party to whom the request is directed serves upon the party requesting the admission ~~either (1) a sworn statement denying~~ *a written answer or objection addressed to the matter, signed by the party or by his attorney, but, unless the court shortens the time,*

New matter is shown in italics; matter to be omitted is lined through

a defendant shall not be required to serve answers or objections before the expiration of 45 days after service of the summons and complaint upon him. If objection is made, the reasons therefor shall be stated. The answer shall specifically *deny* the ~~matters of which an admission is requested~~ *matter* or ~~setting~~ *set* forth in detail the reasons why ~~he~~ *the answering party* cannot truthfully admit or deny ~~those matters~~ *the matter.* ~~or (2) written objections on the ground that some or all of the requested admissions are privileged or irrelevant or that the request is otherwise improper in whole or in part, together with a notice of hearing the objections at the earliest practicable time. If written objections to a part of the request are made, the remainder of the request shall be answered within the period designated in the request.~~ A denial shall fairly meet the substance of the requested admission, and when good faith requires that a party *qualify his answer or* deny only a part ~~or a qualification~~ of ~~a~~ *the* matter of which an admission is requested, he shall specify so much of it as is true and *qualify or* deny ~~only~~ the remainder. *An answering party may not give lack of information or knowledge as a reason for failure to admit or deny unless he states that he has made reasonable inquiry and that the information known or readily obtainable by him is insufficient to enable him to admit or deny. A party who considers that a matter of which an admission has been requested presents a genuine issue for trial may not, on that ground alone, object to the request; he may, subject to the provisions of Rule 37(c), deny the matter or set forth reasons why he cannot admit or deny it.*

The party who has requested the admissions may move to determine the sufficiency of the answers or objections. Unless the court determines that an objection is justified, it shall order that an answer be served. If the court determines that an answer does not comply with the requirements of this rule, it may order either that the matter is admitted or that an amended answer be served. The court may, in lieu of these orders, determine that final disposition of the request be made at a pre-trial conference or at a designated time prior to trial. The provisions of Rule 37(a)(4) apply to the award of expenses incurred in relation to the motion.

(b) Effect of Admission. *Any matter admitted under this rule is conclusively established unless the court on motion permits withdrawal or amendment of the admission. Subject to the provisions of Rule 16 governing amendment of a pre-trial order, the court may permit withdrawal or amendment when the presentation of the merits of the action will be subserved thereby and the party who obtained the admission fails to satisfy the court that withdrawal or amendment will prejudice him in maintaining his action or defense on the merits.* Any admission made by a party

---

New matter is shown in italics; matter to be omitted is lined through

~~pursuant to such request~~ *under this rule* is for the purpose of the pending action only and ~~neither constitutes~~ *is not* an admission by him for any other other purpose nor may *it* be used against him in any other proceeding.

Advisory Committee's Note

Rule 36 serves two vital purposes, both of which are designed to reduce trial time. Admissions are sought, first to facilitate proof with respect to issues that cannot be eliminated from the case, and secondly, to narrow the issues by eliminating those that can be. The changes made in the rule are designed to serve these purposes more effectively. Certain disagreements in the courts about the proper scope of the rule are resolved. In addition, the procedural operation of the rule is brought into line with other discovery procedures, and the binding effect of an admission is clarified. See generally Finman, *The Request for Admissions in Federal Civil Procedure*, 71 Yale L.J. 371 (1962).

Subdivision (a). As revised, the subdivision provides that a request may be made to admit any matters within the scope of Rule 26(b) that relate to statements or opinions of fact or of the application of law to fact. It thereby eliminates the requirement that the matters be "of fact." This change resolves conflicts in the court decisions as to whether a request to admit matters of "opinion" and matters involving "mixed law and fact" is proper under the rule. As to "opinion," *compare, e. g., Jackson Bluff Corp. v. Marcelle*, 20 F.R.D. 139 (E.D.N.Y.1957); *California v. The S. S. Jules Fribourg*, 19 F.R.D. 432 (N.D.Calif.1955), *with e. g., Photon, Inc. v. Harris Intertype, Inc.*, 28 F.R.D. 327 (D.Mass.1961); *Hise v. Lockwood Grader Corp.*, 153 F.Supp. 276 (D.Nebr.1957). As to "mixed law and fact" the majority of courts sustain objections, *e. g., Minnesota Mining and Mfg. Co. v. Norton Co.*, 36 F.R.D. 1 (N.D.Ohio 1964), but *McSparran v. Hanigan*, 225 F.Supp. 628 (E.D.Pa.1963) is to the contrary.

Not only is it difficult as a practical matter to separate "fact" from "opinion," see 4 *Moore's Federal Practice* ¶ 36.04 (2d ed. 1966); *cf.* 2A Barron & Holtzoff, *Federal Practice and Procedure* 317 (Wright ed. 1961), but an admission on a matter of opinion may facilitate proof or narrow the issues or both. An admission of a matter involving the application of law to fact may, in a given case, even more clearly narrow the issues. For example, an admission that an employee acted in the scope of his employment may remove a major issue from the trial. In *McSparran v. Hanigan, supra,* plaintiff admitted that "the premises on which said accident occurred, were occupied or under the control" of one of the defendants, 225 F.Supp. at 636. This admission, involving law as well as fact, removed one of the issues from the lawsuit and thereby reduced the proof required at trial. The amended provision does not authorize requests for admissions of law unrelated to the facts of the case.

Requests for admission involving the application of law to fact may create disputes between the parties which are best resolved in the presence of the judge after much or all of the other discovery has been completed. Power is therefore expressly conferred upon the court to defer decision until a pretrial conference is held or until a designated time prior to trial. On the other hand, the court should not automatically defer decision; in many instances, the importance of the admission lies in enabling the requesting party to avoid the burdensome accumulation of proof prior to the pretrial conference.

Courts have also divided on whether an answering party may properly object to request for admission as to matters which that party regards as "in dispute."

New matter is shown in italics; matter to be omitted is lined through

Compare, e. g., Syracuse Broadcasting Corp. v. Newhouse, 271 F.2d 910, 917 (2d Cir.1959); *Driver v. Gindy Mfg. Corp.,* 24 F.R.D. 473 (E.D.Pa.1959); *with, e. g., McGonigle v. Baxter,* 27 F.R.D. 504 (E.D.Pa.1961); *United States v. Ehbauer,* 13 F.R.D. 462 (W.D.Mo.1952). The proper response in such cases is an answer. The very purpose of the request is to ascertain whether the answering party is prepared to admit or regards the matter as presenting a genuine issue for trial. In his answer, the party may deny, or he may give as his reason for inability to admit or deny the existence of a genuine issue. The party runs no risk of sanctions if the matter is genuinely in issue, since Rule 37(c) provides a sanction of costs only when there are no good reasons for a failure to admit.

On the other hand, requests to admit may be so voluminous and so framed that the answering party finds the task of identifying what is in dispute and what is not unduly burdensome. If so, the responding party may obtain a protective order under Rule 26(c). Some of the decisions sustaining objections on "disputability" grounds could have been justified by the burdensome character of the requests. See, *e. g., Syracuse Broadcasting Corp. v. Newhouse, supra.*

Another sharp split of authority exists on the question whether a party may base his answer on lack of information or knowledge without seeking out additional information. One line of cases has held that a party may answer on the basis of such knowledge as he has at the time he answers. *E. g., Jackson Buff Corp. v. Marcelle,* 20 F.R.D. 139 (E.D.N.Y.1957); *Sladek v. General Motors Corp.,* 16 F.R.D. 104 (S.D.Iowa 1954). A larger group of cases, supported by commentators, has taken the view that if the responding party lacks knowledge, he must inform himself in reasonable fashion. *E. g., Hise v. Lockwood Grader Corp.,* 153 F.Supp. 276 (D.Nebr.1957); *E. H. Tate Co. v. Jiffy Enterprises, Inc.,* 16 F.R.D. 571 (E.D.Pa. 1954); Finman, *supra,* 71 Yale L.J. 371, 404–409; 4 *Moore's Federal Practice* ¶ 36.04 (2d ed. 1966); 2A Barron & Holtzoff, *Federal Practice and Procedure* 509 (Wright ed. 1961).

The rule as revised adopts the majority view, as in keeping with a basic principle of the discovery rules that a reasonable burden may be imposed on the parties when its discharge will facilitate preparation for trial and ease the trial process. It has been argued against this view that one side should not have the burden of "proving" the other side's case. The revised rule requires only that the answering party make reasonable inquiry and secure such knowledge and information as are readily obtainable by him. In most instances, the investigation will be necessary either to his own case or to preparation for rebuttal. Even when it is not, the information may be close enough at hand to be "readily obtainable." Rule 36 requires only that the party state that he has taken these steps. The sanction for failure of a party to inform himself before he answers lies in the award of costs after trial, as provided in Rule 37(c).

The requirement that the answer to a request for admission be sworn is deleted, in favor of a provision that the answer be signed by the party or by his attorney. The provisions of Rule 36 make it clear that admissions function very much as pleadings do. Thus, when a party admits in part and denies in part, his admission is for purposes of the pending action only and may not be used against him in any other proceeding. The broadening of the rule to encompass mixed questions of law and fact reinforces this feature. Rule 36 does not lack a sanction for false answers; Rule 37(c) furnishes an appropriate deterrent.

The existing language describing the available grounds for objection to a request for admission is eliminated as neither necessary nor helpful. The statement that objection may be made to any request which is "improper" adds nothing to the provisions that the party serve an answer or objection addressed to each

---

New matter is shown in italics; matter to be omitted is lined through

matter and that he state his reasons for any objection. None of the other discovery rules sets forth grounds for objection, except so far as all are subject to the general provisions of Rule 26.

Changes are made in the sequence of procedures in Rule 36 so that they conform to the new procedures in Rules 33 and 34. The major changes are as follows:

(1) The normal time for response to a request for admissions is lengthened from 10 to 30 days, conforming more closely to prevailing practice. A defendant need not respond, however, in less than 45 days after service of the summons and complaint upon him. The court may lengthen or shorten the time when special situations require it.

(2) The present requirement that the plaintiff wait 10 days to serve requests without leave of court is eliminated. The revised provision accords with those in Rules 33 and 34.

(3) The requirement that the objecting party move automatically for a hearing on his objection is eliminated, and the burden is on the requesting party to move for an order. The change in the burden of going forward does not modify present law on burden of persuasion. The award of expenses incurred in relation to the motion is made subject to the comprehensive provisions of Rule 37(a)(4).

(4) A problem peculiar to Rule 36 arises if the responding party serves answers that are not in conformity with the requirements of the rule—for example, a denial is not "specific," or the explanation of inability to admit or deny is not "in detail." Rule 36 now makes no provision for court scrutiny of such answers before trial, and it seems to contemplate that defective answers bring about admissions just as effectively as if no answer had been served. Some cases have so held. *E. g., Southern Ry. Co. v. Crosby*, 201 F.2d 878 (4th Cir.1953); *United States v. Laney*, 96 F.Supp. 482 (E.D.S.C.1951).

Giving a defective answer the automatic effect of an admission may cause unfair surprise. A responding party who purported to deny or to be unable to admit or deny will for the first time at trial confront the contention that he has made a binding admission. Since it is not always easy to know whether a denial is "specific" or an explanation is "in detail," neither party can know how the court will rule at trial and whether proof must be prepared. Some courts, therefore, have entertained motions to rule on defective answers. They have at times ordered that amended answers be served, when the defects were technical, and at other times have declared that the matter was admitted. *E. g., Woods v. Stewart*, 171 F.2d 544 (5th Cir.1948); *SEC v. Kaye, Real & Co.*, 122 F.Supp. 639 (S.D.N.Y. 1954); *Sieb's Hatcheries, Inc. v. Lindley*, 13 F.R.D. 113 (W.D.Ark.1952). The rule as revised conforms to the latter practice.

Subdivision (b). The rule does not now indicate the extent to which a party is bound by his admission. Some courts view admissions as the equivalent of sworn testimony. *E. g., Ark-Tenn Distributing Corp. v. Breidt*, 209 F.2d 359 (3d Cir.1954); *United States v. Lemons*, 125 F.Supp. 686 (W.D.Ark.1954); 4 *Moore's Federal Practice* ¶ 36.08 (2d ed. 1966 Supp.). At least in some jurisdictions a party may rebut his own testimony, *e. g., Alamo v. Del Rosario*, 98 F.2d 328 (D.C.Cir.1938), and by analogy an admission made pursuant to Rule 36 may likewise be thought rebuttable. The courts in *Ark-Tenn* and *Lemons, supra*, reasoned in this way, although the results reached may be supported on different grounds. In *McSparran v. Hanigan*, 225 F.Supp. 628, 636–637 (E.D.Pa.1963), the court held that an admission is conclusively binding, though noting the confusion created by prior decisions.

New matter is shown in italics; matter to be omitted is lined through

The new provisions give an admission a conclusively binding effect, for purposes only of the pending action, unless the admission is withdrawn or amended. In form and substance a Rule 36 admission is comparable to an admission in pleadings or a stipulation drafted by counsel for use at trial, rather than to an evidentiary admission of a party. Louisell, *Modern California Discovery* § 8.07 (1963); 2A Barron & Holtzoff, *Federal Practice and Procedure* § 838 (Wright ed. 1961). Unless the party securing an admission can depend on its binding effect, he cannot safely avoid the expense of preparing to prove the very matters on which he has secured the admission, and the purpose of the rule is defeated. Field & McKusick, *Maine Civil Practice* § 36.4 (1959); Finman, *supra*, 71 Yale L.J. 371, 418–426; Comment, 56 Nw.U.L.Rev. 679, 682–683 (1961).

Provision is made for withdrawal or amendment of an admission. This provision emphasizes the importance of having the action resolved on the merits, while at the same time assuring each party that justified reliance on an admission in preparation for trial will not operate to his prejudice. *Cf. Moosman v. Joseph P. Blitz, Inc.,* 358 F.2d 686 (2d Cir.1966).

Rule 37. ~~Refusal~~ *Failure* to Make Discovery: ~~Consequences~~ *Sanctions*

(a) ~~Refusal to Answer.~~ ~~If a party or other deponent refuses to answer any question propounded upon oral examination, the examination shall be completed on other matters or adjourned, as the proponent of the question may prefer. Thereafter, on reasonable notice to all persons affected thereby, he may apply to the court in the district where the deposition is taken for an order compelling an answer. Upon the refusal of a deponent to answer any interrogatory submitted under Rule 31 or upon the refusal of a party to answer any interrogatory submitted under Rule 33, the proponent of the question may on like notice make like application for such an order. If the motion is granted and if the court finds that the refusal was without substantial justification the court shall require the refusing party or deponent and the party or attorney advising the refusal or either of them to pay to the examining party the amount of the reasonable expenses incurred in obtaining the order, including reasonable attorney's fees. If the motion is denied and if the court finds that the motion was made without substantial justification, the court shall require the examining party or the attorney advising the motion or both of them to pay to the refusing party or witness the amount of the reasonable expenses incurred in opposing the motion, including reasonable attorney's fees.~~

(a) Motion for Order Compelling Discovery. A party, upon reasonable notice to other parties and all persons affected thereby, may apply for an order compelling discovery as follows:

(1) Appropriate Court. An application for an order to a party may be made to the court in which the action is pending, or, on

New matter is shown in italics; matter to be omitted is lined through

matters relating to a deposition, to the court in the district where the deposition is being taken. An application for an order to a deponent who is not a party shall be made to the court in the district where the deposition is being taken.

(2) Motion. If a deponent fails to answer a question propounded or submitted under Rule 30 or 31, or a corporation or other entity fails to make a designation under Rule 30(b)(6) or 31(a), or a party fails to answer an interrogatory submitted under Rule 33, or if a party, in response to a request for inspection submitted under Rule 34, fails to respond that inspection will be permitted as requested or fails to permit inspection as requested, the discovering party may move for an order compelling an answer, or a designation, or an order compelling inspection in accordance with the request. When taking a deposition on oral examination, the proponent of the question may complete or adjourn the examination before he applies for an order.

If the court denies the motion in whole or in part, it may make such protective order as it would have been empowered to make on a motion made pursuant to Rule 26(c).

(3) Evasive or Incomplete Answer. For purposes of this subdivision an evasive or incomplete answer is to be treated as a failure to answer.

(4) Award of Expenses of Motion. If the motion is granted, the court shall, after opportunity for hearing, require the party or deponent whose conduct necessitated the motion or the party or attorney advising such conduct or both of them to pay to the moving party the reasonable expenses incurred in obtaining the order, including attorney's fees, unless the court finds that the opposition to the motion was substantially justified or that other circumstances make an award of expenses unjust.

If the motion is denied, the court shall, after opportunity for hearing, require the moving party or the attorney advising the motion or both of them to pay the party or deponent who opposed the motion the reasonable expenses incurred in opposing the motion, including attorney's fees, unless the court finds that the making of the motion was substantially justified or that other circumstances make an award of expenses unjust.

If the motion is granted in part and denied in part, the court may apportion the reasonable expenses incurred in relation to the motion among the parties and persons in a just manner.

(b) Failure to Comply With Order.

(1) ~~Contempt~~ *Sanctions by Court in District Where Deposition is Taken.* If a ~~party or other~~ *deponent* ~~witness refuses~~ *fails* to be

New matter is shown in italics; matter to be omitted is lined through

sworn or ~~refuses~~ to answer ~~any~~ *a* question after being directed to do so by the court in the district in which the deposition is being taken, the ~~refusal~~ *failure* may be considered a contempt of that court.

(2) ~~Other Consequences~~ *Sanctions by Court in Which Action is Pending.* If ~~any~~ *a* party or an officer, *director,* or managing agent of a party *or a person designated under Rule 30(b)(6) or 31(a) to testify on behalf of a party* ~~refuses~~ *fails* to obey an order *to provide or permit discovery, including an order* made under subdivision (a) of this rule ~~requiring him to answer designated questions, or an order made under Rule 34 to produce any document or other thing for inspection, copying, or photographing or to permit it to be done, or to permit entry upon land or other property, or an order made under~~ *or* Rule 35 ~~requiring him to submit to a physical or mental examination~~, the court *in which the action is pending* may make such orders in regard to the ~~refusal~~ *failure* as are just, and among others the following:

~~(i)~~*(A)* An order that the matters regarding which the ~~questions were asked, or the character or description of the thing or land, or the contents of the paper, or the physical or mental condition of the party,~~ *order was made* or any other designated facts shall be taken to be established for the purposes of the action in accordance with the claim of the party obtaining the order;

~~(ii)~~*(B)* An order refusing to allow the disobedient party to support or oppose designated claims or defenses, or prohibiting him from introducing *designated matters* in evidence ~~designated documents or things or items of testimony, or from introducing evidence of physical or mental condition~~;

~~(iii)~~*(C)* An order striking out pleadings or parts thereof, or staying further proceedings until the order is obeyed, or dismissing the action or proceeding or any part thereof, or rendering a judgment by default against the disobedient party;

~~(iv)~~*(D)* In lieu of any of the foregoing orders or in addition thereto, an order ~~directing the arrest of any party or agent of a party for disobeying~~ *treating as a contempt of court the failure to obey* any ~~of such~~ orders except an order to submit to a physical or mental examination~~.~~*;*

(E) Where a party has failed to comply with an order under Rule 35(a) requiring him to produce another for examination, such orders as are listed in paragraphs (A), (B), and (C) of this subdivision, unless the party failing to comply shows that he is unable to produce such person for examination.

New matter is shown in italics; matter to be omitted is lined through

In lieu of any of the foregoing orders or in addition thereto, the court shall require the party failing to obey the order or the attorney advising him or both to pay the reasonable expenses, including attorney's fees, caused by the failure, unless the court finds that the failure was substantially justified or that other circumstances make an award of expenses unjust.

(c) Expenses on ~~Refusal~~ *Failure* **To Admit.** If a party ~~after being served with request under Rule 36,~~ *fails* to admit the genuineness of any documents or the truth of any matters ~~of fact~~ *as requested under Rule 36,* ~~serves a sworn denial thereof~~ and if the party requesting the admissions thereafter proves the genuineness of ~~any such~~ *the* document or the truth of ~~any such~~ *the* matter ~~of fact~~, he may apply to the court for an order requiring the other party to pay him the reasonable expenses incurred in making ~~such~~ *that* proof, including reasonable attorney's fees. ~~Unless the court finds that there were good reasons for the denial or that the admissions sought were of no substantial importance, the order shall be made.~~ *The court shall make the order unless it finds that (1) the request was held objectionable pursuant to Rule 36(a), or (2) the admission sought was of no substantial importance, or (3) the party failing to admit had reasonable ground to believe that he might prevail on the matter, or (4) there was other good reason for the failure to admit.*

(d) Failure of Party To Attend *at Own Deposition* **or Serve Answers** *to Interrogatories or Respond to Request for Inspection.* If a party or an officer, *director,* or managing agent of a party *or a person designated under Rule 30(b)(6) or 31(a) to testify on behalf of a party* ~~wilfully~~ fails *(1)* to appear before the officer who is to take his deposition, after being served with a proper notice, or ~~fails~~ *(2)* to serve answers *or objections* to interrogatories submitted under Rule 33, after proper service of ~~such~~ *the* interrogatories, *or (3) to serve a written response to a request for inspection submitted under Rule 34, after proper service of the request,* the court *in which the action is pending* on motion ~~and notice~~ may ~~strike out all or any part of any pleading of that party, or dismiss the action or proceeding or any part thereof, or enter a judgment by default against that party.~~ *make such orders in regard to the failure as are just, and among others it may take any action authorized under paragraph (A), (B), and (C) of subdivision (b)(2) of this rule. In lieu of any order or in addition thereto, the court shall require the party failing to act or the attorney advising him or both to pay the reasonable expenses, including attorney's fees, caused by the failure, unless the court finds that the failure was substantially justified or that other circumstances make an award of expenses unjust.*

The failure to act described in this subdivision may not be excused on the ground that the discovery sought is objectionable unless the party failing to act has applied for a protective order as provided by Rule 26(c).

(e) ~~Failure To Respond to Letters Rogatory.~~ *Subpoena of Person in Foreign Country.* A subpoena may be issued as provided in Title 28 U.S.C. § 1783, under the circumstances and conditions therein stated.

(f) Expenses Against United States. ~~Expenses and attorney's fees are not to be imposed upon~~ *Except to the extent permitted by statute, expenses and fees may not be awarded against* the United States under this rule.

Advisory Committee's Note

Rule 37 provides generally for sanctions against parties or persons unjustifiably resisting discovery. Experience has brought to light a number of defects in the language of the rule as well as instances in which it is not serving the purposes for which it was designed. See Rosenberg, *Sanctions to Effectuate Pretrial Discovery,* 58 Col.L.Rev. 480 (1958). In addition, changes being made in other discovery rules require conforming amendments to Rule 37.

Rule 37 sometimes refers to a "failure" to afford discovery and at other times to a "refusal" to do so. Taking note of this dual terminology, courts have imported into "refusal" a requirement of "wilfullness." See *Roth v. Paramount Pictures Corp.,* 8 F.R.D. 31 (W.D.Pa.1948); *Campbell v. Johnson,* 101 F.Supp. 705, 707 (S.D.N.Y.1951). In *Societe Internationale v. Rogers,* 357 U.S. 197 (1958), the Supreme Court concluded that the rather random use of these two terms in Rule 37 showed no design to use them with consistently distinctive meanings, that "refused" in Rule 37(b)(2) meant simply a failure to comply, and that wilfullness was relevant only to the selection of sanctions, if any, to be imposed. Nevertheless, after the decision in *Societe,* the court in *Hinson v. Michigan Mutual Liability Co.,* 275 F.2d 537 (5th Cir.1960) once again ruled that "refusal" required wilfullness. Substitution of "failure" for "refusal" throughout Rule 37 should eliminate this confusion and bring the rule into harmony with the *Societe Internationale* decision. See Rosenberg, *supra,* 58 Col.L.Rev. 480, 489–490 (1958).

Subdivision (a). Rule 37(a) provides relief to a party seeking discovery against one who, with or without stated objections, fails to afford the discovery sought. It has always fully served this function in relation to depositions, but the amendments being made to Rules 33 and 34 give Rule 37(a) added scope and importance. Under existing Rule 33, a party objecting to interrogatories must make a motion for court hearing on his objections. The changes now made in Rules 33 and 37(a) make it clear that the interrogating party must move to compel answers, and the motion is provided for in Rule 37(a). Existing Rule 34, since it requires a court order prior to production of documents or things or permission to enter on land, has no relation to Rule 37(a). Amendments of Rules 34 and 37(a) create a procedure similar to that provided for Rule 33.

Subdivision (a)(1). This is a new provision making clear to which court a party may apply for an order compelling discovery. Existing Rule 37(a) refers only to the court in which the deposition is being taken; nevertheless, it has been held that the court where the action is pending has "inherent power" to compel a party

---

New matter is shown in italics; matter to be omitted is lined through

deponent to answer. *Lincoln Laboratories, Inc. v. Savage Laboratories, Inc.*, 27 F.R.D. 476 (D.Del.1961). In relation to Rule 33 interrogatories and Rule 34 requests for inspection, the court where the action is pending is the appropriate enforcing tribunal. The new provision eliminates the need to resort to inherent power by spelling out the respective roles of the court where the action is pending and the court where the deposition is taken. In some instances, two courts are available to a party seeking to compel answers from a party deponent. The party seeking discovery may choose the court to which he will apply, but the court has power to remit the party to the other court as a more appropriate forum.

Subdivision (a)(2). This subdivision contains the substance of existing provisions of Rule 37(a) authorizing motions to compel answers to questions put at depositions and to interrogatories. New provisions authorize motions for orders compelling designation under Rules 30(b) (6) and 31(a) and compelling inspection in accordance with a request made under Rule 34. If the court denies a motion, in whole or part, it may accompany the denial with issuance of a protective order. Compare the converse provision in Rule 26(c).

Subdivision (a)(3). This new provision makes clear that an evasive or incomplete answer is to be considered, for purposes of subdivision (a), a failure to answer. The courts have consistently held that they have the power to compel adequate answers. *E.g., Cone Mills Corp. v. Joseph Bancroft & Sons Co.*, 33 F.R.D. 318 (D.Del.1963). This power is recognized and incorporated into the rule.

Subdivision (a)(4). This subdivision amends the provisions for award of expenses, including reasonable attorney's fees, to the prevailing party or person when a motion is made for an order compelling discovery. At present, an award of expenses is made only if the losing party or person is found to have acted without substantial justification. The change requires that expenses be awarded unless the conduct of the losing party or person is found to have been substantially justified. The test of "substantial justification" remains, but the change in language is intended to encourage judges to be more alert to abuses occurring in the discovery process.

On many occasions, to be sure, the dispute over discovery between the parties is genuine, though ultimately resolved one way or the other by the court. In such cases, the losing party is substantially justified in carrying the matter to court. But the rules should deter the abuse implicit in carrying or forcing a discovery dispute to court when no genuine dispute exists. And the potential or actual imposition of expenses is virtually the sole formal sanction in the rules to deter a party from pressing to a court hearing frivolous requests for or objections to discovery.

The present provision of Rule 37(a) that the court shall require payment if it finds that the defeated party acted without "substantial justification" may appear adequate, but in fact it has been little used. Only a handful of reported cases include an award of expenses, and the Columbia Survey found that in only one instance out of about 50 motions decided under Rule 37(a) did the court award expenses. It appears that the courts do not utilize the most important available sanction to deter abusive resort to the judiciary.

The proposed change provides in effect that expenses should ordinarily be awarded unless a court finds that the losing party acted justifiably in carrying his point to court. At the same time, a necessary flexibility is maintained, since the court retains the power to find that other circumstances make an award of expenses unjust—as where, the prevailing party also acted unjustifiably. The amendment does not significantly narrow the discretion of the court, but rather presses the court to address itself to abusive practices. The present provision that

---

New matter is shown in italics; matter to be omitted is lined through

expenses may be imposed upon either the party or his attorney or both is unchanged. But it is not contemplated that expenses will be imposed upon the attorney merely because the party is indigent.

Subdivision (b). This subdivision deals with sanctions for failure to comply with a court order. The present captions for subsections (1) and (2) entitled, "Contempt" and "Other Consequences," respectively, are confusing. One of the consequences listed in (2) is the arrest of the party, representing the exercise of the contempt power. The contents of the subsections show that the first authorizes the sanction of contempt (and no other) by the court in which the deposition is taken, whereas the second subsection authorizes a variety of sanctions, including contempt, which may be imposed by the court in which the action is pending. The captions of the subsections are changed to reflect their contents.

The scope of Rule 37(b)(2) is broadened by extending it to include any order "to provide or permit discovery," including orders issued under Rules 37(a) and 35. Various rules authorize orders for discovery—*e.g.,* Rule 35(b)(1), Rule 26(c) as revised, Rule 37(d). See Rosenberg, *supra,* 58 Col.L.Rev. 480, 484–486. Rule 37(b)(2) should provide comprehensively for enforcement of all these orders. *Cf. Societe Internationale v. Rogers,* 357 U.S. 197, 207 (1958). On the other hand, the reference to Rule 34 is deleted to conform to the changed procedure in that rule.

A new subsection (E) provides that sanctions which have been available against a party for failure to comply with an order under Rule 35(a) to submit to examination will now be available against him for his failure to comply with a Rule 35(a) order to produce a third person for examination, unless he shows that he is unable to produce the person. In this context, "unable" means in effect "unable in good faith." See *Societe Internationale v. Rogers,* 357 U.S. 197 (1958).

Subdivision (b)(2) is amplified to provide for payment of reasonable expenses caused by the failure to obey the order. Although Rules 37(b)(2) and 37(d) have been silent as to award of expenses, courts have nevertheless ordered them on occasion. *E.g., United Sheeplined Clothing Co. v. Arctic Fur Cap Corp.,* 165 F.Supp. 193 (S.D.N.Y.1958); *Austin Theatre, Inc. v. Warner Bros. Pictures, Inc.,* 22 F.R.D. 302 (S.D.N.Y.1958). The provision places the burden on the disobedient party to avoid expenses by showing that his failure is justified or that special circumstances make an award of expenses unjust. Allocating the burden in this way conforms to the changed provisions as to expenses in Rule 37(a), and is particularly appropriate when a court order is disobeyed.

An added reference to directors of a party is similar to a change made in subdivision (d) and is explained in the note to that subdivision. The added reference to persons designated by a party under Rules 30(b)(6) or 31(a) to testify on behalf of the party carries out the new procedure in those rules for taking a deposition of a corporation or other organization.

Subdivision (c). Rule 37(c) provides a sanction for the enforcement of Rule 36 dealing with requests for admission. Rule 36 provides the mechanism whereby a party may obtain from another party in appropriate instances either (1) an admission, or (2) a sworn and specific denial, or (3) a sworn statement "setting forth in detail the reasons why he cannot truthfully admit or deny." If the party obtains the second or third of these responses, in proper form, Rule 36 does not provide for a pretrial hearing on whether the response is warranted by the evidence thus far accumulated. Instead, Rule 37(c) is intended to provide posttrial relief in the form of a requirement that the party improperly refusing the admission pay the expenses of the other side in making the necessary proof at trial.

Rule 37(c), as now written, addresses itself in terms only to the sworn denial and is silent with respect to the statement of reasons for an inability to admit or

---

New matter is shown in italics; matter to be omitted is lined through

deny. There is no apparent basis for this distinction, since the sanction provided in Rule 37(c) should deter all unjustified failures to admit. This omission in the rule has caused confused and diverse treatment in the courts. One court has held that if a party gives inadequate reasons, he should be treated before trial as having denied the request, so that Rule 37(c) may apply. *Bertha Bldg. Corp. v. National Theatres Corp.*, 15 F.R.D. 339 (E.D.N.Y.1954). Another has held that the party should be treated as having admitted the request. *Heng Hsin Co. v. Stern, Morgenthau & Co.*, 20 Fed.Rules Serv. 36a.52, Case 1 (S.D.N.Y. Dec. 10, 1954). Still another has ordered a new response, without indicating what the outcome should be if the new response were inadequate. *United States Plywood Corp. v. Hudson Lumber Co.*, 127 F.Supp. 489, 497–498 (S.D.N.Y.1954). See generally Finman, *The Request for Admissions in Federal Civil Procedure*, 71 Yale L.J. 371, 426–430 (1962). The amendment eliminates this defect in Rule 37(c) by bringing within its scope all failures to admit.

Additional provisions in Rule 37(c) protect a party from having to pay expenses if the request for admission was held objectionable under Rule 36(a) or if the party failing to admit had reasonable ground to believe that he might prevail on the matter. The latter provision emphasizes that the true test under Rule 37(c) is not whether a party prevailed at trial but whether he acted reasonably in believing that he might prevail.

Subdivision (d). The scope of subdivision (d) is broadened to include responses to requests for inspection under Rule 34, thereby conforming to the new procedures of Rule 34.

Two related changes are made in subdivision (d): the permissible sanctions are broadened to include such orders "as are just"; and the requirement that the failure to appear or respond be "wilful" is eliminated. Although Rule 37(d) in terms provides for only three sanctions, all rather severe, the courts have interpreted it as permitting softer sanctions than those which it sets forth. *E.g., Gill v. Stolow*, 240 F.2d 669 (2d Cir.1957); *Saltzman v. Birrell*, 156 F.Supp. 538 (S.D.N.Y. 1957); 2A Barron & Holtzoff, *Federal Practice and Procedure* 554–557 (Wright ed. 1961). The rule is changed to provide the greater flexibility as to sanctions which the cases show is needed.

The resulting flexibility as to sanctions eliminates any need to retain the requirement that the failure to appear or respond be "wilful." The concept of "wilful failure" is at best subtle and difficult, and the cases do not supply a bright line. Many courts have imposed sanctions without referring to wilfullness. *E.g., Milewski v. Schneider Transportation Co.*, 238 F.2d 397 (6th Cir.1956); *Dictograph Products, Inc. v. Kentworth Corp.*, 7 F.R.D. 543 (W.D.Ky.1947). In addition, in view of the possibility of light sanctions, even a negligent failure should come within Rule 37(d). If default is caused by counsel's ignorance of Federal practice, *cf. Dunn v. Pa. R. R.*, 96 F.Supp. 597 (N.D.Ohio 1951), or by his preoccupation with another aspect of the case, *cf. Maurer-Neuer, Inc. v. United Packinghouse Workers*, 26 F.R.D. 139 (D.Kans.1960), dismissal of the action and default judgment are not justified, but the imposition of expenses and fees may well be. "Wilfullness" continues to play a role, along with various other factors, in the choice of sanctions. Thus, the scheme conforms to Rule 37(b) as construed by the Supreme Court in *Societe Internationale v. Rogers*, 357 U.S. 197, 208 (1958).

A provision is added to make clear that a party may not properly remain completely silent even when he regards a notice to take his deposition or a set of interrogatories or requests to inspect as improper and objectionable. If he desires not to appear or not to respond, he must apply for a protective order. The cases are divided on whether a protective order must be sought. Compare *Collins v.*

New matter is shown in italics; matter to be omitted is lined through

Wayland, 139 F.2d 677 (9th Cir.1944), *cert. den.* 322 U.S. 744; *Bourgeois v. El Paso Natural Gas Co.*, 20 F.R.D. 358 (S.D.N.Y.1957); *Loosley v. Stone*, 15 F.R.D. 373 (S.D.Ill. 1954), with *Scarlatos v. Kulukundis*, 21 F.R.D. 185 (S.D.N.Y.1957); *Ross v. True Temper Corp.*, 11 F.R.D. 307 (N.D.Ohio 1951). Compare also Rosenberg, *supra*, 58 Col.L.Rev. 480, 496 (1958) with 2A Barron & Holtzoff, *Federal Practice and Procedure* 530–531 (Wright ed. 1961). The party from whom discovery is sought is afforded, through Rule 26(c), a fair and effective procedure whereby he can challenge the request made. At the same time, the total non-compliance with which Rule 37(d) is concerned may impose severe inconvenience or hardship on the discovering party and substantially delay the discovery process. *Cf.* 2B Barron & Holtzoff, *Federal Practice and Procedure* 306–307 (Wright ed. 1961) (response to a subpoena).

The failure of an officer or managing agent of a party to make discovery as required by present Rule 37(d) is treated as the failure of the party. The rule as revised provides similar treatment for a director of a party. There is slight warrant for the present distinction between officers and managing agents on the one hand and directors on the other. Although the legal power over a director to compel his making discovery may not be as great as over officers or managing agents, *Campbell v. General Motors Corp.*, 13 F.R.D. 331 (S.D.N.Y.1952), the practical differences are negligible. That a director's interests are normally aligned with those of his corporation is shown by the provisions of old Rule 26(d)(2), transferred to 32(a)(2) (deposition of director of party may be used at trial by an adverse party for any purpose) and of Rule 43(b) (director of party may be treated at trial as a hostile witness on direct examination by any adverse party). Moreover, in those rare instances when a corporation is unable through good faith efforts to compel a director to make discovery, it is unlikely that the court will impose sanctions. *Cf. Societe Internationale v. Rogers*, 357 U.S. 197 (1958).

Subdivision (e). The change in the caption conforms to the language of 28 U.S.C. § 1783, as amended in 1964.

Subdivision (f). Until recently, costs of a civil action could be awarded against the United States only when expressly provided by Act of Congress, and such provision was rarely made. See H.R.Rep.No.1535, 89th Cong., 2d Sess., 2–3 (1966). To avoid any conflict with this doctrine, Rule 37(f) has provided that expenses and attorney's fees may not be imposed upon the United States under Rule 37. See 2A Barron & Holtzoff, *Federal Practice and Procedure* 857 (Wright ed. 1961).

A major change in the law was made in 1966, 80 Stat. 308, 28 U.S.C. § 2412 (1966), whereby a judgment for costs may ordinarily be awarded to the prevailing party in any civil action brought by or against the United States. Costs are not to include the fees and expenses of attorneys. In light of this legislative development, Rule 37(f) is amended to permit the award of expenses and fees against the United States under Rule 37, but only to the extent permitted by statute. The amendment brings Rule 37(f) into line with present and future statutory provisions.

Rule 45. Subpoena

(d) Subpoena for Taking Depositions; Place of Examination.

(1) Proof of service of a notice to take a deposition as provided in Rules ~~30(a)~~ *30(b)* and 31(a) constitutes a sufficient authorization for issuance by the clerk of the district court for the district in

New matter is shown in italics; matter to be omitted is lined through

which the deposition is to be taken of subpoenas for the persons named or described therein. The subpoena may command the person to whom it is directed to produce *and permit inspection and copying of* designated books, papers, documents, or tangible things which constitute or contain ~~evidence relating to any of the~~ matters within the scope of the examination permitted by Rule 26(b), but in that event the subpoena will be subject to the provisions ~~of subdivision (b)~~ of Rule ~~30~~ *26(c)* and subdivision (b) of this ~~Rule 45~~ *rule.*

The person to whom the subpoena is directed may, within 10 days after the service thereof or on or before the time specified in the subpoena for compliance if such time is less than 10 days after service, serve upon the attorney designated in the subpoena written objection to inspection or copying of any or all of the designated materials. If objection is made, the party serving the subpoena shall not be entitled to inspect and copy the materials, except pursuant to an order of the court from which the subpoena was issued. The party serving the subpoena may, if objection has been made, move upon notice to the deponent for an order at any time before or during the taking of the deposition.

Advisory Committee's Note

At present, when a subpoena duces tecum is issued to a deponent, he is required to produce the listed materials at the deposition, but is under no clear compulsion to permit their inspection and copying. This results in confusion and uncertainty before the time the deposition is taken, with no mechanism provided whereby the court can resolve the matter. Rule 45(d)(1), as revised, makes clear that the subpoena authorizes inspection and copying of the materials produced. The deponent is afforded full protection since he can object, thereby forcing the party serving the subpoena to obtain a court order if he wishes to inspect and copy. The procedure is thus analogous to that provided in Rule 34.

The changed references to other rules conform to changes made in those rules. The deletion of words in the clause describing the proper scope of the subpoena conforms to a change made in the language of Rule 34. The reference to Rule 26(b) is unchanged but encompasses new matter in that subdivision. The changes make it clear that the scope of discovery through a subpoena is the same as that applicable to Rule 34 and the other discovery rules.

Rule 69. Execution

(a) In General. Process to enforce a judgment for the payment of money shall be a writ of execution, unless the court directs otherwise. The procedure on execution, in proceedings supplementary to and in aid of a judgment, and in proceedings on and in aid of execution shall be in accordance with the practice and procedure of the state in which the district court is held, existing at the time the remedy is sought, except that any statute

---

New matter is shown in italics; matter to be omitted is lined through

of the United States governs to the extent that it is applicable. In aid of the judgment or execution, the judgment creditor or his successor in interest when that interest appears of record, may ~~examine~~ *obtain discovery from* any person, including the judgment debtor, in the manner provided in these rules ~~for taking depositions~~ or in the manner provided by the practice of the state in which the district court is held.

Advisory Committee's Note

The amendment assures that, in aid of execution on a judgment, all discovery procedures provided in the rules are available and not just discovery via the taking of a deposition. Under the present language, one court has held that Rule 34 discovery is unavailable to the judgment creditor. *M. Lowenstein & Sons, Inc. v. American Underwear Mfg. Co.,* 11 F.R.D. 172 (E.D.Pa.1951). Notwithstanding the language, and relying heavily on legislative history referring to Rule 33, the Fifth Circuit has held that a judgment creditor may invoke Rule 33 interrogatories. *United States v. McWhirter,* 376 F.2d 102 (5th Cir.1967). But the court's reasoning does not extend to discovery except as provided in Rules 26–33. One commentator suggests that the existing language might properly be stretched to all discovery, 7 *Moore's Federal Practice* ¶69.05[1] (2d ed. 1966), but another believes that a rules amendment is needed. 3 Barron & Holtzoff, *Federal Practice and Procedure* 1484 (Wright ed. 1958). Both commentators and the court in *McWhirter* are clear that, as a matter of policy, Rule 69 should authorize the use of all discovery devices provided in the rules.

*

AMENDMENTS OF FEDERAL RULES OF CIVIL PROCE-DURE ADOPTED BY THE SUPREME COURT OF THE UNITED STATES ON APRIL 29, 1980, EFFECTIVE AUGUST 1, 1980, WITH ADVISORY COM-MITTEE'S NOTES THEREON

Rule 4. Process

(a) **Summons: Issuance.** Upon the filing of the complaint the clerk shall forthwith issue a summons and deliver it for service to the marshal or to a̶ *any other* person s̶p̶e̶c̶i̶a̶l̶l̶y̶ ̶a̶p̶p̶o̶i̶n̶t̶e̶d̶ *authorized by Rule 4(c)* to serve it. Upon request of the plaintiff separate or additional summons shall issue against any defendants.

(c) **By Whom Served.** Service of a̶l̶l̶ process shall be made by a United States marshal, by his deputy, or by some person specially appointed by the court for that purpose, except that a subpoena may be served as provided in Rule 45. Special appointments to serve process shall be made freely. w̶h̶e̶n̶ ̶s̶u̶b̶s̶t̶a̶n̶t̶i̶a̶l̶ s̶a̶v̶i̶n̶g̶s̶ ̶i̶n̶ ̶t̶r̶a̶v̶e̶l̶ ̶f̶e̶e̶s̶ ̶w̶i̶l̶l̶ ̶r̶e̶s̶u̶l̶t̶. *Service of process may also be made by a person authorized to serve process in an action brought in the courts of general jurisdiction of the state in which the district court is held or in which service is made.*

Advisory Committee's Note

Subdivision (a). This is a technical amendment to conform this subdivision with the amendment of subdivision (c).

Subdivision (c). The purpose of this amendment is to authorize service of process to be made by any person who is authorized to make service in actions in the courts of general jurisdiction of the state in which the district court is held or in which service is made.

There is a troublesome ambiguity in Rule 4. Rule 4(c) directs that all process is to be served by the marshal, by his deputy, or by a person specially appointed by the court. But Rule 4(d)(7) authorizes service in certain cases "in the manner prescribed by the law of the state in which the district court is held. ..." And Rule 4(e), which authorizes service beyond the state and service in *quasi in rem* cases when state law permits such service, directs that "service may be made ... under the circumstances and in the manner prescribed in the [state] statute or rule." State statutes and rules of the kind referred to in Rule 4(d)(7) and Rule 4(e) commonly designate the persons who are to make the service provided for, *e.g.,* a sheriff or a plaintiff. When that is so, may the persons so designated by state law make service, or is service in all cases to be made by a marshal or by one specially

---

New matter is shown in italics; matter to be omitted is lined through

appointed under present Rule 4(c)? The commentators have noted the ambiguity and have suggested the desirability of an amendment. See 2 *Moore's Federal Practice* ¶4.08 (1974); Wright & Miller, *Federal Practice and Procedure: Civil* § 1092 (1969). And the ambiguity has given rise to unfortunate results. See *United States for the use of Tanos v. St. Paul Mercury Ins. Co.,* 361 F.2d 838 (5th Cir.1966); *Veeck v. Commodity Enterprises, Inc.,* 487 F.2d 423 (9th Cir.1973).

The ambiguity can be resolved by specific amendments to Rules 4(d)(7) and 4(e), but the Committee is of the view that there is no reason why Rule 4(c) should not generally authorize service of process in all cases by anyone authorized to make service in the courts of general jurisdiction of the state in which the district court is held or in which service is made. The marshal continues to be the obvious, always effective officer for service of process.

Rule 5. Service and Filing of Pleadings and Other Papers

(d) Filing. All papers after the complaint required to be served upon a party shall be filed with the court either before service or within a reasonable time thereafter~~.~~, *but the court may on motion of a party or on its own initiative order that depositions upon oral examination and interrogatories, requests for documents, requests for admission, and answers and responses thereto not be filed unless on order of the court or for use in the proceeding.*

Advisory Committee's Note

Subdivision (d). By the terms of this rule and Rule 30(f)(1) discovery materials must be promptly filed, although it often happens that no use is made of the materials after they are filed. Because the copies required for filing are an added expense and the large volume of discovery filings presents serious problems of storage in some districts, the Committee in 1978 first proposed that discovery materials not be filed unless on order of the court or for use in the proceedings. But such materials are sometimes of interest to those who may have no access to them except by a requirement of filing, such as members of a class, litigants similarly situated, or the public generally. Accordingly, this amendment and a change in Rule 30(f)(1) continue the requirement of filing but make it subject to an order of the court that discovery materials not be filed unless filing is requested by the court or is effected by parties who wish to use the materials in the proceeding.

Rule 26. General Provisions Governing Discovery

(f) Discovery Conference. At any time after commencement of an action the court may direct the attorneys for the parties to appear before it for a conference on the subject of discovery. The court shall do so upon motion by the attorney for any party if the motion includes:

> *(1) A statement of the issues as they then appear;*

> *(2) A proposed plan and schedule of discovery;*

> *(3) Any limitations proposed to be placed on discovery;*

New matter is shown in italics; matter to be omitted is lined through

(4) Any other proposed orders with respect to discovery; and

(5) A statement showing that the attorney making the motion has made a reasonable effort to reach agreement with opposing attorneys on the matters set forth in the motion. Each party and his attorney are under a duty to participate in good faith in the framing of a discovery plan if a plan is proposed by the attorney for any party. Notice of the motion shall be served on all parties. Objections or additions to matters set forth in the motion shall be served not later than 10 days after service of the motion.

Following the discovery conference, the court shall enter an order tentatively identifying the issues for discovery purposes, establishing a plan and schedule for discovery, setting limitations on discovery, if any; and determining such other matters, including the allocation of expenses, as are necessary for the proper management of discovery in the action. An order may be altered or amended whenever justice so requires.

Subject to the right of a party who properly moves for a discovery conference to prompt convening of the conference, the court may combine the discovery conference with a pretrial conference authorized by Rule 16.

Advisory Committee's Note

Subdivision (f). This subdivision is new. There has been widespread criticism of abuse of discovery. The Committee has considered a number of proposals to eliminate abuse, including a change in Rule 26(b)(1) with respect to the scope of discovery and a change in Rule 33(a) to limit the number of questions that can be asked by interrogatories to parties.

The Committee believes that abuse of discovery, while very serious in certain cases, is not so general as to require such basic changes in the rules that govern discovery in all cases. A very recent study of discovery in selected metropolitan districts tends to support its belief. P. Connolly, E. Holleman, & M. Kuhlman, *Judicial Controls and the Civil Litigative Process: Discovery* (Federal Judicial Center, 1978). In the judgment of the Committee abuse can best be prevented by intervention by the court as soon as abuse is threatened.

To this end this subdivision provides that counsel who has attempted without success to effect with opposing counsel a reasonable program or plan for discovery is entitled to the assistance of the court.

It is not contemplated that requests for discovery conferences will be made routinely. A relatively narrow discovery dispute should be resolved by resort to Rules 26(c) or 37(a), and if it appears that a request for a conference is in fact grounded in such a dispute, the court may refer counsel to those rules. If the court is persuaded that a request is frivolous or vexatious, it can strike it. See Rules 11 and 7(b)(2).

A number of courts routinely consider discovery matters in preliminary pretrial conferences held shortly after the pleadings are closed. This subdivision

---

New matter is shown in italics; matter to be omitted is lined through

does not interfere with such a practice. It authorizes the court to combine a discovery conference with a pretrial conference under Rule 16 if a pretrial conference is held sufficiently early to prevent or curb abuse.

Rule 28.   Persons Before Whom Depositions May Be Taken

(a) **Within the United States.** Within the United States or within a territory or insular possession subject to the ~~dominion~~ *jurisdiction* of the United States, depositions shall be taken before an officer authorized to administer oaths by the laws of the United States or of the place where the examination is held, or before a person appointed by the court in which the action is pending. A person so appointed has power to administer oaths and take testimony. *The term officer as used in Rules 30, 31 and 32 includes a person appointed by the court or designated by the parties under Rule 29.*

Advisory Committee's Note

The amendments are clarifying.

Rule 30.   Depositions Upon Oral Examination

(b) **Notice of Examination: General Requirements; Special Notice; Non-Stenographic Recording; Production of Documents and Things; Deposition of Organization**~~;~~ *Deposition by Telephone.*

(4) *The parties may stipulate in writing or* [T]*t*he court may upon motion order that the testimony at a deposition be recorded by other than stenographic means~~,~~*.* ~~in which event~~ [t]*T*he *stipulation or* order shall designate *the person before whom the deposition shall be taken,* the manner of recording, preserving and filing the deposition, and may include other provisions to assure that the recorded testimony will be accurate and trustworthy. ~~If the order is made, a~~ *A* party may ~~nevertheless~~ arrange to have a stenographic transcription made at his own expense. *Any objections under subdivision (c), any changes made by the witness, his signature identifying the deposition as his own or the statement of the officer that is required if the witness does not sign, as provided in subdivision (e), and the certification of the officer required by subdivision (f) shall be set forth in a writing to accompany a deposition recorded by non-stenographic means.*

(7) The parties may stipulate in writing or the court may upon motion order that a deposition be taken by telephone. For the purposes of this rule and Rules 28(a), 37(a)(1), 37(b)(1) and 45(d), a deposition taken by telephone is taken in the district and at the

---

New matter is shown in italics;   matter to be omitted is lined through

place where the deponent is to answer questions propounded to him.

(f) Certification and Filing by Officer; Exhibits; Copies; Notice of Filing.

(1) The officer shall certify on the deposition that the witness was duly sworn by him and that the deposition is a true record of the testimony given by the witness. *Unless otherwise ordered by the court,* [H]*he* shall then securely seal the deposition in an envelope indorsed with the title of the action and marked "Deposition of [here insert name of witness]" and shall promptly file it with the court in which the action is pending or send it by registered or certified mail to the clerk thereof for filing.

Documents and things produced for inspection during the examination of the witness, shall, upon the request of a party, be marked for identification and annexed to ~~and returned with~~ the deposition and may be inspected and copied by any party, except that ~~(A)~~ *if* the person producing the materials *desires to retain them he* may ~~substitute~~ *(A) offer* copies to be marked for identification *and annexed to the deposition and to serve thereafter as originals* if he affords to all parties fair opportunity to verify the copies by comparison with the originals, ~~and~~ *or* (B) ~~if the person producing the materials requests their return, the officer shall mark them, give~~ *offer the originals to be marked for identification, after giving to* each party an opportunity to inspect and copy them, ~~and return them to the person producing them, and~~ *in which event* the materials may then be used in the same manner as if annexed to ~~and returned with~~ the deposition. Any party may move for an order that the original be annexed to and returned with the deposition to the court, pending final disposition of the case.

Advisory Committee's Note

Subdivision (b)(4). It has been proposed that electronic recording of depositions be authorized as a matter of course, subject to the right of a party to seek an order that a deposition be recorded by stenographic means. The Committee is not satisfied that a case has been made for a reversal of present practice. The amendment is made to encourage parties to agree to the use of electronic recording of depositions so that conflicting claims with respect to the potential of electronic recording for reducing costs of depositions can be appraised in the light of greater experience. The provision that the parties may stipulate that depositions may be recorded by other than stenographic means seems implicit in Rule 29. The amendment makes it explicit. The provision that the stipulation or order shall designate the person before whom the deposition is to be taken is added to encourage the naming of the recording technician as that person, eliminating the necessity of the presence of one whose only function is to administer the oath. See Rules 28(a) and 29.

New matter is shown in italics; matter to be omitted is lined through

Subdivision (b)(7). Depositions by telephone are now authorized by Rule 29 upon stipulation of the parties. The amendment authorizes that method by order of the court. The final sentence is added to make it clear that when a deposition is taken by telephone it is taken in the district and at the place where the witness is to answer the questions rather than that where the questions are propounded.

Subdivision (f)(1). For the reasons set out in the Note following the amendment of Rule 5(d), the court may wish to permit the parties to retain depositions unless they are to be used in the action. The amendment of the first paragraph permits the court to so order.

The amendment of the second paragraph is clarifying. The purpose of the paragraph is to permit a person who produces materials at a deposition to offer copies for marking and annexation to the deposition. Such copies are a "substitute" for the originals, which are not to be marked and which can thereafter be used or even disposed of by the person who produces them. In the light of that purpose, the former language of the paragraph had been justly termed "opaque." Wright & Miller, *Federal Practice and Procedure: Civil* § 2114.

Rule 32. Use of Depositions in Court Proceedings

(a) **Use of Depositions.** At the trial or upon the hearing of a motion or an interlocutory proceeding, any part or all of a deposition, so far as admissible under the rules of evidence applied as though the witness were then present and testifying, may be used against any party who was present or represented at the taking of the deposition or who had reasonable notice thereof, in accordance with any of the following provisions:

(1) Any deposition may be used by any party for the purpose of contradicting or impeaching the testimony of deponent as a witness., *or for any other purpose permitted by the Federal Rules of Evidence.*

(4) If only part of a deposition is offered in evidence by a party, an adverse party may require him to introduce any other part which ought in fairness to be considered with the part introduced, and any party may introduce any other parts.

Substitution of parties pursuant to Rule 25 does not affect the right to use depositions previously taken; and when an action *has been brought* in any court of the United States or of any State has been dismissed and another action involving the same subject matter is afterward brought between the same parties or their representatives or successors in interest, all depositions lawfully taken and duly filed in the former action may be used in the latter as if originally taken therefor. *A deposition previously taken may also be used as permitted by the Federal Rules of Evidence.*

Advisory Committee's Note

Subdivision (a)(1). Rule 801(d) of the Federal Rules of Evidence permits a prior inconsistent statement of a witness in a deposition to be used as substantive

---

New matter is shown in italics; matter to be omitted is lined through

evidence. And Rule 801(d)(2) makes the statement of an agent or servant admissible against the principal under the circumstances described in the Rule. The language of the present subdivision is, therefore, too narrow.

Subdivision (a)(4). The requirement that a prior action must have been dismissed before depositions taken for use in it can be used in a subsequent action was doubtless an oversight, and the courts have ignored it. See Wright & Miller, *Federal Practice and Procedure: Civil* § 2150. The final sentence is added to reflect the fact that the Federal Rules of Evidence permit a broader use of depositions previously taken under certain circumstances. For example, Rule 804(b)(1) of the Federal Rules of Evidence provides that if a witness is unavailable, as that term is defined by the rule, his deposition in any earlier proceeding can be used against a party to the prior proceeding who had an opportunity and similar motive to develop the testimony of the witness.

Rule 33. Interrogatories to Parties

(c) Option to Produce Business Records. Where the answer to an interrogatory may be derived or ascertained from the business records of the party upon whom the interrogatory has been served or from an examination, audit or inspection of such business records, ~~or from~~ *including* a compilation, abstract or summary ~~based thereon~~ *thereof*, and the burden of deriving or ascertaining the answer is substantially the same for the party serving the interrogatory as for the party served, it is a sufficient answer to such interrogatory to specify the records from which the answer may be derived or ascertained and to afford to the party serving the interrogatory reasonable opportunity to examine, audit or inspect such records and to make copies, compilations, abstracts or summaries. *A specification shall be in sufficient detail to permit the interrogating party to locate and to identify, as readily as can the party served, the records from which the answer may be ascertained.*

Advisory Committee's Note

Subdivision (c). The Committee is advised that parties upon whom interrogatories are served have occasionally responded by directing the interrogating party to a mass of business records or by offering to make all of their records available, justifying the response by the option provided by this subdivision. Such practices are an abuse of the option. A party who is permitted by the terms of this subdivision to offer records for inspection in lieu of answering an interrogatory should offer them in a manner that permits the same direct and economical access that is available to the party. If the information sought exists in the form of compilations, abstracts or summaries then available to the responding party, those should be made available to the interrogating party. The final sentence is added to make it clear that a responding party has the duty to specify, by category and location, the records from which answers to interrogatories can be derived.

New matter is shown in italics; matter to be omitted is lined through

Rule 34. Production of Documents and Things and Entry Upon Land For Inspection and Other Purposes

(b) Procedure. The request may, without leave of court, be served upon the plaintiff after commencement of the action and upon any other party with or after service of the summons and complaint upon that party. The request shall set forth the items to be inspected either by individual item or by category, and describe each item and category with reasonable particularity. The request shall specify a reasonable time, place, and manner of making the inspection and performing the related acts.

The party upon whom the request is served shall serve a written response within 30 days after the service of the request, except that a defendant may serve a response within 45 days after service of the summons and complaint upon that defendant. The court may allow a shorter or longer time. The response shall state, with respect to each item or category, that inspection and related activities will be permitted as requested, unless the request is objected to, in which event the reasons for objection shall be stated. If objection is made to part of an item or category, the part shall be specified. The party submitting the request may move for an order under Rule 37(a) with respect to any objection to or other failure to respond to the request or any part thereof, or any failure to permit inspection as requested.

A party who produces documents for inspection shall produce them as they are kept in the usual course of business or shall organize and label them to correspond with the categories in the request.

Advisory Committee's Note

Subdivision (b). The Committee is advised that, "It is apparently not rare for parties deliberately to mix critical documents with others in the hope of obscuring significance." *Report of the Special Committee for the Study of Discovery Abuse, Section of Litigation of the American Bar Association* (1977) 22. The sentence added by this subdivision follows the recommendation of the *Report*.

Rule 37. Failure to Make *or Cooperate in* Discovery: Sanctions

(b) Failure to Comply with Order.

(2) Sanctions by Court in Which Action is Pending. If a party or an officer, director, or managing agent of a party or a person designated under Rule 30(b)(6) or 31(a) to testify on behalf of a party fails to obey an order to provide or permit discovery,

---

New matter is shown in italics; matter to be omitted is lined through

including an order made under subdivision (a) of this rule or Rule 35, *or if a party fails to obey an order entered under Rule 26(f),* the court in which the action is pending may make such orders in regard to the failure as are just, and among others the following:

(A) An order that the matters regarding which the order was made or any other designated facts shall be taken to be established for the purposes of the action in accordance with the claim of the party obtaining the order;

(B) An order refusing to allow the disobedient party to support or oppose designated claims or defenses, or prohibiting him from introducing designated matters in evidence;

(C) An order striking out pleadings or parts thereof, or staying further proceedings until the order is obeyed, or dismissing the action or proceeding or any part thereof, or rendering a judgment by default against the disobedient party;

(D) In lieu of any of the foregoing orders or in addition thereto, an order treating as a contempt of court the failure to obey any orders except an order to submit to a physical or mental examination;

(E) Where a party has failed to comply with an order under Rule 35(a) requiring him to produce another for examination, such orders as are listed in paragraphs (A), (B), and (C) of this subdivision, unless the party failing to comply shows that he is unable to produce such person for examination.

In lieu of any of the foregoing orders or in addition thereto, the court shall require the party failing to obey the order or the attorney advising him or both to pay the reasonable expenses, including attorney's fees, caused by the failure, unless the court finds that the failure was substantially justified or that other circumstances make an award of expenses unjust.

[(e) Subpoena of Person in Foreign Country.] ~~A subpoena may be issued as provided in Title 28 U.S.C. § 1783, under the circumstances and conditions therein stated.~~

(g) Failure to Participate in the Framing of a Discovery Plan. If a party or his attorney fails to participate in good faith in the framing of a discovery plan by agreement as is required by Rule 26(f), the court may, after opportunity for hearing, require such party or his attorney to pay to any other party the reasonable expenses, including attorney's fees, caused by the failure.

New matter is shown in italics; matter to be omitted is lined through

Subdivision (b)(2). New Rule 26(f) provides that if a discovery conference is held, at its close the court shall enter an order respecting the subsequent conduct of discovery. The amendment provides that the sanctions available for violation of other court orders respecting discovery are available for violation of the discovery conference order.

Subdivision (e). Subdivision (e) is stricken. Title 28, U.S.C. § 1783 no longer refers to sanctions. The subdivision otherwise duplicates Rule 45(e)(2).

Subdivision (g). New Rule 26(f) imposes a duty on parties to participate in good faith in the framing of a discovery plan by agreement upon the request of any party. This subdivision authorizes the court to award to parties who participate in good faith in an attempt to frame a discovery plan the expenses incurred in the attempt if any party or his attorney fails to participate in good faith and thereby causes additional expense.

* * *

Failure of United States to Participate in Good Faith in Discovery. Rule 37 authorizes the court to direct that parties or attorneys who fail to participate in good faith in the discovery process pay the expenses, including attorneys' fees, incurred by other parties as a result of that failure. Since attorneys' fees cannot ordinarily be awarded against the United States (28 U.S.C. § 2412), there is often no practical remedy for the misconduct of its officers and attorneys. However, in the case of a government attorney who fails to participate in good faith in discovery, nothing prevents a court in an appropriate case from giving written notification of that fact to the Attorney General of the United States and other appropriate heads of offices or agencies thereof.

Rule 45. Subpoena

(d) Subpoena for Taking Depositions; Place of Examination.

(1) Proof of service of a notice to take a deposition as provided in Rules 30(b) and 31(a) constitutes a sufficient authorization for the issuance by the clerk of the district court for the district in which the deposition is to be taken of subpoenas for the persons named or described therein. *Proof of service may be made by filing with the clerk of the district court for the district in which the deposition is to be taken a copy of the notice together with a statement of the date and manner of service and of the names of the persons served, certified by the person who made service.* The subpoena may command the person to whom it is directed to produce and permit inspection and copying of designated books, papers, documents, or tangible things which constitute or contain matters within the scope of the examination permitted by Rule 26(b), but in that event the subpoena will be subject to the provisions of Rule 26(c) and subdivision (b) of this rule.

The person to whom the subpoena is directed may, within 10 days after the service thereof or on or before the time specified in

---

New matter is shown in italics; matter to be omitted is lined through

the subpoena for compliance if such time is less than 10 days after service, serve upon the attorney designated in the subpoena written objection to inspection or copying of any or all of the designated materials. If objection is made, the party serving the subpoena shall not be entitled to inspect and copy the materials except pursuant to an order of the court from which the subpoena was issued. The party serving the subpoena may, if objection has been made, move upon notice to the deponent for an order at any time before or during the taking of the deposition.

(e) Subpoena for a Hearing or Trial.

(1) At the request of any party subpoenas for attendance at a hearing or trial shall be issued by the clerk of the district court for the district in which the hearing or trial is held. A subpoena requiring the attendance of a witness at a hearing or trial may be served at any place within the district, or at any place without the district that is within 100 miles of the place of the hearing or trial specified in the subpoena;, *or at a place within the state where a state statute or rule of court permits service of a subpoena issued by a state court of general jurisdiction sitting in the place where the district court is held.* and, *W*when a statute of the United States provides therefor, the court upon proper application and cause shown may authorize the service of a subpoena at any other place.

Advisory Committee's Note

Subdivision (d)(1). The amendment defines the term "proof of service" as used in the first sentence of the present subdivision. For want of a definition, the district court clerks have been obliged to fashion their own, with results that vary from district to district. All that seems required is a simple certification on a copy of the notice to take a deposition that the notice has been served on every other party to the action. That is the proof of service required by Rule 25(d) of both the Federal Rules of Appellate Procedure and the Supreme Court Rules.

Subdivision (e)(1). The amendment makes the reach of a subpoena of a district court at least as extensive as that of the state courts of general jurisdiction in the state in which the district court is held. Under the present rule the reach of a district court subpoena is often greater, since it extends throughout the district. No reason appears why it should be less, as it sometimes is because of the accident of district lines. Restrictions upon the reach of subpoenas are imposed to prevent undue inconvenience to witnesses. State statutes and rules of court are quite likely to reflect the varying degrees of difficulty and expense attendant upon local travel.

*

New matter is shown in italics; matter to be omitted is lined through

CERTAIN OF THE AMENDMENTS OF FEDERAL RULES OF CIVIL PROCEDURE ADOPTED BY THE SUPREME COURT OF THE UNITED STATES ON APRIL 28, 1983, EFFECTIVE AUGUST 1, 1983, WITH ADVISORY COMMITTEE'S NOTES THEREON

[Amendments here omitted: Addition of new Forms 33 and 34.]

Rule 6.   Time

(b) Enlargement.   When by these rules or by a notice given thereunder or by order of court an act is required or allowed to be done at or within a specified time, the court for cause shown may at any time in its discretion (1) with or without motion or notice order the period enlarged if request therefor is made before the expiration of the period originally prescribed or as extended by a previous order, or (2) upon motion made after the expiration of the specified period permit the act to be done where the failure to act was the result of excusable neglect; but it may not extend the time for taking any action under Rules 50(b) *and (c)(2)*, 52(b), 59(b), (d) and (e), 60(b), *and 74(a)*, except to the extent and under the conditions stated in them.

Advisory Committee's Note

Subdivision (b).   The amendment confers finality upon the judgments of magistrates by foreclosing enlargement of the time for appeal except as provided in new Rule 74(a) (20 day period for demonstration of excusable neglect).

Rule 7.   Pleadings Allowed;   Form of Motions

(b) Motions and Other Papers.

(2) The rules applicable to captions, ~~signing,~~ and other matters of form of pleadings apply to all motions and other papers provided for by these rules.

(3) All motions shall be signed in accordance with Rule 11.

Advisory Committee's Note

One of the reasons sanctions against improper motion practice have been employed infrequently is the lack of clarity of Rule 7. That rule has stated only

New matter is shown in italics; matter to be omitted is lined through

generally that the pleading requirements relating to captions, signing, and other matters of form also apply to motions and other papers. The addition of Rule 7(b)(3) makes explicit the applicability of the signing requirement and the sanctions of Rule 11, which have been amplified.

Rule 11. Signing of Pleadings, *Motions, and Other Papers; Sanctions*

Every pleading, *motion, and other paper* of a party represented by an attorney shall be signed by at least one attorney of record in his individual name, whose address shall be stated. A party who is not represented by an attorney shall sign his pleading, *motion, or other paper* and state his address. Except when otherwise specifically provided by rule or statute, pleadings need not be verified or accompanied by affidavit. The rule in equity that the averments of an answer under oath must be overcome by the testimony of two witnesses or of one witness sustained by corroborating circumstances is abolished. The signature of an attorney *or party* constitutes a certificate by him that he has read the pleading, *motion, or other paper*; that to the best of his knowledge, information, and belief ~~there is good ground to support it; and that it is not interposed for delay~~ *formed after reasonable inquiry it is well grounded in fact and is warranted by existing law or a good faith argument for the extension, modification, or reversal of existing law, and that it is not interposed for any improper purpose, such as to harass or to cause unnecessary delay or needless increase in the cost of litigation.* If a pleading, *motion, or other paper* is not signed, *it shall be stricken unless it is signed promptly after the omission is called to the attention of the pleader or movant.* ~~or is signed with intent to defeat the purpose of this rule; it may be stricken as sham and false and the action may proceed as though the pleading had not been served. For a wilful violation of this rule an attorney may be subjected to appropriate disciplinary action. Similar action may be taken if scandalous or indecent matter is inserted.~~ *If a pleading, motion, or other paper is signed in violation of this rule, the court, upon motion or upon its own initiative, shall impose upon the person who signed it, a represented party, or both, an appropriate sanction, which may include an order to pay to the other party or parties the amount of the reasonable expenses incurred because of the filing of the pleading, motion, or other paper, including a reasonable attorney's fee.*

Advisory Committee's Note

Since its original promulgation, Rule 11 has provided for the striking of pleadings and the imposition of disciplinary sanctions to check abuses in the signing of pleadings. Its provisions have always applied to motions and other

---

New matter is shown in italics; matter to be omitted is lined through

papers by virtue of incorporation by reference in Rule 7(b)(2). The amendment and the addition of Rule 7(b)(3) expressly confirms this applicability.

Experience shows that in practice Rule 11 has not been effective in deterring abuses. See 6 Wright & Miller, *Federal Practice and Procedure: Civil* § 1334 (1971). There has been considerable confusion as to (1) the circumstances that should trigger striking a pleading or motion or taking disciplinary action, (2) the standard of conduct expected of attorneys who sign pleadings and motions, and (3) the range of available and appropriate sanctions. See Rodes, Ripple & Mooney, *Sanctions Imposable for Violations of the Federal Rules of Civil Procedure* 64–65, Federal Judicial Center (1981). The new language is intended to reduce the reluctance of courts to impose sanctions, see Moore, *Federal Practice* ¶ 7.05, at 1547, by emphasizing the responsibilities of the attorney and reenforcing those obligations by the imposition of sanctions.

The amended rule attempts to deal with the problem by building upon and expanding the equitable doctrine permitting the court to award expenses, including attorney's fees, to a litigant whose opponent acts in bad faith in instituting or conducting litigation. See, *e.g., Roadway Express, Inc. v. Piper,* 447 U.S. 752 (1980); *Hall v. Cole,* 412 U.S. 1, 5 (1973). Greater attention by the district courts to pleading and motion abuses and the imposition of sanctions when appropriate, should discourage dilatory or abusive tactics and help to streamline the litigation process by lessening frivolous claims or defenses.

The expanded nature of the lawyer's certification in the fifth sentence of amended Rule 11 recognizes that the litigation process may be abused for purposes other than delay. See, *e.g., Browning Debenture Holders' Committee v. DASA Corp.,* 560 F.2d 1078 (2d Cir.1977).

The words "good ground to support" the pleading in the original rule were interpreted to have both factual and legal elements. See, *e.g., Heart Disease Research Foundation v. General Motors Corp.,* 15 Fed.R.Serv.2d 1517, 1519 (S.D.N.Y.1972). They have been replaced by a standard of conduct that is more focused.

The new language stresses the need for some prefiling inquiry into both the facts and the law to satisfy the affirmative duty imposed by the rule. The standard is one of reasonableness under the circumstances. See *Kinee v. Abraham Lincoln Fed. Sav. & Loan Ass'n,* 365 F.Supp. 975 (E.D.Pa.1973). This standard is more stringent than the original good-faith formula and thus it is expected that a greater range of circumstances will trigger its violation. See *Nemeroff v. Abelson,* 620 F.2d 339 (2d Cir.1980).

The rule is not intended to chill an attorney's enthusiasm or creativity in pursuing factual or legal theories. The court is expected to avoid using the wisdom of hindsight and should test the signer's conduct by inquiring what was reasonable to believe at the time the pleading, motion, or other paper was submitted. Thus, what constitutes a reasonable inquiry may depend on such factors as how much time for investigation was available to the signer; whether he had to rely on a client for information as to the facts underlying the pleading, motion, or other paper; whether the pleading, motion, or other paper was based on a plausible view of the law; or whether he depended on forwarding counsel or another member of the bar.

The rule does not require a party or an attorney to disclose privileged communications or work product in order to show that the signing of the pleading, motion, or other paper is substantially justified. The provisions of Rule 26(c), including appropriate orders after *in camera* inspection by the court, remain available to protect a party claiming privilege or work product protection.

New matter is shown in italics; matter to be omitted is lined through

Amended Rule 11 continues to apply to anyone who signs a pleading, motion, or other paper. Although the standard is the same for unrepresented parties, who are obliged themselves to sign the pleadings, the court has sufficient discretion to take account of the special circumstances that often arise in *pro se* situations. See *Haines v. Kerner,* 404 U.S. 519 (1972).

The provision in the original rule for striking pleadings and motions as sham and false has been deleted. The passage has rarely been utilized, and decisions thereunder have tended to confuse the issue of attorney honesty with the merits of the action. See generally Risinger, *Honesty in Pleading and its Enforcement: Some "Striking" Problems with Fed.R.Civ.P. 11,* 61 Minn.L.Rev. 1 (1976). Motions under this provision generally present issues better dealt with under Rules 8, 12, or 56. See *Murchison v. Kirby,* 27 F.R.D. 14 (S.D.N.Y. 1961); 5 Wright & Miller, *Federal Practice and Procedure: Civil* § 1334 (1969).

The former reference to the inclusion of scandalous or indecent matter, which is itself strong indication that an improper purpose underlies the pleading, motion, or other paper, also has been deleted as unnecessary. Such matter may be stricken under Rule 12(f) as well as dealt with under the more general language of amended Rule 11.

The text of the amended rule seeks to dispel apprehensions that efforts to obtain enforcement will be fruitless by insuring that the rule will be applied when properly invoked. The word "sanctions" in the caption, for example, stresses a deterrent orientation in dealing with improper pleadings, motions or other papers. This corresponds to the approach in imposing sanctions for discovery abuses. See *National Hockey League v. Metropolitan Hockey Club,* 427 U.S. 639 (1976) (per curiam). And the words "shall impose" in the last sentence focus the court's attention on the need to impose sanctions for pleading and motion abuses. The court, however, retains the necessary flexibility to deal appropriately with violations of the rule. It has discretion to tailor sanctions to the particular facts of the case, with which it should be well acquainted.

The reference in the former text to wilfulness as a prerequisite to disciplinary action has been deleted. However, in considering the nature and severity of the sanctions to be imposed, the court should take account of the state of the attorney's or party's actual or presumed knowledge when the pleading or other paper was signed. Thus, for example, when a party is not represented by counsel, the absence of legal advice is an appropriate factor to be considered.

Courts currently appear to believe they may impose sanctions on their own motion. See *North American Trading Corp. v. Zale Corp.,* 73 F.R.D. 293 (S.D.N.Y. 1979). Authority to do so has been made explicit in order to overcome the traditional reluctance of courts to intervene unless requested by one of the parties. The detection and punishment of a violation of the signing requirement, encouraged by the amended rule, is part of the court's responsibility for securing the system's effective operation.

If the duty imposed by the rule is violated, the court should have the discretion to impose sanctions on either the attorney, the party the signing attorney represents, or both, or on an unrepresented party who signed the pleading, and the new rule so provides. Although Rule 11 has been silent on the point, courts have claimed the power to impose sanctions on an attorney personally, either by imposing costs or employing the contempt technique. See 5 Wright & Miller, *Federal Practice and Procedure: Civil* § 1334 (1969); 2A Moore, *Federal Practice* ¶ 11.02, at 2104 n. 8. This power has been used infrequently. The amended rule should eliminate any doubt as to the propriety of assessing sanctions against the attorney.

New matter is shown in italics; matter to be omitted is lined through

Even though it is the attorney whose signature violates the rule, it may be appropriate under the circumstances of the case to impose a sanction on the client. See *Browning Debenture Holders' Committee v. DASA Corp., supra.* This modification brings Rule 11 in line with practice under Rule 37, which allows sanctions for abuses during discovery to be imposed upon the party, the attorney, or both.

A party seeking sanctions should give notice to the court and the offending party promptly upon discovering a basis for doing so. The time when sanctions are to be imposed rests in the discretion of the trial judge. However, it is anticipated that in the case of pleadings the sanctions issue under Rule 11 normally will be determined at the end of the litigation, and in the case of motions at the time when the motion is decided or shortly thereafter. The procedure obviously must comport with due process requirements. The particular format to be followed should depend on the circumstances of the situation and the severity of the sanction under consideration. In many situations the judge's participation in the proceedings provides him with full knowledge of the relevant facts and little further inquiry will be necessary.

To assure that the efficiencies achieved through more effective operation of the pleading regimen will not be offset by the cost of satellite litigation over the imposition of sanctions, the court must to the extent possible limit the scope of sanction proceedings to the record. Thus, discovery should be conducted only by leave of the court, and then only in extraordinary circumstances.

Although the encompassing reference to "other papers" in new Rule 11 literally includes discovery papers, the certification requirement in that context is governed by proposed new Rule 26(g). Discovery motions, however, fall within the ambit of Rule 11.

Rule 16. *Pretrial Conferences; Scheduling; Management* ~~Pre-Trial Procedure; Formulating Issues~~

(a) Pretrial Conferences; Objectives. In any action, the court may in its discretion direct the attorneys for the parties *and any unrepresented parties* to appear before it for a conference *or conferences before trial* ~~to consider~~ *for such purposes as*

(1) expediting the disposition of the action;

(2) establishing early and continuing control so that the case will not be protracted because of lack of management;

(3) discouraging wasteful pretrial activities;

(4) improving the quality of the trial through more thorough preparation, and;

(5) facilitating the settlement of the case.

(b) Scheduling and Planning. *Except in categories of actions exempted by district court rule as inappropriate, the judge, or a magistrate when authorized by district court rule, shall, after consulting with the attorneys for the parties and any unrepresented parties, by a scheduling conference, telephone, mail, or other suitable means, enter a scheduling order that limits the time*

New matter is shown in italics; matter to be omitted is lined through

(1) to join other parties and to amend the pleadings;

(2) to file and hear motions; and

(3) to complete discovery.

The scheduling order also may include

(4) the date or dates for conferences before trial, a final pretrial conference, and trial; and

(5) any other matters appropriate in the circumstances of the case.

The order shall issue as soon as practicable but in no event more than 120 days after filing of the complaint. A schedule shall not be modified except by leave of the judge or a magistrate when authorized by district court rule upon a showing of good cause.

(c) Subjects to Be Discussed at Pretrial Conferences. The participants at any conference under this rule may consider and take action with respect to

(1) the *formulation and* simplification of the issues, *including the elimination of frivolous claims or defenses;*

(2) the necessity or desirability of amendments to the pleadings;

(3) the possibility of obtaining admissions of fact and of documents which will avoid unnecessary proof, *stipulations regarding the authenticity of documents, and advance rulings from the court on the admissibility of evidence;*

(4) the avoidance of unnecessary proof and of cumulative evidence;

(5)(4) the ~~limitation of the number of expert~~ *identification of* witnesses *and documents, the need and schedule for filing and exchanging pretrial briefs, and the date or dates for further conferences and for trial;*

(6)(5) the advisability of ~~a preliminary reference of~~ *referring* ~~issues~~ *matters* to a *magistrate or* master ~~for findings to be used as evidence when the trial is to be by jury;~~

(7) the possibility of settlement or the use of extrajudicial procedures to resolve the dispute;

(8) the form and substance of the pretrial order;

(9) the disposition of pending motions;

(10) the need for adopting special procedures for managing potentially difficult or protracted actions that may involve complex issues, multiple parties, difficult legal questions, or unusual proof problems; and

---

New matter is shown in italics; matter to be omitted is lined through

(11)(6) such other matters as may aid in the disposition of the action.

At least one of the attorneys for each party participating in any conference before trial shall have authority to enter into stipulations and to make admissions regarding all matters that the participants may reasonably anticipate may be discussed.

(d) Final Pretrial Conference. Any final pretrial conference shall be held as close to the time of trial as reasonable under the circumstances. The participants at any such conference shall formulate a plan for trial, including a program for facilitating the admission of evidence. The conference shall be attended by at least one of the attorneys who will conduct the trial for each of the parties and by any unrepresented parties.

(e) Pretrial Orders. After any conference held pursuant to this rule, an order shall be entered reciting the action taken. This order shall control the subsequent course of the action unless modified by a subsequent order. The order following a final pretrial conference shall be modified only to prevent manifest injustice.

(f) Sanctions. If a party or party's attorney fails to obey a scheduling or pretrial order, or if no appearance is made on behalf of a party at a scheduling or pretrial conference, or if a party or party's attorney is substantially unprepared to participate in the conference, or if a party or party's attorney fails to participate in good faith, the judge, upon motion or his own initiative, may make such orders with regard thereto as are just, and among others any of the orders provided in Rule 37(b)(2)(B), (C), (D). In lieu of or in addition to any other sanction, the judge shall require the party or the attorney representing him or both to pay the reasonable expenses incurred because of any noncompliance with this rule, including attorney's fees, unless the judge finds that the noncompliance was substantially justified or that other circumstances make an award of expenses unjust.

~~The court shall make an order which recites the action taken at the conference, the amendments allowed to the pleadings, and the agreements made by the parties as to any of the matters considered, and which limits the issues for trial to those not disposed of by admissions or agreements of counsel; and such order when entered controls the subsequent course of the action, unless modified at the trial to prevent manifest injustice. The court in its discretion may establish by rule a pretrial calendar on which actions may be placed for consideration as above provided and may either confine the calendar to jury actions or to non-jury actions or extend it to all actions.~~

New matter is shown in italics; matter to be omitted is lined through

Advisory Committee's Note

Introduction

Rule 16 has not been amended since the Federal Rules were promulgated in 1938. In many respects, the rule has been a success. For example, there is evidence that pretrial conferences may improve the quality of justice rendered in the federal courts by sharpening the preparation and presentation of cases, tending to eliminate trial surprise, and improving, as well as facilitating, the settlement process. See 6 Wright & Miller, *Federal Practice and Procedure: Civil* § 1522 (1971). However, in other respects particularly with regard to case management, the rule has not always been as helpful as it might have been. Thus there has been a widespread feeling that amendment is necessary to encourage pretrial management that meets the needs of modern litigation. See *Report of the National Commission for the Review of Antitrust Laws and Procedures* (1979).

Major criticism of Rule 16 has centered on the fact that its application can result in over-regulation of some cases and under-regulation of others. In simple, run-of-the-mill cases, attorneys have found pretrial requirements burdensome. It is claimed that over-administration leads to a series of mini-trials that result in a waste of an attorney's time and needless expense to a client. Pollack, *Pretrial Procedures More Effectively Handled,* 65 F.R.D. 475 (1974). This is especially likely to be true when pretrial proceedings occur long before trial. At the other end of the spectrum, the discretionary character of Rule 16 and its orientation toward a single conference late in the pretrial process has led to under-administration of complex or protracted cases. Without judicial guidance beginning shortly after institution, these cases often become mired in discovery.

Four sources of criticism of pretrial have been identified. First, conferences often are seen as a mere exchange of legalistic contentions without any real analysis of the particular case. Second, the result frequently is nothing but a formal agreement on minutiae. Third, the conferences are seen as unnecessary and time-consuming in cases that will be settled before trial. Fourth, the meetings can be ceremonial and ritualistic, having little effect on the trial and being of minimal value, particularly when the attorneys attending the sessions are not the ones who will try the case or lack authority to enter into binding stipulations. See generally *McCargo v. Hedrick,* 545 F.2d 393 (4th Cir. 1976); Pollack, *Pretrial Procedures More Effectively Handled,* 65 F.R.D. 475 (1974); Rosenberg, *The Pretrial Conference and Effective Justice* 45 (1964).

There also have been difficulties with the pretrial orders that issue following Rule 16 conferences. When an order is entered far in advance of trial, some issues may not be properly formulated. Counsel naturally are cautious and often try to preserve as many options as possible. If the judge who tries the case did not conduct the conference, he could find it difficult to determine exactly what was agreed to at the conference. But any insistence on a detailed order may be too burdensome, depending on the nature or posture of the case.

Given the significant changes in federal civil litigation since 1938 that are not reflected in Rule 16, it has been extensively rewritten and expanded to meet the challenges of modern litigation. Empirical studies reveal that when a trial judge intervenes personally at an early stage to assume judicial control over a case and to schedule dates for completion by the parties of the principal pretrial steps, the case is disposed of by settlement or trial more efficiently and with less cost and delay than when the parties are left to their own devices. Flanders, *Case Management and Court Management in United States District Courts* 17, Federal Judicial Center (1977). Thus, the rule mandates a pretrial scheduling order.

New matter is shown in italics; matter to be omitted is lined through

However, although scheduling and pretrial conferences are encouraged in appropriate cases, they are not mandated.

Discussion

Subdivision (a); Pretrial Conferences; Objectives. The amended rule makes scheduling and case management an express goal of pretrial procedure. This is done in Rule 16(a) by shifting the emphasis away from a conference focused solely on the trial and toward a process of judicial management that embraces the entire pretrial phase, especially motions and discovery. In addition, the amendment explicitly recognizes some of the objectives of pretrial conferences and the powers that many courts already have assumed. Rule 16 thus will be a more accurate reflection of actual practice.

Subdivision (b); Scheduling and Planning. The most significant change in Rule 16 is the mandatory scheduling order described in Rule 16(b), which is based in part on Wisconsin Civil Procedure Rule 802.10. The idea of scheduling orders is not new. It has been used by many federal courts. See, *e.g.*, Southern District of Indiana, Local Rule 19.

Although a mandatory scheduling order encourages the court to become involved in case management early in the litigation, it represents a degree of judicial involvement that is not warranted in many cases. Thus, subdivision (b) permits each district court to promulgate a local rule under Rule 83 exempting certain categories of cases in which the burdens of scheduling orders exceed the administrative efficiencies that would be gained. See Eastern District of Virginia, Local Rule 12(1). Logical candidates for this treatment include social security disability matters, habeas corpus petitions, forfeitures, and reviews of certain administrative actions.

A scheduling conference may be requested either by the judge, a magistrate when authorized by district court rule, or a party within 120 days after the summons and complaint are filed. If a scheduling conference is not arranged within that time and the case is not exempted by local rule, a scheduling order must be issued under Rule 16(b), after some communication with the parties, which may be by telephone or mail rather than in person. The use of the term "judge" in subdivision (b) reflects the Advisory Committee's judgment that it is preferable that this task should be handled by a district judge rather than a magistrate, except when the magistrate is acting under 28 U.S.C. § 636(c). While personal supervision by the trial judge is preferred, the rule, in recognition of the impracticality or difficulty of complying with such a requirement in some districts, authorizes a district by local rule to delegate the duties to a magistrate. In order to formulate a practicable scheduling order, the judge, or a magistrate when authorized by district court rule, and attorneys are required to develop a timetable for the matters listed in Rule 16(b)(1)–(3). As indicated in Rule 16(b)(4)–(5), the order may also deal with a wide range of other matters. The rule is phrased permissively as to clauses (4) and (5), however, because scheduling these items at an early point may not be feasible or appropriate. Even though subdivision (b) relates only to scheduling, there is no reason why some of the procedural matters listed in Rule 16(c) cannot be addressed at the same time, at least when a scheduling conference is held.

Item (1) assures that at some point both the parties and the pleadings will be fixed, by setting a time within which joinder of parties shall be completed and the pleadings amended.

Item (2) requires setting time limits for interposing various motions that otherwise might be used as stalling techniques.

New matter is shown in italics; matter to be omitted is lined through

Item (3) deals with the problem of procrastination and delay by attorneys in a context in which scheduling is especially important—discovery. Scheduling the completion of discovery can serve some of the same functions as the conference described in Rule 26(f).

Item (4) refers to setting dates for conferences and for trial. Scheduling multiple pretrial conferences may well be desirable if the case is complex and the court believes that a more elaborate pretrial structure, such as that described in the *Manual for Complex Litigation,* should be employed. On the other hand, only one pretrial conference may be necessary in an uncomplicated case.

As long as the case is not exempted by local rule, the court must issue a written scheduling order even if no scheduling conference is called. The order, like pretrial orders under the former rule and those under new Rule 16(c), normally will "control the subsequent course of the action." See Rule 16(e). After consultation with the attorneys for the parties and any unrepresented parties—a formal motion is not necessary—the court may modify the schedule on a showing of good cause if it cannot reasonably be met despite the diligence of the party seeking the extension. Since the scheduling order is entered early in the litigation, this standard seems more appropriate than a "manifest injustice" or "substantial hardship" test. Otherwise, a fear that extensions will not be granted may encourage counsel to request the longest possible periods for completing pleading, joinder, and discovery. Moreover, changes in the court's calendar sometimes will oblige the judge or magistrate when authorized by district court rule to modify the scheduling order.

The district courts undoubtedly will develop several prototype scheduling orders for different types of cases. In addition, when no formal conference is held, the court may obtain scheduling information by telephone, mail, or otherwise. In many instances this will result in a scheduling order better suited to the individual case than a standard order, without taking the time that would be required by a formal conference.

Rule 16(b) assures that the judge will take some early control over the litigation, even when its character does not warrant holding a scheduling conference. Despite the fact that the process of preparing a scheduling order does not always bring the attorneys and judge together, the fixing of time limits serves

> to stimulate litigants to narrow the areas of inquiry and advocacy to those they believe are truly relevant and material. Time limits not only compress the amount of time for litigation, they should also reduce the amount of resources invested in litigation. Litigants are forced to establish discovery priorities and thus to do the most important work first.

Report of the National Commission for the Review of Antitrust Laws and Procedures 28 (1979).

Thus, except in exempted cases, the judge or a magistrate when authorized by district court rule will have taken some action in every case within 120 days after the complaint is filed that notifies the attorneys that the case *will* be moving toward trial. Subdivision (b) is reenforced by subdivision (f), which makes it clear that the sanctions for violating a scheduling order are the same as those for violating a pretrial order.

Subdivision (c); Subjects to be Discussed at Pretrial Conferences. This subdivision expands upon the list of things that may be discussed at a pretrial conference that appeared in original Rule 16. The intention is to encourage better planning and management of litigation. Increased judicial control during the pretrial process accelerates the processing and termination of cases. Flanders, *Case*

New matter is shown in italics; matter to be omitted is lined through

Management and Court Management in United States District Courts, Federal Judicial Center (1977).   See also *Report of the National Commission for the Review of Antitrust Laws and Procedures* (1979).

The reference in Rule 16(c)(1) to "formulation" is intended to clarify and confirm the court's power to identify the litigable issues.   It has been added in the hope of promoting efficiency and conserving judicial resources by identifying the real issues prior to trial, thereby saving time and expense for everyone.   See generally *Meadow Gold Prods. Co. v. Wright,* 278 F.2d 867 (D.C. Cir. 1960).   The notion is emphasized by expressly authorizing the elimination of frivolous claims or defenses at a pretrial conference.   There is no reason to require that this await a formal motion for summary judgment.   Nor is there any reason for the court to wait for the parties to initiate the process called for in Rule 16(c)(1).

The timing of any attempt at issue formulation is a matter of judicial discretion.   In relatively simple cases it may not be necessary or may take the form of a stipulation between counsel or a request by the court that counsel work together to draft a proposed order.

Counsel bear a substantial responsibility for assisting the court in identifying the factual issues worthy of trial.   If counsel fail to identify an issue for the court, the right to have the issue tried is waived.   Although an order specifying the issues is intended to be binding, it may be amended at trial to avoid manifest injustice.   See Rule 16(e).   However, the rule's effectiveness depends on the court employing its discretion sparingly.

Clause (6) acknowledges the widespread availability and use of magistrates. The corresponding provision in the original rule referred only to masters and limited the function of the reference to the making of "findings to be used as evidence" in a case to be tried to a jury.   The new text is not limited and broadens the potential use of a magistrate to that permitted by the Magistrate's Act.

Clause (7) explicitly recognizes that it has become commonplace to discuss settlement at pretrial conferences.   Since it obviously eases crowded court dockets and results in savings to the litigants and the judicial system, settlement should be facilitated at as early a stage of the litigation as possible.   Although it is not the purpose of Rule 16(b)(7) to impose settlement negotiations on unwilling litigants, it is believed that providing a neutral forum for discussing the subject might foster it. See Moore's *Federal Practice* ¶ 16.17; 6 Wright & Miller, *Federal Practice and Procedure: Civil* § 1522 (1971).   For instance, a judge to whom a case has been assigned may arrange, on his own motion or at a party's request, to have settlement conferences handled by another member of the court or by a magistrate. The rule does not make settlement conferences mandatory because they would be a waste of time in many cases.   See Flanders, *Case Management and Court Management in the United States District Courts,* 39, Federal Judicial Center (1977). Requests for a conference from a party indicating a willingness to talk settlement normally should be honored, unless thought to be frivolous or dilatory.

A settlement conference is appropriate at any time.   It may be held in conjunction with a pretrial or discovery conference, although various objectives of pretrial management, such as moving the case toward trial, may not always be compatible with settlement negotiations, and thus a separate settlement conference may be desirable.   See 6 Wright & Miller, *Federal Practice and Procedure: Civil* § 1522, at p. 571 (1971).

In addition to settlement, Rule 16(c)(7) refers to exploring the use of procedures other than litigation to resolve the dispute.   This includes urging the litigants to employ adjudicatory techniques outside the courthouse.   See, for example, the

---

New matter is shown in italics; matter to be omitted is lined through

experiment described in Green, Marks & Olson, *Settling Large Case Litigation: An Alternative Approach,* 11 Loyola of L.A.L.Rev. 493 (1978).

Rule 16(c)(10) authorizes the use of special pretrial procedures to expedite the adjudication of potentially difficult or protracted cases. Some district courts obviously have done so for many years. See Rubin, *The Managed Calendar: Some Pragmatic Suggestions About Achieving the Just, Speedy and Inexpensive Determination of Civil Cases in Federal Courts,* 4 Just.Sys.J. 135 (1976). Clause 10 provides an explicit authorization for such procedures and encourages their use. No particular techniques have been described; the Committee felt that flexibility and experience are the keys to efficient management of complex cases. Extensive guidance is offered in such documents as the *Manual for Complex Litigation.*

The rule simply identifies characteristics that make a case a strong candidate for special treatment. The four mentioned are illustrative, not exhaustive, and overlap to some degree. But experience has shown that one or more of them will be present in every protracted or difficult case and it seems desirable to set them out. See Kendig, *Procedures for Management of Non-Routine Cases,* 3 Hofstra L.Rev. 701 (1975).

The last sentence of subdivision (c) is new. See Wisconsin Civil Procedure Rule 802.11(2). It has been added to meet one of the criticisms of the present practice described earlier and insure proper preconference preparation so that the meeting is more than a ceremonial or ritualistic event. The reference to "authority" is not intended to insist upon the ability to settle the litigation. Nor should the rule be read to encourage the judge conducting the conference to compel attorneys to enter into stipulations or to make admissions that they consider to be unreasonable, that touch on matters that could not normally have been anticipated to arise at the conference, or on subjects of a dimension that normally require prior consultation with and approval from the client.

Subdivision (d); Final Pretrial Conference. This provision has been added to make it clear that the time between any final pretrial conference (which in a simple case may be the *only* pretrial conference) and trial should be as short as possible to be certain that the litigants make substantial progress with the case and avoid the inefficiency of having that preparation repeated when there is a delay between the last pretrial conference and trial. An optimum time of 10 days to two weeks has been suggested by one federal judge. Rubin, *The Managed Calendar: Some Pragmatic Suggestions About Achieving the Just, Speedy and Inexpensive Determination of Civil Cases in Federal Courts,* 4 Just.Sys.J. 135, 141 (1976). The Committee, however, concluded that it would be inappropriate to fix a precise time in the rule, given the numerous variables that could bear on the matter. Thus the timing has been left to the court's discretion.

At least one of the attorneys who will conduct the trial for each party must be present at the final pretrial conference. At this late date there should be no doubt as to which attorney or attorneys this will be. Since the agreements and stipulations made at this final conference will control the trial, the presence of lawyers who will be involved in it is especially useful to assist the judge in structuring the case, and to lead to a more effective trial.

Subdivision (e); Pretrial Orders. Rule 16(e) does not substantially change the portion of the original rule dealing with pretrial orders. The purpose of an order is to guide the course of the litigation and the language of the original rule making that clear has been retained. No compelling reason has been found for major revision, especially since this portion of the rule has been interpreted and clarified by over forty years of judicial decisions with comparatively little difficulty. See 6

New matter is shown in italics; matter to be omitted is lined through

Wright & Miller, *Federal Practice and Procedure: Civil* §§ 1521–30 (1971). Changes in language therefore have been kept to a minimum to avoid confusion.

Since the amended rule encourages more extensive pretrial management than did the original, two or more conferences may be held in many cases. The language of Rule 16(e) recognizes this possibility and the corresponding need to issue more than one pretrial order in a single case.

Once formulated, pretrial orders should not be changed lightly; but total inflexibility is undesirable. See, *e.g., Clark v. Pennsylvania R.R. Co.,* 328 F.2d 591 (2d Cir. 1964). The exact words used to describe the standard for amending the pretrial order probably are less important than the meaning given them in practice. By not imposing any limitation on the ability to modify a pretrial order, the rule reflects the reality that in any process of continuous management what is done at one conference may have to be altered at the next. In the case of the final pretrial order, however, a more stringent standard is called for and the words "to prevent manifest injustice," which appeared in the original rule, have been retained. They have the virtue of familiarity and adequately describe the restraint the trial judge should exercise.

Many local rules make the plaintiff's attorney responsible for drafting a proposed pretrial order, either before or after the conference. Others allow the court to appoint any of the attorneys to perform the task, and others leave it to the court. See Note, *Pretrial Conference: A Critical Examination of Local Rules Adopted by Federal District Courts,* 64 Va.L.Rev. 467 (1978). Rule 16 has never addressed this matter. Since there is no consensus about which method of drafting the order works best and there is no reason to believe that nationwide uniformity is needed, the rule has been left silent on the point. See *Handbook for Effective Pretrial Procedure,* 37 F.R.D. 225 (1964).

Subdivision (f); Sanctions. Original Rule 16 did not mention the sanctions that might be imposed for failing to comply with the rule. However, courts have not hesitated to enforce it by appropriate measures. See, *e.g., Link v. Wabash R. Co.,* 370 U.S. 628 (1962) (district court's dismissal under Rule 41(b) after plaintiff's attorney failed to appear at a pretrial conference upheld); *Admiral Theatre Corp. v. Douglas Theatre,* 585 F.2d 877 (8th Cir. 1978) (district court has discretion to exclude exhibits or refuse to permit the testimony of a witness not listed prior to trial in contravention of its pretrial order).

To reflect that existing practice, and to obviate dependence upon Rule 41(b) or the court's inherent power to regulate litigation, *cf. Societe Internationale Pour Participations Industrielles et Commerciales, S.A. v. Rogers,* 357 U.S. 197 (1958), Rule 16(f) expressly provides for imposing sanctions on disobedient or recalcitrant parties, their attorneys, or both in four types of situations. Rodes, Ripple & Mooney, *Sanctions Imposable for Violations of the Federal Rules of Civil Procedure* 65–67, 80–84, Federal Judicial Center (1981). Furthermore, explicit reference to sanctions reenforces the rule's intention to encourage forceful judicial management.

Rule 16(f) incorporates portions of Rule 37(b)(2), which prescribes sanctions for failing to make discovery. This should facilitate application of Rule 16(f), since courts and lawyers already are familiar with the Rule 37 standards. Among the sanctions authorized by the new subdivision are: preclusion order, striking a pleading, staying the proceeding, default judgment, contempt, and charging a party, his attorney, or both with the expenses, including attorney's fees, caused by noncompliance. The contempt sanction, however, is only available for a violation of a court order. The references in Rule 16(f) are not exhaustive.

New matter is shown in italics; matter to be omitted is lined through

As is true under Rule 37(b)(2), the imposition of sanctions may be sought by either the court or a party. In addition, the court has discretion to impose whichever sanction it feels is appropriate under the circumstances. Its action is reviewable under the abuse-of-discretion standard. See *National Hockey League v. Metropolitan Hockey Club, Inc.*, 427 U.S. 639 (1976).

Rule 26. General Provisions Governing Discovery

(a) Discovery Methods. Parties may obtain discovery by one or more of the following methods: depositions upon oral examination or written questions; written interrogatories; production of documents or things or permission to enter upon land or other property, for inspection and other purposes; physical and mental examinations; and requests for admission. ~~Unless the court orders otherwise under subdivision (e) of this rule, the frequency of use of these methods is not limited.~~

(b) ~~Scope of Discovery~~ *Discovery Scope and Limits.* Unless other wise limited by order of the court in accordance with these rules, the scope of discovery is as follows:

(1) In General. Parties may obtain discovery regarding any matter, not privileged, which is relevant to the subject matter involved in the pending action, whether it relates to the claim or defense of the party seeking discovery or to the claim or defense of any other party, including the existence, description, nature, custody, condition and location of any books, documents, or other tangible things and the identity and location of persons having knowledge of any discoverable matter. It is not ground for objection that the information sought will be inadmissible at the trial if the information sought appears reasonably calculated to lead the discovery of admissible evidence.

The frequency or extent of use of the discovery methods set forth in subdivision (a) shall be limited by the court if it determines that: (i) the discovery sought is unreasonably cumulative or duplicative, or is obtainable from some other source that is more convenient, less burdensome, or less expensive; (ii) the party seeking discovery has had ample opportunity by discovery in the action to obtain the information sought; or (iii) the discovery is unduly burdensome or expensive, taking into account the needs of the case, the amount in controversy, limitations on the parties' resources, and the importance of the issues at stake in the litigation. The court may act upon its own initiative after reasonable notice or pursuant to a motion under subdivision (c).

(g) Signing of Discovery Requests, Responses, and Objections. Every request for discovery or response or objection thereto made by a party represented by an attorney shall be signed by at least one

New matter is shown in italics; matter to be omitted is lined through

*attorney of record in his individual name, whose address shall be
stated. A party who is not represented by an attorney shall sign
the request, response, or objection and state his address. The
signature of the attorney or party constitutes a certification that he
has read the request, response, or objection, and that to the best of
his knowledge, information, and belief formed after a reasonable
inquiry it is: (1) consistent with these rules and warranted by
existing law or a good faith argument for the extension, modification, or reversal of existing law; (2) not interposed for any improper
purpose, such as to harass or to cause unnecessary delay or needless
increase in the cost of litigation; and (3) not unreasonable or
unduly burdensome or expensive, given the needs of the case, the
discovery already had in the case, the amount in controversy, and
the importance of the issues at stake in the litigation. If a request,
response, or objection is not signed, it shall be stricken unless it is
signed promptly after the omission is called to the attention of the
party making the request, response or objection and a party shall
not be obligated to take any action with respect to it until it is
signed.*

*If a certification is made in violation of the rule, the court,
upon motion or upon its own initiative, shall impose upon the
person who made the certification, the party on whose behalf the
request, response, or objection is made, or both, an appropriate
sanction, which may include an order to pay the amount of the
reasonable expenses incurred because of the violation, including a
reasonable attorney's fee.*

Advisory Committee's Note

Excessive discovery and evasion or resistance to reasonable discovery requests
pose significant problems. Recent studies have made some attempt to determine
the sources and extent of the difficulties. See Brazil, *Civil Discovery: Lawyers'
Views of its Effectiveness, Principal Problems and Abuses,* American Bar Founda-
tion (1980); Connolly, Holleman & Kuhlman, *Judicial Controls and the Civil
Litigative Process: Discovery,* Federal Judicial Center (1978); Ellington, *A Study of
Sanctions for Discovery Abuse,* Department of Justice (1979); Schroeder & Frank,
The Proposed Changes in the Discovery Rules, 1978 Ariz.St.L.J. 475.

The purpose of discovery is to provide a mechanism for making relevant
information available to the litigants. "Mutual knowledge of all the relevant facts
gathered by both parties is essential to proper litigation." *Hickman v. Taylor,* 329
U.S. 495, 507 (1947). Thus the spirit of the rules is violated when advocates
attempt to use discovery tools as tactical weapons rather than to expose the facts
and illuminate the issues by overuse of discovery or unnecessary use of defensive
weapons or evasive responses. All of this results in excessively costly and time-
consuming activities that are disproportionate to the nature of the case, the
amount involved, or the issues or values at stake.

Given our adversary tradition and the current discovery rules, is it not
surprising that there are many opportunities, if not incentives, for attorneys to

---

New matter is shown in italics; matter to be omitted is lined through

engage in discovery that, although authorized by the broad, permissive terms of the rules, nevertheless results in delay. See Brazil, *The Adversary Character of Civil Discovery: A Critique and Proposals for Change,* 31 Vand.L.Rev. 1259 (1978). As a result, it has been said that the rules have "not infrequently [been] exploited to the disadvantage of justice." *Herbert v. Lando,* 441 U.S. 153, 179 (1979) (Powell, J., concurring). These practices impose costs on an already overburdened system and impede the fundamental goal of the "just, speedy, and inexpensive determination of every action." Fed.R.Civ.P. 1.

Subdivision (a); Discovery Methods. The deletion of the last sentence of Rule 26(a)(1), which provided that unless the court ordered otherwise under Rule 26(c) "the frequency of use" of the various discovery methods was not to be limited, is an attempt to address the problem of duplicative, redundant, and excessive discovery and to reduce it. The amendment, in conjunction with the changes in Rule 26(b)(1), is designed to encourage district judges to identify instances of needless discovery and to limit the use of the various discovery devices accordingly. The question may be raised by one of the parties, typically on a motion for a protective order, or by the court on its own initiative. It is entirely appropriate to consider a limitation on the frequency of use of discovery at a discovery conference under Rule 26(f) or at any other pretrial conference authorized by these rules. In considering the discovery needs of a particular case, the court should consider the factors described in Rule 26(b)(1).

Subdivision (b); Discovery Scope and Limits. Rule 26(b)(1) has been amended to add a sentence to deal with the problem of over-discovery. The objective is to guard against redundant or disproportionate discovery by giving the court authority to reduce the amount of discovery that may be directed to matters that are otherwise proper subjects of inquiry. The new sentence is intended to encourage judges to be more aggressive in identifying and discouraging discovery overuse. The grounds mentioned in the amended rule for limiting discovery reflect the existing practice of many courts in issuing protective orders under Rule 26(c). See, *e.g., Carlson Cos. v. Sperry & Hutchinson Co.,* 374 F.Supp. 1080 (D.Minn.1974); *Dolgow v. Anderson,* 53 F.R.D. 661 (E.D.N.Y.1971); *Mitchell v. American Tobacco Co.,* 33 F.R.D. 262 (M.D.Pa.1963); *Welty v. Clute,* 1 F.R.D. 446 (W.D.N.Y.1941). On the whole, however, district judges have been reluctant to limit the use of the discovery devices. See, *e.g., Apco Oil Co. v. Certified Transp., Inc.,* 46 F.R.D. 428 (W.D.Mo.1969). See generally 8 Wright & Miller, *Federal Practice and Procedure: Civil* §§ 2036, 2037, 2039, 2040 (1970).

The first element of the standard, Rule 26(b)(1)(i), is designed to minimize redundancy in discovery and encourage attorneys to be sensitive to the comparative costs of different methods of securing information. Subdivision (b)(1)(ii) also seeks to reduce repetitiveness and to oblige lawyers to think through their discovery activities in advance so that full utilization is made of each deposition, document request, or set of interrogatories. The elements of Rule 26(b)(1)(iii) address the problem of discovery that is disproportionate to the individual lawsuit as measured by such matters as its nature and complexity, the importance of the issues at stake in a case seeking damages, the limitations on a financially weak litigant to withstand extensive opposition to a discovery program or to respond to discovery requests, and the significance of the substantive issues, as measured in philosophic, social, or institutional terms. Thus the rule recognizes that many cases in public policy spheres, such as employment practices, free speech, and other matters, may have importance far beyond the monetary amount involved. The court must apply the standards in an even-handed manner that will prevent use of discovery to wage a war of attrition or as a device to coerce a party, whether financially weak or affluent.

New matter is shown in italics; matter to be omitted is lined through

The rule contemplates greater judicial involvement in the discovery process and thus acknowledges the reality that it cannot always operate on a self-regulating basis. See Connolly, Holleman & Kuhlman, *Judicial Controls and the Civil Litigative Process: Discovery* 77, Federal Judicial Center (1978). In an appropriate case the court could restrict the number of depositions, interrogatories, or the scope of a production request. But the court must be careful not to deprive a party of discovery that is reasonably necessary to afford a fair opportunity to develop and prepare the case.

The court may act on motion, or its own initiative. It is entirely appropriate to resort to the amended rule in conjunction with a discovery conference under Rule 26(f) or one of the other pretrial conferences authorized by the rules.

Subdivision (g); Signing of Discovery Requests, Responses, and Objections. Rule 26(g) imposes an affirmative duty to engage in pretrial discovery in a responsible manner that is consistent with the spirit and purposes of Rules 26 through 37. In addition, Rule 26(g) is designed to curb discovery abuse by explicitly encouraging the imposition of sanctions. The subdivision provides a deterrent to both excessive discovery and evasion by imposing a certification requirement that obliges each attorney to stop and think about the legitimacy of a discovery request, a response thereto, or an objection. The term "response" includes answers to interrogatories and to requests to admit as well as responses to production requests.

If primary responsibility for conducting discovery is to continue to rest with the litigants, they must be obliged to act responsibly and avoid abuse. With this in mind, Rule 26(g), which parallels the amendments to Rule 11, requires an attorney or unrepresented party to sign each discovery request, response, or objection. Motions relating to discovery are governed by Rule 11. However, since a discovery request, response, or objection usually deals with more specific subject matter than motions or papers, the elements that must be certified in connection with the former are spelled out more completely. The signature is a certification of the elements set forth in Rule 26(g).

Although the certification duty requires the lawyer to pause and consider the reasonableness of his request, response, or objection, it is not meant to discourage or restrict necessary and legitimate discovery. The rule simply requires that the attorney make a reasonable inquiry into the factual basis of his response, request, or objection.

The duty to make a "reasonable inquiry" is satisfied if the investigation undertaken by the attorney and the conclusions drawn therefrom are reasonable under the circumstances. It is an objective standard similar to the one imposed by Rule 11. See the Advisory Committee Note to Rule 11. See also *Kinee v. Abraham Lincoln Fed. Sav. & Loan Ass'n,* 365 F.Supp. 975 (E.D.Pa.1973). In making the inquiry, the attorney may rely on assertions by the client and on communications with other counsel in the case as long as that reliance is appropriate under the circumstances. Ultimately, what is reasonable is a matter for the court to decide on the totality of the circumstances.

Rule 26(g) does not require the signing attorney to certify the truthfulness of the client's factual responses to a discovery request. Rather, the signature certifies that the lawyer has made a reasonable effort to assure that the client has provided all the information and documents available to him that are responsive to the discovery demand. Thus, the lawyer's certification under Rule 26(g) should be distinguished from other signature requirements in the rules, such as those in Rules 30(e) and 33.

New matter is shown in italics; matter to be omitted is lined through

Nor does the rule require a party or an attorney to disclose privileged communications or work product in order to show that a discovery request, response, or objection is substantially justified. The provisions of Rule 26(c), including appropriate orders after *in camera* inspection by the court, remain available to protect a party claiming privilege or work product protection.

The signing requirement means that every discovery request, response, or objection should be grounded on a theory that is reasonable under the precedents or a good faith belief as to what should be the law. This standard is heavily dependent on the circumstances of each case. The certification speaks as of the time it is made. The duty to supplement discovery responses continues to be governed by Rule 26(e).

Concern about discovery abuse has led to widespread recognition that there is a need for more aggressive judicial control and supervision. *ACF Industries, Inc. v. EEOC,* 439 U.S. 1081 (1979) (certiorari denied) (Powell, J., dissenting). Sanctions to deter discovery abuse would be more effective if they were diligently applied "not merely to penalize those whose conduct may be deemed to warrant such a sanction, but to deter those who might be tempted to such conduct in the absence of such a deterrent." *National Hockey League v. Metropolitan Hockey Club,* 427 U.S. 639, 643 (1976). See also Note, *The Emerging Deterrence Orientation in the Imposition of Discovery Sanctions,* 91 Harv.L.Rev. 1033 (1978). Thus the premise of Rule 26(g) is that imposing sanctions on attorneys who fail to meet the rule's standards will significantly reduce abuse by imposing disadvantages therefor.

Because of the asserted reluctance to impose sanctions on attorneys who abuse the discovery rules, see Brazil, *Civil Discovery: Lawyers' Views of its Effectiveness, Principal Problems and Abuses,* American Bar Foundation (1980); Ellington, *A Study of Sanctions for Discovery Abuse,* Department of Justice (1979), Rule 26(g) makes explicit the authority judges now have to impose appropriate sanctions and requires them to use it. This authority derives from Rule 37, 28 U.S.C. § 1927, and the court's inherent power. See *Roadway Express, Inc. v. Piper,* 447 U.S. 752 (1980); *Martin v. Bell Helicopter Co.,* 85 F.R.D. 654, 661–62 (D.Col.1980); Note, *Sanctions Imposed by Courts on Attorneys Who Abuse the Judicial Process,* 44 U.Chi.L.Rev. 619 (1977). The new rule mandates that sanctions be imposed on attorneys who fail to meet the standards established in the first portion of Rule 26(g). The nature of the sanction is a matter of judicial discretion to be exercised in light of the particular circumstances. The court may take into account any failure by the party seeking sanctions to invoke protection under Rule 26(c) at an early stage in the litigation.

The sanctioning process must comport with due process requirements. The kind of notice and hearing required will depend on the facts of the case and the severity of the sanction being considered. To prevent the proliferation of the sanction procedure and to avoid multiple hearings, discovery in any sanction proceeding normally should be permitted only when it is clearly required by the interests of justice. In most cases the court will be aware of the circumstances and only a brief hearing should be necessary.

Rule 52. Findings by the Court

(a) Effect. In all actions tried upon the facts without a jury or with an advisory jury, the court shall find the facts specially and state separately its conclusions of law thereon, and judgment shall be entered pursuant to Rule 58; and in granting or refusing

New matter is shown in italics; matter to be omitted is lined through

interlocutory injunctions the court shall similarly set forth the findings of fact and conclusions of law which constitute the grounds of its action. Requests for findings are not necessary for purposes of review. Findings of fact shall not be set aside unless clearly erroneous, and due regard shall be given to the opportunity of the trial court to judge of the credibility of the witnesses. The findings of a master, to the extent that the court adopts them, shall be considered as the findings of the court. ~~If an opinion or memorandum of decision is filed, it~~ *It* will be sufficient if the findings of fact and conclusions of law *are stated orally and recorded in open court following the close of the evidence or* appear ~~therein~~ *in an opinion or memorandum of decision filed by the court.* Findings of fact and conclusions of law are unnecessary on decisions of motions under Rules 12 or 56 or any other motion except as provided in Rule 41(b).

Advisory Committee's Note

Rule 52(a) has been amended to revise its penultimate sentence to provide explicitly that the district judge may make the findings of fact and conclusions of law required in nonjury cases orally. Nothing in the prior text of the rule forbids this practice, which is widely utilized by district judges. See Christensen, *A Modest Proposal for Immeasurable Improvement,* 64 A.B.A.J. 693 (1978). The objective is to lighten the burden on the trial court in preparing findings in nonjury cases. In addition, the amendment should reduce the number of published district court opinions that embrace written findings.

Rule 53.   Masters

(a) **Appointment and Compensation.** ~~Each district court with the concurrence of a majority of all the judges thereof may appoint one or more standing masters for its district, and~~ *The* court in which any action is pending may appoint a special master therein. As used in these rules the word "master" includes a referee, an auditor, an examiner, ~~a commissioner,~~ and an assessor. The compensation to be allowed to a master shall be fixed by the court, and shall be charged upon such of the parties or paid out of any fund or subject matter of the action, which is in the custody and control of the court as the court may direct; *provided that this provision for compensation shall not apply when a United States magistrate is designated to serve as a master pursuant to Title 28, U.S.C. § 636(b)(2).* The master shall not retain his report as security for his compensation; but when the party ordered to pay the compensation allowed by the court does not pay it after notice and within the time prescribed by the court, the master is entitled to a writ of execution against the delinquent party.

(b) **Reference.** A reference to a master shall be the exception and not the rule. In actions to be tried by a jury, a reference

---

New matter is shown in italics; matter to be omitted is lined through

shall be made only when the issues are complicated; in actions to be tried without a jury, save in matters of account and of difficult computation of damages, a reference shall be made only upon a showing that some exceptional condition requires it. *Upon the consent of the parties, a magistrate may be designated to serve as a special master without regard to the provisions of this subdivision.*

(c) Powers. The order of reference to the master may specify or limit his powers and may direct him to report only upon particular issues or to do or perform particular acts or to receive and report evidence only and may fix the time and place for beginning and closing the hearings and for the filing of the master's report. Subject to the specifications and limitations stated in the order, the master has and shall exercise the power to regulate all proceedings in every hearing before him and to do all acts and take all measures necessary or proper for the efficient performance of his duties under the order. He may require the production before him of evidence upon all matters embraced in the reference, including the production of all books, papers, vouchers, documents, and writings applicable thereto. He may rule upon the admissibility of evidence unless otherwise directed by the order of reference and has the authority to put witnesses on oath and may himself examine them and may call the parties to the action and examine them upon oath. When a party so requests, the master shall make a record of the evidence offered and excluded in the same manner and subject to the same limitations as provided in ~~Rule 43(e)~~ *the Federal Rules of Evidence* for a court sitting without a jury.

(f) A magistrate is subject to this rule only when the order referring a matter to the magistrate expressly provides that the reference is made under this Rule.

Advisory Committee's Note

Subdivision (a). The creation of full-time magistrates, who serve at government expense and have no nonjudicial duties competing for their time, eliminates the need to appoint standing masters. Thus the prior provision in Rule 53(a) authorizing the appointment of standing masters is deleted. Additionally, the definition of "master" in subdivision (a) now eliminates the superseded office of commissioner.

The term "special master" is retained in Rule 53 in order to maintain conformity with 28 U.S.C. § 636(b)(2), authorizing a judge to designate a magistrate "to serve as a special master pursuant to the applicable provisions of this title and the Federal Rules of Civil Procedure for the United States District Courts." Obviously, when a magistrate serves as a special master, the provisions for compensation of masters are inapplicable, and the amendment to subdivision (a) so provides.

New matter is shown in italics; matter to be omitted is lined through

Although the existence of magistrates may make the appointment of outside masters unnecessary in many instances, see, *e.g., Gautreaux v. Chicago Housing Authority,* 384 F.Supp. 37 (N.D.Ill.1974), mandamus denied *sub nom., Chicago Housing Authority v. Austin,* 511 F.2d 82 (7th Cir. 1975); *Avco Corp. v. American Tel. & Tel. Co.,* 68 F.R.D. 532 (S.D.Ohio 1975), such masters may prove useful when some special expertise is desired or when a magistrate is unavailable for lengthy and detailed supervision of a case.

Subdivision (b). The provisions of 28 U.S.C. § 636(b)(2) not only permit magistrates to serve as masters under Rule 53(b) but also eliminate the exceptional condition requirement of Rule 53(b) when the reference is made with the consent of the parties. The amendment to subdivision (b) brings Rule 53 into harmony with the statute by exempting magistrates, appointed with the consent of the parties, from the general requirement that some exceptional condition requires the reference. It should be noted that subdivision (b) does not address the question, raised in recent decisional law and commentary, as to whether the exceptional condition requirement is applicable when *private masters* who are not magistrates are appointed with the consent of the parties. See Silberman, *Masters and Magistrates Part II: The American Analogue,* 50 N.Y.U.L.Rev. 1297, 1354 (1975).

Subdivision (c). The amendment recognizes the abrogation of Federal Rule 43(c) by the Federal Rules of Evidence.

Subdivision (f). The new subdivision responds to confusion flowing from the dual authority for references of pretrial matters to magistrates. Such references can be made, with or without the consent of the parties, pursuant to Rule 53 or under 28 U.S.C. § 636(b)(1)(A) and (b)(1)(B). There are a number of distinctions between references made under the statute and under the rule. For example, under the statute nondispositive pretrial matters may be referred to a magistrate, without consent, for final determination with reconsideration by the district judge if the magistrate's order is clearly erroneous or contrary to law. Under the rule, however, the appointment of a master, without consent of the parties, to supervise discovery would require some exceptional condition (Rule 53(b)) and would subject the proceedings to the report procedures of Rule 53(e). If an order of reference does not clearly articulate the source of the court's authority the resulting proceedings could be subject to attack on grounds of the magistrate's noncompliance with the provisions of Rule 53. This subdivision therefore establishes a presumption that the limitations of Rule 53 are not applicable unless the reference is specifically made subject to Rule 53.

A magistrate serving as a special master under 28 U.S.C. § 636(b)(2) is governed by the provisions of Rule 53, with the exceptional condition requirement lifted in the case of a consensual reference.

Rule 67. Deposit in Court

In an action in which any part of the relief sought is a judgment for a sum of money or the disposition of a sum of money or the disposition of any other thing capable of delivery, a party, upon notice to every other party, and by leave of court, may deposit with the court all or any part of such sum or thing., *whether or not that party claims all or any part of the sum or thing. The party making the deposit shall serve the order permitting deposit on the clerk of the court.* Money paid into court under

New matter is shown in italics; matter to be omitted is lined through

this rule shall be deposited and withdrawn in accordance with the provisions of Title 28, U.S.C., §§ 2041, and 2042; the Act of June 26, 1934, c. 756, § 23, as amended (48 Stat. 1236, 58 Stat. 845), U.S.C., Title 31, § 725v; or any like statute. *The fund shall be deposited in an interest-bearing account or invested in an interest-bearing instrument approved by the court.*

Advisory Committee's Note

Rule 67 has been amended in three ways. The first change is the addition of the clause in the first sentence. Some courts have construed the present rule to permit deposit only when the party making it claims no interest in the fund or thing deposited. *E.g., Blasin-Stern v. Beech-Nut Life Savers Corp.*, 429 F.Supp. 533 (D.Puerto Rico 1975); *Dinkins v. General Aniline & Film Corp.*, 214 F.Supp. 281 (S.D.N.Y.1963). However, there are situations in which a litigant may wish to be relieved of responsibility for a sum or thing, but continue to claim an interest in all or part of it. In these cases the deposit-in-court procedure should be available; in addition to the advantages to the party making the deposit, the procedure gives other litigants assurance that any judgment will be collectable. The amendment is intended to accomplish that.

The second change is the addition of a requirement that the order of deposit be served on the clerk of the court in which the sum or thing is to be deposited. This is simply to assure that the clerk knows what is being deposited and what his responsibilities are with respect to the deposit. The latter point is particularly important since the rule as amended contemplates that deposits will be placed in interest-bearing accounts; the clerk must know what treatment has been ordered for the particular deposit.

The third change is to require that any money be deposited in an interest-bearing account or instrument approved by the court.

Rule 72.   *Magistrates; Pretrial Matters*

(a) Nondispositive Matters.   A magistrate to whom a pretrial matter not dispositive of a claim or defense of a party is referred to hear and determine shall promptly conduct such proceedings as are required and when appropriate enter into the record a written order setting forth the disposition of the matter.   The district judge to whom the case is assigned shall consider objections made by the parties, provided they are served and filed within 10 days after the entry of the order, and shall modify or set aside any portion of the magistrate's order found to be clearly erroneous or contrary to law.

(b) Dispositive Motions and Prisoner Petitions.   A magistrate assigned without consent of the parties to hear a pretrial matter dispositive of a claim or defense of a party or a prisoner petition challenging the conditions of confinement shall promptly conduct such proceedings as are required.   A record shall be made of all evidentiary proceedings before the magistrate, and a record may be made of such other proceedings as the magistrate deems necessary.   The magistrate shall enter into the record a recommendation for

---

New matter is shown in italics; matter to be omitted is lined through

disposition of the matter, including proposed findings of fact when appropriate. The clerk shall forthwith mail copies to all parties.

A party objecting to the recommended disposition of the matter shall promptly arrange for the transcription of the record, or portions of it as all parties may agree upon or the magistrate deems sufficient, unless the district judge otherwise directs. Within 10 days after being served with a copy of the recommended disposition, a party may serve and file specific, written objections to the proposed findings and recommendations. A party may respond to another party's objections within 10 days after being served with a copy thereof. The district judge to whom the case is assigned shall make a de novo determination upon the record, or after additional evidence, of any portion of the magistrate's disposition to which specific written objection has been made in accordance with this rule. The district judge may accept, reject, or modify the recommended decision, receive further evidence, or recommit the matter to the magistrate with instructions.

Advisory Committee's Note

Subdivision (a). This subdivision addresses court-ordered referrals of non-dispositive matters under 28 U.S.C. § 636(b)(1)(A). The rule calls for a written order of the magistrate's disposition to preserve the record and facilitate review. An oral order read into the record by the magistrate will satisfy this requirement.

No specific procedures or timetables for raising objections to the magistrate's rulings on nondispositive matters are set forth in the Magistrates Act. The rule fixes a 10-day period in order to avoid uncertainty and provide uniformity that will eliminate the confusion that might arise if different periods were prescribed by local rule in different districts. It also is contemplated that a party who is successful before the magistrate will be afforded an opportunity to respond to objections raised to the magistrate's ruling.

The last sentence of subdivision (a) specifies that reconsideration of a magistrate's order, as provided for in the Magistrates Act, shall be by the district judge to whom the case is assigned. This rule does not restrict experimentation by the district courts under 28 U.S.C. § 636(b)(3) involving references of matters other than pretrial matters, such as appointment of counsel, taking of default judgments, and acceptance of jury verdicts when the judge is unavailable.

Subdivision (b). This subdivision governs court-ordered referrals of dispositive pretrial matters and prisoner petitions challenging conditions of confinement, pursuant to statutory authorization in 28 U.S.C. § 636(b)(1)(B). This rule does not extend to habeas corpus petitions, which are covered by the specific rules relating to proceedings under Sections 2254 and 2255 of Title 28.

This rule implements the statutory procedures for making objections to the magistrate's proposed findings and recommendations. The 10-day period, as specified in the statute, is subject to Rule 6(e) which provides for an additional 3-day period when service is made by mail. Although no specific provision appears in the Magistrates Act, the rule specifies a 10-day period for a party to respond to objections to the magistrate's recommendation.

New matter is shown in italics; matter to be omitted is lined through

Implementing the statutory requirements, the rule requires the district judge to whom the case is assigned to make a de novo determination of those portions of the report, findings, or recommendations to which timely objection is made. The term "de novo" signifies that the magistrate's findings are not protected by the clearly erroneous doctrine, but does not indicate that a second evidentiary hearing is required. See *United States v. Raddatz*, 417 U.S. 667 (1980). See also Silberman, *Masters and Magistrates Part II: The American Analogue*, 50 N.Y.U.L.Rev. 1297, 1367 (1975). When no timely objection is filed, the court need only satisfy itself that there is no clear error on the face of the record in order to accept the recommendation. See *Campbell v. United States Dist. Court*, 501 F.2d 196, 206 (9th Cir.1974), cert. denied, 419 U.S. 879, quoted in House Report No. 94–1609, 94th Cong. 2d Sess. (1976) at 3. Compare *Park Motor Mart, Inc. v. Ford Motor Co.*, 616 F.2d 603 (1st Cir.1980). Failure to make timely objection to the magistrate's report prior to its adoption by the district judge may constitute a waiver of appellate review of the district judge's order. See *United States v. Walters*, 638 F.2d 947 (6th Cir.1981).

Rule 73. *Magistrates; Trial by Consent and Appeal Options*

(a) Powers; Procedure. When specially designated to exercise such jurisdiction by local rule or order of the district court and when all parties consent thereto, a magistrate may exercise the authority provided by Title 28, U.S.C. § 636(c) and may conduct any or all proceedings, including a jury or nonjury trial, in a civil case. A record of the proceedings shall be made in accordance with the requirements of Title 28, U.S.C. § 636(c)(7).

(b) Consent. When a magistrate has been designated to exercise civil trial jurisdiction, the clerk shall give written notice to the parties of their opportunity to consent to the exercise by a magistrate of civil jurisdiction over the case, as authorized by Title 28, U.S.C. § 636(c). If, within the period specified by local rule, the parties agree to a magistrate's exercise of such authority, they shall execute and file a joint form of consent or separate forms of consent setting forth such election.

No district judge, magistrate, or other court official shall attempt to persuade or induce a party to consent to a reference of a civil matter to a magistrate under this rule, nor shall a district judge or magistrate be informed of a party's response to the clerk's notification, unless all parties have consented to the referral of the matter to a magistrate.

The district judge, for good cause shown on his own motion or under extraordinary circumstances shown by a party, may vacate a reference of a civil matter to a magistrate under this subdivision.

(c) Normal Appeal Route. In accordance with Title 28, U.S.C. § 636(c)(3), unless the parties otherwise agree to the optional appeal route provided for in subdivision (d) of this rule, appeal from a judgment entered upon direction of a magistrate in proceedings

---

New matter is shown in italics; matter to be omitted is lined through

under this rule will lie to the court of appeals as it would from a judgment of the district court.

(d) Optional Appeal Route. In accordance with Title 28, U.S.C. § 636(c)(4), at the time of reference to a magistrate, the parties may consent to appeal on the record to a judge of the district court and thereafter, by petition only, to the court of appeals.

Advisory Committee's Note

Subdivision (a). This subdivision implements the broad authority of the 1979 amendments to the Magistrates Act, 28 U.S.C. § 636(c), which permit a magistrate to sit in lieu of a district judge and exercise civil jurisdiction over a case, when the parties consent. See McCabe, *The Federal Magistrate Act of 1979,* 16 Harv.J.Legis. 343, 364–79 (1979). In order to exercise this jurisdiction, a magistrate must be specially designated under 28 U.S.C. § 636(c)(1) by the district court or courts he serves. The only exception to a magistrate's exercise of civil jurisdiction, which includes the power to conduct jury and nonjury trials and decide dispositive motions, is the contempt power. A hearing on contempt is to be conducted by the district judge upon certification of the facts and an order to show cause by the magistrate. See 28 U.S.C. § 639(e). In view of 28 U.S.C. § 636(c)(1) and this rule, it is unnecessary to amend Rule 58 to provide that the decision of a magistrate is a "decision by the court" for the purposes of that rule and a "final decision of the district court" for purposes of 28 U.S.C. § 1291 governing appeals.

Subdivision (b). This subdivision implements the blind consent provision of 28 U.S.C. § 636(c)(2) and is designed to ensure that neither the judge nor the magistrate attempts to induce a party to consent to reference of a civil matter under this rule to a magistrate. See House Rep. No. 96–444, 96th Cong. 1st Sess. 8 (1979).

The rule opts for a uniform approach in implementing the consent provision by directing the clerk to notify the parties of their opportunity to elect to proceed before a magistrate and by requiring the execution and filing of a consent form or forms setting forth the election. However, flexibility at the local level is preserved in that local rules will determine how notice shall be communicated to the parties, and local rules will specify the time period within which an election must be made.

The last paragraph of subdivision (b) reiterates the provision in 28 U.S.C. § 636(c)(6) for vacating a reference to the magistrate.

Subdivision (c). Under 28 U.S.C. § 636(c)(3), the normal route of appeal from the judgment of a magistrate—the only route that will be available unless the parties otherwise agree in advance—is an appeal by the aggrieved party "directly to the appropriate United States court of appeals from the judgment of the magistrate in the same manner as an appeal from any other judgment of a district court." The quoted statutory language indicates Congress' intent that the same procedures and standards of appealability that govern appeals from district court judgments govern appeals from magistrates' judgments.

Subdivision (d). 28 U.S.C. § 636(c)(4) offers parties who consent to the exercise of civil jurisdiction by a magistrate an alternative appeal route to that provided in subdivision (c) of this rule. This optional appellate route was provided by Congress in recognition of the fact that not all civil cases warrant the same appellate treatment. In cases where the amount in controversy is not great and there are no difficult questions of law to be resolved, the parties may desire to avoid the expense

New matter is shown in italics; matter to be omitted is lined through

and delay of appeal to the court of appeals by electing an appeal to the district judge. See McCabe, *The Federal Magistrate Act of 1979*, 16 Harv.J.Legis. 343, 388 (1979). This subdivision provides that the parties may elect the optional appeal route at the time of reference to a magistrate. To this end, the notice by the clerk under subdivision (b) of this rule shall explain the appeal option and the corollary restriction on review by the court of appeals. This approach will avoid later claims of lack of consent to the avenue of appeal. The choice of the alternative appeal route to the judge of the district court should be made by the parties in their forms of consent. Special appellate rules to govern appeals from a magistrate to a district judge appear in new Rules 74 through 76.

Rule 74.   Method of Appeal from Magistrate to District Judge under Title 28, U.S.C. § 636(c)(4) and Rule 73(d)

(a) When Taken.   When the parties have elected under Rule 73(d) to proceed by appeal to a district judge from an appealable decision made by a magistrate under the consent provisions of Title 28, U.S.C. § 636(c)(4), an appeal may be taken from the decision of a magistrate by filing with the clerk of the district court a notice of appeal within 30 days of the date of entry of the judgment appealed from; but if the United States or an officer or agency thereof is a party, the notice of appeal may be filed by any party within 60 days of such entry.   If a timely notice of appeal is filed by a party, any other party may file a notice of appeal within 14 days thereafter, or within the time otherwise prescribed by this subdivision, whichever period last expires.

The running of the time for filing a notice of appeal is terminated as to all parties by the timely filing of any of the following motions with the magistrate by any party, and the full time for appeal from the judgment entered by the magistrate commences to run anew from entry of any of the following orders: (1) granting or denying a motion for judgment under Rule 50(b); (2) granting or denying a motion under Rule 52(b) to amend or make additional findings of fact, whether or not an alteration of the judgment would be required if the motion is granted; (3) granting or denying a motion under Rule 59 to alter or amend the judgment; (4) denying a motion for a new trial under Rule 59.

An interlocutory decision or order by a magistrate which, if made by a judge of the district court, could be appealed under any provision of law, may be appealed to a judge of the district court by filing a notice of appeal within 15 days after entry of the decision or order, provided the parties have elected to appeal to a judge of the district court under Rule 73(d).   An appeal of such interlocutory decision or order shall not stay the proceedings before the magistrate unless the magistrate or judge shall so order.

Upon a showing of excusable neglect, the magistrate may extend the time for filing a notice of appeal upon motion filed not

New matter is shown in italics; matter to be omitted is lined through

later than 20 days after the expiration of the time otherwise prescribed by this rule.

(b) Notice of Appeal; Service.   The notice of appeal shall specify the party or parties taking the appeal, designate the judgment, order or part thereof appealed from, and state that the appeal is to a judge of the district court.   The clerk shall mail copies of the notice to all other parties and note the date of mailing in the civil docket.

(c) Stay Pending Appeal.   Upon a showing that the magistrate has refused or otherwise failed to stay the judgment pending appeal to the district judge under Rule 73(d), the appellant may make application for a stay to the district judge with reasonable notice to all parties.   The stay may be conditioned upon the filing in the district court of a bond or other appropriate security.

(d) Dismissal.   For failure to comply with these rules or any local rule or order, the district judge may take such action as is deemed appropriate, including dismissal of the appeal.   The district judge also may dismiss the appeal upon the filing of a stipulation signed by all parties, or upon motion and notice by the appellant.

Advisory Committee's Note

Subdivision (a).   This rule governs appeals from decisions of magistrates exercising consensual civil jurisdiction under Rule 73 when the parties elect to appeal to a judge of the district court under subdivision (d) of that rule.   Congress specified that such an appeal would be "on the record to a judge of the district court in the same manner as on an appeal from a judgment of the district court to a court of appeals."   See 28 U.S.C. § 636(c)(4).   Presumably, Congress intended that the district court follow the same general procedures, including the "clearly erroneous" factual review standard of Civil Rule 52(a), that a court of appeals follows in reviewing a judgment of the district court.   However, Congress also provided that "whenever possible" the local rules of the district court shall endeavor to make appeals expeditious and inexpensive.   See 28 U.S.C. § 636(c)(4).   Since the Federal Rules of Appellate Procedure are designed to cover appeals from a single judge to a three-member appeal tribunal, some modifications have proved desirable in assuring an expeditious appeal from a magistrate to a single district judge.   Rules 74 through 76 provide this set of rules governing appeals from magistrates' exercise of consensual jurisdiction.

The time limits in subdivision (a) generally conform to those in Appellate Rule 4(a), except that the period in which a party may move for leave to file a late notice of appeal on grounds of excusable neglect is 20 days, rather than the 30-day period provided for in the Appellate Rules.

The term "appealable decision" as used in this rule embraces the "final decision" concept of 28 U.S.C. § 1291 and permits an appeal from a magistrate to a district judge in those situations in which an appeal from a district judge to the court of appeals would lie.   That term, along with the specific provision in the rule permitting appeals of certain interlocutory orders, incorporates by reference the provisions of 28 U.S.C. § 1292 and adopts, by analogy to Section 1292(b), a

New matter is shown in italics; matter to be omitted is lined through

certification procedure for otherwise unappealable orders "where the order is based on a controlling question of law as to which there is substantial ground for difference of opinion and an immediate appeal from the order may materially advance the ultimate termination of the litigation." Although no specific certification procedure is set forth, the rule contemplates that a magistrate may certify such an order for appeal, and the district judge, in his discretion, may allow the appeal. In the interest of expediting the trial, interlocutory appeals of any kind will not stay the proceedings unless the magistrate or district judge finds that the nature of the appeal or its relation to the remaining proceedings requires a stay.

Subdivision (b). The provisions governing the content and service of the notice of appeal conform substantially to Rules 3(c) and 3(d) of the Federal Rules of Appellate Procedure.

Subdivision (c). This subdivision represents a simplified version of Rule 8 of the Federal Rules of Appellate Procedure. Under this subdivision, the district judge is in the position of an appellate judge under Rule 8 of the Appellate Rules when the judge below has refused a stay under Rule 62.

In proceedings under 28 U.S.C. § 636(c), an application for a stay of the judgment under Rule 62 initially will be made to the magistrate. The district judge under this rule may hear an application for a stay of the judgment upon a showing that the magistrate has refused to stay the judgment pending appeal to the district judge.

Subdivision (d). The provisions governing dismissal are similar to Rule 3(a) (failure to prosecute) and Rule 42(a) (voluntary dismissal) of the Federal Rules of Appellate Procedure.

Rule 75.　Proceedings on Appeal from Magistrate to District Judge under Rule 73(d)

(a) Applicability.　In proceedings under Title 28, U.S.C. § 636(c), when the parties have previously elected under Rule 73(d) to appeal to a district judge rather than to the court of appeals, this rule shall govern the proceedings on appeal.

(b) Record on Appeal.

(1) Composition.　The original papers and exhibits filed with the clerk of the district court, the transcript of the proceedings, if any, and the docket entries shall constitute the record on appeal. In lieu of this record the parties, within 10 days after the filing of the notice of appeal, may file a joint statement of the case showing how the issues presented by the appeal arose and were decided by the magistrate, and setting forth only so many of the facts averred and proved or sought to be proved as are essential to a decision of the issues presented.

(2) Transcript.　Within 10 days after filing the notice of appeal the appellant shall make arrangements for the production of a transcript of such parts of the proceedings as he deems necessary. Unless the entire transcript is to be included, the appellant, within the time provided above, shall serve on the appellee and file with the court a description of the parts of the transcript which he

intends to present on the appeal. If the appellee deems a transcript of other parts of the proceedings to be necessary, within 10 days after the service of the statement of the appellant, he shall serve on the appellant and file with the court a designation of additional parts to be included. The appellant shall promptly make arrangements for the inclusion of all such parts unless the magistrate, upon motion, exempts the appellant from providing certain parts, in which case the appellee may provide for their transcription.

(3) Statement in Lieu of Transcript. If no record of the proceedings is available for transcription, the parties shall, within 10 days after the filing of the notice of appeal, file a statement of the evidence from the best available means to be submitted in lieu of the transcript. If the parties cannot agree they shall submit a statement of their differences to the magistrate for settlement.

(c) Time for Filing Briefs. Unless a local rule or court order otherwise provides, the following time limits for filing briefs shall apply.

(1) The appellant shall serve and file his brief within 20 days after the filing of the transcript, statement of the case, or statement of the evidence.

(2) The appellee shall serve and file his brief within 20 days after service of the brief of the appellant.

(3) The appellant may serve and file a reply brief within 10 days after service of the brief of the appellee.

(4) If the appellee has filed a cross-appeal, he may file a reply brief limited to the issues on the cross-appeal within 10 days after service of the reply brief of the appellant.

(d) Length and Form of Briefs. Briefs may be typewritten. The length and form of briefs shall be governed by local rule.

(e) Oral Argument. The opportunity for the parties to be heard on oral argument shall be governed by local rule.

Advisory Committee's Note

Subdivision (a). 28 U.S.C. § 636(c)(4) provides that whenever possible the local rules of the district court shall endeavor to make appeals from the magistrate to the district judge expeditious and inexpensive. The provisions of this rule are directed to that end in simplifying the record on appeal and permitting typewritten briefs. The availability of oral argument and the length and form of briefs are matters appropriately left to local rule.

Subdivision (b). The provisions governing the composition of the record and the transcript are adapted from Rule 10 of the Federal Rules of Appellate Procedure. The language requiring the appellant to "make arrangements for the production of a transcript" is broad enough to require the party to order a transcript from the court reporter or to make arrangements to transcribe a taped

New matter is shown in italics; matter to be omitted is lined through

record of the proceedings. The magistrate is to settle any differences regarding the extent of the transcript and to require the appellant to provide for transcription of any additional portions designated by the appellee that are material to the issues on appeal. Naturally, the rule is subject to the operation of 28 U.S.C. § 1915 in the case of a party who is unable to pay such costs.

Although it is not anticipated that an appeal will often be taken from a hearing or trial of which no record was made, the parties do have the option to forego a record in routine matters under 28 U.S.C. § 636(c)(7). In such cases a statement of the evidence will be prepared by the parties (or by the magistrate if the parties cannot agree) from the best available means, including the recollections and notes of the parties and the magistrate.

Subdivision (c). Although the parties, with agreement of the court, can dispense with the filing of briefs, a schedule for the serving and filing of briefs will often be necessary. In lieu of the elaborate provisions of Rules 28 through 32 of the Federal Rules of Appellate Procedure, this rule adopts a simplified approach for the filing and serving of briefs in order to achieve an inexpensive and expeditious appeal from a magistrate's judgment to a district judge. The timing of the appellant's initial brief is tied to the filing of the transcript or statement, instead of the filing of the record (Appellate Rule 31(a)) or the docketing of the appeal, because the rest of the record is already in the hands of the district court clerk and need not be transmitted. This rule does not require payment of a filing fee. Thus the filing of the transcript or statement is all that remains of the traditional concepts of filing the record and docketing the appeal.

The introductory clause of the rule recognizes the desirability of allowing local and individual variations in the filing of briefs, and the numbered clauses prescribe shorter periods than the corresponding intervals allowed by Appellate Rule 31(a). The provision allowing a reply brief for an appellee who has filed a cross-appeal is taken from Appellate Rule 28(c).

Subdivision (d). The use of typewritten briefs is urged as a means of minimizing costs and of expediting appeals from the magistrate to the district judge. The form and length of briefs should be addressed as a matter of local rule in order to avoid resort to the more elaborate provisions of the Federal Rules of Appellate Procedure.

Subdivision (e). The availability of oral argument has been left as a matter for local rule.

Rule 76. *Judgment of the District Judge on the Appeal under Rule 73(d) and Costs*

(a) Entry of Judgment. When the parties have elected under Rule 73(d) to appeal from a judgment of the magistrate to a district judge, the clerk shall prepare, sign, and enter judgment in accordance with the order or decision of the district judge following an appeal from a judgment of the magistrate, unless the district judge directs otherwise. The clerk shall mail to all parties a copy of the order or decision of the district judge.

(b) Stay of Judgments. The decision of the district judge shall be stayed for 10 days during which time a party may petition the district judge for rehearing, and a timely petition shall stay the decision of the district judge pending disposition of a petition for

---

New matter is shown in italics; matter to be omitted is lined through

rehearing. Upon the motion of a party, the decision of the district judge may be stayed in order to allow a party to petition the court of appeals for leave to appeal.

(c) Costs. Except as otherwise provided by law or ordered by the district judge, costs shall be taxed against the losing party; if a judgment of the magistrate is affirmed in part or reversed in part, or is vacated, costs shall be allowed only as ordered by the district judge. The cost of the transcript, if necessary for the determination of the appeal, and the premiums paid for bonds to preserve rights pending appeal shall be taxed as costs by the clerk.

Advisory Committee's Note

Subdivision (a). This subdivision, adapted from Rule 36 of the Federal Rules of Appellate Procedure, directs the clerk to enter judgment in accordance with the order or decision of the district judge affirming, reversing, or modifying the judgment of the magistrate and to mail copies of the order or decision to all parties.

Subdivision (b). This subdivision, adapted from Rule 41 of the Federal Rules of Appellate Procedure, stays the effect of the district judge's decision on an appeal from a judgment of the magistrate. The availability of a rehearing by the district judge is contemplated (see Appellate Rule 40), but no particular form of petition is specified by the rule. The initial 10-day stay and the stay pending disposition of a timely petition for rehearing operate automatically upon the magistrate and all parties. Any other stay is at the discretion of the district judge.

Subdivision (c). This provision for costs on appeal is adapted from Rule 39 of the Federal Rules of Appellate Procedure to achieve the inexpensive appellate process envisioned from district judge review of magistrate action. No filing fee is required since a single clerk's office handles the file throughout, and no bond for costs is required. Ordinarily the only costs will be the costs of the transcript and the premium for any supersedeas bond.

*

New matter is shown in italics; matter to be omitted is lined through

CERTAIN OF THE AMENDMENTS OF FEDERAL RULES OF CIVIL PROCEDURE ADOPTED BY THE SUPREME COURT OF THE UNITED STATES ON APRIL 29, 1985, EFFECTIVE AUGUST 1, 1985, WITH ADVISORY COMMITTEE'S NOTES THEREON

[Amendments here omitted: Changes in Rule 71A, Form 18–A, and Supplemental Rules B, C, and E.]

Rule 6.   Time

(a) Computation.   In computing any period of time prescribed or allowed by these rules, by the local rules of any district court, by order of court, or by any applicable statute, the day of the act, event, or default from which the designated period of time begins to run shall not be included.   The last day of the period so computed shall be included, unless it is a Saturday, a Sunday, or a legal holiday, *or, when the act to be done is the filing of a paper in court, a day on which weather or other conditions have made the office of the clerk of the district court inaccessible,* in which event the period runs until the end of the next day which is not ~~a Saturday, a Sunday, or a legal holiday~~ *one of the aforementioned days.*   When the period of time prescribed or allowed is less than ~~7~~ *11* days, intermediate Saturdays, Sundays, and legal holidays shall be excluded in the computation.   As used in this rule and in Rule 77(c), "legal holiday" includes New Year's Day, *Birthday of Martin Luther King, Jr.,* Washington's Birthday, Memorial Day, Independence Day, Labor Day, Columbus Day, Veterans Day, Thanksgiving Day, Christmas Day, and any other day appointed as a holiday by the President or the Congress of the United States, or by the state in which the district court is held.

Advisory Committee's Note

Rule 6(a) is amended to acknowledge that weather conditions or other events may render the clerk's office inaccessible one or more days.   Parties who are obliged to file something with the court during that period should not be penalized if they cannot do so.   The amendment conforms to changes made in Federal Rule of Criminal Procedure 45(a), effective August 1, 1982.

The Rule also is amended to extend the exclusion of intermediate Saturdays, Sundays, and legal holidays to the computation of time periods less than 11 days.

New matter is shown in italics;   matter to be omitted is lined through

Under the current version of the Rule, parties bringing motions under rules with 10-day periods could have as few as 5 working days to prepare their motions. This hardship would be especially acute in the case of Rules 50(b) and (c)(2), 52(b), and 59(b), (d), and (e), which may not be enlarged at the discretion of the court. See Rule 6(b). If the exclusion of Saturdays, Sundays, and legal holidays will operate to cause excessive delay in urgent cases, the delay can be obviated by applying to the court to shorten the time. See Rule 6(b).

The Birthday of Martin Luther King, Jr., which becomes a legal holiday effective in 1986, has been added to the list of legal holidays enumerated in the Rule.

Rule 45. Subpoena

(d) Subpoena for Taking Depositions; Place of Examination.

(2) ~~A resident of the district in which the deposition is to be taken may be required to attend an examination only in the county wherein he resides or is employed or transacts his business in person, or at such other convenient place as is fixed by an order of court. A nonresident of the district may be required to attend only in the county wherein he is served with a subpoena, or within 40 miles from the place of service, or at such other convenient place as is fixed by an order of court.~~ *A person to whom a subpoena for the taking of a deposition is directed may be required to attend at any place within 100 miles from the place where that person resides, is employed or transacts business in person, or is served, or at such other convenient place as is fixed by an order of court.*

Advisory Committee's Note

Present Rule 45(d)(2) has two sentences setting forth the territorial scope of deposition subpoenas. The first sentence is directed to depositions taken in the judicial district in which the deponent resides; the second sentence addresses situations in which the deponent is not a resident of the district in which the deposition is to take place. The Rule, as currently constituted, creates anomalous situations that often cause logistical problems in conducting litigation.

The first sentence of the present Rule states that a deponent may be required to attend only in the *county* wherein that person resides or is employed or transacts business in person, that is, where the person lives or works. Under this provision a deponent can be compelled, without court order, to travel from one end of that person's home county to the other, no matter how far that may be. The second sentence of the Rule is somewhat more flexible, stating that someone who does not reside in the district in which the deposition is to be taken can be required to attend in the county where the person is served with the subpoena, *or* within 40 miles from the place of service.

Under today's conditions there is no sound reason for distinguishing between residents of the district or county in which a deposition is to be taken and nonresidents, and the Rule is amended to provide that any person may be

New matter is shown in italics; matter to be omitted is lined through

subpoenaed to attend a deposition within a specified radius from that person's residence, place of business, or where the person was served. The 40-mile radius has been increased to 100 miles.

Rule 52. Findings by the Court

(a) **Effect.** In all actions tried upon the facts without a jury or with an advisory jury, the court shall find the facts specially and state separately its conclusions of law thereon, and judgment shall be entered pursuant to Rule 58; and in granting or refusing interlocutory injunctions the court shall similarly set forth the findings of fact and conclusions of law which constitute the grounds of its action. Requests for findings are not necessary for purposes of review. Findings of fact, *whether based on oral or documentary evidence,* shall not be set aside unless clearly erroneous, and due regard shall be given to the opportunity of the trial court to judge of the credibility of the witnesses. The findings of a master, to the extent that the court adopts them, shall be considered as the findings of the court. It will be sufficient if the findings of fact and conclusions of law are stated orally and recorded in open court following the close of the evidence or appear in an opinion or memorandum of decision filed by the court. Findings of fact and conclusions of law are unnecessary on decisions of motions under Rules 12 or 56 or any other motion except as provided in Rule 41(b).

Advisory Committee's Note

Rule 52(a) has been amended (1) to avoid continued confusion and conflicts among the circuits as to the standard of appellate review of findings of fact by the court, (2) to eliminate the disparity between the standard of review as literally stated in Rule 52(a) and the practice of some courts of appeals, and (3) to promote nationwide uniformity. See Note, *Rule 52(a): Appellate Review of Findings of Fact Based on Documentary or Undisputed Evidence,* 49 Va.L.Rev. 506, 536 (1963).

Some courts of appeal have stated that when a trial court's findings do not rest on demeanor evidence and evaluation of a witness' credibility, there is no reason to defer to the trial court's findings and the appellate court more readily can find them to be clearly erroneous. See, *e.g., Marcum v. United States,* 621 F.2d 142, 144–45 (5th Cir. 1980). Others go further, holding that appellate review may be had without application of the "clearly erroneous" test since the appellate court is in as good a position as the trial court to review a purely documentary record. See, *e.g., Atari, Inc. v. North American Philips Consumer Electronics Corp.,* 672 F.2d 607, 614 (7th Cir.), *cert. denied,* 459 U.S. 880 (1982); *Lydle v. United States,* 635 F.2d 763, 765 n. 1 (6th Cir. 1981); *Swanson v. Baker Indus., Inc.,* 615 F.2d 479, 483 (8th Cir. 1980); *Taylor v. Lombard,* 606 F.2d 371, 372 (2d Cir. 1979), *cert. denied,* 445 U.S. 946 (1980); *Jack Kahn Music Co. v. Baldwin Piano & Organ Co.,* 604 F.2d 755, 758 (2d Cir. 1979); *John R. Thompson Co. v. United States,* 477 F.2d 164, 167 (7th Cir. 1973).

New matter is shown in italics; matter to be omitted is lined through

A third group has adopted the view that the "clearly erroneous" rule applies in all nonjury cases even when findings are based solely on documentary evidence or on inferences from undisputed facts. See, *e.g.*, *Maxwell v. Sumner*, 673 F.2d 1031, 1036 (9th Cir.), *cert. denied*, 459 U.S. 976 (1982); *United States v. Texas Education Agency*, 647 F.2d 504, 506–07 (5th Cir. 1981), *cert. denied*, 454 U.S. 1143 (1982); *Constructora Maza, Inc. v. Banco de Ponce*, 616 F.2d 573, 576 (1st Cir. 1980); *In re Sierra Trading Corp.*, 482 F.2d 333, 337 (10th Cir. 1973); *Case v. Morrisette*, 475 F.2d 1300, 1306–07 (D.C. Cir. 1973).

The commentators also disagree as to the proper interpretation of the Rule. *Compare* Wright, *The Doubtful Omniscience of Appellate Courts*, 41 Minn. L. Rev. 751, 769–70 (1957) (language and intent of Rule support view that "clearly errone-ous" test should apply to all forms of evidence), *and* 9 C. Wright & A. Miller, *Federal Practice and Procedure: Civil* § 2587, at 740 (1971) (language of the Rule is clear), *with* 5A J. Moore, *Federal Practice* ¶ 52.04, at 2687–88 (2d ed. 1982) (Rule as written supports broader review of findings based on non-demeanor testimony).

The Supreme Court has not clearly resolved the issue. See *Bose Corp. v. Consumers Union of United States, Inc.*, 104 S.Ct. 1949, 1958 (1984); *Pullman Standard v. Swint*, 456 U.S. 273, 293 (1982); *United States v. General Motors Corp.*, 384 U.S. 127, 141 n. 16 (1966); *United States v. United States Gypsum Co.*, 333 U.S. 364, 394–96 (1948).

The principal argument advanced in favor of a more searching appellate review of findings by the district court based solely on documentary evidence is that the rationale of Rule 52(a) does not apply when the findings do not rest on the trial court's assessment of credibility of the witnesses but on an evaluation of documentary proof and the drawing of inferences from it, thus eliminating the need for any special deference to the trial court's findings. These considerations are outweighed by the public interest in the stability and judicial economy that would be promoted by recognizing that the trial court, not the appellate tribunal, should be the finder of the facts. To permit courts of appeals to share more actively in the fact-finding function would tend to undermine the legitimacy of the district courts in the eyes of litigants, multiply appeals by encouraging appellate retrial of some factual issues, and needlessly reallocate judicial authority.

Rule 83.   Rules by District Courts

Each district court by action of a majority of the judges thereof may from time to time, *after giving appropriate public notice and an opportunity to comment,* make and amend rules governing its practice not inconsistent with these rules. *A local rule so adopted shall take effect upon the date specified by the district court and shall remain in effect unless amended by the district court or abrogated by the judicial council of the circuit in which the district is located.* Copies of rules and amendments so made by any district court shall upon their promulgation be furnished to the ~~Supreme Court of the United States~~ *judicial council and the Administrative Office of the United States Courts and be made available to the public.* In all cases not provided for by rule, the district ~~courts~~ *judges and magistrates* may regulate their practice in any manner not inconsistent with these rules *or those of the district in which they act.*

New matter is shown in italics; matter to be omitted is lined through

Advisory Committee's Note

Rule 83, which has not been amended since the Federal Rules were promulgated in 1938, permits each district to adopt local rules not inconsistent with the Federal Rules by a majority of the judges. The only other requirement is that copies be furnished to the Supreme Court.

The widespread adoption of local rules and the modest procedural prerequisites for their promulgation have led many commentators to question the soundness of the process as well as the validity of some rules. See 12 C. Wright & A. Miller, *Federal Practice and Procedure: Civil* § 3152, at 217 (1973); Caballero, *Is There an Over-Exercise of Local Rule-Making Powers by the United States District Courts?*, 24 Fed. Bar News 325 (1977). Although the desirability of local rules for promoting uniform practice within a district is widely accepted, several commentators also have suggested reforms to increase the quality, simplicity, and uniformity of the local rules. See Note, *Rule 83 and the Local Federal Rules*, 67 Colum. L. Rev. 1251 (1967), and Comment, *The Local Rules of Civil Procedure in the Federal District Courts—A Survey*, 1966 Duke L.J. 1011.

The amended Rule attempts, without impairing the procedural validity of existing local rules, to enhance the local rulemaking process by requiring appropriate public notice of proposed rules and an opportunity to comment on them. Although some district courts apparently consult the local bar before promulgating rules, many do not, which has led to criticism of a process that has district judges consulting only with each other. See 12 C. Wright & A. Miller, *supra*, § 3152, at 217; Blair, *The New Local Rules for Federal Practice in Iowa*, 23 Drake L. Rev. 517 (1974). The new language subjects local rulemaking to scrutiny similar to that accompanying the Federal Rules, administrative rulemaking, and legislation. It attempts to assure that the expert advice of practitioners and scholars is made available to the district court before local rules are promulgated. See Weinstein, *Reform of Court Rule-Making Procedures* 84–87, 127–37, 151 (1977).

The amended Rule does not detail the procedure for giving notice and an opportunity to be heard since conditions vary from district to district. Thus, there is no explicit requirement for a public hearing, although a district may consider that procedure appropriate in all or some rulemaking situations. See generally, Weinstein, *supra*, at 117–37, 151. The new Rule does not foreclose any other form of consultation. For example, it can be accomplished through the mechanism of an "Advisory Committee" similar to that employed by the Supreme Court in connection with the Federal Rules themselves.

The amended Rule provides that a local rule will take effect upon the date specified by the district court and will remain in effect unless amended by the district court or abrogated by the judicial council. The effectiveness of a local rule should not be deferred until approved by the judicial council because that might unduly delay promulgation of a local rule that should become effective immediately, especially since some councils do not meet frequently. Similarly, it was thought that to delay a local rule's effectiveness for a fixed period of time would be arbitrary and that to require the judicial council to abrogate a local rule within a specified time would be inconsistent with its power under 28 U.S.C. § 332 (1976) to nullify a local rule at any time. The expectation is that the judicial council will examine all local rules, including those currently in effect, with an eye toward determining whether they are valid and consistent with the Federal Rules, promote inter-district uniformity and efficiency, and do not undermine the basic objectives of the Federal Rules.

The amended Rule requires copies of local rules to be sent upon their promulgation to the judicial council and the Administrative Office of the United

---

New matter is shown in italics; matter to be omitted is lined through

States Courts rather than to the Supreme Court. The Supreme Court was the appropriate filing place in 1938, when Rule 83 originally was promulgated, but the establishment of the Administrative Office makes it a more logical place to develop a centralized file of local rules. This procedure is consistent with both the Criminal and the Appellate Rules. See Fed. R. Crim. P. 57(a); Fed. R. App. P. 47. The Administrative Office also will be able to provide improved utilization of the file because of its recent development of a Local Rules Index.

The practice pursued by some judges of issuing standing orders has been controversial, particularly among members of the practicing bar. The last sentence in Rule 83 has been amended to make certain that standing orders are not inconsistent with the Federal Rules or any local district court rules. Beyond that, it is hoped that each district will adopt procedures, perhaps by local rule, for promulgating and reviewing single-judge standing orders.

New matter is shown in italics; matter to be omitted is lined through

FEDERAL RULES OF APPELLATE PROCEDURE

(with some omissions)

TABLE OF RULES

Title I. Applicability of Rules

RULES OF APPELLATE PROCEDURE

Appendix of Forms

FEDERAL RULES OF APPELLATE PROCEDURE

(with some omissions)

TITLE I. APPLICABILITY OF RULES

Rule 1.

SCOPE OF RULES

(a) **Scope of Rules.** These rules govern procedure in appeals to United States courts of appeals from the United States district courts and the United States Tax Court; in appeals from bankruptcy appellate panels; in proceedings in the courts of appeals for review or enforcement of orders of administrative agencies, boards, commissions and officers of the United States; and in applications for writs or other relief which a court of appeals or a judge thereof is competent to give. When these rules provide for the making of a motion or application in the district court, the procedure for making such motion or application shall be in accordance with the practice of the district court.

(b) **Rules Not to Affect Jurisdiction.** These rules shall not be construed to extend or limit the jurisdiction of the courts of appeals as established by law.

As amended 1979, 1989.

Rule 2.

SUSPENSION OF RULES

In the interest of expediting decision, or for other good cause shown, a court of appeals may, except as otherwise provided in Rule 26(b), suspend the requirements or provisions of any of these rules in a particular case on application of a party or on its own motion and may order proceedings in accordance with its direction.

TITLE II. APPEALS FROM JUDGMENTS AND ORDERS OF DISTRICT COURTS

Rule 3.

APPEAL AS OF RIGHT—HOW TAKEN

(a) **Filing the Notice of Appeal.** An appeal permitted by law as of right from a district court to a court of appeals shall be taken by filing a notice of appeal with the clerk of the district court within the time allowed by Rule 4. Failure of an appellant to take any step other than the timely filing of a notice of appeal does not affect the validity of the appeal, but is ground only for such action as the court of appeals deems appropriate, which may include dismissal of the appeal. Appeals by permission under 28 U.S.C. § 1292(b) and appeals in bankruptcy shall be taken in the manner prescribed by Rule 5 and Rule 6, respectively.

(b) **Joint or Consolidated Appeals.** If two or more persons are entitled to appeal from a judgment or order of a district court and their interests are such as to make joinder practicable, they may file a joint notice of appeal, or may join in appeal after filing separate timely notices of appeal, and they may thereafter proceed on appeal as a single appellant. Appeals may be consolidated by order of the court of appeals upon its own motion or upon motion of a party, or by stipulation of the parties to the several appeals.

(c) **Content of the Notice of Appeal.** The notice of appeal shall specify the party or parties taking the appeal; shall designate the judgment, order or part thereof appealed from; and shall name the court to which the appeal is taken. Form 1 in the Appendix of Forms is a suggested form of a notice of appeal. An appeal shall not be dismissed for informality of form or title of the notice of appeal.

(d) **Service of the Notice of Appeal.** The clerk of the district court shall serve notice of the filing of a notice of appeal by mailing a copy thereof to counsel of record of each party other than the appellant, or, if a party is not represented by counsel, to the last known address of that party; and the clerk shall transmit forthwith a copy of the notice of appeal and of the docket entries to the clerk of the court of appeals named in the notice. When an appeal is taken by a defendant in a criminal case, the clerk shall also serve a copy of the notice of appeal upon the defendant, either by personal service or by mail addressed to the defendant. The clerk shall note on each copy served the date on which the notice of appeal was filed. Failure of the clerk to serve notice shall not affect the validity of the appeal. Service shall be sufficient notwithstanding the death of a party or the party's counsel. The clerk shall note in the docket the names of the parties to whom the clerk mails copies, with the date of mailing.

(e) **Payment of Fees.** Upon the filing of any separate or joint notice of appeal from the district court, the appellant shall pay to the clerk of the district court such fees as are established by statute, and also the docket fee prescribed by the Judicial Conference of the United States, the latter to be received by the clerk of the district court on behalf of the court of appeals.

As amended 1979, 1986, 1989.

Rule 3.1.

APPEALS FROM JUDGMENTS ENTERED BY MAGISTRATES IN CIVIL CASES [OMITTED]

Rule 4.

APPEAL AS OF RIGHT—WHEN TAKEN

(a) **Appeals in Civil Cases.**

(1) In a civil case in which an appeal is permitted by law as of right from a district court to a court of appeals the notice of appeal required by Rule 3 shall be filed with the clerk of the district court within 30 days after the date of entry of the judgment or order appealed from; but if the United States or an officer or agency thereof is a party, the notice of appeal may be filed by any party within 60 days after such entry. If a notice of appeal is mistakenly filed in the court of appeals, the clerk of the court of appeals shall note thereon the date on which it was received and transmit it to the clerk of the district court and it shall be deemed filed in the district court on the date so noted.

(2) Except as provided in (a)(4) of this Rule 4, a notice of appeal filed after the announcement of a decision or order but before the entry of the judgment or order shall be treated as filed after such entry and on the day thereof.

(3) If a timely notice of appeal is filed by a party, any other party may file a notice of appeal within 14 days after the date on which the first notice of appeal was filed, or within the time otherwise prescribed by this Rule 4(a), whichever period last expires.

(4) If a timely motion under the Federal Rules of Civil Procedure is filed in the district court by any party: (i) for judgment under Rule 50(b); (ii) under Rule 52(b) to amend or make additional findings of fact, whether or not an alteration of the judgment

would be required if the motion is granted; (iii) under Rule 59 to alter or amend the judgment; or (iv) under Rule 59 for a new trial, the time for appeal for all parties shall run from the entry of the order denying a new trial or granting or denying any other such motion. A notice of appeal filed before the disposition of any of the above motions shall have no effect. A new notice of appeal must be filed within the prescribed time measured from the entry of the order disposing of the motion as provided above. No additional fees shall be required for such filing.

(5) The district court, upon a showing of excusable neglect or good cause, may extend the time for filing a notice of appeal upon motion filed not later than 30 days after the expiration of the time prescribed by this Rule 4(a). Any such motion which is filed before expiration of the prescribed time may be ex parte unless the court otherwise requires. Notice of any such motion which is filed after expiration of the prescribed time shall be given to the other parties in accordance with local rules. No such extension shall exceed 30 days past such prescribed time or 10 days from the date of entry of the order granting the motion, whichever occurs later.

(6) A judgment or order is entered within the meaning of this Rule 4(a) when it is entered in compliance with Rules 58 and 79(a) of the Federal Rules of Civil Procedure.

(b) Appeals in Criminal Cases. In a criminal case the notice of appeal by a defendant shall be filed in the district court within 10 days after the entry of (i) the judgment or order appealed from or (ii) a notice of appeal by the Government. A notice of appeal filed after the announcement of a decision, sentence or order but before entry of the judgment or order shall be treated as filed after such entry and on the day thereof. If a timely motion in arrest of judgment or for a new trial on any ground other than newly discovered evidence has been made, an appeal from a judgment of conviction may be taken within 10 days after the entry of an order denying the motion. A motion for a new trial based on the ground of newly discovered evidence will similarly extend the time for appeal from a judgment of conviction if the motion is made before or within 10 days after entry of the judgment. When an appeal by the government is authorized by statute, the notice of appeal shall be filed in the district court within 30 days after the entry of (i) the judgment or order appealed from or (ii) a notice of appeal by any defendant. A judgment or order is entered within the meaning of this subdivision when it is entered in the criminal docket. Upon a showing of excusable neglect the district court may, before or after the time has expired, with or without motion and notice, extend the time for filing a notice of appeal for a period not to exceed 30 days from the expiration of the time otherwise prescribed by this subdivision.

As amended 1979, 1988.

Rule 5.

APPEALS BY PERMISSION UNDER 28 U.S.C. § 1292(b)

(a) Petition for Permission to Appeal. An appeal from an interlocutory order containing the statement prescribed by 28 U.S.C. § 1292(b) may be sought by filing a petition for permission to appeal with the clerk of the court of appeals within 10 days after the entry of such order in the district court with proof of service on all other parties to the action in the district court. An order may be amended to include the prescribed statement at any time, and permission to appeal may be sought within 10 days after entry of the order as amended.

(b) Content of Petition; Answer. The petition shall contain a statement of the facts necessary to an understanding of the controlling question of law determined by the order of the district court; a statement of the question itself; and a statement of the reasons why a substantial basis exists for a difference of opinion on the question and why an immediate appeal may materially advance the termination of the litigation. The petition shall include or have annexed thereto a copy of the order from which appeal is sought and of any findings of fact, conclusions of law and opinion relating thereto. Within 7 days after service of the petition an adverse party may file an answer in opposition. The application and answer shall be submitted without oral argument unless otherwise ordered.

(c) Form of Papers; Number of Copies. All papers may be typewritten. Three copies shall be filed with the original, but the court may require that additional copies be furnished.

(d) Grant of Permission; Cost Bond; Filing of Record. Within 10 days after the entry of an order granting permission to appeal the appellant shall (1) pay to the clerk of the district court the fees established by statute and the docket fee prescribed by the Judicial Conference of the United States and (2) file a bond for costs if required pursuant to Rule 7. The clerk of the district court shall notify the clerk of the court of appeals of the payment of the fees. Upon receipt of such notice the clerk of the court of appeals shall enter the appeal upon the docket. The record shall be transmitted and filed in accordance with Rules 11 and 12(b). A notice of appeal need not be filed.

As amended 1979.

Rule 5.1.

APPEALS BY PERMISSION UNDER 28 U.S.C. § 636(c)(5) [OMITTED]

Rule 6.

APPEALS IN BANKRUPTCY CASES FROM FINAL JUDGMENTS AND ORDERS OF DISTRICT COURTS OR OF BANKRUPTCY APPELLATE PANELS [OMITTED]

Rule 7.

BOND FOR COSTS ON APPEAL IN CIVIL CASES

The district court may require an appellant to file a bond or provide other security in such form and amount as it finds necessary to ensure payment of costs on appeal in a civil case. The provisions of Rule 8(b) apply to a surety upon a bond given pursuant to this rule.

As amended 1979.

Rule 8.

STAY OR INJUNCTION PENDING APPEAL

(a) **Stay Must Ordinarily Be Sought in the First Instance in District Court; Motion for Stay in Court of Appeals.** Application for a stay of the judgment or order of a district court pending appeal, or for approval of a supersedeas bond, or for an order suspending, modifying, restoring or granting an injunction during the pendency of an appeal must ordinarily be made in the first instance in the district court. A motion for such relief may be made to the court of appeals or to a judge thereof, but the motion shall show that application to the district court for the relief sought is not practicable, or that the district court has denied an application, or has failed to afford the relief which the applicant requested, with the reasons given by the district court for its action. The motion shall also show the reasons for the relief requested and the facts relied upon, and if the facts are subject to dispute the motion shall be supported by affidavits or other sworn statements or copies thereof. With the motion shall be filed such parts of the record as are relevant. Reasonable notice of the motion shall be given to all parties. The motion shall be filed with the clerk and normally will be considered by a panel or division of the court, but in exceptional cases where such procedure would be impracticable due to the requirements of time, the application may be made to and considered by a single judge of the court.

(b) Stay May Be Conditioned upon Giving of Bond; Proceedings Against Sureties. Relief available in the court of appeals under this rule may be conditioned upon the filing of a bond or other appropriate security in the district court. If security is given in the form of a bond or stipulation or other undertaking with one or more sureties, each surety submits to the jurisdiction of the district court and irrevocably appoints the clerk of the district court as the surety's agent upon whom any papers affecting the surety's liability on the bond or undertaking may be served. A surety's liability may be enforced on motion in the district court without the necessity of an independent action. The motion and such notice of the motion as the district court prescribes may be served on the clerk of the district court, who shall forthwith mail copies to the sureties if their addresses are known.

(c) Stays in Criminal Cases. Stays in criminal cases shall be had in accordance with the provisions of Rule 38(a) of the Federal Rules of Criminal Procedure.

As amended 1986.

Rule 9.

RELEASE IN CRIMINAL CASES [OMITTED]

Rule 10.

THE RECORD ON APPEAL

(a) Composition of the Record on Appeal. The original papers and exhibits filed in the district court, the transcript of proceedings, if any, and a certified copy of the docket entries prepared by the clerk of the district court shall constitute the record on appeal in all cases.

(b) The Transcript of Proceedings; Duty of Appellant to Order; Notice to Appellee if Partial Transcript Is Ordered.

(1) Within 10 days after filing the notice of appeal the appellant shall order from the reporter a transcript of such parts of the proceedings not already on file as the appellant deems necessary, subject to local rules of the courts of appeals. The order shall be in writing and within the same period a copy shall be filed with the clerk of the district court. If funding is to come from the United States under the Criminal Justice Act, the order shall so state. If no such parts of the proceedings are to be ordered, within the same period the appellant shall file a certificate to that effect.

(2) If the appellant intends to urge on appeal that a finding or conclusion is unsupported by the evidence or is contrary to the evidence, the appellant shall include in the record a transcript of all evidence relevant to such finding or conclusion.

(3) Unless the entire transcript is to be included, the appellant shall, within the 10 days time provided in (b)(1) of this Rule 10, file a statement of the issues the appellant intends to present on the appeal and shall serve on the appellee a copy of the order or certificate and of the statement. If the appellee deems a transcript of other parts of the proceedings to be necessary, the appellee shall, within 10 days after the service of the order or certificate and the statement of the appellant, file and serve on the appellant a designation of additional parts to be included. Unless within 10 days after service of such designation the appellant has ordered such parts, and has so notified the appellee, the appellee may within the following 10 days either order the parts or move in the district court for an order requiring the appellant to do so.

(4) At the time of ordering, a party must make satisfactory arrangements with the reporter for payment of the cost of the transcript.

(c) Statement of the Evidence or Proceedings when No Report Was Made or when the Transcript Is Unavailable. If no report of the evidence or proceedings at a hearing or trial was made, or if a transcript is unavailable, the appellant may prepare a statement of the evidence or proceedings from the best available means, including the appellant's recollection. The statement shall be served on the appellee, who may serve objections or propose amendments thereto within 10 days after service. Thereupon the statement and any objections or proposed amendments shall be submitted to the district court for settlement and approval and as settled and approved shall be included by the clerk of the district court in the record on appeal.

(d) Agreed Statement as the Record on Appeal. In lieu of the record on appeal as defined in subdivision (a) of this rule, the parties may prepare and sign a statement of the case showing how the issues presented by the appeal arose and were decided in the district court and setting forth only so many of the facts averred and proved or sought to be proved as are essential to a decision of the issues presented. If the statement conforms to the truth, it, together with such additions as the court may consider necessary fully to present the issues raised by the appeal, shall be approved by the district court and shall then be certified to the court of appeals as the record on appeal and transmitted thereto by the clerk of the district court within the time provided by Rule 11.

Copies of the agreed statement may be filed as the appendix required by Rule 30.

(e) Correction or Modification of the Record. If any difference arises as to whether the record truly discloses what occurred in the district court, the difference shall be submitted to and settled by that court and the record made to conform to the truth. If anything material to either party is omitted from the record by error or accident or is misstated therein, the parties by stipulation, or the district court either before or after the record is transmitted to the court of appeals, or the court of appeals, on proper suggestion or of its own initiative, may direct that the omission or misstatement be corrected, and if necessary that a supplemental record be certified and transmitted. All other questions as to the form and content of the record shall be presented to the court of appeals.

As amended 1979, 1986.

Rule 11.

TRANSMISSION OF THE RECORD

(a) Duty of Appellant. After filing the notice of appeal the appellant, or in the event that more than one appeal is taken, each appellant, shall comply with the provisions of Rule 10(b) and shall take any other action necessary to enable the clerk to assemble and transmit the record. A single record shall be transmitted.

(b) Duty of Reporter to Prepare and File Transcript; Notice to Court of Appeals; Duty of Clerk to Transmit the Record. Upon receipt of an order for a transcript, the reporter shall acknowledge at the foot of the order the fact that the reporter has received it and the date on which the reporter expects to have the transcript completed and shall transmit the order, so endorsed, to the clerk of the court of appeals. If the transcript cannot be completed within 30 days of receipt of the order the reporter shall request an extension of time from the clerk of the court of appeals and the action of the clerk of the court of appeals shall be entered on the docket and the parties notified. In the event of the failure of the reporter to file the transcript within the time allowed, the clerk of the court of appeals shall notify the district judge and take such other steps as may be directed by the court of appeals. Upon completion of the transcript the reporter shall file it with the clerk of the district court and shall notify the clerk of the court of appeals that the reporter has done so.

When the record is complete for purposes of the appeal, the clerk of the district court shall transmit it forthwith to the clerk of the court of appeals. The clerk of the district court shall number the documents comprising the record and shall transmit with the record a list of documents correspondingly numbered and identified with reasonable definiteness. Documents of unusual bulk or weight, physical exhibits other than documents, and such other parts of the record as the court of appeals may designated by local rule, shall not be transmitted by the clerk unless the clerk is directed to do so by a party or by the clerk of the court of appeals. A party must make advance arrangements with the clerks for the transportation and receipt of exhibits of unusual bulk or weight.

(c) **Temporary Retention of Record in District Court for Use in Preparing Appellate Papers.** Notwithstanding the provisions of (a) and (b) of this Rule 11, the parties may stipulate, or the district court on motion of any party may order, that the clerk of the district court shall temporarily retain the record for use by the parties in preparing appellate papers. In that event the clerk of the district court shall certify to the clerk of the court of appeals that the record, including the transcript or parts thereof designated for inclusion and all necessary exhibits, is complete for purposes of the appeal. Upon receipt of the brief of the appellee, or at such earlier time as the parties may agree or the court may order, the appellant shall request the clerk of the district court to transmit the record.

(d) **Extension of Time for Transmission of the Record; Reduction of Time.** Abrogated Apr. 30, 1979, eff. Aug. 1, 1979.

(e) **Retention of the Record in the District Court by Order of Court.** The court of appeals may provide by rule or order that a certified copy of the docket entries shall be transmitted in lieu of the entire record, subject to the right of any party to request at any time during the pendency of the appeal that designated parts of the record be transmitted.

If the record or any part thereof is required in the district court for use there pending the appeal, the district court may make an order to that effect, and the clerk of the district court shall retain the record or parts thereof subject to the request of the court of appeals, and shall transmit a copy of the order and of the docket entries together with such parts of the original record as the district court shall allow and copies of such parts as the parties may designate.

(f) **Stipulation of Parties that Parts of the Record Be Retained in the District Court.** The parties may agree by written stipulation filed in the district court that designated parts of the record shall be retained in the district court unless thereafter the court of appeals shall order or any party shall request their transmittal. The parts thus designated shall nevertheless be a part of the record on appeal for all purposes.

(g) Record for Preliminary Hearing in the Court of Appeals. If prior to the time the record is transmitted a party desires to make in the court of appeals a motion for dismissal, for release, for a stay pending appeal, for additional security on the bond on appeal or on a supersedeas bond, or for any intermediate order, the clerk of the district court at the request of any party shall transmit to the court of appeals such parts of the original record as any party shall designate.

As amended 1979, 1986.

Rule 12.

DOCKETING THE APPEAL; FILING OF THE RECORD

(a) Docketing the Appeal. Upon receipt of the copy of the notice of appeal and of the docket entries, transmitted by the clerk of the district court pursuant to Rule 3(d), the clerk of the court of appeals shall thereupon enter the appeal upon the docket. An appeal shall be docketed under the title given to the action in the district court, with the appellant identified as such, but if such title does not contain the name of the appellant, the appellant's name, identified as appellant, shall be added to the title.

(b) Filing the Record, Partial Record, or Certificate. Upon receipt of the record transmitted pursuant to Rule 11(b), or the partial record transmitted pursuant to Rule 11(e), (f), or (g), or the clerk's certificate under Rule 11(c), the clerk of the court of appeals shall file it and shall immediately give notice to all parties of the date on which it was filed.

(c) Dismissal for Failure of Appellant to Cause Timely Transmission or to Docket Appeal. Abrogated Apr. 30, 1979, eff. Aug. 1, 1979.

As amended 1979, 1986.

TITLE III.   REVIEW OF DECISIONS OF THE UNITED STATES TAX COURT [OMITTED]

TITLE IV.   REVIEW AND ENFORCEMENT OF ORDERS OF ADMINISTRATIVE AGENCIES, BOARDS, COMMISSIONS AND OFFICERS [OMITTED]

TITLE V.   EXTRAORDINARY WRITS

Rule 21.

WRITS OF MANDAMUS AND PROHIBITION DIRECTED TO A JUDGE OR JUDGES AND OTHER EXTRAORDINARY WRITS

(a) Mandamus or Prohibition to a Judge or Judges; Petition for Writ; Service and Filing. Application for a writ of mandamus or of prohibition directed to a judge or judges shall be made by filing a petition therefor with the clerk of the court of appeals with proof of service on the respondent judge or judges and on all parties to the action in the trial court. The petition shall contain a statement of the facts necessary to an understanding of the issues presented by the application; a statement of the issues presented and of the relief sought; a statement of the reasons why the writ should issue; and copies of any order or opinion or parts of the record which may be essential to an understanding of the matters set forth in the petition. Upon receipt of the prescribed docket fee, the clerk shall docket the petition and submit it to the court.

(b) Denial; Order Directing Answer. If the court is of the opinion that the writ should not be granted, it shall deny the petition. Otherwise, it shall order that an answer to the petition be filed by the respondents within the time fixed by the order. The order shall be served by the clerk on the judge or judges named respondents and on all other parties to the action in the trial court. All parties below other than the petitioner shall also be deemed respondents for all purposes. Two or more respondents may answer jointly. If the judge or judges named respondents do not desire to appear in the proceeding, they may so advise the clerk and all parties by letter, but the petition shall not thereby be taken as admitted. The clerk shall advise the parties of the dates on which briefs are to be filed, if briefs are required, and of the date of oral argument. The proceeding shall be given preference over ordinary civil cases.

(c) Other Extraordinary Writs. Application for extraordinary writs other than those provided for in subdivisions (a) and (b) of this rule shall be made by petition filed with the clerk of the court of appeals with proof of service on the parties named as respondents. Proceedings on such application shall conform, so far as is practicable, to the procedure prescribed in subdivisions (a) and (b) of this rule.

(d) **Form of Papers; Number of Copies.** All papers may be typewritten. Three copies shall be filed with the original, but the court may direct that additional copies be furnished.

TITLE VI.   HABEAS CORPUS; PROCEEDINGS IN FORMA PAUPERIS

Rule 22.

HABEAS CORPUS PROCEEDINGS [OMITTED]

Rule 23.

CUSTODY OF PRISONERS IN HABEAS CORPUS PROCEEDINGS [OMITTED]

Rule 24.

PROCEEDINGS IN FORMA PAUPERIS

(a) **Leave to Proceed on Appeal in Forma Pauperis from District Court to Court of Appeals.** A party to an action in a district court who desires to proceed on appeal in forma pauperis shall file in the district court a motion for leave so to proceed, together with an affidavit, showing, in the detail prescribed by Form 4 of the Appendix of Forms, the party's inability to pay fees and costs or to give security therefor, the party's belief that that party is entitled to redress, and a statement of the issues which that party intends to present on appeal. If the motion is granted, the party may proceed without further application to the court of appeals and without prepayment of fees or costs in either court or the giving of security therefor. If the motion is denied, the district court shall state in writing the reasons for the denial.

Notwithstanding the provisions of the preceding paragraph, a party who has been permitted to proceed in an action in the district court in forma pauperis, or who has been permitted to proceed there as one who is financially unable to obtain an adequate defense in a criminal case, may proceed on appeal in forma pauperis without further authorization unless, before or after the notice of appeal is filed, the district court shall certify that the appeal is not taken in good faith or shall find that the party is otherwise not entitled so to proceed, in which event the district court shall state in writing the reasons for such certification or finding.

If a motion for leave to proceed on appeal in forma pauperis is denied by the district court, or if the district court shall certify that the appeal is not taken in good faith or shall find that the party is otherwise not entitled to proceed in forma pauperis, the clerk shall forthwith serve notice of such action. A motion for leave so to proceed may be filed in the court of appeals within 30 days after service of notice of the action of the district court. The motion shall be accompanied by a copy of the affidavit filed in the district court, or by the affidavit prescribed by the first paragraph of this subdivision if no affidavit has been filed in the district court, and by a copy of the statement of reasons given by the district court for its action.

(b) **Leave to Proceed on Appeal or Review in Forma Pauperis in Administrative Agency Proceedings.** A party to a proceeding before an administrative agency, board, commission or officer (including, for the purpose of this rule, the United States Tax Court) who desires to proceed on appeal or review in a court of appeals in forma pauperis, when such appeal or review may be had directly in a court of appeals, shall file in the court of appeals a motion for leave so to proceed, together with the affidavit prescribed by the first paragraph of (a) of this Rule 24.

(c) **Form of Briefs, Appendices and Other Papers.** Parties allowed to proceed in forma pauperis may file briefs, appendices and other papers in typewritten form, and may request that the appeal be heard on the original record without the necessity of reproducing parts thereof in any form.

As amended 1979, 1986.

TITLE VII.   GENERAL PROVISIONS

Rule 25.

FILING AND SERVICE

(a) **Filing.** Papers required or permitted to be filed in a court of appeals shall be filed with the clerk. Filing may be accomplished by mail addressed to the clerk, but filing shall not be timely unless the papers are received by the clerk within the time fixed for filing, except that briefs and appendices shall be deemed filed on the day of mailing if the most expeditious form of delivery by mail, excepting special delivery, is utilized. If a motion requests relief which may be granted by a single judge, the judge may permit the motion to be filed with the judge, in which event the judge shall note thereon the date of filing and shall thereafter transmit it to the clerk.

(b) Service of All Papers Required. Copies of all papers filed by any party and not required by these rules to be served by the clerk shall, at or before the time of filing, be served by a party or person acting for that party on all other parties to the appeal or review. Service on a party represented by counsel shall be made on counsel.

(c) Manner of Service. Service may be personal or by mail. Personal service includes delivery of the copy to a clerk or other responsible person at the office of counsel. Service by mail is complete on mailing.

(d) Proof of Service. Papers presented for filing shall contain an acknowledgment of service by the person served or proof of service in the form of a statement of the date and manner of service and of the names of the person served, certified by the person who made service. Proof of service may appear on or be affixed to the papers filed. The clerk may permit papers to be filed without acknowledgment or proof of service but shall require such to be filed promptly thereafter.

As amended 1986.

Rule 26.

COMPUTATION AND EXTENSION OF TIME

(a) Computation of Time. In computing any period of time prescribed or allowed by these rules, by an order of court, or by any applicable statute, the day of the act, event, or default from which the designated period of time begins to run shall not be included. The last day of the period so computed shall be included, unless it is a Saturday, a Sunday, or a legal holiday, or, when the act to be done is the filing of a paper in court, a day on which weather or other conditions have made the office of the clerk of the court inaccessible, in which event the period runs until the end of the next day which is not one of the aforementioned days. When the period of time prescribed or allowed is less than 7 days, intermediate Saturdays, Sundays, and legal holidays shall be excluded in the computation. As used in this rule "legal holiday" includes New Year's Day, Birthday of Martin Luther King, Jr., Washington's Birthday, Memorial Day, Independence Day, Labor Day, Columbus Day, Veterans Day, Thanksgiving Day, Christmas Day, and any other day appointed as a holiday by the President or the Congress of the United States. It shall also include a day appointed as a holiday by the state wherein the district court which rendered the judgment or order which is or may be appealed from is situated, or by the state wherein the principal office of the clerk of the court of appeals in which the appeal is pending is located.

(b) Enlargement of Time. The court for good cause shown may upon motion enlarge the time prescribed by these rules or by its order for doing any act, or may permit an act to be done after the expiration of such time; but the court may not enlarge the time for filing a notice of appeal, a petition for allowance, or a petition for permission to appeal. Nor may the court enlarge the time prescribed by law for filing a petition to enjoin, set aside, suspend, modify, enforce or otherwise review, or a notice of appeal from, an order of an administrative agency, board, commission or officer of the United States, except as specifically authorized by law.

(c) Additional Time After Service by Mail. Whenever a party is required or permitted to do an act within a prescribed period after service of a paper upon that party and the paper is served by mail, 3 days shall be added to the prescribed period.

As amended 1971, 1986, 1989.

Rule 26.1.

CORPORATE DISCLOSURE STATEMENT

Any non-governmental corporate body party to a civil or bankruptcy case or agency review proceeding and any non-governmental corporate defendant in a criminal case shall file a statement identifying all parent companies, subsidiaries (except wholly-owned subsidiaries), and affiliates that have issued shares to the public. The statement shall be filed with a party's principal brief or upon filing a motion, response, petition or answer in the court of appeals, whichever first occurs, unless a local rule requires earlier filing. The statement shall be included in front of the table of contents in a party's principal brief even if the statement was previously filed.

Added 1989.

Rule 27.

MOTIONS

(a) Content of Motions; Response. Unless another form is elsewhere prescribed by these rules, an application for an order or other relief shall be made by filing a motion for such order or relief with proof of service on all other parties. The motion shall contain or be accompanied by any matter required by a specific provision of these rules governing such a motion, shall state with particularity the grounds on which it is based, and shall set forth the order or relief sought. If a motion is supported by briefs, affidavits or other papers, they shall be served and filed with the motion. Any party may file a response in opposition to a motion other than one for a procedural order [for which see subdivision (b)] within 7 days after service of the motion, but motions authorized by Rules 8, 9, 18 and 41 may be acted upon after reasonable notice, and the court may shorten or extend the time for responding to any motion.

(b) **Determination of Motions for Procedural Orders.** Notwithstanding the provisions of (a) of this Rule 27 as to motions generally, motions for procedural orders, including any motion under Rule 26(b), may be acted upon at any time, without awaiting a response thereto, and pursuant to rule or order of the court, motions for specified types of procedural orders may be disposed of by the clerk. Any party adversely affected by such action may by application to the court request consideration, vacation or modification of such action.

(c) **Power of a Single Judge to Entertain Motions.** In addition to the authority expressly conferred by these rules or by law, a single judge of a court of appeals may entertain and may grant or deny any request for relief which under these rules may properly be sought by motion, except that a single judge may not dismiss or otherwise determine an appeal or other proceeding, and except that a court of appeals may provide by order or rule that any motion or class of motions must be acted upon by the court. The action of a single judge may be reviewed by the court.

(d) **Form of Papers; Number of Copies.** All papers relating to motions may be typewritten. Three copies shall be filed with the original, but the court may require that additional copies be furnished.

As amended 1979, 1989.

Rule 28.

BRIEFS

(a) **Brief of the Appellant.** The brief of the appellant shall contain under appropriate headings and in the order here indicated:

(1) A table of contents, with page references, and a table of cases (alphabetically arranged), statutes and other authorities

cited, with references to the pages of the brief where they are cited.

(2) A statement of the issues presented for review.

(3) A statement of the case. The statement shall first indicate briefly the nature of the case, the course of proceedings, and its disposition in the court below. There shall follow a statement of the facts relevant to the issues presented for review, with appropriate references to the record (see subdivision (e)).

(4) An argument. The argument may be preceded by a summary. The argument shall contain the contentions of the appellant with respect to the issues presented, and the reasons therefor, with citations to the authorities, statutes and parts of the record relied on.

(5) A short conclusion stating the precise relief sought.

(b) Brief of the Appellee. The brief of the appellee shall conform to the requirements of subdivision (a)(1)–(4), except that a statement of the issues or of the case need not be made unless the appellee is dissatisfied with the statement of the appellant.

(c) Reply Brief. The appellant may file a brief in reply to the brief of the appellee, and if the appellee has cross-appealed, the appellee may file a brief in reply to the response of the appellant to the issues presented by the cross appeal. No further briefs may be filed except with leave of court. All reply briefs shall contain a table of contents, with page references, and a table of cases (alphabetically arranged), statutes and other authorities cited, with references to the pages of the reply brief where they are cited.

(d) References in Briefs to Parties. Counsel will be expected in their briefs and oral arguments to keep to a minimum references to parties by such designations as "appellant" and "appellee". It promotes clarity to use the designations used in the lower court or in the agency proceedings, or the actual names of parties, or descriptive terms such as "the employee," "the injured person," "the taxpayer," "the ship," "the stevedore," etc.

(e) References in Briefs to the Record. References in the briefs to parts of the record reproduced in the appendix filed with the brief of the appellant (see Rule 30(a)) shall be to the pages of the appendix at which those parts appear. If the appendix is prepared after the briefs are filed, references in the briefs to the record shall be made by one of the methods allowed by Rule 30(c). If the record is reproduced in accordance with the provisions of Rule 30(f), or if references are made in the briefs to parts of the record not reproduced, the references shall be to the pages of the parts of the record involved; e.g., Answer p. 7, Motion for Judgment p. 2, Transcript p. 231. Intelligible abbreviations may be used. If reference is made to evidence the admissibility of which is in controversy, reference shall be made to the pages of the appendix or of the transcript at which the evidence was identified, offered, and received or rejected.

(f) Reproduction of Statutes, Rules, Regulations, Etc. If determination of the issues presented requires the study of statutes, rules, regulations, etc. or relevant parts thereof, they shall be reproduced in the brief or in an addendum at the end, or they may be supplied to the court in pamphlet form.

(g) Length of Briefs. Except by permission of the court, or as specified by local rule of the court of appeals, principal briefs shall not exceed 50 pages, and reply briefs shall not exceed 25 pages, exclusive of pages containing the corporate disclosure statement, table of contents, tables of citations and any addendum containing statutes, rules, regulations, etc.

(h) Briefs in Cases Involving Cross Appeals. If a cross appeal is filed, the plaintiff in the court below shall be deemed the appellant for the purposes of this rule and Rules 30 and 31, unless the parties otherwise agree or the court otherwise orders. The brief of the appellee shall contain the issues and argument involved in his appeal as well as the answer to the brief of the appellant.

(i) Briefs in Cases Involving Multiple Appellants or Appellees. In cases involving more than one appellant or appellee, including cases consolidated for purposes of the appeal, any number of either may join in a single brief, and any appellant or appellee may adopt by reference any part of the brief of another. Parties may similarly join in reply briefs.

(j) Citation of Supplemental Authorities. When pertinent and significant authorities come to the attention of a party after the party's brief has been filed, or after oral argument but before decision, a party may promptly advise the clerk of the court, by letter, with a copy to all counsel, setting forth the citations. There shall be a reference either to the page of the brief or to a point argued orally to which the citations pertain, but the letter shall without argument state the reasons for the supplemental citations. Any response shall be made promptly and shall be similarly limited.

As amended 1979, 1986, 1989.

Rule 29.

BRIEF OF AN AMICUS CURIAE

A brief of an amicus curiae may be filed only if accompanied by written consent of all parties, or by leave of court granted on motion or at the request of the court, except that consent or leave shall not be required when the brief is presented by the United States or an officer or agency thereof, or by a State, Territory or Commonwealth. The brief may be conditionally filed with the motion for leave. A motion for leave shall identify the interest of the applicant and shall state the reasons why a brief of an amicus curiae is desirable. Save as all parties otherwise consent, any amicus curiae shall file its brief within the time allowed the party whose position as to affirmance or reversal the amicus brief will support unless the court for cause shown shall grant leave for later filing, in which event it shall specify within what period an opposing party may answer. A motion of an amicus curiae to participate in the oral argument will be granted only for extraordinary reasons.

Rule 30.

APPENDIX TO THE BRIEFS

(a) **Duty of Appellant to Prepare and File; Content of Appendix; Time for Filing; Number of Copies.** The appellant shall prepare and file an appendix to the briefs which shall contain: (1) the relevant docket entries in the proceeding below; (2) any relevant portions of the pleadings, charge, findings or opinion; (3) the judgment, order or decision in question; and (4) any other parts of the record to which the parties wish to direct the particular attention of the court. Except where they have independent relevance, memoranda of law in the district court should not be included in the appendix. The fact that parts of the record are not included in the appendix shall not prevent the parties or the court from relying on such parts.

Unless filing is to be deferred pursuant to the provisions of subdivision (c) of this rule, the appellant shall serve and file the appendix with the brief. Ten copies of the appendix shall be filed with the clerk, and one copy shall be served on counsel for each party separately represented, unless the court shall by rule or order direct the filing or service of a lesser number.

(b) **Determination of Contents of Appendix; Cost of Producing.** The parties are encouraged to agree as to the contents of the appendix. In the absence of agreement, the appellant shall, not later than 10 days after the date on which the record is filed, serve on the appellee a designation of the parts of the record which the appellant intends to include in the appendix and a statement of the issues which the appellant intends to present for review. If the appellee deems it necessary to direct the particular attention of the court to parts of the record not designated by the appellant, the appellee shall, within 10 days after receipt of the designation, serve upon the appellant a designation of those parts. The appellant shall include in the appendix the parts thus designated. In designating parts of the record for inclusion in the appendix, the parties shall have regard for the fact that the entire record is always available to the court for reference and examination and shall not engage in unnecessary designation.

Unless the parties otherwise agree, the cost of producing the appendix shall initially be paid by the appellant, but if the appellant considers that parts of the record designated by the appellee for inclusion are unnecessary for the determination of the issues presented the appellant may so advise the appellee and the appellee shall advance the cost of including such parts. The cost of producing the appendix shall be taxed as costs in the case, but if either party shall cause matters to be included in the appendix unnecessarily the court may impose the cost of producing such parts on the party. Each circuit shall provide by local rule for the imposition of sanctions against attorneys who unreasonably and vexatiously increase the costs of litigation through the inclusion of unnecessary material in the appendix.

(c) Alternative Method of Designating Contents of the Appendix; how References to the Record May Be Made in the Briefs when Alternative Method Is Used. If the court shall so provide by rule for classes of cases or by order in specific cases, preparation of the appendix may be deferred until after the briefs have been filed, and the appendix may be filed 21 days after service of the brief of the appellee. If the preparation and filing of the appendix is thus deferred, the provisions of subdivision (b) of this Rule 30 shall apply, except that the designations referred to therein shall be made by each party at the time each brief is served, and a statement of the issues presented shall be unnecessary.

If the deferred appendix authorized by this subdivision is employed, references in the briefs to the record may be to the pages of the parts of the record involved, in which event the original paging of each part of the record shall be indicated in the appendix by placing in brackets the number of each page at the place in the appendix where that page begins. Or if a party desires to refer in a brief directly to pages of the appendix, that party may serve and file typewritten or page proof copies of the brief within the time required by Rule 31(a), with appropriate references to the pages of the parts of the record involved. In that event, within 14 days after the appendix is filed the party shall serve and file copies of the brief in the form prescribed by Rule 32(a) containing references to the pages of the appendix in place of or in addition to the initial references to the pages of the parts of the record involved. No other changes may be made in the brief as initially served and filed, except that typographical errors may be corrected.

(d) **Arrangement of the Appendix.** At the beginning of the appendix there shall be inserted a list of the parts of the record which it contains, in the order in which the parts are set out therein, with references to the pages of the appendix at which each part begins. The relevant docket entries shall be set out following the list of contents. Thereafter, other parts of the record shall be set out in chronological order. When matter contained in the reporter's transcript of proceedings is set out in the appendix, the page of the transcript at which such matter may be found shall be indicated in brackets immediately before the matter which is set out. Omissions in the text of papers or of the transcript must be indicated by asterisks. Immaterial formal matters (captions, subscriptions, acknowledgments, etc.) shall be omitted. A question and its answer may be contained in a single paragraph.

(e) **Reproduction of Exhibits.** Exhibits designated for inclusion in the appendix may be contained in a separate volume, or volumes, suitably indexed. Four copies thereof shall be filed with the appendix and one copy shall be served on counsel for each party separately represented. The transcript of a proceeding before an administrative agency, board, commission or officer used in an action in the district court shall be regarded as an exhibit for the purpose of this subdivision.

(f) **Hearing of Appeals on the Original Record Without the Necessity of an Appendix.** A court of appeals may by rule applicable to all cases, or to classes of cases, or by order in specific cases, dispense with the requirement of an appendix and permit appeals to be heard on the original record, with such copies of the record, or relevant parts thereof, as the court may require.

As amended 1970, 1986.

Rule 31.

FILING AND SERVICE OF BRIEFS

(a) **Time for Serving and Filing Briefs.** The appellant shall serve and file a brief within 40 days after the date on which the record is filed. The appellee shall serve and file a brief within 30 days after service of the brief of the appellant. The appellant may serve and file a reply brief within 14 days after service of the brief of the appellee, but, except for good cause shown, a reply brief must be filed at least 3 days before argument. If a court of appeals is prepared to consider cases on the merits promptly after briefs are filed, and its practice is to do so, it may shorten the periods prescribed above for serving and filing briefs, either by rule for all cases or for classes of cases, or by order for specific cases.

(b) **Number of Copies to Be Filed and Served.** Twenty-five copies of each brief shall be filed with the clerk, unless the court by order in a particular case shall direct a lesser number, and two copies shall be served on counsel for each party separately represented. If a party is allowed to file typewritten ribbon and carbon copies of the brief, the original and three legible copies shall be filed with the clerk, and one copy shall be served on counsel for each party separately represented.

(c) **Consequence of Failure to File Briefs.** If an appellant fails to file a brief within the time provided by this rule, or within the time as extended, an appellee may move for dismissal of the appeal. If an appellee fails to file a brief, the appellee will not be heard at oral argument except by permission of the court.

As amended 1970, 1986.

Rule 32.

FORM OF BRIEFS, THE APPENDIX AND OTHER PAPERS

(a) **Form of Briefs and the Appendix.** Briefs and appendices may be produced by standard typographic printing or by any duplicating or copying process which produces a clear black image on white paper. Carbon copies of briefs and appendices may not be submitted without permission of the court, except in behalf of parties allowed to proceed in forma pauperis. All printed matter must appear in at least 11 point type on opaque, unglazed paper. Briefs and appendices produced by the standard typographic process shall be bound in volumes having pages 6⅛ by 9¼ inches and type matter 4⅙ by 7⅙ inches. Those produced by any other process shall be bound in volumes having pages not exceeding 8½ by 11 inches and type matter not exceeding 6½ by 9½ inches, with double spacing between each line of text. In patent cases the pages of briefs and appendices may be of such size as is necessary to utilize copies of patent documents. Copies of the reporter's transcript and other papers reproduced in a manner authorized by this rule may be inserted in the appendix; such pages may be informally renumbered if necessary.

If briefs are produced by commercial printing or duplicating firms, or, if produced otherwise and the covers to be described are available, the cover of the brief of the appellant should be blue; that of the appellee, red; that of an intervenor or amicus curiae, green; that of any reply brief, gray. The cover of the appendix, if separately printed, should be white. The front covers of the briefs and of appendices, if separately printed, shall contain: (1) the name of the court and the number of the case; (2) the title of the case (see Rule 12(a)); (3) the nature of the proceeding in the court (e. g., Appeal; Petition for Review) and the name of the court, agency, or board below; (4) the title of the document (e. g., Brief for Appellant, Appendix); and (5) the names and addresses of counsel representing the party on whose behalf the document is filed.

(b) **Form of Other Papers.** Petitions for rehearing shall be produced in a manner prescribed by subdivision (a). Motions and other papers may be produced in like manner, or they may be typewritten upon opaque, unglazed paper $8\frac{1}{2}$ by 11 inches in size. Lines of typewritten text shall be double spaced. Consecutive sheets shall be attached at the left margin. Carbon copies may be used for filing and service if they are legible.

A motion or other paper addressed to the court shall contain a caption setting forth the name of the court, the title of the case, the file number, and a brief descriptive title indicating the purpose of the paper.

Rule 33.

PREHEARING CONFERENCE

The court may direct the attorneys for the parties to appear before the court or a judge thereof for a prehearing conference to consider the simplification of the issues and such other matters as may aid in the disposition of the proceeding by the court. The court or judge shall make an order which recites the action taken at the conference and the agreements made by the parties as to any of the matters considered and which limits the issues to those not disposed of by admissions or agreements of counsel, and such order when entered controls the subsequent course of the proceeding, unless modified to prevent manifest injustice.

ORAL ARGUMENT

(a) **In General; Local Rule.** Oral argument shall be allowed in all cases unless pursuant to local rule a panel of three judges, after examination of the briefs and record, shall be unanimously of the opinion that oral argument is not needed. Any such local rule shall provide any party with an opportunity to file a statement setting forth the reasons why oral argument should be heard. A general statement of the criteria employed in the administration of such local rule shall be published in or with the rule and such criteria shall conform substantially to the following minimum standard:

Oral argument will be allowed unless

(1) the appeal is frivolous; or

(2) the dispositive issue or set of issues has been recently authoritatively decided; or

(3) the facts and legal arguments are adequately presented in the briefs and record and the decisional process would not be significantly aided by oral argument.

(b) **Notice of Argument; Postponement.** The clerk shall advise all parties whether oral argument is to be heard, and if so, of the time and place therefor, and the time to be allowed each side. A request for postponement of the argument or for allowance of additional time must be made by motion filed reasonably in advance of the date fixed for hearing.

(c) **Order and Content of Argument.** The appellant is entitled to open and conclude the argument. The opening argument shall include a fair statement of the case. Counsel will not be permitted to read at length from briefs, records or authorities.

(d) **Cross and Separate Appeals.** A cross or separate appeal shall be argued with the initial appeal at a single argument, unless the court otherwise directs. If a case involves a cross-appeal, the plaintiff in the action below shall be deemed the appellant for the purpose of this rule unless the parties otherwise agree or the court otherwise directs. If separate appellants support the same argument, care shall be taken to avoid duplication of argument.

(e) **Non-Appearance of Parties.** If the appellee fails to appear to present argument, the court will hear argument on behalf of the appellant, if present. If the appellant fails to appear, the court may hear argument on behalf of the appellee, if present.

If neither party appears, the case will be decided on the briefs unless the court shall otherwise order.

(f) Submission on Briefs. By agreement of the parties, a case may be submitted for decision on the briefs, but the court may direct that the case be argued.

(g) Use of Physical Exhibits at Argument; Removal. If physical exhibits other than documents are to be used at the argument, counsel shall arrange to have them placed in the court room before the court convenes on the date of the argument. After the argument counsel shall cause the exhibits to be removed from the court room unless the court otherwise directs. If exhibits are not reclaimed by counsel within a reasonable time after notice is given by the clerk, they shall be destroyed or otherwise disposed of as the clerk shall think best.

As amended 1979, 1986.

Rule 35.

DETERMINATION OF CAUSES BY THE COURT IN BANC

(a) When Hearing or Rehearing in Banc Will Be Ordered. A majority of the circuit judges who are in regular active service may order that an appeal or other proceeding be heard or reheard by the court of appeals in banc. Such a hearing or rehearing is not favored and ordinarily will not be ordered except (1) when consideration by the full court is necessary to secure or maintain uniformity of its decisions, or (2) when the proceeding involves a question of exceptional importance.

(b) Suggestion of a Party for Hearing or Rehearing in Banc. A party may suggest the appropriateness of a hearing or rehearing in banc. No response shall be filed unless the court shall so order. The clerk shall transmit any such suggestion to the members of the panel and the judges of the court who are in regular active service but a vote need not be taken to determine whether the cause shall be heard or reheard in banc unless a judge in regular active service or a judge who was a member of the panel that rendered a decision sought to be reheard requests a vote on such a suggestion made by a party.

(c) Time for Suggestion of a Party for Hearing or Rehearing in Banc; Suggestion Does Not Stay Mandate. If a party desires to suggest that an appeal be heard initially in banc, the suggestion must be made by the date on which the appellee's brief is filed. A suggestion for a rehearing in banc must be made within the time prescribed by Rule 40 for filing a petition for rehearing, whether the suggestion is made in such petition or otherwise.   The pendency of such a suggestion whether or not included in a petition for rehearing shall not affect the finality of the judgment of the court of appeals or stay the issuance of the mandate.

As amended 1979.

Rule 36.

ENTRY OF JUDGMENT

The notation of a judgment in the docket constitutes entry of the judgment.   The clerk shall prepare, sign and enter the judgment following receipt of the opinion of the court unless the opinion directs settlement of the form of the judgment, in which event the clerk shall prepare, sign and enter the judgment following final settlement by the court.   If a judgment is rendered without an opinion, the clerk shall prepare, sign and enter the judgment following instruction from the court.   The clerk shall, on the date judgment is entered, mail to all parties a copy of the opinion, if any, or of the judgment if no opinion was written, and notice of the date of entry of the judgment.

Rule 37.

INTEREST ON JUDGMENTS

Unless otherwise provided by law, if a judgment for money in a civil case is affirmed, whatever interest is allowed by law shall be payable from the date the judgment was entered in the district court.   If a judgment is modified or reversed with a direction that a judgment for money be entered in the district court, the mandate shall contain instructions with respect to allowance of interest.

Rule 38.

DAMAGES FOR DELAY

If a court of appeals shall determine that an appeal is frivolous, it may award just damages and single or double costs to the appellee.

Rule 39.

COSTS

(a) **To Whom Allowed.**   Except as otherwise provided by law, if an appeal is dismissed, costs shall be taxed against the appellant unless otherwise agreed by the parties or ordered by the court; if a judgment is affirmed, costs shall be taxed against the appellant unless otherwise ordered; if a judgment is reversed, costs shall be taxed against the appellee unless otherwise ordered; if a judgment is affirmed or reversed in part, or is vacated, costs shall be allowed only as ordered by the court.

(b) Costs For and Against the United States. In cases involving the United States or an agency or officer thereof, if an award of costs against the United States is authorized by law, costs shall be awarded in accordance with the provisions of subdivision (a); otherwise, costs shall not be awarded for or against the United States.

(c) Costs of Briefs, Appendices, and Copies of Records. By local rule the court of appeals shall fix the maximum rate at which the cost of printing or otherwise producing necessary copies of briefs, appendices, and copies of records authorized by Rule 30(f) shall be taxable. Such rate shall not be higher than that generally charged for such work in the area where the clerk's office is located and shall encourage the use of economical methods of printing and copying.

(d) Bill of Costs; Objections; Costs to Be Inserted in Mandate or Added Later. A party who desires such costs to be taxed shall state them in an itemized and verified bill of costs which the party shall file with the clerk, with proof of service, within 14 days after the entry of judgment. Objections to the bill of costs must be filed within 10 days of service on the party against whom costs are to be taxed unless the time is extended by the court. The clerk shall prepare and certify an itemized statement of costs taxed in the court of appeals for insertion in the mandate, but the issuance of the mandate shall not be delayed for taxation of costs and if the mandate has been issued before final determination of costs, the statement, or any amendment thereof, shall be added to the mandate upon request by the clerk of the court of appeals to the clerk of the district court.

(e) Costs on Appeal Taxable in the District Courts. Costs incurred in the preparation and transmission of the record, the cost of the reporter's transcript, if necessary for the determination of the appeal, the premiums paid for cost of supersedeas bonds or other bonds to preserve rights pending appeal, and the fee for filing the notice of appeal shall be taxed in the district court as costs of the appeal in favor of the party entitled to costs under this rule.

As amended 1979, 1986.

Rule 40.

PETITION FOR REHEARING

(a) **Time for Filing; Content; Answer; Action by Court if Granted.** A petition for rehearing may be filed within 14 days after entry of judgment unless the time is shortened or enlarged by order or by local rule. The petition shall state with particularity the points of law or fact which in the opinion of the petitioner the court has overlooked or misapprehended and shall contain such argument in support of the petition as the petitioner desires to present. Oral argument in support of the petition will not be permitted. No answer to a petition for rehearing will be received unless requested by the court, but a petition for rehearing will ordinarily not be granted in the absence of such a request. If a petition for rehearing is granted the court may make a final disposition of the cause without reargument or may restore it to the calendar for reargument or resubmission or may make such other orders as are deemed appropriate under the circumstances of the particular case.

(b) **Form of Petition; Length.** The petition shall be in a form prescribed by Rule 32(a), and copies shall be served and filed as prescribed by Rule 31(b) for the service and filing of briefs. Except by permission of the court, or as specified by local rule of the court of appeals, a petition for rehearing shall not exceed 15 pages.

As amended 1979.

Rule 41.

ISSUANCE OF MANDATE; STAY OF MANDATE

(a) **Date of Issuance.** The mandate of the court shall issue 21 days after the entry of judgment unless the time is shortened or enlarged by order. A certified copy of the judgment and a copy of the opinion of the court, if any, and any direction as to costs shall constitute the mandate, unless the court directs that a formal mandate issue. The timely filing of a petition for rehearing will stay the mandate until disposition of the petition unless otherwise ordered by the court. If the petition is denied, the mandate shall issue 7 days after entry of the order denying the petition unless the time is shortened or enlarged by order.

(b) **Stay of Mandate Pending Application for Certiorari.** A stay of the mandate pending application to the Supreme Court for a writ of certiorari may be granted upon motion, reasonable notice of which shall be given to all parties. The stay shall not exceed 30 days unless the period is extended for cause shown. If during the period of the stay there is filed with the clerk of the court of appeals a notice from the clerk of the Supreme Court that the party who has obtained the stay has filed a petition for the writ in that court, the stay shall continue until final disposition by the Supreme Court. Upon the filing of a copy of an order of the Supreme Court denying the petition for writ of certiorari the mandate shall issue immediately. A bond or other security may be required as a condition to the grant or continuance of a stay of the mandate.

Rule 42.

VOLUNTARY DISMISSAL

(a) **Dismissal in the District Court.** If an appeal has not been docketed, the appeal may be dismissed by the district court upon the filing in that court of a stipulation for dismissal signed by all the parties, or upon motion and notice by the appellant.

(b) **Dismissal in the Court of Appeals.** If the parties to an appeal or other proceeding shall sign and file with the clerk of the court of appeals an agreement that the proceeding be dismissed, specifying the terms as to payment of costs, and shall pay whatever fees are due, the clerk shall enter the case dismissed, but no mandate or other process shall issue without an order of the court. An appeal may be dismissed on motion of the appellant upon such terms as may be agreed upon by the parties or fixed by the court.

Rule 43.

SUBSTITUTION OF PARTIES

(a) **Death of a Party.** If a party dies after a notice of appeal is filed or while a proceeding is otherwise pending in the court of appeals, the personal representative of the deceased party may be substituted as a party on motion filed by the representative or by any party with the clerk of the court of appeals. The motion of a party shall be served upon the representative in accordance with the provisions of Rule 25. If the deceased party has no representative, any party may suggest the death on the record and proceedings shall then be had as the court of appeals may direct. If a party against whom an appeal may be taken dies after entry of a judgment or order in the district court but before a notice of appeal is filed, an appellant may proceed as if death had not occurred. After the notice of appeal is filed substitution shall be effected in the court of appeals in accordance with this subdivision. If a party entitled to appeal shall die before filing a notice of appeal, the notice of appeal may be filed by that party's personal representative, or, if there is no personal representative, by that party's attorney of record within the time prescribed by these rules. After the notice of appeal is filed substitution shall be effected in the court of appeals in accordance with this subdivision.

(b) Substitution for Other Causes. If substitution of a party in the court of appeals is necessary for any reason other than death, substitution shall be effected in accordance with the procedure prescribed in subdivision (a).

(c) Public Officers; Death or Separation from Office.

(1) When a public officer is a party to an appeal or other proceeding in the court of appeals in an official capacity and during its pendency dies, resigns or otherwise ceases to hold office, the action does not abate and the public officer's successor is automatically substituted as a party. Proceedings following the substitution shall be in the name of the substituted party, but any misnomer not affecting the substantial rights of the parties shall be disregarded. An order of substitution may be entered at any time, but the omission to enter such an order shall not affect the substitution.

(2) When a public officer is a party to an appeal or other proceeding in an official capacity that public officer may be described as a party by the public officer's official title rather than by name; but the court may require the public officer's name to be added.

As amended 1986.

Rule 44.

CASES INVOLVING CONSTITUTIONAL QUESTIONS WHERE UNITED STATES IS NOT A PARTY

It shall be the duty of a party who draws in question the constitutionality of any Act of Congress in any proceeding in a court of appeals to which the United States, or any agency thereof, or any officer or employee thereof, as such officer or employee, is not a party, upon the filing of the record, or as soon thereafter as the question is raised in the court of appeals, to give immediate notice in writing to the court of the existence of said question. The clerk shall thereupon certify such fact to the Attorney General.

Rule 45.

DUTIES OF CLERKS

(a) General Provisions. [Omitted]

(b) The Docket; Calendar; Other Records Required. [Omitted]

(c) Notice of Orders or Judgments. Immediately upon the entry of an order or judgment the clerk shall serve a notice of entry by mail upon each party to the proceeding together with a copy of any opinion respecting the order or judgment, and shall make a note in the docket of the mailing. Service on a party represented by counsel shall be made on counsel.

(d) Custody of Records and Papers. [Omitted]

As amended 1971, 1986.

Rule 46.

ATTORNEYS

(a) Admission to the Bar of a Court of Appeals; Eligibility; Procedure for Admission. An attorney who has been admitted to practice before the Supreme Court of the United States, or the highest court of a state, or another United States court of appeals, or a United States district court (including the district courts for the Canal Zone, Guam and the Virgin Islands), and who is of good moral and professional character, is eligible for admission to the bar of a court of appeals.

An applicant shall file with the clerk of the court of appeals, on a form approved by the court and furnished by the clerk, an application for admission containing the applicant's personal statement showing eligibility for membership. At the foot of the application the applicant shall take and subscribe to the following oath or affirmation:

I, _____, do solemnly swear (or affirm) that I will demean myself as an attorney and counselor of this court, uprightly and according to law; and that I will support the Constitution of the United States.

Thereafter, upon written or oral motion of a member of the bar of the court, the court will act upon the application. An applicant may be admitted by oral motion in open court, but it is not necessary that the applicant appear before the court for the purpose of being admitted, unless the court shall otherwise order.

An applicant shall upon admission pay to the clerk the fee prescribed by rule or order of the court.

(b) Suspension or Disbarment.   When it is shown to the court that any member of its bar has been suspended or disbarred from practice in any other court of record, or has been guilty of conduct unbecoming a member of the bar of the court, the member will be subject to suspension or disbarment by the court.   The member shall be afforded an opportunity to show good cause, within such time as the court shall prescribe, why the member should not be suspended or disbarred.   Upon the member's response to the rule to show cause, and after hearing, if requested, or upon expiration of the time prescribed for a response if no response is made, the court shall enter an appropriate order.

(c) Disciplinary Power of the Court over Attorneys.   A court of appeals may, after reasonable notice and an opportunity to show cause to the contrary, and after hearing, if requested, take any appropriate disciplinary action against any attorney who practices before it for conduct unbecoming a member of the bar or for failure to comply with these rules or any rule of the court.

As amended 1986.

Rule 47.

RULES BY COURTS OF APPEALS

Each court of appeals by action of a majority of the circuit judges in regular active service may from time to time make and amend rules governing its practice not inconsistent with these rules.   In all cases not provided for by rule, the courts of appeals may regulate their practice in any manner not inconsistent with these rules.   Copies of all rules made by a court of appeals shall upon their promulgation be furnished to the Administrative Office of the United States Courts.

Rule 48.

TITLE

These rules may be known and cited as the Federal Rules of Appellate Procedure.

––––––

[The order of the Supreme Court of December 4, 1967, stated that the rules therein set forth, to be known as the Federal Rules of Appellate

Procedure, "be, and they hereby are, prescribed, pursuant to sections 3771 and 3772 of Title 18, United States Code, and sections 2072 and 2075 of Title 28, United States Code, to govern the procedure in appeals to United States courts of appeals from the United States district courts, in the review by United States courts of appeals of decisions of the Tax Court of the United States, in proceedings in the United States courts of appeals for the review or enforcement of orders of administrative agencies, boards, commissions and officers, and in applications for writs or other relief which a United States court of appeals or judge thereof is competent to give."

[The order of December 4, 1967, further stated that the Rules "shall take effect on July 1, 1968, and shall govern all proceedings in appeals and petitions for review or enforcement of orders thereafter brought and in all such proceedings then pending, except to the extent that in the opinion of the court of appeals their application in a particular proceeding then pending would not be feasible or would work injustice, in which case the former procedure may be followed." 389 U.S. 1063, 1065; see 43 F.R.D. 61.]

———

[Rules 30(a) and (c) and 31(a) were amended by the order of the Supreme Court of March 30, 1970, to be effective July 1, 1970. 398 U.S. 971; see 48 F.R.D. 481.]

———

[Rules 26(a) and 45(a) were amended by the order of the Supreme Court of March 1, 1971, to be effective July 1, 1971. 401 U.S. 1029; see 52 F.R.D. 84.]

———

[Rule 9(c) was amended by the order of the Supreme Court of April 24, 1972, to be effective October 1, 1972. 406 U.S. 1005; see 56 F.R.D. 181.]

———

[Rules 1(a), 3(c), (d), and (e), 4(a), 5(d), 6(d), 7, 10(b), 11(a), (b), (c), and (d), 12(a), (b), and (c), 13(a), 24(b), 27(b), 28(g) and (j), 34(a) and (b), 35(b) and (c), 39(c) and (d), and 40(a) and (b) were amended by the order of the Supreme Court of April 30, 1979, to be effective August 1, 1979. 441 U.S. 969; see 16 C. Wright, A. Miller & E. Cooper, Federal Practice and Procedure app. D (Supp.).]

———

[Rule 9(c) was amended October 12, 1984, Pub.L. 98–473, Title II, § 210, 98 Stat. 1987.]

———

[Rules 19, 26(a), 28(c), 30(a) and (b), 39(c), and 45(a) and (b) were amended, and Rules 3.1, 5.1, and 15.1 added, by the order of the Supreme Court of March 10, 1986, to be effective July 1, 1986. That order also neutralized gender-specific language in numerous Rules. 475 U.S. 1153; see 109 F.R.D. 179.]

———

[Rule 4(b) was amended November 18, 1988, Pub.L. 100–690, Title VII, § 7111, 102 Stat. 4419.]

———

[Rules 1(a), 3(a), 6, 26(a), 27(a), and 28(g) were amended, and Rule 26.1 and Form 5 added, by the order of the Supreme Court of April 25, 1989, to be effective December 1, 1989. 490 U.S. 1125; see 124 F.R.D. 361.]

APPENDIX OF FORMS

Form 1.

NOTICE OF APPEAL TO A COURT OF APPEALS FROM A JUDGMENT OR ORDER OF A DISTRICT COURT

United States District Court for the .... District
of ....

File Number ....

A. B., Plaintiff   )
       v.   ) Notice of Appeal
C. D., Defendant)

Notice is hereby given that C. D., defendant above named, hereby appeals to the United States Court of Appeals for the ..... Circuit (from the final judgment) (from the order (describing it)) entered in this action on the ...... day of ....

........, 19....

(S) ....

Attorney for C. D.

....
(Address)

FORMS 2–5 [Omitted]

TABLE OF CONTENTS

SELECTED PROVISIONS OF THE CONSTITUTION OF THE UNITED STATES

SELECTED PROVISIONS OF TITLE 28, UNITED STATES CODE

TABLE OF CONTENTS

TABLE OF CONTENTS

SELECTED PROVISIONS OF OTHER PROCEDURAL STATUTES

*

SELECTED PROVISIONS OF THE CONSTITUTION OF THE UNITED STATES

* * *

ARTICLE. I.

* * *

Section 8. The Congress shall have Power To lay and collect Taxes, Duties, Imposts and Excises, to pay the Debts and provide for the common Defence and general Welfare of the United States; but all Duties, Imposts and Excises shall be uniform throughout the United States;

To borrow Money on the credit of the United States;

To regulate Commerce with foreign Nations, and among the several States, and with the Indian Tribes;

To establish an uniform Rule of Naturalization, and uniform Laws on the subject of Bankruptcies throughout the United States;

To coin Money, regulate the Value thereof, and of foreign Coin, and fix the Standard of Weights and Measures;

To provide for the Punishment of counterfeiting the Securities and current Coin of the United States;

To establish Post Offices and post Roads;

To promote the Progress of Science and useful Arts, by securing for limited Times to Authors and Inventors the exclusive Right to their respective Writings and Discoveries;

To constitute Tribunals inferior to the supreme Court;

To define and punish Piracies and Felonies committed on the high Seas, and Offences against the Law of Nations;

To declare War, grant Letters of Marque and Reprisal, and make Rules concerning Captures on Land and Water;

To raise and support Armies, but no Appropriation of Money to that Use shall be for a longer Term than two Years;

To provide and maintain a Navy;

To make Rules for the Government and Regulation of the land and naval Forces;

To provide for calling forth the Militia to execute the Laws of the Union, suppress Insurrections and repel Invasions;

To provide for organizing, arming, and disciplining, the Militia, and for governing such Part of them as may be employed in the Service of the United States, reserving to the States respectively, the Appointment of the Officers, and the Authority of training the Militia according to the discipline prescribed by Congress;

To exercise exclusive Legislation in all Cases whatsoever, over such District (not exceeding ten Miles square) as may, by Cession of particular States, and the Acceptance of Congress, become the Seat of the Government of the United States, and to exercise like Authority over all Places purchased by the Consent of the Legislature of the State in which the same shall be, for the Erection of Forts, Magazines, Arsenals, dock-Yards, and other needful Buildings;—And

To make all Laws which shall be necessary and proper for carrying into Execution the foregoing Powers, and all other Powers vested by this Constitution in the Government of the United States, or in any Department or Officer thereof.

* * *

ARTICLE. III.

Section 1. The judicial Power of the United States, shall be vested in one supreme Court, and in such inferior Courts as the Congress may from time to time ordain and establish. The Judges, both of the supreme and inferior Courts, shall hold their Offices during good Behaviour, and shall, at stated Times, receive for their Services, a Compensation, which shall not be diminished during their Continuance in Office.

Section 2. The judicial Power shall extend to all Cases, in Law and Equity, arising under this Constitution, the Laws of the United States, and Treaties made, or which shall be made, under their Authority;—to all Cases affecting Ambassadors, other public Ministers and Consuls;—to all Cases of admiralty and maritime Jurisdiction;—to Controversies to which the United States shall be a Party;—to Controversies between two or more States;—between a State and Citizens of another State;—between Citizens of different States;—between Citizens of the same State claiming Lands under Grants of different States, and between a State, or the Citizens thereof, and foreign States, Citizens or Subjects.

In all Cases affecting Ambassadors, other public Ministers and Consuls, and those in which a State shall be Party, the supreme Court shall have original Jurisdiction. In all the other Cases before mentioned, the supreme Court shall have appellate Jurisdiction, both as to Law and Fact, with such Exceptions, and under such Regulations as the Congress shall make.

The Trial of all Crimes, except in Cases of Impeachment, shall be by Jury; and such Trial shall be held in the State where the said Crimes shall have been committed; but when not committed within any State, the Trial shall be at such Place or Places as the Congress may by Law have directed.

* * *

ARTICLE. IV.

Section 1. Full Faith and Credit shall be given in each State to the public Acts, Records, and judicial Proceedings of every other State. And the Congress may by general Laws prescribe the Manner in which such Acts, Records and Proceedings shall be proved, and the Effect thereof.

Section 2. The Citizens of each State shall be entitled to all Privileges and Immunities of Citizens in the several States.

* * *

ARTICLE. VI.

* * *

This Constitution, and the Laws of the United States which shall be made in Pursuance thereof; and all Treaties made, or which shall be made, under the Authority of the United States, shall be the supreme Law of the Land; and the Judges in every State shall be bound thereby, any Thing in the Constitution or Laws of any State to the Contrary notwithstanding.

* * *

AMENDMENT. I.

[1791]

Congress shall make no law respecting an establishment of religion, or prohibiting the free exercise thereof; or abridging the freedom of speech, or of the press; or the right of the people peaceably to assemble, and to petition the Government for a redress of grievances.

AMENDMENT. IV.

The right of the people to be secure in their persons, houses, papers, and effects, against unreasonable searches and seizures, shall not be violated, and no Warrants shall issue, but upon probable cause, supported by Oath or affirmation, and particularly describing the place to be searched, and the persons or things to be seized.

AMENDMENT. V.

No person shall be held to answer for a capital, or otherwise infamous crime, unless on a presentment or indictment of a Grand Jury, except in cases arising in the land or naval forces, or in the Militia, when in actual service in time of War or public danger; nor shall any person be subject for the same offence to be twice put in jeopardy of life or limb; nor shall be compelled in any criminal case to be a witness against himself, nor be deprived of life, liberty, or property, without due process of law; nor shall private property be taken for public use, without just compensation.

AMENDMENT. VI.

In all criminal prosecutions, the accused shall enjoy the right to a speedy and public trial, by an impartial jury of the State and district wherein the crime shall have been committed, which district shall have been previously ascertained by law, and to be informed of the nature and cause of the accusation; to be confronted with the Witnesses against him; to have compulsory process for obtaining witnesses in his favor, and to have the Assistance of Counsel for his defence.

UNITED STATES CONSTITUTION

AMENDMENT. VII.

In suits at common law, where the value in controversy shall exceed twenty dollars, the right of trial by jury shall be preserved, and no fact tried by a jury, shall be otherwise re-examined in any Court of the United States, than according to the rules of the common law.

AMENDMENT. IX.

The enumeration in the Constitution, of certain rights, shall not be construed to deny or disparage others retained by the people.

AMENDMENT. X.

The powers not delegated to the United States by the Constitution, nor prohibited by it to the States, are reserved to the States respectively, or to the people.

AMENDMENT. XI.

[1795*]

The Judicial power of the United States shall not be construed to extend to any suit in law or equity, commenced or prosecuted against one of the United States by Citizens of another State, or by Citizens or Subjects of any Foreign State.

AMENDMENT. XIV.

[1868]

Section 1. All persons born or naturalized in the United States, and subject to the jurisdiction thereof, are citizens of the United States and of the State wherein they reside. No State shall make or enforce any law which shall abridge the privileges or immunities of citizens of the United States; nor shall any State deprive any person of life, liberty, or property, without due process of law; nor deny to any person within its jurisdiction the equal protection of the laws.

Section 2. Representatives shall be apportioned among the several States according to their respective numbers, counting the whole number of persons in each State, excluding Indians not taxed. But when the right to vote at any election for the choice of electors for President and Vice President of the United States, Representatives in Congress, the Executive and Judicial officers of a State, or the members of the Legislature thereof, is denied to any of the male inhabitants of such State, being twenty-one years of age, and citizens of the United States, or in any way abridged, except for participation in rebellion, or other crime, the basis of representation therein shall be reduced in the proportion which the number of such male citizens shall bear to the whole number of male citizens twenty-one years of age in such State.

Section 3. No person shall be a Senator or Representative in Congress, or elector of President and Vice President, or hold any office, civil or military, under the United States, or under any State, who, having

* Official announcement of ratification was not made until January 8, 1798, in a message from the President to Congress.

previously taken an oath, as a member of Congress, or as an officer of the United States, or as a member of any State legislature, or as an executive or judicial officer of any State, to support the Constitution of the United States, shall have engaged in insurrection or rebellion against the same, or given aid or comfort to the enemies thereof. But Congress may by a vote of two-thirds of each House, remove such disability.

Section 4. The validity of the public debt of the United States, authorized by law, including debts incurred for payment of pensions and bounties for services in suppressing insurrection or rebellion, shall not be questioned. But neither the United States nor any State shall assume or pay any debt or obligation incurred in aid of insurrection or rebellion against the United States, or any claim for the loss or emancipation of any slave; but all such debts, obligations and claims shall be held illegal and void.

Section 5. The Congress shall have power to enforce, by appropriate legislation, the provisions of this article.

*

SELECTED PROVISIONS OF TITLE 28, UNITED STATES CODE

§ 41. Number and composition of circuits

The thirteen judicial circuits of the United States are constituted as follows:

Circuits	Composition
District of Columbia	District of Columbia.
First	Maine, Massachusetts, New Hampshire, Puerto Rico, Rhode Island.
Second	Connecticut, New York, Vermont.
Third	Delaware, New Jersey, Pennsylvania, Virgin Islands.
Fourth	Maryland, North Carolina, South Carolina, Virginia, West Virginia.
Fifth	District of the Canal Zone, Louisiana, Mississippi, Texas.
Sixth	Kentucky, Michigan, Ohio, Tennessee.
Seventh	Illinois, Indiana, Wisconsin.
Eighth	Arkansas, Iowa, Minnesota, Missouri, Nebraska, North Dakota, South Dakota.
Ninth	Alaska, Arizona, California, Idaho, Montana, Nevada, Oregon, Washington, Guam, Hawaii.
Tenth	Colorado, Kansas, New Mexico, Oklahoma, Utah, Wyoming.
Eleventh	Alabama, Florida, Georgia.
Federal	All Federal judicial districts.

As amended Oct. 31, 1951, c. 655, § 34, 65 Stat. 723; Oct. 14, 1980, Pub.L. 96–452, § 2, 94 Stat. 1994; Apr. 2, 1982, Pub.L. 97–164, Title I, § 101, 96 Stat. 25.

§ 133. Appointment and number of district judges

(a) The President shall appoint, by and with the advice and consent of the Senate, district judges for the several judicial districts, as follows:

Districts	Judges
Alabama:	
Northern	7
Middle	3
Southern	3
Alaska	3
Arizona	8
Arkansas:	

Districts	Judges
Eastern	5
Western	3
California:	
Northern	14
Eastern	6
Central	27
Southern	8
Colorado	7
Connecticut	8
Delaware	4
District of Columbia	15
Florida:	
Northern	4
Middle	11
Southern	16
Georgia:	
Northern	11
Middle	4
Southern	3
Hawaii	3
Idaho	2
Illinois:	
Northern	22
Central	3
Southern	3
Indiana:	
Northern	5
Southern	5
Iowa:	
Northern	2
Southern	3
Kansas	5
Kentucky:	
Eastern	4
Western	4
Eastern and Western *	1
Louisiana:	
Eastern	13
Middle	2
Western	7
Maine	3
Maryland	10
Massachusetts	13
Michigan:	
Eastern	15
Western	4
Minnesota	7
Mississippi:	

* A district judge may be appointed to serve in more than one district.—Ed.

Districts	Judges
Northern	3
Southern	6
Missouri:	
Eastern	6
Western	5
Eastern and Western	2
Montana	3
Nebraska	3
Nevada	4
New Hampshire	3
New Jersey	17
New Mexico	5
New York:	
Northern	4
Southern	28
Eastern	15
Western	4
North Carolina:	
Eastern	4
Middle	4
Western	3
North Dakota	2
Ohio:	
Northern	11
Southern	8
Oklahoma:	
Northern	3
Eastern	1
Western	6
Northern, Eastern, and Western	1
Oregon	6
Pennsylvania:	
Eastern	22
Middle	6
Western	10
Puerto Rico	7
Rhode Island	3
South Carolina	9
South Dakota	3
Tennessee:	
Eastern	5
Middle	4
Western	5
Texas:	
Northern	12
Southern	18
Eastern	7
Western	10
Utah	5
Vermont	2

Districts	Judges
Virginia:	
Eastern	9
Western	4
Washington:	
Eastern	4
Western	7
West Virginia:	
Northern	3
Southern	5
Wisconsin:	
Eastern	4
Western	2
Wyoming	3.

(b)(1) In any case in which a judge of the United States (other than a senior judge) assumes the duties of a full-time office of Federal judicial administration, the President shall appoint, by and with the advice and consent of the Senate, an additional judge for the court on which such judge serves. If the judge who assumes the duties of such full-time office leaves that office and resumes the duties as an active judge of the court, then the President shall not appoint a judge to fill the first vacancy which occurs thereafter in that court.

(2) For purposes of paragraph (1), the term "office of Federal judicial administration" means a position as Director of the Federal Judicial Center, Director of the Administrative Office of the United States Courts, or administrative assistant to the Chief Justice. Latest amendment Dec. 1, 1990, Pub.L. 101–650, Title II, § 203(d), Title III, § 303, 104 Stat. 5101, 5105.

§ 144. Bias or prejudice of judge

Whenever a party to any proceeding in a district court makes and files a timely and sufficient affidavit that the judge before whom the matter is pending has a personal bias or prejudice either against him or in favor of any adverse party, such judge shall proceed no further therein, but another judge shall be assigned to hear such proceeding.

The affidavit shall state the facts and the reasons for the belief that bias or prejudice exists, and shall be filed not less than ten days before the beginning of the term at which the proceeding is to be heard, or good cause shall be shown for failure to file it within such time. A party may file only one such affidavit in any case. It shall be accompanied by a certificate of counsel of record stating that it is made in good faith. As amended May 24, 1949, c. 139, § 65, 63 Stat. 99.

§ 331. Judicial Conference of the United States

The Chief Justice of the United States shall summon annually the chief judge of each judicial circuit, the chief judge of the Court of International Trade, and a district judge from each judicial circuit to a conference at such time and place in the United States as he may designate. He shall preside at such conference which shall be known as the Judicial Conference of the United States. Special sessions of the

Conference may be called by the Chief Justice at such times and places as he may designate.

* * *

The Conference shall make a comprehensive survey of the condition of business in the courts of the United States and prepare plans for assignment of judges to or from circuits or districts where necessary. It shall also submit suggestions and recommendations to the various courts to promote uniformity of management procedures and the expeditious conduct of court business. The Conference is authorized to exercise the authority provided in section 372(c) of this title as the Conference, or through a standing committee. If the Conference elects to establish a standing committee, it shall be appointed by the Chief Justice and all petitions for review shall be reviewed by that committee. The Conference or the standing committee may hold hearings, take sworn testimony, issue subpoenas and subpoenas duces tecum, and make necessary and appropriate orders in the exercise of its authority. Subpoenas and subpoenas duces tecum shall be issued by the clerk of the Supreme Court or by the clerk of any court of appeals, at the direction of the Chief Justice or his designee and under the seal of the court, and shall be served in the manner provided in rule 45(c) of the Federal Rules of Civil Procedure for subpoenas and subpoenas duces tecum issued on behalf of the United States or an officer or any agency thereof. The Conference may also prescribe and modify rules for the exercise of the authority provided in section 372(c) of this title. All judicial officers and employees of the United States shall promptly carry into effect all orders of the Judicial Conference or the standing committee established pursuant to this section.

The Conference shall also carry on a continuous study of the operation and effect of the general rules of practice and procedure now or hereafter in use as prescribed by the Supreme Court for the other courts of the United States pursuant to law. Such changes in and additions to those rules as the Conference may deem desirable to promote simplicity in procedure, fairness in administration, the just determination of litigation, and the elimination of unjustifiable expense and delay shall be recommended by the Conference from time to time to the Supreme Court for its consideration and adoption, modification or rejection, in accordance with law.

The Judicial Conference shall review rules prescribed under section 2071 of this title by the courts, other than the Supreme Court and the district courts, for consistency with Federal law. The Judicial Conference may modify or abrogate any such rule so reviewed found inconsistent in the course of such a review.

* * *

The Chief Justice shall submit to Congress an annual report of the proceedings of the Judicial Conference and its recommendations for legislation. As amended July 9, 1956, c. 517, § 1(d), 70 Stat. 497; Aug. 28, 1957, Pub.L. 85–202, 71 Stat. 476; July 11, 1958, Pub.L. 85–513, 72 Stat. 356; Sept. 19, 1961, Pub.L. 87–253, §§ 1, 2, 75 Stat. 521; Oct. 15, 1980, Pub.L. 96–458, § 4, 94 Stat. 2040; Apr. 2, 1982, Pub.L. 97–164, Title I,

§ 111, 96 Stat. 29; Oct. 14, 1986, Pub.L. 99–466, § 1, 100 Stat. 1190; Nov. 19, 1988, Pub.L. 100–702, Title IV, § 402(b), 102 Stat. 4650.

§ 332. Judicial councils of circuits

(a)(1) The chief judge of each judicial circuit shall call, at least twice in each year and at such places as he or she may designate, a meeting of the judicial council of the circuit, consisting of the chief judge of the circuit, who shall preside, and an equal number of circuit judges and district judges of the circuit, as such member [sic] is determined by majority vote of all such judges of the circuit in regular active services.

(2) Members of the council shall serve for terms established by a majority vote of all judges of the circuit in regular active service.

* * *

(d)(1) Each judicial council shall make all necessary and appropriate orders for the effective and expeditious administration of justice within its circuit. Any general order relating to practice and procedure shall be made or amended only after giving appropriate public notice and an opportunity for comment. Any such order so relating shall take effect upon the date specified by such judicial council. Copies of such orders so relating shall be furnished to the Judicial Conference and the Administrative Office of the United States Courts and be made available to the public. Each council is authorized to hold hearings, to take sworn testimony, and to issue subpoenas and subpoenas duces tecum. Subpoenas and subpoenas duces tecum shall be issued by the clerk of the court of appeals, at the direction of the chief judge of the circuit or his designee and under the seal of the court, and shall be served in the manner provided in rule 45(c) of the Federal Rules of Civil Procedure for subpoenas and subpoenas duces tecum issued on behalf of the United States or an officer or agency thereof.

(2) All judicial officers and employees of the circuit shall promptly carry into effect all orders of the judicial council. In the case of failure to comply with an order made under this subsection or a subpoena issued under section 372(c) of this title, a judicial council or a special committee appointed under section 372(c)(4) of this title may institute a contempt proceeding in any district court in which the judicial officer or employee of the circuit who fails to comply with the order made under this subsection shall be ordered to show cause before the court why he or she should not be held in contempt of court.

(3) Unless an impediment to the administration of justice is involved, regular business of the courts need not be referred to the council.

(4) Each judicial council shall periodically review the rules which are prescribed under section 2071 of this title by district courts within its circuit for consistency with rules prescribed under section 2072 of this title. Each council may modify or abrogate any such rule found inconsistent in the course of such a review.

* * *

As amended Nov. 13, 1963, Pub.L. 88–176, § 3, 77 Stat. 331; Jan. 5, 1971, Pub.L. 91–647, 84 Stat. 1907; Oct. 15, 1980, Pub.L. 96–458, § 2(a)–(d)(1), 94

Stat. 2035; Oct. 1, 1988, Pub.L. 100–459, Title IV, § 407, 102 Stat. 2213; Nov. 19, 1988, Pub.L. 100–702, Title IV, § 403(a)(2), (b), Title X, §§ 1018, 1020(a)(1), 102 Stat. 4651, 4670, 4671; Dec. 1, 1990, Pub.L. 101–650, Title III, §§ 323, 325(b)(1), Title IV, § 403, 104 Stat. 5120, 5121, 5124.

§ 333. Judicial conferences of circuits

The chief judge of each circuit shall summon biennially, and may summon annually, the circuit, district, and bankruptcy judges of the circuit, in active service, to a conference at a time and place that he designates, for the purpose of considering the business of the courts and advising means of improving the administration of justice within such circuit. He shall preside at such conference, which shall be known as the Judicial Conference of the circuit. The judges of the District Court of Guam, the District Court of the Virgin Islands, and the District Court of the Northern Mariana Islands shall also be summoned biennially, and may be summoned annually, to the conferences of their respective circuits.

Every judge summoned shall attend, and unless executed by the chief judge, shall remain throughout the conference.

The court of appeals for each circuit shall provide by its rules for representation and active participation at such conference by members of the bar of such circuit. As amended Dec. 29, 1950, c. 1185, 64 Stat. 1128; Oct. 31, 1951, c. 655, § 38, 65 Stat. 723; July 7, 1958, Pub.L. 85–508, § 12(e), 72 Stat. 348; Nov. 6, 1978, Pub.L. 95–598, Title II, § 210, 92 Stat. 2661; Dec. 1, 1990, Pub.L. 101–650, Title III, § 320, 104 Stat. 5117.

§ 455. Disqualification of justice, judge, or magistrate

(a) Any justice, judge, or magistrate of the United States shall disqualify himself in any proceeding in which his impartiality might reasonably be questioned.

(b) He shall also disqualify himself in the following circumstances:

(1) Where he has a personal bias or prejudice concerning a party, or personal knowledge of disputed evidentiary facts concerning the proceeding;

(2) Where in private practice he served as lawyer in the matter in controversy, or a lawyer with whom he previously practiced law served during such association as a lawyer concerning the matter, or the judge or such lawyer has been a material witness concerning it;

(3) Where he has served in governmental employment and in such capacity participated as counsel, adviser or material witness concerning the proceeding or expressed an opinion concerning the merits of the particular case in controversy;

(4) He knows that he, individually or as a fiduciary, or his spouse or minor child residing in his household, has a financial interest in the subject matter in controversy or in a party to the proceeding, or any other interest that could be substantially affected by the outcome of the proceeding;

(5) He or his spouse, or a person within the third degree of relationship to either of them, or the spouse of such a person:

   (i) Is a party to the proceeding, or an officer, director, or trustee of a party;

   (ii) Is acting as a lawyer in the proceeding;

   (iii) Is known by the judge to have an interest that could be substantially affected by the outcome of the proceeding;

   (iv) Is to the judge's knowledge likely to be a material witness in the proceeding.

(c) A judge should inform himself about his personal and fiduciary financial interests, and make a reasonable effort to inform himself about the personal financial interests of his spouse and minor children residing in his household.

(d) For the purposes of this section the following words or phrases shall have the meaning indicated:

   (1) "proceeding" includes pretrial, trial, appellate review, or other stages of litigation;

   (2) the degree of relationship is calculated according to the civil law system;

   (3) "fiduciary" includes such relationships as executor, administrator, trustee, and guardian;

   (4) "financial interest" means ownership of a legal or equitable interest, however small, or a relationship as director, adviser, or other active participant in the affairs of a party, except that:

      (i) Ownership in a mutual or common investment fund that holds securities is not a "financial interest" in such securities unless the judge participates in the management of the fund;

      (ii) An office in an educational, religious, charitable, fraternal, or civic organization is not a "financial interest" in securities held by the organization;

      (iii) The proprietary interest of a policyholder in a mutual insurance company, of a depositor in a mutual savings association, or a similar proprietary interest, is a "financial interest" in the organization only if the outcome of the proceeding could substantially affect the value of the interest;

      (iv) Ownership of government securities is a "financial interest" in the issuer only if the outcome of the proceeding could substantially affect the value of the securities.

(e) No justice, judge, or magistrate shall accept from the parties to the proceeding a waiver of any ground for disqualification enumerated in subsection (b). Where the ground for disqualification arises only under subsection (a), waiver may be accepted provided it is preceded by a full disclosure on the record of the basis for disqualification.

(f) Notwithstanding the preceding provisions of this section, if any justice, judge, magistrate, or bankruptcy judge to whom a matter has been assigned would be disqualified, after substantial judicial time has been devoted to the matter, because of the appearance or discovery, after the matter was assigned to him or her, that he or she individually or as a fiduciary, or his or her spouse or minor child residing in his or her household, has a financial interest in a party (other than an interest that could be substantially affected by the outcome), disqualification is not required if the justice, judge, magistrate, bankruptcy judge, spouse or minor child, as the case may be, divests himself or herself of the interest that provides the grounds for the disqualification. As amended Dec. 5, 1974, Pub.L. 93–512, § 1, 88 Stat. 1609; Nov. 6, 1978, Pub.L. 95–598, Title II, § 214(a), (b), 92 Stat. 2661; Nov. 19, 1988, Pub.L. 100–702, Title X, § 1007, 102 Stat. 4667.

§ 636. Jurisdiction, powers, and temporary assignment

(a) Each United States magistrate serving under this chapter shall have within the territorial jurisdiction prescribed by his appointment—

(1) all powers and duties conferred or imposed upon United States commissioners by law or by the Rules of Criminal Procedure for the United States District Courts;

(2) the power to administer oaths and affirmations, issue orders pursuant to section 3142 of title 18 concerning release or detention of persons pending trial, and take acknowledgments, affidavits, and depositions;

(3) the power to conduct trials under section 3401, title 18, United States Code, in conformity with and subject to the limitations of that section, and

(4) the power to enter a sentence for a misdemeanor or infraction with the consent of the parties.

(b)(1) Notwithstanding any provision of law to the contrary—

(A) a judge may designate a magistrate to hear and determine any pretrial matter pending before the court, except a motion for injunctive relief, for judgment on the pleadings, for summary judgment, to dismiss or quash an indictment or information made by the defendant, to suppress evidence in a criminal case, to dismiss or to permit maintenance of a class action, to dismiss for failure to state a claim upon which relief can be granted, and to involuntarily dismiss an action. A judge of the court may reconsider any pretrial matter under this subparagraph (A) where it has been shown that the magistrate's order is clearly erroneous or contrary to law.

(B) a judge may also designate a magistrate to conduct hearings, including evidentiary hearings, and to submit to a judge of the court proposed findings of fact and recommendations for the disposition, by a judge of the court, of any motion excepted in subparagraph (A), of applications for posttrial relief made by individuals convicted of criminal offenses and of prisoner petitions challenging conditions of confinement.

(C) the magistrate shall file his proposed findings and recommendations under subparagraph (B) with the court and a copy shall forthwith be mailed to all parties.

Within ten days after being served with a copy, any party may serve and file written objections to such proposed findings and recommendations as provided by rules of court. A judge of the court shall make a de novo determination of those portions of the report or specified proposed findings or recommendations to which objection is made. A judge of the court may accept, reject, or modify, in whole or in part, the findings or recommendations made by the magistrate. The judge may also receive further evidence or recommit the matter to the magistrate with instructions.

(2) A judge may designate a magistrate to serve as a special master pursuant to the applicable provisions of this title and the Federal Rules of Civil Procedure for the United States district courts. A judge may designate a magistrate to serve as a special master in any civil case, upon consent of the parties, without regard to the provisions of rule 53(b) of the Federal Rules of Civil Procedure for the United States district courts.

(3) A magistrate may be assigned such additional duties as are not inconsistent with the Constitution and laws of the United States.

(4) Each district court shall establish rules pursuant to which the magistrates shall discharge their duties.

(c) Notwithstanding any provision of law to the contrary—

(1) Upon the consent of the parties, a full-time United States magistrate or à part-time United States magistrate who serves as a full-time judicial officer may conduct any or all proceedings in a jury or nonjury civil matter and order the entry of judgment in the case, when specially designated to exercise such jurisdiction by the district court or courts he serves. Upon the consent of the parties, pursuant to their specific written request, any other part-time magistrate may exercise such jurisdiction, if such magistrate meets the bar membership requirements set forth in section 631(b)(1) and the chief judge of the district court certifies that a full-time magistrate is not reasonably available in accordance with guidelines established by the judicial council of the circuit. When there is more than one judge of a district court, designation under this paragraph shall be by the concurrence of a majority of all the judges of such district court, and when there is no such concurrence, then by the chief judge.

(2) If a magistrate is designated to exercise civil jurisdiction under paragraph (1) of this subsection, the clerk of court shall, at the time the action is filed, notify the parties of the availability of a magistrate to exercise such jurisdiction. The decision of the parties shall be communicated to the clerk of court. Thereafter, either the district court judge or the magistrate may again advise the parties of the availability of the magistrate, but in so doing, shall also advise the parties that they are free to withhold consent without adverse substantive consequences. Rules of court for the reference of civil

matters to magistrates shall include procedures to protect the voluntariness of the parties' consent.

(3) Upon entry of judgment in any case referred under paragraph (1) of this subsection, an aggrieved party may appeal directly to the appropriate United States court of appeals from the judgment of the magistrate in the same manner as an appeal from any other judgment of a district court. In this circumstance, the consent of the parties allows a magistrate designated to exercise civil jurisdiction under paragraph (1) of this subsection to direct the entry of a judgment of the district court in accordance with the Federal Rules of Civil Procedure. Nothing in this paragraph shall be construed as a limitation of any party's right to seek review by the Supreme Court of the United States.

(4) Notwithstanding the provisions of paragraph (3) of this subsection, at the time of reference to a magistrate, the parties may further consent to appeal on the record to a judge of the district court in the same manner as on an appeal from a judgment of the district court to a court of appeals. Wherever possible the local rules of the district court and the rules promulgated by the conference shall endeavor to make such appeal inexpensive. The district court may affirm, reverse, modify, or remand the magistrate's judgment.

(5) Cases in the district courts under paragraph (4) of this subsection may be reviewed by the appropriate United States court of appeals upon petition for leave to appeal by a party stating specific objections to the judgement. Nothing in this paragraph shall be construed to be a limitation on any party's right to seek review by the Supreme Court of the United States.

(6) The court may, for good cause shown on its own motion, or under extraordinary circumstances shown by any party, vacate a reference of a civil matter to a magistrate under this subsection.

(7) The magistrate shall, subject to guidelines of the Judicial Conference, determine whether the record taken pursuant to this section shall be taken by electronic sound recording, by a court reporter, or by other means.

(d) The practice and procedure for the trial of cases before officers serving under this chapter, and for the taking and hearing of appeals to the district courts, shall conform to rules promulgated by the Supreme Court pursuant to section 2072 of this title.

(e) In a proceeding before a magistrate, any of the following acts or conduct shall constitute a contempt of the district court for the district wherein the magistrate is sitting: (1) disobedience or resistance to any lawful order, process, or writ; (2) misbehavior at a hearing or other proceeding, or so near the place thereof as to obstruct the same; (3) failure to produce, after having been ordered to do so, any pertinent document; (4) refusal to appear after having been subpenaed or, upon appearing, refusal to take the oath or affirmation as a witness, or, having taken the oath or affirmation, refusal to be examined according to law; or (5) any other act or conduct which if committed before a judge of the district court would constitute contempt of such court. Upon the commission of any such act or conduct, the magistrate shall forthwith certify the facts to a judge of the district court and may serve or cause to be served upon any person whose behavior is brought into question under this section an order requiring such person to appear before a judge of that court upon a day certain to show cause why he should not be adjudged in contempt by reason of the facts so certified. A judge of the district court shall thereupon, in a summary manner, hear the evidence as to the act or conduct complained of and, if it is such as to warrant punishment, punish such person in the same manner and to the same extent as for a contempt committed before a judge of the court, or commit such person upon the conditions applicable in the case of defiance of the process of the district court or misconduct in the presence of a judge of that court.

* * *

As amended Oct. 17, 1968, Pub.L. 90–578, Title I, § 101, 82 Stat. 1113; Mar. 1, 1972, Pub.L. 92–239, § 2, 86 Stat. 47; Oct. 21, 1976, Pub.L. 94–577, § 1, 90 Stat. 2729; Oct. 28, 1977, Pub.L. 95–144, § 2, 91 Stat. 1220; Oct. 10, 1979, Pub.L. 96–82, § 2, 93 Stat. 643; Oct. 12, 1984, Pub.L. 98–473, Title II, § 208, 98 Stat. 1986; Nov. 8, 1984, Pub.L. 98–620, Title IV, § 402(29)(B), 98 Stat. 3359; Nov. 14, 1986, Pub.L. 99–651, Title II, § 201(a)(2), 100 Stat. 3647; Nov. 15, 1988, Pub.L. 100–659, § 4(c), 102 Stat. 3918; Nov. 18, 1988, Pub.L. 100–690, Title VII, § 7322, 102 Stat. 4467; Nov. 19, 1988, Pub.L. 100–702, Title IV, § 404(b)(1), Title X, § 1014, 102 Stat. 4651, 4669; Dec. 1, 1990, Pub.L. 101–650, Title III, § 308(a), 104 Stat. 5112.

§ 1251. Original jurisdiction

(a) The Supreme Court shall have original and exclusive jurisdiction of all controversies between two or more States.

(b) The Supreme Court shall have original but not exclusive jurisdiction of:

> (1) All actions or proceedings to which ambassadors, other public ministers, consuls, or vice consuls of foreign states are parties;

> (2) All controversies between the United States and a State;

> (3) All actions or proceedings by a State against the citizens of another State or against aliens. As amended Sept. 30, 1978, Pub.L. 95–393, § 8(b), 92 Stat. 810.

§ 1253. Direct appeals from decisions of three-judge courts

Except as otherwise provided by law, any party may appeal to the Supreme Court from an order granting or denying, after notice and hearing, an interlocutory or permanent injunction in any civil action, suit or proceeding required by any Act of Congress to be heard and determined by a district court of three judges.

§ 1254. Courts of appeals; certiorari; certified questions

Cases in the courts of appeals may be reviewed by the Supreme Court by the following methods:

438

(1) By writ of certiorari granted upon the petition of any party to any civil or criminal case, before or after rendition of judgment or decree;

(2) By certification at any time by a court of appeals of any question of law in any civil or criminal case as to which instructions are desired, and upon such certification the Supreme Court may give binding instructions or require the entire record to be sent up for decision of the entire matter in controversy. As amended June 27, 1988, Pub.L. 100–352, § 2, 102 Stat. 662.

§ 1257. State courts; certiorari

(a) Final judgments or decrees rendered by the highest court of a State in which a decision could be had, may be reviewed by the Supreme Court by writ of certiorari where the validity of a treaty or statute of the United States is drawn in question or where the validity of a statute of any State is drawn in question on the ground of its being repugnant to the Constitution, treaties, or laws of the United States, or where any title, right, privilege, or immunity is specially set up or claimed under the Constitution or the treaties or statutes of, or any commission held or authority exercised under, the United States.

(b) For the purposes of this section, the term "highest court of a State" includes the District of Columbia Court of Appeals. As amended July 29, 1970, Pub.L. 91–358, 84 Stat. 590; June 27, 1988, Pub.L. 100–352, § 3, 102 Stat. 662.

§ 1291. Final decisions of district courts

The courts of appeals (other than the United States Court of Appeals for the Federal Circuit) shall have jurisdiction of appeals from all final decisions of the district courts of the United States, the United States District Court for the District of the Canal Zone, the District Court of Guam, and the District Court of the Virgin Islands, except were a direct review may be had in the Supreme Court. The jurisdiction of the United States Court of Appeals for the Federal Circuit shall be limited to the jurisdiction described in sections 1292 (c) and (d) and 1295 of this title. As amended Oct. 31, 1951, c. 655, § 48, 65 Stat. 726; July 7, 1958, Pub.L. 85–508, § 12(e), 72 Stat. 348; Apr. 2, 1982, Pub.L. 97–164, Title I, § 124, 96 Stat. 36.

§ 1292. Interlocutory decisions

(a) Except as provided in subsections (c) and (d) of this section, the courts of appeals shall have jurisdiction of appeals from:

(1) Interlocutory orders of the district courts of the United States, the United States District Court for the District of the Canal Zone, the District Court of Guam, and the District Court of the Virgin Islands, or of the judges thereof, granting, continuing, modifying, refusing or dissolving injunctions, or refusing to dissolve or modify injunctions, except where a direct review may be had in the Supreme Court;

(2) Interlocutory orders appointing receivers, or refusing orders to wind up receiverships or to take steps to accomplish the purposes thereof, such as directing sales or other disposals of property;

(3) Interlocutory decrees of such district courts or the judges thereof determining the rights and liabilities of the parties to admiralty cases in which appeals from final decrees are allowed.

(b) When a district judge, in making in a civil action an order not otherwise appealable under this section, shall be of the opinion that such order involves a controlling question of law as to which there is substantial ground for difference of opinion and that an immediate appeal from the order may materially advance the ultimate termination of the litigation, he shall so state in writing in such order. The Court of Appeals which would have jurisdiction of an appeal of such action may thereupon, in its discretion, permit an appeal to be taken from such order, if application is made to it within ten days after the entry of the order: *Provided, however,* That application for an appeal hereunder shall not stay proceedings in the district court unless the district judge or the Court of Appeals or a judge thereof shall so order.

(c) The United States Court of Appeals for the Federal Circuit shall have exclusive jurisdiction—

   (1) of an appeal from an interlocutory order or decree described in subsection (a) or (b) of this section in any case over which the court would have jurisdiction of an appeal under section 1295 of this title; and

   (2) of an appeal from a judgment in a civil action for patent infringement which would otherwise be appealable to the United States Court of Appeals for the Federal Circuit and is final except for an accounting.

(d)(1) When the chief judge of the Court of International Trade issues an order under the provisions of section 256(b) of this title, or when any judge of the Court of International Trade, in issuing any other interlocutory order, includes in the order a statement that a controlling question of law is involved with respect to which there is a substantial ground for difference of opinion and that an immediate appeal from that order may materially advance the ultimate termination of the litigation, the United States Court of Appeals for the Federal Circuit may, in its discretion, permit an appeal to be taken from such order, if application is made to that Court within ten days after the entry of such order.

(2) When any judge of the United States Claims Court, in issuing an interlocutory order, includes in the order a statement that a controlling question of law is involved with respect to which there is a substantial ground for difference of opinion and that an immediate appeal from that order may materially advance the ultimate termination of the litigation, the United States Court of Appeals for the Federal Circuit may, in its discretion, permit an appeal to be taken from such order, if application is made to that Court within ten days after the entry of such order.

(3) Neither the application for nor the granting of an appeal under this subsection shall stay proceedings in the Court of International Trade or in the Claims Court, as the case may be, unless a stay is ordered by a judge of the Court of International Trade or of the Claims Court or by the

United States Court of Appeals for the Federal Circuit or a judge of that court.

(4)(A) The United States Court of Appeals for the Federal Circuit shall have exclusive jurisdiction of an appeal from an interlocutory order of a district court of the United States, the District Court of Guam, the District Court of the Virgin Islands, or the District Court for the Northern Mariana Islands, granting or denying, in whole or in part, a motion to transfer an action to the United States Claims Court under section 1631 of this title.

(B) When a motion to transfer an action to the Claims Court is filed in a district court, no further proceedings shall be taken in the district court until 60 days after the court has ruled upon the motion. If an appeal is taken from the district court's grant or denial of the motion, proceedings shall be further stayed until the appeal has been decided by the Court of Appeals for the Federal Circuit. The stay of proceedings in the district court shall not bar the granting of preliminary or injunctive relief, where appropriate and where expedition is reasonably necessary. However, during the period in which proceedings are stayed as provided in this subparagraph, no transfer to the Claims Court pursuant to the motion shall be carried out. As amended Oct. 31, 1951, c. 655, § 49, 65 Stat. 726; July 7, 1958, Pub.L. 85–508, § 12(e), 72 Stat. 348; Sept. 2, 1958, Pub.L. 85–919, 72 Stat. 1770; Apr. 2, 1982, Pub.L. 97–164, Title I, § 125, 96 Stat. 36; Nov. 8, 1984, Pub.L. 98–620, Title IV, § 412, 98 Stat. 3362; Nov. 19, 1988, Pub.L. 100–702, Title V, § 501, 102 Stat. 4652.

§ 1295. Jurisdiction of the United States Court of Appeals for the Federal Circuit

(a) The United States Court of Appeals for the Federal Circuit shall have exclusive jurisdiction—

(1) of an appeal from a final decision of a district court of the United States, the United States District Court for the District of the Canal Zone, the District Court of Guam, the District Court of the Virgin Islands, or the District Court for the Northern Mariana Islands, if the jurisdiction of that court was based, in whole or in part, on section 1338 of this title, except that a case involving a claim arising under any Act of Congress relating to copyrights, exclusive rights in mask works, or trademarks and no other claims under section 1338(a) shall be governed by sections 1291, 1292, and 1294 of this title;

(2) of an appeal from a final decision of a district court of the United States, the United States District Court for the District of the Canal Zone, the District Court of Guam, the District Court of the Virgin Islands, or the District Court for the Northern Mariana Islands, if the jurisdiction of that court was based, in whole or in part, on section 1346 of this title, except that jurisdiction of an appeal in a case brought in a district court under section 1346(a)(1), 1346(b), 1346(e), or 1346(f) of this title or under section 1346(a)(2) when the claim is founded upon an Act of Congress or a regulation of an

executive department providing for internal revenue shall be governed by sections 1291, 1292, and 1294 of this title;

(3) of an appeal from a final decision of the United States Claims Court;

(4) of an appeal from a decision of—

(A) the Board of Patent Appeals and Interferences of the Patent and Trademark Office with respect to patent applications and interferences, at the instance of an applicant for a patent or any party to a patent interference, and any such appeal shall waive the right of such applicant or party to proceed under section 145 or 146 of title 35;

(B) the Commissioner of Patents and Trademarks or the Trademark Trial and Appeal Board with respect to applications for registration of marks and other proceedings as provided in section 21 of the Trademark Act of 1946 (15 U.S.C. 1071); or

(C) a district court to which a case was directed pursuant to section 145 or 146 of title 35;

(5) of an appeal from a final decision of the United States Court of International Trade;

(6) to review the final determinations of the United States International Trade Commission relating to unfair practices in import trade, made under section 337 of the Tariff Act of 1930 (19 U.S.C. 1337);

(7) to review, by appeal on questions of law only, findings of the Secretary of Commerce under U.S. note 6 to subchapter X of chapter 98 of the Harmonized Tariff Schedule of the United States (relating to importation of instruments or apparatus);

(8) of an appeal under section 71 of the Plant Variety Protection Act (7 U.S.C. 2461);

(9) of an appeal from a final order or final decision of the Merit Systems Protection Board, pursuant to sections 7703(b)(1) and 7703(d) of title 5; and

(10) of an appeal from a final decision of an agency board of contract appeals pursuant to section 8(g)(1) of the Contract Disputes Act of 1978 (41 U.S.C. 607(g)(1)).

(b) The head of any executive department or agency may, with the approval of the Attorney General, refer to the Court of Appeals for the Federal Circuit for judicial review any final decision rendered by a board of contract appeals pursuant to the terms of any contract with the United States awarded by that department or agency which the head of such department or agency has concluded is not entitled to finality pursuant to the review standards specified in section 10(b) of the Contract Disputes Act of 1978 (41 U.S.C. 609(b)). The head of each executive department or agency shall make any referral under this section within one hundred and twenty days after the receipt of a copy of the final appeal decision.

(c) The Court of Appeals for the Federal Circuit shall review the matter referred in accordance with the standards specified in section 10(b) of the Contract Disputes Act of 1978. The court shall proceed with judicial review on the administrative record made before the board of contract appeals on matters so referred as in other cases pending in such court, shall determine the issue of finality of the appeal decision, and shall, if appropriate, render judgment thereon, or remand the matter to any administrative or executive body or official with such direction as it may deem proper and just. Added Apr. 2, 1982, Pub.L. 97–164, Title I, § 127(a), 96 Stat. 37; as amended Nov. 8, 1984, Pub.L. 98–622, Title II, § 205(a), 98 Stat. 3388; Aug. 23, 1988, Pub.L. 100–418, Title I, § 1214(a)(3), 102 Stat. 1156; Nov. 19, 1988, Pub.L. 100–702, Title X, § 1020(a)(3), 102 Stat. 4671.

§ 1331. Federal question

The district courts shall have original jurisdiction of all civil actions arising under the Constitution, laws, or treaties of the United States. As amended July 25, 1958, Pub.L. 85–554, § 1, 72 Stat. 415; Oct. 21, 1976, Pub.L. 94–574, § 2, 90 Stat. 2721; Dec. 1, 1980, Pub.L. 96–486, § 2(a), 94 Stat. 2369.

§ 1332. Diversity of citizenship; amount in controversy; costs

(a) The district courts shall have original jurisdiction of all civil actions where the matter in controversy exceeds the sum or value of $50,000, exclusive of interest and costs, and is between—

    (1) citizens of different States;

    (2) citizens of a State and citizens or subjects of a foreign state;

    (3) citizens of different States and in which citizens or subjects of a foreign state are additional parties; and

    (4) a foreign state, defined in section 1603(a) of this title, as plaintiff and citizens of a State or of different States.

For the purposes of this section, section 1335, and section 1441, an alien admitted to the United States for permanent residence shall be deemed a citizen of the State in which such alien is domiciled.

(b) Except when express provision therefor is otherwise made in a statute of the United States, where the plaintiff who files the case originally in the Federal courts is finally adjudged to be entitled to recover less than the sum or value of $50,000, computed without regard to any setoff or counterclaim to which the defendant may be adjudged to be entitled, and exclusive of interest and costs, the district court may deny costs to the plaintiff and, in addition, may impose costs on the plaintiff.

(c) For the purposes of this section and section 1441 of this title—

    (1) a corporation shall be deemed to be a citizen of any State by which it has been incorporated and of the State where it has its principal place of business, except that in any direct action against the insurer of a policy or contract of liability insurance, whether incorporated or unincorporated, to which action the insured is not joined as a party-defendant, such insurer shall be deemed a citizen of

the State of which the insured is a citizen, as well as of any State by which the insurer has been incorporated and of the State where it has its principal place of business; and

(2) the legal representative of the estate of a decedent shall be deemed to be a citizen only of the same State as the decedent, and the legal representative of an infant or incompetent shall be deemed to be a citizen only of the same State as the infant or incompetent.

(d) The word "States", as used in this section, includes the Territories, the District of Columbia, and the Commonwealth of Puerto Rico. As amended July 26, 1956, c. 740, 70 Stat. 658; July 25, 1958, Pub.L. 85–554, § 2, 72 Stat. 415; Aug. 14, 1964, Pub.L. 88–439, § 1, 78 Stat. 445; Oct. 21, 1976, Pub.L. 94–583, § 3, 90 Stat. 2891; Nov. 19, 1988, Pub.L. 100–702, Title II, §§ 201–203, 102 Stat. 4646.

§ 1333. Admiralty, maritime and prize cases

The district courts shall have original jurisdiction, exclusive of the courts of the States, of:

(1) Any civil case of admiralty or maritime jurisdiction, saving to suitors in all cases all other remedies to which they are otherwise entitled.

(2) Any prize brought into the United States and all proceedings for the condemnation of property taken as prize. As amended May 24, 1949, c. 139, § 79, 63 Stat. 101.

§ 1335. Interpleader

(a) The district courts shall have original jurisdiction of any civil action of interpleader or in the nature of interpleader filed by any person, firm, or corporation, association, or society having in his or its custody or possession money or property of the value of $500 or more, or having issued a note, bond, certificate, policy of insurance, or other instrument of value or amount of $500 or more, or providing for the delivery or payment or the loan of money or property of such amount or value, or being under any obligation written or unwritten to the amount of $500 or more, if

(1) Two or more adverse claimants, of diverse citizenship as defined in section 1332 of this title, are claiming or may claim to be entitled to such money or property, or to any one or more of the benefits arising by virtue of any note, bond, certificate, policy or other instrument, or arising by virtue of any such obligation; and if (2) the plaintiff has deposited such money or property or has paid the amount of or the loan or other value of such instrument or the amount due under such obligation into the registry of the court, there to abide the judgment of the court, or has given bond payable to the clerk of the court in such amount and with such surety as the court or judge may deem proper, conditioned upon the compliance by the plaintiff with the future order or judgment of the court with respect to the subject matter of the controversy.

(b) Such an action may be entertained although the titles or claims of the conflicting claimants do not have a common origin, or are not identical, but are adverse to and independent of one another.

§ 1337. Commerce and antitrust regulations; amount in controversy, costs

(a) The district courts shall have original jurisdiction of any civil action or proceeding arising under any Act of Congress regulating commerce or protecting trade and commerce against restraints and monopolies: *Provided, however,* That the district courts shall have original jurisdiction of an action brought under section 11707 of title 49, only if the matter in controversy for each receipt or bill of lading exceeds $10,000, exclusive of interest and costs.

(b) Except when express provision therefor is otherwise made in a statute of the United States, where a plaintiff who files the case under section 11707 of title 49, originally in the Federal courts is finally adjudged to be entitled to recover less than the sum or value of $10,000, computed without regard to any setoff or counterclaim to which the defendant may be adjudged to be entitled, and exclusive of any interest and costs, the district court may deny costs to the plaintiff and, in addition, may impose costs on the plaintiff.

(c) The district courts shall not have jurisdiction under this section of any matter within the exclusive jurisdiction of the Court of International Trade under chapter 95 of this title. As amended Oct. 20, 1978, Pub.L. 95–486, § 9(a), 92 Stat. 1633; Oct. 10, 1980, Pub.L. 96–417, Title V, § 505, 94 Stat. 1743; Jan. 12, 1983, Pub.L. 97–449, § 5(f), 96 Stat. 2442.

§ 1338. Patents, plant variety protection, copyrights, mask works, trade-marks, and unfair competition

(a) The district courts shall have original jurisdiction of any civil action arising under any Act of Congress relating to patents, plant variety protection, copyrights and trade-marks. Such jurisdiction shall be exclusive of the courts of the states in patent, plant variety protection and copyright cases.

(b) The district courts shall have original jurisdiction of any civil action asserting a claim of unfair competition when joined with a substantial and related claim under the copyright, patent, plant variety protection or trade-mark laws.

(c) Subsections (a) and (b) apply to exclusive rights in mask works under chapter 9 of title 17 to the same extent as such subsections apply to copyrights. As amended Dec. 24, 1970, Pub.L. 91–577, Title III, § 143(b), 84 Stat. 1559; Nov. 19, 1988, Pub.L. 100–702, Title X, § 1020(a)(4), 102 Stat. 4671.

§ 1343. Civil rights and elective franchise

(a) The district courts shall have original jurisdiction of any civil action authorized by law to be commenced by any person:

(1) To recover damages for injury to his person or property, or because of the deprivation of any right or privilege of a citizen of the United States, by any act done in furtherance of any conspiracy mentioned in section 1985 of Title 42;

445

(2) To recover damages from any person who fails to prevent or to aid in preventing any wrongs mentioned in section 1985 of Title 42 which he had knowledge were about to occur and power to prevent;

(3) To redress the deprivation, under color of any State law, statute, ordinance, regulation, custom or usage, of any right, privilege or immunity secured by the Constitution of the United States or by any Act of Congress providing for equal rights of citizens or of all persons within the jurisdiction of the United States;

(4) To recover damages or to secure equitable or other relief under any Act of Congress providing for the protection of civil rights, including the right to vote.

(b) For purposes of this section—

(1) the District of Columbia shall be considered to be a State; and

(2) any Act of Congress applicable exclusively to the District of Columbia shall be considered to be a statute of the District of Columbia. As amended Sept. 3, 1954, c. 1263, § 42, 68 Stat. 1241; Sept. 9, 1957, Pub.L. 85–315, Part III, § 121, 71 Stat. 637; Dec. 29, 1979, Pub.L. 96–170, § 2, 93 Stat. 1284.

§ 1345. United States as plaintiff

Except as otherwise provided by Act of Congress, the district courts shall have original jurisdiction of all civil actions, suits or proceedings commenced by the United States, or by any agency or officer thereof expressly authorized to sue by Act of Congress.

§ 1346. United States as defendant

(a) The district courts shall have original jurisdiction, concurrent with the United States Claims Court, of:

(1) Any civil action against the United States for the recovery of any internal-revenue tax alleged to have been erroneously or illegally assessed or collected, or any penalty claimed to have been collected without authority or any sum alleged to have been excessive or in any manner wrongfully collected under the internal-revenue laws;

(2) Any other civil action or claim against the United States, not exceeding $10,000 in amount, founded either upon the Constitution, or any Act of Congress, or any regulation of an executive department, or upon any express or implied contract with the United States, or for liquidated or unliquidated damages in cases not sounding in tort, except that the district courts shall not have jurisdiction of any civil action or claim against the United States founded upon any express or implied contract with the United States or for liquidated or unliquidated damages in cases not sounding in tort which are subject to sections 8(g)(1) and 10(a)(1) of the Contract Disputes Act of 1978. For the purpose of this paragraph, an express or implied contract with the Army and Air Force Exchange Service, Navy Exchanges, Marine Corps Exchanges, Coast Guard Exchanges, or Exchange Councils of the National Aeronautics and Space Administration shall be considered an express or implied contract with the United States.

(b) Subject to the provisions of chapter 171 of this title, the district courts, together with the United Stated District Court for the District of the Canal Zone and the District Court of the Virgin Islands, shall have exclusive jurisdiction of civil actions on claims against the United States, for money damages, accruing on and after January 1, 1945, for injury or loss of property, or personal injury or death caused by the negligent or wrongful act or omission of any employee of the government while acting within the scope of his office or employment, under circumstances where the United States, if a private person, would be liable to the claimant in accordance with the law of the place where the act or omission occurred.

(c) The jurisdiction conferred by this section includes jurisdiction of any set-off, counterclaim, or other claim or demand whatever on the part of the United States against any plaintiff commencing an action under this section.

(d) The district courts shall not have jurisdiction under this section of any civil action or claim for a pension.

(e) The district courts shall have original jurisdiction of any civil action against the United States provided in section 6226, 6228(a), 7426, or 7428 (in the case of the United States district court for the District of Columbia) or section 7429 of the Internal Revenue Code of 1954.

(f) The district courts shall have exclusive original jurisdiction of civil actions under section 2409a to quiet title to an estate or interest in real property in which an interest is claimed by the United States. As amended Apr. 25, 1949, c. 92, § 2(a), 63 Stat. 62; May 24, 1949, c. 139, § 80(a, b), 63 Stat. 101; Oct. 31, 1951, c. 655, § 50(b), 65 Stat. 727; July 30, 1954, c. 648, § 1, 68 Stat. 589; July 7, 1958, Pub.L. 85–508, § 12(e), 72 Stat. 348; Aug. 30, 1964, Pub.L. 88–519, 78 Stat. 699; Nov. 2, 1966, Pub.L. 89–719, Title II, § 202(a), 80 Stat. 1148; July 23, 1970, Pub.L. 91–350, 84 Stat. 449; Oct. 25, 1972, Pub.L. 92–562, § 1, 86 Stat. 1176; Oct. 4, 1976, Pub.L. 94–455, Title XII, § 1204(c)(1), Title XIII, § 1306(b)(7), 90 Stat. 1697, 1719; Nov. 1, 1978, Pub.L. 95–563, § 14(a), 92 Stat. 2389; Apr. 2, 1982, Pub.L. 97–164, Title I, § 129, 96 Stat. 39; Sept. 3, 1982, Pub.L. 97–248, Title IV, § 402(c)(17), 96 Stat. 669.

§ 1359. Parties collusively joined or made

A district court shall not have jurisdiction of a civil action in which any party, by assignment or otherwise, has been improperly or collusively made or joined to invoke the jurisdiction of such court.

§ 1361. Action to compel an officer of the United States to perform his duty

The district courts shall have original jurisdiction of any action in the nature of mandamus to compel an officer or employee of the United States or any agency thereof to perform a duty owed to the plaintiff. Added Oct. 5, 1962, Pub.L. 87–748, § 1(a), 76 Stat. 744.

§ 1367. Supplemental jurisdiction

(a) Except as provided in subsections (b) and (c) or as expressly provided otherwise by Federal statute, in any civil action of which the district courts have original jurisdiction, the district courts shall have supplemental jurisdiction over all other claims that are so related to claims in the action within such original jurisdiction that they form part of the same case or controversy under Article III of the United States Constitution. Such supplemental jurisdiction shall include claims that involve the joinder or intervention of additional parties.

(b) In any civil action of which the district courts have original jurisdiction founded solely on section 1332 of this title, the district courts shall not have supplemental jurisdiction under subsection (a) over claims by plaintiffs against persons made parties under Rule 14, 19, 20, or 24 of the Federal Rules of Civil Procedure, or over claims by persons proposed to be joined as plaintiffs under Rule 19 of such rules, or seeking to intervene as plaintiffs under Rule 24 of such rules, when exercising supplemental jurisdiction over such claims would be inconsistent with the jurisdictional requirements of section 1332.

(c) The district courts may decline to exercise supplemental jurisdiction over a claim under subsection (a) if—

(1) the claim raises a novel or complex issue of State law,

(2) the claim substantially predominates over the claim or claims over which the district court has original jurisdiction,

(3) the district court has dismissed all claims over which it has original jurisdiction, or

(4) in exceptional circumstances, there are other compelling reasons for declining jurisdiction.

(d) The period of limitations for any claim asserted under subsection (a), and for any other claim in the same action that is voluntarily dismissed at the same time as or after the dismissal of the claim under subsection (a), shall be tolled while the claim is pending and for a period of 30 days after it is dismissed unless State law provides for a longer tolling period.

(e) As used in this section, the term "State" includes the District of Columbia, the Commonwealth of Puerto Rico, and any territory or possession of the United States.   Added Dec. 1, 1990, Pub.L. 101–650, Title III, § 310(a), 104 Stat. 5113.

§ 1391. Venue generally

(a) A civil action wherein jurisdiction is founded only on diversity of citizenship may, except as otherwise provided by law, be brought only in (1) a judicial district where any defendant resides, if all defendants reside in the same State, (2) a judicial district in which a substantial part of the events or omissions giving rise to the claim occurred, or a substantial part of property that is the subject of the action is situated, or (3) a judicial district in which the defendants are subject to personal jurisdiction at the time the action is commenced.

(b) A civil action wherein jurisdiction is not founded solely on diversity of citizenship may, except as otherwise provided by law, be brought only if [sic] (1) a judicial district where any defendant resides, if all defendants reside in the same State, (2) a judicial district in which a substantial part of the events or omissions giving rise to the claim occurred, or a substantial part of property that is the subject of the action is situated, or (3) a judicial district in which any defendant may be found, if there is no district in which the action may otherwise be brought.

(c) For purposes of venue under this chapter, a defendant that is a corporation shall be deemed to reside in any judicial district in which it is subject to personal jurisdiction at the time the action is commenced. In a State which has more than one judicial district and in which a defendant that is a corporation is subject to personal jurisdiction at the time an action is commenced, such corporation shall be deemed to reside in any district in that State within which its contacts would be sufficient to subject it to personal jurisdiction if that district were a separate State, and, if there is no such district, the corporation shall be deemed to reside in the district within which it has the most significant contacts.

(d) An alien may be sued in any district.

(e) A civil action in which a defendant is an officer or employee of the United States or any agency thereof acting in his official capacity or under color of legal authority, or an agency of the United States, or the United States, may, except as otherwise provided by law, be brought in any judicial district in which (1) a defendant in the action resides, (2) a substantial part of the events or omissions giving rise to the claim occurred, or a substantial part of property that is the subject of the action is situated, or (3) the plaintiff resides if no real property is involved in the action. Additional persons may be joined as parties to any such action in accordance with the Federal Rules of Civil Procedure and with such other venue requirements as would be applicable if the United States or one of its officers, employees, or agencies were not a party.

The summons and complaint in such an action shall be served as provided by the Federal Rules of Civil Procedure except that the delivery of the summons and complaint to the officer or agency as required by the rules may be made by certified mail beyond the territorial limits of the district in which the action is brought.

(f) A civil action against a foreign state as defined in section 1603(a) of this title may be brought—

(1) in any judicial district in which a substantial part of the events or omissions giving rise to the claim occurred, or a substantial part of property that is the subject of the action is situated;

(2) in any judicial district in which the vessel or cargo of a foreign state is situated, if the claim is asserted under section 1605(b) of this title;

(3) in any judicial district in which the agency or instrumentality is licensed to do business or is doing business, if the action is brought against an agency or instrumentality of a foreign state as defined in section 1603(b) of this title; or

(4) in the United States District Court for the District of Columbia if the action is brought against a foreign state or political subdivision thereof. As amended Oct. 5, 1962, Pub.L. 87–748, § 2, 76 Stat. 744; Dec. 23, 1963, Pub.L. 88–234, 77 Stat. 473; Nov. 2, 1966,

Pub.L. 89–714, §§ 1, 2, 80 Stat. 1111; Oct. 21, 1976, Pub.L. 94–574, § 3, 90 Stat. 2721; Oct. 21, 1976, Pub.L. 94–583, § 5, 90 Stat. 2897; Nov. 19, 1988, Pub.L. 100–702, Title X, § 1013, 102 Stat. 4669; Dec. 1, 1990, Pub.L. 101–650, Title III, § 311, 104 Stat. 5114.

§ 1392. Defendants or property in different districts in same State

(a) Any civil action, not of a local nature, against defendants residing in different districts in the same State, may be brought in any of such districts.

(b) Any civil action, of a local nature, involving property located in different districts in the same State, may be brought in any of such districts.

§ 1397. Interpleader

Any civil action of interpleader or in the nature of interpleader under section 1335 of this title may be brought in the judicial district in which one or more of the claimants reside.

§ 1400. Patents and copyrights

(a) Civil actions, suits, or proceedings arising under any Act of Congress relating to copyrights or exclusive rights in mask works may be instituted in the district in which the defendant or his agent resides or may be found.

(b) Any civil action for patent infringement may be brought in the judicial district where the defendant resides, or where the defendant has committed acts of infringement and has a regular and established place of business.   As amended Nov. 19, 1988, Pub.L. 100–702, Title X, § 1020(a)(5), 102 Stat. 4671.

§ 1401. Stockholder's derivative action

Any civil action by a stockholder on behalf of his corporation may be prosecuted in any judicial district where the corporation might have sued the same defendants.

§ 1402. United States as defendant

(a) Any civil action in a district court against the United States under subsection (a) of section 1346 of this title may be prosecuted only:

(1) Except as provided in paragraph (2), in the judicial district where the plaintiff resides;

(2) In the case of a civil action by a corporation under paragraph (1) of subsection (a) of section 1346, in the judicial district in which is located the principal place of business or principal office or agency of the corporation; or if it has no principal place of business or principal office or agency in any judicial district (A) in the judicial district in which is located the office to which was made the return of the tax in respect of which the claim is made, or (B) if no return was made, in the judicial district in which lies the District of Columbia.   Notwithstanding the foregoing provisions of this paragraph a district court, for the convenience

of the parties and witnesses, in the interest of justice, may transfer any such action to any other district or division.

(b) Any civil action on a tort claim against the United States under subsection (b) of section 1346 of this title may be prosecuted only in the judicial district where the plaintiff resides or wherein the act or omission complained of occurred.

(c) Any civil action against the United States under subsection (e) of section 1346 of this title may be prosecuted only in the judicial district where the property is situated at the time of levy, or if no levy is made, in the judicial district in which the event occurred which gave rise to the cause of action.

(d) Any civil action under section 2409a to quiet title to an estate or interest in real property in which an interest is claimed by the United States shall be brought in the district court of the district where the property is located or, if located in different districts, in any of such districts. As amended Sept. 2, 1958, Pub.L. 85–920, 72 Stat. 1770; Nov. 2, 1966, Pub.L. 89–719, Title II, § 202(b), 80 Stat. 1149; Oct. 25, 1972, Pub.L. 92–562, § 2, 86 Stat. 1176; Apr. 2, 1982, Pub.L. 97–164, Title I, § 131, 96 Stat. 39.

§ 1404. Change of venue

(a) For the convenience of parties and witnesses, in the interest of justice, a district court may transfer any civil action to any other district or division where it might have been brought.

(b) Upon motion, consent or stipulation of all parties, any action, suit or proceeding of a civil nature or any motion of hearing thereof, may be transferred, in the discretion of the court, from the division in which pending to any other division in the same district. Transfer of proceedings in rem brought by or on behalf of the United States may be transferred under this section without the consent of the United States where all other parties request transfer.

(c) A district court may order any civil action to be tried at any place within the division in which it is pending.

(d) As used in this section, "district court" includes the United States District Court for the District of the Canal Zone; and "district" includes the territorial jurisdiction of that court. As amended Oct. 18, 1962, Pub.L. 87–845, § 9, 76A Stat. 699.

§ 1406. Cure or waiver of defects

(a) The district court of a district in which is filed a case laying venue in the wrong division or district shall dismiss, or if it be in the interest of justice, transfer such case to any district or division in which it could have been brought.

(b) Nothing in this chapter shall impair the jurisdiction of a district court of any matter involving a party who does not interpose timely and sufficient objection to the venue.

(c) As used in this section, "district court" includes the United States District Court for the District of the Canal Zone; and "district" includes the territorial jurisdiction of that court. As amended May 24, 1949, c. 139, § 81, 63 Stat. 101; Sept. 13, 1960, Pub.L. 86–770, § 1, 74 Stat. 912; Oct. 18, 1962, Pub.L. 87–845, § 10, 76A Stat. 699; Apr. 2, 1982, Pub.L. 97–164, Title I, § 132, 96 Stat. 39.

§ 1407. Multidistrict litigation

(a) When civil actions involving one or more common questions of fact are pending in different districts, such actions may be transferred to any district for coordinated or consolidated pretrial proceedings. Such transfers shall be made by the judicial panel on multidistrict litigation authorized by this section upon its determination that transfers for such proceedings will be for the convenience of parties and witnesses and will promote the just and efficient conduct of such actions. Each action so transferred shall be remanded by the panel at or before the conclusion of such pretrial proceedings to the district from which it was transferred unless it shall have been previously terminated: *Provided, however,* That the panel may separate any claim, cross-claim, counter-claim, or third-party claim and remand any of such claims before the remainder of the action is remanded.

(b) Such coordinated or consolidated pretrial proceedings shall be conducted by a judge or judges to whom such actions are assigned by the judicial panel on multidistrict litigation. For this purpose, upon request of the panel, a circuit judge or a district judge may be designated and assigned temporarily for service in the transferee district by the Chief Justice of the United States or the chief judge of the circuit, as may be required, in accordance with the provisions of chapter 13 of this title. With the consent of the transferee district court, such actions may be assigned by the panel to a judge or judges of such district. The judge or judges to whom such actions are assigned, the members of the judicial panel on multidistrict litigation, and other circuit and district judges designated when needed by the panel may exercise the powers of a district judge in any district for the purpose of conducting pretrial depositions in such coordinated or consolidated pretrial proceedings.

(c) Proceedings for the transfer of an action under this section may be initiated by—

(i) the judicial panel on multidistrict litigation upon its own initiative, or

(ii) motion filed with the panel by a party in any action in which transfer for coordinated or consolidated pretrial proceedings under this section may be appropriate. A copy of such motion shall be filed in the district court in which the moving party's action is pending.

The panel shall give notice to the parties in all actions in which transfers for coordinated or consolidated pretrial proceedings are contemplated, and such notice shall specify the time and place of any hearing to determine whether such transfer shall be made. Orders of the panel to set a hearing and other orders of the panel issued prior to the order either directing or denying transfer shall be filed in the office of the clerk of the district court in which a transfer hearing is to be or has been held. The panel's order of transfer shall be based upon a record of such hearing at which material evidence may be offered by any party to an action pending in any district that would be affected by the proceedings under this section, and shall be supported by findings of fact and conclusions of law based upon such record. Orders of transfer and such other orders as the panel may make thereafter shall be filed in the office of the clerk of the district court of the transferee district and shall be effective when thus filed. The clerk of the transferee district court shall forthwith transmit a certified copy of the panel's order to transfer to the clerk of the district court from which the action is being transferred. An order denying transfer shall be filed in each district wherein there is a case pending in which the motion for transfer has been made.

(d) The judicial panel on multidistrict litigation shall consist of seven circuit and district judges designated from time to time by the Chief Justice of the United States, no two of whom shall be from the same circuit. The concurrence of four members shall be necessary to any action by the panel.

(e) No proceedings for review of any order of the panel may be permitted except by extraordinary writ pursuant to the provisions of title 28, section 1651, United States Code. Petitions for an extraordinary writ to review an order of the panel to set a transfer hearing and other orders of the panel issued prior to the order either directing or denying transfer shall be filed only in the court of appeals having jurisdiction over the district in which a hearing is to be or has been held. Petitions for an extraordinary writ to review an order to transfer or orders subsequent to transfer shall be filed only in the court of appeals having jurisdiction over the transferee district. There shall be no appeal or review of an order of the panel denying a motion to transfer for consolidated or coordinated proceedings.

(f) The panel may prescribe rules for the conduct of its business not inconsistent with Acts of Congress and the Federal Rules of Civil Procedure.

(g) Nothing in this section shall apply to any action in which the United States is a complainant arising under the antitrust laws. "Antitrust laws" as used herein include those acts referred to in the Act of October 15, 1914, as amended (38 Stat. 730; 15 U.S.C. 12), and also include the Act of June 19, 1936 (49 Stat. 1526; 15 U.S.C. 13, 13a, and 13b) and the Act of September 26, 1914, as added March 21, 1938 (52 Stat. 116, 117; 15 U.S.C. 56); but shall not include section 4A of the Act of October 15, 1914, as added July 7, 1955 (69 Stat. 282; 15 U.S.C. 15a).

(h) Notwithstanding the provisions of section 1404 or subsection (f) of this section, the judicial panel on multidistrict litigation may consolidate and transfer with or without the consent of the parties, for both pretrial purposes and for trial, any action brought under section 4C of the Clayton Act. Added Apr. 29, 1968, Pub.L. 90–296, § 1, 82 Stat. 109; as amended Sept. 30, 1976, Pub.L. 94–435, Title III, § 303, 90 Stat. 1396.

§ 1441. Actions removable generally

(a) Except as otherwise expressly provided by Act of Congress, any civil action brought in a State court of which the district courts of the

United States have original jurisdiction, may be removed by the defendant or the defendants, to the district court of the United States for the district and division embracing the place where such action is pending. For purposes of removal under this chapter, the citizenship of defendants sued under fictitious names shall be disregarded.

(b) Any civil action of which the district courts have original jurisdiction founded on a claim or right arising under the Constitution, treaties or laws of the United States shall be removable without regard to the citizenship or residence of the parties. Any other such action shall be removable only if none of the parties in interest properly joined and served as defendants is a citizen of the State in which such action is brought.

(c) Whenever a separate and independent claim or cause of action within the jurisdiction conferred by section 1331 of this title, is joined with one or more otherwise non-removable claims or causes of action, the entire case may be removed and the district court may determine all issues therein, or, in its discretion, may may [sic] remand all matters in which State law predominates.

(d) Any civil action brought in a State court against a foreign state as defined in section 1603(a) of this title may be removed by the foreign state to the district court of the United States for the district and division embracing the place where such action is pending. Upon removal the action shall be tried by the court without jury. Where removal is based upon this subsection, the time limitations of section 1446(b) of this chapter may be enlarged at any time for cause shown.

(e) The court to which such civil action is removed is not precluded from hearing and determining any claim in such civil action because the State court from which such civil action is removed did not have jurisdiction over that claim. As amended Oct. 21, 1976, Pub.L. 94–583, § 6, 90 Stat. 2898; June 19, 1986, Pub.L. 99–336, § 3, 100 Stat. 637; Nov. 19, 1988, Pub.L. 100–702, Title X, § 1016(a), 102 Stat. 4669; Dec. 1, 1990, Pub.L. 101–650, Title III, § 312, 104 Stat. 5114.

§ 1442. Federal officers sued or prosecuted

(a) A civil action or criminal prosecution commenced in a State court against any of the following persons may be removed by them to the district court of the United States for the district and division embracing the place wherein it is pending:

(1) Any officer of the United States or any agency thereof, or person acting under him, for any act under color of such office or on account of any right, title or authority claimed under any Act of Congress for the apprehension or punishment of criminals or the collection of the revenue.

(2) A property holder whose title is derived from any such officer, where such action or prosecution affects the validity of any law of the United States.

(3) Any officer of the courts of the United States, for any Act under color of office or in the performance of his duties;

(4) Any officer of either House of Congress, for any act in the discharge of his official duty under an order of such House.

(b) A personal action commenced in any State court by an alien against any citizen of a State who is, or at the time the alleged action accrued was, a civil officer of the United States and is a nonresident of such State, wherein jurisdiction is obtained by the State court by personal service of process, may be removed by the defendant to the district court of the United States for the district and division in which the defendant was served with process.

§ 1443. Civil rights cases

Any of the following civil actions or criminal prosecutions, commenced in a State court may be removed by the defendant to the district court of the United States for the district and division embracing the place wherein it is pending:

(1) Against any person who is denied or cannot enforce in the courts of such State a right under any law providing for the equal civil rights of citizens of the United States, or of all persons within the jurisdiction thereof;

(2) For any act under color of authority derived from any law providing for equal rights, or for refusing to do any act on the ground that it would be inconsistent with such law.

§ 1445. Nonremovable actions

(a) A civil action in any State court against a railroad or its receivers or trustees, arising under section 51 to 60 of Title 45, may not be removed to any district court of the United States.

(b) A civil action in any State court against a common carrier or its receivers or trustees to recover damages for delay, loss, or injury of shipments, arising under section 11707 of Title 49, may not be removed to any district court of the United States unless the matter in controversy exceeds $10,000, exclusive of interest and costs.

(c) A civil action in any State court arising under the workmen's compensation laws of such State may not be removed to any district court of the United States. As amended July 25, 1958, Pub.L. 85–554, § 572 Stat. 415; Oct. 17, 1978, Pub.L. 95–473, § 2(a)(3)(A), 92 Stat. 1465; Oct. 20, 1978, Pub.L. 95–486, § 9(b), 92 Stat. 1634.

§ 1446. Procedure for removal

(a) A defendant or defendants desiring to remove any civil action or criminal prosecution from a State court shall file in the district court of the United States for the district and division within which such action is pending a notice of removal signed pursuant to Rule 11 of the Federal Rules of Civil Procedure and containing a short and plain statement of the grounds for removal, together with a copy of all process, pleadings, and orders served upon such defendant or defendants in such action.

(b) The notice of removal of a civil action or proceeding shall be filed within thirty days after the receipt by the defendant, through service or otherwise, of a copy of the initial pleading setting forth the claim for relief upon which such action or proceeding is based, or within thirty days after the service of summons upon the defendant if such initial pleading has then been filed in court and is not required to be served on the defendant, whichever period is shorter.

If the case stated by the initial pleading is not removable, a notice of removal may be filed within thirty days after receipt by the defendant, through service or otherwise, of a copy of an amended pleading, motion, order or other paper from which it may first be ascertained that the case is one which is or has become removable, except that a case may not be removed on the basis of jurisdiction conferred by section 1332 of this title more than 1 year after commencement of the action.

(c)(1) A petition for removal of a criminal prosecution shall be filed not later than thirty days after the arraignment in the State court, or at any time before trial, whichever is earlier, except that for good cause shown the United States district court may enter an order granting the petitioner leave to file the petition at a later time.

(2) A petition for removal of a criminal prosecution shall include all grounds for such removal. A failure to state grounds which exist at the time of the filing of the petition shall constitute a waiver of such grounds, and a second petition may be filed only on grounds not existing at the time of the original petition. For good cause shown, the United States district court may grant relief from the limitations of this paragraph.

(3) The filing of a petition for removal of a criminal prosecution shall not prevent the State court in which such prosecution is pending from proceeding further, except that a judgment of conviction shall not be entered unless the petition is first denied.

(4) The United States district court to which such petition is directed shall examine the petition promptly. If it clearly appears on the face of the petition and any exhibits annexed thereto that the petition for removal should not be granted, the court shall make an order for its summary dismissal.

(5) If the United States district court does not order the summary dismissal of such petition, it shall order an evidentiary hearing to be held promptly and after such hearing shall make such disposition of the petition as justice shall require. If the United States district court determines that such petition shall be granted, it shall so notify the State court in which prosecution is pending, which shall proceed no further.

(d) Promptly after the filing of such petition for the removal of a civil action and bond the defendant or defendants shall give written notice thereof to all adverse parties and shall file a copy of the petition with the clerk of such State court, which shall effect the removal and the State court shall proceed no further unless and until the case is remanded.

(e) If the defendant or defendants are in actual custody on process issued by the State court, the district court shall issue its writ of habeas corpus, and the marshal shall thereupon take such defendant or defendants into his custody and deliver a copy of the writ to the clerk of such State court. As amended May 24, 1949, c. 139, § 83, 63 Stat. 101; Sept. 29, 1965, Pub.L. 89–215, 79 Stat. 887; July 30, 1977, Pub.L. 95–78, § 3, 91

Stat. 321; Nov. 19, 1988, Pub.L. 100–702, Title X, § 1016(b), 102 Stat. 4669.

§ 1447. Procedure after removal generally

(a) In any case removed from a State court, the district court may issue all necessary orders and process to bring before it all proper parties whether served by process issued by the State court or otherwise.

(b) It may require the petitioner to file with its clerk copies of all records and proceedings in such State court or may cause the same to be brought before it by writ of certiorari issued to such State court.

(c) A motion to remand the case on the basis of any defect in removal procedure must be made within 30 days after the filing of the notice of removal under section 1446(a). If at any time before final judgment it appears that the district court lacks subject matter jurisdiction, the case shall be remanded. An order remanding the case may require payment of just costs and any actual expenses, including attorney fees, incurred as a result of the removal. A certified copy of the order of remand shall be mailed by the clerk to the clerk of the State court. The State court may thereupon proceed with such case.

(d) An order remanding a case to the State court from which it was removed is not reviewable on appeal or otherwise, except that an order remanding a case to the State court from which it was removed pursuant to section 1443 of this title shall be reviewable by appeal or otherwise.

(e) If after removal the plaintiff seeks to join additional defendants whose joinder would destroy subject matter jurisdiction, the court may deny joinder, or permit joinder and remand the action to the State court. As amended May 24, 1949, c. 139, § 84, 63 Stat. 102; July 2, 1964, Pub.L. 88–352, Title IX, § 901, 78 Stat. 266; Nov. 19, 1988, Pub.L. 100–702, Title X, § 1016(c), 102 Stat. 4670.

§ 1448. Process after removal

In all cases removed from any State court to any district court of the United States in which any one or more of the defendants has not been served with process or in which the service has not been perfected prior to removal, or in which process served proves to be defective, such process or service may be completed or new process issued in the same manner as in cases originally filed in such district court.

This section shall not deprive any defendant upon whom process is served after removal of his right to move to remand the case.

§ 1449. State court record supplied

Where a party is entitled to copies of the records and proceedings in any suit or prosecution in a State court, to be used in any district court of the United States, and the clerk of such State court, upon demand, and the payment or tender of the legal fees, fails to deliver certified copies, the district court may, on affidavit reciting such facts, direct such record to be supplied by affidavit or otherwise. Thereupon such proceedings, trial, and judgment may be had in such district court, and all such process awarded, as if certified copies had been filed in the district court. As amended May 24, 1949, c. 139, § 85, 63 Stat. 102.

§ 1450. Attachment or sequestration; securities

Whenever any action is removed from a State court to a district court of the United States, any attachment or sequestration of the goods or estate of the defendant in such action in the State court shall hold the goods or estate to answer the final judgment or decree in the same manner as they would have been held to answer final judgment or decree had it been rendered by the State court.

All bonds, undertakings, or security given by either party in such action prior to its removal shall remain valid and effectual notwithstanding such removal.

All injunctions, orders, and other proceedings had in such action prior to its removal shall remain in full force and effect until dissolved or modified by the district court.

§ 1631. Transfer to cure want of jurisdiction

Whenever a civil action is filed in a court as defined in section 610 of this title or an appeal, including a petition for review of administrative action, is noticed for or filed with such a court and that court finds that there is a want of jurisdiction, the court shall, if it is in the interest of justice, transfer such action or appeal to any other such court in which the action or appeal could have been brought at the time it was filed or noticed, and the action or appeal shall proceed as if it had been filed in or noticed for the court to which it is transferred on the date upon which it was actually filed in or noticed for the court from which it is transferred. Added Apr. 2, 1982, Pub.L. 97–164, Title III, § 301(a), 96 Stat. 55.

§ 1651. Writs

(a) The Supreme Court and all courts established by Act of Congress may issue all writs necessary or appropriate in aid of their respective jurisdictions and agreeable to the usages and principles of law.

(b) An alternative writ or rule nisi may be issued by a justice or judge of a court which has jurisdiction. As amended May 24, 1949, c. 139, § 90, 63 Stat. 102.

§ 1652. State laws as rules of decision

The laws of the several states, except where the Constitution or treaties of the United States or Acts of Congress otherwise require or provide, shall be regarded as rules of decision in civil actions in the courts of the United States, in cases where they apply.

§ 1653. Amendment of pleadings to show jurisdiction

Defective allegations of jurisdiction may be amended, upon terms, in the trial or appellate courts.

§ 1654. Appearance personally or by counsel

In all courts of the United States the parties may plead and conduct their own cases personally or by counsel as, by the rules of such courts, respectively, are permitted to manage and conduct causes therein. As amended May 24, 1949, c. 139, § 91, 63 Stat. 103.

§ 1655. Lien enforcement; absent defendants

In an action in a district court to enforce any lien upon or claim to, or to remove any incumbrance or lien or cloud upon the title to, real or personal property within the district, where any defendant cannot be served within the State, or does not voluntarily appear, the court may order the absent defendant to appear or plead by a day certain.

Such order shall be served on the absent defendant personally if practicable, wherever found, and also upon the person or persons in possession or charge of such property, if any. Where personal service is not practicable, the order shall be published as the court may direct, not less than once a week for six consecutive weeks.

If an absent defendant does not appear or plead within the time allowed, the court may proceed as if the absent defendant had been served with process within the State, but any adjudication shall, as regards the absent defendant without appearance, affect only the property which is the subject of the action. When a part of the property is within another district, but within the same state, such action may be brought in either district.

Any defendant not so personally notified may, at any time within one year after final judgment, enter his appearance, and thereupon the court shall set aside the judgment and permit such defendant to plead on payment of such costs as the court deems just.

§ 1657. Priority of civil actions

(a) Notwithstanding any other provision of law, each court of the United States shall determine the order in which civil actions are heard and determined, except that the court shall expedite the consideration of any action brought under chapter 153 or section 1826 of this title, any action for temporary or preliminary injunctive relief, or any other action if good cause therefor is shown. For purposes of this subsection, "good cause" is shown if a right under the Constitution of the United States or a Federal Statute (including rights under section 552 of title 5) would be maintained in a factual context that indicates that a request for expedited consideration has merit.

(b) The Judicial Conference of the United States may modify the rules adopted by the courts to determine the order in which civil actions are heard and determined, in order to establish consistency among the judicial circuits. Added Nov. 8, 1984, Pub.L. 98–620, Title IV, § 401(a), 98 Stat. 3356.

§ 1658. Time limitations on the commencement of civil actions arising under Acts of Congress

Except as otherwise provided by law, a civil action arising under an Act of Congress enacted after the date of the enactment of this section may not be commenced later than 4 years after the cause of action accrues. Added Dec. 1, 1990, Pub.L. 101–650, Title III, § 313(a), 104 Stat. 5114.

§ 1693. Place of arrest in civil action

Except as otherwise provided by Act of Congress, no person shall be arrested in one district for trial in another in any civil action in a district court.

§ 1694. Patent infringement action

In a patent infringement action commenced in a district where the defendant is not a resident but has a regular and established place of business, service of process, summons or subpoena upon such defendant may be made upon his agent or agents conducting such business.

§ 1695. Stockholder's derivative action

Process in a stockholder's action in behalf of his corporation may be served upon such corporation in any district where it is organized or licensed to do business or is doing business.

§ 1738. State and Territorial statutes and judicial proceedings; full faith and credit

The Acts of the legislature of any State, Territory, or Possession of the United States, or copies thereof, shall be authenticated by affixing the seal of such State, Territory or Possession thereto.

The records and judicial proceedings of any court of any such State, Territory or Possession, or copies thereof, shall be proved or admitted in other courts within the United States and its Territories and Possessions by the attestation of the clerk and seal of the court annexed, if a seal exists, together with a certificate of a judge of the court that the said attestation is in proper form.

Such Acts, records and judicial proceedings or copies thereof, so authenticated, shall have the same full faith and credit in every court within the United States and its Territories and Possessions as they have by law or usage in the courts of such State, Territory or Possession from which they are taken.

§ 1738A. Full faith and credit given to child custody determinations

(a) The appropriate authorities of every State shall enforce according to its terms, and shall not modify except as provided in subsection (f) of this section, any child custody determination made consistently with the provisions of this section by a court of another State.

(b) As used in this section, the term—

 (1) "child" means a person under the age of eighteen;

(2) "contestant" means a person, including a parent, who claims a right to custody or visitation of a child;

(3) "custody determination" means a judgment, decree, or other order of a court providing for the custody or visitation of a child, and includes permanent and temporary orders, and initial orders and modifications;

(4) "home State" means the State in which, immediately preceding the time involved, the child lived with his parents, a parent, or a person acting as parent, for at least six consecutive months, and in the case of a child less than six months old, the State in which the child lived from birth with any of such persons. Periods of temporary absence of any of such persons are counted as part of the six-month or other period;

(5) "modification" and "modify" refer to a custody determination which modifies, replaces, supersedes, or otherwise is made subsequent to, a prior custody determination concerning the same child, whether made by the same court or not;

(6) "person acting as a parent" means a person, other than a parent, who has physical custody of a child and who has either been awarded custody by a court or claims a right to custody;

(7) "physical custody" means actual possession and control of a child; and

(8) "State" means a State of the United States, the District of Columbia, the Commonwealth of Puerto Rico, or a territory or possession of the United States.

(c) A child custody determination made by a court of a State is consistent with the provisions of this section only if—

(1) such court has jurisdiction under the law of such State; and

(2) one of the following conditions is met:

(A) such State (i) is the home State of the child on the date of the commencement of the proceeding, or (ii) had been the child's home State within six months before the date of the commencement of the proceeding and the child is absent from such State because of his removal or retention by a contestant or for other reasons, and a contestant continues to live in such State;

(B)(i) it appears that no other State would have jurisdiction under subparagraph (A), and (ii) it is in the best interest of the child that a court of such State assume jurisdiction because (I) the child and his parents, or the child and at least one contestant, have a significant connection with such State other than mere physical presence in such State, and (II) there is available in such State substantial evidence concerning the child's present or future care, protection, training, and personal relationships;

(C) the child is physically present in such State and (i) the child has been abandoned, or (ii) it is necessary in an emergency to protect the child because he has been subjected to or threatened with mistreatment or abuse;

461

(D)(i) it appears that no other State would have jurisdiction under subparagraph (A), (B), (C), or (E), or another State has declined to exercise jurisdiction on the ground that the State whose jurisdiction is in issue is the more appropriate forum to determine the custody of the child, and (ii) it is in the best interest of the child that such court assume jurisdiction; or

(E) the court has continuing jurisdiction pursuant to subsection (d) of this section.

(d) The jurisdiction of a court of a State which has made a child custody determination consistently with the provisions of this section continues as long as the requirement of subsection (c)(1) of this section continues to be met and such State remains the residence of the child or of any contestant.

(e) Before a child custody determination is made, reasonable notice and opportunity to be heard shall be given to the contestants, any parent whose parental rights have not been previously terminated and any person who has physical custody of a child.

(f) A court of a State may modify a determination of the custody of the same child made by a court of another State, if—

(1) it has jurisdiction to make such a child custody determination; and

(2) the court of the other State no longer has jurisdiction, or it has declined to exercise such jurisdiction to modify such determination.

(g) A court of a State shall not exercise jurisdiction in any proceeding for a custody determination commenced during the pendency of a proceeding in a court of another State where such court of that other State is exercising jurisdiction consistently with the provisions of this section to make a custody determination. Added Dec. 28, 1980, Pub.L. 96–611, § 8(a), 94 Stat. 3569.

§ 1746. Unsworn declarations under penalty of perjury

Wherever, under any law of the United States or under any rule, regulation, order, or requirement made pursuant to law, any matter is required or permitted to be supported, evidenced, established, or proved by the sworn declaration, verification, certificate, statement, oath, or affidavit, in writing of the person making the same (other than a deposition, or an oath of office, or an oath required to be taken before a specified official other than a notary public), such matter may, with like force and effect, be supported, evidenced, established, or proved by the unsworn declaration, certificate, verification, or statement, in writing of such person which is subscribed by him, as true under penalty of perjury, and dated, in substantially the following form:

(1) If executed without the United States: "I declare (or certify, verify, or state) under penalty of perjury under the laws of the United

States of America that the foregoing is true and correct. Executed on (date).

(Signature)".

(2) If executed within the United States, its territories, possessions, or commonwealths: "I declare (or certify, verify, or state) under penalty of perjury that the foregoing is true and correct. Executed on (date).

(Signature)".

Added Oct. 18, 1976, Pub.L. 94–550, § 1(a), 90 Stat. 2534.

§ 1861. Declaration of policy

It is the policy of the United States that all litigants in Federal courts entitled to trial by jury shall have the right to grand and petit juries selected at random from a fair cross section of the community in the district or division wherein the court convenes. It is further the policy of the United States that all citizens shall have the opportunity to be considered for service on grand and petit juries in the district courts of the United States, and shall have an obligation to serve as jurors when summoned for that purpose. As amended Sept. 9, 1957, Pub.L. 85–315, Part V, § 152, 71 Stat. 638; Mar. 27, 1968, Pub.L. 90–274, § 101, 82 Stat. 53.

§ 1870. Challenges

In civil cases, each party shall be entitled to three peremptory challenges. Several defendants or several plaintiffs may be considered as a single party for the purposes of making challenges, or the court may allow additional peremptory challenges and permit them to be exercised separately or jointly.

All challenges for cause or favor, whether to the array or panel or to individual jurors, shall be determined by the court. As amended Sept. 16, 1959, Pub.L. 86–282, 73 Stat. 565.

§ 1914. District court; filing and miscellaneous fees; rules of court

(a) The clerk of each district court shall require the parties instituting any civil action, suit or proceeding in such court, whether by original process, removal or otherwise, to pay a filing fee of $120, except that on application for a writ of habeas corpus the filing fee shall be $5.

(b) The clerk shall collect from the parties such additional fees only as are prescribed by the Judicial Conference of the United States.

(c) Each district court by rule or standing order may require advance payment of fees. As amended Nov. 6, 1978, Pub.L. 95–598, Title II, § 244, 92 Stat. 2671; June 19, 1986, Pub.L. 99–336, § 4(a), 100 Stat. 637; Oct. 18, 1986, Pub.L. 99–500, Title I, § 101(b) [Title IV, § 407(a)], 100 Stat. 1783–64; Oct. 30, 1986, Pub.L. 99–591, Title I, § 101(b) [Title IV, § 407(a)], 100 Stat. 3341–64.

463

§ 1915. Proceedings in forma pauperis

(a) Any court of the United States may authorize the commencement, prosecution or defense of any suit, action or proceeding, civil or criminal, or appeal therein, without prepayment of fees and costs or security therefor, by a person who makes affidavit that he is unable to pay such costs or give security therefor. Such affidavit shall state the nature of the action, defense or appeal and affiant's belief that he is entitled to redress.

An appeal may not be taken in forma pauperis if the trial court certifies in writing that it is not taken in good faith.

(b) Upon the filing of an affidavit in accordance with subsection (a) of this section, the court may direct payment by the United States of the expenses of (1) printing the record on appeal in any civil or criminal case, if such printing is required by the appellate court; (2) preparing a transcript of proceedings before a United States magistrate in any civil or criminal case, if such transcript is required by the district court, in the case of proceedings conducted under section 636(b) of this title or under section 3401(b) of title 18, United States Code; and (3) printing the record on appeal of such printing is required by the appellate court, in the case of proceedings conducted pursuant to section 636(c) of this title. Such expenses shall be paid when authorized by the Director of the Administrative Office of the United States Courts.

(c) The officers of the court shall issue and serve all process, and perform all duties in such cases. Witnesses shall attend as in other cases, and the same remedies shall be available as are provided for by law in other cases.

(d) The court may request an attorney to represent any such person unable to employ counsel and may dismiss the case if the allegation of poverty is untrue, or if satisfied that the action is frivolous or malicious.

(e) Judgment may be rendered for costs at the conclusion of the suit or action as in other cases, but the United States shall not be liable for any of the costs thus incurred. If the United States has paid the cost of a stenographic transcript or printed record for the prevailing party, the same shall be taxed in favor of the United States. As amended May 24, 1949, c. 139, § 98, 63 Stat. 104; Oct. 31, 1951, c. 655, § 51(b, c), 65 Stat. 727; Sept. 21, 1959, Pub.L. 86–320, 73 Stat. 590; Oct. 10, 1979, Pub.L. 96–82, § 6, 93 Stat. 645.

§ 1919. District courts; dismissal for lack of jurisdiction

Whenever any action or suit is dismissed in any district court or the Court of International Trade for want of jurisdiction, such court may order the payment of just costs. As amended Oct. 10, 1980, Pub.L. 96–417, Title V, § 510, 94 Stat. 1743.

§ 1920. Taxation of costs

A judge or clerk of any court of the United States may tax as costs the following:

(1) Fees of the clerk and marshal;

(2) Fees of the court reporter for all or any part of the stenographic transcript necessarily obtained for use in the case;

(3) Fees and disbursements for printing and witnesses;

(4) Fees for exemplification and copies of papers necessarily obtained for use in the case;

(5) Docket fees under section 1923 of this title;

(6) Compensation of court appointed experts, compensation of interpreters, and salaries, fees, expenses, and costs of special interpretation services under section 1828 of this title.

A bill of costs shall be filed in the case and, upon allowance, included in the judgment or decree. As amended Oct. 28, 1978, Pub.L. 95–539, § 7, 92 Stat. 2044.

§ 1924. Verification of bill of costs

Before any bill of costs is taxed, the party claiming any item of cost or disbursement shall attach thereto an affidavit, made by himself or by his duly authorized attorney or agent having knowledge of the facts, that such item is correct and has been necessarily incurred in the case and that the services for which fees have been charged were actually and necessarily performed.

§ 1927. Counsel's liability for excessive costs

Any attorney or other person admitted to conduct cases in any court of the United States or any Territory thereof who so multiplies the proceedings in any case unreasonably and vexatiously may be required by the court to satisfy personally the excess costs, expenses, and attorneys' fees reasonably incurred because of such conduct. As amended Sept. 12, 1980, Pub.L. 96–349, § 3, 94 Stat. 1156.

§ 1961. Interest

(a) Interest shall be allowed on any money judgment in a civil case recovered in a district court. Execution therefor may be levied by the marshal, in any case where, by the law of the State in which such court is held, execution may be levied for interest on judgments recovered in the courts of the State. Such interest shall be calculated from the date of the entry of the judgment, at a rate equal to the coupon issue yield equivalent (as determined by the Secretary of the Treasury) of the average accepted auction price for the last auction of fifty-two week United States Treasury bills settled immediately prior to the date of the judgment. The Director of the Administrative Office of the United States Courts shall distribute notice of that rate and any changes in it to all Federal judges.

(b) Interest shall be computed daily to the date of payment except as provided in section 2516(b) of this title and section 1304(b) of title 31, and shall be compounded annually.

(c)(1) This section shall not apply in any judgment of any court with respect to any internal revenue tax case. Interest shall be allowed in such cases at the underpayment rate or overpayment rate (whichever is appropriate) established under section 6621 of the Internal Revenue Code of 1954.

(2) Except as otherwise provided in paragraph (1) of this subsection, interest shall be allowed on all final judgments against the United States in the United States Court of Appeals for the Federal circuit, at the rate provided in subsection (a) and as provided in subsection (b).

(3) Interest shall be allowed, computed, and paid on judgments of the United States Claims Court only as provided in paragraph (1) of this subsection or in any other provision of law.

(4) This section shall not be construed to affect the interest on any judgment of any court not specified in this section. As amended Apr. 2, 1982, Pub.L. 97–164, Title III, § 302(a), 96 Stat. 55; Sept. 13, 1982, Pub.L. 97–258, § 2(m)(1), 96 Stat. 1062; Jan. 12, 1983, Pub.L. 97–452, § 2(d)(1), 96 Stat. 2478; Oct. 22, 1986, Pub.L. 99–514, Title XV, § 1511(c)(17), 100 Stat. 2745.

§ 1963. Registration of judgments of the district courts and the Court of International Trade

A judgment in an action for the recovery of money or property entered in any district court or in the Court of International Trade may be registered by filing a certified copy of such judgment in any other district or, with respect to the Court of International Trade, in any judicial district, when the judgment has become final by appeal or expiration of the time for appeal or when ordered by the court that entered the judgment for good cause shown. Such a judgment entered in favor of the United States may be so registered any time after judgment is entered. A judgment so registered shall have the same effect as a judgment of the district court of the district where registered and may be enforced in like manner.

A certified copy of the satisfaction of any judgment in whole or in part may be registered in like manner in any district in which the judgment is a lien. As amended Aug. 23, 1954, c. 837, 68 Stat. 772; July 7, 1958, Pub.L. 85–508, § 12(o), 72 Stat. 349; Nov. 19, 1988, Pub.L. 100–702, Title X, § 1002, 102 Stat. 4664; Nov. 29, 1990, Pub.L. 101–647, Title XXXVI, § 3628, 104 Stat. 4965.

§ 2071. Rule-making power generally

(a) The Supreme Court and all courts established by Act of Congress may from time to time prescribe rules for the conduct of their business. Such rules shall be consistent with Acts of Congress and rules of practice and procedure prescribed under section 2072 of this title.

(b) Any rule prescribed by a court, other than the Supreme Court, under subsection (a) shall be prescribed only after giving appropriate public notice and an opportunity for comment. Such rule shall take effect upon the date specified by the prescribing court and shall have such effect on pending proceedings as the prescribing court may order.

(c)(1) A rule of a district court prescribed under subsection (a) shall remain in effect unless modified or abrogated by the judicial council of the relevant circuit.

(2) Any other rule prescribed by a court other than the Supreme Court under subsection (a) shall remain in effect unless modified or abrogated by the Judicial Conference.

(d) Copies of rules prescribed under subsection (a) by a district court shall be furnished to the judicial council, and copies of all rules prescribed by a court other than the Supreme Court under subsection (a) shall be furnished to the Director of the Administrative Office of the United States Courts and made available to the public.

(e) If the prescribing court determines that there is an immediate need for a rule, such court may proceed under this section without public notice and opportunity for comment, but such court shall promptly thereafter afford such notice and opportunity for comment.

(f) No rule may be prescribed by a district court other than under this section. As amended May 24, 1949, c. 139, § 102, 63 Stat. 104; Nov. 19, 1988, Pub.L. 100–702, Title IV, § 403(a)(1), 102 Stat. 4650.

§ 2072. Rules of procedure and evidence; power to prescribe

(a) The Supreme Court shall have the power to prescribe general rules of practice and procedure and rules of evidence for cases in the United States district courts (including proceedings before magistrates thereof) and courts of appeals.

(b) Such rules shall not abridge, enlarge or modify any substantive right. All laws in conflict with such rules shall be of no further force or effect after such rules have taken effect.

(c) Such rules may define when a ruling of a district court is final for the purposes of appeal under section 1291 of this title. As amended May 24, 1949, c. 139, § 103, 63 Stat. 104; July 18, 1949, c. 343, § 2, 63 Stat. 446; May 10, 1950, c. 174, § 2, 64 Stat. 158; July 7, 1958, Pub.L. 85–508, § 12(m), 72 Stat. 348; Nov. 6, 1966, Pub.L. 89–773, § 1, 80 Stat. 1323; Nov. 19, 1988, Pub.L. 100–702, Title IV, § 401(a), 102 Stat. 4648; Dec. 1, 1990, Pub.L. 101–650, Title III, § 315, 104 Stat. 5115.

§ 2073. Rules of procedure and evidence; method of prescribing

(a)(1) The Judicial Conference shall prescribe and publish the procedures for the consideration of proposed rules under this section.

(2) The Judicial Conference may authorize the appointment of committees to assist the Conference by recommending rules to be prescribed under section 2072 of this title. Each such committee shall consist of members of the bench and the professional bar, and trial and appellate judges.

(b) The Judicial Conference shall authorize the appointment of a standing committee on rules of practice, procedure, and evidence under subsection (a) of this section. Such standing committee shall review each recommendation of any other committees so appointed and recommend to the Judicial Conference rules of practice, procedure, and evidence and such changes in rules proposed by a committee appointed under subsection (a)(2) of this section as may be necessary to maintain consistency and otherwise promote the interest of justice.

(c)(1) Each meeting for the transaction of business under this chapter by any committee appointed under this section shall be open to the public, except when the committee so meeting, in open session and with a majority present, determines that it is in the public interest that all or part of the remainder of the meeting on that day shall be closed to the public, and states the reason for so closing the meeting. Minutes of each meeting for the transaction of business under this chapter shall be maintained by the committee and made available to the public, except that any portion of such minutes, relating to a closed meeting and made available to the public, may contain such deletions as may be necessary to avoid frustrating the purposes of closing the meeting.

(2) Any meeting for the transaction of business under this chapter, by a committee appointed under this section, shall be preceded by sufficient notice to enable all interested persons to attend.

(d) In making a recommendation under this section or under section 2072, the body making that recommendation shall provide a proposed rule, an explanatory note on the rule, and a written report explaining the body's action, including any minority or other separate views.

(e) Failure to comply with this section does not invalidate a rule prescribed under section 2072 of this title. Added Nov. 19, 1988, Pub.L. 100–702, Title IV, § 401(a), 102 Stat. 4648.

§ 2074. Rules of procedure and evidence; submission to Congress; effective date

(a) The Supreme Court shall transmit to the Congress not later than May 1 of the year in which a rule prescribed under section 2072 is to become effective a copy of the proposed rule. Such rule shall take effect no earlier than December 1 of the year in which such rule is so transmitted unless otherwise provided by law. The Supreme Court may fix the extent such rule shall apply to proceedings then pending, except that the Supreme Court shall not require the application of such rule to further proceedings then pending to the extent that, in the opinion of the court in which such proceedings are pending, the application of such rule in such proceedings would not be feasible or would work injustice, in which event the former rule applies.

(b) Any such rule creating, abolishing, or modifying an evidentiary privilege shall have no force or effect unless approved by Act of Congress. Added Nov. 19, 1988, Pub.L. 100–702, Title IV, § 401(a), 102 Stat. 4648.

§ 2077. Publication of rules; advisory committees

(a) The rules for the conduct of the business of each court of appeals, including the operating procedures of such court, shall be published. Each court of appeals shall print or cause to be printed necessary copies of the rules. The Judicial Conference shall prescribe the fees for sales of copies under section 1913 of this title, but the Judicial Conference may provide for free distribution of copies to members of the bar of each court and to other interested persons.

(b) Each court, except the Supreme Court, that is authorized to prescribe rules of the conduct of such court's business under section 2071 of this title shall appoint an advisory committee for the study of the rules of practice and internal operating procedures of such court and, in the case of an advisory committee appointed by a court of appeals, of the rules of the judicial council of the circuit. The advisory committee shall make recommendations to the court concerning such rules and procedures. Members of the committee shall serve without compensation, but the Director may pay travel and transportation expenses in accordance with section 5703 of title 5. Added Apr. 2, 1982, Pub.L. 97–164, Title II, § 208(a), 96 Stat. 54; as amended Nov. 19, 1988, Pub.L. 100–702, Title IV, § 401(b), 102 Stat. 4650; Dec. 1, 1990, Pub.L. 101–650, Title IV, § 406, 104 Stat. 5124.

§ 2106. Determination

The Supreme Court or any other court of appellate jurisdiction may affirm, modify, vacate, set aside or reverse any judgment, decree, or order of a court lawfully brought before it for review, and may remand the cause and direct the entry of such appropriate judgment, decree, or order, or require such further proceedings to be had as may be just under the circumstances.

§ 2111. Harmless error

On the hearing of any appeal or writ of certiorari in any case, the court shall give judgment after an examination of the record without regard to errors or defects which do not affect the substantial rights of the parties. Added May 24, 1949, c. 139, § 110, 63 Stat. 105.

§ 2201. Creation of remedy

(a) In a case of actual controversy within its jurisdiction, except with respect to Federal taxes other than actions brought under section 7428 of the Internal Revenue Code of 1986, a proceeding under section 505 or 1146 of title 11, or in any civil action involving an antidumping or countervailing duty proceeding regarding a class or kind of Canadian merchandise, as determined by the administering authority, any court of the United States, upon the filing of an appropriate pleading, may declare the rights and other legal relations of any interested party seeking such declaration, whether or not further relief is or could be sought. Any such declaration shall have the force and effect of a final judgment or decree and shall be reviewable as such.

(b) For limitations on actions brought with respect to drug patents see section 505 or 512 of the Federal Food, Drug, and Cosmetic Act. As amended May 24, 1949, c. 139, § 111, 63 Stat. 105; Aug. 28, 1954, c. 1033, 68 Stat. 890; July 7, 1958, Pub.L. 85–508, § 12(p), 72 Stat. 349; Oct. 4, 1976, Pub.L. 94–455, Title XIII, § 1306(b)(8), 90 Stat. 1719; Nov. 6, 1978, Pub.L. 95–598, Title II, § 249, 92 Stat. 2672; Sept. 24, 1984, Pub.L. 98–417, Title I, § 106, 98 Stat. 1597; Sept. 28, 1988, Pub.L. 100–449, Title IV, § 402(c), 102 Stat. 1884; Nov. 16, 1988, Pub.L. 100–670, Title I, § 107(b), 102 Stat. 3984.

§ 2202. Further relief

Further necessary or proper relief based on a declaratory judgment or decree may be granted, after reasonable notice and hearing, against any adverse party whose rights have been determined by such judgment.

§ 2283. Stay of State court proceedings

A court of the United States may not grant an injunction to stay proceedings in a State court except as expressly authorized by Act of Congress, or where necessary in aid of its jurisdiction, or to protect or effectuate its judgments.

§ 2284. Three-judge court; when required; composition; procedure

(a) A district court of three judges shall be convened when otherwise required by Act of Congress, or when an action is filed challenging the constitutionality of the apportionment of congressional districts or the apportionment of any statewide legislative body.

(b) In any action required to be heard and determined by a district court of three judges under subsection (a) of this section, the composition and procedure of the court shall be as follows:

(1) Upon the filing of a request for three judges, the judge to whom the request is presented shall, unless he determines that three judges are not required, immediately notify the chief judge of the circuit, who shall designate two other judges, at least one of whom shall be a circuit judge. The judges so designated, and the judge to whom the request was presented, shall serve as members of the court to hear and determine the action or proceeding.

(2) If the action is against a State, or officer or agency thereof, at least five days' notice of hearing of the action shall be given by registered or certified mail to the Governor and attorney general of the State.

(3) A single judge may conduct all proceedings except the trial, and enter all orders permitted by the rules of civil procedure except as provided in this subsection. He may grant a temporary restraining order on a specific finding, based on evidence submitted, that specified irreparable damage will result if the order is not granted, which order, unless previously revoked by the district judge, shall remain in force only until the hearing and determination by the district court of three judges of an application for a preliminary injunction. A single judge shall not appoint a master, or order a reference, or hear and determine any application for a preliminary or permanent injunction or motion to vacate such an injunction, or enter judgment on the merits. Any action of a single judge may be reviewed by the full court at any time before final judgment. As amended June 11, 1960, Pub.L. 86–507, § 1(19), 74 Stat. 201; Aug. 12, 1976, Pub.L. 94–381, § 3, 90 Stat. 1119; Nov. 8, 1984, Pub.L. 98–620, Title IV, § 402(29)(E), 98 Stat. 3359.

§ 2361. Process and procedure

In any civil action of interpleader or in the nature of interpleader under section 1335 of this title, a district court may issue its process for all claimants and enter its order restraining them from instituting or prosecuting any proceeding in any State or United States court affecting the property, instrument or obligation involved in the interpleader action until further order of the court. Such process and order shall be returnable at such time as the court or judge thereof directs, and shall be addressed to and served by the United States marshals for the respective districts where the claimants reside or may be found.

Such district court shall hear and determine the case, and may discharge the plaintiff from further liability, make the injunction permanent, and make all appropriate orders to enforce its judgment. As amended May 24, 1949, c. 139, § 117, 63 Stat. 105.

§ 2403. Intervention by United States or a State; constitutional question

(a) In any action, suit or proceeding in a court of the United States to which the United States or any agency, officer or employee thereof is not a party, wherein the constitutionality of any Act of Congress affecting the public interest is drawn in question, the court shall certify such fact to the Attorney General, and shall permit the United States to intervene for presentation of evidence, if evidence is otherwise admissible in the case, and for argument on the question of constitutionality. The United States shall, subject to the applicable provisions of law, have all the rights of a party and be subject to all liabilities of a party as to court costs to the extent necessary for a proper presentation of the facts and law relating to the question of constitutionality.

(b) In any action, suit, or proceeding in a court of the United States to which a State or any agency, officer, or employee thereof is not a party, wherein the constitutionality of any statute of that State affecting the public interest is drawn in question, the court shall certify such fact to the attorney general of the State, and shall permit the State to intervene for presentation of evidence, if evidence is otherwise admissible in the case, and for argument on the question of constitutionality. The State shall, subject to the applicable provisions of law, have all the rights of a party and be subject to all liabilities of a party as to court costs to the extent necessary for a proper presentation of the facts and law relating to the question of constitutionality. As amended Aug. 12, 1976, Pub.L. 94–381, § 5, 90 Stat. 1120.

§ 2412. Costs and fees

(a) Except as otherwise specifically provided by statute, a judgment for costs, as enumerated in section 1920 of this title, but not including the fees and expenses of attorneys, may be awarded to the prevailing party in any civil action brought by or against the United States or any agency or any official of the United States acting in his or her official capacity in any court having jurisdiction of such action. A judgment for costs when taxed against the United States shall, in an amount established by statute, court rule, or order, be limited to reimbursing in whole or in part the prevailing party for the costs incurred by such party in the litigation.

(b) Unless expressly prohibited by statute, a court may award reasonable fees and expenses of attorneys, in addition to the costs which may be awarded pursuant to subsection (a), to the prevailing party in any civil action brought by or against the United States or any agency or any official of the United States acting in his or her official capacity in any court having jurisdiction of such action. The United States shall be liable for such fees and expenses to the same extent that any other party would be liable under the common law or under the terms of any statute which specifically provides for such an award.

(c)(1) Any judgment against the United States or any agency and any official of the United States acting in his or her official capacity for costs pursuant to subsection (a) shall be paid as provided in sections 2414 and 2517 of this title and shall be in addition to any relief provided in the judgment.

(2) Any judgment against the United States or any agency and any official of the United States acting in his or her official capacity for fees and expenses of attorneys pursuant to subsection (b) shall be paid as provided in sections 2414 and 2517 of this title, except that if the basis for the award is a finding that the United States acted in bad faith, then the award shall be paid by any agency found to have acted in bad faith and shall be in addition to any relief provided in the judgment.

(d)(1)(A) Except as otherwise specifically provided by statute, a court shall award to a prevailing party other than the United States fees and other expenses, in addition to any costs awarded pursuant to subsection (a), incurred by that party in any civil action (other than cases sounding in tort), including proceedings for judicial review of agency action, brought by or against the United States in any court having jurisdiction of that action, unless the court finds that the position of the United States was substantially justified or that special circumstances make an award unjust.

(B) A party seeking an award of fees and other expenses shall, within thirty days of final judgment in the action, submit to the court an application for fees and other expenses which shows that the party is a prevailing party and is eligible to receive an award under this subsection, and the amount sought, including an itemized statement from any attorney or expert witness representing or appearing in behalf of the party stating the actual time expended and the rate at which fees and other expenses are computed. The party shall also allege that the position of the United States was not substantially justified. Whether or not the position of the United States was substantially justified shall be determined on the basis of the record (including the record with respect to the action or failure to act by the agency upon which the civil action is based) which is made in the civil action for which fees and other expenses are sought.

(C) The court, in its discretion, may reduce the amount to be awarded pursuant to this subsection, or deny an award, to the extent that the prevailing party during the course of the proceedings engaged in conduct which unduly and unreasonably protracted the final resolution of the matter in controversy.

(2) For the purposes of this subsection—

(A) "fees and other expenses" includes the reasonable expenses of expert witnesses, the reasonable cost of any study, analysis, engineering report, test, or project which is found by the court to be necessary for the preparation of the party's case, and reasonable attorney fees (The amount of fees awarded under this subsection shall be based upon prevailing market rates for the kind and quality of the services furnished, except that (i) no expert witness shall be compensated at a rate in excess of the highest rate of compensation for expert witnesses paid by the United States; and (ii) attorney fees shall not be awarded in excess of $75 per hour unless the court determines that an increase in the cost of living or a special factor, such as the limited availability of qualified attorneys for the proceedings involved, justifies a higher fee.);

(B) "party" means (i) an individual whose net worth did not exceed $2,000,000 at the time the civil action was filed, or (ii) any owner of an unincorporated business, or any partnership, corporation, association, unit of local government, or organization, the net worth of which did not exceed $7,000,000 at the time the civil action was filed, and which had not more than 500 employees at the time the civil action was filed; except that an organization described in section 501(c)(3) of the Internal Revenue Code of 1954 (26 U.S.C. 501(c)(3)) exempt from taxation under section 501(a) of such Code, or a cooperative association as defined in section 15(a) of the Agricultural Marketing Act (12 U.S.C. 1141j(a)), may be a party regardless of the net worth of such organization or cooperative association;

(C) "United States" includes any agency and any official of the United States acting in his or her official capacity;

(D) "position of the United States" means, in addition to the position taken by the United States in the civil action, the action or failure to act by the agency upon which the civil action is based; except that fees and expenses may not be awarded to a party for any portion of the litigation in which the party has unreasonably protracted the proceedings;

(E) "civil action brought by or against the United States" includes an appeal by a party, other than the United States, from a decision of a contracting officer rendered pursuant to a disputes clause in a contract with the Government or pursuant to the Contract Disputes Act of 1978;

(F) "court" includes the United States Claims Court;

(G) "final judgment" means a judgment that is final and not appealable, and includes an order of settlement; and

(H) "prevailing party", in the case of eminent domain proceedings, means a party who obtains a final judgment (other than by settlement), exclusive of interest, the amount of which is at least as close to the highest valuation of the property involved that is attested to at trial on behalf of the property owner as it is to the highest valuation of the property involved that is attested to at trial on behalf of the Government.

473

(3) In awarding fees and other expenses under this subsection to a prevailing party in any action for judicial review of an adversary adjudication, as defined in subsection (b)(1)(C) of section 504 of title 5, United States Code, or an adversary adjudication subject to the Contract Disputes Act of 1978, the court shall include in that award fees and other expenses to the same extent authorized in subsection (a) of such section, unless the court finds that during such adversary adjudication the position of the United States was substantially justified, or that special circumstances make an award unjust.

(4) Fees and other expenses awarded under this subsection to a party shall be paid by any agency over which the party prevails from any funds made available to the agency by appropriation or otherwise.

(5) The Director of the Administrative Office of the United States Courts shall include in the annual report prepared pursuant to section 604 of this title, the amount of fees and other expenses awarded during the preceding fiscal year pursuant to this subsection. The report shall describe the number, nature, and amount of the awards, the claims involved in the controversy, and any other relevant information which may aid the Congress in evaluating the scope and impact of such awards.

(e) The provisions of this section shall not apply to any costs, fees, and other expenses in connection with any proceeding to which section 7430 of the Internal Revenue Code of 1954 applies (determined without regard to subsections (b) and (f) of such section). Nothing in the preceding sentence shall prevent the awarding under subsection (a) of section 2412 of title 28, United States Code, of costs enumerated in section 1920 of such title (as in effect on October 1, 1981).

(f) If the United States appeals an award of costs or fees and other expenses made against the United States under this section and the award is affirmed in whole or in part, interest shall be paid on the amount of the award as affirmed. Such interest shall be computed at the rate determined under section 1961(a) of this title, and shall run from the date of the award through the day before the date of the mandate of affirmance. As amended July 18, 1966, Pub.L. 89–507, § 1, 80 Stat. 308; Oct. 21, 1980, Pub.L. 96–481, Title II, § 204(a), (c), 94 Stat. 2327, 2329; Sept. 3, 1982, Pub.L. 97–248, Title II, § 292(c), 96 Stat. 574; Aug. 5, 1985, Pub.L. 99–80, §§ 2, 6, 99 Stat. 184, 186.

SELECTED PROVISIONS OF OTHER PROCEDURAL STATUTES

TITLE 15, UNITED STATES CODE

§ 4. Jurisdiction of courts; duty of United States attorneys; procedure

The several district courts of the United States are invested with jurisdiction to prevent and restrain violations of sections 1 to 7 [Sherman Antitrust Act] of this title; and it shall be the duty of the several United States attorneys, in their respective districts, under the direction of the Attorney General, to institute proceedings in equity to prevent and restrain such violations. Such proceedings may be by way of petition setting forth the case and praying that such violation shall be enjoined or otherwise prohibited. When the parties complained of shall have been duly notified of such petition the court shall proceed, as soon as may be, to the hearing and determination of the case; and pending such petition and before final decree, the court may at any time make such temporary restraining order or prohibition as shall be deemed just in the premises.

§ 5. Bringing in additional parties

Whenever it shall appear to the court before which any proceeding under section 4 of this title may be pending, that the ends of justice require that other parties should be brought before the court, the court may cause them to be summoned, whether they reside in the district in which the court is held or not; and subpoenas to that end may be served in any district by the marshal thereof.

§ 15. Suits by persons injured

(a) Amount of recovery; prejudgment interest

Except as provided in subsection (b) of this section, any person who shall be injured in his business or property by reason of anything forbidden in the antitrust laws may sue therefor in any district court of the United States in the district in which the defendant resides or is found or has an agent, without respect to the amount in controversy, and shall recover threefold the damages by him sustained, and the cost of suit, including a reasonable attorney's fee. The court may award under this section, pursuant to a motion by such person promptly made, simple interest on actual damages for the period beginning on the date of service of such person's pleading setting forth a claim under the antitrust laws and ending on the date of judgment, or for any shorter period therein, if the court finds that the award of such interest for such period is just in the circumstances. In determining whether an award of interest under

475

this section for any period is just in the circumstances, the court shall consider only—

(1) whether such person or the opposing party, or either party's representative, made motions or asserted claims or defenses so lacking in merit as to show that such party or representative acted intentionally for delay, or otherwise acted in bad faith;

(2) whether, in the course of the action involved, such person or the opposing party, or either party's representative, violated any applicable rule, statute, or court order providing for sanctions for dilatory behavior or otherwise providing for expeditious proceedings; and

(3) whether such person or the opposing party, or either party's representative, engaged in conduct primarily for the purpose of delaying the litigation or increasing the cost thereof.

(b) Amount of damages payable to foreign states and instrumentalities of foreign states

* * *

§ 15a. Suits by United States; amount of recovery; prejudgment interest

Whenever the United States is hereafter injured in its business or property by reason of anything forbidden in the antitrust laws it may sue therefor in the United States district court for the district in which the defendant resides or is found or has an agent, without respect to the amount in controversy, and shall recover threefold the damages by it sustained and the cost of suit. The court may award under this section, pursuant to a motion by the United States promptly made, simple interest on actual damages for the period beginning on the date of service of the pleading of the United States setting forth a claim under the antitrust laws and ending on the date of judgment, or for any shorter period therein, if the court finds that the award of such interest for such period is just in the circumstances. In determining whether an award of interest under this section for any period is just in the circumstances, the court shall consider only—

(1) whether the United States or the opposing party, or either party's representative, made motions or asserted claims or defenses so lacking in merit as to show that such party or representative acted intentionally for delay or otherwise acted in bad faith;

(2) whether, in the course of the action involved, the United States or the opposing party, or either party's representative, violated any applicable rule, statute, or court order providing for sanctions for dilatory behavior or otherwise providing for expeditious proceedings;

(3) whether the United States or the opposing party, or either party's representative, engaged in conduct primarily for the purpose of delaying the litigation or increasing the cost thereof; and

(4) whether the award of such interest is necessary to compensate the United States adequately for the injury sustained by the United States.

§ 15b. Limitation of actions

Any action to enforce any cause of action under sections 15, 15a, or 15c of this title shall be forever barred unless commenced within four years after the cause of action accrued. No cause of action barred under existing law on the effective date [1956] of this Act shall be revived by this Act.

§ 15c. Actions by State attorneys general

* * *

§ 16. Judgments

(a) Prima facie evidence; collateral estoppel

A final judgment or decree heretofore or hereafter rendered in any civil or criminal proceeding brought by or on behalf of the United States under the antitrust laws to the effect that a defendant has violated said laws shall be prima facie evidence against such defendant in any action or proceeding brought by any other party against such defendant under said laws as to all matters respecting which said judgment or decree would be an estoppel as between the parties thereto: *Provided*, That this section shall not apply to consent judgments or decrees entered before any testimony has been taken. Nothing contained in this section shall be construed to impose any limitation on the application of collateral estoppel, except that, in any action or proceeding brought under the antitrust laws, collateral estoppel effect shall not be given to any finding made by the Federal Trade Commission under the antitrust laws or under section 45 of this title which could give rise to a claim for relief under the antitrust laws.

* * *

(i) Suspension of limitations

Whenever any civil or criminal proceeding is instituted by the United States to prevent, restrain, or punish violations of any of the antitrust laws, but not including an action under section 15a of this title, the running of the statute of limitations in respect of every private or State right of action arising under said laws and based in whole or in part on any matter complained of in said proceeding shall be suspended during the pendency thereof and for one year thereafter: *Provided, however,* That whenever the running of the statute of limitations in respect of a cause of action arising under section 15 or 15c of this title is suspended hereunder, any action to enforce such cause of action shall be forever barred unless commenced either within the period of suspension or within four years after the cause of action accrued.

§ 22. District in which to sue corporation

Any suit, action, or proceeding under the antitrust laws against a corporation may be brought not only in the judicial district whereof it is an inhabitant, but also in any district wherein it may be found or transacts business; and all process in such cases may be served in the district of which it is an inhabitant, or wherever it may be found.

§ 23. Suits by United States; subpoenas for witnesses

In any suit, action, or proceeding brought by or on behalf of the United States subpoenas for witnesses who are required to attend a court of the United States in any judicial district in any case, civil or criminal, arising under the antitrust laws may run into any other district: *Provided*, That in civil cases no writ of subpoena shall issue for witnesses living out of the district in which the court is held at a greater distance than one hundred miles from the place of holding the same without the permission of the trial court being first had upon proper application and cause shown.

§ 25. Restraining violations; procedure

The several district courts of the United States are invested with jurisdiction to prevent and restrain violations of this [Clayton Antitrust] Act, and it shall be the duty of the several United States attorneys, in their respective districts, under the direction of the Attorney General, to institute proceedings in equity to prevent and restrain such violations. Such proceedings may be by way of petition setting forth the case and praying that such violation shall be enjoined or otherwise prohibited. When the parties complained of shall have been duly notified of such petition, the court shall proceed, as soon as may be, to the hearing and determination of the case; and pending such petition, and before final decree, the court may at any time make such temporary restraining order or prohibition as shall be deemed just in the premises. Whenever it shall appear to the court before which any such proceeding may be pending that the ends of justice require that other parties should be brought before the court, the court may cause them to be summoned whether they reside in the district in which the court is held or not, and subpoenas to that end may be served in any district by the marshal thereof.

§ 26. Injunctive relief for private parties; exception; costs

Any person, firm, corporation, or association shall be entitled to sue for and have injunctive relief, in any court of the United States having jurisdiction over the parties, against threatened loss or damage by a violation of the antitrust laws, including sections 13, 14, 18, and 19 of this title, when and under the same conditions and principles as injunctive relief against threatened conduct that will cause loss or damage is granted by courts of equity, under the rules governing such proceedings, and upon the execution of proper bond against damages for an injunction improvidently granted and a showing that the danger of irreparable loss or damage is immediate, a preliminary injunction may issue: *Provided*, That nothing herein contained shall be construed to entitle any person, firm, corporation, or association, except the United States, to bring suit in equity for injunctive relief against any common carrier subject to the provisions of subtitle IV of Title 49, in respect of any matter subject to the

SELECTED PROVISIONS

regulation, supervision, or other jurisdiction of the Interstate Commerce Commission. In any action under this section in which the plaintiff substantially prevails, the court shall award the cost of suit, including a reasonable attorney's fee, to such plaintiff.

TITLE 42, UNITED STATES CODE

§ 1983. Civil action for deprivation of rights

Every person who, under color of any statute, ordinance, regulation, custom, or usage, of any State or Territory or the District of Columbia, subjects, or causes to be subjected, any citizen of the United States or other person within the jurisdiction thereof to the deprivation of any rights, privileges, or immunities secured by the Constitution and laws, shall be liable to the party injured in an action at law, suit in equity, or other proper proceeding for redress. For the purposes of this section, any Act of Congress applicable exclusively to the District of Columbia shall be considered to be a statute of the District of Columbia.

§ 1988. Proceedings in vindication of civil rights; attorney's fees

The jurisdiction in civil and criminal matters conferred on the district courts by the provisions of this Title, and of Title "CIVIL RIGHTS," and of Title "CRIMES," for the protection of all persons in the United States in their civil rights, and for their vindication, shall be exercised and enforced in conformity with the laws of the United States, so far as such laws are suitable to carry the same into effect; but in all cases where they are not adapted to the object, or are deficient in the provisions necessary to furnish suitable remedies and punish offenses against law, the common law, as modified and changed by the constitution and statutes of the State wherein the court having jurisdiction of such civil or criminal cause is held, so far as the same is not inconsistent with the Constitution and laws of the United States, shall be extended to and govern the said courts in the trial and disposition of the cause, and, if it is of a criminal nature, in the infliction of punishment on the party found guilty. In any action or proceeding to enforce a provision of sections 1981, 1982, 1983, 1985, and 1986 of this title, title IX of Public Law 92–318, or title VI of the Civil Rights Act of 1964, the court, in its discretion, may allow the prevailing party, other than the United States, a reasonable attorney's fee as part of the costs.

CALIFORNIA

Code of Civil Procedure

§ 410.10. Basis

A court of this state may exercise jurisdiction on any basis not inconsistent with the Constitution of this state or of the United States.

Fed.Rules Civ.Proc. 1991 Pamph. FP—16   479

OTHER PROCEDURAL STATUTES

NEW YORK

Judiciary Law

§ 140–b. General jurisdiction of supreme court

The general jurisdiction in law and equity which the supreme court possesses under the provisions of the constitution [art. VI, § 7] includes all the jurisdiction which was possessed and exercised by the supreme court of the colony of New York at any time, and by the court of chancery in England on the fourth day of July, seventeen hundred seventy-six, with the exceptions, additions and limitations created and imposed by the constitution and laws of the state. Subject to those exceptions and limitations the supreme court of the state has all the powers and authority of each of those courts and may exercise them in like manner.

Civil Practice Law and Rules

Article 2—Limitations of Time

§ 201. Application of article

An action, including one brought in the name or for the benefit of the state, must be commenced within the time specified in this article unless a different time is prescribed by law or a shorter time is prescribed by written agreement. No court shall extend the time limited by law for the commencement of an action.

§ 202. Cause of action accruing without the state

An action based upon a cause of action accruing without the state cannot be commenced after the expiration of the time limited by the laws of either the state or the place without the state where the cause of action accrued, except that where the cause of action accrued in favor of a resident of the state the time limited by the laws of the state shall apply.

§ 203. Method of computing periods of limitation generally

(a) **Accrual of cause of action and interposition of claim.** The time within which an action must be commenced, except as otherwise expressly prescribed, shall be computed from the time the cause of action accrued to the time the claim is interposed.

(b) **Claim in complaint.** A claim asserted in the complaint is interposed against the defendant or a co-defendant united in interest with him when:

1. the summons is served upon the defendant; or

2. first publication of the summons against the defendant is made pursuant to an order, and publication is subsequently completed; or

3. an order for a provisional remedy other than attachment is granted, if, within thirty days thereafter, the summons is served upon the defendant or first publication of the summons against the defendant is made pursuant to an order and publication is subsequently completed, or, where the defendant dies within thirty days after the order is granted and before the summons is served upon him or publication is completed, if the

summons is served upon his executor or administrator within sixty days after letters are issued; for this purpose seizure of a chattel in an action to recover a chattel is a provisional remedy; or

4. an order of attachment is granted, if the summons is served in accordance with the provisions of section 6213; or

5. the summons is delivered to the sheriff of that county outside the city of New York or is filed with the clerk of that county within the city of New York in which the defendant resides, is employed or is doing business, or if none of the foregoing is known to the plaintiff after reasonable inquiry, then of the county in which the defendant is known to have last resided, been employed or been engaged in business, or in which the cause of action arose; or if the defendant is a corporation, of a county in which it may be served or in which the cause of action arose; provided that:

(i) the summons is served upon the defendant within sixty days after the period of limitation would have expired but for this provision; or

(ii) first publication of the summons against the defendant is made pursuant to an order within sixty days after the period of limitation would have expired but for this provision and publication is subsequently completed; or

(iii) the summons is served upon the defendant's executor or administrator within sixty days after letters are issued, where the defendant dies within sixty days after the period of limitation would have expired but for this provision and before the summons is served upon him or publication is completed.

6. in an action to be commenced in a court not of record, the summons is delivered for service upon the defendant to any officer authorized to serve it in a county, city or town in which the defendant resides, is employed or is doing business, or if none of the foregoing be known to the plaintiff after reasonable inquiry, then in a county, city or town in which defendant is known to have last resided, been employed or been engaged in business, or, where the defendant is a corporation, in a county, city or town in which it may be served, if the summons is served upon the defendant within sixty days after the period of limitation would have expired but for this provision; or, where the defendant dies within sixty days after the period of limitation would have expired but for this provision and before the summons is served upon him, if the summons is served upon his executor or administrator within sixty days after letters are issued.

(c) **Defense or counterclaim.** A defense or counterclaim is interposed when a pleading containing it is served. A defense or counterclaim is not barred if it was not barred at the time the claims asserted in the complaint were interposed, except that if the defense or counterclaim arose from the transactions, occurrences, or series of transactions or occurrences, upon which a claim asserted in the complaint depends, it is not barred to the extent of the demand in the complaint notwithstanding that it was barred at the time the claims asserted in the complaint were interposed.

(d) Effect upon defense or counterclaim of termination of action because of death or by dismissal or voluntary discontinuance. Where a defendant has served an answer containing a defense or counterclaim and the action is terminated because of the plaintiff's death or by dismissal or voluntary discontinuance, the time which elapsed between the commencement and termination of the action is not a part of the time within which an action must be commenced to recover upon the claim in the defense or counterclaim or the time within which the defense or counterclaim may be interposed in another action brought by the plaintiff or his successor in interest.

(e) Claim in amended pleading. A claim asserted in an amended pleading is deemed to have been interposed at the time the claims in the original pleading were interposed, unless the original pleading does not give notice of the transactions, occurrences, or series of transactions or occurrences, to be proved pursuant to the amended pleading.

(f) Time computed from actual or imputed discovery of facts. Except as provided in article 2 of the uniform commercial code or in section two hundred fourteen–a of this chapter, where the time within which an action must be commenced is computed from the time when facts were discovered or from the time when facts could with reasonable diligence have been discovered, or from either of such times, the action must be commenced within two years after such actual or imputed discovery or within the period otherwise provided, computed from the time the cause of action accrued, whichever is longer.

§ 204. Stay of commencement of action; demand for arbitration

* * *

§ 205. Termination of action

(a) New action by plaintiff. If an action is timely commenced and is terminated in any other manner than by a voluntary discontinuance, a dismissal of the complaint for neglect to prosecute the action, or a final judgment upon the merits, the plaintiff, or, if he dies, and the cause of action survives, his executor or administrator, may commence a new action upon the same transaction or occurrence or series of transactions or occurrences within six months after the termination provided that the new action would have been timely commenced at the time of commencement of the prior action.

(b) Defense or counterclaim. Where the defendant has served an answer and the action is terminated in any manner, and a new action upon the same transaction or occurrence or series of transactions or occurrences is commenced by the plaintiff or his successor in interest, the assertion of any cause of action or defense by the defendant in the new action shall be timely if it was timely asserted in the prior action.

(c) Application. This section also applies to a proceeding brought under the workmen's compensation law.

482

SELECTED PROVISIONS

§ 206. Computing periods of limitation in particular actions

[Treatment of actions where a demand is necessary to entitle a person to commence the action and of actions based on misconduct of an agent, on breach of a covenant of seizin or against incumbrances, or on account.]

§ 207. Defendant's absence from state or residence under false name

If, when a cause of action accrues against a person, he is without the state, the time within which the action must be commenced shall be computed from the time he comes into or returns to the state. If, after a cause of action has accrued against a person, he departs from the state and remains continuously absent therefrom for four months or more, or he resides within the state under a false name which is unknown to the person entitled to commence the action, the time of his absence or residence within the state under such a false name is not a part of the time within which the action must be commenced. This section does not apply:

1. while there is in force a designation, voluntary or involuntary, made pursuant to law, of a person to whom a summons may be delivered within the state with the same effect as if served personally within the state; or

2. while a foreign corporation has one or more officers or other persons in the state on whom a summons against such corporation may be served; or

3. while jurisdiction over the person of the defendant can be obtained without personal delivery of the summons to him within the state.

§ 208. Infancy, insanity

If a person entitled to commence an action is under a disability because of infancy or insanity at the time the cause of action accrues, and the time otherwise limited for commencing the action is three years or more and expires no later than three years after the disability ceases, or the person under the disability dies, the time within which the action must be commenced shall be extended to three years after the disability ceases or the person under the disability dies, whichever event first occurs; if the time otherwise limited is less than three years, the time shall be extended by the period of disability. The time within which the action must be commenced shall not be extended by this provision beyond ten years after the cause of action accrues, except, in any action other than for medical, dental or podiatric malpractice, where the person was under a disability due to infancy. This section shall not apply to an action to recover a penalty or forfeiture, or against a sheriff or other officer for an escape.

§ 209. War

* * *

§ 210. Death of claimant or person liable; cause of action accruing after death and before grant of letters

(a) **Death of claimant.** Where a person entitled to commence an action dies before the expiration of the time within which the action must be commenced and the cause of action survives, an action may be commenced by his representative within one year after his death.

(b) **Death of person liable.** The period of eighteen months after the death, within or without the state, of a person against whom a cause of action exists is not a part of the time within which the action must be commenced against his executor or administrator.

(c) **Cause of action accruing after death and before grant of letters.** In an action by an executor or administrator to recover personal property wrongfully taken after the death and before the issuance of letters, or to recover damages for taking, detaining or injuring personal property within that period, the time within which the action must be commenced shall be computed from the time the letters are issued or from three years after the death, whichever event first occurs. Any distributee, next of kin, legatee or creditor who was under a disability prescribed in section 208 at the time the cause of action accrued, may, within two years after the disability ceases, commence an action to recover such damages or the value of such property as he would have received upon a final distribution of the estate if an action had been timely commenced by the executor or administrator.

§ 211. Actions to be commenced within twenty years

(a) **On a bond.** An action to recover principal or interest upon a written instrument evidencing an indebtedness of the state of New York or of any person, association or public or private corporation, originally sold by the issuer after publication of an advertisement for bids for the issue in a newspaper of general circulation and secured only by a pledge of the faith and credit of the issuer, regardless of whether a sinking fund is or may be established for its redemption, must be commenced within twenty years after the cause of action accrues. This subdivision does not apply to actions upon written instruments evidencing an indebtedness of any corporation, association or person under the jurisdiction of the public service commission, the commissioner of transportation, the interstate commerce commission, the federal communications commission, the civil aeronautics board, the federal power commission, or any other regulatory commission or board of a state or of the federal government. This subdivision applies to all causes of action, including those barred on April eighteenth, nineteen hundred fifty, by the provisions of the civil practice act then effective.

(b) **On a money judgment.** A money judgment is presumed to be paid and satisfied after the expiration of twenty years from the time when the party recovering it was first entitled to enforce it. This presumption is conclusive, except as against a person who within the twenty years acknowledges an indebtedness, or makes a payment, of all or part of the amount recovered by the judgment, or his heir or personal representative, or a person whom he otherwise represents. Such an acknowledgment must be in writing and signed by the person to be charged. Property acquired by an enforcement order or by levy upon an execution is a payment, unless the person to be charged shows that it did not include property claimed by him. If such an acknowledgment or payment is made, the judgment is conclusively presumed to be paid and satisfied as against any person after the expiration of twenty years after the last acknowledgment or payment made by him. The presumption created by this subdivision may be availed of under an allegation that the action was not commenced within the time limited.

(c) **By state for real property.** The state will not sue a person for or with respect to real property, or the rents or profits thereof, by reason of the right or title of the state to the same, unless the cause of action accrued, or the state, or those from whom it claims, have received the rents and profits of the real property or of some part thereof, within twenty years before the commencement of the action.

(d) **By grantee of state for real property.** An action shall not be commenced for or with respect to real property by a person claiming by virtue of letters patent or a grant from the state, unless it might have been maintained by the state, as prescribed in this section, if the patent or grant had not been issued or made.

(e) **For support, alimony or maintenance.** An action or proceeding to enforce any temporary order, permanent order or judgment of any court of competent jurisdiction which awards support, alimony or maintenance, regardless of whether or not arrears have been reduced to a money judgment, must be commenced within twenty years from the date of a default in payment. This section shall only apply to orders which have been entered subsequent to the date upon which this section shall become effective.

§ 212. **Actions to be commenced within ten years**

(a) **Possession necessary to recover real property.** An action to recover real property or its possession cannot be commenced unless the plaintiff, or his predecessor in interest, was seized or possessed of the premises within ten years before the commencement of the action.

(b) **Annulment of letters patent.** Where letters patent or a grant of real property, issued or made by the state, are declared void on the ground of fraudulent suggestion or concealment, forfeiture, mistake or ignorance of a material fact, wrongful detaining or defective title, an action to recover the premises may be commenced by the state or by a subsequent patentee or grantee, or his successor in interest, within ten years after the determination is made.

(c) **To redeem from a mortgage.** An action to redeem real property from a mortgage with or without an account of rents and profits may be commenced by the mortgagor or his successors in interest, against the mortgagee in possession, or against the purchaser of the mortgaged premises at a foreclosure sale in an action in which the mortgagor or his successors in interest were not excluded from their interest in the mortgaged premises, or against a successor in interest of either, unless the mortgagee, purchaser or successor was continuously possessed of the

485

premises for ten years after the breach or non-fulfillment of a condition or covenant of the mortgage, or the date of recording of the deed of the premises to the purchaser.

§ 213. Actions to be commenced within six years: where not otherwise provided for; on contract; on sealed instrument; on bond or note, and mortgage upon real property; by state based on misappropriation of public property; based on mistake; by corporation against director, officer or stockholder; based on fraud

The following actions must be commenced within six years:

1.   an action for which no limitation is specifically prescribed by law;

2.   an action upon a contractual obligation or liability, express or implied, except as provided in section two hundred thirteen-a of this article or article 2 of the uniform commercial code or article 36–B of the general business law;

3.   an action upon a sealed instrument;

4.   an action upon a bond or note, the payment of which is secured by a mortgage upon real property, or upon a bond or note and mortgage so secured, or upon a mortgage of real property, or any interest therein;

5.   an action by the state based upon the spoliation or other misappropriation of public property; the time within which the action must be commenced shall be computed from discovery by the state of the facts relied upon;

6.   an action based upon mistake;

7.   an action by or on behalf of a corporation against a present or former director, officer or stockholder for an accounting, or to procure a judgment on the ground of fraud, or to enforce a liability, penalty or forfeiture, or to recover damages for waste or for an injury to property or for an accounting in conjunction therewith;

8.   an action based upon fraud; the time within which the action must be commenced shall be computed from the time the plaintiff or the person under whom he claims discovered the fraud, or could with reasonable diligence have discovered it.

§ 213–a. Actions to be commenced within four years: residential rent overcharge

An action on a residential rent overcharge shall be commenced within four years of such overcharge.

§ 214. Actions to be commenced within three years: for non-payment of money collected on execution; for penalty created by statute; to recover chattel; for injury to property; for personal injury; for malpractice other than medical, dental or podiatric malpractice; to annul a marriage on the ground of fraud

The following actions must be commenced within three years:

1. an action against a sheriff, constable or other officer for the non-payment of money collected upon an execution;

2. an action to recover upon a liability, penalty or forfeiture created or imposed by statute except as provided in sections 213 and 215;

3. an action to recover a chattel or damages for the taking or detaining of a chattel;

4. an action to recover damages for an injury to property;

5. an action to recover damages for a personal injury except as provided in sections 214-b and 215;

6. an action to recover damages for malpractice, other than medical, dental or podiatric malpractice; and

7. an action to annul a marriage on the ground of fraud; the time within which the action must be commenced shall be computed from the time the plaintiff discovered the facts constituting the fraud, but if the plaintiff is a person other than the spouse whose consent was obtained by fraud, the time within which the action must be commenced shall be computed from the time, if earlier, that that spouse discovered the facts constituting the fraud.

§ 214–a. Action for medical, dental or podiatric malpractice to be commenced within two years and six months; exceptions

An action for medical, dental or podiatric malpractice must be commenced within two years and six months of the act, omission or failure complained of or last treatment where there is continuous treatment for the same illness, injury or condition which gave rise to the said act, omission or failure; provided, however, that where the action is based upon the discovery of a foreign object in the body of the patient, the action may be commenced within one year of the date of such discovery or of the date of discovery of facts which would reasonably lead to such discovery, whichever is earlier. For the purpose of this section the term "continuous treatment" shall not include examinations undertaken at the request of the patient for the sole purpose of ascertaining the state of the patient's condition. For the purpose of this section the term "foreign object" shall not include a chemical compound, fixation device or prosthetic aid or device.

§ 214–b. Action to recover damages for personal injury caused by contact with or exposure to phenoxy herbicides

Notwithstanding any provision of law to the contrary, an action to recover damages for personal injury caused by contact with or exposure to phenoxy herbicides while serving as a member of the armed forces of the United States in Indo-China from January first, nineteen hundred sixty-two through May seventh, nineteen hundred seventy-five, may be commenced within two years from the date of the discovery of such injury, or within two years from the date when through the exercise of reasonable diligence the cause of such injury should have been discovered, whichever is later.

§ 214–c. Certain actions to be commenced within three years of discovery

1. In this section: "exposure" means direct or indirect exposure by absorption, contact, ingestion, inhalation or injection.

2. Notwithstanding the provisions of section 214, the three year period within which an action to recover damages for personal injury or injury to property caused by the latent effects of exposure to any substance or combination of substances, in any form, upon or within the body or upon or within property must be commenced shall be computed from the date of discovery of the injury by the plaintiff or from the date when through the exercise of reasonable diligence such injury should have been discovered by the plaintiff, whichever is earlier.

3. For the purposes of sections fifty-e and fifty-i of the general municipal law, section thirty-eight hundred thirteen of the education law and the provisions of any general, special or local law or charter requiring as a condition precedent to commencement of an action or special proceeding that a notice of claim be filed or presented within a specified period of time after the claim or action accrued, a claim or action for personal injury or injury to property caused by the latent effects of exposure to any substance or combination of substances, in any form, upon or within the body or upon or within property shall be deemed to have accrued on the date of discovery of the injury by the plaintiff or on the date when through the exercise of reasonable diligence the injury should have been discovered, whichever is earlier.

4. Notwithstanding the provisions of subdivisions two and three of this section, where the discovery of the cause of the injury is alleged to have occurred less than five years after discovery of the injury or when with reasonable diligence such injury should have been discovered, whichever is earlier, an action may be commenced or a claim filed within one year of such discovery of the cause of the injury; provided, however, if any such action is commenced or claim filed after the period in which it would otherwise have been authorized pursuant to subdivision two or three of this section the plaintiff or claimant shall be required to allege and prove that technical, scientific or medical knowledge and information sufficient to ascertain the cause of his injury had not been discovered, identified or determined prior to the expiration of the period within which the action or claim would have been authorized and that he has otherwise satisfied the requirements of subdivisions two and three of this section.

5. This section shall not be applicable to any action for medical or dental malpractice.

6. This section shall be applicable to acts, omissions or failures occurring prior to, on or after July first, nineteen hundred eighty-six, except that this section shall not be applicable to any act, omission or failure:

(a) which occurred prior to July first, nineteen hundred eighty-six, and

(b) which caused or contributed to an injury that either was discovered or through the exercise of reasonable diligence should have been discovered prior to such date, and

(c) an action for which was or would have been barred because the applicable period of limitation had expired prior to such date.

§ 215. **Actions to be commenced within one year: against sheriff, coroner or constable; for escape of prisoner; for assault, battery, false imprisonment, malicious prosecution, libel or slander; for violation of right of privacy; for penalty given to informer; on arbitration award**

The following actions shall be commenced within one year:

1. an action against a sheriff, coroner or constable, upon a liability incurred by him by doing an act in his official capacity or by omission of an official duty, except the non-payment of money collected upon an execution;

2. an action against an officer for the escape of a prisoner arrested or imprisoned by virtue of a civil mandate;

3. an action to recover damages for assault, battery, false imprisonment, malicious prosecution, libel, slander, false words causing special damages, or a violation of the right of privacy under section fifty-one of the civil rights law;

4. an action to enforce a penalty or forfeiture created by statute and given wholly or partly to any person who will prosecute; if the action is not commenced within the year by a private person, it may be commenced on behalf of the state, within three years after the commission of the offense, by the attorney-general or the district attorney of the county where the offense was committed; and

5. an action upon an arbitration award.

6. An action to recover any overcharge of interest or to enforce a penalty for such overcharge.

7. an action by a tenant pursuant to subdivision three of section two hundred twenty-three-b of the real property law.

8. Whenever it is shown that a criminal action against the same defendant has been commenced with respect to the event or occurrence from which a claim governed by this section arises, the plaintiff shall have at least one year from the termination of the criminal action as defined in section 1.20 of the criminal procedure law in which to commence the civil action, notwithstanding that the time in which to commence such action has already expired or has less than a year remaining.

§ 217. **Proceeding against body or officer; actions complaining about conduct that would constitute a union's breach of its duty of fair representation; four months**

1. Unless a shorter time is provided in the law authorizing the proceeding, a proceeding against a body or officer must be commenced within four months after the determination to be reviewed becomes final and binding upon the petitioner or the person whom he represents in law

or in fact, or after the respondent's refusal, upon the demand of the petitioner or the person whom he represents, to perform its duty; or with leave of the court where the petitioner or the person whom he represents, at the time such determination became final and binding upon him or at the time of such refusal, was under a disability specified in section 208, within two years after such time.

2. (a) Any action or proceeding against an employee organization subject to article fourteen of the civil service law or article twenty of the labor law which complains that such employee organization has breached its duty of fair representation regarding someone to whom such employee organization has a duty shall be commenced within four months of the date the employee or former employee knew or should have known that the breach has occurred, or within four months of the date the employee or former employee suffers actual harm, whichever is later.

(b) Any action or proceeding by an employee or former employee against an employer subject to article fourteen of the civil service law or article twenty of the labor law, an essential element of which is that an employee organization breached its duty of fair representation to the person making the complaint, shall be commenced within four months of the date the employee or former employee knew or should have known that the breach has occurred, or within four months of the date the employee or former employee suffers actual harm, whichever is later.

Article 3—Jurisdiction and Service, Appearance and Choice of Court

§ 301. Jurisdiction over persons, property or status

A court may exercise such jurisdiction over persons, property, or status as might have been exercised heretofore.

§ 302. Personal jurisdiction by acts of non-domiciliaries

(a) **Acts which are the basis of jurisdiction.** As to a cause of action arising from any of the acts enumerated in this section, a court may exercise personal jurisdiction over any non-domiciliary, or his executor or administrator, who in person or through an agent:

1. transacts any business within the state or contracts anywhere to supply goods or services in the state; or

2. commits a tortious act within the state, except as to a cause of action for defamation of character arising from the act; or

3. commits a tortious act without the state causing injury to person or property within the state, except as to a cause of action for defamation of character arising from the act, if he

(i) regularly does or solicits business, or engages in any other persistent course of conduct, or derives substantial revenue from goods used or consumed or services rendered, in the state, or

(ii) expects or should reasonably expect the act to have consequences in the state and derives substantial revenue from interstate or international commerce; or

4. owns, uses or possesses any real property situated within the state.

(b) Personal jurisdiction over non-resident defendant in matrimonial actions or family court proceedings. A court in any matrimonial action or family court proceeding involving a demand for support, alimony, maintenance, distributive awards or special relief in matrimonial actions may exercise personal jurisdiction over the respondent or defendant notwithstanding the fact that he or she no longer is a resident or domiciliary of this state, or over his or her executor or administrator, if the party seeking support is a resident of or domiciled in this state at the time such demand is made, provided that this state was the matrimonial domicile of the parties before their separation, or the defendant abandoned the plaintiff in this state, or the claim for support, alimony, maintenance, distributive awards or special relief in matrimonial actions accrued under the laws of this state or under an agreement executed in this state.

(c) Effect of appearance. Where personal jurisdiction is based solely upon this section, an appearance does not confer such jurisdiction with respect to causes of action not arising from an act enumerated in this section.

§ 303. Designation of attorney as agent for service

The commencement of an action in the state by a person not subject to personal jurisdiction is a designation by him of his attorney appearing in the action or of the clerk of the court if no attorney appears, as agent, during the pendency of the action, for service of a summons pursuant to section 308, in any separate action in which such a person is a defendant and another party to the action is a plaintiff if such separate action would have been permitted as a counterclaim had the action been brought in the supreme court.

§ 307. Personal service upon the state

* * *

§ 308. Personal service upon a natural person

Personal service upon a natural person shall be made by any of the following methods:

1. by delivering the summons within the state to the person to be served; or

2. by delivering the summons within the state to a person of suitable age and discretion at the actual place of business, dwelling place or usual place of abode of the person to be served and by either mailing the summons to the person to be served at his or her last known residence or by mailing the summons by first class mail to the person to be served at his or her actual place of business in an envelope bearing the legend "personal and confidential" and not indicating on the outside thereof, by return address or otherwise, that the communication is from an attorney or concerns an action against the person to be served, such delivery and mailing to be effected within twenty days of each other; proof of such

service shall be filed with the clerk of the court designated in the summons within twenty days of either such delivery or mailing, whichever is effected later; service shall be complete ten days after such filing; proof of service shall identify such person of suitable age and discretion and state the date, time and place of service, except in matrimonial actions where service hereunder may be made pursuant to an order made in accordance with the provisions of subdivision a of section two hundred thirty-two of the domestic relations law; or

3. by delivering the summons within the state to the agent for service of the person to be served as designated under rule 318, except in matrimonial actions where service hereunder may be made pursuant to an order made in accordance with the provisions of subdivision a of section two hundred thirty-two of the domestic relations law;

4. where service under paragraphs one and two cannot be made with due diligence, by affixing the summons to the door of either the actual place of business, dwelling place or usual place of abode within the state of the person to be served and by either mailing the summons to such person at his or her last known residence or by mailing the summons by first class mail to the person to be served at his or her actual place of business in an envelope bearing the legend "personal and confidential" and not indicating on the outside thereof, by return address or otherwise, that the communication is from an attorney or concerns an action against the person to be served, such affixing and mailing to be effected within twenty days of each other; proof of such service shall be filed with the clerk of the court designated in the summons within twenty days of either such affixing or mailing, whichever is effected later; service shall be complete ten days after such filing, except in matrimonial actions where service hereunder may be made pursuant to an order made in accordance with the provisions of subdivision a of section two hundred thirty-two of the domestic relations law;

5. in such manner as the court, upon motion without notice, directs, if service is impracticable under paragraphs one, two and four of this section.

§ 309. Personal service upon an infant, incompetent or conservatee

* * *

§ 310. Personal service upon a partnership

* * *

§ 311. Personal service upon a corporation or governmental subdivision

Personal service upon a corporation or governmental subdivision shall be made by delivering the summons as follows:

1. upon any domestic or foreign corporation, to an officer, director, managing or general agent, or cashier or assistant cashier or to any other agent authorized by appointment or by law to receive service;

* * *

§ 312. Personal service upon a court, board or commission

* * *

§ 312–a. Personal service by mail

(a) Service. As an alternative to the methods of personal service authorized by section 307, 308, 310, 311 or 312 of this article, a summons and complaint, or summons and notice, or notice of petition and petition may be served by the plaintiff, the plaintiff's attorney or an employee of the attorney by mailing to the person or entity to be served, by first class mail, postage prepaid, a copy of the summons and complaint, or summons and notice or notice of petition and petition, together with two copies of a statement of service by mail and acknowledgement of receipt in the form set forth in subdivision (d) of this section, with a return envelope, postage prepaid, addressed to the sender.

(b) Completion of service and time to answer.

1. The defendant, defendant's attorney or an employee of the attorney must complete the acknowledgement of receipt and mail or deliver a copy of it within thirty (30) days from the date of receipt. An action is commenced and service is complete on the date the signed acknowledgement of receipt is mailed or delivered to the sender. The signed acknowledgement of receipt shall constitute proof of service.

2. Where a complaint or petition is served with the summons or notice of petition, the defendant shall serve an answer within twenty days after the date the signed acknowledgement of receipt is mailed or delivered to the sender.

(c) Affirmation. The acknowledgement of receipt of service shall be subscribed and affirmed as true under penalties of perjury and shall have the same force and effect as an affidavit.

(d) Form. The statement of service by mail and the acknowledgement of receipt of such service shall be in substantially the following form:

Statement of Service by Mail and
Acknowledgement of Receipt by Mail of
Summons and Complaint or Summons and Notice
or Notice of Petition and Petition

[CAPTION]

STATEMENT OF SERVICE BY MAIL

To: (Insert the name and address of the person or entity to be served.) The enclosed summons and complaint, or summons and notice, or notice of petition and petition are served pursuant to section 312–a of the Civil Practice Law and Rules.

To avoid being charged with the expense of service upon you, you must sign, date and complete the acknowledgement part of this form and mail or deliver one copy of the completed form to the sender within thirty

493

(30) days from the date you receive it. If you wish to consult an attorney, you should do so as soon as possible before the thirty (30) days expire.

If you do not complete and return the form to the sender within thirty (30) days, you (or the party on whose behalf you are being served) may be required to pay expenses incurred in serving the summons and complaint, or summons and notice, or notice of petition and petition in any other manner permitted by law, and the cost of such service as permitted by law may be entered as a judgment against you.

If you have received a complaint or petition with this statement, the return of this statement and acknowledgement does not relieve you of the necessity to answer the complaint or petition. The time to answer expires twenty (20) days after the day you mail or deliver this form to the sender. If you wish to consult with an attorney, you should do so as soon as possible before the twenty (20) days expire.

If you are served on behalf of a corporation, unincorporated association, partnership or other entity, you must indicate under your signature your relationship to the entity. If you are served on behalf of another person and you are authorized to receive process, you must indicate under your signature your authority.

It is a crime to forge a signature or to make a false entry on this statement or on the acknowledgement.

_____

Signature

_____

Print name

_____

Address

ACKNOWLEDGEMENT OF RECEIPT OF SUMMONS AND COMPLAINT OR SUMMONS AND NOTICE OR NOTICE OF PETITION AND PETITION

I received a summons and complaint, or summons and notice, or notice of petition and petition in the above-captioned matter at (insert address). PLEASE CHECK ONE OF THE FOLLOWING;

IF 2 IS CHECKED, COMPLETE AS INDICATED:

1. / /I am not in military service.

2. / /I am in military service, and my rank, serial number and branch of service are as follows:

_____

Rank

_____

Serial number

_____

Branch of Service

Date:

(Date this Acknowledgement is executed)

I affirm the above as true under penalty of perjury.

_____

Signature

_____

Print name

_____

Relationship to entity/Authority to Receive Service of Process

(e) Subsequent service. Where a duly executed acknowledgement is not returned, upon the subsequent service of process in another manner permitted by law, the summons or notice of petition or paper served with the summons or notice of petition shall indicate that an attempt previously was made to effect service pursuant to this section.

(f) Disbursements. Where the signed acknowledgement of receipt is not returned within thirty (30) days after receipt of the documents mailed pursuant to subdivision (a) of this section, the reasonable expense of serving process by an alternative method shall be taxed by the court as a disbursement to the party serving process, if that party is awarded costs in the action or proceeding.

§ 313. Service without the state giving personal jurisdiction

A person domiciled in the state or subject to the jurisdiction of the courts of the state under section 301 or 302, or his executor or administrator, may be served with the summons without the state, in the same manner as service is made within the state, by any person authorized to make service within the state who is a resident of the state or by any person authorized to make service by the laws of the state, territory, possession or country in which service is made or by any duly qualified attorney, solicitor, barrister, or equivalent in such jurisdiction.

§ 314. Service without the state not giving personal jurisdiction in certain actions

Service may be made without the state by any person authorized by section 313 in the same manner as service is made within the state:

1. in a matrimonial action; or

2. where a judgment is demanded that the person to be served be excluded from a vested or contingent interest in or lien upon specific real or personal property within the state; or that such an interest or lien in favor of either party be enforced, regulated, defined or limited; or otherwise affecting the title to such property, including an action of interpleader or defensive interpleader; or

3. where a levy upon property of the person to be served has been made within the state pursuant to an order of attachment or a chattel of such person has been seized in an action to recover a chattel.

§ 315. Service by publication authorized

The court, upon motion without notice, shall order service of a summons by publication in an action described in section 314 if service cannot be made by another prescribed method with due diligence.

Rule 316. Service by publication [method]

* * *

§ 317. Defense by person to whom summons not personally delivered

A person served with a summons other than by personal delivery to him or to his agent for service designated under rule 318, within or without the state, who does not appear may be allowed to defend the action within one year after he obtains knowledge of entry of the judgment, but in no event more than five years after such entry, upon a finding of the court that he did not personally receive notice of the summons in time to defend and has a meritorious defense. If the defense is successful, the court may direct and enforce restitution in the same manner and subject to the same conditions as where a judgment is reversed or modified on appeal. This section does not apply to an action for divorce, annulment or partition.

Rule 318. Designation of agent for service

A person may be designated by a natural person, corporation or partnership as an agent for service in a writing, executed and acknowledged in the same manner as a deed, with the consent of the agent endorsed thereon. The writing shall be filed in the office of the clerk of the county in which the principal to be served resides or has its principal office. The designation shall remain in effect for three years from such filing unless it has been revoked by the filing of a revocation, or by the death, judicial declaration of incompetency or legal termination of the agent or principal.

Rule 320. Defendant's appearance

(a) **Requirement of appearance.** The defendant appears by serving an answer or a notice of appearance, or by making a motion which has the effect of extending the time to answer. An appearance shall be made within twenty days after service of the summons, except that if the summons was served on the defendant by delivering it to an official of the state authorized to receive service in his behalf or if it was served pursuant to section 303, subdivision two, three, four or five of section 308, or sections 313, 314 or 315, the appearance shall be made within thirty days after service is complete. If the complaint is not served with the summons, the time to appear may be extended as provided in subdivision (b) of section 3012.

(b) When appearance confers personal jurisdiction, generally. Subject to the provisions of subdivision (c), an appearance of the defendant is equivalent to personal service of the summons upon him, unless an objection to jurisdiction under paragraph eight of subdivision (a) of rule 3211 is asserted by motion or in the answer as provided in rule 3211.

(c) When appearance confers personal jurisdiction, in certain actions; limited appearance. When the court's jurisdiction is not based upon personal service on the defendant, an appearance is not equivalent to personal service upon the defendant:

1. in a case specified in subdivision (3) of section 314, if jurisdiction is based solely upon a levy on defendant's property within the state pursuant to an order of attachment; or

2. in any other case specified in section 314, if an objection to jurisdiction under paragraphs eight [personal jurisdiction] or nine [non-personal jurisdiction] of subdivision (a) of rule 3211, or both, is asserted by motion or in the answer as provided in rule 3211, unless the defendant proceeds with the defense after asserting the objection to jurisdiction and the objection is not ultimately sustained.

(d) Appearance after first publication. Where the defendant appears during the period of publication of a summons against him, the service by publication shall be deemed completed by the appearance.

Rule 327. Inconvenient forum

(a) When the court finds that in the interest of substantial justice the action should be heard in another forum, the court, on the motion of any party, may stay or dismiss the action in whole or in part on any conditions that may be just. The domicile or residence in this state of any party to the action shall not preclude the court from staying or dismissing the action.

(b) Notwithstanding the provisions of subdivision (a) of this rule, the court shall not stay or dismiss any action on the ground of inconvenient forum, where the action arises out of or relates to a [big commercial] contract, agreement or undertaking to which section 5–1402 of the general obligations law applies, and the parties to the contract have agreed that the law of this state shall govern their rights or duties in whole or in part.

Article 5—Venue

§ 501. Contractual provisions fixing venue

Subject to the provisions of subdivision two of section 510, written agreement fixing place of trial, made before an action is commenced, shall be enforced upon a motion for change of place of trial.

§ 502. Conflicting venue provisions

Where, because of joinder of claims or parties, there is a conflict of provisions under this article, the court, upon motion, shall order as the place of trial one proper under this article as to at least one of the parties or claims.

OTHER PROCEDURAL STATUTES

§ 503. Venue based on residence

(a) Generally. Except where otherwise prescribed by law, the place of trial shall be in the county in which one of the parties resided when it was commenced; or, if none of the parties then resided in the state, in any county designated by the plaintiff. A party resident in more than one county shall be deemed a resident of each such county.

(b) Executor, administrator, trustee, committee, conservator, general or testamentary guardian, or receiver. An executor, administrator, trustee, committee, conservator, general or testamentary guardian, or receiver shall be deemed a resident of the county of his appointment as well as the county in which he actually resides.

(c) Corporation. A domestic corporation, or a foreign corporation authorized to transact business in the state, shall be deemed a resident of the county in which its principal office is located; except that such a corporation, if a railroad or other common carrier, shall also be deemed a resident of the county where the cause of action arose.

(d) Unincorporated association, partnership, or individually-owned business. A president or treasurer of an unincorporated association, suing or being sued on behalf of the association, shall be deemed a resident of any county in which the association has its principal office, as well as the county in which he actually resides. A partnership or an individually-owned business shall be deemed a resident of any county in which it has its principal office, as well as the county in which the partner or individual owner suing or being sued actually resides.

(e) Assignee. In an action for a sum of money only, brought by an assignee other than an assignee for the benefit of creditors or a holder in due course of a negotiable instrument, the assignee's residence shall be deemed the same as that of the original assignor at the time of the original assignment.

(f) Consumer credit transaction. In an action arising out of a consumer credit transaction where a purchaser, borrower or debtor is a defendant, the place of trial shall be the residence of a defendant, if one resides within the state or the county where such transaction took place, if it is within the state, or, in other cases, as set forth in subdivision (a).

§ 504. Actions against counties, cities, towns, villages, school districts and district corporations

* * *

§ 505. Actions involving public authorities

* * *

§ 506. Where special proceeding commenced

* * *

SELECTED PROVISIONS

§ 507. Real property actions

The place of trial of an action in which the judgment demanded would affect the title to, or the possession, use or enjoyment of, real property shall be in the county in which any part of the subject of the action is situated.

§ 508. Actions to recover a chattel

The place of trial of an action to recover a chattel may be in the county in which any part of the subject of the action is situated at the time of the commencement of the action.

§ 509. Venue in county designated

Notwithstanding any provision of this article, the place of trial of an action shall be in the county designated by the plaintiff, unless the place of trial is changed to another county by order upon motion, or by consent as provided in subdivision (b) of rule 511.

§ 510. Grounds for change of place of trial

The court, upon motion, may change the place of trial of an action where:

1. the county designated for that purpose is not a proper county; or

2. there is reason to believe that an impartial trial cannot be had in the proper county; or

3. the convenience of material witnesses and the ends of justice will be promoted by the change.

Rule 511. Change of place of trial

(a) **Time for motion or demand.** A demand under subdivision (b) for change of place of trial on the ground that the county designated for that purpose is not a proper county shall be served with the answer or before the answer is served. A motion for change of place of trial on any other ground shall be made within a reasonable time after commencement of the action.

(b) **Demand for change of place of trial upon ground of improper venue, where motion made.** The defendant shall serve a written demand that the action be tried in a county he specifies as proper. Thereafter, the defendant may move to change the place of trial within fifteen days after service of the demand, unless within five days after such service plaintiff serves a written consent to change the place of trial to that specified by the defendant. Defendant may notice such motion to be heard as if the action were pending in the county he specified, unless plaintiff within five days after service of the demand serves an affidavit showing either that the county specified by the defendant is not proper or that the county designated by him is proper.

(c) **Stay of proceedings.** No order to stay proceedings for the purpose of changing the place of trial shall be granted unless it appears from the papers that the change is sought with due diligence.

(d) Order, subsequent proceedings and appeal. Upon filing of consent by the plaintiff or entry of an order changing the place of trial by the clerk of the county from which it is changed, the clerk shall forthwith deliver to the clerk of the county to which it is changed all papers filed in the action and certified copies of all minutes and entries, which shall be filed, entered or recorded, as the case requires, in the office of the latter clerk. Subsequent proceedings shall be had in the county to which the change is made as if it had been designated originally as the place of trial, except as otherwise directed by the court. An appeal from an order changing the place of trial shall be taken in the department in which the motion for the order was heard and determined.

RULES OF EVIDENCE FOR UNITED STATES COURTS AND MAGISTRATES

TABLE OF CONTENTS

RULES OF EVIDENCE

RULES OF EVIDENCE

*

RULES OF EVIDENCE
FOR UNITED STATES COURTS
AND MAGISTRATES

ARTICLE I. GENERAL PROVISIONS

Rule 101.

SCOPE

These rules govern proceedings in the courts of the United States and before United States bankruptcy judges and United States magistrates, to the extent and with the exceptions stated in rule 1101.

As amended 1987, 1988.

Rule 102.

PURPOSE AND CONSTRUCTION

These rules shall be construed to secure fairness in administration, elimination of unjustifiable expense and delay, and promotion of growth and development of the law of evidence to the end that the truth may be ascertained and proceedings justly determined.

Rule 103.

RULINGS ON EVIDENCE

(a) **Effect of erroneous ruling.** Error may not be predicated upon a ruling which admits or excludes evidence unless a substantial right of the party is affected, and

(1) *Objection.* In case the ruling is one admitting evidence a timely objection or motion to strike appears of record, stating the specific ground of objection if the specific ground was not apparent from the context; or

(2) *Offer of proof.* In case the ruling is one excluding evidence, the substance of the evidence was made known to the judge

by offer or was apparent from the context within which questions were asked.

(b) Record of offer and ruling. The court may add any other or further statement which shows the character of the evidence, the form in which it was offered, the objection made, and the ruling thereon. It may direct the making of an offer in question and answer form.

(c) Hearing of jury. In jury cases, proceedings shall be conducted, to the extent practicable, so as to prevent inadmissible evidence from being suggested to the jury by any means, such as making statements or offers of proof or asking questions in the hearing of the jury.

(d) Plain error. Nothing in this rule precludes taking notice of plain errors affecting substantial rights although they were not brought to the attention of the court.

Rule 104.

PRELIMINARY QUESTIONS

(a) Questions of admissibility generally. Preliminary questions concerning the qualification of a person to be a witness, the existence of a privilege, or the admissibility of evidence shall be determined by the court, subject to the provisions of subdivision (b). In making its determination is not bound by the rules of evidence except those with respect to privileges.

(b) Relevancy conditioned on fact. When the relevancy of evidence depends upon the fulfillment of a condition of fact, the judge shall admit it upon, or subject to, the introduction of evidence sufficient to support a finding of the fulfillment of the condition.

(c) Hearing of jury. Hearings on the admissibility of confessions shall in all cases be conducted out of the hearing of the jury. Hearings on other preliminary matters shall be so conducted when the interests of justice require, or when an accused is a witness and so requests.

(d) Testimony by accused. The accused does not, by testifying upon a preliminary matter, become subject to cross-examination as to other issues in the case.

(e) Weight and credibility. This rule does not limit the right of a party to introduce before the jury evidence relevant to weight or credibility.

As amended 1987.

Rule 105.

LIMITED ADMISSIBILITY

When evidence which is admissible as to one party or for one purpose but not admissible as to another party or for another purpose is admitted, the court, upon request, shall restrict the evidence to its proper scope and instruct the jury accordingly.

Rule 106.

REMAINDER OF OR RELATED WRITINGS OR RECORDED STATEMENTS

When a writing or recorded statement or part thereof is introduced by a party, an adverse party may require the introduction at that time of any other part or any other writing or recorded statement which ought in fairness to be considered contemporaneously with it.

As amended 1987.

ARTICLE II.   JUDICIAL NOTICE

Rule 201.

JUDICIAL NOTICE OF ADJUDICATIVE FACTS

(a) **Scope of rule.**   This rule governs only judicial notice of adjudicative facts.

(b) **Kinds of facts.**   A judicially noticed fact must be one not subject to reasonable dispute in that it is either (1) generally known within the territorial jurisdiction of the trial court or (2) capable of accurate and ready determination by resort to sources whose accuracy cannot reasonably be questioned.

(c) **When discretionary.**   A court may take judicial notice, whether requested or not.

(d) **When mandatory.**   A court shall take judicial notice if requested by a party and supplied with the necessary information.

(e) **Opportunity to be heard.**   A party is entitled upon timely request to an opportunity to be heard as to the propriety of taking judicial notice and the tenor of the matter noticed.   In the absence of prior notification, the request may be made after judicial notice has been taken.

(f) **Time of taking notice.**   Judicial notice may be taken at any stage of the proceeding.

(g) **Instructing jury.** In a civil action or proceeding, the court shall instruct the jury to accept as conclusive any fact judicially noticed. In a criminal case, the court shall instruct the jury that it may, but is not required to, accept as conclusive any fact judicially noticed.

ARTICLE III.   PRESUMPTIONS IN CIVIL ACTIONS AND PROCEEDINGS

Rule 301.

PRESUMPTIONS IN GENERAL IN CIVIL ACTIONS AND PROCEEDINGS

In all civil actions and proceedings not otherwise provided for by Act of Congress or by these rules, a presumption imposes on the party against whom it is directed the burden of going forward with evidence to rebut or meet the presumption, but does not shift to such party the burden of proof in the sense of the risk of nonpersuasion, which remains throughout the trial upon the party on whom it was originally cast.

Rule 302.

APPLICABILITY OF STATE LAW IN CIVIL ACTIONS AND PROCEEDINGS

In civil actions and proceedings, the effect of a presumption respecting a fact which is an element of a claim or defense as to which state law supplies the rule of decision is determined in accordance with state law.

ARTICLE IV.   RELEVANCY AND ITS LIMITS

Rule 401.

DEFINITION OF "RELEVANT EVIDENCE"

"Relevant evidence" means evidence having any tendency to make the existence of any fact that is of consequence to the determination of the action more probable or less probable than it would be without the evidence.

Rule 402.

RELEVANT EVIDENCE GENERALLY ADMISSIBLE; IRRELEVANT EVIDENCE INADMISSIBLE

All relevant evidence is admissible, except as otherwise provided by the Constitution of the United States, by Act of Congress, by these rules, or by other rules prescribed by the Supreme Court pursuant to statutory authority. Evidence which is not relevant is not admissible.

Rule 403.

EXCLUSION OF RELEVANT EVIDENCE ON GROUNDS OF PREJUDICE, CONFUSION, OR WASTE OF TIME

Although relevant, evidence may be excluded if its probative value is substantially outweighed by the danger of unfair prejudice, confusion of the issues, or misleading the jury, or by considerations of undue delay, waste of time, or needless presentation of cumulative evidence.

Rule 404.

CHARACTER EVIDENCE NOT ADMISSIBLE TO PROVE CONDUCT; EXCEPTIONS; OTHER CRIMES

(a) Character evidence generally. Evidence of a person's character or a trait of character is not admissible for the purpose of proving action in conformity therewith on a particular occasion, except:

(1) *Character of accused.* Evidence of a pertinent trait of character offered by an accused, or by the prosecution to rebut the same;

(2) *Character of victim.* Evidence of a pertinent trait of character of the victim of the crime offered by an accused, or by the prosecution to rebut the same, or evidence of a character trait of peacefulness of the victim offered by the prosecution in a homicide case to rebut evidence that the victim was the first aggressor;

(3) *Character of witness.* Evidence of the character of a witness, as provided in Rules 607, 608, and 609.

(b) Other crimes, wrongs, or acts. Evidence of other crimes, wrongs, or acts is not admissible to prove the character of a person in order to show action in conformity therewith. It may, however, be admissible for other purposes, such as proof of motive, opportunity, intent, preparation, plan, knowledge, identity, or absence of mistake or accident.

As amended 1987.

Rule 405.

METHODS OF PROVING CHARACTER

(a) Reputation or opinion. In all cases in which evidence of character or a trait of character of a person is admissible, proof may be made by testimony as to reputation or by testimony in the form of an opinion. On cross-examination, inquiry is allowable into relevant specific instances of conduct.

(b) Specific instances of conduct. In cases in which character or a trait of character of a person is an essential element of a charge, claim, or defense, proof may also be made of specific instances of that person's conduct.

As amended 1987.

Rule 406.

HABIT; ROUTINE PRACTICE

Evidence of the habit of a person or of the routine practice of an organization, whether corroborated or not and regardless of the presence of eyewitnesses, is relevant to prove that the conduct of the person or organization on a particular occasion was in conformity with the habit or routine practice.

Rule 407.

SUBSEQUENT REMEDIAL MEASURES

When, after an event, measures are taken which, if taken previously, would have made the event less likely to occur, evidence of the subsequent measures is not admissible to prove negligence or culpable conduct in connection with the event. This rule does not require the exclusion of evidence of subsequent measures when offered for another purpose, such as proving ownership, control, or feasibility of precautionary measures, if controverted, or impeachment.

Rule 408.

COMPROMISE AND OFFERS TO COMPROMISE

Evidence of (1) furnishing or offering or promising to furnish, or (2) accepting or offering or promising to accept, a valuable consideration in compromising or attempting to compromise a claim which was disputed as to either validity or amount, is not admissible to prove liability for or invalidity of the claim or its amount. Evidence of conduct or statements made in compromise negotiations is likewise not admissible. This rule does not require the exclusion of any evidence otherwise discoverable merely because it is presented in the course of compromise negotiations. This rule also does not require exclusion when the evidence is offered for another purpose, such as proving bias or prejudice of a witness, negativing a contention of undue delay, or proving an effort to obstruct a criminal investigation or prosecution.

Rule 409.

PAYMENT OF MEDICAL AND SIMILAR EXPENSES

Evidence of furnishing or offering or promising to pay medical, hospital, or similar expenses occasioned by an injury is not admissible to prove liability for the injury.

Rule 410.

INADMISSIBILITY OF PLEAS, PLEA DISCUSSIONS, AND RELATED STATEMENTS

Except as otherwise provided in this rule, evidence of the following is not, in any civil or criminal proceeding, admissible against the defendant who made the plea or was a participant in the plea discussions:

(1) a plea of guilty which was later withdrawn;

(2) a plea of nolo contendere;

(3) any statement made in the course of any proceedings under Rule 11 of the Federal Rules of Criminal Procedure or comparable state procedure regarding either of the foregoing pleas; or

(4) any statement made in the course of plea discussions with an attorney for the prosecuting authority which do not result in a plea of guilty or which result in a plea of guilty later withdrawn.

However, such a statement is admissible (i) in any proceeding wherein another statement made in the course of the same plea or plea discussions has been introduced and the statement ought in fairness be considered contemporaneously with it, or (ii) in a criminal proceeding for perjury or false statement if the statement was made by the defendant under oath, on the record and in the presence of counsel.

As amended 1975, 1980.

<h2 align="center">Rule 411.</h2>

<h2 align="center">LIABILITY INSURANCE</h2>

Evidence that a person was or was not insured against liability is not admissible upon the issue whether the person acted negligently or otherwise wrongfully. This rule does not require the exclusion of evidence of insurance against liability when offered for another purpose, such as proof of agency, ownership, or control, or bias or prejudice of a witness.

As amended 1987.

<h2 align="center">Rule 412.</h2>

<h2 align="center">SEX OFFENSE CASES; RELEVANCE OF VICTIM'S
PAST BEHAVIOR</h2>

(a) Notwithstanding any other provision of law, in a criminal case in which a person is accused of an offense under chapter 109A of title 18, United States Code, reputation or opinion evidence of the past sexual behavior of an alleged victim of such offense is not admissible.

(b) Notwithstanding any other provision of law, in a criminal case in which a person is accused of an offense under chapter 109A of title 18, United States Code, evidence of a victim's past sexual behavior other than reputation or opinion evidence is also not admissible, unless such evidence other than reputation or opinion evidence is—

    (1) admitted in accordance with subdivisions (c)(1) and (c)(2) and is constitutionally required to be admitted; or

    (2) admitted in accordance with subdivision (c) and is evidence of—

        (A) past sexual behavior with persons other than the accused, offered by the accused upon the issue of whether the accused was or was not, with respect to the alleged victim, the source of semen or injury; or

514

(B) past sexual behavior with the accused and is offered by the accused upon the issue of whether the alleged victim consented to the sexual behavior with respect to which such offense is alleged.

(c)(1) If the person accused of committing an offense under chapter 109A of title 18, United States Code intends to offer under subdivision (b) evidence of specific instances of the alleged victim's past sexual behavior, the accused shall make a written motion to offer such evidence not later than fifteen days before the date on which the trial in which such evidence is to be offered is scheduled to begin, except that the court may allow the motion to be made at a later date, including during trial, if the court determines either that the evidence is newly discovered and could not have been obtained earlier through the exercise of due diligence or that the issue to which such evidence relates has newly arisen in the case. Any motion made under this paragraph shall be served on all other parties and on the alleged victim.

(2) The motion described in paragraph (1) shall be accompanied by a written offer of proof. If the court determines that the offer of proof contains evidence described in subdivision (b), the court shall order a hearing in chambers to determine if such evidence is admissible. At such hearing the parties may call witnesses, including the alleged victim, and offer relevant evidence. Notwithstanding subdivision (b) of rule 104, if the relevancy of the evidence which the accused seeks to offer in the trial depends upon the fulfillment of a condition of fact, the court, at the hearing in chambers or at a subsequent hearing in chambers scheduled for such purpose, shall accept evidence on the issue of whether such condition of fact is fulfilled and shall determine such issue.

(3) If the court determines on the basis of the hearing described in paragraph (2) that the evidence which the accused seeks to offer is relevant and that the probative value of such evidence outweighs the danger of unfair prejudice, such evidence shall be admissible in the trial to the extent an order made by the court specifies evidence which may be offered and areas with respect to which the alleged victim may be examined or cross-examined.

(d) For purposes of this rule, the term "past sexual behavior" means sexual behavior other than the sexual behavior with respect to which an offense under chapter 109A of title 18, United States Code is alleged.

Added 1978; as amended 1988.

515

ARTICLE V.   PRIVILEGES

Rule 501.

GENERAL RULE

Except as otherwise required by the Constitution of the United States or provided by Act of Congress or in rules prescribed by the Supreme Court pursuant to statutory authority, the privilege of a witness, person, government, State, or political subdivision thereof shall be governed by the principles of the common law as they may be interpreted by the courts of the United States in the light of reason and experience. However, in civil actions and proceedings, with respect to an element of a claim or defense as to which State law supplies the rule of decision, the privilege of a witness, person, government, State, or political subdivision thereof shall be determined in accordance with State law.

ARTICLE VI.   WITNESSES

Rule 601.

GENERAL RULE OF COMPETENCY

Every person is competent to be a witness except as otherwise provided in these rules. However, in civil actions and proceedings, with respect to an element of a claim or defense as to which State law supplies the rule of decision, the competency of a witness shall be determined in accordance with State law.

Rule 602.

LACK OF PERSONAL KNOWLEDGE

A witness may not testify to a matter unless evidence is introduced sufficient to support a finding that the witness has personal knowledge of the matter. Evidence to prove personal knowledge may, but need not, consist of the witness' own testimony. This rule is subject to the provisions of rule 703, relating to opinion testimony by expert witnesses.

As amended 1987, 1988.

Rule 603.

OATH OR AFFIRMATION

Before testifying, every witness shall be required to declare that the witness will testify truthfully, by oath or affirmation administered in a form calculated to awaken the witness' conscience and impress the witness' mind with the duty to do so.

As amended 1987.

Rule 604.

INTERPRETERS

An interpreter is subject to the provisions of these rules relating to qualification as an expert and the administration of an oath or affirmation to make a true translation.

As amended 1987.

Rule 605.

COMPETENCY OF JUDGE AS WITNESS

The judge presiding at the trial may not testify in that trial as a witness. No objection need be made in order to preserve the point.

Rule 606.

COMPETENCY OF JUROR AS WITNESS

(a) At the trial. A member of the jury may not testify as a witness before that jury in the trial of the case in which the juror is sitting. If the juror is called so to testify, the opposing party shall be afforded an opportunity to object out of the presence of the jury.

(b) Inquiry into validity of verdict or indictment. Upon an inquiry into the validity of a verdict or indictment, a juror may not testify as to any matter or statement occurring during the course of the jury's deliberations or to the effect of anything upon that or any other juror's mind or emotions as influencing the juror to assent to or dissent from the verdict or indictment or concerning the juror's mental processes in connection therewith, except that a juror may testify on the question whether extraneous prejudicial information was improperly brought to the jury's attention or whether any outside influence was improperly brought to bear upon any juror. Nor may a juror's affidavit or evidence of any statement by the juror concerning a matter about which the juror would be precluded from testifying be received for these purposes.

As amended 1975, 1987.

Rule 607.

WHO MAY IMPEACH

The credibility of a witness may be attacked by any party, including the party calling the witness.

As amended 1987.

Rule 608.

EVIDENCE OF CHARACTER AND CONDUCT OF WITNESS

(a) Opinion and reputation evidence of character. The credibility of a witness may be attacked or supported by evidence in the form of opinion or reputation, but subject to these limitations: (1) the evidence may refer only to character for truthfulness or untruthfulness, and (2) evidence of truthful character is admissible only after the character of the witness for truthfulness has been attacked by opinion or reputation evidence or otherwise.

(b) Specific instances of conduct. Specific instances of the conduct of a witness, for the purpose of attacking or supporting the witness' credibility, other than conviction of crime as provided in rule 609, may not be proved by extrinsic evidence. They may, however, in the discretion of the court, if probative of truthfulness or untruthfulness, be inquired into on cross-examination of the witness (1) concerning the witness' character for truthfulness or untruthfulness, or (2) concerning the character for truthfulness or untruthfulness of another witness as to which character the witness being cross-examined has testified.

The giving of testimony, whether by an accused or by any other witness, does not operate as a waiver of the accused's or the witness' privilege against self-incrimination when examined with respect to matters which relate only to credibility.

As amended 1987, 1988.

Rule 609.

IMPEACHMENT BY EVIDENCE OF CONVICTION OF CRIME

(a) General rule. For the purpose of attacking the credibility of a witness,

    (1) evidence that a witness other than an accused has been convicted of a crime shall be admitted, subject to Rule

403, if the crime was punishable by death or imprisonment in excess of one year under the law under which the witness was convicted, and evidence that an accused has been convicted of such a crime shall be admitted if the court determines that the probative value of admitting this evidence outweighs its prejudicial effect to the accused; and

(2) evidence that any witness has been convicted of a crime shall be admitted if it involved dishonesty or false statement, regardless of the punishment.

(b) Time limit. Evidence of a conviction under this rule is not admissible if a period of more than ten years has elapsed since the date of the conviction or of the release of the witness from the confinement imposed for that conviction, whichever is the later date, unless the court determines, in the interests of justice, that the probative value of the conviction supported by specific facts and circumstances substantially outweighs its prejudicial effect. However, evidence of a conviction more than 10 years old as calculated herein, is not admissible unless the proponent gives to the adverse party sufficient advance written notice of intent to use such evidence to provide the adverse party with a fair opportunity to contest the use of such evidence.

(c) Effect of pardon, annulment, or certificate of rehabilitation. Evidence of a conviction is not admissible under this rule if (1) the conviction has been the subject of a pardon, annulment, certificate of rehabilitation, or other equivalent procedure based on a finding of the rehabilitation of the person convicted, and that person has not been convicted of a subsequent crime which was punishable by death or imprisonment in excess of one year, or (2) the conviction has been the subject of a pardon, annulment, or other equivalent procedure based on a finding of innocence.

(d) Juvenile adjudications. Evidence of juvenile adjudications is generally not admissible under this rule. The court may, however, in a criminal case allow evidence of a juvenile adjudication of a witness other than the accused if conviction of the offense would be admissible to attack the credibility of an adult and the court is satisfied that admission in evidence is necessary for a fair determination of the issue of guilt or innocence.

(e) Pendency of appeal. The pendency of an appeal therefrom does not render evidence of a conviction inadmissible. Evidence of the pendency of an appeal is admissible.

As amended 1987, 1990.

Rule 610.

RELIGIOUS BELIEFS OR OPINIONS

Evidence of the beliefs or opinions of a witness on matters of religion is not admissible for the purpose of showing that by reason of their nature the witness' credibility is impaired or enhanced.

As amended 1987.

Rule 611.

MODE AND ORDER OF INTERROGATION AND PRESENTATION

(a) **Control by court.** The court shall exercise reasonable control over the mode and order of interrogating witnesses and presenting evidence so as to (1) make the interrogation and presentation effective for the ascertainment of the truth, (2) avoid needless consumption of time, and (3) protect witnesses from harassment or undue embarrassment.

(b) **Scope of cross-examination.** Cross-examination should be limited to the subject matter of the direct examination and matters affecting the credibility of the witness. The court may, in the exercise of discretion, permit inquiry into additional matters as if on direct examination.

(c) **Leading questions.** Leading questions should not be used on the direct examination of a witness except as may be necessary to develop the witness' testimony. Ordinarily leading questions should be permitted on cross-examination. When a party calls a hostile witness, an adverse party, or a witness identified with an adverse party, interrogation may be by leading questions.

As amended 1987.

Rule 612.

WRITING USED TO REFRESH MEMORY

Except as otherwise provided in criminal proceedings by section 3500 of title 18, United States Code, if a witness uses a writing to refresh memory for the purpose of testifying, either—

    (1) while testifying, or

    (2) before testifying, if the court in its discretion determines it is necessary in the interests of justice,

an adverse party is entitled to have the writing produced at the hearing, to inspect it, to cross-examine the witness thereon, and to introduce in evidence those portions which relate to the testimony of the witness. If it is claimed that the writing contains matters not related to the subject matter of the testimony the court shall examine the writing in camera, excise any portions not so related, and order delivery of the remainder to the party entitled thereto. Any portion withheld over objections shall be preserved and made available to the appellate court in the event of an appeal. If a writing is not produced or delivered pursuant to order under this rule, the court shall make any order justice requires, except that in criminal cases when the prosecution elects not to comply, the order shall be one striking the testimony or, if the court in its discretion determines that the interests of justice so require, declaring a mistrial.

As amended 1987.

Rule 613.

PRIOR STATEMENTS OF WITNESSES

(a) **Examining witness concerning prior statement.** In examining a witness concerning a prior statement made by the witness, whether written or not, the statement need not be shown nor its contents disclosed to the witness at that time, but on request the same shall be shown or disclosed to opposing counsel.

(b) **Extrinsic evidence of prior inconsistent statement of witness.** Extrinsic evidence of a prior inconsistent statement by a witness is not admissible unless the witness is afforded an opportunity to explain or deny the same and the opposite party is afforded an opportunity to interrogate the witness thereon, or the interests of justice otherwise require. This provision does not apply to admissions of a party-opponent as defined in rule 801(d)(2).

As amended 1987, 1988.

Rule 614.

CALLING AND INTERROGATION OF WITNESSES BY COURT

(a) **Calling by court.** The court may, on its own motion or at the suggestion of a party, call witnesses, and all parties are entitled to cross-examine witnesses thus called.

(b) **Interrogation by court.** The court may interrogate witnesses, whether called by itself or by a party.

(c) **Objections.**   Objections to the calling of witnesses by the court or to interrogation by it may be made at the time or at the next available opportunity when the jury is not present.

Rule 615.

EXCLUSION OF WITNESSES

At the request of a party the court shall order witnesses excluded so that they cannot hear the testimony of other witnesses, and it may make the order of its own motion.   This rule does not authorize exclusion of (1) a party who is a natural person, or (2) an officer or employee of a party which is not a natural person designated as its representative by its attorney, or (3) a person whose presence is shown by a party to be essential to the presentation of the party's cause.

As amended 1987, 1988.

ARTICLE VII.   OPINIONS AND EXPERT TESTIMONY

Rule 701.

OPINION TESTIMONY BY LAY WITNESSES

If the witness is not testifying as an expert, the witness' testimony in the form of opinions or inferences is limited to those opinions or inferences which are (a) rationally based on the perception of the witness and (b) helpful to a clear understanding of the witness' testimony or the determination of a fact in issue.

As amended 1987.

Rule 702.

TESTIMONY BY EXPERTS

If scientific, technical, or other specialized knowledge will assist the trier of fact to understand the evidence or to determine a fact in issue, a witness qualified as an expert by knowledge, skill, experience, training, or education, may testify thereto in the form of an opinion or otherwise.

Rule 703.

BASES OF OPINION TESTIMONY BY EXPERTS

The facts or data in the particular case upon which an expert bases an opinion or inference may be those perceived by or made known to the expert at or before the hearing. If of a type reasonably relied upon by experts in the particular field in forming opinions or inferences upon the subject, the facts or data need not be admissible in evidence.

As amended 1987.

Rule 704.

OPINION ON ULTIMATE ISSUE

(a) Except as provided in subdivision (b), testimony in the form of an opinion or inference otherwise admissible is not objectionable because it embraces an ultimate issue to be decided by the trier of fact.

(b) No expert witness testifying with respect to the mental state or condition of a defendant in a criminal case may state an opinion or inference as to whether the defendant did or did not have the mental state or condition constituting an element of the crime charged or of a defense thereto. Such ultimate issues are matters for the trier of fact alone.

As amended 1984.

Rule 705.

DISCLOSURE OF FACTS OR DATA UNDERLYING EXPERT OPINION

The expert may testify in terms of opinion or inference and give reasons therefor without prior disclosure of the underlying facts or data, unless the judge requires otherwise. The expert may in any event be required to disclose the underlying facts or data on cross-examination.

As amended 1987.

Rule 706.

COURT APPOINTED EXPERTS

(a) **Appointment.** The court may on its own motion or on the motion of any party enter an order to show cause why expert witnesses should not be appointed, and may request the parties to submit nominations. The court may appoint any expert witnesses agreed upon by the parties, and may appoint witnesses of its own selection. An expert witness shall not be appointed by the court unless the witness consents to act. A witness so appointed shall be informed of the witness' duties by the court in writing, a copy of which shall be filed with the clerk, or at a conference in which the parties shall have opportunity to participate. A witness so appointed shall advise the parties of the witness' findings, if any; the witness' deposition may be taken by any party; and the witness may be called to testify by the court or any party. The witness shall be subject to cross-examination by each party, including a party calling the witness.

(b) Compensation. Expert witnesses so appointed are entitled to reasonable compensation in whatever sum the court may allow. The compensation thus fixed is payable from funds which may be provided by law in criminal cases and civil actions and proceedings involving just compensation under the Fifth Amendment. In other civil actions and proceedings the compensation shall be paid by the parties in such proportion and at such time as the court directs, and thereafter charged in like manner as other costs.

(c) Disclosure of appointment. In the exercise of its discretion, the court may authorize disclosure to the jury of the fact that the court appointed the expert witness.

(d) Parties' experts of own selection. Nothing in this rule limits the parties in calling expert witnesses of their own selection.

As amended 1987.

ARTICLE VIII. HEARSAY

Rule 801.

DEFINITIONS

The following definitions apply under this article:

(a) Statement. A "statement" is (1) an oral or written assertion or (2) nonverbal conduct of a person, if it is intended by the person as an assertion.

(b) Declarant. A "declarant" is a person who makes a statement.

(c) Hearsay. "Hearsay" is a statement, other than one made by the declarant while testifying at the trial or hearing, offered in evidence to prove the truth of the matter asserted.

(d) Statements which are not hearsay. A statement is not hearsay if—

(1) *Prior statement by witness.* The declarant testifies at the trial or hearing and is subject to cross-examination concerning the

statement, and the statement is (A) inconsistent with the declarant's testimony, and was given under oath subject to the penalty of perjury at a trial, hearing, or other proceeding, or in a deposition, or (B) consistent with the declarant's testimony and is offered to rebut an express or implied charge against the declarant of recent fabrication or improper influence or motive, or (C) one of identification of a person made after perceiving the person; or

(2) *Admission by party-opponent.* The statement is offered against a party and is (A) the party's own statement, in either an individual or a representative capacity or (B) a statement of which the party has manifested an adoption or belief in its truth, or (C) a statement by a person authorized by the party to make a statement concerning the subject, or (D) a statement by the party's agent or servant concerning a matter within the scope of the agency or employment, made during the existence of the relationship, or (E) a statement by a coconspirator of a party during the course and in furtherance of the conspiracy.

As amended 1975, 1987.

Rule 802.

HEARSAY RULE

Hearsay is not admissible except as provided by these rules or by other rules prescribed by the Supreme Court pursuant to statutory authority or by Act of Congress.

Rule 803.

HEARSAY EXCEPTIONS; AVAILABILITY OF DECLARANT IMMATERIAL

The following are not excluded by the hearsay rule, even though the declarant is available as a witness:

(1) **Present sense impression.** A statement describing or explaining an event or condition made while the declarant was perceiving the event or condition, or immediately thereafter.

(2) **Excited utterance.** A statement relating to a startling event or condition made while the declarant was under the stress of excitement caused by the event or condition.

(3) **Then existing mental, emotional, or physical condition.** A statement of the declarant's then existing state of mind, emotion, sensation, or physical condition (such as intent, plan, motive, design, mental feeling, pain, and bodily health), but not including a statement of memory or belief to prove the fact

remembered or believed unless it relates to the execution, revocation, identification, or terms of declarant's will.

(4) Statements for purposes of medical diagnosis or treatment. Statements made for purposes of medical diagnosis or treatment and describing medical history, or past or present symptoms, pain, or sensations, or the inception or general character of the cause or external source thereof insofar as reasonably pertinent to diagnosis or treatment.

(5) Recorded recollection. A memorandum or record concerning a matter about which a witness once had knowledge but now has insufficient recollection to enable the witness to testify fully and accurately, shown to have been made or adopted by the witness when the matter was fresh in the witness' memory and to reflect that knowledge correctly. If admitted, the memorandum or record may be read into evidence but may not itself be received as an exhibit unless offered by an adverse party.

(6) Records of regularly conducted activity. A memorandum, report, record, or data compilation, in any form, of acts, events, conditions, opinions, or diagnoses, made at or near the time by, or from information transmitted by, a person with knowledge, if kept in the course of a regularly conducted business activity and if it was the regular practice of that business activity to make the memorandum, report, record, or data compilation, all as shown by the testimony of the custodian or other qualified witness, unless the source of information or the method or circumstances of preparation indicate lack of trustworthiness. The term "business" as used in this paragraph includes business, institution, association, profession, occupation, and calling of every kind, whether or not conducted for profit.

(7) Absence of entry in records kept in accordance with the provisions of paragraph (6). Evidence that a matter is not included in the memoranda reports, records, or data compilations, in any form, kept in accordance with the provisions of paragraph (6), to prove the nonoccurrence or nonexistence of the matter, if the matter was of a kind of which a memorandum, report, record, or data compilation was regularly made and preserved, unless the sources of information or other circumstances indicate lack of trustworthiness.

(8) Public records and reports. Records, reports, statements, or data compilations, in any form, of public offices or agencies, setting forth (A) the activities of the office or agency, or (B) matters observed pursuant to duty imposed by law as to which matters there was a duty to report, excluding, however, in criminal cases matters observed by police officers and other law enforcement personnel, or (C) in civil actions and proceedings and against the Government in criminal cases, factual findings resulting from an investigation made pursuant to authority granted by law, unless the sources of information or other circumstances indicate lack of trustworthiness.

(9) Records of vital statistics. Records or data compilations, in any form, of births, fetal deaths, deaths, or marriages, if the report thereof was made to a public office pursuant to requirements of law.

(10) Absence of public record or entry. To prove the absence of a record, report, statement, or data compilation, in any form, or the nonoccurrence or nonexistence of a matter of which a record, report, statement, or data compilation, in any form, was regularly made and preserved by a public office or agency, evidence in the form of a certification in accordance with Rule 902, or testimony, that diligent search failed to disclose the record, report, statement, or data compilation, or entry.

(11) Records of religious organizations. Statements of births, marriages, divorces, deaths, legitimacy, ancestry, relationship by blood or marriage, or other similar facts of personal or family history, contained in a regularly kept record of a religious organization.

(12) Marriage, baptismal, and similar certificates. Statements of fact contained in a certificate that the maker performed a marriage or other ceremony or administered a sacrament, made by a clergyman, public official, or other person authorized by the rules or practices of a religious organization or by law to perform the act certified, and purporting to have been issued at the time of the act or within a reasonable time thereafter.

(13) Family records. Statements of fact concerning personal or family history contained in family Bibles, genealogies, charts, engravings on rings, inscription on family portraits, engravings on urns, crypts, or tombstones, or the like.

(14) Records of documents affecting an interest in property. The record of a document purporting to establish or affect an interest in property, as proof of the content of the original recorded document and its execution and delivery by each person by whom it purports to have been executed, if the record is a record of a public office and an applicable statute authorized the recording of documents of that kind in that office.

(15) Statements in documents affecting an interest in property. A statement contained in a document purporting to establish or affect an interest in property if the matter stated was relevant to the purpose of the document, unless dealings with the property since the documentwas made have been inconsistent with the truth of the statement or the purport of the document.

(16) Statements in ancient documents. Statements in a document in existence 20 years or more whose authenticity is established.

(17) Market reports, commercial publications. Market quotations, tabulations, lists, directories, or other published compilations, generally used and relied upon by the public or by persons in particular occupations.

(18) Learned treatises. To the extent called to the attention of an expert witness upon cross-examination or relied upon by the expert witness in direct examination, statements contained in published treatises, periodicals, or pamphlets on a subject of history, medicine, or other science or art, established as a reliable authority by the testimony or admission of the witness or by other expert testimony or by judicial notice. If admitted, the statements may be read into evidence but may not be received as exhibits.

(19) Reputation concerning personal or family history. Reputation among members of a person's family by blood, adoption, or marriage, or among a person's associates, or in the community, concerning a person's birth, adoption, marriage, divorce, death, legitimacy, relationship by blood, adoption, or marriage, ancestry, or other similar fact of personal or family history.

(20) Reputation concerning boundaries or general history. Reputation in a community, arising before the controversy, as to boundaries of or customs affecting lands in the community, and reputation as to events of general history important to the community or state or nation in which located.

(21) Reputation as to character. Reputation of a person's character among associates or in the community.

(22) Judgment of previous conviction. Evidence of a final judgment, entered after a trial or upon a plea of guilty (but not upon a plea of nolo contendere), adjudging a person guilty of a crime punishable by death or imprisonment in excess of one year, to prove any fact essential to sustain the judgment, but not including, when offered by the government in a criminal prosecution for purposes other than impeachment, judgments against persons other than the accused. The pendency of an appeal may be shown but does not affect admissibility.

(23) Judgment as to personal, family, or general history, or boundaries. Judgments as proof of matters of personal, family or general history, or boundaries, essential to the judgment, if the same would be provable by evidence of reputation.

(24) Other exceptions. A statement not specifically covered by any of the foregoing exceptions but having equivalent circumstantial guarantees of trustworthiness, if the court determines that (A) the statement is offered as evidence of a material fact; (B) the statement is more probative on the point for which it is offered than any other evidence which the proponent can procure through reasonable efforts; and (C) the general purposes of these rules and the interests of justice will best be served by admission of the statement into evidence. However, a statement may not be admitted under this exception unless the proponent of it makes known to the adverse party sufficiently in advance of the trial or hearing to provide the adverse party with a fair opportunity to prepare to meet it, the proponent's intention to offer the statement and the particulars of it, including the name and address of the declarant.

As amended 1975, 1987.

Rule 804.

HEARSAY EXCEPTIONS; DECLARANT UNAVAILABLE

(a) Definition of unavailability. "Unavailability as a witness" includes situations in which the declarant—

(1) is exempted by ruling of the court on the ground of privilege from testifying concerning the subject matter of the declarant's statement; or

(2) persists in refusing to testify concerning the subject matter of the declarant's statement despite an order of the court to do so; or

(3) testifies to a lack of memory of the subject matter of the declarant's statement; or

(4) is unable to be present or to testify at the hearing because of death or then existing physical or mental illness or infirmity; or

(5) is absent from the hearing and the proponent of a statement has been unable to procure the declarant's attendance (or in the case of a hearsay exception under subdivision (b)(2), (3), or (4), the declarant's attendance or testimony) by process or other reasonable means.

A declarant is not unavailable as a witness if exemption, refusal, claim of lack of memory, inability, or absence is due to the procurement or wrongdoing of the proponent of a statement for the purpose of preventing the witness from attending or testifying.

(b) Hearsay exceptions. The following are not excluded by the hearsay rule if the declarant is unavailable as a witness:

(1) *Former testimony.* Testimony given as a witness at another hearing of the same or a different proceeding, or in a deposition taken in compliance with law in the course of the same or another proceeding, if the party against whom the testimony is now offered, or, in a civil action or proceeding, a predecessor in interest, had an opportunity and similar motive to develop the testimony by direct, cross, or redirect examination.

(2) *Statement under belief of impending death.* In a prosecution for homicide or in a civil action or proceeding, a statement made by a declarant while believing that the declarant's death was imminent, concerning the cause or circumstances of what the declarant believed to be impending death.

(3) *Statement against interest.* A statement which was at the time of its making so far contrary to the declarant's pecuniary or proprietary interest, or so far tended to subject the declarant to civil or criminal liability, or to render invalid a claim by the declarant against another, that a reasonable person in the declarant's position would not have made the statement unless believing it to be true. A statement tending to expose the declarant to criminal liability and offered to exculpate the accused is not admissible unless corroborating circumstances clearly indicate the trustworthiness of the statement.

(4) *Statement of personal or family history.* (A) A statement concerning the declarant's own birth, adoption, marriage, divorce, legitimacy, relationship by blood, adoption, or marriage, ancestry, or other similar fact of personal or family history, even though declarant had no means of acquiring personal knowledge of the matter stated; or (B) a statement concerning the foregoing matters, and death also, of another person, if the declarant was related to the other by blood, adoption, or marriage or was so intimately associated with the other's family as to be likely to have accurate information concerning the matter declared.

(5) *Other exceptions.* A statement not specifically covered by any of the foregoing exceptions but having equivalent circumstantial guarantees of trustworthiness, if the court determines that (A) the statement is offered as evidence of a material fact; (B) the statement is more probative on the point for which it is offered than any other evidence which the proponent can procure through reasonable efforts; and (C) the general purposes of these rules and the interests of justice will best be served by admission of the statement into evidence.

However, a statement may not be admitted under this exception unless the proponent of it makes known to the adverse party sufficiently in advance of the trial or hearing to provide the adverse party with a fair opportunity to prepare to meet it, the proponent's intention to offer the statement and the particulars of it, including the name and address of the declarant.

As amended 1975, 1987, 1988.

Rule 805.

HEARSAY WITHIN HEARSAY

Hearsay included within hearsay is not excluded under the hearsay rule if each part of the combined statements conforms with an exception to the hearsay rule provided in these rules.

Rule 806.

ATTACKING AND SUPPORTING CREDIBILITY OF DECLARANT

When a hearsay statement, or a statement defined in Rule 801(d)(2), (C), (D), or (E), has been admitted in evidence, the credibility of the declarant may be attacked, and if attacked may be supported, by any evidence which would be admissible for those purposes if declarant had testified as a witness. Evidence of a statement or conduct by the declarant at any time, inconsistent with the declarant's hearsay statement, is not subject to any requirement that the declarant may have been afforded an opportunity to deny or explain. If the party against whom a hearsay statement has been admitted calls the declarant as a witness, the party is entitled to examine the declarant on the statement as if under cross-examination.

As amended 1987.

ARTICLE IX. AUTHENTICATION AND IDENTIFICATION

Rule 901.

REQUIREMENT OF AUTHENTICATION OR IDENTIFICATION

(a) **General provision.** The requirement of authentication or identification as a condition precedent to admissibility is satisfied by evidence sufficient to support a finding that the matter in question is what its proponent claims.

(b) Illustrations. By way of illustration only, and not by way of limitation, the following are examples of authentication or identification conforming with the requirements of this rule:

(1) Testimony of witness with knowledge. Testimony that a matter is what it is claimed to be.

(2) Nonexpert opinion on handwriting. Nonexpert opinion as to the genuineness of handwriting, based upon familiarity not acquired for purposes of the litigation.

(3) Comparison by trier or expert witness. Comparison by the trier of fact or by expert witnesses with specimens which have been authenticated.

(4) Distinctive characteristics and the like. Appearance, contents, substance, internal patterns, or other distinctive characteristics, taken in conjunction with circumstances.

(5) Voice identification. Identification of a voice, whether heard firsthand or through mechanical or electronic transmission or recording, by opinion based upon hearing the voice at any time under circumstances connecting it with the alleged speaker.

(6) Telephone conversations. Telephone conversations, by evidence that a call was made to the number assigned at the time by the telephone company to a particular person or business, if (A) in the case of a person, circumstances, including self-identification, show the person answering to be the one called, or (B) in the case of a business, the call was made to a place of business and the conversation related to business reasonably transacted over the telephone.

(7) Public records or reports. Evidence that a writing authorized by law to be recorded or filed and in fact recorded or filed in a public office, or a purported public record, report, statement, or data compilation, in any form, is from the public office where items of this nature are kept.

(8) Ancient documents or data compilation. Evidence that a document or data compilation, in any form, (A) is in such condition as to create no suspicion concerning its authenticity, (B) was in a place where it, if authentic, would likely be, and (C) has been in existence 20 years or more at the time it is offered.

(9) Process or system. Evidence describing a process or system used to produce a result and showing that the process or system produces an accurate result.

(10) Methods provided by statute or rule. Any method of authentication or identification provided by Act of Congress or by other rules prescribed by the Supreme Court pursuant to statutory authority.

Rule 902.

SELF–AUTHENTICATION

Extrinsic evidence of authenticity as a condition precedent to admissibility is not required with respect to the following:

(1) Domestic public documents under seal. A document bearing a seal purporting to be that of the United States, or of any state, district, commonwealth, territory, or insular possession thereof, or the Panama Canal Zone, or the Trust Territory of the Pacific Islands, or of a political subdivision, department, officer, or agency thereof, and a signature purporting to be an attestation or execution.

(2) Domestic public documents not under seal. A document purporting to bear the signature in the official capacity of an officer or employee of any entity included in paragraph (1) hereof, having no seal, if a public officer having a seal and having official duties in the district or political subdivision of the officer or employee certifies under seal that the signer has the official capacity and that the signature is genuine.

(3) Foreign public documents. A document purporting to be executed or attested in an official capacity by a person authorized by the laws of a foreign country to make the execution or attestation, and accompanied by a final certification as to the genuineness of the signature and official position (A) of the executing or attesting person, or (B) of any foreign official whose certificate of genuineness of signature and official position relates to the execution or attestation or is in a chain of certificates of genuineness of signature and official position relating to the execution or attestation. A final certification may be made by a secretary of an embassy or legation, consul general, consul, vice consul, or consular agent of the United States, or a diplomatic or consular official of the foreign country assigned or accredited to the United States. If reasonable opportunity has been given to all parties to investigate the authenticity and accuracy of official documents, the court may, for good cause shown, order that they be treated as presumptively authentic without final certification or permit them to be evidenced by an attested summary with or without final certification.

(4) Certified copies of public records. A copy of an official record or report or entry therein, or of a document authorized by law to be recorded or filed and actually recorded or filed in a public office, including data compilations in any form, certified as correct by the custodian or other person authorized to make the certification, by certificate complying with paragraph (1), (2), or (3) of this Rule or complying with any Act of Congress or rule prescribed by the Supreme Court pursuant to statutory authority.

(5) Official publications. Books, pamphlets, or other publications purporting to be issued by public authority.

(6) Newspapers and periodicals. Printed materials purporting to be newspapers or periodicals.

(7) Trade inscriptions and the like. Inscriptions, signs, tags, or labels purporting to have been affixed in the course of business and indicating ownership, control, or origin.

(8) Acknowledged documents. Documents accompanied by a certificate of acknowledgment executed in the manner provided by law by a notary public or other officer authorized by law to take acknowledgments.

(9) Commercial paper and related documents. Commercial paper, signatures thereon, and documents relating thereto to the extent provided by general commercial law.

(10) Presumptions under Acts of Congress. Any signature, document, or other matter declared by Act of Congress to be presumptively or prima facie genuine or authentic.

As amended 1987, 1988.

Rule 903.

SUBSCRIBING WITNESS' TESTIMONY UNNECESSARY

The testimony of a subscribing witness is not necessary to authenticate a writing unless required by the laws of the jurisdiction whose laws govern the validity of the writing.

ARTICLE X.   CONTENTS OF WRITINGS, RECORDINGS, AND PHOTOGRAPHS

Rule 1001.

DEFINITIONS

For purposes of this article the following definitions are applicable:

(1) Writings and recordings. "Writings" and "recordings" consist of letters, words, or numbers, or their equivalent, set down by handwriting, typewriting, printing, photostating, photographing, magnetic impulse, mechanical or electronic recording, or other form of data compilation.

(2) Photographs. "Photographs" include still photographs, X-ray films, and motion pictures.

(3) **Original.** An "original" of a writing or recording is the writing or recording itself or any counterpart intended to have the same effect by a person executing or issuing it. An "original" of a photograph includes the negative or any print therefrom. If data are stored in a computer or similar device, any printout or other output readable by sight, shown to reflect the data accurately, is an "original."

(4) **Duplicate.** A "duplicate" is a counterpart produced by the same impression as the original, or from the same matrix, or by means of photography, including enlargements and miniatures, or by mechanical or electronic re-recording, or by chemical reproduction, or by other equivalent techniques which accurately reproduces the original.

Rule 1002.

REQUIREMENT OF ORIGINAL

To prove the content of a writing, recording, or photograph, the original writing, recording, or photograph is required, except as otherwise provided in these rules or by Act of Congress.

Rule 1003.

ADMISSIBILITY OF DUPLICATES

A duplicate is admissible to the same extent as an original unless (1) a genuine question is raised as to the authenticity of the original or (2) in the circumstances it would be unfair to admit the duplicate in lieu of the original.

Rule 1004.

ADMISSIBILITY OF OTHER EVIDENCE OF CONTENTS

The original is not required, and other evidence of the contents of a writing, recording, or photograph is admissible if—

(1) **Originals lost or destroyed.** All originals are lost or have been destroyed, unless the proponent lost or destroyed them in bad faith; or

(2) **Original not obtainable.** No original can be obtained by any available judicial process or procedure; or

(3) **Original in possession of opponent.** At a time when an original was under the control of the party against whom offered, that party was put on notice, by the pleadings or otherwise, that

the contents would be a subject of proof at the hearing, and that party does not produce the original at the hearing; or

(4) Collateral matters.   The writing, recording, or photograph is not closely related to a controlling issue.

As amended 1987.

Rule 1005.

PUBLIC RECORDS

The contents of an official record, or of a document authorized to be recorded or filed and actually recorded or filed, including data compilations in any form, if otherwise admissible, may be proved by copy, certified as correct in accordance with Rule 902 or testified to be correct by a witness who has compared it with the original. If a copy which complies with the foregoing cannot be obtained by the exercise of reasonable diligence, then other evidence of the contents may be given.

Rule 1006.

SUMMARIES

The contents of voluminous writings, recordings, or photographs which cannot conveniently be examined in court may be presented in the form of a chart, summary, or calculation. The originals, or duplicates, shall be made available for examination or copying, or both, by other parties at reasonable time and place. The court may order that they be produced in court.

Rule 1007.

TESTIMONY OR WRITTEN ADMISSION OF PARTY

Contents of writings, recordings, or photographs may be proved by the testimony or deposition of the party against whom offered or by that party's written admission, without accounting for the nonproduction of the original.

As amended 1987.

Rule 1008.

FUNCTIONS OF COURT AND JURY

When the admissibility of other evidence of contents of writings, recordings, or photographs under these rules depends upon the fulfillment of a condition of fact, the question whether the condition has been fulfilled is ordinarily for the court to determine in accordance with the provisions of Rule 104. However, when an issue is raised (a) whether the asserted writing ever existed, or (b) whether another writing, recording, or photograph produced at the trial is the original, or (c) whether other evidence of contents correctly reflects the contents, the issue is for the trier of fact to determine as in the case of other issues of fact.

ARTICLE XI. MISCELLANEOUS RULES

Rule 1101.

APPLICABILITY OF RULES

(a) **Courts and magistrates.** These rules apply to the United States district courts, the District Court of Guam, the District Court of the Virgin Islands, the District Court for the Northern Mariana Islands, the United States courts of appeals, the United States Claims Court, and to United States bankruptcy judges and United States magistrates, in the actions, cases, and proceedings and to the extent hereinafter set forth. The terms "judge" and "court" in these rules include United States bankruptcy judges and United States magistrates.

(b) **Proceedings generally.** These rules apply generally to civil actions and proceedings, including admiralty and maritime cases, to criminal cases and proceedings, to contempt proceedings except those in which the court may act summarily, and to proceedings and cases under title 11, United States Code.

(c) **Rule of privilege.** The rule with respect to privileges applies at all stages of all actions, cases, and proceedings.

(d) **Rules inapplicable.** The rules (other than with respect to privileges) do not apply in the following situations:

(1) *Preliminary questions of fact.* The determination of questions of fact preliminary to admissibility of evidence when the issue is to be determined by the court under rule 104.

(2) *Grand jury.* Proceedings before grand juries.

(3) *Miscellaneous proceedings.* Proceedings for extradition or rendition; preliminary examinations in criminal cases; sentencing, or granting or revoking probation; issuance of warrants for arrest, criminal summonses, and search warrants; and proceedings with respect to release on bail or otherwise.

(e) **Rules applicable in part.** In the following proceedings these rules apply to the extent that matters of evidence are not provided for in the statutes which govern procedure therein or in other rules prescribed by the Supreme Court pursuant to statutory authority; the trial of minor and petty offenses by United States magistrates; review of agency actions when the facts are subject to trial de novo under section 706(2)(F) of title 5, United States Code; review of orders of the Secretary of Agriculture under section 2 of the Act entitled "An Act to authorize association of producers of agricultural products" approved February 18, 1922 (7 U.S.C. 292), and under sections 6 and 7(c) of the Perishable Agricultural Commodities Act, 1930 (7 U.S.C. 499f, 499g(c)); naturalization and revocation of naturalization under sections 310–318 of the Immigration and Nationality Act (8 U.S.C. 1421–1429); prize proceedings in admiralty under sections 7651–7681 of title 10, United States Code; review of orders of the Secretary of the Interior under section 2 of the Act entitled "An Act authorizing associations of producers of aquatic products" approved June 25, 1931 (15 U.S.C. 522); review of orders of petroleum control boards under section 5 of the Act entitled "An Act to regulate interstate and foreign commerce in petroleum and its products by prohibiting the shipment in such commerce of petroleum and its products produced in violation of State law, and for other purposes", approved February 22, 1935 (15 U.S.C. 715d); actions for fines, penalties, or forfeitures under part V of title IV of the Tariff Act of 1930 (19 U.S.C. 1581–1624), or under the Anti-Smuggling Act (19 U.S.C. 1701–1711); criminal libel for condemnation, exclusion of imports, or other proceedings under the Federal Food, Drug, and Cosmetic Act (21 U.S.C. 301–392); disputes between seamen under sections 4079, 4080, and 4081 of the Revised Statutes (22 U.S.C. 256–258); habeas corpus under sections 2241–2254 of title 28, United States Code; motions to vacate, set aside or correct sentence under section 2255 of title 28, United States Code; actions for penalties for refusal to transport destitute seamen under section 4578 of the Revised Statutes (46 U.S.C. 679); actions against the United States under the Act entitled "An Act authorizing suits against the United States in admiralty for damage caused by and salvage service rendered to public vessels belonging to the United States, and for other purposes", approved March 3, 1925 (46 U.S.C. 781–790), as implemented by section 7730 of title 10, United States Code.

As amended 1975, 1979, 1982, 1987, 1988.

Rule 1102.

AMENDMENTS

Amendments to the Federal Rules of Evidence may be made as provided in section 2076 of title 28 of the United States Code.

Rule 1103.

TITLE

These rules may be known and cited as the Federal Rules of Evidence.

[The Act of Congress of January 2, 1975, Pub.L. 93–595, § 1, 88 Stat. 1926, stated that the rules therein set forth, to be known as the Federal Rules of Evidence, "shall take effect on the one hundred and eightieth day beginning after the date of the enactment of this Act. These rules apply to actions, cases, and proceedings brought after the rules take effect. These rules also apply to further procedure in actions, cases, and proceedings then pending, except to the extent that application of the rules would not be feasible, or would work injustice, in which event former evidentiary principles apply." The Rules became effective July 1, 1975. For legislative history, see M. Graham, Handbook of Federal Evidence.]

[Rule 801(d) was amended October 16, 1975, Pub.L. 94–113, § 1, 89 Stat. 576, to be effective October 31, 1975.]

[Technical corrections to Rules 606(b), 803(23), 804(b), and 1101(e), and an amendment to Rule 410, were made December 12, 1975, Pub.L. 94–149, § 1, 89 Stat. 805.]

[Rule 412 was added October 28, 1978, Pub.L. 95–540, § 2, 92 Stat. 2046, to be effective November 28, 1978.]

[Rule 1101(a) and (b) was amended November 6, 1978, Pub.L. 95–598, Title II, § 251, 92 Stat. 2673, to be effective October 1, 1979.]

[Rule 410 was amended by the order of the Supreme Court of April 30, 1979. 441 U.S. 1005. The effective date of this amendment was delayed by Congress July 31, 1979, Pub.L. 96–42, 93 Stat. 326, until December 1, 1980.]

———

[Rule 1101(a) was amended April 2, 1982, Pub.L. 97–164, Title I, § 142, 96 Stat. 45, to be effective October 1, 1982.]

———

[Rule 704 was amended October 12, 1984, Pub.L. 98–473, Title II, § 406, 98 Stat. 2067.]

———

[Rules 101 and 1101(a) were amended, and gender-specific language was neutralized in numerous Rules, by the order of the Supreme Court of March 2, 1987, to be effective October 1, 1987.   480 U.S. 1023.]

———

[Technical corrections to Rules 101, 602, 608(b), 613(b), 615, 902(3), and 1101(a) and (e) were made by the order of the Supreme Court of April 25, 1988, to be effective November 1, 1988.   485 U.S. 1049.]

———

[Rules 412, 804(a), and 1101(a) were amended November 18, 1988, Pub.L. 100–690, Title VII, §§ 7046, 7075, 102 Stat. 4400, 4405.]

———

[Rule 609(a) was amended by the order of the Supreme Court of January 26, 1990, to be effective December 1, 1990. ___ U.S. ___.]

INDEX

References are to Federal Rule of Civil Procedure (C),
Federal Rule of Appellate Procedure (A),
Section of 28 U.S.C. (§), or Federal
Rule of Evidence (E)

ADMIRALTY
Appeal, interlocutory, § 1292(a)(3).
Procedure, special, C 9(h), C 81(a).
Subject-matter jurisdiction, § 1333.
Venue, C 82.

ADMISSIONS
Evidential, E 801(d).
Judicial, C 8, C 36.
Requests for, C 36, C 37(c).

AMENDMENT
Findings, C 52(b).
Judgment, C 59(e).
Pleadings, C 15.
    Jurisdictional allegations, § 1653.
    Omitted counterclaims, C 13(f).
    Relation back, C 15(c).
Process, C 4(h).
Rules, see Federal Rules.

ANSWER
    See also Counterclaims; Defenses;
        Pleadings.
Generally, C 7(a), C 12(a), C 81(c).

APPEAL
Amicus curiae, A 29.
Appendix to briefs, A 30, A 32(a).
Argument, oral, A 34.
Attorney General, notice to, A 44.
Attorneys,
    Admission of, A 46(a).
    Discipline of, A 46(c).
    Suspension or disbarment of, A
      46(b).
Bond, C 62, A 7, A 8(b).
Briefs, A 28.
    Appendix to, A 30, A 32(a).
    Filing and serving, A 31.
    Form of, A 32(a).
    Length of, A 28(g).
    Submission on, A 34(f).

APPEAL—Cont'd
Briefs—Cont'd
    Types of,
      Amicus curiae, A 29.
      Appellant's, A 28(a).
      Appellee's, A 28(b).
      Reply, A 28(c).
Caption of case, A 12(a).
Clerks, duties of, A 45.
Conference, prehearing, A 33.
Corporate disclosure statement, A 26.1.
Costs, A 39.
    Bond for, A 7.
Dismissal, voluntary, A 42.
Disposition, § 2106.
Docketing of, A 12(a).
Extraordinary writs, A 21.
Federal Rules of Appellate Procedure,
    Scope of, A 1.
    Suspension of, A 2.
    Title of, A 48.
Filing of papers, A 25(a).
Final decisions, § 1291, § 2072(c).
Frivolous, A 38.
Harmless error, § 2111.
In banc, A 35.
In forma pauperis, A 24.
Interest during, A 37.
Interlocutory decisions, § 1292.
Judgment,
    Entry of, A 36, A 45(c).
    Interest on, A 37.
Local rules, A 47.
Magistrate, see Magistrate.
Mandamus, A 21.
Mandate,
    Issuance of, A 41(a).
    Stay of, A 35(c), A 41.
Motions, A 27.
Notice of, A 3.
Oral argument, A 34.
Orders, entry of, A 45(c).

541

INDEX

INDEX

INJUNCTIONS
Anti–Injunction Act, § 2283.
Appeal, interlocutory, § 1292(a)(1).
Expedited proceedings, C 65, § 1657(a).
Findings and conclusions, C 52(a).
General provision, C 65.
Interpleader, statutory, § 2361.
Stay, C 62.

INSTRUCTIONS
Jury, C 51.

INSURANCE
Direct action, § 1332(c)(1).
Discovery, C 26(b)(2).
Evidence, E 411.

INTEREST
Appeal, during, A 37.
General provision, § 1961.
Jurisdictional amount, see Subject–Matter Jurisdiction.

INTERNATIONAL LITIGATION
Discovery, C 28(b).
Foreign law, determining, C 44.1.
Foreign official record, proving, C 44(a)(2).
Service of process, C 4(i).
Subject-matter jurisdiction, § 1332.
Subpoena, C 45(e)(2).
Venue, § 1391(d).

INTERPLEADER
Rule, C 22(1), C 67.
Statutory, C 22(2).
    Injunction, § 2361.
    Service of process, § 2361.
    Subject-matter jurisdiction, § 1335.
    Venue, § 1397.

INTERROGATORIES
Discovery, C 33.
Jury verdict, C 49(b).

INTERVENTION
Class actions, C 23(d).
General provision, C 24.
United States or state as intervenor, § 2403.

INVOLUNTARY DISMISSAL
See Dismissal.

INVOLUNTARY PLAINTIFF
Joinder, C 19(a).

JOINDER
    See also Class Actions; Impleader; Interpleader; Intervention; Shareholders' Derivative Actions.
Claims, C 18.
Consolidation, C 42(a).
Joint trial, C 42(a).
Multidistrict litigation, § 1407.

JOINDER—Cont'd
Parties,
    Bulge service, C 4(f).
    Collusive, § 1359.
    Compulsory, C 19.
    Counterclaims and cross-claims, C 13(h).
    Defenses to, C 12, C 21.
    Involuntary plaintiff, C 19(a).
    Permissive, C 20.
Separate judgments, C 13(i), C 54(b).
Separate trials, C 13(i), C 14(a), C 20(b), C 42(b).
Severance, C 14(a), C 21.

JUDGE
Appearing as witness, E 605.
Calling and interrogating witnesses, E 614, E 706.
Disability of, C 63.
Disqualification of, § 144, § 455.
District judges, appointment and number of, § 133.
Trial by, see Nonjury Trial.

JUDGMENT
Appellate, A 36.
Declaratory, C 57, §§ 2201–2202.
Default, see Default.
Definition of, C 54(a).
Demand for, C 8(a), C 54(c).
Enforcement of, see Enforcement of Judgments.
Entry of, C 58, C 77(d), C 79.
Form of, C 54(a), C 58, C 65(d).
N.o.v., C 50.
Offer of, C 68.
Pleading of, C 9(e).
Registration of, § 1963.
Relief from, C 59(e), C 60.
Separate, C 13(i), C 54(b).
Stay of, see Stays.
Summary, see Summary Judgments.

JUDICIAL CONFERENCE
Circuit's, § 333.
United States', § 331, § 1657(b), § 1914(b).

JUDICIAL COUNCIL
Circuit's, C 83, § 332, § 2077(b).

JURISDICTION
Courts of appeals', see Courts of Appeals.
Jurisdictional amount, see Subject–Matter Jurisdiction.
Subject matter, see Subject–Matter Jurisdiction.
Supreme Court's, see Supreme Court.
Territorial, see Territorial Jurisdiction.

JURY TRIAL
Advisory jury, C 39(c).

546

INDEX

INDEX

APPENDIX

L. RALPH MECHAM
DIRECTOR

JAMES E. MACKLIN, JR.
DEPUTY DIRECTOR

ADMINISTRATIVE OFFICE OF THE
UNITED STATES COURTS

WASHINGTON, D.C. 20544

19 NOV 1990

TO THE HONORABLE, THE CHIEF JUSTICE AND THE ASSOCIATE
JUSTICES OF THE SUPREME COURT OF THE UNITED STATES:

By direction of the Judicial Conference of the
United States, pursuant to the authority conferred by
28 U.S.C. § 331, I have the honor to transmit herewith
for the consideration of the Court proposed amendments
to the Federal Rules of Civil Procedure, and amendments
to the Supplemental Rules for Certain Admiralty and
Maritime Claims. The Judicial Conference recommends
that these amendments be approved by the Court and
transmitted to the Congress pursuant to law.

The changes recommended by the Conference include:
proposed new Civil Rule 4.1, proposed amendments to
Rules 4, 5, 12, 15, 16, 24, 26, 28, 30, 34, 35, 41, 44,
45, 47, 48, 50, 52, 53, 63, 71A, 72, and 77; proposed
new Chapter headings VIII and IX; proposed amendments
to the Appendix of Forms; and proposed amendments to
Rules C and E of the Supplemental Rules for Certain
Admiralty and Maritime Claims. The proposed amendments
are accompanied by Advisory Committee Notes.

For your assistance in considering these proposed
amendments, I am also transmitting an excerpt from the
Report of the Committee on Rules of Practice and
Procedure to the Judicial Conference and the Report of
the Advisory Committee on the Federal Rules of Civil
Procedure.

L. Ralph Mecham

Enclosures

A TRADITION OF SERVICE TO THE FEDERAL JUDICIARY

[G4127]

551

TO THE CHIEF JUSTICE OF THE UNITED STATES AND
MEMBERS OF THE JUDICIAL CONFERENCE OF THE UNITED
STATES

I.   Amendments to the Rules of Practice and Procedure

   B.   Federal Rules of Civil Procedure

   The Advisory Committee on the Federal Rules of Civil Procedure
has submitted to your Committee proposed new Civil Rule 4.1; proposed
amendments to Civil Rules 4, 5, 12, 15, 16, 24, 26, 28, 30, 34, 35, 41,
44, 45, 47, 48, 50, 52, 53, 63, 71A, 72, and 77; proposed new Chapter
headings VIII and IX; proposed amendments to the Appendix of Forms;
and proposed amendments to Admiralty Rules C and E.   Most of these
amendments were approved for publication by your Committee at its July
1989 meeting; some had been approved earlier.

   The amendments to Rule 4 would result in a reorganization of the
provisions of Rule 4 to eliminate overlapping provisions, to remove
certain disconnected provisions to a new Rule 4.1, and to make the
organization of this frequently amended rule more rational and easily
accessible to practitioners. A number of substantive changes were made
to accomplish the following: (1) authorize the use of any means of
service provided by the state in which a defendant is served, as well as by
the forum state: (2) permit nationwide exercise of personal jurisdiction in
Federal question cases unless Congress otherwise provides; (3) clarify and
extend the cost-saving practice of securing waivers of actual service of
process; (4) call attention to the Hague Convention and other pertinent
treaties; (5) reduce the risk that a plaintiff may lose a meritorious claim
against the United States for failure to serve process properly on it; (6)
allow the United States to effect service more economically and further
reduce the use of United States marshals for service of process.
Proposed new Civil Rule 4.1 would contain provisions eliminated from the
old Rule 4 to achieve greater textual clarity.

1   [G4128]

The proposed amendment to Rule 5(d) would require that a person making service under the Rule certify the means of service. The proposed amendment to Rule 5(e), like the proposed amendment to Appellate Rule 25(a), is a reaction to the recommendation of the Judicial Improvements Committee that the rules permit local rules that would allow filing by electronic means if use of such means were approved by the Judicial Conference. The proposed amendment is consistent with the proposed appellate rule that any local rules must be consistent with any standards established by the Judicial Conference. Since it would not be effective until and unless the Judicial Conference first acts, your Committee approved this amendment even though it has not been submitted for public comment. Finally, another proposed amendment to Rule 5(e) would foreclose the local practice in some districts of requiring the clerk to reject for filing, instruments that do not conform to specified standards.

The proposed amendment to Rule 12 is necessary to conform with the proposed amendments to Rule 4. It also provides additional time to answer for defendants who waive service of process.

Rule 15 would be amended to prevent parties against whom claims are made from taking unjust advantage of otherwise inconsequential pleading errors to sustain a limitations defense. It would compel a different result in cases like <u>Schiavone v. Fortune</u>, 106 S.Ct. 2379 (1986).

The proposed amendment to Rule 16(b) would establish that the time for the scheduling order be within 60 days after the appearance of any defendant. The proposed revision of Rule 16(d) is derivative from the proposals to be made with respect to Rules 50 and 52. It would call attention to the appropriate uses of Rules 42, 50, 52, and 56 at the pretrial stage to reduce the scope of discovery or of trial. The proposed amendment to Rule 24 would merely conform the rule to a controlling statute requiring notice to a state Attorney General when the constitutionality of state legislation is challenged.

Two amendments of Rule 26 are proposed. The first is to subdivision (a) and would create a preference for internationally agreed methods of discovery when such methods are available. The second revision would add a paragraph to subdivision (b) to impose on parties asserting privileges a duty to disclose information that would enable adversaries to resist the claims of privilege. The proposed amendment to Rule 28 is intended to conform the rule to the Hague Convention on the Taking of Evidence Abroad.

2   [G4129]

The proposal to amend Rule 30 would conform the rule to the revision of Rule 4 by postponing depositions in actions in which the defendant has waived service of process. More extensive amendments to Rule 30 were temporarily withdrawn by the Advisory Committee in light of the comments received.

The proposed amendment to Rule 34 would reflect the change effected by the proposed revision to Rule 45; it provides for a subpoena to compel non-parties to produce documents and things and to submit to inspections on premises. The proposed amendment to Rule 35 reflects changes in the rule made by Congress in 1988 permitting clinical psychologists to perform mental examinations conducted pursuant to that rule. The proposed amendment would extend the scope of professions authorized to conduct such examinations by permitting examinations by suitably licensed or certified examiners.

Rule 41 would be revised to delete the provision for its use as a method of evaluating the sufficiency of the evidence presented at trial by a plaintiff. This language would be replaced by a new provision found in Rule 52(c) that would be more broadly useful. The proposed amendment to Rule 44 would take advantage of the Hague Public Documents Convention. The rule would also be amended to delete references to specific jurisdictions no longer subject to the sovereignty of the United States.

The proposed amendment of Rule 45 would substantially re-write the rule. The aims of revision are (1) to clarify and enlarge the protections afforded non-parties who are subject to subpoenas; (2) to facilitate access outside the deposition procedure to documents and things in the possession of non-parties; (3) to facilitate service of subpoenas at places distant from the district in which the action is pending; (4) to enable the court to compel a witness found within its state to attend trial; and (5) to clarify the text of the rule. The amendment would, _inter alia,_ permit the issuance of subpoenas by attorneys as officers of the court, including attorneys in distant districts.

The proposed amendment to Rule 47 would eliminate the institution of the "alternate" juror. This, together with the amendment of Rule 48, would permit all jurors who sit through the case to participate in the verdict. In addition to providing that all jurors who hear the evidence would be permitted to participate in the verdict, Rule 48 would be revised to conform the rule to existing practice in requiring at least six jurors. The proposed amendment would limit the number of jurors seated to twelve.

The proposed amendments to Rule 50 would serve several purposes. One is to enable the court to render judgment at any time during a jury trial when it becomes clear a party is entitled to such judgment. A second is to abandon familiar terminology that carries the burden of anachronisms suggested by the text of the present subdivision 50(a). A third is to articulate the standard for entry of judgment as a matter of law with sufficient clarity that an uninstructed reader of the rule can gain some understanding of its function. The standard is not changed from the present law. In addition, Rule 52 would be amended to add subdivision (c) authorizing the court to enter judgment at any time during a non-jury trial when it becomes clear a party is entitled to such judgment. This provision is a companion to the proposed revision of Rule 50. The two proposals are also reflected in the language that would be added to Rule 16. Their shared purpose is to reduce the number of long trials. Judges using these devices as intended may schedule the course of a trial in such manner as to reach first any dispositive issues on which either party may fail to carry a burden of production or proof.

The proposed amendment to Rule 53 would impose on special masters the duty to distribute their reports to the parties. This would reduce dependence on the office of the clerks to perform this service.

Substantial proposed amendments to Rule 56 were temporarily withdrawn by the Advisory Committee in light of the comments received.

The proposed amendment to Rule 63 would facilitate the use of a substitute judge in the event the trial judge is unable to proceed. A substitute judge at a bench trial would be required to recall material witnesses who are available to testify again if such recall would not be an undue burden.

The proposed amendment to Rule 71A would conform that rule to the revised Rule 4. The revision to Rule 71A was not circulated for public comment, but since the amendment is technical, your Committee approved the change without publication. Rule 72 would be amended to eliminate discrepancy in the present rule in measuring the time for objection to a magistrate's action. The proposed revision of Rule 77 would conform that rule to the proposed revision of Appellate Rule 4, which will enable the district courts to deal with the increasingly frequent

4   [G4131]

problem of parties receiving no notice of judgments from which appeals might be taken.

The proposed amendments to chapter headings VIII and IX are designed to clarify the organization of the rules. The proposed revisions to the Appendix of Forms would delete Form 18A and replace it with new Forms 1A and 1B to accommodate the waiver of service provisions of amended Rule 4.

Finally, proposed amendments to Admiralty Rules C and E would conform those rules to Rule 4, as amended, by reducing the required use of United States marshals.

Except as noted above, the above-referenced new rule, amendments, chapter headings, and revisions to the forms were approved for public comment by your Committee and were published in October 1989. Hearings were held in Chicago and San Francisco. Minor changes were made in response to the comments received. Your Committee approves the proposed rule and amendments.

The above-proposed rule and amendments to the Federal Rules of Civil Procedure, the proposed amended chapter headings and amendments to the Appendix of Forms of the Federal Rules of Civil Procedure and the proposed amendments to the Supplemental Rules for Certain Admiralty and Maritime Claims are set out in Appendix B and are accompanied by Advisory Committee Notes and a report explaining their purpose and intent.

> **Recommendation 3:** That the Judicial Conference approve new Rule 4.1 and amendments to Rules 4, 5, 12, 15, 16, 24, 26, 28, 30, 34, 35, 41, 44, 45, 47, 48, 50, 52, 53, 63, 71A, 72, and 77 of the Federal Rules of Civil Procedure; new chapter headings VIII and IX and amendments to the Appendix of Forms to the Federal Rules of Civil Procedure; and amendments to Rules C and E of the Supplemental Rules for Certain Admiralty and Maritime Claims and transmit them to the Supreme Court for its consideration with a recommendation that they be approved by the Court and transmitted to Congress pursuant to law.

[G4132]

5

COMMITTEE ON RULES OF PRACTICE AND PROCEDURE

OF THE

JUDICIAL CONFERENCE OF THE UNITED STATES

WASHINGTON. D.C. 20544

JOSEPH F WEIS JR
CHAIRMAN

JAMES E MACKLIN JR
SECRETARY

June 19, 1990

CHAIRMEN OF ADVISORY COMMITTEES

JON O NEWMAN
APPELLATE RULES

JOHN F GRADY
CIVIL RULES

LELAND C NIELSEN
CRIMINAL RULES

LLOYD D GEORGE
BANKRUPTCY RULES

TO: HON. JOSEPH F. WEIS, JR, CHAIR, STANDING COMMITTEE ON RULES OF PRACTICE AND PROCEDURE

FROM: JOHN F. GRADY, CHAIR, ADVISORY COMMITTEE ON CIVIL RULES

I have the honor to report the recommendation of the Civil Rules Committee that the Supreme Court of the United States be advised to promulgate a substantial package of amendments to the Federal Rules of Civil Procedure.

These recommendations are based upon many extensive comments by the bench and bar on the package of proposals published for comment in October, 1989. Minor revisions have been made to many of the proposed amendments then published, and three of the proposals, the amendments to Rules 30, 38 and 56, have been temporarily withdrawn pending republication of more substantial revisions.

It is the hope of the Civil Rules Committee that so much of this package as your committee may approve will be transmitted to the Judicial Conference of the United States for consideration at its fall meeting, and that the rules might be promulgated with an effective date in 1991.

RULE 4.

This rule would be almost entirely re-written, to serve the following aims:

First, the revise rule authorizes the use of any means of service provided not only by the law of the forum state, but also of the state in which a defendant is served.

Second, the revised rule clarifies and extends the cost-saving practice of securing the assent of the defendant to dispense with actual service of the summons and complaint. This practice was introduced to the rule in 1983 by an act of Congress authorizing "service-by-mail," a procedure that effects economic service with cooperation of the defendant. Defendants magnifying costs of service by requiring

[G4133]

557

expensive service not necessary to achieve full notice of an action brought against them are required to bear the wasteful costs. This provision is made available in actions against defendants who cannot be served in the districts in which the actions are brought.

Third, the revision reduces the hazard of commencing an action against the United States or its officers, agencies, and corporations. A party failing to effect service on all the offices of the United States as required by the rule is assured adequate time to cure defects of service.

Fourth, the revision calls attention to the important effect of the Hague Convention and other treaties bearing on service of documents abroad and favors the use of internationally agreed means of service. In some respects, such treaties have facilitated service in foreign countries but are not fully known to the bar.

Fifth, the revision enables the United States to effect service more economically and further reduces the use of United States marshals in the performance of routine duties of service.

Finally, the revised rule extends the reach of federal courts to impose jurisdiction over the person of all defendants against whom federal law claims are made who can be constitutionally subject to the jurisdiction of the courts of the United States. The present territorial limits on the effectiveness of service to subject a defendant to the jurisdiction of the court over the defendant's person are retained for all actions in which there is a state in which personal jurisdiction can be asserted consistently with state law and the Fourteenth Amendment. But a new provision makes those limits inapplicable to cases in which there is no state in which the defendant can be sued.

The revised rule is reorganized to make its provisions more accessible to those not familiar with all of them. Additional subdivisions in this rule allow for more captions; several overlaps among subdivisions are eliminated; and several disconnected provisions are removed, to be relocated in a new Rule 4.1.

RULE 4.1.

This is a new rule. The purpose in creating a new rule is to separate those few provisions of the former Rule 4 bearing on matters other than service of a summons to allow greater textual clarity in Rule 4. The new rule would provide nationwide service of orders of civil commitment enforcing decrees or injunctions issued to compel compliance with federal law. The rule makes no change in the practice with respect to the enforcement of injunctions or decrees not involving the enforcement of federally-created rights.

RULE 5.

This rule would be revised in three significant respects. The first is to require that the person making service under the rule file a certificate of service. The second is to make provisional authorization for the use of FAX to file papers with district courts.

[G4134]

The third is to foreclose the practice of some districts requiring the clerk to reject for filing instruments that do not conform to specified standards.

RULE 12.

Amendment of this rule is necessary to conform to the revision of Rule 4. The revision provides additional time for answer by defendants who waive service of process.

RULE 14.

This rule would be amended to assure that third party defendants are provided with copies of current pleadings in actions to which they are joined as parties.

RULE 15.

The revision of this rule would prevent parties against whom claims are made from taking unjust advantage of otherwise inconsequential pleading errors to sustain a limitations defense. It extends the relation back of amendments that change the party or the naming of the party.

RULE 16.

An amendment to subdivision (b) is proposed with respect to the time for scheduling. The present rule requires that this be done within 120 days after filing, but it is possible that the defendant may not have been served by then. The Civil Rules Committee proposes that the time for scheduling be within 60 days after the appearance of a defendant.

The revision of subdivision (d) calls attention to the appropriate uses that may be made of Rules 42, 50, 52, and 56 at the pretrial stage to reduce the compass of discovery or of trial. The revision is related to concurrent amendments of Rules 50 and 52.

RULE 24.

This revision would conform the rule to a controlling statute requiring notice to a state Attorney General when the constitutionality of state legislation is challenged.

RULE 26.

Two revisions of this rule are proposed. The first is to subdivision (a) and creates a preference for internationally agreed methods of discovery when such methods are available. The second revision is to add a paragraph to subdivision (b) to impose
[G4135]

559

on parties asserting privileges a duty to disclose information enabling adversaries to resist such claims of privileges.

RULE 28.

The amendments to this rule conform the rule to the Hague Evidence Convention.

RULE 30.

This rule would be revised to conform to the revision of Rule 4, to postpone depositions in actions in which the defendant has waived service of process.

RULE 34.

This amendment would reflect the change effected by the proposed revision of Rule 45 to provide for subpoenas to compel non-parties to produce documents and things and to submit to inspections of premises.

RULE 35.

The revision adds a requirement that a professional appointed pursuant to this rule must be suitably licensed or certified. It is occasioned by a 1988 Congressional amendment of the rule. The requirement that the examiner be suitably licensed is intended to authorize the court to consider the appropriateness of the credentials of any specialist whom the court is asked to appoint pursuant to this rule.

RULE 41.

This rule would be revised to delete the provision for its use as a method of evaluating the sufficiency of the evidence presented at trial by a plaintiff. This language would be replaced by a new provision found in Rule 52(c) that would be more broadly useful.

RULE 44.

The revision of this rule would make appropriate use of the Hague Documents Convention and would delete an obsolete reference.

RULE 45.

This rule would be completely re-written. The purposes of this revision are (1) to clarify and enlarge the protections afforded persons who are required to assist the

[G4136]

court by giving information or evidence; (2) to facilitate access outside the deposition procedure provided by Rule 30 to documents and other information in the possession of persons who are not parties; (3) to facilitate service of subpoenas for depositions or productions of evidence at places distant from the district in which an action is proceeding; (4) to enable the court to compel a witness found within the state in which the court sits to attend trial; (5) to clarify the organization of the text of the rule.

RULE 47.

This revision would eliminate the use of alternate jurors, a practice that proceeded from the premise that a jury should number precisely twelve. It would also allow the court to excuse a juror during deliberations if the juror could not continue.

RULE 48.

This revision specifies that a jury may render a verdict with as few as six remaining members, and limits the number to twelve.

RULE 50.

This rule would be revised for several purposes. One is to enable the court to render judgment at any time during a jury trial that it is clear that a party is entitled to such judgment. A second is to abandon familiar terminology that carries a burden of anachronisms suggested by the text of the present subdivision 50(a). A third is to articulate the standard for entry of judgment as a matter of law with sufficient clarity that an uninstructed reader of the rule can gain some understanding of its function. The standard is not changed from the present law.

Likewise retained is the provision requiring that a motion for judgment be made prior to submission if it is to be renewed after verdict. The Civil Rules Committee determined that there was sufficient reason to retain that requirement although some persons have argued for its deletion; the requirement does protect against possible surprise.

RULE 52.

This rule would be revised to add subdivision (c) authorizing the court to enter judgment at any time during a non-jury trial that it became clear that a party is entitled to such judgment. This provision is a companion to the revision of Rule 50, and replaces the deleted provisions of Rule 41. The two proposals are also reflected in the language added to Rule 16. Their shared purpose is to reduce the number of long trials. Judges using these devices as intended may schedule the course of a trial in such manner as to reach first any dispositive issues on which either party is likely to fail to carry a burden of production or proof. [G4137]

RULE 53.

This rule would be revised to impose on special masters the duty to distribute their reports to the parties. This would reduce dependence on the office of the clerks to perform this service.

RULE 63.

This proposed revision would provide for a substitute judge. Such a judge at a bench trial would be required to recall material witnesses who are available to testify again.

CHAPTER HEADINGS VIII AND IX.

These revisions clarify the organization of the rules.

RULE 71A.

This revision would delete an incorrect reference to Rule 4. It has not been published for comment, but is merely technical in nature.

RULE 72.

This revision would clarify an ambiguity regarding the time for objection to a magistrate's report.

RULE 77.

This revision is proposed to conform to a proposed revision of the Federal Rules of Appellate Procedure which will enable the district courts to deal with the increasingly frequent problem of the party receiving no notice of an unfavorable judgment from which an appeal might be taken.

APPENDIX OF FORMS

This revision would delete the present Form 18A, and replace it with new Forms 1A and 1B that accurately reflect the proposed new Rule 4. These forms have been published for comment. [G4138]

ADMIRALTY RULE C.

This revision conforms to the amendment of Rule 4 by reducing the required use of United States marshals.

ADMIRALTY RULE E.

This revision conforms to the amendment of Rule 4 by reducing the required use of United States marshals.

[G4139]

PROPOSED AMENDMENTS
TO THE
FEDERAL RULES OF CIVIL PROCEDURE*

Special Note: If paragraph (k)(2) of the proposed
revision of Rule 4 is disapproved by the Congress, it is
nevertheless recommended that the rule be approved with
the deletion of the paragraph, which is separable from
the revised rule, and the numerical designation (1) from
the preceding paragraph of subdivision (k).

Rule 4 ~~Process~~ Summons

1   (a) ~~SUMMONS: ISSUANCE. Upon the filing of the~~

2   ~~complaint, the clerk shall forthwith issue a~~

3   ~~summons and deliver the summons to the plaintiff or~~

4   ~~the plaintiff's attorney, who shall be responsible~~

5   ~~for prompt service of the summons and a copy of the~~

6   ~~complaint. Upon request of the plaintiff separate~~

7   ~~or additional summons shall issue against any~~

8   ~~defendants.~~

9   ~~(b) SAME:~~ FORM. The summons shall be signed

10   by the clerk, be under the seal of the court,

11   contain the name of the court and the names of the

12   parties, be directed to the defendant, state the

13   name and address of the plaintiff's attorney, if

---

*New matter is underlined; matter to be omitted is
lined through. [G4140]

564

14   any, otherwise the plaintiff's address, and the

15   time within which these rules require the defendant

16   to appear and defend, and shall notify the

17   defendant that in case of the defendant's failure

18   to do so judgment by default will be rendered

19   against the defendant for the relief demanded in

20   the complaint. ~~When, under Rule 4(e), service is~~

21   ~~made pursuant to a statute or rule of court of a~~

22   ~~state, the summons, or notice, or order in lieu of~~

23   ~~summons shall correspond as nearly as may be to~~

24   ~~that required by the statute or rule.~~ The court

25   may allow a summons to be amended.

26   (b)   ISSUANCE.   Upon the filing of the

27   complaint, the plaintiff may present a summons to

28   the clerk for signature and seal.   If in proper

29   form, the clerk shall sign and seal the summons and

30   issue it to the plaintiff for service on the

31   defendant.   A summons or a copy of the summons if

32   it is addressed to multiple defendants shall be

33   issued for each defendant to be served.

34   (c)   SERVICE WITH COMPLAINT; BY WHOM MADE.

                                                    [G4141]

35   (1) ~~Process, other than a subpoena or a~~

36 ~~summons and complaint, shall be served by a~~

37 ~~United States marshal or deputy United States~~

38 ~~marshal, or by a person specially appointed for~~

39 ~~that purpose~~ A summons shall be served together

40 with a copy of the complaint. The plaintiff

41 shall be responsible for service of a summons

42 and complaint within the time allowed under

43 subdivision (m) of this rule and shall furnish

44 the person effecting service with such copies

45 of the summons and complaint as are necessary.

46   (2)(A) ~~A summons and complaint shall,~~

47 ~~except as provided in subparagraphs (B) and (C)~~

48 ~~of this paragraph, be served~~ Service may be

49 effected by any person who is not a party and

50 is not less than 18 years of age~~.~~, provided

51 that the court may at the request of the

52 plaintiff direct that service be effected by a

53 person or officer (who may be a United States

54 marshal or deputy United States marshal)

55 specially appointed by the court for that

[G4142]

566

56   purpose.   A special appointment shall be made

57   when the plaintiff is

58   ~~(B) A summons and complaint shall, at the~~

59   ~~request of the party seeking service or such~~

60   ~~party's attorney, be served by a United States~~

61   ~~marshal or deputy United States marshal, or by~~

62   ~~a person specially appointed by the court for~~

63   ~~that purpose, only~~

64   ~~(i) on behalf of a party~~ authorized

65   to proceed in forma pauperis pursuant to

66   Title 28, U.S.C. § 1915, or ~~of~~ a seaman

67   authorized to proceed under Title 28,

68   U.S.C. § 1916~~,~~.

69   ~~(ii) on behalf of the United States~~

70   ~~or an officer or agency of the United~~

71   ~~States, or~~

72   ~~(iii) pursuant to an order issued~~

73   ~~by the court stating that a United States~~

74   ~~marshal or deputy United States marshal,~~

75   ~~or a person specially appointed for that~~

76   ~~purpose, is required to serve the summons~~

77   ~~and complaint in order that service be~~

                                                [G4143]

78 ~~properly effected in that particular~~
79 ~~action.~~
80 ~~(C) A summons and complaint may be served~~
81 ~~upon a defendant of any class referred to in~~
82 ~~paragraph (1) or (3) of subdivision (d) of this~~
83 ~~rule~~
84 ~~(i) pursuant to the law of the~~
85 ~~State in which the district court is held~~
86 ~~for the service of summons or other like~~
87 ~~process upon such defendant in an action~~
88 ~~brought in the courts of general~~
89 ~~jurisdiction of that State, or~~
90 ~~(ii) by mailing a copy of the~~
91 ~~summons and of the complaint (by~~
92 ~~first-class mail, postage prepaid) to the~~
93 ~~person to be served, together with two~~
94 ~~copies of a notice and acknowledgment~~
95 ~~conforming substantially to form 18-A and~~
96 ~~a return envelope, postage prepaid,~~
97 ~~addressed to the sender. If no~~
98 ~~acknowledgment of service under this~~
99 ~~subdivision of this rule is received by~~

[G4144]

100   ~~the sender within 20 days after the date~~

101   ~~of mailing, service of such summons and~~

102   ~~complaint shall be made under subparagraph~~

103   ~~(A) or (B) of this paragraph in the manner~~

104   ~~prescribed by subdivision (d)(1) or~~

105   ~~(d)(3).~~

106   ~~(D) Unless good cause is shown for not~~

107   ~~doing so the court shall order the payment of~~

108   ~~the costs of personal service by the person~~

109   ~~served if such person does not complete and~~

110   ~~return within 20 days after mailing, the notice~~

111   ~~and acknowledgment of receipt of summons.~~

112   ~~(E) The notice and acknowledgment of~~

113   ~~receipt of summons and complaint shall be~~

114   ~~executed under oath or affirmation.~~

115   ~~(3) The court shall freely make special~~

116   ~~appointments to serve summonses and complaints~~

117   ~~under paragraph (2)(B) of this subdivision of~~

118   ~~this rule and all other process under paragraph~~

119   ~~(1) of this subdivision of this rule.~~

120   (d)   ~~SUMMONS AND COMPLAINT: PERSON TO BE~~

121   ~~SERVED.~~ <u>WAIVER OF SERVICE; DUTY TO SAVE COSTS OF</u>

[G4145]

569

122 <u>SERVICE; REQUEST TO WAIVE.</u> ~~The summons and~~
123 ~~complaint shall be served together. The plaintiff~~
124 ~~shall furnish the person making service with such~~
125 ~~copies as are necessary. Service shall be made as~~
126 ~~follows:~~

127   (1) A defendant who waives service of a
128 summons does not thereby waive any objection to
129 the venue or to the jurisdiction of the court
130 over the person of the defendant.

131   (2) An individual, corporation, or
132 association subject to service under
133 subdivisions (e), (f), or (h) of this rule, who
134 receives notice of an action in the manner
135 provided in this paragraph has a duty to avoid
136 unnecessary costs of service of a summons. To
137 avoid costs, the plaintiff may notify the
138 defendant of the commencement of the action and
139 request that the defendant waive service of a
140 summons. If the notice and request

141   (A) is in writing and addressed to an
142 individual who is the defendant or who could be
143 served pursuant to subdivision (h) of this rule

[G4146]

144 as representative of an entity that is the
145 defendant; and

146   (B) is dispatched through first-class mail
147 or other reliable means; and

148   (C) is accompanied by a copy of the
149 complaint and identifies the court in which it
150 has been filed; and

151   (D) informs the defendant, by means of a
152 text prescribed in an official form promulgated
153 pursuant to Rule 84, of the consequences of
154 compliance and of a failure to comply with the
155 request; and

156   (E) sets forth the date on which the
157 request is sent; and

158   (F) allows the defendant a reasonable time
159 to return the waiver, which shall be at least
160 30 days from the date on which the request is
161 sent, or 60 days from such date if the
162 defendant is addressed outside any judicial
163 district of the United States; and   [G4147]

164   (G) provides the defendant with an extra

165   copy of the notice and request and a prepaid

166   means of compliance in writing;

167   and the defendant fails to comply with the

168   request, the court shall impose the costs of

169   effecting service on the defendant unless good

170   cause for the failure be shown.

171   (3) A defendant timely returning a waiver

172   so requested shall not be required to serve an

173   answer to the complaint until 60 days from the

174   date on which the request of waiver of service

175   was sent, or 90 days from such date if the

176   defendant was addressed outside any judicial

177   district of the United States.

178   (4) When a waiver of service is filed by

179   the plaintiff with the court, the action shall

180   proceed as if a summons and complaint had been

181   served at the time of filing of the waiver and

182   no proof of service shall be required.

183   (5) The costs to be imposed on a

184   defendant under paragraph (2) for failure to

185   comply with a request for a waiver of service

[G4148]

186   of a summons shall include the costs of service

187   under subdivision (e), (f) or (h) of this rule

188   and   the   costs,   including   a   reasonable

189   attorney's   fee,   of   any   motion   required   to

190   collect such costs of service.

191   (1 e)   SERVICE UPON INDIVIDUALS WITHIN A

192   JUDICIAL DISTRICT OF THE UNITED STATES. Unless

193   otherwise   provided   by   federal   law,   service

194   Uupon an individual other than an infant or an

195   incompetent person, from whom a waiver has not

196   been obtained and filed, may be effected in any

197   judicial district of the United States:

198   (1) pursuant to the law of the State in

199   which the district court is held, or in which

200   service   is   effected,   for   the   service   of   a

201   summons   upon   such   defendant   in   an   action

202   brought in the courts of general jurisdiction

203   of such State; or

204   (2) by delivering a copy of the summons

205   and   of   the   complaint   to   the   individual

206   personally or by leaving copies thereof at the

207   individual's dwelling house or usual place of

                                                    [G4149]

208   abode with some person of suitable age and
209   discretion then residing therein or by
210   delivering a copy of the summons and of the
211   complaint to an agent authorized by appointment
212   or by law to receive service of process.
213   (f) SERVICE UPON INDIVIDUALS IN A FOREIGN
214   COUNTRY. Unless otherwise provided by federal law,
215   service upon an individual other than an infant or
216   an incompetent person, from whom a waiver has not
217   been obtained and filed, may be effected in a
218   foreign country:
219   (1) by any internationally agreed means
220   reasonably calculated to give notice, such as
221   those means authorized by the Hague Convention
222   on the Service Abroad of Judicial and
223   Extrajudicial Documents; or
224   (2) if there is no internationally agreed
225   means of service or the applicable
226   international agreement allows other means of
227   service, provided that service is reasonably
228   calculated to give notice:

[G4150]

229   (A) in the manner prescribed by the law of

230   the foreign country for service in that country

231   in an action in any of its courts of general

232   jurisdiction; or

233   (B) as directed by the foreign authority

234   in response to a letter rogatory or letter of

235   request; or

236   (C) unless prohibited by the law of the

237   foreign country, by

238   (i) delivery to the individual

239   personally of copies of the summons and of

240   the complaint; or

241   (ii) any form of mail requiring a

242   signed receipt, to be addressed and

243   dispatched by the clerk of the court to

244   the party to be served; or

245   (iii) diplomatic or consular officers

246   when authorized by the United States

247   Department of State; or

248   (3) by whatever means may be directed by

249   the court, including service by means not

250   authorized by international agreement or not

[G4151]

251 consistent with the law of a foreign country,

252 if the court finds that internationally agreed

253 means or the law of the foreign country (A)

254 will not provide a lawful means by which

255 service can be effected, or (B) in cases of

256 urgency, will not permit service of process

257 within the time required by the circumstances.

258   (2 g) SERVICE UPON INFANTS AND INCOMPETENT

259 PERSONS. Service Uupon an infant or an incompetent

260 person by serving the summons and complaint shall

261 be effected in a judicial district of the United

262 States in the manner prescribed by the law of the

263 state in which the service is made for the service

264 of summons or like process upon any such defendant

265 in an action brought in the courts of general

266 jurisdiction of that state. Service upon an infant

267 or an incompetent person shall be effected in a

268 foreign country in the manner prescribed by

269 subparagraphs (2)(A) or (2)(B) of subdivision (f)

270 of this rule or by such means as the court may

271 direct. [G4152]

272   (3 h)   SERVICE   UPON   CORPORATIONS   AND

273 ASSOCIATIONS. Unless otherwise provided by federal

274 law, service Uupon a domestic or foreign

275 corporation or upon a partnership or other

276 unincorporated association which is subject to suit

277 under a common name, and from whom a waiver of

278 service has not been obtained and filed, shall be

279 effected:

280   (1) in a judicial district of the United

281   States in the manner prescribed for individuals

282   by paragraph (e)(1) of this rule or by

283   delivering a copy of the summons and of the

284   complaint to an officer, a managing or general

285   agent, or to any other agent authorized by

286   appointment or by law to receive service of

287   process and, if the agent is one authorized by

288   statute to receive service and the statute so

289   requires, by also mailing a copy to the

290   defendant, or

291   (2) in a foreign country in any manner

292   prescribed for individuals by subdivision (f)

[G4153]

293   of this rule, except personal delivery as

294   provided in clause (f)(2)(C)(i).

295   (4 i) SERVICE UPON THE UNITED STATES, AND

296 ITS AGENCIES, CORPORATIONS OR OFFICERS.

297   (1) Service Uupon the United States,

298   shall be effected by delivering a copy of the

299   summons and of the complaint to the United

300   States attorney for the district in which the

301   action is brought or to an assistant United

302   States attorney or clerical employee designated

303   by the United States attorney in a writing

304   filed with the clerk of the court or by sending

305   a copy of the summons and of the complaint by

306   registered or certified mail addressed to the

307   civil process clerk at the office of the United

308   States attorney and by sending a copy of the

309   summons and of the complaint by registered or

310   certified mail to the Attorney General of the

311   United States at Washington, District of

312   Columbia, and in any action attacking the

313   validity of an order of an officer or agency of

314   the United States not made a party, by also

[G4154]

315   sending a copy of the summons and of the

316   complaint by registered or certified mail to

317   such officer or agency.

318   (5 2) Service Uupon an officer, or

319   agency, or corporation of the United States,

320   shall be effected by serving the United States

321   in the manner prescribed by paragraph (1) of

322   this subdivision and by sending a copy of the

323   summons and of the complaint by registered or

324   certified mail to such officer, or agency, or

325   corporation. If the agency is a corporation

326   the copy shall be delivered as provided in

327   paragraph (3) of this subdivision of this rule.

328   (3) The court shall allow a reasonable

329   time for service of process under this

330   subdivision for the purpose of curing the

331   failure to serve multiple officers of the

332   United States, its agencies and corporations,

333   if the plaintiff has effected service on either

334   the United States attorney or the Attorney

335   General of the United States.   [G4155]

336 (~~6~~ j) SERVICE UPON FOREIGN, STATE OR LOCAL
337 GOVERNMENTS.

338 (1) Service upon a foreign state or
339 political subdivision thereof shall be effected
340 pursuant to 28 U.S.C. § 1608.

341 (2) Service ~~U~~upon a state or municipal
342 corporation or other governmental organization
343 thereof subject to suit~~,~~ shall be effected by
344 delivering a copy of the summons and of the
345 complaint to the chief executive officer
346 thereof or by serving the summons and complaint
347 in the manner prescribed by the law of that
348 state for the service of summons upon any such
349 defendant.

350 ~~(e) SUMMONS: SERVICE UPON PARTY NOT~~
351 ~~INHABITANT OF OR FOUND WITHIN STATE. Whenever a~~
352 ~~statute of the United States or an order of court~~
353 ~~thereunder provides for service of a summons, or of~~
354 ~~a notice, or of an order in lieu of summons upon a~~
355 ~~party not an inhabitant of or found within the~~
356 ~~state in which the district court is held, service~~
357 ~~may be made under the circumstances and in the~~

[G4156]

580

358 ~~manner prescribed by the statute or order, or, if~~
359 ~~there is no provision therein prescribing the~~
360 ~~manner of service, in a manner stated in this rule.~~
361 ~~Whenever a statute or rule of court of the state in~~
362 ~~which the district court is held provides (1) for~~
363 ~~service of a summons, or of a notice, or of an~~
364 ~~order in lieu of summons upon a party not an~~
365 ~~inhabitant of or found within the state, or (2) for~~
366 ~~service upon or notice to him to appear and respond~~
367 ~~or defend in an action by reason of the attachment~~
368 ~~or garnishment or similar seizure of his property~~
369 ~~located within the state, service may in either~~
370 ~~case be made under the circumstances and in the~~
371 ~~manner prescribed in the statute or rule.~~

372   (~~f~~ k)   TERRITORIAL LIMITS OF EFFECTIVE SERVICE.
373 ~~All process other than a subpoena may be served~~
374 ~~anywhere within the territorial limits of the state~~
375 ~~in which the district court is held, and, when~~
376 ~~authorized by a statute of the United States or by~~
377 ~~these rules, beyond the territorial limits of that~~
378 ~~state. In addition, persons who are brought in as~~
379 ~~parties pursuant to Rule 14, or as additional~~

[G4157]

380 ~~parties to a pending action or a counterclaim or~~
381 ~~cross-claim therein pursuant to Rule 19, may be~~
382 ~~served in the manner stated in paragraphs (1)-(6)~~
383 ~~of subdivision (d) of this rule at all places~~
384 ~~outside the state but within the United States that~~
385 ~~are not more than 100 miles from the place in which~~
386 ~~the action is commenced, or to which it is assigned~~
387 ~~or transferred for trial; and persons required to~~
388 ~~respond to an order of commitment for civil~~
389 ~~contempt may be served at same places. A subpoena~~
390 ~~may be served within the territorial limits~~
391 ~~provided in Rule 45.~~
392 <u>(1) Service of a summons or filing a</u>
393 <u>waiver of service is effective to establish</u>
394 <u>jurisdiction over the person of a defendant</u>
395 <u>(A) who could be subjected to the</u>
396 <u>jurisdiction of a court of general jurisdiction</u>
397 <u>in the state in which the district court is</u>
398 <u>held, or</u>
399 <u>(B) who is a party joined under Rule 14 or</u>
400 <u>Rule 19 and served at a place within a judicial</u>
401 <u>district of the United States and not more than</u>

[G4158]

402 100 miles from the place from which the summons

403 issues, or

404   (C) who is subject to the federal

405 interpleader jurisdiction under 28 U. S. C. §

406 1335, or

407   (D) when authorized by a statute of the

408 United States.

409   (2) Unless a statute of the United

410 States otherwise provides, or the Constitution

411 in a specific application otherwise requires,

412 service of a summons or filing a waiver of

413 service is also effective to establish

414 jurisdiction with respect to claims arising

415 under federal law over the person of any

416 defendant who is not subject to the

417 jurisdiction of the courts of general

418 jurisdiction of any state.

419 (g l) ~~RETURN~~ PROOF OF SERVICE. If service is

420 not waived, ~~T~~the person ~~serving the process~~

421 effecting service shall make proof ~~of service~~

422 thereof to the court ~~promptly and in any event~~

423 ~~within the time during which the person served must~~

[G4159]

424   ~~respond to the process.~~ If service is made by a

425   person other than a United States marshal or deputy

426   United States marshal, such person shall make

427   affidavit thereof. <u>If service is made outside any</u>

428   <u>judicial district of the United States, proof may</u>

429   <u>be made pursuant to any applicable treaty or</u>

430   <u>convention, or if service is made pursuant to</u>

431   <u>paragraphs (2) or (3) of subdivision (f) of this</u>

432   <u>rule, proof of service shall include a receipt</u>

433   <u>signed by the addressee or other evidence of</u>

434   <u>delivery to the addressee satisfactory to the</u>

435   <u>court.</u> ~~If service is made under subdivision~~

436   ~~(c)(2)(C)(ii) of this rule, return shall be made by~~

437   ~~the sender's filing with the court the~~

438   ~~acknowledgment received pursuant to such~~

439   ~~subdivision.~~ Failure to make proof of service does

440   not affect the validity of the service. <u>The court</u>

441   <u>may allow proof of service to be amended.</u>

442   ~~(h) AMENDMENT. At any time in its discretion~~

443   ~~and upon such terms as it deems just, the court~~

444   ~~may allow any process or proof of service thereof~~

445   ~~to be amended, unless it clearly appears that~~

[G4160]

446   ~~material prejudice would result to the substantial~~
447   ~~rights of the party against whom the process~~
448   ~~issued.~~
449   ~~(i) ALTERNATIVE PROVISIONS FOR SERVICE IN A~~
450   ~~FOREIGN COUNTRY.~~
451   ~~(1) Manner. When the federal or state~~
452   ~~law referred to in subdivision (e) of this rule~~
453   ~~authorizes service upon a party not an~~
454   ~~inhabitant of or found within the state in~~
455   ~~which the district court is held, and service~~
456   ~~is to be effected upon the party in a foreign~~
457   ~~country, it is also sufficient if service of~~
458   ~~the summons and complaint is made: (A) in the~~
459   ~~manner prescribed by the law of the foreign~~
460   ~~country for service in that country in an~~
461   ~~action in any of its courts of general~~
462   ~~jurisdiction; of (B) as directed by the foreign~~
463   ~~authority in response to a letter rogatory,~~
464   ~~when service in either case is reasonably~~
465   ~~calculated to give actual notice;or (C) upon an~~
466   ~~individual, by delivery to him personally, and~~
467   ~~upon a corporation or partnership or~~

[G4161]

585

468   ~~association, by delivery to an officer, a~~
469   ~~managing or general agent; or (D) by any form~~
470   ~~of mail, requiring a signed receipt, to be~~
471   ~~addressed and dispatched by the clerk of the~~
472   ~~court to the party to be served; or (E) as~~
473   ~~directed by order of the court. Service under~~
474   ~~(C) or (E) above may be made by any person who~~
475   ~~is not a party and is not less than 18 years of~~
476   ~~age or who is designated by order of the~~
477   ~~district court or by the foreign court. On~~
478   ~~request, the clerk shall deliver the summons to~~
479   ~~the plaintiff for transmission to the person or~~
480   ~~the foreign court or officer who will make the~~
481   ~~service.~~

482   ~~(2) Return. Proof of service may be made~~
483   ~~as prescribed by subdivision (g) of this rule,~~
484   ~~or by the law of the foreign country, or by~~
485   ~~order of the court. When service is made~~
486   ~~pursuant to subparagraph (1)(D) of this~~
487   ~~subdivision, proof of service shall include a~~
488   ~~receipt signed by the addressee or other~~

[G4162]

489   ~~evidence of delivery to the addressee~~

490   ~~satisfactory to the court.~~

491   (~~j~~ m) ~~SUMMONS:~~ TIME LIMIT FOR SERVICE.   If

492   service   of the summons and complaint is not made

493   upon a defendant within 120 days after the filing

494   of the complaint ~~and the party on whose behalf such~~

495   ~~service was required cannot show good cause why~~

496   ~~such service was not made within that period~~, the

497   court ~~action~~ shall ~~be dismissed as to that~~

498   ~~defendant without prejudice~~ upon ~~the court's~~ its

499   own initiative after notice to ~~such party or upon~~

500   ~~motion~~ the plaintiff dismiss the action without

501   prejudice as to that defendant or direct that

502   service be effected within a specified time,

503   provided however that if the plaintiff shows good

504   cause for the failure, the court shall extend the

505   time for service for an appropriate period.   This

506   subdivision shall not apply to service in a foreign

507   country pursuant to subdivision (~~i~~f) of this rule.

508   (n)   SEIZURE OF PROPERTY; SERVICE OF SUMMONS

509   NOT FEASIBLE.   [G4163]

510   (1) If a statute of the United States so
511   provides, the court may assert jurisdiction
512   over property.   Notice to claimants of the
513   property shall then be sent in the manner
514   provided by the statute or by service of a
515   summons under this rule.
516   (2) Upon a showing that the plaintiff
517   cannot with reasonable efforts serve the
518   defendant with a summons in any manner
519   authorized by this rule, the court may assert
520   jurisdiction over any assets of the defendant
521   found within the district by seizing the assets
522   under the circumstances and in the manner
523   provided by the law of the state in which the
524   district court sits.

COMMITTEE NOTES

Purposes of Revision.   The general purpose of this revision is to facilitate the service of the summons and complaint.   The revised rule explicitly authorizes a means for service of the summons and complaint on any defendant.   While the means of service so authorized always provides appropriate notice to persons against whom claims are made, effective service under this rule does not assure that personal jurisdiction has been established over the defendant served.   [G4164]

First, the revised rule authorizes the use of any means of service provided not only by the law of the forum state, but also of the state in which a defendant is served, unless the defendant is a minor or incompetent.

Second, the revised rule clarifies and extends the cost-saving practice of securing the assent of the defendant to dispense with actual service of the summons and complaint. This practice was introduced to the rule in 1983 by an act of Congress authorizing "service-by-mail," a procedure that effects economic service with cooperation of the defendant. Defendants magnifying costs of service by requiring expensive service not necessary to achieve full notice of an action brought against them are required to bear the wasteful costs. This provision is made available in actions against defendants who cannot be served in the districts in which the actions are brought.

Third, the revision reduces the hazard of commencing an action against the United States or its officers, agencies, and corporations. A party failing to effect service on all the offices of the United States as required by the rule is assured adequate time to cure defects of service.

Fourth, the revision calls attention to the important effect of the Hague Convention and other treaties bearing on service of documents in foreign countries and favors the use of internationally agreed means of service. In some respects, such treaties have facilitated service in foreign countries but are not fully known to the bar.

Fifth, the revision corrects a hiatus in the enforcement of federal law by providing nationwide territorial jurisdiction over defendants who are subject to the jurisdictional reach of no state.

Finally, the revised rule extends the reach of federal courts to impose jurisdiction over the person of all defendants against whom federal law claims are made who can be constitutionally subject to the jurisdiction of the courts of the United States. The present
[G4165]

territorial limits on the effectiveness of service to subject a defendant to the jurisdiction of the court over the defendant's person are retained for all actions in which there is a state in which personal jurisdiction can be asserted consistently with state law and the Fourteenth Amendment. But a new provision makes those limits inapplicable to cases in which there is no state in which the defendant can be sued.

The revised rule is reorganized to make its provisions more accessible to those not familiar with all of them. Additional subdivisions in this rule allow for more captions; several overlaps among subdivisions are eliminated; and several disconnected provisions are removed, to be relocated in a new Rule 4.1.

The Caption of the Rule. Rule 4 was entitled "Service of Process" and applied to the service not only of summons, but also other process as well, although these are not specified by the present rule. The service of process in eminent domain proceedings is governed by Rule 71A. The service of a subpoena is governed by Rule 45, and service of papers such as orders, motions, notices, pleadings, and other documents is governed by Rule 5.

The revised rule is entitled "Summons" and applies only to that form of legal process. Unless service of the summons is waived as provided in subdivision (d), a summons must be served whenever a person is joined as a party against whom a claim is made. Those few provisions of the present rule which bear specifically on the service of process other than a summons are relocated in Rule 4.1 in order to simplify the text of this rule.

Subdivision (a). The revised subdivision (a) contains most of the language of the former subdivision (b). The second sentence of the former subdivision (b) has been stricken, so that the federal court summons will be in all cases the same. Few states now employ distinctive requirements of form for a summons and the applicability of such requirements in federal court can only serve as a trap for an unwary party or attorney.
[G4166]

A sentence is added to this subdivision authorizing an amendment of a summons. This sentence replaces the rarely used former subdivision 4(h). See 4A WRIGHT & MILLER, FEDERAL PRACTICE AND PROCEDURE § 1131 (2d ed. 1987).

Subdivision (b). The revised subdivision (b) replaces the former subdivision (a). The revised text makes clear that the responsibility for filling in the summons falls on the plaintiff, not the clerk of court. If there are multiple defendants, the plaintiff may secure issuance of a summons for each defendant, or may serve copies of a single original bearing the names of multiple defendants, so long as the addressee of the summons is effectively identified.

Subdivision (c). Paragraph (1) of the revised subdivision retains language from the former subdivision (d)(1). Paragraph (2) retains language from the former subdivision (a), and adds an appropriate caution regarding the time limit on service set forth in subdivision (m).

The 1983 revision of Rule 4 relieved the marshals' offices of much of the burden of serving summons. Subdivision (c) now extends that reduced dependence on the marshal's office in actions in which the party seeking service is the United States. The United States, like other civil litigants, would be permitted to designate any person who is 18 years of age and not a party to serve its summons.

The court remains obligated to provide through special appointment of a marshal, a deputy, or some other person, for the service of a summons in two classes of cases specified by statute, actions brought in forma pauperis or by a seaman. 28 U.S.C. §§ 1915, 1916. The court also retains discretion to provide for official service on motion of a party. Where a law enforcement presence appears to be necessary or advisable to keep the peace, the court should appoint a marshal or deputy or other official person to make the service. The Department of Justice may also call upon the Marshals
[G4167]

Service to perform services in actions brought by the United States. 28 U. S. C. § 651.

Subdivision (d). This text is new, but is substantially derived from the former subparagraph (c)(2)(C) and (D) added to the rule by Congress in 1983. The aims of the provision are to eliminate the costs of service of a summons on many parties and to foster cooperation among adversaries and counsel. This device should be useful in dealing with furtive defendants or those who are outside the United States and can be actually served only at substantial and unnecessary expense.

The former text described this process as service-by-mail. This language misled some plaintiffs into thinking that service could be effected by mail without the affirmative cooperation of the defendant. E.g., Gulley v. The Mayo Foundation, 886 F. 2d 161 (8th cir. 1989). It is more accurate to describe the communication sent to the defendant as a request for a waiver of formal service.

An individual or corporate defendant may be requested to waive service of a summons wherever or however that defendant might be served. The United States is not expected to waive service for the reason that its mail receiving facilities are inadequate to assure that the notice is actually received by the correct person in the Department of Justice. The same principle is applied to agencies, corporations, and officers of the United States and to other governments subject to service under subdivision (j). Infants or incompetent persons are likewise not required to waive service because they are not presumed to understand the request and its consequences and must generally be served through fiduciaries.

The former rule was held to limit the acknowledgment procedure to cases in which the defendant could have been served within the forum state. CASAD, JURISDICTION IN CIVIL CASES (1986 Supp.), S5-13 and cases cited. But see United States v. Union Indemnity Ins. Co., 4 F.R.Serv. 3d 578 (E.D.N.Y. 1986). As Professor Casad observed,

[G4168]

there was no reason not to use this form of service
outside the state, and there are many instances in which
it has in fact been so used.

Paragraph (d)(1) is explicit that a timely waiver of
service of a summons and complaint does not prejudice the
right of a defendant to object by means of a motion
authorized by Rule 12(b)(2) to the absence of
jurisdiction over the defendant's person, or to assert
any other defense that may be available. All that is
eliminated are issues of the sufficiency of the summons
and the sufficiency of the method by which it is served.

A defendant failing to comply with a request for
waiver shall be given an opportunity to show good cause
for the failure, but sufficient cause should be rare.
It is not a good cause for failure to waive service that
the claim is unjust or that the court lacks jurisdiction.
It would, however, be sufficient cause not to shift the
cost of service if the defendant did not receive the
request or was insufficiently literate in English to
understand it.

Because the transmission of the waiver does not
purport to effect service except by consent, the
transmission of a request for consent sent to a foreign
country gives no reasonable offense to foreign
sovereignty, even to foreign governments that have
withheld their assent to service by mail.   See
Heidenberg, Service of Process and Gathering Information
Relative to a Lawsuit Brought in West Germany, 9 INT'L
LAW 725, 78-29 (1975). Because of the unreliability of
some foreign mail services, the longer period of 60 days
is provided for a return of a notice and request for
waiver sent to a foreign country.   The time limit of
subdivision (m) is not applicable to such service.

Paragraph (d)(2) states what the present rule
implies, that there is a duty to avoid costs associated
with the service of a summons not needed to inform the
defendant regarding the commencement of an action. The
text of the rule also sets forth the requirements for a
Notice and Request for Waiver sufficient to put the
cost-shifting provision in place. These requirements are
[G4169]

illustrated in Forms 1A and 1B, which replace the former
Form 18A.

Subparagraph (d)(2)(A) is explicit that a request
for waiver of service by a corporate defendant must be
addressed to a person qualified to receive service. The
general mail rooms of large organizations cannot be
required to identify the appropriate individual recipient
for an institutional summons.

Subparagraph (d)(2)(B) permits the use of
alternatives to the United States mails in sending the
Notice and Request. While private messenger services or
electronic communications are not likely to be as
inexpensive as the mail, they may be equally reliable and
on occasion more convenient to the plaintiff. Especially
with respect to transmissions to foreign countries,
alternative means may be desirable, for in some
countries, facsimile transmission is the most efficient
means of communication. If electronic means such as
facsimile transmission are employed, the sender should
maintain a record of the transmission to assure proof of
transmission if receipt is denied, but a party receiving
such a transmission has a duty to cooperate and cannot
avoid liability for the resulting cost of formal service
if the transmission is prevented at the point of receipt.

Paragraph (d)(3) extends the time for answer to
assure that a defendant will not gain any delay by
failing to waive service of the summons. Absent this
extension, the defendant would be rewarded with
additional time for answer under Rule 12(a) if the waiver
is not returned, or if its return is postponed as long
as the Notice and Request allows.

Paragraph (d)(4) clarifies the effective date of
service when service is waived; the provision is needed
to resolve an issue arising when applicable law requires
service of process to toll the statute of limitations.
E.g., Morse v. Elmira Country Club, 752 F.2d 35 (2d Cir.
1984). Cf. Walker v. Armco Steel Corp., 446 U.S. 740
(1980). It is also important to clarify the effective
date for the purposes of Rules 12(a), 30(a), and 33(a).
[G4170]

The former provision set forth in subdivision (c)(2)(C)(ii) of this rule may have been misleading to some parties. Some plaintiffs not reading the rule carefully supposed that service of the summons by ordinary mail was effective on receipt by the defendant, not only to establish the jurisdiction of the court over the defendant's person, but to toll the statute of limitations in actions in which service of the summons was required to toll the limitations period. The revised rule is clear that no tolling effect results from the dispatch of a Notice and Request that is not returned and filed, nor can the action proceed as it could if a summons had actually been served.

State limitations law may toll an otherwise applicable statute at the time when the defendant receives notice of the action. Nevertheless, the device of requested waiver of service is not suitable to circumstances in which the statute of limitations is about to run. Unless there is ample time, the plaintiff should proceed directly to the formal methods of service identified in subdivisions (e), (f) or (h).

Requested waiver should also be avoided when the time for service under subdivision (m) will expire before the ate on which the waiver must be returned. While a

plaintiff has been allowed additional time for service in that situation, e.g., Prather v. Raymond Constr. Co., 570 F. Supp. 278 (N.D.Ga., 1983), the court could refuse a request for additional time unless the defendant appears to have evaded service pursuant to subdivision (e) or (h).

Paragraph (d)(5) is a cost-shifting provision retained from the former rule. The costs that may be imposed on the defendant could include, for example, costs of translation or the cost of the time of a process server required to make contact with a defendant residing in guarded apartment houses or residential developments. The paragraph is explicit that the costs of enforcing the cost-shifting provision are themselves recoverable from a defendant who fails to return the waiver. In the absence of such a provision, the purpose of the rule

[G4171]

would be frustrated by the cost of its enforcement, which is likely to be high in relation to the small benefit secured by the plaintiff.

Subdivision (e). This subdivision displaced the former paragraph (d)(1) and clause (c)(2)(C)(i). It provides means for the service of summons on individuals in any judicial district. Together with subdivision (f), it provides for service on persons anywhere.

Service of the summons under this subdivision does not conclusively establish the jurisdiction of the court over the person of the defendant. A defendant may invoke the territorial limits of the court's reach set forth in subdivision (k), including of course constitutional limitations that may be imposed by the Due Process Clause of the Fifth Amendment.

Paragraph (e)(1) authorizes service in any judicial district in conformity with state law. This paragraph sets forth the language of former clause (c)(2)(C)(i) which authorized the use of the law of the state in which the district court sits, but adds as an alternative the use of the law of the state in which the service is effected.

Paragraph (e)(2) retains the text of the former paragraph (d)(1) and authorizes the use of the familiar methods of personal or abode service or service on an authorized agent in any judicial district.

To conform to these provisions, the former subdivision (e) bearing on proceedings against parties not found within the state is stricken. Likewise stricken is the first sentence of the former subdivision (f) restricting the authority of the federal process server to the state in which the district court sits.

Subdivision (f). This subdivision provides for service on individuals who are in a foreign country, replacing the former subdivision (i) that was added to Rule 4 in 1963. Reflecting the pattern of Rule 4 in incorporating state-law limitations on the exercise of jurisdiction over persons, the former subdivision (i)

[G4172]

limited service outside the United States to cases in which such extraterritorial service was authorized by state or federal law. The new rule eliminates the requirement of explicit authorization. On occasion, service in a foreign country was held to be improper for lack of such statutory authority. E.g. <u>Martens v. Winder</u>, 341 F.2d 197 (9th Cir.), <u>cert. denied 382</u> U.S. 937 (1965). Such authority was, however, found to exist by implication. E.g., <u>SEC v. VTR, Inc.</u>, 39 F.R.D. 19 (S.D.N.Y. 1966). Given the substantial increase in the number of international transactions and events that are the subject of litigation in federal courts, it is appropriate to infer a general legislative authority to effect service on defendants in a foreign country.

A secondary effect of this provision for service of a federal summons in any judicial district is to facilitate the use of federal long-arm law applicable to actions brought to enforce the national law against defendants who cannot be served under local state law. Such a provision is set forth in paragraph (2) of subdivision (k) of this rule applicable only to persons not subject to the territorial jurisdiction of any state.

Paragraph (f)(1) gives effect to the Hague Convention on the Service Abroad of Judicial and Extrajudicial Documents, which entered into force for the United States on February 10, 1969. See 28 U.S.C.A., F. R. Civ. P. 4 (1986 Supp.). This Convention is an important means of dealing with problems of service in a foreign country. <u>See generally</u> RISTAU 1 INTERNATIONAL JUDICIAL ASSISTANCE 118-176 (1984). The use of the Convention is mandatory when available. See <u>Volkswagenwerk Aktiengesellschaft v. Schlunk</u>, 108 S. Ct. 722 (1988); Weis, <u>The Federal Rules and the Hague Conventions: Concerns of Conformity and Comity</u>, 50 U. PITT. L. REV. 903 (1989). Therefore, this paragraph provides that the methods of service appropriate under an applicable treaty shall be employed if available when service is to be effected outside a judicial district of the United States, and if the applicable treaty so requires. [G4173]

The Hague Service Convention furnishes safeguards against the abridgment of rights of parties through inadequate notice. Article 15 provides for verification of actual notice or a demonstration that process was served by a method prescribed by the internal laws of the foreign state before a default judgment may be entered. Article 16 of the Convention also enables the judge to extend the time for appeal after judgment if the defendant shows either a lack of adequate notice to defend or to appeal the judgment, or has disclosed a prima facie case on the merits.

The Hague Convention does not provide a time within which a Central Authority must effect service, but Article 15 does provide that alternate methods may be used if a Central Authority does not respond within six months. Generally, a Central Authority can be expected to respond much more quickly than that limit might permit, but there have been occasions when the signatory state was dilatory or refused to cooperate for substantive reasons. In such cases, resort may be had to the provision set forth in paragraph (f)(3).

Two minor changes in the text reflect the Hague Convention. First, the term "letter of request" has been added. Although these words are synonymous with "letter rogatory," "letter of request" is preferred in modern usage. The provision should not be interpreted to authorize use of a letter of request when there is in fact no treaty obligation on the receiving country to honor such a request from this country or when the United States does not extend diplomatic recognition to the foreign nation. Second, the passage formerly found in subparagraph (i)(1)(B), "when service in either case is reasonably calculated to give actual notice," has been relocated.

Paragraph (f)(2) provides alternative methods for use when internationally agreed methods are not intended to be exclusive, or where there is no international agreement applicable. It contains most of the language formerly set forth in subdivision (i) of the rule.
[G4174]

Service by methods that are violations of foreign
law are not generally authorized. Subparagraphs (A) and
(B) prescribe the more appropriate methods of conforming
to local practice or using a local authority.

Subparagraph (f)(2)(C) prescribes other methods
authorized by the former rule, and a new one set forth
in clause (iii). This clause allows American consular
and diplomatic officers to serve process in a foreign
country pursuant to State Department rules. There is a
statutory provision for this in the Foreign Sovereign
Immunities Act, 28 U.S.C. § 1608(a)(4).

Paragraph (f)(3) authorizes the court to approve
additional methods of service to be employed when
circumstances justify. In approving exceptional service
in urgent circumstances, the paragraph tracks the text
of the Hague Convention. Other circumstances that might
justify the use of additional methods include the failure
of the foreign country's Central Authority to effect
service within the six-month period provided by the
Convention, or the refusal of the Central Authority to
serve a complaint seeking punitive damages or to enforce
the antitrust laws of the United States. In such cases,
the court shall direct the method of service and may
approve means that are not authorized by international
agreement or that are contrary to foreign law. Inasmuch
as our Constitution requires that reasonable notice be
given, an earnest effort should be made to devise a
method of communication that is consistent with due
process and minimizes offense to foreign law. A court
may in some instances specially authorize use of ordinary
mail.   Cf. Levin v. Ruby Trading Corporation, 248 F.
Sup.. 537 (S.D.N.Y. 1965).

Subdivision (g). This subdivision retains the text
of the former paragraph (d)(2). Provision is made for
service upon an infant or incompetent person in a foreign
country.

Subdivision (h). This provision retains the text of
the present paragraph (d)(3), with changes reflecting
those made in subdivision (e). Provision is also
explicitly made for service on a corporation or

[G4175]

association in a foreign country as formerly provided in subdivision (i).

Frequent use should be made of the Notice and Request procedure set forth in subdivision (d) in actions against corporations. Care must be taken, however, to address the request to an individual officer or authorized agent of the corporation. It is not effective use of the Notice and Request procedure if the mail is sent undirected to the mail room of the organization.

Subdivision (i). This subdivision retains much of the text of former paragraphs (d)(4) and (5). Paragraph (i)(1) provides for service of a summons on the United States; it amends former paragraph (d)(4) to permit the United States attorney to be served by registered or certified mail. The rule does not authorize the use of the Notice and Request procedure of revised subdivision (d) when the United States is the defendant. To assure proper handling of mail in the Department of Justice, the authorized mail service must be specifically addressed to the civil process clerk of the office of the United States Attorney.

Paragraph (i)(2) replaces the former paragraph (d)(5). Paragraph (i)(3) saves the plaintiff from the hazard of losing a substantive right because of failure to comply with the complex requirements of service under this subdivision. That risk has proved to be more than nominal. E.g., Whale v. United States, 792 F. 2d 951 (9th cir. 1986). This provision may be read in connection with the provisions of subdivision (c) of Rule 15 to preclude loss of substantive rights by a plaintiff against the United States or its agencies, corporations, or officers resulting from a failure correctly to identify and serve all the persons who should be named or served in order to assert such rights.

Subdivision (j). This subdivision retains the text of the former paragraph (d)(6) without material change. The waiver-of-service provision is also inapplicable to actions against governments served pursuant to this subdivision. [G4176]

The revision adds a new paragraph (j)(1) referring to the statute governing service of a summons on a foreign state or political subdivision, the Foreign Sovereign Immunities Act of 1976, 28 U.S.C. § 1608. The caption of the subdivision reflects that change.

Subdivision (k). This subdivision replaces the former subdivision (f), with no change in the title. Paragraph (k)(1) retains the substance of the former rule in explicitly authorizing the exercise of personal jurisdiction over persons who could be reached under state long-arm law, the "100-mile bulge" provision added in 1963, or the federal interpleader act. Subparagraph (k)(1)(D) is new, but merely calls attention to federal legislation that may provide for nationwide or even world-wide service of process in cases arising under particular federal laws. Congress has provided for nationwide service of process and full exercise of territorial jurisdiction by all district courts with respect to specified federal actions. See CASAD, JURISDICTION IN CIVIL ACTIONS, chap. 5 (1983).

Paragraph (2) is new. It authorizes the exercise of territorial jurisdiction over the person of any defendant against whom is made a claim arising under any federal law if that person is subject to personal jurisdiction in no state. This addition is a companion to the amendments made in revised subdivisions (e) and (f) that provide for service of a summons and complaint anywhere in the world.

This paragraph corrects a hiatus in the enforcement of federal law. Under the former rule, a problem was presented when the defendant was a non-resident of the United States having contacts with the United States sufficient to justify the application of United States law and to satisfy federal standards of forum selection, but having insufficient contact with any single state to support jurisdiction under state long-arm legislation or meet the requirements of the Fourteenth Amendment limitation on state court territorial jurisdiction. In such cases, the defendant was shielded from the enforcement of federal law by the fortuity of a favorable

[G4177]

limitation on the power of state courts which was incorporated into the federal practice by the former rule. In this respect, the revision responds to the suggestion of the Supreme Court made in <u>Omni Capital Intern. v. Rudolf Wolff & Co., Ltd.</u>, 108 S.Ct. 404, 411 (1987). This paragraph provides a federal reach in actions not subject to such nationwide service provisions if it is needed to enable the federal courts to enforce the national law.

There remain Constitutional limitations on the exercise of territorial jurisdiction of federal courts over persons outside the United States. These arise from the Fifth Amendment rather than from the Fourteenth Amendment, which limits state-court reach and which was incorporated into federal practice by the reference to state law in the text of the former subdivision (e) that is deleted by this revision. The Fifth Amendment requires that any defendant have affiliating contacts with the United States sufficient to justify the exercise of personal jurisdiction over that party. Cf. <u>Wells Fargo & Co. v. Wells Fargo Express Co.</u>, 556 F.2d 406, 418 (9th Cir. 1977). There may also be a further Fifth Amendment constraint in that a plaintiff's forum selection might be so inconvenient to a defendant that it would be a denial of the "fair play and substantial justice" required by the due process clause, even though the defendant had significant affiliating contacts with the United States. See <u>DeJames v. Magnificent Carriers, 654 F.2d. 280, 286 n.3 (3d Cir. 1981). Compare World Wide Volkswagen Corp. v. Woodson, 444 U.S. 286, 293-294 (1980); Insurance Corp of Ireland v. Compagnie des Bauxites des Guinee, 456 U.S. 692, 702-703 (1982); Asahi Metal Indus v. Superior Court of Cal., Solano County, 107 S. Ct. 1026, 1033-1035 (1987). See generally Lusardi, Nationwide Service of Process: Due Process Limitations on the Power of the Sovereign</u>, 33 VILL. L. REV. 1 (1988).

This provision does not affect the operation of federal venue legislation. <u>See generally</u> 28 U.S.C. § 1391. Nor does it affect the operation of federal law providing for the change of venue. 28 U. S. C. §§ 1404, 1406. The availability of § 1404 providing for transfer for fairness and convenience precludes any conflict

[G4178]

between the full exercise of territorial jurisdiction
permitted by this rule and the Fifth Amendment
requirement of "fair play and substantial justice."

The district court should be especially scrupulous
to protect aliens who reside in a foreign country from
forum selections so onerous that injustice could result.
"[G]reat care and reserve should be exercised when
extending our notions of personal jurisdiction into the
international field." Asahi Metal Ind. v. Superior Court
of Cal., Solano County, 107 S. CT. 1026, 1035 (1987),
quoting United States v. First National City Bank, 379
U. S. 378, 404 (1965) (Harlan, J., dissenting).

This narrow extension of the federal reach is
inapplicable to cases in which federal jurisdiction rests
on the diversity of citizenship of the parties. This is
perhaps a necessary application of the principle of Erie
Railroad Co. v. Tompkins, 304 U.S. 64 (1938). Cf.
Arrowsmith v. United Press International, 320 F.2d 219
(2d Cir. 1963). The extension of the federal reach under
this rule is also applicable only to defendants against
whom a federal claim is made.

Subdivision (1). This subdivision assembles in one
place all the provisions of the present rule bearing on
proof of service. No material change in the rule is
effected. The provision that proof of service can be
amended by leave of court is retained from the former
subdivision (h). See generally 4A WRIGHT & MILLER,
FEDERAL PRACTICE AND PROCEDURE § 1132 (2d ed. 1987).

Subdivision (m). This subdivision retains much of
the language of the present subdivision (j).

The new subdivision explicitly provides that the
court shall allow additional time for service if there
is good cause for the plaintiff's failure to effect it
in the prescribed 120 days, and authorizes the court to
relieve a plaintiff of the consequences of an application
of this subdivision even if there is no good cause shown.
Such relief was formerly available in some cases, partly
in reliance on Rule 6(b), and it was not the purpose of
the former rule to be rigorous in the imposition of a
[G4179]

dismissal for slowness in effecting service. Relief may be justified, for example, in a case in which the applicable statute of limitations would bar the refiled action, or the defendant was evading service or concealing a defect in attempted service. E.g., Ditkof v. Owens-Illinois, Inc., 114 F. R. D. 104 (E.D.Mich. 1987). A specific instance of good cause is set forth in paragraph (i)(3) of this rule, which provides for extensions if necessary to correct oversights in compliance with the requirements of multiple service in actions against the United States or its officers, agencies, and corporations. The district court should also take care to protect pro se plaintiffs from consequences of confusion or delay attending the resolution of an in forma pauperis petition. Robinson v. America's Best Contacts and Eyeglasses, 876 F. 2d. 596 (7th cir. 1989).

The 1983 revision of this subdivision referred to the "party on whose behalf such service was required," rather than to the "plaintiff," a term used generically elsewhere in this rule to refer to any party initiating a claim against a person who is not a party to the action. To simplify the text, the revision returns to the usual practice in the rule of referring simply to "the plaintiff" even though its principles apply with equal force to defendants who may assert claims against non-parties under Rules 13(h), 14, 19, 20, or 21.

Subdivision (n). This subdivision provides for in rem and quasi-in-rem jurisdiction. Paragraph (n)(1) saves the rule from superseding 28 U.S.C. § 1655 or any similar provisions bearing on seizures or liens.

Paragraph (n)(2) provides for other uses of quasi-in-rem jurisdiction, but limits its use to necessitous circumstances. Provisional remedies may be employed as a means to secure jurisdiction over the property of a defendant whose person is not within reach of the court, but occasions for the use of this provision should be rare, as where the defendant is a fugitive or assets are in imminent danger of disappearing. Until 1963, it was not possible under Rule 4 to assert jurisdiction in a federal court over the property of a

[G4180]

defendant not personally served.   The 1963 amendment to
subdivision   (e)   authorized   the   use   of   state   law
procedures authorizing such seizures of assets as a basis
for   jurisdiction.   Given   the   liberal   availability   of
long-arm jurisdiction, the exercise of power quasi-in-rem
has become an anachronism.   Circumstances too spare to
affiliate the defendant to the forum state sufficiently
to support long-arm jurisdiction over the defendant's
person are also inadequate to support seizure of the
defendant's assets fortuitously found within the state.
<u>Shaffer v. Heitner</u>, 433 U.S. 186 (1977).

Rule 4.1   Service of Other Process

1   (a)   GENERALLY.   Process, other than a summons

2   as provided in Rule 4 or subpoena as provided in

3   Rule 45, shall be served by a United States marshal

4   or a deputy United States marshal, or by a person

5   specially appointed for that purpose, who shall

6   make proof of service as provided in Rule 4(l).

7   Such process may be served anywhere within the

8   territorial limits of the state in which the

9   district court is held, and, when authorized by a

10   statute   of   the   United   States,   beyond   the

11   territorial limits of that state.

12   (b)   ENFORCEMENT OF ORDERS: COMMITMENT FOR

13   CIVIL CONTEMPT.   An order of civil commitment of a

14   person held to be in contempt of a decree or

[G4181]

15   injunction issued to enforce the laws of the United

16   States may be served and enforced in any district.

17   Orders of civil contempt enforcing other decrees or

18   injunctions shall be served in the state in which

19   is located the court issuing the order to be

20   enforced or elsewhere within the United States if

21   not more than 100 miles from the place at which the

22   order to be enforced was issued.

COMMITTEE NOTE

This is a new rule. Its purpose is to separate those few provisions of the former Rule 4 bearing on matters other than service of a summons to allow greater textual clarity in Rule 4. Subdivision (a) contains no new language.

Subdivision (b) replaces the final clause of the penultimate sentence of the former subdivision 4(f), a clause added to the rule in 1963. The new rule provides for nationwide service of orders of civil commitment enforcing decrees or injunctions issued to compel compliance with federal law. The rule makes no change in the practice with respect to the enforcement of injunctions or decrees not involving the enforcement of federally-created rights.

Service of process is not required to notify a party of a decree or injunction, or of an order that the party show cause why that party should not be held in contempt of such an order. With respect to a party who has once been served with a summons, the service of the decree or injunction itself or of an order to show cause can be made pursuant to Rule 5. Thus, for example, an injunction may be served on a party through that person's attorney. Chagras v. United States, 369 F. 2d 643 (5th

[G4182]

cir. 1966).   The same is true for service of an order to show cause. <u>Waffenschneider v. Mackay</u>, 763 F. 2d 711 (5th cir. 1985).

The new rule does not affect the reach of the court to impose criminal contempt sanctions.   Nationwide enforcement of federal decrees and injunctions is already available with respect to criminal contempt: a federal court may effect the arrest of a criminal contemnor anywhere in the United States, 28 U.S.C. § 3041, and a contemnor when arrested may be subject to removal to the district in which punishment may be imposed. F. R. Crim. Pro. 40. Thus, the present law permits criminal contempt enforcement against a contemnor wherever that person may be found.

The effect of the revision is to provide a choice of civil or criminal contempt sanctions in those situations to which it applies. Contempt proceedings, whether civil or criminal, must be brought in the court that was allegedly defied by a contumacious act. <u>Ex parte Bradley</u>, 74 U.S. 366 (1869). This is so even if the offensive conduct or inaction occurred outside the district of the court in which the enforcement proceeding must be conducted. <u>E.g.</u>, <u>McCartney v. United States</u>, 291 Fed. 497 (8th cir.), <u>cert. denied</u> 263 U.S. 714 (1923). For this purpose, the rule as before does not distinguish between parties and other persons subject to contempt sanctions by reason of their relation or connection to parties.

Rule 5. Service and Filing of Pleadings and Other Papers

* * * * *

1   (d) FILING; CERTIFICATE OF SERVICE. All papers

2   after the complaint required to be served upon a

3   party, together with a certificate of service,

4   shall be filed with the court ~~either before service~~

[G4183]

5   ~~or~~ within a reasonable time ~~thereafter~~ <u>service</u>, but

6   the court may on motion of a party or on its own

7   initiative order that depositions upon oral

8   examination and interrogatories, requests for

9   documents, requests for admission, and answers and

10   responses thereto not be filed unless on order of

11   the court or for use in the proceeding.

12   (e) FILING WITH THE COURT DEFINED. The filing

13   of ~~pleadings and other~~ papers with the court as

14   required by these rules shall be made by filing

15   them with the clerk of the court, except that the

16   judge may permit the papers to be filed with the

17   judge, in which event the judge shall note thereon

18   the filing date and forthwith transmit them to the

19   office of the clerk. <u>Papers may be filed by</u>

20   <u>facsimile transmission if permitted by rules of the</u>

21   <u>district court, provided that the rules are</u>

22   <u>authorized by and consistent with standards</u>

23   <u>established by the Judicial Conference of the</u>

24   <u>United States. The clerk shall not refuse to</u>

25   <u>accept for filing any paper presented for that</u>

26   <u>purpose solely because it is not presented in</u>

[G4184]

27   <u>proper form as required by these rules or any local</u>

28   <u>rules or practices.</u>

COMMITTEE NOTES

<u>Subdivision (d).</u>   This subdivision is amended to require that the person making service under the rule certify that service has been effected.   Such a requirement has generally been imposed by local rule.

Having such information on file may be useful for many purposes, including proof of service if an issue arises concerning the effectiveness of the service.   The certificate will generally specify the date as well as the manner of service, but parties employing private delivery services may sometimes be unable to specify the date of delivery.   In the latter circumstance, a specification of the date of transmission of the paper to the delivery service may be sufficient for the purposes of this rule.

<u>Subdivision (e).</u> The words "<u>pleading and other</u>" are stricken as unnecessary.   Pleadings are papers within the meaning of the rule.   The revision also accommodates the development of the use of facsimile transmission for filing.

Several local district rules have directed the office of the clerk to refuse to accept for filing papers not conforming to certain requirements of form imposed by local rules or practice.   This is not a suitable role for the office of the clerk, and the practice exposes litigants to the hazards of time bars; for these reasons, such rules are proscribed by this revision.   The enforcement of these rules and of the local rules is a role for a judicial officer.   A clerk may of course advise a party or counsel that a particular instrument is not in proper form, and may be directed to so inform the court.   [G4185]

609

Rule 12.   Defenses and Objections -- When and How Presented -- By Pleading or Motion -- Motion for Judgment on Pleadings

1   (a) WHEN PRESENTED.

2   (1)   Unless   a   different   time   is

3   prescribed   in   a   statute   of   the   United

4   States, A a defendant shall serve an answer

5   (A) within 20 days after the service of

6   the   summons   and   complaint   upon   that

7   defendant, or

8   (B) if service of the summons has been

9   waived   on   request   made   pursuant   to   Rule

10   4(d), within 60 days from the date on which

11   the request of waiver was sent, or 90 days

12   from   such   date   if   the   defendant   was

13   addressed outside any judicial district of

14   the United States except when service is

15   made under Rule 4(e) and a different time is

16   prescribed in the order of court under the

17   statute of the United States or in the

18   statute or rule of court of the state.

19   (2)   A party served with a pleading

20   stating   a   cross-claim   against   that   party

[G4186]

610

21   shall serve an answer thereto within 20 days

22   after the service upon that party.   The

23   plaintiff   shall   serve   a   reply   to   a

24   counterclaim in the answer within 20 days

25   after service of the answer, or, if a reply

26   is   ordered   by   the   court,   within   20   days

27   after service of the order, unless the order

28   otherwise directs.   The United States or an

29   officer or   agency thereof shall serve an

30   answer to the complaint or to a cross-claim,

31   or a reply to a counterclaim, within 60 days

32   after the   service   upon   the   United   States

33   attorney of the pleading in which the claim

34   is asserted.

35   (3)   The service of a motion permitted

36   under this rule alters these periods of time

37   as follows, unless a different time is fixed

38   by order of the court:

39   (1 A) if the court denies the motion or

40   postpones its disposition until the trial on

41   the merits, the responsive pleading shall be

[G4187]

611

42   served within 10 days after notice of the

43   court's action; or

44   (2 B) if the court grants a motion for

45   a more definite statement, the responsive

46   pleading shall be served within 10 days

47   after the service of the more definite

48   statement.

49   * * * * * *

COMMITTEE NOTE

Subdivision (a) is revised by the addition of subparagraph (a)(1)(B) to reflect amendments to Rule 4. A defendant who waives service of process on request made pursuant to Rule 4(d) is protected against any resulting abbreviation of the time for answer. Pursuant to Rule 4(d)(3), the defendant is allowed 60 days from the date of dispatch of the notice and request, or 90 days if the defendant is addressed outside any judicial district of the United States.

The time of dispatch appears on the face of the request for waiver and is hence a date readily known to both parties. It is therefore the date used to measure the return day for the waiver form, so that the plaintiff can know on a day certain that service of process will be necessary, and is accordingly also a useful date for measuring the time for answer. The defendant who returns the waiver is given additional time for answer in order to assure that the defendant loses nothing by waiving service of process. [G4188]

The subdivision is also amended to strike a reference to a subdivision of Rule 4 that has been deleted from that rule. It is also amended to strike the reference to state law with respect to the time for answer. This amendment accords with the amendment to Rule 4 in providing nationwide uniformity with respect to the form and content of a summons: 20 days after service of the summons is the time normally required for answer wherever the district court may sit.

Rule 15. Amended and Supplemental Pleadings

* * * * *

1   (C) RELATION BACK OF AMENDMENTS. An amendment of

2   a pleading relates back to the date of the original

3   pleading when

4   (1) relation back is permitted by the law

5   that provides the statute of limitations

6   applicable to the action, or

7   (2) ~~Whenever~~ the claim or defense asserted

8   in the amended pleading arose out of the

9   conduct, transaction, or occurrence set forth or

10   attempted to be set forth in the original

11   pleading, ~~the amendment relates back to the date~~

12   ~~of the original pleading.~~ or

13   (3) ~~An~~ the amendment ~~changing~~ changes the

14   party or the naming of the party against whom a

[G4189]

15   claim is asserted ~~relates back~~ if the foregoing

16   provision <u>(2)</u> is satisfied and, within the

17   period provided by ~~law~~ <u>Rule 4(m)</u> for ~~commencing~~

18   ~~the action against~~ <u>service of the summons and</u>

19   <u>complaint,</u> the party to be brought in by

20   amendment~~, that party~~ (~~1~~ <u>A</u>) has received such

21   notice of the institution of the action that the

22   party will not be prejudiced in maintaining a

23   defense on the merits, and (~~2~~ <u>B</u>) knew or should

24   have known that, but for a mistake concerning

25   the identity of the proper party, the action

26   would have been brought against the party.

27   The delivery or mailing of process to the

28   United States Attorney, or United States

29   Attorney's designee, or the Attorney General of

30   the United States, or an agency or officer who

31   would have been a proper defendant if named,

32   satisfies the requirement of ~~clauses~~

33   <u>subparagraphs</u> (~~1~~ <u>A</u>) and (~~2~~ <u>B</u>) ~~here~~of <u>this</u>

34   <u>paragraph (3)</u> with respect to the United States

35   or any agency or officer thereof to be brought

36   into the action as a defendant.   [G4190]

* * * * *

COMMITTEE NOTE

The rule has been revised to prevent parties against whom claims are made from taking unjust advantage of otherwise inconsequential pleading errors to sustain a limitations defense.

Paragraph (c)(1). This provision is new. It is intended to make it clear that the rule does not apply to preclude any relation back that may be permitted under the applicable limitations law. Generally, the applicable limitations law will be state law. If federal jurisdiction is based on the citizenship of the parties, the primary reference is the law of the state in which the district court sits. Walker v. Armco Steel Corp., 446 U.S. 740 (1980). If federal jurisdiction is based on a federal question, the reference may be to the law of the state governing relations between the parties. E.g., Board of Regents v. Tomanio, 446 U. S. 478 (1980). In some circumstances, the controlling limitations law may be federal law. E.g., West v. Conrail, Inc. 107 S. Ct. 1538 (1987). Cf. Burlington Northern R. Co. v. Woods, 480 U. S. 1 (1987); Stewart Organization v. Ricoh, 108 S. Ct. 2239 (1988). Whatever may be the controlling body of limitations law, if that law affords a more forgiving principle of relation back than the one provided in this rule, it should be available to save the claim. Accord, Marshall v. Mulrenin, 508 F. 2d 39 (1st cir. 1974). If Schiavone v. Fortune, 106 S. Ct. 2379 (1986) implies the contrary, this paragraph is intended to make a material change in the rule.

Paragraph (c)(3). This paragraph has been revised to change the result in Schiavone v. Fortune, supra, with respect to the problem of a misnamed defendant. An intended defendant who is notified of an action within the period allowed by Rule 4(m) for service of a summons and complaint may not under the revised rule defeat the action on account of a defect in the pleading with respect to the defendant's name, provided that the requirements of clauses (A) and (B) have been met. If

[G4191]

the notice requirement is met within the Rule 4(m) period, a complaint may be amended at any time to correct a formal defect such as a misnomer or misidentification. On the basis of the text of the former rule, the Court reached a result in <u>Schiavone v. Fortune</u> that was inconsistent with the liberal pleading practices secured by Rule 8. See Bauer, Schiavone: <u>An Un-Fortune-ate Illustration of the Supreme Court's Role as Interpreter of the Federal Rules of Civil Procedure</u>, 63 NOTRE DAME L. REV. 720 (1988); Brussack, <u>Outrageous Fortune: The Case for Amending Rule 15(c) Again</u>, 61 S. CAL. L. REV. 671 (1988); Lewis, <u>The Excessive History of Federal Rule 15(c) and Its Lessons for Civil Rules Revision</u>, 86 MICH. L. REV. 1507 (1987).

In allowing a name-correcting amendment within the time allowed by Rule 4(m), this rule allows not only the 120 days specified in that rule, but also any additional time resulting from any extension ordered by the court pursuant to that rule, as may be granted, for example, if the defendant is a fugitive from service of the summons.

This revision, together with the revision of Rule 4(i) with respect to the failure of a plaintiff in an action against the United States to effect timely service on all the appropriate officials, is intended to produce results contrary to those reached in <u>Gardner v. Gartman</u>, 880 F. 2d 797 (4th cir. 1989), <u>Rys v. U. S. Postal Service</u>, 886 F. 2d 443 (1st cir. 1989), <u>Martin's Food & Liquor, Inc. v. U. S. Dept. of Agriculture</u>, 14 F. R. S. 3d 86 (N. D. Ill. 1988). <u>But cf. Montgomery v. United States Postal Service</u>, 867 F. 2d 900 (5th cir. 1989), <u>Warren v. Department of the Army</u>, 867 F. 2d 1156 (8th cir. 1989); <u>Miles v. Department of the Army</u>, 881 F. 2d 777 (9th cir. 1989), <u>Barsten v. Department of the Interior</u>, 896 F. 2d 422 (9th cir. 1990); <u>Brown v. Georgia Dept. of Revenue</u>, 881 F. 2d 1018 (11th cir. 1989).

[G4192]

Rule 16. Pretrial Conferences; Scheduling; Management

* * * * *

1   (b) SCHEDULING AND PLANNING.   Except in

2 categories of actions exempted by district court

3 rule as inappropriate, the judge, or a magistrate

4 when authorized by district court rule, shall,

5 after consulting with the attorneys for the parties

6 and any unrepresented parties, by a scheduling

7 conference, telephone, mail, or other suitable

8 means, enter a scheduling order that limits the

9 time

10   (1) to join other parties and to amend the

11 pleadings;

12   (2) to file and hear motions; and

13   (3) to complete discovery.

14 The scheduling order also may include

15   (4) the date or dates for conferences

16   before trial, a final pretrial conference, and

17   trial; and

18   (5) any other matters appropriate in the

19   circumstances of the case.

20 The order shall issue as soon as practicable but in

21 no event more than ~~120~~ 60 days after ~~filing of the~~

22 ~~complaint~~ the appearance of a defendant.   A

[G4193]

617

23   schedule shall not be modified except by leave of

24   the judge or a magistrate when authorized by

25   district court rule upon a showing of good cause.

26   (c)   SUBJECTS TO BE DISCUSSED AT PRETRIAL

27   CONFERENCES. The participants at any conference

28   under this rule may consider and take action with

29   respect to

30   (1) the formulation and simplification of

31   the issues, including the elimination of

32   frivolous claims or defenses;

33   (2) the necessity or desirability of

34   amendments to the pleadings;

35   (3) the possibility of obtaining admissions

36   of fact and of documents which will avoid

37   unnecessary proof, stipulations regarding the

38   authenticity of documents, and advance rulings

39   from the court on the admissibility of evidence;

40   (4) the avoidance of unnecessary proof and

41   of cumulative evidence;

42   (5) the identification of witnesses and

43   documents, the need and schedule for filing and

44   exchanging pretrial briefs, and the date or

45   dates for further conferences and for trial;

[G4194]

46 (6) the advisability of referring matters

47 to a magistrate or master;

48 (7) the possibility of settlement or the

49 use of extrajudicial procedures to resolve the

50 dispute;

51 (8) the form and substance of the pretrial

52 order;

53 (9) the disposition of pending motions;

54 (10) the need for adopting special

55 procedures for managing potentially difficult or

56 protracted actions that may involve complex

57 issues, multiple parties, difficult legal

58 questions, or unusual proof problems; and

59 (11) an order for a separate trial pursuant

60 to Rule 42(b) with respect to a claim,

61 counterclaim, or cross-claim or with respect to

62 any particular issue of fact arising in the

63 case;

64 (12) an order directing a party or parties

65 to present evidence early in the trial with

66 respect to a manageable issue that could on the

67 evidence be the basis for a judgment as a matter

68 of law entered pursuant to Rule 50(a) or a

[G4195]

69   judgment on partial findings pursuant to Rule

70   52(c); and

71   (1̶1̶3) such other matters as may aid in the

72   disposition of the action.

73 At least one of the attorneys for each party

74 participating in any conference before trial shall

75 have authority to enter into stipulations and to

76 make admissions regarding all matters that the

77 participants may reasonably anticipate may be

78 discussed.

79   In addition, in order to avoid unnecessary

80 costs of trial, the court may consider whether on

81 its own initiative with adequate notice

82   (14) facts or law should be summarily

83   established pursuant to Rule 56(a) to define the

84   issues remaining for trial; or

85   (15) summary judgment should be entered

86   pursuant to Rule 56(b) with respect to any

87   pending claim, counterclaim, or cross claim.

* * * * *

COMMITTEE NOTES

Subdivision (b). The purpose of this amendment is to provide an appropriate time for the initial scheduling order required by the rule. The former rule allowed 120 days from the date of filing of the complaint. This was

[G4196]

not an appropriate time because Rule 4(n) allows 120 days for service of the summons, and the scheduling order should not be made until at least one defendant has been served and appeared in the action. The revision allows only 60 days, but measures the time from the date of a defendant's appearance.

Subdivision (c). This subdivision is amended to reflect changes in Rules 50 and 56. Paragraphs (11) and (12) are added to call attention to the revision of Rule 50 and to the appropriateness of scheduling the trial to facilitate the use of the authority of the court to enter judgment as a matter of law as soon as it appears that this is the proper disposition of a claim or action.

New paragraphs (14) and (15) are added to call attention to the revision of Rule 56 and to the appropriateness of establishing facts or law that may serve to limit the needs of the parties to present proof at trial.

In combination, these provisions are intended to enable the district courts to obviate the need for long trials resulting from the needs of parties to present evidence that may be immaterial to the result.

[G4197]

Rule 24.   Intervention

* * * * *

1   (c) PROCEDURE.   A person desiring to intervene

2   shall serve a motion to intervene upon the parties

3   as provided in Rule 5.   The motion shall state the

4   grounds therefor and shall be accompanied by a

5   pleading setting forth the claim or defense for

6   which intervention is sought.   The same procedure

7   shall be followed when a statute of the United

8   States gives a right to intervene.   When the

9   constitutionality of an act of Congress affecting

10   the public interest is drawn in question in any

11   action in which the United States or an officer,

12   agency, or employee thereof is not a party, the

13   court shall notify the Attorney General of the

14   United States as provided in Title 28, U.S.C. §

15   2403. <u>When the constitutionality of any statute of</u>

16   <u>a State affecting the public interest is drawn in</u>

17   <u>question in any action in which that State or any</u>

18   <u>agency, officer, or employee thereof is not a</u>

19   <u>party, the court shall notify the attorney general</u>

20   <u>of the State as provided in Title 28, U.S.C. §</u>

[G4198]

21   2403. A party challenging the constitutionality of

22   legislation should call the attention of the court

23   to its consequential duty, but failure to do so is

24   not a waiver of any constitutional right otherwise

25   timely asserted.

COMMITTEE NOTE

Language is added to bring Rule 24(c) into conformity with the statute cited, resolving some confusion reflected in district court rules. As the text provides, counsel challenging the constitutionality of legislation in an action in which the appropriate government is not a party should call the attention of the court to its duty to notify the appropriate governmental officers. The statute imposes the burden of notification on the court, not the party making the constitutional challenge, partly in order to protect against any possible waiver of constitutional rights by parties inattentive to the need for notice. For this reason, the failure of a party to call the court's attention to the matter cannot be treated as a waiver.

Rule 26. General Provisions Governing Discovery

1   (a)   DISCOVERY METHODS.   Parties may obtain

2   discovery by one or more of the following methods:

3   depositions upon oral examination or written

4   questions; written interrogatories; production of

5   documents or things or permission to enter upon

6   land or other property, for inspection and other

[G4199]

7   purposes; physical and mental examinations; and
8   requests for admission. Discovery at a place
9   within a country having a treaty with the United
10 States applicable to such discovery shall be
11 conducted by methods authorized by the treaty
12 unless the court determines that those methods are
13 inadequate or inequitable and authorizes other
14 discovery methods not prohibited by the treaty.
15   (b) DISCOVERY SCOPE AND LIMITS.
16   * * * * *
17   (5) Claims of Privilege or Protection of
18 Trial Preparation Materials. When information
19 is withheld from discovery on a claim that it is
20 privileged or subject to protection as trial
21 preparation materials, the claim shall be made
22 expressly and shall be supported by a
23 description of the nature of the documents,
24 communications, or things not produced that is
25 sufficient to enable the demanding party to
26 contest the claim.

                  * * * * *   [G4200]

COMMITTEE NOTES

Subdivision (a). Language is added to this subdivision to reflect a policy of balanced accommodation to international agreements bearing on methods of discovery. Cf. Societe Nationale v. U. S. Dist. Ct., S. D. Iowa, 107 S. Ct. 2542, 2557-2568 (1987). Attorneys and judges should be cognizant of the adverse consequence for international relations of unduly intrusive discovery methods that offend the sensibilities of those governing other countries. See generally Weis, The Federal Rules and the Hague Conventions: Concerns of Conformity and Comity, 50 U. PITT. L. REV. 903 (1989); Alley & Prescott, Recent Developments in the United States Under the Hague Evidence Convention, 2 LEIDEN J. INT'L LAW 19 (1989). If certain methods of discovery have been approved for international use, positive international relations require that these methods be preferred, and that other methods should not be employed in discovery at places in foreign countries, at least if the approved methods are adequate to meet the need of the litigant for timely access to the information.

The rule of comity stated in this rule does not apply to discovery of documents and things from parties who are subject to the court's personal jurisdiction, and who may be required to produce such materials at the place of trial. E.g. Insurance Corp. of Ireland v. Campagnie des Bauxites, 456 U. S. 694 (1982). The rule also does not apply to the taking of depositions of parties or persons controlled by parties who may be deposed within the United States. However, comity may be employed in matters to which the requirement of the rule does not apply. Cf. Societe Nationale v. U. S. Dist. Ct., S. D. Iowa, 107 S. Ct. 2542 (1987).

Nor does the rule require comity where the discovery methods available by treaty are "inadequate or inequitable." This provision allows the court to make a discreet judgment on the facts as to the sufficiency of the internationally agreed discovery methods. Illustratively, a party should be required to make first resort under the Hague Convention despite a partial Article 23 reservation by the country in which discovery

[G4601]

is sought, but not if that country has imposed a blanket
reservation as an obstacle to discovery.

The rule also directs the court to authorize the use
of other discovery methods as may be needed to assure
that discovery is not "inequitable." International
litigants should not be placed in a favored position as
compared to American litigants similarly situated,
especially in commercial matters with respect to which
the similar American litigants may be their economic
competitors. Especially, an international litigant using
the provisions of Rule 26-37 should not be permitted to
use the Hague Convention or a similar international
agreement or even the law of the party's own country to
create obstacles to equivalent discovery by an adversary.

Indeed, the court is not precluded by the rule from
authorizing, to assure that discovery is adequate and
equitable, the use of discovery methods that may violate
the laws of another country. Cf. Societe Internationale
v. Rogers, 357 U. S. 197 (1958). Where the impediment
to discovery is imposed by public authority not at the
request of the international litigant or the non-party
from whom information is sought, accommodation may be
necessary to reconcile the requirement of this rule that
discovery be equitable to foreign law. But in no
circumstance can the court authorize discovery methods
that violate the mandate of a treaty that is the law of
the United States.

Subdivision (b). A new paragraph (b)(5) is added.
Its purpose is to provide a party whose discovery is
constrained by a claim of privilege or work product
protection with information sufficient to evaluate such
a claim and to resist if it seems unjustified. The party
claiming a privilege or protection cannot decide the
limits of that party's own entitlement.

A party receiving a discovery request who claims a
privilege or protection but fails to disclose the claim
is at risk of waiving the privilege or protection and may
be subject to sanctions under Rule 37(b)(2). A party
claiming a privilege or protection who fails to provide
adequate information about the claim to the party seeking

[G4602]

the information may be compelled to do so by motion made pursuant to Rule 37(a). Such motions and responses to motions are subject to the sanctions provisions of Rules 7 and 11.

A party receiving a discovery request that is too broad may be faced with a burdensome task to provide full information regarding all that party's claims to privilege or work product protection. Such a party is entitled to a protective order under subdivision (c) of this rule. The issue of the sufficiency of a disclosure is appropriate for resolution at a pretrial conference conducted under Rule 16(b), and may require an examination of documents in camera.

Rule 28. Persons Before Whom Depositions May Be Taken

* * * * *

1   (b)   IN FOREIGN COUNTRIES.   Subject to the

2   provisions of Rule 26(a) ~~In a foreign country~~,

3   depositions may be taken in a foreign country (1)

4   pursuant to any applicable treaty or convention, or

5   (2) pursuant to a letter of request (whether or not

6   captioned a letter rogatory), or (3) on notice

7   before a person authorized to administer oaths in

8   the place in which the examination is held, either

9   by the law thereof or by the law of the United

10   States, or (~~2~~ 4) before a person commissioned by

11   the court, and a person so commissioned shall have

[G4603]

12   the power by virtue of his commission to administer

13   any necessary oath and take testimony~~, or (3)~~

14   ~~pursuant to a letter rogatory~~. A commission or a

15   letter ~~rogatory~~ <u>of request</u> shall be issued on

16   application and notice and on terms that are just

17   and appropriate. It is not requisite to the

18   issuance of a commission or a letter ~~rogatory~~ <u>of</u>

19   <u>request</u> that the taking of the deposition in any

20   other manner is impracticable or inconvenient; and

21   both a commission and a letter ~~rogatory~~ <u>of request</u>

22   may be issued in proper cases. A notice or

23   commission may designate the person before whom the

24   deposition is to be taken either by name or by

25   descriptive title. A letter ~~rogatory~~ <u>of request</u>

26   may be addressed "To the Appropriate Authority in

27   [here name the country]." <u>When a letter of request</u>

28   <u>or any other device is used pursuant to any</u>

29   <u>applicable treaty or convention it shall be</u>

30   <u>captioned in the form prescribed by that treaty or</u>

31   <u>convention.</u> Evidence obtained in response to a

32   letter ~~rogatory~~ <u>of request</u> need not be excluded

33   merely for the reason that it is not a verbatim

[G4604]

34   transcript or that the testimony was not taken

35   under oath or for any similar departure from the

36   requirements for depositions taken within the

37   United States under these rules.

38   * * * * *

COMMITTEE NOTE

This revision is intended to make effective use of the Hague Convention on the Taking of Evidence Abroad in Civil or Commercial Matters, and of any similar treaties which the United States may enter into in the future, as sources of additional methods for taking depositions abroad. Pursuant to revised Rule 26(a), the party taking the deposition is obliged to conform to an applicable treaty or convention if an effective deposition can be taken by such internationally approved means, even though a verbatim transcript is not available or testimony cannot be taken under oath.

The term "letter of request" has been substituted in the rule for the former term, "letter rogatory" because it is the primary method provided by the Hague Convention. A letter rogatory is essentially a form of letter of request. There are several other minor changes that are designed merely to carry out the intent of the other alterations.

Rule 30. Depositions Upon Oral Examination

1   (a) WHEN DEPOSITIONS MAY BE TAKEN. After

2   commencement of the action, any party may take the

3   testimony of any person, including a party, by

[G4605]

629

4   deposition upon oral examination. Leave of court,

5   granted with or without notice, must be obtained

6   only if the plaintiff seeks to take a deposition

7   prior to the expiration of 30 days after service of

8   the summons and complaint upon any defendant or

9   ~~service made under Rule 4(e)~~, <u>if service has been</u>

10 <u>waived pursuant to Rule 4(d), 70 days after the</u>

11 <u>date on which the request for waiver was sent or</u>

12 <u>100 days if the defendant was addressed outside any</u>

13 <u>judicial district of the United States</u>, except that

14 leave is not required (1) if a defendant has served

15 a notice of taking deposition or otherwise sought

16 discovery, or (2) if special notice is given as

17 provided in subdivision (b)(2) of this rule. The

18 attendance of witnesses may be compelled by

19 subpoena as provided in Rule 45. The deposition of

20 a person confined in prison may be taken only by

21 leave of court on such terms as the court

22 prescribes.

* * * * *   [G4606]

COMMITTEE NOTE

Subdivision (a). The revision deletes the reference to Rule 4(e), a provision that has itself been deleted.

The revision also adds a provision conforming this rule to Rules 4(d) and 12(a), as amended, providing a grace period for all defendants wherever served; those who waive service, like those who are served, are protected from depositions until 10 days after the date on which the answer must be filed.

Rule 34. Production of Documents and Things and Entry Upon Land for Inspection and Other Purposes

* * * * *

1   (c) PERSONS NOT PARTIES. ~~This rule does not~~

2 ~~preclude an independent action against a person not~~

3 ~~a party for production of documents and things and~~

4 ~~permission to enter upon land~~ A person not a party

5 to the action may be compelled to produce documents

6 and things or to submit to an inspection as

7 provided in Rule 45.

COMMITTEE NOTE

This amendment reflects the change effected by revision of Rule 45 to provide for subpoenas to compel non-parties to produce documents and things and to submit to inspections of premises. The deletion of the text of the former paragraph is not intended to preclude an independent action for production of documents or things or for permission to enter upon land, but such actions may no longer be necessary in light of this revision.

[G4607]

Rule 35. Physical and Mental Examinations of Persons

1   (a) ORDER FOR EXAMINATION. When the mental or

2   physical condition (including the blood group) of

3   a party or of a person in the custody or under the

4   legal control of a party, is in controversy, the

5   court in which the action is pending may order the

6   party to submit to a physical ~~examination by a~~

7   ~~physician,~~ or mental examination by a ~~physician or~~

8   ~~psychologist~~ <u>suitably licensed or certified</u>

9   <u>examiner</u> or to produce for examination the person

10 in the party's custody or legal control. The order

11 may be made only on motion for good cause shown and

12 upon notice to the person to be examined and to all

13 parties and shall specify the time, place, manner,

14 conditions, and scope of the examination and the

15 person or persons by whom it is to be made.

16   (b)   REPORT   OF   ~~EXAMINING   PHYSICIAN   OR~~

17 ~~PSYCHOLOGIST~~ <u>EXAMINER</u>.

18   (1) If requested by the party against whom

19   an order is made under Rule 35(a) or the person

20   examined, the party causing the examination to be

21   made shall deliver to the requesting party a copy

[G4608]

632

22 of the detailed written report of the ~~examining~~
23 ~~physician or psychologist~~ examiner setting out
24 the ~~physician's~~ examiner's findings, including
25 results of all tests made, diagnoses and
26 conclusions, together with like reports of all
27 earlier examinations of the same condition.
28 After delivery the party causing the examination
29 shall be entitled upon request to receive from
30 the party against whom the order is made a like
31 report of any examination, previously or
32 thereafter made, of the same condition, unless,
33 in the case of a report of examination of a
34 person not a party, the party shows that the
35 party is unable to obtain it. The court on
36 motion may make an order against a party
37 requiring delivery of a report on such terms as
38 are just, and if an ~~physician or psychologist~~
39 examiner fails or refuses to make a report the
40 court may exclude the ~~physician~~ examiner's
41 testimony if offered at trial.
42   (2) * * * * *
43   (3) This subdivision applies to examinations
44 made by agreement of the parties, unless the
45 agreement expressly provides otherwise. This
      [G4609]

46   subdivision does not preclude discovery of a

47   report of an ~~examining physician or psychologist~~

48   examiner or the taking of a deposition of the

49   ~~physician psychologist~~ examiner in accordance

50   with the provisions of any other rule.

51   ~~(c) DEFINITIONS.   For the purpose of this rule,~~

52   ~~a psychologist is a psychologist licensed or~~

53   ~~certified by a State or the District of Columbia.~~

COMMITTEE NOTE

The revision authorizes the court to require physical or mental examinations conducted by any person who is suitably licensed or certified.

The rule was revised in 1988 by Congressional enactment to authorize mental examinations by licensed clinical pyschologists. This revision extends that amendment to include other certified or licensed professionals, such as dentists or occupational therapists, who are not physicians or clinical psychologists, but who may be well-qualified to give valuable testimony about the physical or mental condition that is the subject of dispute.

The requirement that the examiner be suitably licensed or certified is a new requirement. The court is thus expressly authorized to assess the credentials of the examiner to assure that no person is subjected to a court-ordered examination by an examiner whose testimony would be of such limited value that it would be unjust to require the person to undergo the invasion of privacy associated with the examination. This authority is not wholly new, for under the former rule, the court retained discretion to refuse to order an examination, or to restrict an examination. 8 WRIGHT & MILLER, FEDERAL PRACTICE & PROCEDURE § 2234 (1986 Supp.). The revision is intended to encourage the exercise of

[G4610]

this discretion, especially with respect to examinations by persons having narrow qualifications.

The court's responsibility to determine the suitability of the examiner's qualifications applies even to a proposed examination by a physician. If the proposed examination and testimony calls for an expertise that the proposed examiner does not have, it should not be ordered, even if the proposed examiner is a physician. The rule does not, however, require that the license or certificate be conferred by the jurisdiction in which the examination is conducted.

Rule 41. Dismissal of Actions

* * * * *

1   (b) INVOLUNTARY DISMISSAL: EFFECT THEREOF. For

2   failure of the plaintiff to prosecute or to comply

3   with these rules or any order of court, a defendant

4   may move for dismissal of an action or of any claim

5   against the defendant. ~~After the plaintiff, in an~~

6   ~~action tried by the court without a jury, has~~

7   ~~completed the presentation of evidence, the~~

8   ~~defendant, without waiving the right to offer~~

9   ~~evidence in the event the motion is not granted,~~

10   ~~may move for a dismissal on the ground that upon~~

11   ~~the facts and the law the plaintiff has shown no~~

12   ~~right to relief. The court as trier of the facts~~

13   ~~may then determine them and render judgment against~~

14   ~~the plaintiff or may decline to render any judgment~~

15   ~~until the close of all the evidence. If the court~~

[G4611]

16   ~~renders judgment on the merits against the~~
17   ~~plaintiff, the court shall make findings as~~
18   ~~provided in Rule 52(a).~~ Unless the court in its
19   order for dismissal otherwise specifies, a
20   dismissal under this subdivision and any dismissal
21   not provided for in this rule, other than a
22   dismissal for lack of jurisdiction, for improper
23   venue, or for failure to join a party under Rule
24   19, operates as an adjudication upon the merits.

* * * * *

COMMITTEE NOTE

Language is deleted that authorized the use of this rule as a means of terminating a non-jury action on the merits when the plaintiff has failed to carry a burden of proof in presenting the plaintiff's case. The device is replaced by the new provisions of Rule 52(c), which authorize entry of judgment against the defendant as well as the plaintiff, and earlier than the close of the case of the party against whom judgment is rendered. A motion to dismiss under Rule 41 on the ground that a plaintiff's evidence is legally insufficient should now be treated as a motion for judgment on partial findings as provided in Rule 52(c).

Rule 44. Proof of Official Record

1   (a) AUTHENTICATION.

2   (1) Domestic. An official record kept
3   within the United States, or any state, district,
[G4612]

4   <u>or</u> commonwealth, ~~territory, or insular possession~~

5   ~~thereof,~~ or within ~~the Panama Canal Zone, the~~

6   ~~Trust Territory of the Pacific Islands, or the~~

7   ~~Ryukyu Islands~~ <u>a territory subject to the</u>

8   <u>administrative or judicial jurisdiction of the</u>

9   <u>United States</u>, or an entry therein, when

10   admissible for any purpose, may be evidenced by

11   an official publication thereof or by a copy

12   attested by the officer having the legal custody

13   of the record, or by the officer's deputy, and

14   accompanied by a certificate that such officer

15   has the custody. The certificate may be made by

16   a judge of a court of record of the district or

17   political sub-division in which the record is

18   kept, authenticated by the seal of the court, or

19   may be made by any public officer having a seal

20   of office and having official duties in the

21   district or political subdivision in which the

22   record is kept, authenticated by the seal of the

23   officer's office.

24   (2) Foreign. A foreign official record, or

25   an entry therein, when admissible for any

26   purpose, may be evidenced by an official

27   publication thereof; or a copy thereof, attested

[G4613]

637

28   by a person authorized to make the attestation,

29   and accompanied by a final certification as to

30   the genuineness of the signature and official

31   position (i) of the attesting person, or (ii) of

32   any foreign official whose certificate of

33   genuineness of signature and official position

34   relates to the attestation or is in a chain of

35   certificates of genuineness of signature and

36   official position relating to the attestation.

37   A final certification may be made by a secretary

38   of embassy or legation, consul general, vice

39   consul, or consular agent of the United States,

40   or a diplomatic or consular official of the

41   foreign country assigned or accredited to the

42   United States. If reasonable opportunity has

43   been given to all parties to investigate the

44   authenticity and accuracy of the documents, the

45   court may, for good cause shown, (i) admit an

46   attested copy without final certification or (ii)

47   permit the foreign official record to be

48   evidenced by an attested summary with or without

49   a final certification. <u>The final certification</u>

50   <u>is unnecessary if the record and the attestation</u>

51   <u>are   certified   as   provided   in   a   treaty   or</u>

[G4614]

52   convention to which the United States and the

53   foreign country in which the official record is

54   located are parties.

* * * * *

COMMITTEE NOTE

The amendment to paragraph (a)(1) strikes the references to specific territories, two of which are no longer subject to the jurisdiction of the United States, and adds a generic term to describe governments having a relationship with the United States such that their official records should be treated as domestic records.

The amendment to paragraph (a)(2) adds a sentence to dispense with the final certification by diplomatic officers when the United States and the foreign country where the record is located are parties to a treaty or convention that abolishes or displaces the requirement. In that event the treaty or convention is to be followed. This changes the former procedure for authenticating foreign official records only with respect to records from countries that are parties to the Hague Convention Abolishing the Requirement of Legalization for Foreign Public Documents. Moreover, it does not affect the former practice of attesting the records, but only changes the method of certifying the attestation.

The Hague Public Documents Convention provides that the requirement of a final certification is abolished and replaced with a model apostille, which is to be issued by officials of the country where the records are located. See Hague Public Documents Convention, Arts. 2-4. The apostille certifies the signature, official position, and seal of the attesting officer. The authority who issues the apostille must maintain a register or card index showing the serial number of the apostille and other relevant information recorded on it. A foreign court can then check the serial number and information on the apostille with the issuing authority in order to guard against the use of fraudulent apostilles. This system provides a reliable method for maintaining the integrity of the authentication process, and the apostille can be accorded greater weight than the
[G4615]

normal authentication procedure because foreign officials are more likely to know the precise capacity under their law of the attesting officer than would an American official. See generally Comment, <u>The United States and the Hague Convention Abolishing the Requirement of Legalization for Foreign Public Documents</u>, 11 HARV. INT'L L.J. 476, 482, 488 (1970).

Rule 45.   Subpoena

1   (a) ~~FOR ATTENDANCE OF WITNESSES;~~ FORM; ISSUANCE.

2   <u>(1)</u> Every subpoena shall ~~be issued by the~~

3   ~~clerk under the seal of the court, shall~~

4   <u>(A)</u> state the name of the court <u>from</u>

5   <u>which it is issued;</u> and

6   <u>(B) state</u> the title of the action<u>, the</u>

7   <u>name of the court in which it is pending, and</u>

8   <u>its civil action number;</u> and

9   <u>(C)</u> command each person to whom it is

10   directed to attend and give testimony <u>or to</u>

11   <u>produce and permit inspection and copying of</u>

12   <u>designated books, documents or tangible</u>

13   <u>things in the possession, custody or control</u>

14   <u>of that person, or to permit inspection of</u>

15   <u>premises,</u> at a time and place therein

16   specified<u>; and</u>

17   <u>(D) set forth the text of subdivisions(c)</u>

18   <u>and (d) of this rule.</u>   [G4616]

19 A command to produce evidence or to permit
20 inspection may be joined with a command to appear
21 at trial or hearing or at deposition, or may be
22 issued separately.

23   (2) A subpoena commanding attendance at a
24 trial or hearing shall issue from the court for
25 the district in which the hearing or trial is to
26 be held. A subpoena for attendance at a
27 deposition shall issue from the court for the
28 district designated by the notice of deposition
29 as the district in which the deposition is to be
30 taken. If separate from a subpoena commanding
31 the attendance of a person, a subpoena for
32 production or inspection shall issue from the
33 court for the district in which the production or
34 inspection is to be made.

35   (3) The clerk shall issue a subpoena, ~~or a~~
36 ~~subpoena for the production of documentary~~
37 ~~evidence,~~ signed ~~and sealed~~ but otherwise in
38 blank, to a party requesting it, who shall ~~fill~~
39 complete it ~~in~~ before service. An attorney as
40 officer of the court may also issue and sign a
41 subpoena on behalf of   [G4617]

42   <u>(A) a court in which the attorney is</u>

43   <u>authorized to practice; or</u>

44   <u>(B) a court for a district in which a</u>

45   <u>deposition or production is compelled by the</u>

46   <u>subpoena, if the deposition or production</u>

47   <u>pertains to an action pending in a court in</u>

48   <u>which the attorney is authorized to practice.</u>

49   (b) ~~FOR PRODUCTION OF DOCUMENTARY EVIDENCE. A~~

50   ~~subpoena may also command the person to whom it is~~

51   ~~directed to produce the books, papers, documents, or~~

52   ~~tangible things designated therein; but the court,~~

53   ~~upon motion made promptly and in any event at or~~

54   ~~before the time specified in the subpoena for~~

55   ~~compliance therewith, may (1) quash or modify the~~

56   ~~subpoena if it is unreasonable or oppressive or (2)~~

57   ~~condition denial of the motion upon the advancement~~

58   ~~by the person in whose behalf the subpoena is~~

59   ~~issued of the reasonable cost of producing the~~

60   ~~books, papers, documents, or tangible things.~~

61   ~~(e)~~ SERVICE

62   <u>(1)</u> A subpoena may be served by ~~the marshal,~~

63   ~~a deputy marshal, or by~~ any person who is not a

64   party and is not less than 18 years of age.

65   Service of a subpoena upon a person named therein

[G4618]

66   shall be made by delivering a copy thereof to

67   such person and, if the person's attendance is

68   commanded, by tendering to that person the fees

69   for one day's attendance and the mileage allowed

70   by law. When the subpoena is issued on behalf of

71   the United States or an officer or agency

72   thereof, fees and mileage need not be tendered.

73   Prior notice of any commanded production of

74   documents and things or inspection of premises

75   before trial shall be served on each party in the

76   manner prescribed by Rule 5(b).

77   (d) SUBPOENA FOR TAKING DEPOSITIONS; PLACE OF

78   EXAMINATION.

79   (1) Proof of service of a notice to take a

80   deposition as provided in Rules 30(b) and 31(a)

81   constitutes a sufficient authorization for the

82   issuance by the clerk of the district court for

83   the district in which the deposition is to be

84   taken of subpoenas for the persons named or

85   described therein. Proof of service may be made

86   by filing with the clerk of the district court

87   for the district in which the deposition is to be

88   taken a copy of the notice together with a

89   statement of the date and manner of service and

[G4619]

90 ~~of the names of the persons served, certified by~~

91 ~~the person who made service.   The subpoena may~~

92 ~~command the person to whom it is directed to~~

93 ~~produce and permit inspection and copying of~~

94 ~~designated books, papers, documents, or tangible~~

95 ~~things which constitute or contain matters within~~

96 ~~the scope of the examination permitted by Rule~~

97 ~~26(b), but in that event the subpoena will be~~

98 ~~subject to the provisions of Rule 26(c) and~~

99 ~~subdivision (b) of this rule.~~

100 ~~The person to whom the subpoena is directed~~

101 ~~may, within 10 days after the service thereof or on~~

102 ~~or before the time specified in the subpoena for~~

103 ~~compliance if such time is less than 10 days after~~

104 ~~service, serve upon the attorney designated in the~~

105 ~~subpoena written objection to inspection or copying~~

106 ~~of any or all of the designated materials.   If~~

107 ~~objection is made, the party serving the subpoena~~

108 ~~shall not be entitled to inspect and copy the~~

109 ~~materials except pursuant to an order of the court~~

110 ~~from which the subpoena was issued.   The party~~

111 ~~serving the subpoena may, if objection has been~~

112 ~~made, move upon notice to the deponent for an order~~

[G4620]

113 ~~at any time before or during the taking of the~~

114 ~~deposition.~~

115 ~~(2) A person to whom a subpoena for the~~

116 ~~taking of a deposition is directed may be~~

117 ~~required to attend at any place within 100 miles~~

118 ~~from the place where that person resides, is~~

119 ~~employed or transacts business in person, or is~~

120 ~~served, or at such other convenient place as is~~

121 ~~fixed by an order of court.~~

122 ~~(c) SUBPOENA FOR A HEARING OR TRIAL.~~

123 ~~(1) At the request of any party subpoenas~~

124 ~~for attendance at a hearing or trial shall be~~

125 ~~issued by the clerk of the district court for the~~

126 ~~district in which the hearing or trial is held.~~

127 <u>(2) Subject to the provisions of clause (ii)</u>

128 <u>of subparagraph (c)(3)(A) of this rule,</u> ~~A~~ <u>a</u>

129 subpoena ~~requiring the attendance of a witness at~~

130 ~~a hearing or trial~~ may be served at any place

131 within the district <u>of the court by which it is</u>

132 <u>issued</u>, or at any place without the district that

133 is within 100 miles of the place of the

134 <u>deposition,</u> hearing, ~~or~~ trial, <u>production, or</u>

135 <u>inspection</u> specified in the subpoena or at any

136 place within the state where a state statute or
[G4621]

645

137   rule of court permits service of a subpoena

138   issued by a state court of general jurisdiction

139   sitting in the place ~~where the district court is~~

140   ~~held~~ of the deposition, hearing, trial,

141   production or inspection specified in the

142   subpoena. When a statute of the United States

143   provides therefor, the court upon proper

144   application and cause shown may authorize the

145   service of a subpoena at any other place.

146   ~~(2)~~ A subpoena directed to a witness in a foreign

147   country who is a national or resident of the

148   United States shall issue under the circumstances

149   and in the manner and be served as provided in

150   Title 28, U.S.C. § 1783.

151   (3) Proof of service when necessary shall be

152   made by filing with the clerk of the court by

153   which the subpoena is issued a statement of the

154   date and manner of service and of the names of

155   the persons served, certified by the person who

156   made the service.

157   (c) PROTECTION OF PERSONS SUBJECT TO SUBPOENAS.

158   (1) A party or an attorney responsible for

159   the issuance and service of a subpoena shall take

160   reasonable steps to avoid imposing undue burden

[G4622]

161 or expense on a person subject to that subpoena.

162 The court on behalf of which the subpoena was

163 issued shall enforce this duty and impose upon

164 the party or attorney in breach of this duty an

165 appropriate sanction, which may include, but is

166 not limited to, lost earnings and a reasonable

167 attorney's fee.

168   (2)(A) A person commanded to produce and

169 permit inspection and copying of designated

170 books, papers, documents or tangible things or

171 inspection of premises need not appear in person

172 at the place of production or inspection unless

173 commanded to appear for deposition, hearing or

174 trial.

175   (B) Subject to paragraph (d)(2) of this

176 rule, a person commanded to produce and permit

177 inspection and copying may, within 14 days after

178 service of the subpoena or before the time

179 specified for compliance if such time is less

180 than 14 days after service, serve upon the party

181 or attorney designated in the subpoena written

182 objection to inspection or copying of any or all

183 of the designated materials or of the premises.

184 If objection is made, the party serving the

[G4623]

185   subpoena shall not be entitled to inspect and

186   copy the materials or inspect the premises except

187   pursuant to an order of the court by which the

188   subpoena was issued. If objection has been made,

189   the party serving the subpoena may, upon notice

190   to the person commanded to produce, move at any

191   time for an order to compel the production. Such

192   an order to compel production shall protect any

193   person who is not a party or an officer of a

194   party from significant expense resulting from the

195   inspection and copying commanded.

196   (3)(A) On timely motion, the court by which

197   a subpoena was issued shall quash or modify the

198   subpoena if it

199   (i) fails to allow reasonable time for

200   compliance;

201   (ii) requires a person who is not a party

202   or an officer of a party to travel to a place

203   more than 100 miles from the place where that

204   person resides, is employed or regularly

205   transacts business in person, except that,

206   subject   to   the   provisions   of   clause

207   (c)(3)(B)(iii) of this rule, such a person

208   may in order to attend trial be commanded to

[G4624]

209   <u>travel from any such place within the state</u>

210   <u>in which the trial is held, or</u>

211   <u>(iii) requires disclosure of privileged</u>

212   <u>or other protected matter and no exception or</u>

213   <u>waiver applies, or</u>

214   <u>(iv) subjects a person to undue burden.</u>

215   <u>(B) If a subpoena</u>

216   <u>(i) requires disclosure of a trade secret</u>

217   <u>or other confidential research, development,</u>

218   <u>or commercial information, or</u>

219   <u>(ii) requires disclosure of an unretained</u>

220   <u>expert's opinion or information not</u>

221   <u>describing specific events or occurrences in</u>

222   <u>dispute and resulting from the expert's study</u>

223   <u>made not at the request of any party, or</u>

224   <u>(iii) requires a person who is not a</u>

225   <u>party or an officer of a party to incur</u>

226   <u>substantial expense to travel more than 100</u>

227   <u>miles to attend trial,</u>

228 <u>the court may, to protect a person subject to or</u>

229 <u>affected by the subpoena, quash or modify the</u>

230 <u>subpoena or, if the party in whose behalf the</u>

231 <u>subpoena is issued shows a substantial need for the</u>

232 <u>testimony or material that cannot be otherwise met</u>

[G4625]

233 without undue hardship and assures that the person

234 to whom the subpoena is addressed will be

235 reasonably compensated, the court may order

236 appearance or production only upon specified

237 conditions.

238   (d) DUTIES IN RESPONDING TO SUBPOENA.

239   (1) A person responding to a subpoena to

240   produce documents shall produce them as they are

241   kept in the usual course of business or shall

242   organize and label them to correspond with the

243   categories in the demand.

244   (2) When information subject to a subpoena

245   is withheld on a claim that it is privileged or

246   subject to protection as trial preparation

247   materials, the claim shall be made expressly and

248   shall be supported by a description of the nature

249   of the documents, communications, or things not

250   produced that is sufficient to enable the

251   demanding party to contest the claim.

252   (f e) CONTEMPT. Failure by any person without

253 adequate excuse to obey a subpoena served upon that

254 person may be deemed a contempt of the court from

255 which the subpoena issued. An adequate cause for

256 failure to obey exists when a subpoena purports to

[G4626]

257   require a non-party to attend or produce at a place

258   not within the limits provided by clause (ii) of

259   subparagraph (c)(3)(A).

COMMITTEE NOTES

   Purposes of Revision. The purposes of this revision
are (1) to clarify and enlarge the protections afforded
persons who are required to assist the court by giving
information or evidence; (2) to facilitate access outside
the deposition procedure provided by Rule 30 to documents
and other information in the possession of persons who
are not parties; (3) to facilitate service of subpoenas
for depositions or productions of evidence at places
distant from the district in which an action is
proceeding; (4) to enable the court to compel a witness
found within the state in which the court sits to attend
trial; (5) to clarify the organization of the text of the
rule.

   <u>Subdivision (a)</u>.   This subdivision is amended in
seven significant respects.

   First, Paragraph (a)(3) modifies the requirement that
a subpoena be issued by the clerk of court.   Provision
is made for the issuance of subpoenas by attorneys as
officers of the court.   This revision perhaps culminates
an evolution.   Subpoenas were long issued by specific
order of the court.   As this became a burden to the
court, general orders were made authorizing clerks to
issue subpoenas on request.   Since 1948, they have been
issued in blank by the clerk of any federal court to any
lawyer, the clerk serving as stationer to the bar.   In
allowing counsel to issue the subpoena, the rule is
merely a recognition of present reality.

   Although the subpoena is in a sense the command of
the attorney who completes the form, defiance of a
subpoena is nevertheless an act in defiance of a court
order and exposes the defiant witness to contempt
sanctions.   In <u>ICC v. Brimson</u>, 154 U.S. 447 (1894), the
Court upheld a statute directing federal courts to issue
[G4627]

subpoenas to compel testimony before the ICC.   In <u>CAB v.
Hermann</u>, 353 U.S. 322 (1957), the Court approved as
established practice the issuance of administrative
subpoenas as a matter of absolute agency right.   And in
<u>NLRB v. Warren Co.</u>, 350 U.S. 107 (1955), the Court held
that the lower court had no discretion to withhold
sanctions against a contemnor who violated such
subpoenas.   The 1948 revision of Rule 45 put the attorney
in a position similar to that of the administrative
agency, as a public officer entitled to use the court's
contempt power to investigate facts in dispute.   Two
courts of appeals have touched on the issue and have
described lawyer-issued subpoenas as mandates of the
court.   <u>Waste Conversion, Inc. v. Rollins Environmental
Services (NJ), Inc.</u>,   893 F. 2d. 605 (3d cir, 1990);
<u>Fisher v. Marubent Cotton Corp.</u>, 526 F. 2d 1338, 1340
(8th cir., 1975).   Cf. <u>Young v. United States ex rel
Vuitton et Fils S.A.</u>, 481 U. S. 787, 821 (1987)(Scalia,
J., concurring).   This revision makes the rule explicit
that the attorney acts as an officer of the court in
issuing and signing subpoenas.

Necessarily accompanying the evolution of this power
of the lawyer as officer of the court is the development
of increased responsibility and liability for the misuse
of this power.   The latter development is reflected in
the provisions of subdivision (c) of this rule, and also
in the requirement imposed by paragraph (3) of this
subdivision that the attorney issuing a subpoena must
sign it.

Second, Paragraph (a)(3) authorizes attorneys in
distant districts to serve as officers authorized to
issue commands in the name of the court.   Any attorney
permitted to represent a client in a federal court, even
one admitted pro haec vice, has the same authority as a
clerk to issue a subpoena from any federal court for the
district in which the subpoena is served and enforced.
In authorizing attorneys to issue subpoenas from distant
courts, the amended rule effectively authorizes service
of a subpoena anywhere in the United States by an
attorney representing any party.   This change is intended
to ease the administrative burdens of inter-district law
practice.   The former rule resulted in delay and expense
caused by the need to secure forms from clerks' offices
some distance from the place at which the action

[G4628]

proceeds. This change does not enlarge the burden on the witness.

Pursuant to Paragraph (a)(2), a subpoena for a deposition must still issue from the court in which the deposition or production would be compelled. Accordingly, a motion to quash such a subpoena if it overbears the limits of the subpoena power must, as under the previous rule, be presented to the court for the district in which the deposition would occur. Likewise, the court in whose name the subpoena is issued is responsible for its enforcement.

Third, in order to relieve attorneys of the need to secure an appropriate seal to affix to a subpoena issued as an officer of a distant court, the requirement that a subpoena be under seal is abolished by the provisions of Paragraph (a)(1).

Fourth, Paragraph (a)(1) authorizes the issuance of a subpoena to compel a non-party to produce evidence independent of any deposition. This revision spares the necessity of a deposition of the custodian of evidentiary material required to be produced. A party seeking additional production from a person subject to such a subpoena may serve an additional subpoena requiring additional production at the same time and place.

Fifth, Paragraph (a)(2) makes clear that the person subject to the subpoena is required to produce materials in that person's control whether or not the materials are located within the district or within the territory within which the subpoena can be served. The non-party witness is subject to the same scope of discovery under this rule as that person would be as a party to whom a request is addressed pursuant to Rule 34.

Sixth, Paragraph (a)(1) requires that the subpoena include a statement of the rights and duties of witnesses by setting forth in full the text of the new subdivisions (c) and (d).

Seventh, the revised rule authorizes the issuance of a subpoena to compel the inspection of premises in the possession of a non-party. Rule 34 has authorized such inspections of premises in the possession of a party as discovery compelled under Rule 37, but prior practice

[G4629]

required an independent proceeding to secure such relief ancillary to the federal proceeding when the premises were not in the possession of a party. Practice in some states has long authorized such use of a subpoena for this purpose without apparent adverse consequence.

Subdivision (b). Paragraph (b)(1) retains the text of the former subdivision (c) with minor changes.

The reference to the United States marshal and deputy marshal is deleted because of the infrequency of the use of these officers for this purpose. Inasmuch as these officers meet the age requirement, they may still be used if available.

A provision requiring service of prior notice pursuant to Rule 5 of compulsory pretrial production or inspection has been added to paragraph (b)(1). The purpose of such notice is to afford other parties an opportunity to object to the production or inspection, or to serve a demand for additional documents or things. Such additional notice is not needed with respect to a deposition because of the requirement of notice imposed by Rule 30 or 31. But when production or inspection is sought independently of a deposition, other parties may need notice in order to monitor the discovery and in order to pursue access to any information that may or should be produced.

Paragraph (b)(2) retains language formerly set forth in subdivision (e) and extends its application to subpoenas for depositions or production.

Paragraph (b)(3) retains language formerly set forth in paragraph (d)(1) and extends its applications to subpoenas for trial or hearing or production.

Subdivision (c). This provision is new and states the rights of witnesses. It is not intended to diminish rights conferred by Rules 26-37 or any other authority.

Paragraph (c)(1) gives specific application to the principle stated in Rule 26(g) and specifies liability for earnings lost by a non-party witness as a result of a misuse of the subpoena. No change in existing law is thereby effected. Abuse of a subpoena is an actionable tort, <u>Board of Ed. v. Farmingdale Classroom Teach. Ass'n</u>,
[G4630]

38 N.Y.2d 397, 380 N.Y.S.2d 635, 343 N.E.2d 278 (1975), and the duty of the attorney to the non-party is also embodied in Model Rule of Professional Conduct 4.4. The liability of the attorney is correlative to the expanded power of the attorney to issue subpoenas. The liability may include the cost of fees to collect attorneys' fees owed as a result of a breach of this duty.

Paragraph (c)(2) retains language from the former subdivision (b) and paragraph (d)(1). The 10-day period for response to a subpoena is extended to 14 days to avoid the complex calculations associated with short time periods under Rule 6 and to allow a bit more time for such objections to be made.

A non-party required to produce documents or materials is protected against significant expense resulting from involuntary assistance to the court. This provision applies, for example, to a non-party required to provide a list of class members. The court is not required to fix the costs in advance of production, although this will often be the most satisfactory accommodation to protect the party seeking discovery from excessive costs. In some instances, it may be preferable to leave uncertain costs to be determined after the materials have been produced, provided that the risk of uncertainty is fully disclosed to the discovering party. See, e.g., United States v. Columbia Broadcasting Systems, Inc., 666 F.2d 364 (9th Cir. 1982).

Paragraph (c)(3) explicitly authorizes the quashing of a subpoena as a means of protecting a witness from misuse of the subpoena power. It replaces and enlarges on the former subdivision (b) of this rule and tracks the provisions of Rule 26(c). While largely repetitious, this rule is addressed to the witness who may read it on the subpoena, where it is required to be printed by the revised paragraph (a)(1) of this rule.

Subparagraph (c)(3)(A) identifies those circumstances in which a subpoena must be quashed or modified. It restates the former provisions with respect to the limits of mandatory travel that are set forth in the former paragraphs (d)(2) and (e)(1), with one important change. Under the revised rule, a federal court can compel a witness to come from any place in the state to attend trial, whether or not the local state law so provides.
[G4631]

This extension is subject to the qualification provided
in the next paragraph, which authorizes the court to
condition enforcement of a subpoena compelling a
non-party witness to bear substantial expense to attend
trial. The traveling non-party witness may be entitled
to reasonable compensation for the time and effort
entailed.

Clause (c)(3)(A)(iv) requires the court to protect
all persons from undue burden imposed by the use of the
subpoena power. Illustratively, it might be unduly
burdensome to compel an adversary to attend trial as a
witness if the adversary is known to have no personal
knowledge of matters in dispute, especially so if the
adversary would be required to incur substantial travel
burdens.

Subparagraph (c)(3)(B) identifies circumstances in
which a subpoena should be quashed unless the party
serving the subpoena shows a substantial need and the
court can devise an appropriate accommodation to protect
the interests of the witness. An additional circumstance
in which such action is required is a request for costly
production of documents; that situation is expressly
governed by subparagraph (b)(2)(B).

Clause (c)(3)(B)(i) authorizes the court to quash,
modify, or condition a subpoena to protect the person
subject to or affected by the subpoena from unnecessary
or unduly harmful disclosures of confidential
information. It corresponds to Rule 26(c)(7).

Clause (c)(3)(B)(ii) provides appropriate protection
for the intellectual property of the non-party witness;
it does not apply to the expert retained by a party,
whose information is subject to the provisions of Rule
26(b)(4). A growing problem has been the use of
subpoenas to compel the giving of evidence and
information by unretained experts. Experts are not
exempt from the duty to give evidence, even if they
cannot be compelled to prepare themselves to give
effective testimony, e.g., Carter-Wallace, Inc. v. Otte,
474 F.2d 529 (2d Cir. 1972), but compulsion to give
evidence may threaten the intellectual property of
experts denied the opportunity to bargain for the value
of their services. See generally Maurer, Compelling the
Expert Witness: Fairness and Utility Under the Federal

[G4632]

Rules of Civil Procedure, 19 GA.L.REV. 71 (1984); Note, Discovery and Testimony of Unretained Experts, 1987 DUKE L.J. 140. Arguably the compulsion to testify can be regarded as a "taking" of intellectual property. The rule establishes the right of such persons to withhold their expertise, at least unless the party seeking it makes the kind of showing required for a conditional denial of a motion to quash as provided in the final sentence of subparagraph (c)(3)(B); that requirement is the same as that necessary to secure work product under Rule 26(b)(3) and gives assurance of reasonable compensation. The Rule thus approves the accommodation of competing interests exemplified in United States v. Columbia Broadcasting Systems Inc., 666 F.2d 364 (9th Cir. 1982). See also Wright v. Jeep Corporation, 547 F. Supp. 871 (E.D. Mich. 1982).

As stated in Kaufman v. Edelstein, 539 F.2d 811, 822 (2d Cir. 1976), the district court's discretion in these matters should be informed by "the degree to which the expert is being called because of his knowledge of facts relevant to the case rather than in order to give opinion testimony; the difference between testifying to a previously formed or expressed opinion and forming a new one; the possibility that, for other reasons, the witness is a unique expert; the extent to which the calling party is able to show the unlikelihood that any comparable witness will willingly testify; and the degree to which the witness is able to show that he has been oppressed by having continually to testify...."

Clause (c)(3)(B)(iii) protects non-party witnesses who may be burdened to perform the duty to travel in order to provide testimony at trial. The provision requires the court to condition a subpoena requiring travel of more than 100 miles on reasonable compensation.

Subdivision (d). This provision is new. Paragraph (d)(1) extends to non-parties the duty imposed on parties by the last paragraph of Rule 34(b), which was added in 1980.

Paragraph (d)(2) is new and corresponds to the new Rule 26(b)(5). Its purpose is to provide a party whose discovery is constrained by a claim of privilege or work product protection with information sufficient to evaluate such a claim and to resist if it seems

[G4633]

unjustified.   The   person   claiming   a   privilege   or
protection cannot decide the limits of that party's own
entitlement.

A party receiving a discovery request who asserts a
privilege or protection but fails to disclose that claim
is at risk of waiving the privilege or protection.   A
person claiming a privilege or protection who fails to
provide adequate information about the privilege or
protection claim to the party seeking the information is
subject to an order to show cause why the person should
not be held in contempt under subdivision (e).   Motions
for such orders and responses to motions are subject to
the sanctions provisions of Rules 7 and 11.

A person served a subpoena that is too broad may be
faced with a burdensome task to provide full information
regarding all that person's claims to privilege or work
product protection.   Such a person is entitled to
protection that may be secured through an objection made
pursuant to paragraph (c)(2).

Subdivision (e). This provision retains most of the
language of the former subdivision (f).

"Adequate cause" for a failure to obey a subpoena
remains undefined.   In at least some circumstances, a
non-party might be guilty of contempt for refusing to
obey a subpoena even though the subpoena manifestly
overreaches the appropriate limits of the subpoena power.
E.g., Walker v. City of Birmingham, 388 U.S. 307 (1967).
But, because the command of the subpoena is not in fact
one uttered by a judicial officer, contempt should be
very sparingly applied when the non-party witness has
been overborne by a party or attorney.   The language
added to subdivision (f) is intended to assure that
result where a non-party has been commanded, on the
signature of an attorney, to travel greater distances
than can be compelled pursuant to this rule.   [G4634]

Rule 47. Selection of Jurors

* * * * *

1   (b)   ~~ALTERNATE JURORS. The court may direct~~
2   ~~that not more than six jurors in addition to the~~
3   ~~regular jury be called and impanelled to sit as~~
4   ~~alternate jurors. Alternate jurors in the order in~~
5   ~~which they are called shall replace jurors who,~~
6   ~~prior to the time the jury retires to consider its~~
7   ~~verdict, become or are found to be unable or~~
8   ~~disqualified to perform their duties. Alternate~~
9   ~~jurors shall be drawn in the same manner, shall~~
10   ~~have the same qualifications, shall be subject to~~
11   ~~the same examination and challenges, shall take the~~
12   ~~same oath, and shall have the same functions,~~
13   ~~powers, facilities, and privileges as the regular~~
14   ~~jurors. An alternate juror who does not replace a~~
15   ~~regular juror shall be discharged after the jury~~
16   ~~retires to consider its verdict. Each side is~~
17   ~~entitled to 1 peremptory challenge in addition to~~
18   ~~those otherwise allowed by law if 1 or 2 alternate~~
19   ~~jurors are to be impanelled, 2 peremptory~~
20   ~~challenges if 3 or 4 alternate jurors are to be~~
21   ~~impanelled, and 3 peremptory challenges if 5 or 6~~
22   ~~alternate jurors are to be impanelled. The~~
[G4635]

23   ~~additional peremptory challenges may be used~~

24   ~~against an alternate juror only, and the other~~

25   ~~peremptory challengesallowed by law shall not be~~

26   ~~used against an alternate juror.~~

27   PEREMPTORY CHALLENGES. The court shall allow the

28   number of   peremptory challenges provided by 28

29   U.S. C. § 1870.

30   (c)   EXCUSE.   The   court   may   for   good   cause

31   excuse   a   juror   from   service   during   trial   or

32   deliberation.

COMMITTEE NOTE

Subdivision (b). The former provision for alternate
jurors is stricken and the institution of the alternate
juror abolished.

The   former   rule   reflected   the   long-standing
assumption that a jury would consist of exactly twelve
members.   It provided for additional jurors to be used
as substitutes for jurors who are for any reason excused
or disqualified from service after the commencement of
the   trial.   Additional   jurors   were   traditionally
designated at the outset of the trial, and excused at the
close of the evidence if they had not been promoted to
full service on account of the elimination of one of the
original jurors.

The use of alternate jurors has been a source of
dissatisfaction with the jury system because of the
burden it places on alternates who are required to listen
to   the   evidence   but   denied   the   satisfaction   of
participating in its evaluation.

Subdivision (c). This provision makes it clear that
the court may in appropriate circumstances excuse a juror
during the jury deliberations without causing a mistrial.
[G4636]

Sickness, family emergency or juror miscondct that might occasion a mistrial are examples of appropriate grounds for excusing a juror. It is not grounds for the dismissal of a juror that the juror refuses to join with fellow jurors in reaching a unanimous verdict.

Rule 48. ~~Juries of Less Than Twelve--Majority Verdict~~ **Number** of **Jurors--Participation** in Verdict

1 ~~The parties may stipulate that the jury shall~~

2 ~~consist of any number less than twelve or that a~~

3 ~~verdict or a finding of a stated majority of the~~

4 ~~jurors shall be taken as the verdict or finding of~~

5 ~~the jury.~~

6 The court shall seat a jury of not fewer than six

7 and not more than twelve members and all jurors

8 shall participate in the verdict unless excused

9 from service by the court pursuant to Rule 47(c).

10 Unless the parties otherwise stipulate, (1) the

11 verdict shall be unanimous and (2) no verdict shall

12 be taken from a jury reduced in size to fewer than

13 six members.

COMMITTEE NOTE

The former rule was rendered obsolete by the adoption in many districts of local rules establishing six as the standard size for a civil jury.

It appears that the minimum size of a jury consistent with the Seventh Amendment is six. Cf. Ballew v.
[G4637]

<u>Georgia</u>, 435 U.S. 223 (1978) (holding that a conviction based on a jury of less than six is a denial of due process of law). If the parties agree to trial before a smaller jury, a verdict can be taken, but the parties should not other than in exceptional circumstances be encouraged to waive the right to a jury of six, not only because of the constitutional stature of the right, but also because smaller juries are more erratic and less effective in serving to distribute responsibility for the exercise of judicial power.

Because the institution of the alternate juror has been abolished by the proposed revision of Rule 47, it will ordinarily be prudent and necessary, in order to provide for sickness or disability among jurors, to seat more than six jurors. The use of jurors in excess of six increases the representativeness of the jury and harms no interest of a party. <u>Ray v. Parkside Surgery Center</u>, 13 F. R. Serv. 585 (6th cir. 1989).

If the court takes the precaution of seating a jury larger than six, an illness occurring during the deliberation period will not result in a mistrial, as it did formerly, because all seated jurors will participate in the verdict and a sufficient number will remain to render a unanimous verdict of six or more.

In exceptional circumstances, as where a jury suffers depletions during trial and deliberation that are greater than can reasonably be expected, the parties may agree to be bound by a verdict rendered by fewer than six jurors. The court should not, however, rely upon the availability of such an agreement, for the use of juries smaller than six is problematic for reasons fully explained in <u>Ballew v. Georgia</u>, supra.

Rule 50. ~~Motion for a Directed Verdict and for~~ Judgment ~~Notwithstanding the Verdict~~ as a Matter of Law in Actions Tried by Jury; Alternative Motion for New Trial; Conditional Rulings

1   (a)   ~~MOTION FOR DIRECTED VERDICT: WHEN MADE;~~

2   ~~EFFECT. A party who moves for a directed verdict~~

[G4638]

3   ~~at the close of the evidence offered by an opponent~~

4   ~~may offer evidence in the event that the motion is~~

5   ~~not granted, without having reserved the right so~~

6   ~~to do and to the same extent as if the motion had~~

7   ~~not been made. A motion for a directed verdict~~

8   ~~which is not granted is not a waiver of trial by~~

9   ~~jury even though all parties to the action have~~

10 ~~moved for directed verdicts.   A motion for a~~

11 ~~directed verdict shall state the specific grounds~~

12 ~~therefor. The order of the court granting a motion~~

13 ~~for a directed verdict is effective without any~~

14 ~~assent of the jury.~~

15 <u>JUDGMENT AS A MATTER OF LAW</u>

16   <u>(1) If during a trial by jury a party has</u>

17 <u>been fully heard with respect to an issue and</u>

18 <u>there is no legally sufficient evidentiary basis</u>

19 <u>for a reasonable jury to have found for that</u>

20 <u>party with respect to that issue, the court may</u>

21 <u>grant a motion for judgment as a matter of law</u>

22 <u>against that party on any claim, counterclaim,</u>

23 <u>cross-claim, or third party claim that cannot</u>

24 <u>under the controlling law be maintained without</u>

25 <u>a favorable finding on that issue.</u>   [G4639]

26   <u>(2) Motions for judgment as a matter of law</u>

27   <u>may be made at any time before submission of the</u>

28   <u>case to the jury. Such a motion shall specify</u>

29   <u>the judgment sought and the law and the facts on</u>

30   <u>which the moving party is entitled to the</u>

31   <u>judgment.</u>

32   (b) <u>RENEWAL OF MOTION FOR JUDGMENT AFTER TRIAL;</u>

33   ALTERNATIVE MOTION FOR <u>NEW TRIAL</u> ~~JUDGMENT~~

34   ~~NOTWITHSTANDING THE VERDICT~~. Whenever a motion for

35   a ~~directed verdict~~ <u>judgment as a matter of law</u> made

36   at the close of all the evidence is denied or for

37   any reason is not granted, the court is deemed to

38   have submitted the action to the jury subject to a

39   later determination of the legal questions raised

40   by the motion. <u>Such a motion may be renewed by</u>

41   <u>service and filing</u>—~~N~~<u>n</u>ot later than 10 days after

42   entry of judgment~~, a party who has moved for a~~

43   ~~directed verdict may move to have the verdict and~~

44   ~~any judgment entered thereon set aside and to have~~

45   ~~judgment entered in accordance with the party's~~

46   ~~motion for a directed verdict; or if a verdict was~~

47   ~~not returned such party, within 10 days after the~~

48   ~~jury has been discharged, may move for judgment in~~

49   ~~accordance with the party's motion for a directed~~

[G4640]

50   ~~verdict~~. A motion for a new trial <u>under Rule 59</u>

51   may be joined with <u>a renewal of the</u> ~~this~~ motion <u>for</u>

52   <u>judgment as a matter of law</u>, or a new trial may be

53   ~~prayed for~~ <u>requested</u> in the alternative.   If a

54   verdict was returned<u>,</u> the court may<u>, in disposing</u>

55   <u>of the renewed motion,</u> allow the judgment to stand

56   or may reopen the judgment and either order a new

57   trial or direct the entry of judgment as <u>a matter</u>

58   <u>of law</u> ~~if the requested verdict had been directed~~.

59   If no verdict was returned<u>,</u> the court may<u>, in</u>

60   <u>disposing of the renewed motion,</u> direct the entry

61   of judgment as <u>a matter of law</u> ~~if the requested~~

62   ~~verdict had been directed~~ or may order a new trial.

63   (C) SAME: CONDITIONAL RULINGS ON GRANT OF MOTION

64   FOR JUDGMENT AS A MATTER OF LAW.

65   (1) If the <u>renewed</u> motion for judgment

66   ~~notwithstanding the verdict, provided for in~~

67   ~~subdivision (b) of this rule,~~ <u>as a matter of law</u>

68   is granted, the court shall also rule on the

69   motion for a new trial, if any, by determining

70   whether it should be granted if the judgment is

71   thereafter vacated or reversed, and shall specify

72   the grounds for granting or denying the motion

73   for the new trial.   If the motion for a new

                                        [G4641]

74   trial is thus conditionally granted, the order

75   thereon does not affect the finality of the

76   judgment. In case the motion for a new trial has

77   been conditionally granted and the judgment is

78   reversed on appeal, the new trial shall proceed

79   unless the appellate court has otherwise ordered.

80   In case the motion for a new trial has been

81   conditionally denied, the appellee on appeal may

82   assert error in that denial; and if the judgment

83   is reversed on appeal, subsequent proceedings

84   shall be in accordance with the order of the

85   appellate court.

86   (2) The party ~~whose verdict has been set~~

87   ~~aside on motion for judgment notwithstanding the~~

88   ~~verdict~~ against whom judgment as a matter of law

89   has been rendered may serve a motion for a new

90   trial pursuant to Rule 59 not later than 10 days

91   after entry of the judgment ~~notwithstanding the~~

92   ~~verdict~~.

93   (d) SAME: DENIAL OF MOTION FOR JUDGMENT AS A

94   MATTER OF LAW.   If the motion for judgment

95   ~~notwithstanding the verdict~~ as a matter of law is

96   denied, the party who prevailed on that motion may,

97   as appellee, assert grounds entitling the party to

[G4642]

666

98   a new trial in the event the appellate court

99   concludes that the trial court erred in denying the

100 motion for judgment ~~notwithstanding the verdict~~.

101 If the appellate court reverses the judgment,

102 nothing in this rule precludes it from determining

103 that the appellee is entitled to a new trial, or

104 from directing the trial court to determine whether

105 a new trial shall be granted.

COMMITTEE NOTE

Subdivision (a). The revision of this subdivision aims to facilitate the exercise by the court of its responsibility to assure the fidelity of its judgment to the controlling law, a responsibility imposed by the Due Process Clause of the Fifth Amendment. Cf. Galloway v. United States, 319 U. S. 372 (1943).

The revision abandons the familiar terminology of direction of verdict for several reasons. The term is misleading as a description of the relationship between judge and jury. It is also freighted with anachronisms some of which are the subject of the text of former subdivision (a) of this rule that is deleted in this revision. Thus, it should not be necessary to state in the text of this rule that a motion made pursuant to it is not a waiver of the right to jury trial, and only the antiquities of directed verdict practice suggest that it might have been. The term "judgment as a matter of law" is an almost equally familiar term and appears in the text of Rule 56; its use in Rule 50 calls attention to the relationship between the two rules. Finally, the change enables the rule to refer to preverdict and post-verdict motions with a terminology that does not conceal the common identity of two motions made at different times in the proceeding. [G4643]

If a motion is denominated a motion for directed verdict or for judgment notwithstanding the verdict, the party's error is merely formal. Such a motion should be treated as a motion for judgment as a matter of law in accordance with this rule.

Paragraph (a)(1) articulates the standard for the granting of a motion for judgment as a matter of law. It effects no change in the existing standard. That existing standard was not expressed in the former rule, but was articulated in long-standing case law. See generally Cooper, Directions for Directed Verdicts: A Compass for Federal Courts, 55 MINN. L. REV. 903 (1971). The expressed standard makes clear that action taken under the rule is a performance of the court's duty to assure enforcement of the controlling law and is not an intrusion on any responsibility for factual determinations conferred on the jury by the Seventh Amendment or any other provision of federal law. Because this standard is also used as a reference point for entry of summary judgment under 56(a), it serves to link the two related provisions.

The revision authorizes the court to perform its duty to enter judgment as a matter of law at any time during the trial, as soon as it is apparent that either party is unable to carry a burden of proof that is essential to that party's case. Thus, the second sentence of paragraph (a)(1) authorizes the court to consider a motion for judgment as a matter of law as soon as a party has completed a presentation on a fact essential to that party's case. Such early action is appropriate when economy and expedition will be served. In no event, however, should the court enter judgment against a party who has not been apprised of the materiality of the dispositive fact and been afforded an opportunity to present any available evidence bearing on that fact. In order further to facilitate the exercise of the authority provided by this rule, Rule 16 is also revised to encourage the court to schedule an order of trial that proceeds first with a presentation on an issue that is likely to be dispositive, if such an issue is identified in the course of pretrial. Such scheduling can be appropriate where the court is uncertain whether favorable action should be taken under Rule 56. Thus, the revision affords the court the alternative of denying a motion for summary judgment while scheduling a separate

[G4644]

trial of the issue under Rule 42(b) or scheduling the trial to begin with a presentation on that essential fact which the opposing party seems unlikely to be able to maintain.

Paragraph (a)(2) retains the requirement that a motion for judgment be made prior to the close of the trial, subject to renewal after a jury verdict has been rendered. The purpose of this requirement is to assure the responding party an opportunity to cure any deficiency in that party's proof that may have been overlooked until called to the party's attention by a late motion for judgment. Cf. Farley Transp. Co. v. Santa Fe Trail Transp. Co., 786 F.2d 1342 (9th Cir. 1986) ("If the moving party is then permitted to make a later attack on the evidence through a motion for judgment notwithstanding the verdict or an appeal, the opposing party may be prejudiced by having lost the opportunity to present additional evidence before the case was submitted to the jury"); Benson v. Allphin, 786 F.2d 268 (7th Cir. 1986) ("the motion for directed verdict at the close of all the evidence provides the nonmovant an opportunity to do what he can to remedy the deficiencies in his case ..."); McLaughlin v. The Fellows Gear Shaper Co., 4 F.R.Serv. 3d 607 (3d Cir. 1986) (per Adams, J., dissenting: "This Rule serves important practical purposes in ensuring that neither party is precluded from presenting the most persuasive case possible and in preventing unfair surprise after a matter has been submitted to the jury"). At one time, this requirement was held to be of constitutional stature, being compelled by the Seventh Amendment. Cf. Slocum v New York Insurance Co., 228 U.S. 364 (1913). But cf. Baltimore & Carolina Line v. Redman, 295 U.S. 654 (1935).

The second sentence of paragraph (a)(2) does impose a requirement that the moving party articulate the basis on which a judgment as a matter of law might be rendered. The articulation is necessary to achieve the purpose of the requirement that the motion be made before the case is submitted to the jury, so that the responding party may seek to correct any overlooked deficiencies in the proof. The revision thus alters the result in cases in which courts have used various techniques to avoid the requirement that a motion for a directed verdict be made as a predicate to a motion for judgment notwithstanding the verdict. E.g., Benson v. Allphin, 788 F. 2d. 268
[G4645]

(7th cir. 1986) ("this circuit has allowed something less than a formal motion for directed verdict to preserve a party's right to move for judgment notwithstanding the verdict"). <u>See generally</u> 9 WRIGHT & MILLER, FEDERAL PRACTICE AND PROCEDURE § 2537 (1971 and Supp.). The information required with the motion may be supplied by explicit reference to materials and argument previously supplied to the court.

This subdivision deals only with the entry of judgment and not with the resolution of particular factual issues as a matter of law. The court may, as before, properly refuse to instruct a jury to decide an issue if a reasonable jury could on the evidence presented decide that issue in only one way.

<u>Subdivision (b)</u>. This provision retains the concept of the former rule that the post-verdict motion is a renewal of an earlier motion made at the close of the evidence. One purpose of this concept was to avoid any question arising under the Seventh Amendment. <u>Montgomery Ward & Co. v. Duncan</u>, 311 U.S. 243 (1940). It remains useful as a means of defining the appropriate issue posed by the post-verdict motion. A post-trial motion for judgment can be granted only on grounds advanced in the pre-verdict motion. <u>E.g., Kutner Buick, Inc. v. American Motors Corp.</u>, 848 F. 2d 614 (3d cir. 1989).

Often it appears to the court or to the moving party that a motion for judgment as a matter of law made at the close of the evidence should be reserved for a post-verdict decision. This is so because a jury verdict for the moving party moots the issue and because a preverdict ruling gambles that a reversal may result in a new trial that might have been avoided. For these reasons, the court may often wisely decline to rule on a motion for judgment as a matter of law made at the close of the evidence, and it is not inappropriate for the moving party to suggest such a postponement of the ruling until after the verdict has been rendered.

In ruling on such a motion, the court should disregard any jury determination for which there is no legally sufficient evidentiary basis enabling a reasonable jury to make it. The court may then decide such issues as a matter of law and enter judgment if all other material issues have been decided by the jury on

[G4646]

the basis of legally sufficient evidence, or by the court as a matter of law.

The revised rule is intended for use in this manner with Rule 49. Thus, the court may combine facts established as a matter of law either before trial under Rule 56 or at trial on the basis of the evidence presented with other facts determined by the jury under instructions provided under Rule 49 to support a proper judgment under this rule.

This provision also retains the former requirement that a post-trial motion under the rule must be made within 10 days after entry of a contrary judgment. The renewed motion must be served and filed as provided by Rule 5. A purpose of this requirement is to meet the requirements of F. R. App. P. 4(a)(4).

Subdivision (c). Revision of this subdivision conforms the language to the change in diction set forth in subdivision (a) of this revised rule.

Subdivision (d). Revision of this subdivision conforms the language to that of the previous subdivisions.

Rule 52. Findings by the Court; Judgment on Partial Findings

1   (a) EFFECT. In all actions tried upon the facts

2   without a jury or with an advisory jury, the court

3   shall find the facts specially and state separately

4   its conclusions of law thereon, and judgment shall

5   be entered pursuant to Rule 58; and in granting or

6   refusing interlocutory injunctions the court shall

7   similarly set forth the findings of fact and

8   conclusions of law which constitute the grounds of

9   its action. Requests for findings are not

[G4647]

10   necessary for purposes of review.   Findings of

11   fact, whether based on oral or documentary

12   evidence, shall not be set aside unless clearly

13   erroneous, and due regard shall be given to the

14   opportunity of the trial court to judge of the

15   credibility of the witnesses.   The findings of a

16   master, to the extent that the court adopts them,

17   shall be considered as the findings of the court.

18   It will be sufficient if the findings of fact and

19   conclusions of law are stated orally and recorded

20   in open court following the close of the evidence

21   or appear in an opinion or memorandum of decision

22   filed by the court.   Findings of fact and

23   conclusions of law are unnecessary on decisions of

24   motions under Rule 12 or 56 or any other motion

25   except as provided in ~~Rule 41(b)~~ subdivision (c) of

26   this rule.

27   (b) AMENDMENT.* * * * *

28   (c) JUDGMENT ON PARTIAL FINDINGS.   If during a

29   trial without a jury a party has been fully heard

30   with respect to an issue and the court finds

31   against the party on that issue, the court may

32   enter judgment as a matter of law against that

33   party on any claim, counterclaim, cross-claim or

[G4648]

34 <u>third-party claim that cannot under the controlling</u>

35 <u>law be maintained or defeated without a favorable</u>

36 <u>finding on that issue, or the court may decline to</u>

37 <u>render any judgment until the close of all the</u>

38 <u>evidence. Such a judgment shall be supported by</u>

39 <u>findings of fact and conclusions of law as required</u>

40 <u>by subdivision (a) of this rule.</u>

COMMITTEE NOTE

Subdivision (c) is added. It parallels the revised Rule 50(a), but is applicable to non-jury trials. It authorizes the court to enter judgment at any time that it can appropriately make a dispositive finding of fact on the evidence.

The new subdivision replaces part of Rule 41(b), which formerly authorized a dismissal at the close of the plaintiff's case if the plaintiff had failed to carry an essential burden of proof. Accordingly, the reference to Rule 41 formerly made in subdivision (a) of this rule is deleted.

As under the former Rule 41(b), the court retains discretion to enter no judgment prior to the close of the evidence.

Judgment entered under this rule differs from a summary judgment under Rule 56 in the nature of the evaluation made by the court. A judgment on partial findings is made after the court has heard all the evidence bearing on the crucial issue of fact, and the finding is reversible only if the appellate court finds it to be "clearly erroneous." A summary judgment, in contrast, is made on the basis of facts established on account of the absence of contrary evidence or presumptions; such establishments of fact are rulings on

[G4649]

questions of law as provided in Rule 56(a) and are not shielded by the "clear error" standard of review.

Rule 53. Masters

* * * * *

1   (e) REPORT.

2   (1) Contents and Filing. The master shall

3   prepare a report upon the matters submitted to

4   the master by the order of reference and, if

5   required to make findings of fact and conclusions

6   of law, the master shall set them forth in the

7   report. The master shall file the report with

8   the clerk of the court and serve on all parties

9   notice of the filing. I~~i~~n an action to be tried

10   without a jury, unless otherwise directed by the

11   order of reference, the master shall file with ~~it~~

12   the report a transcript of the proceedings and of

13   the evidence and the original exhibits. ~~The~~

14   ~~clerk shall forthwith mail to all parties notice~~

15   ~~of the filing.~~ Unless otherwise directed by the

16   order of reference, the master shall serve a copy

17   of the report on each party.

* * * * *   [G4650]

COMMITTEE NOTE

The purpose of the revision is to expedite proceedings before a master. The former rule required only a filing of the master's report, with the clerk then notifying the parties of the filing. To receive a copy, a party would then be required to secure it from the clerk. By transmitting directly to the parties, the master can save some efforts of counsel. Some local rules have previously required such action by the master.

Rule 63. ~~Disability~~ Inability of a Judge to Proceed

1 If ~~by reason of death, sickness or other~~
2 ~~disability, a judge before whom an action has been~~
3 ~~tried~~ a trial or hearing has been commenced and the
4 judge is unable to ~~perform the duties to be~~
5 ~~performed by the court under these rules~~ proceed,
6 ~~after a verdict is returned or findings of fact and~~
7 ~~conclusions of law are filed, then~~ any other judge
8 ~~regularly sitting in or assigned to the court in~~
9 ~~which the action was tried~~ may ~~perform those~~
10 ~~duties;~~ proceed with it ~~but if such other judge is~~
11 ~~satisfied that such other judge cannot perform~~
12 ~~those duties because such other judge did not~~
13 ~~preside at the trial or for any other reason, such~~
14 ~~other judge may in such other judge's discretion~~
15 ~~grant a new trial~~ upon certifying familiarity with
16 the record and determining that the proceedings in

[G4651]

675

17   the case may be completed without prejudice to the

18   parties. In a hearing or trial without a jury, the

19   successor judge shall at the request of a party

20   recall any witness whose testimony is material and

21   disputed and who is available to testify again

22   without undue burden. The successor judge may also

23   recall any other witness.

COMMITTEE NOTE

The revision substantially displaces the former rule. The former rule was limited to the disability of the judge, and made no provision for disqualification or possible other reasons for the withdrawal of the judge during proceedings.   In making provision for other circumstances, the revision is not intended to encourage judges to discontinue participation in a trial for any but compelling reasons. Cf. United States v. Lane, 708 F. 2d 1394, 1395-1397 (9th cir. 1983).   Manifestly, a substitution should not be made for the personal convenience of the court, and the reasons for a substitution should be stated on the record.

The former rule made no provision for the withdrawal of the judge during the trial, but was limited to disqualification after trial. Several courts concluded that the text of the former rule prohibited substitution of a new judge prior to the points described in the rule, thus requiring a new trial, whether or not a fair disposition was within reach of a substitute judge. E.g., Whalen v. Ford Motor Credit Co., 684 F.2d 272 (4th Cir. 1982, en banc) cert. denied, 459 U.S. 910 (1982) (jury trial); Arrow-Hart, Inc. v. Philip Carey Co., 552 F.2d 711 (6th Cir. 1977) (non-jury trial). See generally Comment, The Case of the Dead Judge: Fed.R.Civ.P. 63: Whalen v. Ford Motor Credit Co., 67 MINN. L. REV. 827 (1983).

The increasing length of federal trials has made it likely that the number of trials interrupted by the

[G4652]

disability of the judge will increase. An efficient mechanism for completing these cases without unfairness is needed to prevent unnecessary expense and delay. To avoid the injustice that may result if the substitute judge proceeds despite unfamiliarity with the action, the new Rule provides, in language similar to Federal Rule of Criminal Procedure 25(a), that the successor judge must certify familiarity with the record and determine that the case may be completed before that judge without prejudice to the parties. This will necessarily require that there be available a transcript or a videotape of the proceedings prior to substitution. If there has been a long but incomplete jury trial, the prompt availability of the transcript or videotape is crucial to the effective use of this rule, for the jury cannot long be held while an extensive transcript is prepared without prejudice to one or all parties.

The revised text authorizes the substitute judge to make a finding of fact at a bench trial based on evidence heard by a different judge. This may be appropriate in limited circumstances. First, if a witness has become unavailable, the testimony recorded at trial can be considered by the successor judge pursuant to F. R. Ev. 804, being equivalent to a recorded deposition available for use at trial pursuant to Rule 32. For this purpose, a witness who is no longer subject to a subpoena to compel testimony at trial is unavailable. Secondly, the successor judge may determine that particular testimony is not material or is not disputed, and so need not be reheard. The propriety of proceeding in this manner may be marginally affected by the availability of a videotape record; a judge who has reviewed a trial on videotape may be entitled to greater confidence in his or her ability to proceed.

The court would, however, risk error to determine the credibility of a witness not seen or heard who is available to be recalled. Cf. <u>Anderson v. City of Bessemer City NC</u>, 470 U. S. 564, 575 (1985); <u>Marshall v. Jerrico Inc</u>, 446 U. S. 238, 242 (1980). See also <u>United States v. Radatz</u>, 447 U.S. 667 (1980).   [G4653]

VIII.   PROVISIONAL AND FINAL REMEDIES ~~AND SPECIAL~~
             ~~PROCEEDINGS~~

COMMITTEE NOTE

The purpose of the revision is to divide this chapter
of the Rules into two. No substantive change is
effected.

IX.   SPECIAL PROCEEDINGS

Committee Note

This chapter heading is to be inserted between Rule
71 and Rule 71A.

Rule 71A.   Condemnation Of Property

* * * * *

1   (d) PROCESS.

2   * * * * *

3   (3) Service of Notice.

4   (i) Personal Service.   Personal service

5   of the notice (but without copies of the

6   complaint) shall be made in accordance with Rule

7   4 ~~(c) and (d)~~ upon a defendant who resides within

8   the United States or its territories or insular

9   possessions and whose residence is known.

10   * * * * *   [G4654]

11   (4) Return; Amendment. Proof of service of

12   the notice shall be made and amendment of the

13   notice or proof of its service allowed in the

14   manner provided for the return and amendment of

15   the summons under Rule 4 ~~(g) and (h)~~.

* * * * *

COMMITTEE NOTE

   The references to the subdivisions of Rule 4 are
deleted in light of the revision of that rule.

   Rule 72. Magistrates; Pretrial Orders

1   (a)   NONDISPOSITIVE MATTERS.   A magistrate to

2   whom a pretrial matter not dispositive of a claim

3   or defense of a party is referred to hear and

4   determine shall promptly conduct such proceedings

5   as are required and when appropriate enter into the

6   record   a   written   order   setting   forth   the

7   disposition of the matter. <u>Within 10 days after</u>

8   <u>being served with a copy of the magistrate's order,</u>

9   <u>a party may serve and file objections to the order;</u>

10   <u>a party may not thereafter assign as error a defect</u>

11   <u>in the magistrate's order to which objection was</u>

12   <u>not timely made.</u> The district judge to whom the

[G4655]

13   case is assigned shall consider <u>such</u> objections

14   ~~made by the parties, provided they are served and~~

15   ~~filed within 10 days after entry of the order,~~ and

16   shall modify or set aside any portion of the

17   magistrate's order found to be clearly erroneous or

18   contrary to law.

* * * * *

COMMITTEE NOTE

This amendment is intended to eliminate a discrepancy in measuring the 10 days for serving and filing objections to a magistrate's action under subdivisions (a) and (b) of this Rule. The rule as promulgated in 1983 required objections to the magistrate's handling of nondispositive matters to be served and filed within 10 days of entry of the order, but required objections to dispositive motions to be made within 10 days of being served with a copy of the recommended disposition. Subdivision (a) is here amended to conform to subdivision (b) to avoid any confusion or technical defaults, particularly in connection with magistrate orders that rule on both dispositive and nondispositive matters.

The amendment is also intended to assure that objections to magistrate's orders that are not timely made shall not be considered. <u>Compare</u> Rule 51.

Rule 77. District Courts and Clerks

* * * * *

(d) NOTICE OF ORDER OR JUDGMENTS.

1   Immediately upon the entry of an order or judgment

2   the clerk shall serve a notice of the entry by mail

3   in the manner provided for in Rule 5 upon each

[G4656]

4   party who is not in default for failure to appear,

5   and shall make a note in the docket of the mailing.

6   ~~Such mailing is sufficient notice for all purposes~~

7   ~~for which notice of the entry of an order is~~

8   ~~required by these rules; but~~ a̶Any party may in

9   addition serve a notice of such entry in the manner

10 provided in Rule 5 for the service of papers. Lack

11 of notice of the entry by the clerk does not affect

12 the time to appeal or relieve or authorize the

13 court to relieve a party for failure to appeal

14 within the time allowed, except as permitted in

15 Rule 4(a) of the Federal Rules of Appellate

16 Procedure.

COMMITTEE NOTE

This revision is a companion to the concurrent amendment to Rule 4 of the Federal Rules of Appellate Procedure. The purpose of the revisions is to permit district courts to ease strict sanctions now imposed on appellants whose notices of appeal are filed late because of their failure to receive notice of entry of a judgment. See, e.g. Tucker v. Commonwealth Land Title Ins. Co., 800 F.2d 1054 (11th Cir. 1986); Ashby Enterprises, Ltd. v. Weitzman, Dym & Associates, 780 F.2d 1043 (D.C. Cir. 1986); In re OPM Leasing Services, Inc., 769 F.2d 911 (2d Cir. 1985); Spika v. Village of Lombard, Ill., 763 F.2d 282 (7th Cir. 1985); Hall v. Community Mental Health Center of Beaver County, 772 F.2d 42 (3d Cir. 1985); Wilson v. Atwood v. Stark, 725 F.2d 255 (5th Cir. en banc), cert dismissed, 105 S.Ct. 17 (1984); Case v. BASF Wyandotte, 727 F.2d 1034 (Fed. Cir. 1984), cert. denied, 105 S.Ct. 386 (1984); Hensley v. Chesapeake &

[G4657]

Ohio R.R.Co., 651 F.2d 226 (4th Cir. 1981); Buckeye Cellulose Corp. v. Electric Construction Co., 569 F.2d 1036 (8th Cir. 1978).

Failure to receive notice may have increased in frequency with the growth in the caseload in the clerks' offices. The present strict rule imposes a duty on counsel to maintain contact with the court while a case is under submission. Such contact is more difficult to maintain if counsel is outside the district, as is increasingly common, and can be a burden to the court as well as counsel.

The effect of the revisions is to place a burden on prevailing parties who desire certainty that the time for appeal is running. Such parties can take the initiative to assure that their adversaries receive effective notice. An appropriate procedure for such notice is provided in Rule 5.

The revised rule lightens the responsibility but not the workload of the clerk's offices, for the duty of that office to give notice of entry of judgment must be maintained. [G4658]

APPENDIX OF FORMS

* * * * *

Form 1A. Notice of Lawsuit and Request for Waiver of
Service of Summons

To: [Fill in the name of the person to be served by a
summons if service is necessary], on behalf of
---------[Name of any entity on whose behalf that person
may be notified of the action].

A lawsuit has been commenced against [you or the
entity on whose behalf you are addressed]. A copy of the
complaint is attached to this notice. It has been filed
in [name of district court]. It has been assigned docket
number ----.

The purpose of this Notice and Request is to save the
cost of service on you of a summons in that action. I
hereby request that you sign the enclosed waiver. The
cost of service will be avoided if I receive a signed
copy of this form before ------------ [at least 30 days
after the date designated below as the date on which this
Notice and Request is sent, or 60 days if addressee is

[G4659]

683

not in any judicial district of the United States].   I
enclose a stamped and addressed envelope [or other means
of cost-free return] for your use.   An extra copy of the
waiver is also attached for your records.

   If you comply with this request and return this form,
it will be filed with the court and no summons will be
served on you, but the action will proceed as if you had
been served on the date of filing.   You will not be
required to answer the complaint until ------- [60 days
from the date designated below as the date on which this
notice is sent, or 90 days if the addressee is not in any
judicial district].

   If you do not comply, I will effect service in a
manner authorized by the Federal Rules of Civil Procedure
and will ask the court to require you [or the party on
whose behalf you are served] to pay the full costs of
such service.   In that connection, please read the
statement of your duty to waive the service of the
summons which is set forth in officially prescribed
language on the reverse side   [or at the foot]   of the
waiver form.   [G4660]

I affirm that this request is being sent to you on behalf of the claimant this ------- day of -----, 19--.

Signature of Plaintiff's Attorney

Form 1B.   Waiver of Service of Summons

TO: [plaintiff's name and address]

I acknowledge receipt of your request that I waive service of a summons in the action of ---------- [caption of action] which is case number ------ [docket number] on the docket of the United States District Court for the -----------[name of district].   I have also received a copy of the complaint in the action, two copies of an instrument by which I can waive service of a summons and which formally explains the Duty to Waive Service, and a means by which I can return the signed waiver to you without cost to me.

I agree to save the cost of service on me of a summons and an additional copy of the complaint in this lawsuit

[G4661]

and I do not require that you serve me in the manner provided by Rule 4.

I retain any defenses or objections I [or the entity on whose behalf I am addressed] may have to the lawsuit or the jurisdiction or venue of the court except any defense based on a defect in the summons or in the service of the summons.

I understand that a judgment may be entered against me [or the party on whose behalf I am addressed] if I do not answer the complaint within the time allowed by Rule 12(a) of the Federal Rules of Civil Procedure, but that on no account will a judgment be entered before the date specified for my answer in your request for this waiver.

Signature of Addressee

Date:-----------------

Relationship to Defendant, if responding on behalf of an entity:--------------

To be printed on reverse side of the waiver form provided by the Administrative Office of the United States Courts, or set forth at the foot of the waiver instrument if the form is not used: [G4662]

THE DUTY TO WAIVE SERVICE OF A SUMMONS

Rule 4 of the Federal Rules of Civil Procedure requires all parties to cooperate in saving the cost of service of the summons and complaint. A defendant who is notified of an action and asked for a waiver of service of a summons will be required to bear the cost of such service unless good cause be shown for the failure to sign such a waiver.

It is not good cause for a failure to waive service that a party believes that the complaint is unfounded or that the action has been brought in an improper place or in a court that lacks jurisdiction over the subject matter of the action or over your person or property. A party who waives service of the summons retains any defenses or objections except any that might relate to the summons or to the service of the summons and complaint, and may later object to the jurisdiction of the court or the place where the action has been brought.

[G4663]

A defendant who waives service of a summons must serve on the plaintiff an answer to the complaint. The answer should also be filed with the court. If the answer is not served within the time allowed by Rule 12(a), a default judgment may be taken against that defendant. A defendant is allowed more time to answer if service is waived than if the summons is actually served.

COMMITTEE NOTE

These Forms 1A and 1B reflect the revision of Rule 4. They replace Form 18-A.

Form 18-A. [Abrogated]

[G4664]

SUPPLEMENTAL RULES FOR CERTAIN ADMIRALTY AND MARITIME CLAIMS

* * * * *

RULE C.   Actions in Rem: Special Provisions

* * * * *

1   (3)   JUDICIAL AUTHORIZATION AND PROCESS.   Except

2   in actions by the United States for forfeitures or

3   federal   statutory   violations,   the   verified

4   complaint and any supporting papers shall be

5   reviewed by the court and, if the conditions for an

6   action is rem appear to exist, an order so stating

7   and authorizing a warrant for the arrest of the

8   vessel or other property that is the subject of the

9   action shall issue and be delivered to the clerk

10   who shall prepare the warrant ~~and deliver it~~.   If

11   the property is a vessel or a vessel and tangible

12   property on board the vessel, the warrant shall be

13   delivered to the marshal for service.   If other

14   property, tangible or intangible is the subject of

15   the action, the warrant shall be delivered by the

16   clerk to a person or organization authorized to

[G4665]

17   <u>enforce it, who may be a marshal, a person or</u>

18   <u>organization contracted with by the United States,</u>

19   <u>a person specially appointed by the court for that</u>

20   <u>purpose, or, if the action is brought by the United</u>

21   <u>States, any officer or employee of the United</u>

22   <u>States.</u> If the property that is the subject of the

23   action consists in whole or in part of freight, or

24   the proceeds of property sold, or other intangible

25   property, the clerk shall issue a summons directing

26   any person having control of the funds to show

27   cause why they should not be paid into court to

28   abide the judgment. Supplemental process enforcing

29   the court's order may be issued by the clerk upon

30   application without further order of the court. If

31   the plaintiff or the plaintiff's attorney certifies

32   that exigent circumstances make review by the court

33   impracticable, the clerk shall issue a summons and

34   warrant for the arrest and the plaintiff shall have

35   the burden on a post-arrest hearing under Rule

36   E(4)(f) to show that exigent circumstances existed.

37   In actions by the United States for forfeitures for

38   federal statutory violations, the clerk, upon
                                                    [G4666]

39   filing of the complaint, shall forthwith issue a

40   summons and warrant for the arrest of the vessel or

41   other property without requiring a certification of

42   exigent circumstances.

43   * * * * *

44   (5) ANCILLARY PROCESS. In any action in rem in

45   which process has been served as provided by this

46   rule, if any part of the property that is the

47   subject of the action has not been brought within

48   the control of the court because it has been

49   removed or sold, or because it is intangible

50   property in the hands of a person who has not been

51   served with process, the court may, on motion,

52   order any person having possession or control of

53   such property or its proceeds to show cause why it

54   should not be delivered into the custody of the

55   marshal or other person or organization having a

56   warrant for the arrest of the property, or paid

57   into court to abide the judgment; and, after

58   hearing, the court may enter such judgment as law

59   and justice may require.   [G4667]

COMMITTEE NOTE

These amendments are designed to conform the rule to Fed.R.Civ.P. 4, as amended. As with recent amendments to Rule 4, it is intended to relieve the Marshals Service of the burden of using its limited personnel and facilities for execution of process in routine circumstances. Doing so may involve a contractual arrangement with a person or organization retained by the govnernment to perform these services, or the use of other government officers and employees, or the special appointment by the court of persons available to perform suitably.

The seizure of a vessel, with or without cargo, remains a task assigned to the Marshal. Successful arrest of a vessel frequently requires the enforcement presence of an armed government official and the cooperation of the United States Coast Guard and other governmental authorities. If the marshal is called upon to seize the vessel, it is expected that the same officer will also be responsible for the seizure of any property on board the vessel at the time of seizure that is to be the object of arrest or attachment.

RULE E. Actions in Rem and Quasi in Rem: General Provisions

* * * * *

1   (4) EXECUTION OF PROCESS; MARSHAL'S RETURN;

2   CUSTODY OF PROPERTY; PROCEDURES FOR RELEASE.

3   (a) In General. Upon issuance and

4   delivery of the process, or, in the case of

5   summons with process of attachment and

6   garnishment, when it appears that the defendant

[G4668]

7   cannot be found within the district, the

8   marshal <u>or other person or organization having</u>

9   <u>a warrant</u> shall forthwith execute the process

10   in accordance with this subdivision (4), making

11   due and prompt return.

12   (b) Tangible Property. If tangible

13   property is to be attached or arrested, the

14   marshal <u>or other person or organization having</u>

15   <u>the warrant</u> shall take it into the marshal's

16   possession for safe custody. If the character

17   or situation of the property is such that the

18   taking of actual possession is impracticable,

19   the marshal <u>or other person executing the</u>

20   <u>process</u> shall ~~execute the process by~~ affix~~ing~~

21   a copy thereof to the property in a conspicuous

22   place and ~~by leaving~~ <u>leave</u> a copy of the

23   complaint and process with the person having

24   possession or the person's agent. In

25   furtherance of the marshal's custody of any

26   vessel the marshal is authorized to make a

27   written request to the collector of customs not

28   to grant clearance to such vessel until

[G4669]

693

29   notified by the marshal or deputy marshal or by

30   the clerk that the vessel has been released in

31   accordance with these rules.

32   (c) Intangible Property.   If intangible

33   property is to be attached or arrested the

34   marshal or other person or organization having

35   the warrant shall execute the process by

36   leaving with the garnishee or other obligor a

37   copy of the complaint and process requiring the

38   garnishee   or   other   obligor   to   answer   as

39   provided in Rules B(3)(a) and C(6);   or the

40   marshal   may   accept   for   payment   into   the

41   registry of the court the amount owed to the

42   extent of the amount claimed by the plaintiff

43   with interest and costs, in which event the

44   garnishee   or   other   obligor   shall   not   be

45   required to answer unless alias process shall

46   be served.

47   (d) Directions With Respect to Property in

48   Custody.   The   marshal   or   other   person   or

49   organization having the warrant may at any time

50   apply to the court for directions with respect

51 to property that has been attached or arrested,

52 and shall give notice of such application to

53 any or all of the parties as the court may

54 direct.

55   * * * * *

56 (5) RELEASE OF PROPERTY.

57   * * * * *

58   (c) Release by Consent or Stipulation;

59 Order of Court or Clerk; Costs. Any vessel,

60 cargo, or other property in the custody of the

61 marshal or other person or organization having

62 the warrant may be released forthwith upon the

63 marshal's acceptance and approval of a

64 stipulation, bond, or other security, signed by

65 the party on whose behalf the property is

66 detained or the party's attorney and expressly

67 authorizing such release, if all costs and

68 charges of the court and its officers shall

69 have first been paid. Otherwise no property in

70 the custody of the marshal, other person or

71 organization having the warrant, or other

72 officer of the court shall be released without

[G4671]

695

73   an order of the court; but such order may be

74   entered as of course by the clerk, upon the

75   giving of approved security as provided by law

76   and these rules, or upon the dismissal or

77   discontinuance of the action; but the marshal

78   or other person or organization having the

79   warrant shall not deliver any property so

80   released until the costs and charges of the

81   officers of the court shall first have been

82   paid.

83   * * * * *

84   (9) DISPOSITION OF PROPERTY; SALES

85   * * * * *

86   (b) Interlocutory Sales. If property that

87   has been attached or arrested is perishable, or

88   liable to deterioration, decay, or injury by

89   being detained in custody pending the action,

90   or if the expense of keeping the property is

91   excessive or disproportionate, or if there is

92   unreasonable delay in securing the release of

93   property, the court, on application of any

94   party or of the marshal, or other person or

[G4672]

95   <u>organization having the warrant,</u> may order the

96   property or any portion thereof to be sold;

97   and the proceeds, or so much thereof as shall

98   be adequate to satisfy any judgment, may be

99   ordered brought into court to abide the event

100   of the action; or the court may, upon motion

101   of the defendant or claimant, order delivery of

102   the property to the defendant or claimant, upon

103   the giving of security in accordance with these

104   rules.

105   (c) Sales, Proceeds.   All sales of

106   property shall be made by the marshal or a

107   deputy marshal, or <u>by other person or</u>

108   <u>organization having the warrant, or by any</u>

109   other ~~proper officer~~ <u>person</u> assigned by the

110   court where the marshal <u>or other person or</u>

111   <u>organization having the warrant</u> is a party in

112   interest; and the proceeds of sale shall be

113   forthwith paid into the registry of the court

114   to be disposed of according to law.

                                                    [G4673]

COMMITTEE NOTE

These amendments are designed to conform this rule to Fed. R. Civ. P. 4, as amended. They are intended to relieve the Marshals Service of the burden of using its limited personnel and facilities for execution of process in routine circumstances. Doing so may involve a contractual arrangement with a person or organization retained by the government to perform these services, or the use of other government officers and employees, or the special appointment by the court of persons available to perform suitably. [G4674]

NOTICE

By order of April 30, 1991, the Supreme Court promulgated the foregoing amendments to Civil Rules 5, 15, 24, 34, 35, 41, 44, 45, 47, 48, 50, 52, 53, 63, 72, and 77 and to Supplemental Rules C and E--but not the proposed changes to Civil Rules 4, 4.1, 12, 16, 26, 28, 30, and 71A. Pursuant to 28 U.S.C. § 2074, the promulgated amendments will become effective December 1, 1991, unless Congress intercedes by statute.

†